Religion, Economics and Social Thought

Religion, Economics and Social Thought

Contributors include:

Gregory Baum
Martin E. Marty
Richard Neuhaus
Michael Novak
Edward Scott
John H. Yoder

Edited by:
Walter Block
Irving Hexham

THE FRASER
INSTITUTE

Proceedings of an International Symposium on Religion, Economics and Social Thought, held August 2–4, 1982 in Vancouver, British Columbia, Canada. This event is part of the program of Liberty Fund Inc., under the direction of its President, Dr. Neil McLeod. It was managed by the Centre for the Study of Economics and Religion, a division of the Fraser Institute. It was organized by CSER Director, Dr. Walter Block, Professor Paul Heyne of the University of Washington, Seattle and Professor Anthony Waterman of St. John's College, the University of Manitoba.

Canadian Cataloguing in Publication Data

Main entry under title:
Religion, economics and social thought

Based on the proceedings of the International
Symposium on Religion, Economics and Social
Thought, held Aug. 2–4, 1982 in Vancouver, B.C.
Includes index.
ISBN 0-88975-076-9

1. Economics - Religious aspects - Congresses.
2. Religion and politics - Congresses. 3.
Religion and sociology - Congresses. 4.
Capitalism - Religious aspects - Congresses.
I. Block, Walter, 1941–   II. Hexham,
Irving. III. Baum, Gregory, 1923–
IV. International Symposium on Religion,
Economics and Social Thought (1982 : Vancouver,
B.C.) V. Fraser Institute (Vancouver, B.C.)
HB72.R44 1986   291.1'785   C86-091079-2

Printed in Singapore

Contents

PART SIX
ISLAMIC SOCIAL THOUGHT

Participants

Dr. Muhammad Abdul-Rauf
Rector, International Islamic University, Malaysia. Author of *Marriage in Islam, The Islamic View of the Woman and the Family* and *A Muslim's Reflection on Democratic Capitalism.* Contributor to scholarly journals on Islamic history and civilization.

Dr. Imad A. Ahmad
Islamic scholar and theologian, International Islamic Weekend School. Contributor to numerous political, scholarly, and Libertarian journals.

Dr. Gregory Baum
Professor of Catholic Theology, St. Michael's College, University of Toronto, cross-appointed to the Sociology Department. Author of *Catholics and Canadian Socialism; The Priority of Labour;* and *Ethics and Economics.*

Dr. Robert Benne
Professor of Religion, Roanoke College, Salem, Virginia. Author of *Wandering in the Wilderness—Christians and the New Culture; Defining America: A Christian Critique;* and *The Ethic of Democratic Capitalism.*

Dr. John C. Bennett
President Emeritus and Reinhold Niebuhr Professor of Social Ethics Emeritus, Union Theological Seminary, New York City; Minister of the United Church of Christ. Author of *Christian Ethics and Social Policy; Christians and the State; Foreign Policy in Christian Perspective;* and *The Radical Imperative.* Senior contributing editor of *Christianity and Crisis.*

Dr. John Berthrong
Interfaith Dialogue Secretary, Division of World Outreach, United Church of Canada. Author of articles and reviews on Chinese philosophy and religion, contemporary issues in interfaith dialogue, and the theology of pluralism.

Dr. Walter Block
Director, Centre for the Study of Economics and Religion; Senior Economist, The Fraser Institute. Author of *Amending the Combines Investigation Act; Focus: On Economics and the Canadian Bishops* and *Focus: On Employment Equity.* Editor of *Zoning: Its Cost and Relevance; Rent Control: Myths and Realities; Discrimination, Affirmative Action, and Equal Opportunity; Morality of the Market* and *Theology, Third World Development and Economic Justice.*

Dr. Susan Feigenbaum
Associate Professor of Economics, Claremont McKenna College and Claremont Graduate School. Contributor to numerous economics journals on the roles of government and the marketplace.

Dr. Marilyn Friedman
Professor of Philosophy and Ethics, Bowling Green State University in Bowling Green, Ohio. Contributor to numerous philosophical and scholarly journals.

Dr. Bob Goudzwaard
Professor of Economics, Free University of Amsterdam, Holland. Rector of Educational Institute Dutch Christian Labour Association. Former MP, Dutch Parliament. Author of *Aid for the Overdeveloped West; Capitalism and Progress; The Christian and the Modern Business Enterprise;* and *A Christian Political Option.*

Dr. Irving Hexham
Professor, Department of Religious Studies, University of Calgary, Alberta. Author of *The Irony of Apartheid* and numerous academic articles; co-author, with Karla Poewe, of *Understanding Cults and New Religions.*

Dr. Paul Heyne
Lecturer in Economics, University of Washington, Seattle. Author of *Private Keepers of the Public Interest* and *The Economic Way of Thinking.* Contributor to numerous journals of economics and theology.

Dr. P. J. Hill
Professor of Economics, Montana State University, Author of *Establishing Property Rights in Energy: Efficient Processes; Birth of a Transfer Society;* and *Growth and Welfare.*

Dr. Roger Hutchinson
Professor of Church and Society, Emmanual College, Toronto School of Theology, University of Toronto. Author of numerous articles on social ethics.

Dr. Hanna E. Kassis
Professor of Religious Studies, University of British Columbia, Vancouver. Author of *A Concordance of the Qur'an* and a contributor to several learned periodicals in North America and abroad.

Dr. Clark A. Kucheman
Arthur V. Stoughton Professor of Christian Ethics, Claremont McKenna College, and Professor of Religion, Claremont Graduate School. Author of numerous articles on moral philosophy and economic justice in scholarly journals and co-author of *The Life of Choice.*

Dr. Martin E. Marty
Fairfax M. Cone Distinguished Service Professor of the History of Modern Christianity at the University of Chicago and Associate Editor of *The Christian Century.* Author of *Pilgrims in Their Own Land.*

Dr. Richard Neuhaus
Editor, *Lutheran Forum;* Director, The Rockford Institute Center on Religion and Society. Author of *In Defense of People; Christian Faith and Public Policy; Freedom for Ministry; Movement and Revolution* (with Peter Berger); *The Naked Public Square: Religion and Democracy in America.*

Dr. Ronald Preston
Emeritus Professor Social and Pastoral Theology, University of Manchester, and Canon Emeritus of Manchester Cathedral. Author of *Religion and the Persistence of Capitalism; Explorations in Theology 9; Church and Society in the Late Twentieth Century;* and contributor (mainly on social ethics) to theological journals.

Dr. Michael Novak
George Frederick Jewett Chair in Religion, Philosophy, and Public Policy at the American Enterprise Institute, Washington, D.C.; Founding Editor, *Catholicism in Crisis.* Author of *Freedom with Justice: Catholic Social Thought and Liberal Institutions; The Spirit of Democratic Capitalism; Confession of a Catholic;* and numerous other works.

Dr. Ellis Rivkin
Adolph S. Ochs Professor of Jewish History, Hebrew Union College-Jewish Institute of Religion, Cincinnati Campus. Author of *Leon da Modena and the Kol Sakhal; The Shaping of Jewish History; A Hidden Revolution; What Crucified Jesus?* Guggenheim Fellow (1962), and contributor to *American Historical Review, Jewish Quarterly Review, Hebrew Union College Annual, Commentary* and other publications.

Reverend James A. Sadowsky, S. J.
Professor, Department of Philosophy, Fordham University. Book review editor of *International Philosophical Quarterly* and author of a recent publication in the series *Taking Thought for the Poor.*

The Most Reverend Edward Scott
Primate of the Anglican Church of Canada; Moderator of the Central Committee of the World Council of Churches. Archbishop Scott was admitted as a Companion of the Order of Canada in 1978 and has received many honorary doctoral degrees from Canadian colleges.

Mr. Arthur A. Shenfield
Professor of Economics, University of London and University of Chicago Graduate School of Business, and lately Ludwig von Mises Distinguished Professor of Economics, Hillsdale College. Author of *Capitalism Under the Test of Ethics* and former President of the Mont Pelerin Society.

Dr. Meir Tamari
Economic Research Department, Bank of Israel, Jerusalem. Author of *Jewish Moral and Ethical Issues in Economics.*

Dr. Stephen Tonsor
Professor of History, University of Michigan. Author of *Historical Theology; What Is Christian Education?;* and *The Church-Related College*. Contributor to *Catholic Historical Review, Modern Age*.

Dr. Anthony Waterman
Fellow of St. John's College, Winnipeg and Professor of Economics, University of Manitoba. Formerly Chairman, Anglican National Task Force on the Economy. Author of *Poverty in Canada: A Christian Perspective* and contributor to both economic and theological literature.

Dr. John H. Yoder
Professor of Theology, University of Notre Dame. Author of *The Politics of Jesus* and *The Priestly Kingdom*.

Preface

Ethics and public policy

This book is an attempt to bridge the gap between two academic disciplines, economics and theology. As such it may be appropriate to reflect upon the approach of this new interdisciplinary study, "economics-theology."

One drawback with economics as a specialized field of study is that in many cases public policy recommendations do not follow directly from its analysis, however rigorous. It is for this reason that economists often disagree as to the implications of economic findings, even if not on the findings themselves. This "value-free" aspect of economics, we hasten to add, is only a shortcoming from the perspective of public policy decision-making. From the vantage point of economics as a science, the attempt at value-freedom is of course an advantage, even a prerequisite.

The branch of theology which attempts to deal with man's relation with his fellow man has no such disadvantage. On the contrary, values are central to the whole enterprise, not banished from the outset, as in the discipline of economics. But this benefit comes only at the cost of other advantages. Lacking an economic perspective, the findings of moral theology are no more capable than are those of economics of affording, *by themselves*, a reliable basis for public policy formation. It is perhaps for this reason that theologians, too, find themselves so sharply divided on policy prescriptions.

Ethical principles of some kind are necessary for sound public policy, but are not sufficient. Economic analysis is necessary, but not sufficient. The two together, we believe, are necessary and sufficient for the construction of a normative social theory which relates to what are usually thought of as the "economic" aspects of human existence.

This book, however, is more than the thin end of the wedge for an interdisciplinary study of "economics-theology." It is also an at-

tempt to draw into dialogue both economic and theological representatives from all points on the political spectrum.

The Canadian Conference of Bishops is on record as calling for just
this sort of dialogue. In their "Ethical Reflections on the Economic
Crisis" (reprinted in the Fraser Institute publication, *Focus: On Economics and the Canadian Bishops*, pp. 68–76) the bishops call for "a
real public debate about economic visions and industrial strategies involving choices about values and priorities for the future direction of
the country." Our volume may be regarded in some respects as a response to their call for meaningful dialogue.

It is an important mission to which we are called by the bishops.
Given widely divergent opinions on public policy issues, we can either talk or fight. Surely the former is preferable. But discourse is not
enough. Dialogue, meaningful dialogue, is necessary, if we are not to
pass each other as "dark ships in the night."

A bridge

This book is thus an attempt to bridge several gaps: between economists and theologians; between "Conservatives" and "Liberals";
between Marxists and free market advocates; between centralists
and decentralists. It is an attempt to ensure that hitherto separate universes of discourse are brought into hailing distance of each other.

The present book, like its companion volume *The Morality of the
Market: Religious and Economic Perspectives*, is based on the proceedings of a conference held by the Liberty Fund in conjunction
with the Centre for the Study of Economics and Religion, a division
of the Fraser Institute. It is remarkable in its coverage of divergent
and even conflicting points of view on economic, political and
theological issues. It is unusual, too, in that the participants come to
grips with the views of opposing schools of thought on numerous issues. This was partly a function of the "round-table" discussion
style, and partly a result of choosing paper-givers and commentators
on the basis of their different perspectives.

The purpose of the conference was to present representative accounts of the principal traditions of theological social thought in
Christianity, Judaism and Islam, and to expose these to criticism
from both theologians and social scientists. The chief objective of the
book is therefore to inform. What have the Christian churches, and
the other great religious traditions, believed and taught about the way

human societies ought to arrange their economic affairs? Its secondary objective is to stimulate critical thinking about those traditions, particularly about their relevance—if any—to the industrialized, secular, pluralistic and international world of late-twentieth century capitalism.

The conference organizers (Walter Block of the Fraser Institute, Paul Heyne of the University of Washington, and Anthony Waterman of St. John's College, Winnipeg) began with a broad and somewhat crude classification of the multifarious traditions: this classification shaped the conference and has determined the form of the present book. First and foremost come the many Christian traditions: not because of any bias on the part of the organizers, but simply because Christianity dominated the intellectual life of Western civilization from St. Augustine to Karl Marx. Because of this dominance, all serious thinking about any question was carried out in terms of Christian categories. All dispute (with very few exceptions) was dispute between Christian and Christian. Hence the very great variety of disagreement among Christians, to which our classification does little more than pay lip service. In Islam and Judaism by contrast, especially the latter, external pressures put a premium upon agreement.

Within Christianity, of course, the most venerable and fully-worked-out body of social thought is that of the Church of Rome. The organizers' decision to exclude the Eastern Orthodox tradition, though perhaps justifiable, is the most serious lacuna in this book. In practice, any detailed account of pre-modern Catholic thought was also excluded, for Father James Sadowsky's paper on "classical" social doctrine actually begins with the encyclical *Rerum Novarum* of 1891. According to that document, a "natural" right to private property exists which the state cannot remove. The putative evils of capitalism, attacked by Leo XIII and Pius XI, are actually caused—Father Sadowsky argues—by state intervention. "What was wrong with Roman Catholic social thought in the nineteenth century was not so much its ethics, as its lack of understanding of how the free market can work."

Liberation Theology

It is paradoxical that Gregory Baum's paper on the recent shift to the Left in Roman Catholic teaching, which he identifies as taking place since 1971, reveals that the intellectual process which led to this shift began with the rediscovery by Jacques Maritain of the medieval tradition of Catholic social thought. But in Latin America by the end of the 1960s many influential Catholics had come to believe that the human goals implicit in Christianity can only be realised by a definitely socialist economic and political order. The "Liberation Theology" which articulates this conviction was clearly to be seen in the encyclical *Octogesima Adveniens* (1971) and at the episcopal synod in Rome of the same year. Recent utterances by the U.S. and Canadian bishops have increasingly depended upon this way of thinking.

Outside the Roman Church, the earliest post-medieval tradition of social thought is that which emerged in Great Britain towards the end of the eighteenth century. The intellectual alliance of Protestant Christianity with the newly developed political economy of Adam Smith and Thomas Malthus (himself an Anglican priest) turned out to have strongly conservative social and political implications. Poverty and inequality are inevitable in this view, and more or less unaffected by legislated changes in social and economic institutions. This life is a state of "discipline and trial" for eternity; charity can not, and must not, be compulsory; and the institutions of private property, marriage, wage-labour and competition are on the whole more beneficial than harmful. Anthony Waterman's paper shows the origins of this tradition in Malthus's first *Essay on Population* (1798) and its development by J. B. Sumner, Thomas Chalmers and others. Paul Heyne's traces its propagation in the United States (in Chalmers's version) through the writings of Francis Wayland (1798–1865), Baptist Minister and President of Brown University from 1827 to 1855.

As confidence in *laissez-faire* waned during the nineteenth century, Protestant social thinking began to turn towards socialism. Ronald Preston traces the beginnings of this movement in mid-Victorian England and outlines its subsequent development. By the end of the nineteenth century it was acceptable in the Church of England, almost fashionable, to profess socialist beliefs, and the Lambeth Conference of 1897 commended socialism in general terms. The twentieth century has seen much development and much internal schism among Christian socialist bodies in Britain, Canada, the United States and several other countries, but this philosophy still claims the allegiance of many theologians.

Christian socialism made its presence felt in North America not so much by the intellectual conversion of the social and ecclesiastical

elite as by a grass-roots movement known as the "Social Gospel."
One of the most distinguished and influential figures in that movement was the theologian Reinhold Niebuhr. The other paper in this
section, that by Roger Hutchinson, explores the implications for
Christian socialist thought of Niebuhr's rejection of his early Marxism. Awareness of the pervasiveness of sin in all human arrangements, while consistent with the political pursuit of social justice, is a
safeguard against uncritical reliance upon particular programmes and
ideologies.

The fourth section of this book—the very existence of which is an
admission of failure on the part of the organizers—is a catchall for
three of the more important aspects of Christian social thought which
could not be fitted in to the first three classes. They have nothing in
common save their unclassifiability.

A miscellany

The first paper, by Bob Goudzwaard, describes what is theologically
a highly exclusive and somewhat peripheral tradition: that of Dutch
Neo-Calvinism. Groen van Prinsterer (1801–1876) and Abraham
Kuyper (1837–1920) were the Fathers of a spiritual and political
awakening of the Dutch Church and people. Kuyper founded the
Free (Calvinistic) University of Amsterdam, and a newspaper, a political party and the Christian labour movement. Kuyper's practical
application of Reformed Christianity was "anti-revolutionary" not
"counter-revolutionary"; and more successfully than most other
nineteenth century Christian traditions promotes the solidarity of employers and employees in a capitalist society.

The third paper, by Canada's Anglican Archbishop Edward Scott,
describes the totally inclusive attempts of the World Council of Churches to say something meaningful on behalf of all Christians and
Christian bodies. The World Council is composed of some three hundred different Christian churches, each with its own understanding of
authority and order. The work of the General Secretariat on behalf of
the Assembly is wide-ranging, and public statements on social issues
are only a small part of its business. Member churches have the right
to dissent from public statements and to criticize them. Issues are
presented by member churches and consensus is sought on the proper
application of Christian principles. Yet despite the immense possibil-

ity of disagreement and dispute, a broad "ecumenical consensus" has generally been obtained on such matters as "racism, militarism and human rights."

The remaining paper in this section, an account of minority thinking by John H. Yoder, amounts to a comprehensive rejection of all other formulations of Christian social thought reported in this book. For if, as Yoder suggests, it is not possible in principle to see the social system as a whole, then "letting the world go to the dogs in its own way is a proper thing to do." Yoder illustrates his theme by examining selected examples from a "thin strand of Christian cultural tradition": early monachism, the *patarini* of medieval Milan, the movements begun by St. Francis of Assissi (c. 1200) and by Waldo (c. 1180), the Czech Brethren of the Hussite Reformation, and the various Anabaptist sects which emerged during the "Second Reformation" in the sixteenth century. The vision of Christian community and voluntary Christian poverty common to all of these "represent an incarnate proclamation of the Lordship of Christ to all possible worlds in which food and shelter are needed."

The fifth section contains two accounts of Judaic attempts to relate the ethical doctrines of the Hebrew religion, first framed for a small agricultural nation in ancient Palestine, to the vastly different social and economic conditions of the Diaspora. Meir Tamari shows how Talmudic teaching was developed to accommodate the needs of Jewish mercantile communities in medieval Europe. Secondly, Ellis Rivkin attempts a general survey, from the standpoint of Reform Judaism, of the evolution of Judaic social thought over a vast sweep of history from Moses to twentieth century America.

Medieval Jewish communities practised price control in the sale of wine, meat and other items essential to ritual observances. The Talmudic law of *ona'ah* was developed in a way closely parallel to the contemporary Christian doctrine of the "just price," despite the attempt of Maimonides (1135–1204) to limit it to the basic necessities. Competition, free entry and location of firms were limited by "the religious considerations of mercy, justice and the general well-being of the community" embodied in the *Herem Hayishuv* and the *Marufia*. All of these doctrinal developments, Tamari suggests, were the result of the special circumstances of Jewish communities in medieval Europe, under which "it was no longer true that competition was the best means of maximizing communal welfare."

Adversity

Whereas Meir Tamari's paper is a detailed case-study intended to throw light on the *method* by which Judaic social teaching evolves in response to changing economic conditions, Ellis Rivkin's is a "broad-brush" history of that evolution. To Adam and Eve, "God gave dominion over all that He had created." The expulsion from Eden and the curse of Adam are omitted from Rivkin's theology: "God had not doomed humankind to eternal scarcity. Scarcity was a vibrant challenge, and not a tragic destiny." The remainder of his story is therefore one of continual human victory over temporary adversity, though he points out that the treatment of Jewish minorities during the Middle Ages and later fluctuated with the state of the economy. However, "whenever capitalism spread and triumphed, Jews were emancipated." As a direct consequence—according to Rivkin—a "radically new form of Judaism" (i.e., Reform Judaism) could thus emerge, which could say "'Yes' to modernization and Westernization; 'Yes' to capitalism's promise of overcoming scarcity; 'Yes' to the free-choosing, risk-taking individual; and 'Yes' to scientific and critical thinking."

Though by comparison with Judaism, Islam has played but an insignificant part in the social ethics of capitalist civilization, an Islamic contribution by Imad Ahmad was included in the conference and is printed in this book. There are three reasons for this. In the first place, migration has brought increasing numbers of Muslims to live and work in the midst of Western, formerly Christian societies. The cause of mutual understanding is served by information about the ethical beliefs of immigrant minorities. Secondly, the rise of Islamic nationalism, and the economic power of certain Islamic states, has made the study of Islam a matter of practical importance to contemporary capitalism. Thirdly and most importantly, the religious basis of Islamic social thought, like that of Christianity and Judaism, has its ultimate source in the same events: the call of Abraham and the revelation to Moses upon Sinai. A view of the similarities and differences to be found in the Islamic version of this common tradition is certain to be instructive and enlightening to Christian and Judaic readers.

The most obvious difference, it would seem from Ahmad's paper and the remarks of his commentators, is the altogether different treatment in Islam of the sacred texts. Although four main schools of interpretation are distinguished, the literal text of the Holy *Qu'ran* (believed to be the actual speech of God dictated to, and faithfully recorded by, the Prophet) is given a definitive importance that no Christian or Jewish theologian has ever been able to ascribe to the literal text of the Bible. For whereas the *Qu'ran* is a unified document specific to a time and place, the Bible is a library of books from widely different times and places, bearing the marks of constant revision and full of ambiguity and internal inconsistency, even contradiction. As against the speculative, open-ended and evolutionary nature of Christian and Judaic social thought therefore, that of Islam is more purely exegetical and juridical. In many practical details however, such as the importance of contracts, the existence of property rights, the propriety of accepting interest, and the obligation to pay taxes (*Zakat*) for social welfare, Islamic doctrine appears to approximate the contemporaneous teachings of Christianity and Judaism.

The arguments, confrontations and strongly held positions maintained in this book range widely over the spheres of economics, politics, sociology and theology. The Fraser Institute is pleased to publish the findings of our panel of scholars as a signal contribution to each of these fields. However, due to the independence of each participant, their views may or may not conform, severally or collectively to the views of the members of the Fraser Institute.

Walter Block
Irving Hexham

PART ONE

CATHOLIC SOCIAL THOUGHT

Chapter 1

Classical Social Doctrine in the Roman Catholic Church

James A. Sadowsky

What I call the "classical" social doctrine is that which prevailed among Roman Catholic thinkers from the encyclical *Rerum Novarum*[1] (1891) until the middle of the twentieth century. An "encyclical" is a papal letter addressed to the bishops in the Roman Catholic Church articulating the pope's position on some matter that is of importance to the Church. While what is set forth in encyclicals possesses great authority, it does not in and of itself possess the force of definitive Catholic doctrine. Positions can change with the passage of time. That this is so will become obvious from Dr. Baum's account of the developments that have occurred since the Second World War.

I have chosen to write about this encyclical of Leo XIII because more than any other single document it guided the thinking of Catholics on socio-economic questions during the first half of our century: most treatises on these questions were inspired by *Rerum Novarum*.

The encyclical *Rerum Novarum*

As stated, the encyclical was written in 1891. Marx had died in 1883, and Engels was to die in 1895. The important treatises on classical economics had already been completed, and the age of Austrian economics had begun with the publication of Menger's *Principles* in 1871.

Our encyclical does not pay much attention to any of the writings of the great economists. Yet if one wishes to understand the workings of the market, that is exactly what one has to do. What Leo XIII was striving to do was to improve the living conditions of the worker, and quite properly so. But to do so one must know what causes the poor conditions and what brings about the good. A doctor has to know whether to intervene in the course of nature or to let nature take its own course. Leo assumed that poor working conditions and poverty were in large measure due to a lack of good will on the part of employers. If that is the case, then it is appropriate to remedy that lack. But suppose that this is not so. Or suppose there is ill will, but that it is being exercised in some other, unnoticed direction. The question is whether the evil is accomplished through market forces alone, or by their being sabotaged by governments acting on behalf of favoured businessmen. We shall return to these questions after presenting the main points of the encyclical.

Here is Pope Leo's summary of the problem that he thought needed his attention:

> After the trade guilds had been destroyed in the last century, and no protection was substituted in their place, and when public institutions and legislation had cast off traditional religious teaching, it gradually came about that the present age handed over the workers, each alone and defenceless, to the inhumanity of employers and the unbridled greed of competitors ... and in addition the whole process of production as well as trade in every kind of goods has been brought almost entirely under the power of a few, so that a very few exceedingly rich men have laid a yoke almost of slavery on the unnumbered masses of non-owning workers. (6)

No socialist, no liberation theologian could have brought forth a stronger indictment. But if one is expecting the pope to propose the socialist remedy as his own, one is heading for a severe disappointment:

> To cure this evil, the Socialists, exciting the envy of the poor toward the rich, contend that it is necessary to do away with private possession of goods and in its place to make the goods of individuals common to all, and that the men who preside over a municipality or who direct the entire State should act as administrators of these goods. They hold that, by such a transfer of pri-

vate goods from private individuals to the community, they can cure the present evil through dividing wealth and benefits equally among the citizens. (7)

But their program is so unsuited for terminating the conflict that it actually injures the workers themselves. Moreover, it is highly unjust, because it violates the rights of lawful owners, perverts the functions of the State, and throws governments into utter confusion. (8)

If the worker cannot use his wages to buy property, which under socialism he could not do, his right to dispose of his wages as he sees fit is taken from him. His holdings are "nothing but his wages under a different form." (9) In other words, socialism dooms the worker to remaining forever under the very wage system it deplores. " . . . inasmuch as the Socialists seek to transfer the goods of private persons to the community at large, they make the lot of all wage earners worse, because of abolishing the freedom to dispose of wages they take away from them by this very act the hope and the opportunity of increasing their property and of securing advantages for themselves." (9)

Private property

But even more important is the claim that a regime of private property is demanded by human nature itself. Unlike the animals, man must plan for the future. He can do so only if he is able to possess the fruit of his labours in a permanent and stable fashion. (10, 11) It is in the power of man

> to choose the things which he considers best adapted to benefit him not only in the present but also in the future. Whence it follows that dominion not only over the fruits of the earth but also over the earth itself ought to rest in man, since he sees that things necessary for the future are furnished him out of the produce of the earth. The needs of every man are subject, as it were, to constant recurrences, so that, satisfied today, they make new demands tomorrow. Therefore nature necessarily gave man something stable and perpetually lasting on which he can count for continuous support. But nothing can give continuous support of this kind save the earth with its great abundance. (12)

The ownership of the earth by man in general means only that God did not assign any particular part of the earth to any one person, but left the limits of private possessions to be fixed by the industry of man and the institutions of peoples. To use the technical phrase, ownership in the original state was negatively rather than positively common: owned by no one but capable of being converted into property by anyone. (14)

How does one convert the unowned into property? By working on that, which up to that time, has not been owned. By so doing one "appropriates that part of physical nature to himself which he has cultivated." He stamps his own image on the work of his hands in such a way that "no one in any way should be permitted to violate this right." (15)

Those who would deny to the individual the ownership of the soil he cultivates while conceding to him the produce that results from that activity forget that the modifications he introduces into the soil are inseparable from it: he cannot own one without owning the other. (16) To use another example, it is nonsense to say that a person owns the statue he has carved but not the substance he has hewn into that form. There is no way in which he can carry away the statue while leaving behind the stone.

In sum, here is Leo's indictment of socialism:

> From all these conversations, it is perceived that the fundamental principle of Socialism which would make all possessions public property is to be utterly rejected because it injures the very ones it seeks to help, contravenes the natural rights of individual persons, and throws the functions of the State and public peace into confusion. Let it be regarded, therefore, as established that in seeking help for the masses this principle before all is to be considered as basic, namely, that private ownership must be preserved inviolate. (23)

Running through the encyclical is the theme that man's natural right of possessing and transmitting property by inheritance must remain intact and cannot be taken away by the State; "for man precedes the State," (6) and, "the domestic household is antecedent as well in idea as in fact, to the gathering of men into a community."(10)

At most, the State could modify the use of private property but never take away the basic right to its ownership and ordinary exercise.

Forty years afterwards Pius XI indicated his agreement with this teaching in *Quadragesimo Anno:*

Hence the prudent Pontiff had already declared it unlawful for the state to exhaust the means of individuals by crushing taxes and tributes. "The right to possess private property is derived from nature, not from man; and the state has by no means the right to abolish it, but only to control its use and bring it into harmony with the interests of the public good." (35) However, when the civil authority adjusts ownership to meet the needs of the public good it acts not as the enemy, but as the friend of private owners; for thus it effectively prevents the possession of private property, by Nature's Author in His Wisdom for the sustaining of human life, from creating intolerable burdens and so rushing to its own destruction. It does not therefore abolish, but protects private ownership; and, far from weakening the right of private property, it gives new strength.[2]

So it would seem that both for Leo XIII and Pius XI socialism in the sense of the generalized ownership of the means of production is out of the question. But they do allow for interventionism. The question is: how much interventionism?

Monopoly and state ownership

Leo XIII does not discuss the extent of legitimate nationalization of property; but Michael Cronin, who was in general a highly regarded interpreter of Catholic ethics, lays down the limits of state ownership in a fashion that I think would have won the agreement of both Leo XIII and Pius XI:

> If State nationalisation should reach a point where the pressure of State restriction begins to be felt by private persons, so that it can no longer be said that these persons have ample and full opportunity for private enterprise and investment, or if such a point has even been definitely approached so that there is danger to the private person's right of free enterprise and investment, then the State has already passed the limits of lawful monopoly. Also, if there be anything which is of such fundamental importance to the economic life of the community that to nationalise it would give the State a kind of modified ownership over all wealth, gravely hamper the freedom of private owners in every department of commerce, and so introduce conditions almost equivalent to those of socialism, then nationalisation in such a case would seem to be forbidden as imperilling the liberty and welfare of the community.[3]

Cronin would allow the state to set up a monopoly only for very grave reasons, and only after full compensation has been made to existing owners.

> There is all the difference in the world between monopolies owned by private individuals and monopolies set up by the State. The private individual or company which establishes a monopoly succeeds in doing so, not by forbidding a particular line of business to others, but as a result of open competition and by utilising the lawful expedients which competition brings into play; and supposing that only lawful expedients are utilised, a private company has quite as good a right to acquire a monopoly in open competition with others, as an individual has to win a race or to secure a prize by examination. But, on the other hand, when the State contemplates setting up a monopoly in any line of business, it forbids all others from entering that line of business, and thus effects a serious encroachment on the liberty of the subject. Such encroachment can only be justified by very grave reasons of public policy and necessity.[4]

Cronin's thinking on the subject of monopolies represents a high degree of sophistication. Few have been aware of the distinction between the type of "monopoly" that results from the consumers' refusing to deal with more than one producer of a good, and the "monopoly" that results when the State uses force to ban all but one producer of the good. Here we must digress on the nature of competition.

If the State's ban on competition brings about a result that would not otherwise have occurred, this means that those consumers who would have preferred to buy from some other firm are now prevented from doing so. Injury is done both to those firms that would have entered the market and to the consumers who would have preferred an alternative. In the absence of governmental interference the consumers are able to choose between a single seller and many. It is well to note that the monopoly Adam Smith deplored was precisely that which was brought about and kept in being by the power of the State. The term "monopoly" was never used in his day to designate the sole producer of a commodity, except when that uniqueness was caused by state intervention.

One often hears that the free market envisaged by Smith and his contemporaries no longer exists. Now if this means that there is far more government intervention in the economy than Smith would have accepted, then of course the claim is true. But this is not what the charge generally intends. Instead, the market is said to be unfree because the size of firms is far greater than Smith supposed they ought to be. According to this view, Smith thought that for the market to be free, and for prices to be "competitive," it must consist of firms so small that the withdrawal of a single one could have no effect upon the price of a given product.

Never mind that it is a logical impossibility for a firm to be that small. The whole thing is creative history. Nowhere does Smith attribute the success and freedom of markets to the smallness of the firms that make up an industry. For him the freedom of the market consisted of but one thing: the absence of government interference. As to the size of the firm that would result from the freedom of the market, he was perfectly willing to let the chips fall where they might. In his mind competition existed whenever there was legal freedom to enter the market.[5] As long as the market was free in his sense *all* prices were *eo ipso* competitive. The only time there would be a monopoly price, as distinct from a competitive price, was when the monopoly resulted from state action: thereby bringing about a price different from that which would have been obtained in the absence of government interference.[6] In any case, as long as governments permit free trade across national boundaries, one is not the single seller of a good unless one is the only seller of that good in the entire world. Otherwise the only hardware store on the north-west corner of Q Street would have to be declared a monopoly. As long as there are two in the entire world, the price differential can hardly exceed the transportation costs.

There is small likelihood of there being any great number of genuine market-formed monopolies: exceedingly few cases where we could speak of the only seller in the entire world. And even in such cases, a firm must meet certain conditions if it is to remain a monopoly. Above all, it must sell its goods at a price lower than the price at which its *potential* competitors could afford to sell. Once it ceases to do so, the potential competitors turn into *actual* competitors.

Papal criticism of capitalism

Most critics of capitalism in our own day tend to regard competition as a beneficial force. They recognize that it makes for lower prices, better quality, and increased protection for employers. If anything, their complaint is that business is not sufficiently competitive. In the light of this it may seem strange to see Catholic authorities of the last century blaming the economic evils of their day on competition. Leo XIII, for example, says that "the present age handed over the workers, each alone and defenceless, to the inhumanity of employers and the unbridled greed of competitors." (6) Pius XI makes the following remarks:

> In the first place, then, it is patent that in our days not alone is wealth accumulated, but immense power and despotic economic domination is concentrated in the hands of a few, and that those few are frequently not the owners, but only the trustees and directors of invested funds who administer them at their good pleasure.
>
> This power becomes particularly irrestible when exercised by those who, because they hold and control money, are able to govern credit and control its allotment, for that reason supplying so to speak the life-blood to the entire economic body, and grasping, as it were, in their hands the very soul of production, so that no one dares breathe against their will.
>
> This accumulation of power the characteristic note of the modern economic order, is a natural result of limitless free competition, which permits the survival of those only who are the strongest, which often means those who fight most relentlessly, who pay least heed to the dictates of conscience.[7]

One of the great problems we encounter when dealing with what purports to be a criticism of capitalism is that of discovering exactly what kind of capitalism is being criticized. An attack against one kind may be totally irrelevant when directed against another kind.

For our purposes we can distinguish between two kinds of capitalism: *laissez-faire* capitalism and State capitalism. The advocates of *laissez-faire* capitalism want the activities of the State to be restricted to the punishment of fraud and violence and the protection of property rights. The State, is not a participant in the economy except as customer. This implies no intervention either on behalf of or against any business interest. According to this creed the only thing that the State is capable of doing for business in general is to follow a strictly hands-off policy.

Laissez-faire capitalism excludes all subsidies and tax-exemptions, and in particular, it entails completely privatized money and a de-regulated banking system. Money is any good which will exchange for all other goods, and is decided by the market.

Money

Most foes of *laissez-faire* and many of its champions have failed to notice that in actual fact the money supply is entirely under the control of the State. It alone is allowed to issue money; and under legal tender laws, all are forced to accept it as payment for the goods we sell. This enables the government of a closed economy to increase the money supply at will. If there is no corresponding increase in production, each unit of money buys less than would otherwise have been the case. It is this phenomenon that people call inflation. Not only does it have the effect of large scale counterfeiting; it greatly inhibits money from performing its function as a calculating device that enables us to compare the relative prices of different goods. If it continues long enough, money becomes worth so little, and calculation so difficult, that people abandon it altogether and flee into barter, as happened in the Germany of the twenties.[8] None of this could occur if the monetary system were in the hands of the people. The market would choose by a process of trial and error some commodity whose supply could not readily be increased. One possibility would be gold. Suppose, however, someone finally discovers the philosopher's stone. The supply of the money commodity starts to increase; money prices start rising; calculation becomes more and more difficult. Absent legal tender laws, people are free to use or not to use the gold as the medium of exchange. Little by little, they start switching to some other metal that is less susceptible to increase, such as platinum. The inflation is nipped in the bud. Thus we see that, left to its own devices, the market has a built-in mechanism that stops any inflation before it can get off the ground. According to *laissez-faire* doctrine, government does not have to provide us with a sound currency. All it has to do is to let us alone.

What is the source of investment in a society where money is privatized? It can come only from pre-existent money. If money is to be available for investment, those who have it must reduce the portion they spend on consumption. Ultimately, the course of investment depends on the decisions of thousands of individuals who decide how much to invest and to whom they shall entrust their money. Lending institutions must either give satisfaction or go out of business.

It is, therefore, hard to see that "trustees and directors of invested funds can administer at their good pleasure" when in the last analysis those funds are supplied by those who limit their own consumption. Either the money ends up in the production of goods that future consumers want or it does not. If it does, then society in general is the winner: either because the prices it has to pay are lower, or because the quality of goods has been improved. If it does not, the goods will not be purchased and the investments will have become unprofitable. Surely people will not continue to entrust their money to organizations that go on making such mistakes?

But if banks are able to create money, there is an exogenous source of investment. Banks do not lend out pre-existent money; they create it. Thus a considerable amount of investment can and does take place apart from the voluntary decisions of people to abstain from consumption. This causes the phenomenon of "forced savings." People in general are forced to "save" more than they would otherwise have done. Of course, this is saving only in the sense of non-consumption, not in the sense of accumulation. There will be fewer goods available to the people (goods of *their* choosing), and in any case their money will be worth less. Here then we have individuals who by virtue of State-granted power are able to determine to a large extent both the form and amount of investment, and who by so doing bring about a state of affairs different from what would have obtained in the absence of this power. This state of affairs existed in the time of Leo XIII and in that of Pius XI; it continues in our own day. The popes were not wrong in identifying this sinister force with such enormous power over the economy. What they and so many others failed to see was that this power could not have existed without the benefit of State interference. The problem (for the defence of capitalism) is that the regimes that follow such policies get labelled as "capitalistic" *tout court*. To the extent, however, that a state of affairs exists by virtue of governmental intervention, that state of affairs is not strictly capitalistic. It is a mixture of capitalism and interventionism. If in such a regime there is economic misery, we must always ask whether the misery is caused by the *capitalism* or by the *intervention*. All too often people cry for more intervention as the cure when in fact the disease was brought about by prior intervention. Surely in such a case the solution is to stop intervening? More often than not, the solution to a problem is not to pass, but to repeal a law.

Does capitalism contain the seeds of its own transformation?

Of course, there are those who think that "pro-business" intervention is itself part of the immanent logic of capitalism, that the chicken of State capitalism automatically develops from the egg of *laissez-faire*.

Pius XI seems to have something of this sort in mind when he says that

> This concentration of power has led to a threefold struggle for domination. First, there is the struggle for dictatorship in the economic sphere itself; then the fierce battle to acquire control of the State, so that its resources and authority may be abused in the economic struggles; finally the clash between the states themselves. This latter arises from two causes: because the nations apply their power and political influence, regardless of circumstances to promote the economic advantages of their citizens; and because, vice versa, economic forces and economic domination are used to decide political controversies between peoples.[9]

There is no doubt that this describes the history of so-called capitalistic regimes. Certainly many business men have struggled in order to achieve domination of the State and in many instances have succeeded. Not only have they thus committed aggression against their own people; they have influenced their governments to commit aggression against others as well. The point to be made is that none of these monstrosities results from capitalism *per se*.

Capitalism is the *only* economic system that can be conceived of as existing without a State. It is, for example, the economic system described by Locke as existing in the state of nature—Society without the State. True, the society he depicts is a rather primitive one, but this is logically accidental. I, for one, find no reason to believe that this state of nature could not have elaborate technologies and gigantic corporations. (Notice that the requirement that corporations should be chartered is a purely legal and not a conceptual requirement.

Without it the corporation could exist but would simply be illegal: without the charter it *can* but *may* not exist.)

It should also be pointed out that it is conceptually possible to have (*pace* Locke) a legal system and a protection system in the absence of a State.[10] The point here is not to advocate the abolition of the State but simply to show that capitalism can be *conceived* as existing without it. All other forms of economic order, interventionism, fascism, involuntary communism, require a state apparatus for their very existence. Voluntary communism, as practiced in monasteries and communes, is subsumed under capitalism since it is compatible with the right to private property.

The abuses rightly deplored by Pius XI require the existence of the State if they are to be institutionalized. Not any State, but the type of State that does claim the authority to do this sort of thing for special interests. Again we call attention to the fact that the State cannot benefit *all* business interests. Since they are in competition with each other, what benefits one interest is bound to be harmful to some other.

As long as there are States in a position to render favours to special interests, they will try to obtain them. Often they will succeed. It is naive to expect otherwise. The usual reaction to this state of affairs is to seek similar favours for the interest group that had suffered as a result of the previous intervention. The *laissez-faire* solution is not to compensate one wrong with another wrong but rather to make it constitutionally impossible for the State to do these things in the first place. But it is important to realise that capitalism on its own is incapable of bringing about the conditions that Pius XI so rightly deplores. One can only regret that he and so many others blame capitalism for what results from unnoticed interventionism. How many, for example notice that government regulation and taxes put marginal firms out of business, thereby lessening competition and raising prices? How strange that people expect monopoly-creating governments to save us from monopolies!

The encyclicals and the labour market

I now turn to what the encyclicals have to say concerning the treatment of employees. In general, they reject the ideal that wealth and positions should be equally distributed. On this let us hear Leo XIII:

> Therefore, let it be laid down in the first place that a condition of human existence must be borne with, namely, that in civil society the lowest cannot be made equal with the highest. Socialists, of course, agitate the contrary, but all struggling against nature is in vain. There are truly very great and many natural differences among men. Neither the talents, nor the skill, nor the health, nor the capacities of all are the same, and unequal fortune follows of itself upon necessary inequality in respect to these endowments. And clearly this condition of things is adapted to benefit both individuals and the community; for to carry on its affairs community life requires varied aptitudes and diverse services, and to perform those diverse services men are impelled most by differences in individual property holdings. (26)

Secondly, there is the rejection of any notion of class war:

> It is a capital evil with respect to the question We are discussing to take for granted that the one class of society is of itself hostile to the other, as if nature had set rich and poor against each other to fight fiercely in implacable war. This is so abhorrent to the reason and truth that the exact opposite is true; for just as the human body whose different members harmonise with each other, whence arises that disposition of parts and proportion in the human figure rightly called symmetry, so likewise nature has commanded in the case of the State that the two classes mentioned should agree harmoniously and should properly form equally balanced counterparts to each other. Each needs the other completely: neither capital can do without labour, nor labour without capital ... (28)

Workers are

> ... To perform entirely and conscientiously whatever work has been voluntarily and equitably agreed upon; not in any way to injure the property or to harm the person of employers; in protecting their own interests, to refrain from violence and never to engage in rioting; not to associate with vicious men who craftily hold out exaggerated hopes and who make huge promises, a

course usually ending in vain regrets in the destruction of wealth.
(30)

But it is precisely the notion of "voluntary and equitable agreements" that has traditionally caused problems for Catholic thinkers just as it does for many other in our own day. Both Leo XIII and Pius XI objected to the "liberal" understanding of freedom of contract ("liberal" here being understood in its traditional, nineteenth-century sense). The advocates of *laissez-faire* considered a contract to be free as long as no one was using physical force or threatening it in order to bring the contract about. The fact that one of the parties had an irresistible desire for what the other contracting party was offering was not considered to impair the freedom of the contract as long as the other party had not brought about that need by theft, fraud, or violence. If, for example, someone had entered a marriage because he found the woman to be irresistible, liberals would not have regarded this as destroying the essential freedom of the marriage contract—this despite the fact that the woman had taken advantage of the man's need for her. Perhaps it will be said that she created this need by her charm and beauty. But, this, the liberals would have said, is not so. She did not create his need for charm and beauty; she is simply offering to satisfy that need. Had the victim not wanted charm and beauty in the first place, all her efforts would have been in vain.

Perhaps the threat of withholding the offered benefit unless the other party agrees to the terms of the contract constitutes the coercion. Louis Napoleon is said to have tried to make Eugenie de Montijo his lover. According to the story, she told him that the way to her boudoir was through the church door. The liberals would have denied that the terms imposed by Eugenie made the subsequent matrimonial contract a coercive one.

Necessities

They applied these principles to all contracts, even the so-called necessitous ones. Consider the case of the starving man. Does he have a prior right to my food? If the answer is yes, I must give it to him without laying down conditions: the question of the contract does not arise. But suppose the answer is no. While I may well be acting indecently if I refuse his request for food, I am, by supposition, not violat-

ing his right. How then do I violate his right by giving him the food under onerous conditions? How is he any more coerced than he would
be if I had no food to offer him? If anything, my offering to give him a
meal for his onerous labour makes him less coerced than he was before. Before the offering he could only starve. After, he has the alternative of starvation or work. Does not the existence of an alternative
make him *freer* than he was before? The fact that by being generous I
could have offered an even greater range of alternatives does not constitute a lessening of his freedom but only a failure to increase it. So,
the liberal would say, neither the offering of a good that cannot be
resisted, nor the refusal to confer it without the performance of an
onerous task, makes the worker any less free than he would have
been had the question of making the contract never arisen.

To this a Marxist would reply that the necessity of work or starvation is imposed upon the worker by the capitalistic system itself: the
very existence of this system is in violation of his rights. It is because
"capitalists have a monopoly over the means of production" that the
wretched alternative of work or starve is presented to whose who are
excluded from the means of production.

Now of course the capitalists have a monopoly on the means of
production, but only in the sense that husbands have a monopoly on
wives and farmers on agriculture. Indeed, the only ones who have
wives are husbands. But this is not because someone has passed a law
that prevents non-husbands from having wives. If there is a law, the
law is a purely semantic one. It is contradictory to say that one is a
non-husband and yet has a wife. And this is so only because "husband" is defined as "one who has a wife." It is not a question of who
is allowed to do what but rather of the names we give to people and to
the things they do. This law has no effect upon the real world; it does
nothing to limit the number of people who have wives.

Similarly by "capitalist" we mean "an owner of the means of production." If we keep this in mind, our stirring sentence reduces to:
"The only owners of the means of production are the owners of the
means of production." In other words, by the very fact that you acquire ownership over a means of production you become a capitalist.
That is to say: A is A.

The question is not whether one has to become a capitalist in order
to have some ownership of the means of production but whether in a
laissez-faire regime there is any obstacle imposed that prevents non-
capitalists from becoming capitalists. All non-capitalists have to do is

to reduce their present consumption and start investing. To which it is said that workers cannot reduce their consumption. Now once again, we have to be careful not to define "worker" as "one who must consume all his earnings." In that case, we simply ask whether one has to remain a worker. The fact is that in the nineteenth century when workers had far less to consume than their counterparts today, a good number did become capitalists. It is all too often the *unwillingness* to restrict consumption, a grasshopper attitude, that prevents workers from becoming capitalists. But even in our own day we see, especially among immigrants from Asia, an amazing willingness to defer present consumption. We find these people living initially in conditions that we should judge to be absolutely impossible. Yet before we know it, they are operating successful businesses. We should probably see far more of this than we in fact do were it not for all the government regulations that make it so difficult for the poor to engage in business: laws against peddling, sanitary regulations, etc. These, of course, cannot be blamed on *laissez-faire*.

But this apart, the necessity of doing *some* work or starving unless you have kind friends or relatives is one that comes from nature itself. The point to be made, however, is that to the extent the economy was free, living standards rose during the nineteenth century. How else are we to explain the enormous rise in population? Far more people were surviving until the age of reproduction. The amount of work that had to be done in order to avoid starvation was steadily diminishing. The increasing flow of goods was raising the real income of workers, enabling them to buy a greater quantity of goods with their wages.[11] This in turn increased the relative value of leisure to the employees: it became more and more difficult to get them to work the same number of hours at the old wage-rates. The result of all this was that the working day was gradually shortened. The laws that were enacted to shorten the hours did little more than ratify the *fait accompli*. To have enacted a law in 1801 that required no more than eight hours of work would have brought on mass starvation: the amount of production in such a period could not have sustained the lives of all these workers. The working day in fact turns out to be nothing but the number of hours that the majority of people are willing to work. And what determines the amount of time that people are willing to work is the amount of goods produced in conjunction with peoples' leisure preferences. (There is, after all, some truth to the claim that capitalism tends to generate unemployment; but the unemployment that it generates is *voluntary*.)

Capitalism and the real wage

Perhaps it is worth while to say something about the charge that under capitalism the wages tend to remain just low enough to secure the "reproduction of the worker." Now there is a sense in which this is false and a sense in which it is true. If it is supposed to refer to the purely *biological* reproduction of the person who happens to be the worker, then it is clearly false. It has already been remarked that wages have risen far above subsistence level in areas where the economy is more or less free. It is true in the sense that if the task is to continue being done, wages cannot fall below the level required for the reproduction of the worker *qua* worker. All that it means is that the wages have to be high enough to attract workers, and will be no higher than what is required to do that. How high will it have to be? Since the "law" is nothing but a truism, it cannot tell us.

What was the response of the encyclicals to this liberal theory of freedom of contract and theory of wages? Leo XIII makes a distinction between the labour contract and other contracts. He makes the point that, unlike other products, labour cannot be separated from the person who performs it:

> ... in man labour has two marks, as it were, implanted by nature, so that it is truly *personal*, because work energy inheres in the person and belongs completely to him by whom it is expended and for whose use it is destined by nature; and secondly, that it is *necessary*, because man has need of the fruit of his labours to preserve his life, and nature itself, which must be most strictly obeyed, commands him to preserve it. If labour should be considered only under the aspect that it is personal, there is no doubt that it would be entirely in the worker's power to set the amount of the agreed wage at too low a level ... But this matter must be judged far differently, if with the factor of *personality* we combine the factor of *necessity*, from which the former is separable in thought but not in reality. In fact, to preserve one's life is a duty common to all individuals, and to neglect this duty is a crime. Hence arises necessarily the right of securing the things to sustain life, and only a wage earned by his labour gives a poor man the means to acquire these things. (62)

Perhaps Cronin makes clearer what Leo XIII is getting at:

> ... The man who gives up his whole labour-day to another, puts at the disposal of that other all those energies with which nature

has equipped him for the supplying of his own needs. Therefore, the just wage payable in return for the use of those energies, the only wage which can justly be represented as the equivalent of those energies, is a *wage capable of supplying the same needs* which our human energies are meant to supply. And the minimum just wage will be a wage capable of supplying the minimum essentials of those needs, the essentials of human life. This, then, is the first measure and test of the minimum just wage. It is a measure which is based on the nature of labour itself and its essential function.[12]

This suggests the idea of opportunity cost. Presumably, the worker is to expect of his employer at least what he could have obtained by expending his energies on his own behalf instead of on behalf of an employer. All well and good. But isn't that what is happening? Why is our man not self-employed in the first place? Surely it is because he thinks that his employer is giving him more than he would have received by going into business himself? In other words, we have to ask ourselves where he would be if there were no employers around. One gets the idea from Cronin that job-offers make people poorer than they would have been in the absence of such offers!

Low wages

To be sure, our worker is in dire need. And certainly from a Christian point of view we ought to help him meet those needs. Why, however, should it be precisely the *employer* on whom this obligation falls rather than upon *anyone else?* The employer is not worsening but bettering the condition of his employee.

But perhaps it will be said that the necessary condition of these low wages is the inability of the worker to obtain a suitable income elsewhere. Now it is certainly true that one is not ordinarily going to take a low-paying job if the alternative income is sufficiently high. This is in fact the reason why all sorts of menial jobs are not accepted today. Welfare is a mighty source of voluntary unemployment: it has provided numerous persons with an alternative income. But if the theory we are discussing were correct, the fact that people have this alternative ought to cause employers to offer a correspondingly higher wage to induce people to take the jobs. Why are they not rushing in to outbid welfare? The answer is simple. The consumers who in the last analysis pay the costs of doing business would not be willing to pay the resulting higher prices; and when this happens, the job goes out of existence.

What many do not see is that it is the consumer who puts the cap on wages. Essentially the employer is a middleman. By buying elsewhere, or by not buying at all, the consumer vetoes the choice of an over-generous or extravagant employer. Unless the government forces the consumer to buy the good at the higher price, there is no way that employers can increase wages and still remain in business. The faceless "exploiter" of the worker is none other than the consumer. The only choice, according to this line of argument, is market wages or unemployment.

Given an understanding of the market, the debate about the living wage need never have occurred. The fact is that if employers are unable to pay a living wage, the market itself will force them to do so. And if they cannot, they are not obliged to do so. *Nemo tenetur ad impossibile*. It is, of course, impossible to stay in business for any length of time and pay a living wage unless one is making a profit. Let us now suppose that it is possible to make a profit while paying a living wage but that the existing firms are not doing so, i.e., not paying the living wage. This means, (if we assume freedom of entry) that it will be profitable for *other* firms to enter that market and lure the workers from the recalcitrant firms by offering to pay a higher wage. This process will go on until the wage rises to the level of the living wage. The only "fair" way to keep these would-be entrants out of the market is for the firms already there to offer a living wage in the first place. The best ally of the worker will be the competition for workers that exists among businessmen. Of course, a government can try to manipulate the market and force some firms to pay the living wage when this is not produced by market conditions. But in that case those who are receiving it are doing so at the expense of those who because of their unemployment are receiving no wages at all.

Conclusion

What was wrong with Roman Catholic social thought in the nineteenth century was not so much its ethics, as its lack of understanding of how the free market can work. The concern for the worker was entirely legitimate, but concern can accomplish little without knowledge of the causes and the cures of the disease.

Like so many others, Catholic thinkers were unaware of the

amount of government intervention in their day. Though considerably less than in our own day, it was considerable. This fact prevented them from asking whether the problems they saw were due to intervention or to the lack of it. The tendency, therefore, was to blame whatever went wrong on the market itself. And when this happens, the temptation is to demand more and more intervention—the very cause of the problem in the first place.

Frequently our ethical judgements of an action are based on what the effects of that action are perceived to be. Most people, for example, will be for or against government intervention depending on what they think this sort of thing will achieve. But this makes it all the more important that we should know what those effects are. I doubt that Catholic thinkers would have judged the market as they did had they known its workings better.

NOTES

1. *Rerum Novarum:* Encyclical Letter on the Condition of the Workingman. St. Paul Editions, Jamaica Plains, Massachusetts. The numbers in parentheses refer to the paragraph numbers in the official translation of the text.

2. Pius XI, *Quadragesimo Anno,* Encyclical Letter *On Social Reconstruction,* Jamaica Plains, Massachusetts: St. Paul Editions, p. 26.

3. Michael Cronin, *The Science of Ethics* (New York: Benzinger Brothers, 1917), II, p. 279.

4. Cronin, *op. cit.*, p. 277.

5. On this see Paul J. McNulty, "Economic Theory and the Meaning of Competition" in *The Competitive Economy* ed. Yale Brozen (Morristown, N.J.: General Learning Press 1975) pp. 64–75.

6. Cf. Dominick T. Armentano, *Antitrust and Monopoly,* (New York: John Wiley and Sons, 1982) pp. 13–31. This work contains an excellent critique of the attempt to distinguish between a competitive and monopoly price on the unhampered market. He shows that the only "market"

price is the one that has been bizarrely called the "monopoly" price.

7. Pius XI, p. 50

8. See Murray Rothbard, *What Has the Government Done to Our Money?*, (Novato, California: Liberty Press 1962). This book is the best little introduction to money I know.

9. Pius XI, p. 51.

10. For one of the increasing number of such discussions see John T. Sanders, *The Ethical Argument Against Government*, (Washington, D.C.: University Press of America 1980) pp. 177–193.

11. Cf. F. A. Hayek, *Capitalism and the Historians* (Chicago: The University of Chicago Press 1954)

12. Cronin, II p. 346

Comment

Clark A. Kucheman

Basically, Father Sadowsky's challenging and informative essay is a defence of *laissez-faire* capitalism against a number of criticisms made by Pope Leo XIII in the encyclical *Rerum Novarum* (1891) and by Pope Pius XI in the encyclical *Quadragesimo Anno* (1931). The popes were mistaken, both in their criticisms and in their policy proposals, Father Sadowsky maintains, because they did not understand the functioning of *laissez-faire* —as opposed to "State"—capitalism. "What was wrong with Roman Catholic social thought in the nineteenth century," he explains, "was not so much its ethics as its lack of understanding of how the free market can work. The concern for the worker was entirely legitimate, but concern can accomplish little without knowledge of the causes and the cures of the disease." And in the final analysis, both then and now, according to Father Sadowsky, the cause of capitalism's disease is governmental intervention, and its cure is therefore the ending of governmental intervention.

Certainly I agree with Father Sadowsky in "doubt[ing] that Catholic thinkers would have judged the market as they did had they known its workings better." (p. 22). Many of the encyclicals' criticisms and proposals—including those to which Father Sadowsky refers and, I would add, especially Pope Pius XI's proposal for a "corporative system"[1]—reflect at least in part faulty understanding of the competitive market's functioning. I also agree that much governmental intervention is for the illegitimate purpose of "render[ing] favors to special interests," such as in the United States to agriculture and merchant shipping. But I do not agree with what seems to be Father Sadowsky's assumption that market competition suffices by itself to implement human rights. Instead, and in spite of the fact that it makes me very nervous as a Unitarian-Universalist to side with a pope, I agree with Pope Pius XI in saying that "free competition, . . . though justified and quite useful within certain limits, cannot be an adequate controlling principle in economic affairs."[2] It may well be true that "capitalism is the only system that can be conceived of as existing without a State." But capitalism *ought* not to exist without governmental intervention for the purpose of implementing the moral rights of human beings.

Ends and means

What moral rights? According to Pope John XXIII—the favorite pope of Unitarian-Universalists—"human beings have the natural right to free initiative in the economic field," first of all, including "the right to private property, even of productive goods."[3] Or as I prefer to put it, in my quasi-Kantian language, individual human beings have the moral right to act on ends they will for themselves without being coerced to serve ends willed arbitrarily by others. And—at least if it is truly competitive, and if we can ignore neighborhood effects—market capitalism does function in harmony with this right. For it is an arrangement wherein individuals pursue ends they will for themselves in voluntary, not coercive, interaction with others.[4]

But this negative right to freedom from coercion is not the only moral right of individual human beings, according to Pope John XXIII. In addition,

> Every man has the right to life, to bodily integrity, and to the means which are necessary and suitable for the proper development of life; these are primarily food, clothing, shelter, rest, medical care, and finally the necessary social services. Therefore a human being also has the right to security in cases of sickness, inability to work, widowhood, old age, unemployment, or in any other case in which he is deprived of the means of subsistence through no fault of his own.[5]

Moreover, as Pope John XXIII says elsewhere, "vigilance should be exercised and effective steps taken that class differences arising from disparity of wealth not be increased, but lessened so far as possible," and hence "the economic prosperity of any people is to be assessed not so much from the sum total of goods and wealth possessed as from the distribution of goods according to norms of justice, so that everyone in the community can develop and perfect himself."[6]

Now I think everyone will agree that the competitive market does not suffice to implement the positive right of individuals to "the means which are necessary and suitable for the proper development of life." In the competitive market individuals' incomes are determined not by what they need in order to "develop and perfect" themselves but, instead, by supply and demand. If an individual has little or nothing to offer in the competitive market that is scarce in relation to the demand for it, then his or her income—and consequently his or her access to "the means which are necessary and suitable for the proper development of life"—will be little or nothing as well. And if we take the poverty line as an indicator, then roughly 12 per cent of the population of the United States lack what they need in order to "develop and perfect" themselves as human beings.

Nor does the market reduce "class differences arising from disparity of wealth." Even if in the long run the unhampered market makes the poor richer, it does not enrich both the rich and the poor to the same degree. Percentage-wise, the disparity of incomes has not increased; indeed, it has decreased somewhat in recent years. In absolute terms, however, the disparity between the rich and the poor has increased. "As average incomes have risen," Lester Thurow and Robert Lucas pointed out a few years ago, "real income gaps have expanded when measured in constant dollars. Where the real income gap was $10,565 between the average income of the poorest and richest quintile of the population in 1949 it was $19,071 in 1969."[7] Furthermore, the percentage gain of the lowest fifth from 4.1 per cent in 1948 to 5.6 per cent of per capita household income in 1977 was brought about by governmental intervention rather than by the "unhampered market." "Without income transfers," Thurow explains, "the share of income going to the bottom quintile of households would have been more than cut in half during the post-World War II period. Governmental actions prevented this from happening and actually caused a substantial gain in the income position of the poor."[8]

Limitations

It would appear, therefore, to quote Pope Pius XI again, that "free competition, . . . though justified and quite useful within certain limits, cannot be an adequate controlling principle in economic affairs." It is "justified and quite useful" as a way of implementing the moral right of individuals to what Pope John XXIII refers to as "free initiative in the economic field," but it "cannot be an adequate controlling principle in economic affairs" because by itself it does not provide to everyone conditions of life on the basis of which they can "develop and perfect" themselves as human beings.

The issue here is on the level of ethical, not economic, analysis. While we may disagree on the level of economic analysis—about Professor Thurow's interpretation of income statistics, for example—we cannot disagree that poverty exists, nor that the "unhampered market" cannot by itself guarantee that everyone will have an above-poverty income. The question at issue is not the factual one of whether there are human beings who are "deprived of the means of subsistence through no fault of [their] own." Instead, the question at issue is the morally normative one of whether human beings have a right to be provided with "the means which are necessary and suitable for the proper development of life"—above-poverty incomes, adequate medical care, and so on—when they are unable to do so for themselves. For if they really do have this positive moral right, then justice requires governmental intervention to redistribute income, directly or indirectly, from the rich to the poor.

According to Pope John XXIII, human beings have moral rights and duties, including this particular right and duty corresponding to it, because they are rational—intelligent—and consequently free, persons. "Every human being is a person" in that "his nature is endowed with intelligence and free will," and "by virtue of this," Pope John XXIII argues, "he has rights and duties of his own, flowing directly and simultaneously from his very nature, which are therefore universal, inviolable, and inalienable."[9]

While I do not accept the natural law theory of moral obligation on which the pope's formulation depends, I nevertheless agree that we human beings have moral duties and rights, including the ones in question, because we are "endowed with intelligence and free will."

Borrowing from the German Idealism of Immanuel Kant, G. W. F. Hegel, and Paul Tillich, rather than from the natural theory of St. Thomas Aquinas, I would argue in the following manner.

To be a *person* is by definition to be self-determining. We human beings are persons if and in the degree to which we are self-determining *sub*jects, not other-determined *ob*jects. So when are we self-determining? We are not self-determining if we simply follow whatever desires or wants we happen to have. In Hegel's words, "The natural man, whose motions follow the rule only of his appetites, is not his own master. Be he self-willed as he may, the constituents of his will and opinion are not his own, and his freedom is merely formal."[10] For as selves, egos, we are other than and transcend everything external, including even our most strongly felt desires. "When I say 'I'," as Hegel explains, "I *eo ipso* abandon all my particular characteristics, my disposition, natural endowment, knowledge, and age. The ego is quite empty, a mere point, simple, yet active in this simplicity. The variegated canvas of the world is before me; I stand against it."[11] As selves, we are "mere point[s]" for whom everything else is an external object about which we actively think and will. We are self-determining, then, not when we obey a desire, but rather, when we obey the inner laws of our own thinking and willing selves, namely, the laws of logic, that is, the laws of valid thinking. "Thinking and the laws of thinking are one and the same,"[12] as Paul Tillich points out, and consequently we are self-determining when we think and will in obedience to these laws. Fully to be a person is thus to be rationally self-determining. We are persons if and in the degree to which we govern our thinking and our willing—our thinking about what ends to pursue, in other words—by the laws of logic.

Potentialities

As we exist, we human beings are not fully actual persons. Instead, we are potential and partially actual persons. We are potential persons in that we are capable of rational thinking and willing, and we are partially actual persons in that—and in the extent to which—we do in fact think and will rationally. But we have a moral *duty* to think and will rationally. Since we cannot deny that we ought (whether we want to or not) to think and will rationally without presupposing at the same time that we ought to, personhood is morally obligatory. Whether we want to or not, we ought to govern our thinking and willing by the principles of logic and, consequently, to develop our capacities for so doing. As potential and partially actual persons, we human beings have moral duties, imposed on us by the inner laws of our own thinking, to actualize our potential personhood in rational thinking and willing. In so far as we are capable of doing so, we ought as a matter of self-imposed duty to become and be rationally self-determining persons.

So what does this moral duty to become and be rationally self-determining have to do with the specific economic duties and rights at issue here?

Notice first that the duty to govern our thinking and willing by the "laws of thinking" prohibits us from acting in ways that we cannot without contradiction will that others who are relevantly similar to us should act. Since we violate a fundamental "law of thinking," namely, the law of contradiction, if we assert a right for ourselves that we at the same time deny to others, and since all human beings are relevantly similar to one another as potential and partially actual persons, we have self-imposed moral duties, in Kant's words, "never to act except in such a way that [we] can also will that [our] maxim should become a universal law."[13]

Now, since we necessarily assert a right to act on ends we will for ourselves, including the morally obligatory end of actualizing ourselves as rationally self-determining persons, we thereby have self-imposed duties on this principle of universalizability to act only on policies of action which respect this same right in others. We may not treat other human beings always as mere means to our own private ends, either by coercing them or by depriving them of the means by which they can act on ends they will for themselves, because we cannot will to be treated by others in this way; we cannot will that our own will should be overridden in this way by others. Hence we have duties, to which others have corresponding rights, to treat other human beings always as potential and partially actual persons who think and will for themselves and never as mere things without the capacity for thinking and willing by leaving them at liberty to act on ends they will for themselves. Every individual human being has a moral right to develop and express his or her capacity for rational self-determination by acting on ends he or she wills for himself or herself independently of coercion or manipulation to serve ends willed arbitrarily by others.

This moral right of course entails what Pope John XXIII refers to as "the natural right to free initiative in the economic field" and "the right to private property, even of productive goods." It is what requires us to have market capitalism as our overall economic organization. For at least in principle, if not always in fact, a market capitalist arrangement is one wherein everyone can act on ends of his or her own in voluntary, not coercive, interaction with others.

Conditions of life

The moral right of every individual human being to be treated always as a potential and partially actual person and never as a mere thing is not only a negative right not to be coerced or manipulated to serve others' arbitrary ends, however. It is also a positive right to what Pope John XXIII refers to as "the means which are necessary and suitable for the proper development of life." It is a right to conditions of life on the basis of which self-determination is possible, and market capitalism does not by itself suffice to assure these conditions of life to everyone.

There can be a right only if there is a corresponding duty, to be sure. So why do we have a duty to provide "the means which are necessary and suitable for the proper development of life" to others who are unable to do so for themselves?

Part of the answer is that the principle of universalizability requires us to act at least sometimes to promote others' welfare above our own. We have duties on this principle to treat other human beings always as thinking and willing persons who set and pursue ends of their own and never as mere things that neither think nor will and consequently have no ends of their own. We do treat other human beings as mere things, however, if we act *always* to give our own private ends priority over others' ends, i.e., if we *never* act to promote others' welfare above our own. Hence we have duties to promote the welfare of others along with our own and, at least on occasion, to give others' welfare—their ends—priority over our own.

This is of course so far not a duty to perform any specific actions. It requires only that we have a general intention to promote the welfare of others along with our own. We must put others' welfare above our own at least sometimes, but for the most part we fulfill our duties on this principle so long as we are not always self-interested in our action. We do not have a duty to provide a dish of ice cream for anyone who happens to have a yen for ice cream, for example; we do not act contrary to duty if we give our own private ends priority over this end. The duty to promote others' welfare along with our own *does* require us to perform specific actions, however, if not performing them would deprive others of the conditions of personhood itself. If I can rescue someone from a burning house without sacrificing my own life in the process, for example—say, by calling the fire department— then my not acting to do so is itself an action, and it is contrary to my duty. The other has a moral right against me to be saved from the burning house. My act of not acting treats him or her not as a person but as a mere thing whose welfare does not count against my own.

This, then, is the reason why we have moral duties, when we are able and in a position to do so, to provide others who cannot do so for themselves with "the means which are necessary and suitable for the proper development of life." Since our act of not acting to provide at least the minimal material conditions "which are necessary and suitable" for developing and expressing rational self-determination— personhood—for others who cannot do so for themselves is contrary to our self-imposed moral duties, those who are in need having corresponding rights against us.

Governmental intervention is therefore justified as the mechanism by which to implement these positive rights. And those of us who are coerced to pay for anti-poverty programs, medical care, food stamps, and the like, cannot complain that we are being treated as things rather than as persons. On the contrary, we are being treated precisely as persons who have self-imposed moral duties to do so.

NOTES

1. This is a proposal to reorganize the economy into vocational groups, each of which would control the economic activities of its members. The various vocational groups would then be organized into broader groups until the economy as a whole is effectively coordinated. It was presented initially, I believe, in the encyclical *Quadragesimo Anno*.

2. *Quadragesimo Anno*, in *Seven Great Encyclicals* (Glen Rock, New Jersey: Paulist Press, 1963), paragraph 88, p. 150.

3. *Pacem in Terris*, in *Seven Great Encyclicals*, paragraphs 18 and 21, p. 293.

4. This statement needs to be qualified. Even if the market were truly competitive and had no significant coercive neighborhood effects, it would still function in violation of this right. For the market could reflect people's tastes, and, if enough people had a distaste, say, for the services of blacks or women, then the result would be—as it in fact has been and is—to deny "free initiative" to those who are affected.

5. *Pacem in Terris*, paragraph 11, p. 291.

6. *Mater et Magistra*, in *Seven Great Encyclicals*, paragraphs 73 and 74, p. 235.

7. *The American Distribution of Income* (Washington, D.C.: United States Government Printing Office, 1972), p. 1.

8. *The Zero-Sum Society* (New York: Basic Books, Inc., 1980), p. 156.

9. *Pacem in Terris*, paragraph 9, p. 291.

10. *Hegel's Logic*, tr. William Wallace (Oxford: Clarendon, 1975), p. 38.

11. *Hegel's Philosophy of Right*, tr. T. M. Knox (Oxford: Clarendon, 1962), p. 226.

12. *Gesammelte Werke*, Vol. I: *Fruhe Hauptwerke* (Stuttgart: Evangelisches Verlagswerk, 1959), p. 129.

13. *Groundwork of the Metaphysic of Morals,* tr. H. J. Paton (New York: Harper and Row, 1964), p. 70.

Discussion

Edited by: Irving Hexham

James Sadowsky: I want to point out that in my paper I did not deal with John XXIII or any of his successors. I didn't intend to go beyond the classical social doctrine of the Church. I don't think that Pius XI and Leo XIII would have written what John XXIII wrote.

When I talk about the word "right," I use it in a very strict sense. When I say that John has the right to do X, this means that no one may use physical force or the threat thereof in order to stop him. In other words, all rights are, by definition, morally enforceable. One has the right to enforce it. So if I claim that I have a right to something, that means that I may use force in order to obtain it.

It is important to assert this because people use the term "rights" in different ways. It may well be that in some usages, people have a right to superfluous food. When I deny that they do, I assert that although I may have a Christian duty to give food to the poor, if it is not a right they may use force or the threat thereof to take it from me.

Now I maintain that all rights are negative. If I am the only person in the world, then there is no way in which my rights can be violated, because there is no one else who can use force against me. (I ignore the case of animals violating my rights.) The test of whether you have a right to something is whether anybody else in the world is required to implement it. If you say, for example, "I have a right to a job," what does that entail? According to my usage, it means that somebody else must take positive action in order to provide you with employment. And if he does not, then you may use physical force to bring it about. This is a very strong meaning to the use of the term "right."

It strikes me that the positive rights my commentator discusses are all rights that cannot be implemented unless there are other people around besides myself. In other words, if I have the right to medical care, the corollary of that is that I may either directly or indirectly point a gun at this person and force him to give me that medical care. The least I can say about the claim that rights of this sort exist, is that this is unproven. In another part of this paper the Kantian postulate that no one may use anyone else as a means to an end is cited. But surely it is using somebody as a means to an end if I can force him to perform services in my behalf.

Surely it is selective slavery to do that. But this is precisely what occurs in the philosophy of positive rights. Here, other persons are used as a means.

It is argued that the market will reflect people's tastes, that if enough people have a distaste for the services of blacks or women, then the result will be to deny free initiative to those who are affected.

But this is simply not true. First of all the market does not deal directly with the people. It deals with their products. Dealing with products, one is necessarily colour blind.

Secondly, the idea that on a free market blacks would be paid less than whites, supposing that their services are identical, is again nonsense. If for example a white insists on a higher salary for performing the same services as a black, no one is going to be willing to pay the white a higher salary when he can get the same services from a black at a lower salary. What will happen is that if whites or males, whatever the group may be, hold out for a higher salary their services will remain unsold.

Walter Block: I would argue somewhat differently. Racial discrimination and prejudice certainly exists even in a *laissez-faire* market situation. But it costs money to discriminate. If one is willing to pay the price such behaviour can exist. In the long run the market will tend to eliminate racial discrimination in jobs. But in the short run, if one is willing to pay the price, the market will not necessarily destroy racial discrimination or discrimination of any other kind.

Marilyn Friedman: Your phrase was that no one in his right mind would pay whites a higher salary than blacks. The presumption there is that all participants in the market are in their right mind. You seem to be defining "right mind"as a mind which is either free of prejudice or which does not act on prejudice if it is economically disadvantageous. How many minds are "right" in that sense?

Secondly, I wondered how important the word "arbitrarily" was in one sentence: "But individual human beings have the moral right to act on ends they will for themselves, without being coerced to serve ends willed arbitrarily by others." What about, "ends willed non-arbitrarily by others"?

Clark Kucheman: I mean somebody else's private purposes. Coercion for the sake of compelling somebody to perform his or her own duty is something quite different. It is subjection to another's arbitrary private purpose that violates rights.

Walter Block: I want to argue that if you say rights are positive, that we have a right to food, clothing, shelter, or whatever, you make rights dependent upon income levels of the society.

For example, when Jim Sadowsky was on his island by himself, if this island was not rich enough to satisfy his right to food, then his rights are violated. That seems to me to do an injustice to the way we use the word "rights." By stipulation, there was no one there who could have violated his rights. In this view, whether your rights are abrogated or not would depend upon what kind of island you land on. Did the caveman have a right to food, clothing and shelter of the sort that we now enjoy? Hardly.

I think it is incorrect to interpret rights in this positive sense. In the classical literature, rights were negative. We had a right not to be violated. We had a right not to be murdered, raped, or pillaged.

Here is a second distinction between rights in a positive and negative sense. Merely by an act of will, all violations of negative rights could be ended, forthwith. That is, all four and a half billion of us people could suddenly decide to stop all invasive behaviour. But even with the best will in the world, we cannot end "positive right" violations all at once. This would require great increments of income, wealth, or resources. This is just unavailable to us.

And there is a third distinction as well. Positive rights are akin to a zero or negative sum game. If I have more food or shelter at your expense, you necessarily have less. But this does not apply to negative rights. If I am not robbed, this does not mean that you will be. In a society that respects negative rights, neither of us will be victimized.

Susan Feigenbaum: Only in the presence of a perfectly competitive labour market and fairly competitive entry into producer markets will discrimination be competed away, unless it is a consumption activity of the entrepreneur.

I am a little concerned about distinguishing between the impact of the market mechanism on income distribution versus the impact of initial property rights distribution and endowments on wealth or income distribution. I would disagree that it is supply and demand that determines individuals' income and wellbeing. Instead, it's the initial distribution of endowments and redistributions of endowments. There are several places where this point is illustrated. For example, the observation that the market enriches the wealthy more than it enriches the poor might be explained by differing initial physical and human capital endowments.

Finally, with respect to government actions preventing the poor from getting poorer, we should think a little bit about the impact of policies like agricultural price controls on the income and well-being of the poor in society. There are indirect transfers occurring as a result of such types of government intervention.

Gregory Baum: The whole rights language, it seems to me, is different in different traditions. We use the word "classical" very often to indicate the one we like the best. I don't see what is classical about this. (laughter) In the Roman Catholic tradition, the whole human rights language was not developed. Instead there was a concept of material rights. For instance, the right to eat in pre-modern society meant that you could steal if you were hungry. It was not a sin. You could always take food because it was believed that God created food for everybody; not just for people who had the money to pay for it.

There are simply different intellectual and moral traditions. It is improper to adopt the word "classical" for one's own.

Richard Neuhaus: I am a little uneasy with Jim Sadowsky's rigorous enthusiasm about the possibility of market mechanisms in all areas of law. This is almost a libertarian approach. I am not sure if one might or might not call it classical.

The idea of the state as a moral actor is missing. The state in terms of democratic theory is a response to the mores or operative values of a society. It has a role in trying to respond to those needs which are recognized as being communal or collective in character.

I share the uneasiness with the movement from negative to positive rights. I wonder whether we wouldn't do better to talk about claims which we are morally obligated to acknowledge. Thus the state is one agency within this society that articulates and to a degree acts upon those moral claims which we acknowledge that others have.

We can look at human needs, recognize miseries, and demonstrate that the political democratic processes of consensus will respond to what is manifestly miserable.

Clark Kucheman assumed a response ought to be redistributive in some way or another. He said "take from the rich and give to the poor." Surely there are cases in which people are so devoid of human capital, are so incapable by virtue of manifest physical handicap, the blind, the feeble-minded, etc., that taking care of them is their moral claim which we communally acknowledge and exercise in part through the state. That is a question of redistribution.

But, if we are talking about poverty—why isn't the response, "How do we incorporate these people into a wealth-producing system of productivity?" The whole question of the intervention is not the intervention of the state versus the non-intervention of the state, but *how* does the state intervene in devising policies which actually empower people to become productive, wealth-producing members of society.

Clark Kucheman: I agree. Somebody has to have a duty if somebody else is to have a right.

What I tried to do in the paper was to argue that people have duties to provide some help for other people who cannot provide it for themselves. And it is by virtue of this, that they have rights.

If people are compelled to contribute to some purpose, including anti-poverty programs that would empower people, it is still redistribution. You're still taxing people to pay for programs from which other people will benefit.

People who are coerced are not treated as mere things because they are being compelled to act on a purpose they really do set for themselves in the sense that they have a duty to do it. They may not want it, but it is their purpose nevertheless because it's their duty. That's why I keep using the word "self-imposed duty" rather than an "externally imposed duty."

Anthony Waterman: I want to develop a point raised briefly by Gregory Baum about what is and what isn't a classical doctrine. I want to talk about "rights," and I want to focus on a particular right mentioned in the paper, and most forcibly asserted in *Rerum Novarum:* the right to own private property. As I understand *Rerum Novarum,* the entire argument turns upon whether or not a natural right exists to own property. And all that Father Sadowsky has called "classical, Roman Catholic teaching" really belongs to that tradition: the idea there is a natural and indeed an inalienable right as Leo puts it, to private property.

It has been argued since 1950 that the conception of a natural right to property is an importation into Catholic theology. It is in fact a Protestant innovation, curiously enough, and over the last 90 years it has been successively squeezed out again.

So, it might be a mistake to take *Rerum Novarum* as an example of classical Roman Catholic social teaching. It might be a horrible aberration instead.

According to de Sousberghe, the story of its writing went like this. *Rerum Novarum* was drafted by d'Azeglio who in turn was influenced by Lacordière, who in turn was influenced through the French *philosophes* by Locke. And the fact is that this doctrine of private property in *Rerum Novarum* is essentially a bowdlerized version of Locke's doctrine, a kind of strawman version of Locke that you get, for example, caricatured in C. B. MacPherson's book on *Possessive Individualism.*

If de Sousberghe was right about all this, then what has happened subsequently is both interesting and relevant. Successive encyclicals, ostensibly issued to celebrate and honour *Rerum Novarum,* have in fact successively watered down this doctrine, and the latest one, *Laborem Exercens,* actually repudiates it. (laughter)

I would like to suggest that insofar as *Rerum Novarum* is taken to be representative of Catholic social thought, it ought not to be thought "classical," in the sense of belonging to a continuing tradition going back to scholastics and the Fathers, but rather as a peculiar nineteenth century innovation resulting essentially from a cultural break in Catholicism caused by the impact of the French revolution.

P. J. Hill: With regard to the issue of discrimination, the question is not "Does discrimination occur?" but "Under what sorts of institutional arrangements is it least likely to occur?" I would agree that under the marketplace, people can discriminate and they do. They discriminate on all sorts of bases, whether or not we think them to be legitimate.

I would argue that historically, discrimination on a basis that many of us think would be illegitimate has been most likely to occur when the coercive state has been in place, because then it has the power to use its biases or the biases of the people in power in some very unfortunate ways. And so, despite the fact that discrimination can occur in the marketplace, I would suggest that it is less likely to be all pervasive and less likely to have the pernicious effects that it can have if the state does not support it.

Walter Block: Consider this analogy. "Mother nature" seems to give weak animals a blessing, a compensating advantage. The skunk has its smell, the deer has its speed, the chamelion has the ability to change colours. In much the same way, "Mother economics" also gives her less fortunate children a saving grace, a balance. And who are the unfortunate children in economics? They are the ones with poor work skills who are discriminated against—women, blacks, youth, minorities, handicapped, etc. What is the saving grace that on the marketplace such weak economic actors have, instead of the smell or the speed or the ability to change colour? It is the ability to work for lower wages than other people.

This tends to reduce any degree of discrimination that exists. The degree of economically effective prejudice is reduced in this way. It is one thing for a discriminator to favour a white over a black when he has to pay each the same amount. But suppose he has to pay the white twice as much. Then the profit motive works against discrimination. In contrast, if we insist by law that the wages have to be equal, the employer can discriminate without any cost to himself at all. This is cut-rate discrimination—discrimination on the cheap.

One of the benefits of the free market is that discrimination costs something, and the more it costs, the less likely people are to indulge themselves. However, there is one unhappy occurrence in this situation; this is the fact that government has unwisely passed legislation which diminishes the ability of the weak economic actor to work for lower pay. It is as if government were to take away the deer's speed or the chamelion's ability to change colour. It does this by mandating that wages shall be equal. For example, equal pay for equal work is something that many people in society favour. However well-intended, this certainly doesn't favour the weak economic actor, the people at the bottom of the employment hierarchy.

Minimum wage legislation is another case in point. It legally prohibits the minority person from undercutting his competition, from being able to work for a lower wage, and from getting the job. Such legislation makes it very hard for people to get on the first rungs of the employment ladder. And when they cannot obtain work, they are consigned to a life of idleness. They are not able to increase their human capital or their skills.

I would add that we don't need so-called perfectly competitive conditions to make this work. That is just a red herring. All we need is the absence of laws that interfere with the natural economic process, whereby the weak economic actor can clutch onto the realm of economics.

This is why we have unemployment rates for black teenagers in the United States at ghastly levels of 40 and 50 per cent and a similar problem besets Canadian youth as well.

Hanna Kassis: We speak of rights; natural rights; inalienable rights; we speak of moral duty; we speak of a sense of responsibility; but what bothers me is that I cannot understand what the authority is behind a person having a right; or there being a natural right. As far as I know, I don't know that I have any right by virtue of anything other than maybe the consensus of the community. This bothers me because the consensus of the community could change, or the decision of the majority of the community could also change. And what is today a right, moral responsibility or duty would become tomorrow a social crime. Consider an example from the history of the province of British Columbia. Not long ago certain things were not allowed in regard to the Chinese and East Indians but today these practices would be found in contempt of the laws of the community. In other words, what was not a right before is a right now. What is now a right to be enjoyed by the Chinese and the East Indians in this province was previously a violation of the law.

What we have here is talk about rights. But nobody is defining the authority behind these rights that makes them inalienable rights.

In the Islamic tradition a person has a right by virtue of the fact that God has said so and there is no question to be asked about it. It is not a decision of the community, the consensus of the community, the majority of the community or anybody else.

Arthur Shenfield: I'd like to ask Mr. Kucheman two questions. First, what is the extent of the duty that a man has to provide for his fellow man—food and shelter, medical services, and so on? Is the duty of an American limited to supplying those things to a fellow American? Or does he have a like duty to supply those things to a Canadian, or an Ethiopian, or an African pygmy?

If the answer is that he does have a duty to supply those things to people other than Americans, is his duty to them less than his duty to Americans, or not? If it is less, why is it less? If it is not less, then can you picture the extent of the so-called duty that you are imposing upon the Americans?

The second question is this: If it is wrong for the rich to get richer, faster than the poor, why wasn't it wrong for them to have become rich in the first place?

Clark Kucheman: Well, there are so many things here, I think one consideration is that we are an organized community of citizens in the United States, you know, with some relation to each other that we do not have to an Ethiopian, because we have no control over the Ethiopian.

Arthur Shenfield: But surely this duty is based on common humanity.

Clark Kucheman: I think there is a duty to all human beings. That's right. The question is how to carry it out.

Arthur Shenfield: Why is it thus?

Clark Kucheman: I think the duty is stronger to people who are closer to us. One time I was getting off the bus in Chicago and a wineo got off behind me and began to fall under the wheels of the bus. I think my duty to him, and his right against me, was very strong. Now there might have been hundreds of other people in the neighborhood who were falling under the wheels of buses, but I had no access to them; so I had no duty toward them in the same way that I had toward this particular person.

So, I agree. I do have a duty to Ethiopians along with other citizens of the United States. But I think the degree of strength of that duty is quite different because my relation is so distant.

Arthur Shenfield: I don't think I could do that on a scale. I would like to offer the general principle "Be persons and respect others as persons." People really operate on this basis. They know that to treat somebody else simply as a tool for their own private purposes is wrong. Because we are then treating a human being not as a person but as a mere thing.

That is how I would argue for the positive right to help others who cannot help themselves. If you do not, you treat them as if they were mere things without purposes of their own. And you can't will that as universal law.

Bob Goudzwaard: I was puzzled by a remark in Father Sadowsky's paper about capitalism. Capitalism is the only economic system that can be seen as existing without states. Father Sadowsky said that it's the only economic system that can be conceived without a state.

The background is the definition of capitalism itself. If you take the static form of a market society, perhaps in theory you can say such a thing. But capitalism, I think, has a dynamic feature. It is not only the concept of a free market, but also combined with that is a possibility of free entry and the free use of technology in the market. This has led in history to a change of the phenomenon from a lot of small enterprises competing with each other, to the introduction of mass production, oligopoly. In such a situation the government has to intervene just to uphold the possibility of competition. To some extent, the crisis of the 1930s of growing unemployment in market economies forced the government to intervene.

My question is to Father Sadowsky. Is his definition of capitalism too static? In my opinion the system itself evolves in time. It can begin as a conservative system and end as a collectivistic one.

Ellis Rivkin: I think we ought to take into account the historical overlay. We cannot ignore the historical burdens that the capitalist system had to confront in the evolution and development of the capitalist system. Capitalism began with pre-existing economic, social and political systems that were very antithetical and very obstructive to its subsequent development. So there was never a real opportunity for pure capitalism. It had to grope and deal with already existing state systems and value systems that were not particularly helpful in its development.

The result was that there are certain kinds of impediments to the free entry of individuals into the marketplace. It is very unlikely that this would have been the case had capitalism started out without a firm pre-capitalist grounding. One example of this was the development within the United States of a plantation system built on slavery which was a form of capitalism.

Now by virtue of that historical overlay, the blacks did not have an opportunity to move into a freer kind of market. But this was not because capitalism per se blocked this, it was simply this was the kind of arrangement that historically emerged out of that kind of twilight world of the older order. As a result we are dealing with a whole range of discriminations that didn't follow from the capitalist dynamic but from the fact of the historical genesis of capitalism.

Secondly, capitalism arose within systems already existing in nation states, which were pre-capitalist. When Adam Smith wrote his book, *The Wealth of Nations,* he already took that for granted. He didn't write about the wealth of humanity. The pre-existing state systems with all of their powerful interests in retaining as much of the old order as was politically possible were well known. There was also a whole series of obstructions to what would have been an optimal capitalist kind of development. This presumably would have required no nation states at all.

Since the role of government derives from the protection of its economic system against competing nation states, there was a whole pre-capitalist superimposition on free capitalism.

This lead me to another point: what would the world be like if there were simply capitalism? Secondly, what is the role of the state in the capitalist system? Is it simply a matter of building an infrastructure that guarantees free access to the market? The state as capitalist should be judged only to the degree that it intervenes to remove the blockages to free entry which exist by virtue of either pre-capitalist obstructions and limitations of the legal system, or by virtue of earlier forms of capitalism such as a planter capitalism.

Richard Neuhaus: We live in a society of many different communities, many of which are much more effectively, efficiently and likely to be able to respond to human need than is a governmental program. The government, or the state is nonetheless a necessary moral actor in making sure that these interactions are given free play.

Hanna Kassis's point is an extremely important one. He asked "by what authority?" If one believes that religion or values are at the heart of culture, politics is a function of culture and at the heart of culture is religion.

Indeed, the definition of rights, or of claims, is fickle, changeable and dangerous. But this is true of any society. And I think that is the game in which we are involved. Economics is simply one factor within what is essentially a continuing democratic process of letting cultural values reflect the beliefs of the people.

Robert Benne: I wanted to get back to what I considered to be at least the fundamental question in Jim Sadowsky's paper. Paul Tillich, in a marvelous book called *The World Situation* identified the principle of harmony as the one which drove the Enlightenment. Harmony in economic life meant the free market system. In political life it meant representative democracy. In education it meant liberal education. From the human exercise of reason it was believed a beautiful harmonious system would emerge.

Running through this paper was a very heavy dose of harmony thinking when it came to economic life. But not when it came to political life. Political life was always driven by narrow interest. But somehow a free market system would be characterized by beautiful harmony if only the state would disengage.

It seems to me that the principle of harmony assumes that humans are relatively equal in terms of power and rationale. There are two places in the paper where those assumptions are made.

One is that the length of the working day was simply the preference of people to labour instead of taking leisure. Now that assumes that the people are not in dire circumstances, driven by necessity. People driven by necessity do not make preferences like that as they are not free enough to make preferences. They are driven by necessity.

The other point is where he talked about multi-nationals paying as high a wage as they possibly can in underdeveloped countries. But this ignores the huge imbalances of power by which, sometimes at least, monopoly situations can be made in which people genuinely can be exploited economically.

Meir Tamari: I think there is a danger of using the market mechanism as a social and political philosophy, rather than as a technical, economic term. We seem to forget that the market mechanism is simply a method of organizing the supply of economic goods. It is not a value structure and it is not equivalent to a value judgement. Society in every generation has its own value structures derived from religion or lack of religion. That affects everything, including the economic situation. Because of that, it is simply not true that this mechanism of production and distribution is able to solve something which society doesn't want solved.

For instance, I don't think we could prove that child labour in the eighteenth and nineteenth centuries, which made admirable economic sense, would ever have been done away with economically. But society decided it didn't want this practice to continue.

I am not so sure that the example of South Africa is a proof that economic factors will lead to a change in the wage structure. I don't know how to isolate the pressure which is being brought to bear on South Africa to change its wage structure. I am not able to differentiate the internal and external pressures which cause those wages to change.

We assume that economic systems are simply a method to satisfy the need to eat, or to drink, or to be clothed. In doing so I think we have been ignoring very important findings of modern managerial analyses which show that people in corporations do things which are not aimed simply at increasing profitability.

People's need to increase economic goods seems to be a mental and a moral need, not just a physical need. Therefore this cannot be solved simply by the market mechanism. The question of nepotism introduces all sorts of decisions into the company which have nothing to do with making or losing money. The fact is that the market mechanism may be the most efficient way of organizing the market. But there are many other human factors involved. These are controlled by society, religion, or culture.

Inefficient people do exist in the world as do people who are incapable. They might be thought not to have a place in the economic structure. But society is obligated to look after them. Therefore religion leads to a distortion of the market mechanism in order to cater to those people.

James Sadowsky: First of all an historical point to Dr. Waterman's thesis.

It is interesting, but surely the idea of private property as a natural right pre-exists Locke and is found in the "De Legibus" of Francis Suarez. It's practically the same teaching, and evidently not original with Suarez either. He's passing on something that he himself perceives. The doctrine is not quite so new as Waterman would have us believe.

Secondly, I think a lot of people have the wrong idea about Adam Smith. Smith did not say that firms *had* to be very small, only that they be free to compete at whatever size they were. In my paper, I answered all of these objections, and I did so beautifully and eloquently. (laughter)

Now about redistribution. First of all I don't think you can derive coercive redistributionism out of Kantian thinking. It may be wrong not to help a person but I don't see how I am violating the Kantian norm by refraining. If it is wrong for me to force somebody to distribute his wealth, then how can I give to the state an authority which I do not have?

Finally, most of what creates the need for all this redistribution is the problem of unemployment. You can't deal with the problem of unemployment unless you are willing to face up to the question of excessive wage rates. Once you get rid of the institutional pressures— imposed by government—that bring about excessive wage rates, you will have gone very far in eliminating at least involuntary unemployment, and the necessity for most welfare.

Chapter 2

Recent Roman Catholic Social Teaching: A
Shift to the Left

Gregory Baum

The historical fact on my mind as I write this paper is the growing unemployment in Canada and its grave social and personal consequences. As a Catholic I have a special affinity with the Catholics of Latin America who, like Bishop Romero of El Salvador, have declared themselves in solidarity with the oppressed; I also have a special sympathy for the struggling and now partially defeated proletariat of Poland.

In this paper I wish to render an account of the shift to the left that has taken place in the social teaching of the Roman Catholic Church. In my opinion the year 1971 is a turning point. As early as the 1960s the Popes John XXIII and Paul VI became increasingly aware of the problems and aspirations of the peoples of the Third World. In the encyclical *Populorum Progressio* (1968) we are told that transnational corporations have become so large and so powerful that their impact on the economy of nations is often greater than that of the legitimate government. While in the past Catholic social teaching warned people against the excessive power of the state (and offered this as one reason for opposing socialism) *Populorum Progressio* reveals greater fear of the excessive power of the transnationals and hence regards the power of governments as an important counterweight.[1] Then, in 1971, two Roman documents registered a clear shift of perspective.

Turning point 1971

In a letter entitled *Octogesima Adveniens*, addressed to Cardinal Maurice Roy, Archbishop of Quebec, at the time President of the Pontifical Commission on Justice and Peace, Pope Paul VI offered new reflections on the demands of justice in the contemporary world. In this connection he recognized that many Catholics had become socialists (para. 32). They have done so, the Pope explained, out of fidelity to Christian values and from the conviction that this is the movement of history. What was the Pope's reaction to this? He removed the ecclesiastical taboo from socialism. We recall that Pope Pius XI, in the 1931 encyclical, *Quadragesimo Anno*, written at the height of the depression, while severely critical of monopoly capitalism, had explicitly and uncompromisingly condemned socialism in its revolutionary and democratic forms. One could not be a sincere Catholic and an authentic socialist at the same time. This condemnation of socialism profoundly influenced the social orientation of the Catholic hierarchy and the political consciousness of the Catholic People.[2] In the early 1960s Pope John XXIII admitted that historical movements undergo transformations and that socialism could therefore change its nature and become a suitable partner for dialogue and eventual cooperation. This remained vague. It was only in 1971 that the ecclesiastical censure was removed from socialism. Pope Paul VI argued that there are many kinds of socialism. Catholics must adopt a nuanced position. The Pope warned Catholics against those versions of socialism that are wedded to a total philosophy. Socialism that is doctrinaire and seeks ideological purity cannot be reconciled with Christian faith. The Christian receives the total picture from divine revelation, not from a secular philosophy. But forms of socialism that remain ideologically pluralistic may well be acceptable to Christians. What Paul VI had in mind, the reader gathers from the text, was the emergence of new forms of socialism in Africa and other parts of the Third World, in which Catholics had become actively involved. What Catholics must do in these movements is to protect their pluralism and their openness.

Social sin

In the same letter, *Octogesima Adveniens*, Paul VI offers a new perspective on Marxism. He argues that Marxism refers to several distinct phenomena (para. 32). It is useful to distinguish between Marxism as a secular philosophy, Marxism as a form of political organization, and Marxism as a sociological approach. As secular philosophy Marxism must be rejected. Ecclesiastical documents of the past have made this point many times. What is meant by Marxism as political organization? From the letter it appears that the Pope had in mind the political structure of Soviet bloc Marxist-Leninism. Christians must repudiate this Marxism because of its totalitarian and oppressive character. However, Marxism understood as a form of social analysis, as a sociology of oppression, may well be useful for Christians committed to social justice. The letter warns the reader that a Marxist analysis of society may be one-sided and reductionist. This happens whenever the economic infrastructure is regarded as the one historical factor that accounts for society as a whole, including its culture. But if a class analysis of society is done carefully, free of ideological commitment, then it may be of great use for Christians. This positive evaluation of Marxist analysis has been picked up by several national hierarchies in their pastoral letters, among them the Canadian bishops.[3]

In the same year 1971 the Synod of Bishops held in Rome published a document entitled *Justice in the World,* which gave expression to a remarkable doctrinal development. The document recognized the reality of "social sin" (paras. 2–5). Over the centuries Christian theology has tended to understand sin largely in personal terms. Individuals sin. They violate the divine commandment, they turn against God's will. In the Scriptures, however, we also find the notion of social sin: the people of Israel called by God to constitute a just society were accused of sin whenever they reconciled themselves to the oppression of the poor and unprotected. In recent decades, Christian theologians have tried to recover the social dimension of sin. Structures are called sinful when they are the causes of oppression and dehumanization. Large-scale unemployment is a social sin. Colonial domination is a social sin. And because *Justice in the World* accepts this wider notion of sin it is obliged also to expand its understanding of Christian redemption. If Jesus is the one sent by God to save us from sin, then this includes the personal and the social dimension of sin. What follows from this is that salvation too has a social dimension. *Justice in the World* explicitly affirms that the redemption which Jesus Christ has brought includes the liberation of people from the oppressive conditions of their lives (para. 6). This is a new position in Catholic teaching. A theological movement that took place especially in Third World countries has here influenced the Church's official teaching. The Good News has a socio-political thrust. Jesus Christ promises victory over sin and death and this includes the liberation of people from oppressive structures. *Justice in the World* insists that the preaching of the Good News from the pulpit includes as an integral part the public demand for social justice (para. 6). In its missionary activity the Church in a single affirmation proclaims the Gospel and defends human rights and economic justice.

The reason why I regard the year 1971 as a turning point is that a significant shift in the Church's social teaching is accompanied by a parallel and related shift in its properly theological teaching. The Church's social teaching here assumes a new location in the communication and assimilation of the Christian Gospel. It has moved to the centre of attention. The link between Christian faith and social justice has been extraordinarily tightened. Christian self-understanding has undergone an important transformation. To be a Christian today means to be a critic of society in the name of social justice.

I have suggested that the shift in Vatican teaching has occurred because of the influence exerted by the churches in the Third World. If I had the space I would analyze the social teaching of the important Latin American Bishops' Conference held at Medellin, Columbia, (1968), in which the liberationist perspective was adopted for the first time in an ecclesiastical document. Since 1971 various national hierarchies in the Roman Catholic Church have taken the social justice mission seriously and published pastoral directives that manifest the same shift to the left. Allow me to offer a brief analysis of some of the Labour Day Messages sent by the Canadian Catholic bishops in the 1970s.[4]

Canadian Labour Day Messages

In the 1976 message entitled "From Words to Action," the Canadian bishops argue that the present economic system fails to serve the great majority of people. Why? Because capitalism widens the gap between the rich and the poor, especially between rich and poor countries, and it allows the control of resources and production to slip into the hands of an ever-shrinking economic elite (para. 3). The bishops ask for "a New Economic Order." The vocabulary, we note, is here taken from the debates at the United Nations. The bishops explain to Catholics that Christian faith today demands social justice. But what can the Christian community do about this? The pastoral statement outlines several steps that Christians should take (para. 9). The first one is of a spiritual nature. The bishops ask that Catholics reread the Scriptures to hear in it God's call to social justice. Even familiar biblical and liturgical texts often reveal new meaning when they are read with new questions in mind. Once we permit ourselves to be touched by poverty and oppression in society we read the Scriptures in a new light and hear almost·on every page God's call for social justice. Secondly, the bishops ask that Catholics listen to the voice of the victims of society. If we talk only to people of our own kind we cannot come to profound self-knowledge. The cultural mainstream tries to hide from people the sin and destruction operative in society. Only as we listen to the victims of society do we find out the truth about ourselves. The native peoples, the unemployed, women, those who live in disadvantaged regions, the non-white population, and so forth—all have a message that enables us to recognize the truth about ourselves as Canadian society. Fourthly, the bishops ask that Catholics analyze the historical causes of oppression in society. In one way or another, the various forms of victimhood are related to the economic system which excludes certain sectors of the population from the wealth of society. The bishops themselves often engage in this kind of economic analysis. In one of their letters they argue that in order to understand the causes of oppression in our society a "Marxist analysis," if utilized in a nuanced fashion, can be very useful. Finally, the Labor Day statement urges Catholics to become politically active to overcome these causes of oppression in society.

What do the Canadian bishops mean when they recommend that people engage in the transformation of society? They reply to this question in the 1977 Labour Day statement, "A Society to be Transformed." Christians committed to social justice, they write, involve themselves in Canadian society in three ways (para. 18). Some, thinking that capitalism can be reformed, involve themselves in political organizations that seek to make the present economic system more just. Others, no longer believing that capitalism can respond to today's needs, involve themselves in socialist projects. The bishops do not specify what precisely they have in mind. Are they thinking of the left wing of the New Democratic Party? Are they thinking of various socialist organizations in Quebec? Finally, there are Christians who engage themselves in the construction of a society beyond capitalism and socialism. What do the bishops have in mind here? They are thinking of several movements in Canada inspired by the vision of a cooperative, self-governing society which offers an alternative to capitalism and socialism. The cooperative movement and movements for workers' joint ownership of the industries point in this direction. The Catholic Church in Quebec has supported a number of such ventures. The ecological movement with its stress on self-limitation also turns away from the growth-orientation associated with both capitalism and socialism. The peace movement, the anti-nuclear movement, the search for a new "life-style," and the quest for greater participation in various levels of the social order all point to a new vision of society.

In "From Words to Action" the Canadian bishops clearly recognize that only a minority of Catholics follow this new understanding of the Christian message (para. 7). They regard this as a significant minority for it summons the entire Church to greater fidelity. The bishops admit that this minority is often criticized within the Catholic community, especially by its more powerful and affluent members, and in this situation they regard it as their duty to defend and encourage this small group (para. 10). The great majority of Catholics receives their understanding of society not from church teaching but from the cultural mainstream. In Canadian society the shift to the left of official church teaching only affects a relatively small number.

International Aspects

Let me give another example of the shift to the left in the social teaching of the Canadian bishops. In a recent pastoral letter, "On Unemployment," (1980), the bishops engage in a critical analysis of the structure of capital in Canada. They argue that large-scale unemployment is the source of so much misery that the Church cannot be silent about it. What is the cause of present-day unemployment? Some people wrongly blame the victims for the present situation. They say that the workers are at fault because they do not want to work or because they ask for too high wages. Other people say it is the fault of the immigrants who are taking away the jobs; others again blame women who have joined the labour force and seek employment. The bishops regard these false explanations as dangerous because they easily create or encourage prejudice against certain groups of people.

If we want to understand the cause of unemployment we must examine the structure of capital. In a few paragraphs the pastoral letter outlines five characteristics of capital in this country. First, the letter mentions the concentration of capital in ever larger corporations, which gives them enormous power, often power greater than that of the elected government. This concentration also tends to divide countries and even continents into industrial centres and dependent hinterlands thus leading to patterns of regional disparity and marginalization. Secondly, the letter mentions the internationalization of capital. The transnational corporations are able to move units of production away from Canada to parts of the world where labour is as yet unorganized and therefore cheap and unprotected. They are also able to move capital investment from Canada to countries where they anticipate greater profit. In this manner they undermine the industrial development of Canada and eliminate vast numbers of jobs. The letter then speaks of the foreign ownership of many Canadian industries. When the head office of a corporation is outside the country it is unlikely that its planning of production and employment will be made with the good of Canadian society in mind. The letter then points to the colonial structure of production in Canada. Colonies are looked upon by the mother country as suppliers of natural resources, but they are not allowed to develop their secondary industries. This industrial pattern, inherited from the colonial period, has not been overcome in Canada. Secondary production remains undeveloped. We do not produce the goods we need, we have to import a large percentage of them, and therefore the satisfaction of the people's needs does not generate Canadian jobs. Finally the letter points out that new industries are often based on such capital-intensive technology that they do not need a great number of workers. New industries are planned not to serve the community but to maximize efficiency and production. While the pastoral letter treats these matters very briefly, it clearly tells the Catholic people that the analysis of capital in Canada is the first, indispensable step toward gaining an understanding of poverty, discrimination and marginalization in this country.

Faith and justice

An interesting document to illustrate the shift to the left that has taken place in the Canadian Catholic Church is the handbook, entitled *Witness to Justice*, produced by the Bishops' Commission for Social Affairs (Ottawa, 1979), which offers to schools, parishes, youth organizations, study clubs, labour groups and farmers' associations a set of working instruments to help them analyze Canadian society from a social-justice point of view. Part I is entitled "Faith and Justice." The chapters explain the shift in the understanding of the biblical message. Christ's preaching of God's coming kingdom has again become important in the Church. Each chapter refers to biblical texts, the Church's official teaching, and appropriate books and articles on the topic. Part II is called "Justice in Canada." Here the chapters deal with such topics as the economic order, continuing poverty, industrial exploitation, regional disparity, northern development, and minority discrimination. Again each chapter offers a bibliography drawn from church publications and secular political science literature. Part III is entitled "Justice in the Third World." Here the chapters deal with underdevelopment, the global economy, self-reliant development, foreign aid, international trade, world hunger, human rights and military armament. Again each chapter refers to church statements and secular literature. The entire handbook stresses what it calls "the Canadian paradox." What is this paradox? "In the *first* place, Canada is a relatively affluent, developed country enjoying the wealth and comforts of modern industrialized society. Yet it is also clear that Canada suffers under economic, social and cultural injustices that characterize the underdeveloped countries of the Third World. In the *second* place, Canada occupies within the global economy a position similar to that of some Third World countries and therefore shares similar economic and political problems. Yet Canadian governments and corporations also participate along with other industrialized states in the exploitation of certain Third World countries."

It is perhaps worth mentioning in this context that the Canadian bishops, along with other Canadian church leaders, have been sympathetic to the revolutionary movements in Latin America which enjoy a strong Catholic participation. According to church teaching, revolutionary movements are legitimate "where there is manifest, long-standing tyranny which would do great damage to fundamental personal rights and dangerous harm to the common good of the country" (Paul VI, *Populorum Progressio,* para. 31). The Canadian bishops have dared to differ in their interpretation of these events, especially in Nicaragua and El Salvador, from the American and Canadian governments. Thanks to the Catholic participation in these revolutionary struggles, the bishops of the U.S.A. and Canada do not depend on the reports made available through newspapers and government sources; they have their own sources of information. What the American and Canadian bishops fear is that increasing American intervention and repression create the need for greater unity and control in the revolutionary movements, undermine their ideological pluralism and respect for Christian values, and encourage the more ideologically committed Marxists to exercise unchallenged leadership. It is both tragic and ironic that the government of the United States adopts policies out of fear of communism which weaken the pluralism of revolutionary movements and thus encourage communism in Third World countries.

John Paul II's Encyclical on labour

After these remarks on the social approach of the Canadian bishops, let me return again to the social teaching at the centre of the Roman Catholic Church, in particular to Pope John Paul II's recent encyclical *Laborem Exercens* (1981).[5] The encyclical argues that the principal cause of the present world crisis and the multiple forms of oppression is the conflict between capital and labour (para. 11). According to the Pope's analysis, labour movements and progressive governments in Western society in the twentieth century had tamed the original liberal, *laissez-faire* capitalism and produced a moderate form of capitalism, "neo-capitalism" in the terms of the encyclical (para. 8), in which capital was no longer independent but made to serve, at least to a certain degree, the needs of workers and society as a whole. Recent developments, the Pope argues, have changed the structure of capital, undermined the relative advantages of neo-capitalism, and produced an economic order that causes world-wide poverty, oppression and misery (para. 8). Capital has again assumed priority over labour. According to the encyclical, this is true also in the communist countries. There capital in the hands of the state bureaucracy is used not to serve the working people but to promote the government's political purposes (para. 11). The important principle of economics which the encyclical lays down is "the priority of labour over capital" (para. 12).

What does this principle mean? The priority of labour over capital means that capital must be made to serve labour, that is to say serve the workers in the industry, serve the extension and development of the industry, and finally serve the whole of labouring society. The encyclical argues that in contemporary society because of the inter-connectedness of the industries and the various public services, including schools and administration, the whole of society is involved in production. The encyclical argues that crises in the economic system and in particular the present crisis, is due to the violation of labour's priority over capital. Pope John Paul insists that the nationalization of industries, though sometimes necessary, is no guarantee in and by itself that capital will be made to serve labour. For it is possible that the government bureaucracy runs the industries not to serve the workers but to maximize its power (paras. 11, 14). The Pope from Poland knows what he is talking about. Whenever an economic system, he argues, violates the priority of labour then, by whatever name it may wish to be known, it is a form of capitalism (para. 7). In other words, the collectivist system of the Soviet bloc countries is, in the eyes of Pope John Paul, not socialism but a form of state capitalism.

How does this position differ from Marxism? In Marxism, the encyclical argues, the principal question is the *ownership* of capital while what actually counts is the *use* of capital (para. 14). The private ownership of the means of production is quite acceptable as is the public ownership of these means—under the one condition that capital is used to serve labour. "The only legitimate title to the possession of capital—whether in the form of private ownership or in the form of public or collective ownership—is that it serve labour" (para. 14). The Christian tradition, we are told, has always defended the right to private property. At the same time, the Christian tradition has not regarded this right as an absolute. "The right to private property is subordinated to the right to common use, to the fact that goods are meant for everyone" (para. 14).

How can society achieve and protect the priority of labour over capital? Nationalization, as we have seen, offers no such guarantee. The only assurance society can have, the encyclical argues, is that the workers themselves become co-owners and co-policy-makers of the industries (para. 14). Pope John Paul II strongly advocates the democratization of the work place. He encourages all efforts and all experiments in this direction, in Western as well as in Eastern societies. Only when the workers themselves become the co-owners of the giant workbench at which they labour will society be able to establish the priority of labour over capital.

After offering this principle of de-centralization, the democratization of the work place, the encyclical presents a counter-principle of centralization, namely the central planning of the economy (para. 18). Pope John Paul argues that because of modern technological developments not only the industries are involved in production but society as a whole. Society provides public services, trains people for industrial labour, and creates the conditions that make industrial production possible. And since production must serve the whole of society, the economy must be planned. The encyclical insists that this planning be done not simply by government—the Pope from Poland knows the dangers of this—but by an agency that involves the government as well as representatives from various regions, trades and industries (para. 14). Out of the creative tension between the de-centralizing and centralizing principles will emerge a society that is rationally planned while at the same time allowing freedom for groups and individuals to exercise their initiative and assume their responsibility.

Laborem Exercens **in relation to traditional doctrine**

How does the social teaching of Pope John Paul II differ from the traditional corporatism advocated by previous popes, in particular by Pius XI in his 1931 *Quadragesimo Anno?* The theory of corporatism envisaged that all classes, especially labourer and capitalist, subordinate themselves to the norms of justice that served the common good of society. The reconstruction of society was here largely a spiritual task: workers and capitalists were asked to recognize a set of values that demanded universal allegiance. For Pope John Paul II the entry into justice is a much more combative affair. He tells us that the dynamic principle of contemporary society is the worker's movement struggling for social justice, i.e., struggling to gain control over the use of capital (paras. 8, 20). While the workers' struggle as such is not *against* the ruling class but *for* social justice (this is an echo of corporatist theory), in actual fact as soon as those who control capital are unwilling to concede justice, the workers' movement must turn against this decision-making class (para. 8). In this struggle the rest of the citizens are not neutral observers. Pope John Paul preaches solidarity *of* the workers and solidarity *with* the workers. Those who love justice must be on their side. This call for solidarity bursts the corporatist framework. Pope John Paul II even applies his social theory to the Third World. In Third World countries the poor are not workers, they are on the whole excluded from production, but even there the overcoming of oppression will only be possible through the solidarity *of* the poor struggling, accompanied by solidarity *with* the poor by all those who love justice, including the Church itself (para. 8). The key for the understanding of *Laborem Exercens* is the Pope's own identification with the Polish union movement, *Solidarity*, which in 1981 appeared as a powerful instrument for the transformation of Polish society.

Allow me at this point to give a precise definition of a term I have used throughout this paper. When I speak of the "shift to the left" in Catholic social teaching I mean the introduction of new arguments critical of contemporary capitalism, the new recognition of socialism as a Catholic option, the doctrinal link established between Christian faith and human emancipation, and the declaration of the Church's solidarity with the struggling poor. One should mention incidentally that this shift to the left in the Church's teaching does not mean that Popes and bishops necessarily act in accordance with these principles.

Laborem Exercens is a truly startling document. It presents us with a socialist vision of society, but one that is decidedly non-Marxist, i.e., at odds with official Marxism. As soon as one speaks of Marxism it is important to distinguish between official Marxism, i.e., the ideology of the Soviet bloc countries and the communist parties, and various forms of revisionist Marxism or neo-Marxism which differ considerably from Marxist orthodoxy and often claim to be in keeping with the original social thought of Marx himself. I wish to indicate five points according to which the social teaching of *Laborem Exercens* differs from official Marxism.

Laborem Exercens **in relation to Marxism**

First, for Pope John Paul II, the struggle for justice and the control of capital in which the workers are engaged and which all those who love justice must join in solidarity is both material and spiritual. It is grounded in the self-interest of the oppressed as well as in the commitment to justice, freedom, solidarity and universal concern. The struggle has a moral character, it embodies a spiritual dimension. It is a sign of God's presence in history. God as the Gracious Presence in history enlightens and empowers people to transform the world in accordance with justice. In Marxism, the dynamic that moves history forward is not the hidden God but a law that can be grasped scientifically and that expresses itself in *necessary* class conflict until the final resolution in a classless society.

Secondly, the encyclical is willing to speak of the socialization of capital only if people remain freely and responsibly involved in the shaping of society and contribute to the building of their world. One can speak of socialism only if the "subject" character of society is guaranteed (para. 15). If people cease to be subjects of their society, they become objects in the social process and are prevented from realizing themselves as human beings. This vision is at odds with what is sometimes called a "zoo" understanding of socialism, that is to say a social system where a group of people at the top provide for the material and cultural needs of the masses. For the encyclical, even a planned economy must protect the "subject" character of society. This differs considerably from official Marxism, even though Marx's original social theory was very much concerned with the "subject" character of human being and favoured a social revolution that would allow people to become subjects of their own history. But since for Marx the subjectivity of man was not grounded in a metaphysical principle, it quickly gave way under the influence of the objective, technical and scientific aspect of his own theory.

The third difference we already mentioned. For Pope John Paul II the "ownership-question" is not crucial for justice in society as it was for Marx; but rather the "use-question," that is to say the use of capital in the service of labour and the labouring society.

Fourthly, a radical difference exists between papal social teaching and the official Marxism in regard to the emphasis on de-centralization, the democratization of the work place, the responsible role of workers in the running of the industries and the function of labour unions in the transformation of society. In 1981 Pope John Paul II identified himself with the position of the *Solidarity* union in Poland. There is a radical difference between the totalitarianism of Russian-style communism and the stress of *Laborem Exercens* on de-centralization, pluralism, and workers' participation.

Fifthly, the very word "labour" refers to different realities in Marxism and in papal teaching. For Marx and Marxism the word usually refers to industrial labour. Marx had the idea that because of the development of industrial technology the vast majority of people would eventually become engaged in industrial production. He did not foresee the emergence of the white-collar workers. In Marxism industrial labour is regarded as "productive," while the labour of the service industries and of clerical and scientific tasks is regarded as "unproductive," as living off the wealth produced by industrial labour. *Laborem Exercens* rejects the distinction between productive and unproductive labour. It argues instead that society is produced and reproduced by the labour of people in every field and on all levels, including industrial, agricultural, clerical, governmental, administrative, scientific and intellectual workers. There is, for the Pope, no room for a leisure class in society.

After this relatively brief account of the shift to the left on the part of the Church's official teaching, we turn to a number of important questions raised by this recent ecclesiastical development. We must ask, first of all, how this rather surprising development can be explained sociologically.

Reasons for the ecclesiastical evolution

A number of authors hostile to the recent development have tried to account for the shift to the left in terms of influence exerted by dissatisfied and power-hungry intellectual church workers, hired by the bishops to engage in the Church's social ministry. Edward Norman, in his *Christianity and the World Order,* follows the controversial theory of "the new class."[6] Some neo-conservative sociologists argue that teachers, social workers, intellectuals, community organizers and other social activists, (including church workers), hired by public institutions, large or small, constitute "a new class" that has become an agent of instability in society.[7] Giving in to their own restlessness and their yearning for power, they exaggerate the alienation suffered by the ordinary people, spread dissatisfaction and the spirit of revolt, undermine the cohesion and stability of the present order, and advocate socialist ideals. Conservative social thinkers have always tended to explain unrest and dissatisfaction in society through the influence of subversive agents. Thus Edmund Burke believed that the French Revolution was caused by the cultural influence of the French philosophers. This theory, however, is not very convincing. On the contrary, what seems altogether remarkable to me and in need of explanation is that in Western society which at this time is suffering from massive unemployment and reduction of welfare, ordinary people who are suffering great hardship express so little impatience for the reconstruction of society. The theory of the new class offers no explanation whatever why Catholic bishops and the Pope himself should have become more radical in their social teaching.

What historical factors do account for the shift in the Church's teaching? Perhaps the most important one is the end of the colonial age after World War II and the emergence of new peoples who claim a share of the world's resources. These developments profoundly affected the churches in the Third World. Since Latin America is largely a Catholic society, at least nominally, the developments on that continent exerted considerable influence on the Catholic Church at its centre. On a previous page, we already mentioned the 1971 Synod of Bishops and Pope Paul VI's letter, *Octogesima Adveniens*.

To understand the situation of the Church in Latin America we have to glance at the history of the Church in European society. In the nineteenth century the Church in Europe tended to identify itself with the *ancien regime*, with the aristocratic order still largely based on landed property, and therefore opposed the emergence of modern, secular, liberal, democratic society. This resistance to the modern, secular state still inspired the critical papal teaching from Leo XIII to Pius XI. Corporatist theory, promoted especially by Pius XI, was an attempt to adapt a medieval ideal to modern times. In the name of an idealized cooperative society of the past, corporatism rejected secularization, egalitarianism, and socialism as well as parliamentary democracy and *laissez-faire* capitalism. It was only during World War II that Pius XII, in his famous Christmas address of 1944, clearly affirmed modern democracy and reform capitalism as the social ideal most in keeping with Catholic values. A new Catholic social philosophy emerged, strongly influenced by Jacques Maritain, which allowed the Church to shift its allegiance to the liberal sector of society and offer its support to the Christian democratic parties, newly founded in several Catholic countries, especially in Latin America. On that continent the Catholic Church had been strongly identified with the traditional families, land-owners and military, and the conservative vision of society. Now the progressive sector of the Church, often supported by the bishops, affirmed economic progress, industrial development and neo-capitalism as advocated by the Christian democratic parties. Catholic Bishops and Catholic social thinkers saw this as a third way or middle way between *laissez-faire* capitalism and materialistic socialism. What happened in the 1960s in many Latin American countries was that some Catholics, identified with the great majority of the poor, became convinced that the neo-capitalist middle way of the Christian democratic parties offered no solution to the problems of poverty and underdevelopment. They opted for "liberation." They believed that Latin American societies must sever their link with international capitalism, and begin their own self-reliant development, rationally planned, based on their own human resources. They envisaged a socialist society. Some priests and eventually some bishops joined this (relatively) radical movement.

Still divided

The new liberationist approach proved so powerful in the Latin American Church that it influenced certain paragraphs of the pastoral conclusions published by the episcopal conferences, first at Medellin in 1968 and then at Puebla in 1979. Today, the Catholic Church in Latin America is still greatly divided. There is still a sector that is identified with "traditionalism"; there is a modernizing sector which thinks of itself as "progressive" and supports the Christian democratic parties; and there is a "radical" sector identified with the liberationist movements on the continent. This latter, backed by a considerable number of bishops and strengthened by a remarkable body of theological and spiritual literature, often referred to as "Theology of Liberation," has had an appreciable influence on the world-wide church, including the centre of the Roman Catholic magisterium. We mentioned in particular the 1971 Synod of Bishops and Pope Paul VI's *Octogesima Adveniens*. In *Laborem Exercens* Pope John Paul II also reveals his own option for the poor. "In order to achieve social justice in the various parts of the world, in various countries and in the relationships between them, there is a need for ever new movements of solidarity of the workers and with the workers. This solidarity must be present whenever it is called for by the social degrading of the subject of work, by exploitation of the workers and by the growing areas of poverty and even hunger. The

Church is firmly committed to this cause for she considers it her mission, her service, a proof of her fidelity to Christ, so that she can truly be 'the church of the poor'"(para. 8).

A second consideration to explain the Church's shift to the left is drawn from the sociology of organization. When the credibility of an organization is questioned by the public, then the officers are often willing to make decisions that reveal the fidelity of the organization to its own symbols, even if these decisions should be impractical and inefficient as far as their short-range consequences are concerned. The officers believe that by enhancing the credibility of the organization they act responsibly even though the organization will profit from this only in the long run. There are times, it is argued, when the truly practical thing to do is not to be "practical" in the narrow sense.

Talcott Parsons claimed that church organizations have to be particularly concerned about "symbolic adequacy."[8] At moments of crisis in particular, they must ask themselves whether their collective life reflects the values and symbols that constitute the substance of their message. In the present secular age with grave and urgent questions pressing in upon us, the credibility of the Church has been widely questioned. The churches recognize that they must be relevant if they want to be heard. At Vatican II the Roman Catholic Church accommodated itself very considerably to modern society. To demonstrate its relevance it endorsed many liberal ideals, which it defended with appropriate theological arguments. In some instances, this led to such an identification with modern culture that the Church was in danger of losing its identity. The time had come for ecclesiastical decisions that would manifest the Church's fidelity to the life and message of Jesus Christ and thereby create an appropriate distance from the cultural mainstream.

In practice

But what does symbolic fidelity mean in practice? It could mean what it has often meant in the past, namely a renewed dedication to the sacred. The Church could define itself more clearly through liturgical worship, God-centredness, and other-worldly spirituality. In traditional society, the sacred had universal significance. Every sector of society regarded the sacred as a superior order. The sacred held society together. It affected the lives of people and groups on every level. But in modern times, thanks to the advance of secularization, the sacred is no longer universally relevant. Vast numbers of people do not refer themselves to a sacred dimension. If the Church seeks its identity and symbolic fidelity in terms of the sacred, then it easily ceases to have universal relevance, and becomes simply a religious sect with appeal to religious people. There are many Christian groups that are willing to define themselves in terms of the sacred, even if this means that they become a small remnant. Yet the Roman Church has always understood itself as bearing a message of universal significance. Hence in line with this Catholic tradition, the ecclesiastical decision-makers sought symbols of fidelity to the message of Jesus Christ that would bring out his universal significance. Inspired by an important trend in contemporary theology, church teaching focused on Jesus's own preaching of the coming of the Kingdom, on the judgement of God pronounced on an unjust and oppressive society, and on the solidarity of Jesus himself with the little ones, the excluded, the poor. By committing itself to the "social-justice" dimension of divine redemption, the Church sought to reveal its fidelity to its founder and at the same time to manifest the universality of the Gospel. Social justice touches every aspect of human society. By making it the primary concern in Western capitalist societies, the Church finds itself at odds with the preoccupation of the upper and middle classes and the mainstream of contemporary culture. The shift to the left, therefore, offers considerable organizational advantages, especially in the long run. The Church achieves greater symbolic adequacy, reveals its universal significance, and draws new boundaries that protect its identity, even though the upheaval has many negative short-range consequences, such as the alienation of the upper classes accustomed to the Church's blessing of the existing order.

The impact of the new teaching

This leads me to another question raised by this recent ecclesiastical development. What is the impact of the new social teaching on Catholics? In Canada the impact is small. On a previous page we have seen that the Canadian bishops themselves recognize that only a minority of Catholics follow this new way of "Social Justice," even though they praise this minority as significant. Who makes up this minority? It would be possible to render a detailed account of the various small communities, centres of research, action teams, pastoral projects, educational workshops, and collectives publishing newspapers, brochures and information sheets—all of which are dedicated to the Church's new social orientation.[9] Some are concerned with concrete issues such as northern development or nuclear armament, others focus more generally on the critique of capitalism and the Church's new economic teaching, while others again are made up of people who suffer under oppressive conditions and who now struggle for a new deal from society. The great majority of these groups and centres are cross-denominational. Protestants and Catholics cooperate spontaneously. Despite (or because of) the manifold activities of these groups and centres, there has not emerged from them a single political thrust. This holds true for Canada and for the United States.

A question of much greater importance, however, is how the new church teaching is received in countries which experience massive ideological division. Here Catholics find themselves confronted by the choice between reformist parties supported by the middle classes, and socialist parties supported by workers and the lower classes. Catholics who opt for the socialist parties often call themselves the "Catholic Left." The question I wish to raise is how the Catholic Left reacts to the Church's new social teaching. While a question of this kind would demand careful research into the conditions of various European and Third-World countries, it can be said in general that the Catholic Left has been critical of church teaching. They say that despite the shift to the left here recorded, church teaching is still idealistic, still simply offering a beautiful theory of what ought to be, without any foundation in actual historical conditions. The fact is that in many countries Catholics must choose between middle-class reformist and popular socialist parties. A middle ground is not available. Because the Church's social teaching, while critical of capitalism and advocating socialist ideals, still condemns Marxism as a philosophy and political strategy, still opposes socialist movements that make no room for spiritual values, still warns people against mindless cooperation with Marxists, the Church—in their eyes—is still advocating a "third way" between the two choices that face them in their country. Since the terms of the social struggle are defined by an antecedent history, there is no room for a third way. To the Catholic Left the Church's social teaching, despite its "progressive" sound, expresses the refusal to endorse the existing socialist movements, and hence actually favours a policy that supports the existing capitalist order. In some parts the bishops clearly say that the new social teaching still accords with the reform program of the Christian democratic parties. In countries such as Italy and France, or in Chile prior to the rightist coup, the Catholic Left quarrelled with the Church's official teaching and defined its social vision quite independently. There are Christian socialist voices in Canada that have expressed the same reservations in regard to the social teaching of the Canadian bishops.

Liberation theology

It is useful at this point to ask how Latin American "liberation theology" is related to the new social teaching of the Church. Since liberation theology has produced a considerable body of literature, I do not have the space in this paper to make a detailed analysis. I am prepared to argue that liberation theology and the new social teaching are closely related. Both see a close link between faith and justice, both opt for solidarity with the poor and oppressed, both perceive the central conflict of society in terms of the domination of capital over labour, and both assert that the redemption Jesus Christ has brought includes emancipation from oppression.

How do the two differ? Liberation theology includes in its critical examination the Church itself. Church teaching locates the source of oppression in the present system and the worldly culture that accompanies it, and it presumes that the Church has, and has always had, the answer to the disorder in society. Liberation theology on the other hand raises the critical question whether and to what extent the Church itself has been part of the oppressive structures. Has church culture or church polity legitimated injustice in the past? Only after this extended critical phase, only after an "ideology critique" of the Catholic tradition, do liberation theologians spell out the liberating meaning of the Gospel for their times. This self-critical stance has often been criticized by Church authorities. In all honesty, however, this approach of liberation theology seems rationally consistent and evangelical.

There are other differences between liberation theology and the new social teaching I have already mentioned. Liberation theology argues that in Latin American countries, people are confronted by a choice between two historically defined realities, on the one hand the inherited elite structure, deeply tied into international capitalism, and on the other the people's struggle for a self-reliant, participatory socialism. Between these two there is no third choice. Liberation theologians understand the Church's teaching, and above all the actual involvement of the bishops and sometimes even the Pope as pleading for a third way. By doing this, liberation theologians argue, the Church, despite its progressive teaching, easily becomes the protector of the existing order. There are, of course, a good number of bishops who identify themselves with the thrust of liberation theology. There are also many public gestures by national hierarchies and by the Pope himself that have encouraged the struggle for liberation.

Occasionally church authorities have accused liberation theology of offering a reductionist interpretation of the Christian Gospel. This is not a well-founded criticism. Liberation theology is not a secular social theory that seeks to enlist religious sentiment in its support; it is in the most proper sense a Christian theology, a reflection on the meaning and power of the revelatory events recorded in the Scriptures.[10] In substance, I repeat, liberation theology and the new social teaching are closely related and intertwined.

Concluding from the above reflections I have the impression that the impact of the Church's new social teaching is quite limited. The great majority of Catholics belonging to the upper and middle classes are confused and embarrassed by the new teaching whenever it is explained to them. In Canada and the U.S.A. the minority which permits itself to be inspired by this teaching represents largely church people, that is to say people who have, or have had, a special relation to church organizations. No single political thrust has emerged from them. But even in countries where there exists a significant Catholic Left, the impact of the new social teaching is indirect. The only parts of the world where the influence of the new teaching is considerable is where the bishops themselves encourage the formation of "base communities": small cells of Catholic families united as action groups and liturgical communities. Brazil is perhaps the best example of this ecclesiastical policy. If church leaders want to promote radical social teaching then this can be effective only if they are also willing to engage themselves in constructing a new organizational base for this. The wide network of base communities then may become the social bearer of the new teaching and the core of a social movement that might give it historical reality.

Longer-run effects of the shift to the left

At the same time my evaluation of the long-range effect of the Church's shift to the left is quite different. To grasp the function the new teaching may play in the future, I must mention several historical developments taking place at this time. There can be no doubt that Western capitalist society is undergoing a crisis of considerable proportions. The emergence of new nations, formerly colonized or dependent, who demand their rightful place among the nations and access to the world's resources, and the recent discovery that the world's natural resources are limited and the ecological balance in fact gravely threatened, have produced new historical conditions. They demand that the orientation toward industrial growth, characteristic of capitalist society, must come to an end. As resources become scarcer and, more especially, as the industrialized nations experience a decline (in part because of the policies of international capital), the ruling elites try to organize society so that the main burden will lie on the shoulders of the lower classes. This will eventually create enormous social unrest. People will struggle within the democratic system they have inherited for a society that moves into slower growth in a democratic way, distributing the burden in appropriate proportion. The Western nations will soon face the political choice between domination or democracy. To respond to the conditions of the future, society will be in need of self-limiting principles, principles that only the great moral and religious traditions can provide. While for the present the individualistic religion promoted by evangelical church groups still exerts considerable influence, the time may soon come when more social forms of religion become relevant. The Church's social teaching may then come into its own.

Secondly, the brutal crushing of *Solidarity,* the Polish workers' movement, has again reminded the world of the totalitarian character of Soviet-style communism. More than that, it has brought out more than any other event the inherent contradiction in the communist system: it presents itself as a socialist society and yet it does not allow the proletariat to organize into unions and exercise responsible leadership. The Polish tragedy has ushered in a new crisis of Marxism in Western Europe. This has affected the communist parties in these countries. More than that, a great many intellectuals who until now have found valuable inspiration in Marxism have come to the realization that today Marxism, even in its revised forms, is unable to deal with many of the burning issues of contemporary society.[11] Marxism has no wisdom in regard to the ecological crisis. It has been oriented toward industrial growth as much as capitalism. Marxism has very little to say on issues of national and ethnic identity; it does not respond to the movements of liberation organized by oppressed peoples, especially the racially oppressed; it appreciates the woman's movement in a very limited way; it has almost nothing to offer to questions such as moral integrity, the meaning of life, the search for inwardness, and the promotion of family, love and fidelity, all issues of utmost importance for those struggling for a just society. In France, in particular, a great number of intellectuals have turned away from Marxism in search of a new social philosophy that could respond to the human needs created by the historical conditions of our times. Some of them have become interested in religion, the greater number have not. But the questions they ask and the values they seek have an affinity with the religious traditions.

A relevant force

Thirdly, in the last decade we have observed in many Third-World countries the emergence of social religion on a large and sometimes frightening scale. The politics of Iran have drawn the world's attention to this development. But there are many other countries in Asia and Africa where religion has emerged as a socially and politically relevant force. The observer gets the impression that these Third-World peoples seeking their own self-reliant development want to avoid the pattern of American capitalism and Russian communism: they want to create a socialist society adapted to their particular historical circumstances and grounded in their own cultural tradition. Since their cultural tradition is largely religious, they hope that the revival and reinterpretation of this religion will enable them to become a modern, partially industrialized society in an original way, avoiding the pitfalls of Western industrial society. We find movements of religious socialism among Muslims, Hindus and Buddhists. It is perhaps not so surprising that Third-World countries of Catholic tradition, in Latin America and the Philippines, also conceive their religion in social terms and seek to build socialist societies around sacred values. Again, these developments suggest that the Church's new social teaching may well achieve historical importance.

Finally, I wish to argue that universal solidarity, especially solidarity with the poor, is a value that is ultimately religious. Universal solidarity transcends the aspirations of rational or enlightened self-interest. Some may wish to argue that social peace is so important for industry and commerce, and hence for the well being of all, that it is rational and enlightened to prevent people at the bottom from becoming trouble-makers. Universal solidarity, such a person may argue, has therefore a functional value. Yet this argument is not convincing. The social philosopher Hannah Arendt once expressed her fear that the new industrial developments in Third-World countries had achieved such technological sophistication that very few labourers would be needed and a great majority of the people would have no function in the process of production and exchange. They would be strictly marginal. She feared that political forces would emerge that would try to eliminate these superfluous people. Social peace can be achieved by making the poor disappear. There seem to be no strong rational grounds why people in the developed countries, the middle class as well as workers and unemployed, should be concerned about the dispossessed of the Third World. Universal Solidarity is rational only for those who recognize something sacred in humanity. People are God's creatures. There is a transcendent element in every human life. This consideration points to the future political relevance of social religion, in this case the new social Catholicism.

In the light of these remarks it seems to me that the shift to the left in the Catholic Church's social teaching will have an important impact on civilization in the long run. It is therefore practical in the best sense. It is prophetic: it deals now with social issues that will become crucial for vast numbers in the future.

NOTES

1. *Populorum Progressio*, paras. 8, 9, 20, 33, 58, 60.

2. For a detailed account of papal teaching on socialism, see G. Baum, *Catholics and Canadian Socialism*, Toronto: Lorimer, 1980, pp. 71–92.

3. "A Society to be Transformed," Labour Day Message 1977, para. 16.

4. The Labour Day Messages of the Canadian bishops are the important sources of Catholic social teaching in Canada. In this paper I only refer to three of them, "From Words to Action" (1976), "A Society to be Transformed," (1977), and "On Unemployment," (1980). Since the present paper was written, the Canadian bishops published two pastoral letters that attracted wide attention, "Ethical Reflections of the Economic Crisis" (1983) and "Ethical Choices and Political Challenges" (1984), which moved in the same radical direction. See G. Baum and D. Cameron, *Ethics and Economics*, Toronto: Lorimer, 1984. On his visit to Canada, Pope John Paul II strongly supported the social teaching of the Canadian bishops. See Dan Donovan, *A Lasting Impact*, Ottawa: Novalis, 1985, pp. 83–105. In 1984 the Vatican published an Instruction which warned against the excesses of Latin American liberation theology and their "insufficiently critical use" of Marxism. A few months later, John Paul II, on his visit to Edmonton, Alberta, supported the Latin American bishops in their use of dependency theory. "Poor people and poor nations—poor in different ways, not only lacking food, but also deprived of freedom and other human rights—will sit in judgement on those people who take these goods away from them, amassing to themselves the imperialistic monopoly of economic and political supremacy at the expense of others."

5. Cf. G. Baum, *The Priority of Labor: Commentary on John Paul II's "Laborem Exercens,"* New York: Paulist Press, 1982.

6. For a critical review of E. Norman's *Christianity and the World Order*, (Oxford University Press, 1978) see G. Baum, "Attack on the New Social Gospel," *The Ecumenist*, 17 (Sept.—Oct., 1979) pp. 81–84.

7. Peter Steinfels, *The Neo-Conservatives*, New York: Simon & Schuster, 1979 pp. 188–213.

8. Talcott Parsons, *The Structure of Social Action*, New York: The Free Press, 1968, p. 158.

9. Cf., Tony Clarke, "Communities of Justice," *The Ecumenist*, 19 (Jan.–Feb., 1981) pp. 17–25.

10. Cf. G. Baum, "Liberation Theology and the 'Supernatural,'" *The Ecumenist*, 19 (Sept.–Oct., 1981), pp. 81–87.

11. Cf., *Les Cahiers du Socialisme*, 9 (Winter, 1982), pp. 122–142.

Comment

Robert Benne

Let me enter a caveat at the very beginning of my response. I am assuming the accuracy of Dr. Baum's account of the various Catholic documents that he discusses. I leave it to those who are far more expert than I to quarrel with his interpretation of Roman Catholic social thought. There may be such in this audience. If so, I invite them to rise to the occasion.

Assuming the above, I want to develop my response to the Catholic shift to the left and to Baum's obvious approval of this shift as well as his interpretation of its meaning.

Areas of general agreement

Initially I wish to point to areas of agreement and appreciation, but I will do so with some critical reflection which I hope will challenge Dr. Baum to further response.

First, I agree that what Baum calls the Catholic shift to the left "will have an important impact on civilization in the long run." The Roman Catholic church has enormous importance in affecting the shape of the developing world and has increasing significance in aggressively entering debate on social-political issues. I believe that the last few years have marked an important turning point in the Catholic approach to public issues in the United States. No longer is the church defensively guarding its own interest and the interest of its members (which, by the way, put it on the side of the democratic centre and left), but now has the courage and confidence to speak out and act on many issues of over-arching national and world importance. So, this "moral weight" will certainly have its effect. The "preferential option for the poor" is of world-historical importance, and, if flexibly and imaginatively applied, will work its way out in important world-wide gains for the poor. I have great appreciation for this witness. The poor are certainly with us, and it is the church's vocation to identify with them and call attention to their cause, a cause which goes beyond charity toward a fuller justice. This vocation is in line with the biblical vision of justice and thus gives the Catholic shift to the left its noteworthy moral weight.

I would go further in affirming with the paper that identification with the excluded, the poor and the struggling has generally meant support of the political left. Dr. Baum argues that the "shift to the left . . . means the declaration of the church's solidarity with the struggling poor." I believe it is historically incontestable that social and economic rights have been won by the political left, and where the winning of those rights constitutes an unfinished agenda, the left will be a viable option. Therefore, I am pleased along with Baum that "ecclesiastical censure was removed from socialism."

However, I have two issues for further discussion. One has to do with the traditions of political rights—constitutional democracy—and civil rights that have not had such a close identification with the political left. Where do these fit in the vision of the Pope, the Canadian bishops, and Gregory Baum? These traditions are often borne by the "bourgeois" elements of any society and in the long run are very important for the prospects of the poor. In fact, representative democracy may be the best lever the poor have for gaining those very economic and social rights, while yet preserving a context of political and civil liberty. Does Baum's shift to the left skip from a religious tradition that legitimated an authoritarian, semi-feudal political economy (the traditional right) to an authoritarian left, without stopping to cherish and bear forward the political values historically associated with the economic and political middle?

A second issue has more to do with the economic sphere. While I do agree that most of the social and economic rights have been won by the left, I do not agree that the left is solely or even primarily responsible for the actual well-being of the workers. The general and dramatic upswing in the income of the working classes in the Western world in the last two centuries has been brought about primarily by a productive and expanding economy. This effect, while often unintentional, is hastened by the distributive pressure of the left. But without a productive economy, often presided over by liberals and conservatives, those distributive efforts would be much less successful. Certainly the Social Democrats and the unions played an important part in winning a better life for German workers after World War II, but without the lively economy administered by that crusty old Catholic, Konrad Adenauer, the gains would have been much less, and with less liberty. U.S. workers probably experienced the sharpest upturn in their standard of living in the 1950s, when a moderate republican was in the White House.

Distinctions

Second, I affirm the very useful distinctions listed by Dr. Baum as he distinguishes the Catholic turn to the left from "official Marxism." These five points seem to represent an infusion of religiously-based human values into the mix so that the oppressions of official Marxist-Leninism are avoided, at least theoretically. One can even discern in the insistence on "the subject character of society" a commitment to democracy, to *democratic* socialism. Now, if these distinctions are taken seriously, do they not rule out affiliation with certain elements of the revolutionary left (those who do not recognize such distinctions)? I wish Baum would address this question. For later in the paper he shows his approval of those liberation movements that reject any third way. It seems to me that the "third way" may in fact represent the kind of distinctions Baum applauds earlier in the paper. Certainly there is a plurality of viewpoints in most liberation movements. Isn't it proper for the church and for Dr. Baum to insist on these distinctions? (By the way, I think it a gross error to describe the "massive ideological division" faced by Third World countries as a choice between "middle class reformist" parties and "socialist populism"). And in making those critical choices, shouldn't the church insist upon the criteria that Baum himself considers important in the Catholic turn toward the left? Don't these criteria rule out religious cooperation with some elements of the revolutionary left?

Third, I concur with Dr. Baum on the reasons for the church's turn to the left. Certainly, the church's presence and participation in countries where the poor and/or colonialized were caught up in a revolution of rising expectations was crucial in its movement from right to left, from legitimating the old order to an openness to the new. Its renewed commitment to biblical symbols of justice pressed for identification with the poor and dependent, and once it identified with them the involvement in liberation movements and theologies followed naturally. I further agree that such an evolution will be useful and profitable in the long run, if the church maintains its critical faculties. It would be terribly foolish to write off this momentous turn to machinations of a New Class. Baum must read more neo-conservative literature than I do, though, for I don't recall any effort to explain the Catholic church's preferential option for the poor as a New Class stratagem, particularly in the context of the world discussion. Neo-conservatives have generally pointed to New Class phenomena in developed countries, where the educational apparatus churns out many "critical" persons to fill the large public sector. It would seem to be a useful Marxist insight to recognize that such persons have an "interest" which may be a good target for healthy criticism.

Finally, I want to reinforce Baum's argument that "universal solidarity, especially with the poor, is a value that is ultimately religious ... and that it transcends the aspirations of rational or enlightened self-interest." Mainstream economic thinking seems so blind to such motivations that it continually ignores or misunderstands the fervour of religious and quasi-religious impulses. Its cool rationality rarely enlists the social idealism of the morally passionate, leaving the field to "radical" economic analysis that may be more morally appealing, even if poor economics.

Is socialism the ethical form of Christianity?

While it is evident that I share some of the general thrust of the paper, there are points at which I take serious exception. But before I get into those major criticisms, let me rehearse the main components of the Catholic turn to the left, as assessed by Dr. Baum. It is the removal by the church of its censure of socialism as a Christian option. It is the Pope's critical analysis of reform-capitalism and his constructive proposal of decentralized, worker co-ownership and management of the means of production. It is the Canadian bishops' seemingly Marxist analysis of Canadian economic troubles. It is the solidarity of some elements of the church with "liberation" movements around the world. It is Baum's hearty endorsement of these developments, and his wish to press further. He opts for liberation theology's application of Marx's notion of *praxis* to the church's identity and inheritance itself; he affirms the tendency of those in liberation movements in developing countries to reject any "third way" between what he calls "middle class reformist" and "popular socialist" parties. (Baum seems to discern nothing further right than the Christian Democratic parties. I'm not sure Robert D'Aubuisson is a middle-class reformist or a Christian Democrat). And finally, he is eager to adopt a third way in the developed countries, something along the lines of the Pope's proposal that goes beyond both reform capitalism and orthodox Marxism, which are both in terminal crisis.

That seems to be the full-blown form of Gregory Baum's own turn to the left. For him at this time and place, socialism is applied Christianity. The social justice mandated by the Gospel must take the form of a decentralized, participatory socialism that will emerge out of the *praxis* of workers. To paraphrase Tillich: Socialism is the ethical form of Christianity; Christian values—duly reformed by the insights of the young Marx—are the substance of socialism. There is a theonomous relation between true—religiously grounded—human values and socialism.

Now, the more particular form of the argument is quite disturbing to me for both theological and social-scientific reason. These two rubrics provide the handles upon which to fasten my major criticisms.

My *theological* reservation has to do with the near fusion of the central symbols of the Christian faith with one option in social ethics, a fusion that is detrimental both to the central symbols and to social ethics. The near fusion, already stated in one form above, can be alternatively expressed: Salvation is conterminous with liberation; liberation is the *praxis* of socialism; therefore, salvation is the *praxis* of socialism. That may be overstated, but Baum makes little effort to prevent such a tight linkage between the Gospel and a particular social ethical option.

Oppression and salvation

I agree that God's salvation, when fully wrought, will certainly include the liberation of all people from oppressive structures. Salvation, eschatologically viewed, includes all of life brought into God's lively harmony. And there are proleptic signs of that harmony now. But none presently fulfill the promise, not even our personal appropriation and response to the Gospel. Further, every effort at social, political, and economic liberation in history is shot through with the ambiguities of sin and finitude. This does not mean that Christians must not choose concrete options nor does it mean that some options are not ruled out.

But it is clearly the purpose of Dr. Baum's paper to recommend one option. By the logic of his argument he claims salvific potency for one particular political option and embodiment. "The Good News has a socio-political thrust.... To be a Christian today means to be a critic of society in the name of social justice." Formally speaking, many can agree with those statements. After reading the paper, however, it is clear what specific socio-political thrust and version of social justice Baum has in mind. Faith means *one* social ethical option. By identifying with it, one moves with and carries forward the salvific potencies of God. Outside socialist *praxis* there is no salvation. This is a re-emergence of Pelagianism which, though ethically potent, is religiously and theologically destructive; more especially in view of Baum's willingness to give up on the sacred (the religious) in favour of historical liberation (the secular).

In contrast to this view, I would like to maintain a distinction—though certainly no separation—between the central symbols of redemption and social ethical options. I would do so primarily for the sake of the Gospel itself—its substance and universality. I wish to maintain a specificity and transcendence to the Christian revelation that I believe is seriously eroded by Baum's fusion of faith and socialism. There is a domestication of the Gospel going on here in his accommodation of it to *praxis,* and its substance is being compromised.

I believe, moreover, he is limiting the Gospel to those with the right political orientation. But on the contrary, the salvific grace of God is given to all sinners, even hidebound Republicans like my father, if they only accept it in humble repentance. I'm not sure Baum can include those who do not earn God's grace by correct political beliefs and practice. Much liberation theology, in my view, falls under the same strictures.

Furthermore, I want to maintain the distinction between the central symbols of redemption and social ethical options for the sake of the freedom and dignity of the Christian laity. Has it occurred to Gregory Baum that there may be responsible, intelligent Christian people in the Christian Democratic parties of Latin America? In my view, Eduardo Frei claims as much honour and respect as a Christian politician as Baum's heroes further to the left. As the old saw has it, Christians of good will can disagree on policy questions— within limits, of course. There is and ought to be much more authentic pluralism in the Christian laity than Baum allows with his fusion of faith and socialism. Let me quote a relevant passage from the Chicago Declaration of Christian Concern, a statement by Catholic lay people:

> During the last decade especially, many priests have acted as if the primary responsibility in the Church for uprooting injustice, ending wars and defending human rights rested with them as ordained ministers. As a result they bypassed the laity to pursue social causes on their own rather than enabling lay Christians to shoulder their own responsibilities. These priests and religious have sought to impose their own agendas for the world upon the laity. Indeed, if in the past the Church has suffered from a tendency to clericalism on the right, it may now face the threat of a revived clericalism—on the left.

If Baum takes the Christian laity of Canada and the United States seriously as intelligent and mature Christians, and does not write them off as comfortable middle-class denizens of the mainstream, he will find his linkage of faith and one ethical option severely strained. The laity, even those most hungering for peace and justice, simply do not move in the political direction that he thinks they should. And for good reasons, to which I now turn.

Inadequacy of Marxian analysis

The Pope and the Canadian bishops (if they are being interpreted correctly by Dr. Baum), and Dr. Baum himself have fallen into a kind of economic fundamentalism. The economic analysis they espouse, far from being a "new argument critical of contemporary capitalism," is a rehearsal of a rather tired set of raw Marxist categories of dubious interpretative and prescriptive usefulness. Their approach reminds me of one of my philosophy instructors who taught us that all philosophies could be understood from the perspective of two categories—

optimism and pessimism. Now this was a provocative point of view, and perhaps even helpful at a very elementary level, but it had two serious deficiences. It forced highly complex and nuanced systems of thought into two simple categories that were finally not illuminative of the thinkers under discussion. It also didn't tell you much about the objects of the study—the philosophers in question. I tried this lecturer's approach in the Graduate Record Exam in philosophy when I came across questions about a philosopher I didn't know well. My answer that "he was an optimist" didn't get me many points.

I submit that the economic analysis portrayed in the paper suffers the same kind of shortcoming—it forces economic interpretation into two gross categories (capital and labour) and thereby fails to tell much about a highly complex economic reality. The economic approach of the paper reduces the many prisms of economic analysis down to two and then expects to perceive accurately a highly variegated and dynamic economic reality through those two prisms.

> The source of economic woe is capital's priority over labour.
> The solution of economic problems is labour's priority over capital.

Everyone in the paper seems to believe that capital must be made to serve labour, and that labour must gain control over capital by worker co-ownership and management of the means of production. The technical and moral problems of political economy will be overcome by this approach.

I have a serious problem in understanding what is meant by labour and capital, and further, by the elimination of other elements among the factors of production. But let's stick with "labour" and "capital." Dr. Baum himself begins to unravel the categories when he distinguishes the Pope's approach from orthodox Marxism. "*Laborem Exercens* rejects the distinction between productive and unproductive labour. It argues instead that society is produced and reproduced by the labour of people in every field and on all levels, including industrial, agricultural, clerical, service-oriented, administrative, scientific and intellectual workers." Now if one goes this far, why wouldn't one include entrepreneurs, bankers, managers in every kind of enterprise, investors, pension fund directors, speculators, etc.? All of them perform useful specialized tasks in the complex productive process. I submit that this reading of "labour" includes most of us, barring a very small leisure class and very large pensioned population. How can it be that all of us are dominated by some mysterious capital? Democracy and markets cannot be working at all if this is the case. No, this crude juxtapositioning of labour and capital may have some small use in understanding countries with a small number of people owning most of the land and productive apparatus, but it gives very little help at all in understanding developed economies. I suspect that the American and Canadian economies have so many interdependent connections and interactions that no one fully understands them, let alone is able to press the proper levers to control things. I would prefer an economic analysis with more prisms than the Pope's to understand and shape the economies we are involved in.

Who are the capitalists?

One could ask the same questions coming from the other direction: what is capital? Who owns and controls it? My reading of economics indicates that the savings of ordinary people are immensely significant in capital formation, that the giant pension funds of the workers will soon provide over half the equity capital of the economy, that an ever-higher percentage of the GNP is going to labour rather than to rent and capital, and that stock holders have really not been doing too well in recent years. And what would the Pope make of a favourite phrase of contemporary economists—"investment in human capital?"

Once these tidy categories fall, so do many of the doctrinaire assumptions rampant in the paper: that capital is becoming more concentrated; that multinational companies have complete freedom to move where and as they wish; that capital always oppresses labour and not vice-versa, or that labour does not oppress labour; that central planning is a good thing and that it is possible without a sharp dimunition in economic efficiency and human liberty, that international capital investments have predominantly adverse effects, that Canada can really be compared with an underdeveloped, Third World country; and that there are no other reasons for holding capital than to serve labour.

If all, or at least some, of these assumptions are questioned, as I believe they must be in any fair appropriation of the economic science of the day, then the analysis and prescriptions of Gregory Baum, the

Canadian bishops, and even the Pope himself dissolve into thin air. A more accurate economic analysis—with more prisms—will lead to a more flexible and less doctrinaire approach to policy. I do not wish to call into question the intentions that any of these parties hold. Nor do I question their claim to solidarity with the oppressed. But I do think their economic analysis and prescriptions are woefully inadequate. As economic science, they may have the virtue of simplicity—one of the criteria of assessment—but they do not meet the criteria of adequacy (ability to account for the data), scope (range of theory), and verifiability (testability and confirmation). If economic reality is more complex than Catholic social thought avers, then the good guys and the bad guys are hard to identify. The dialectic is blunted and policy questions become open to fair moral discourse without anyone easily grabbing the high moral ground. This is not to say that there is not a moral dimension to policy questions. There most certainly is, but those policy questions involve trade-offs that imply moral ambiguity from beginning to end.

One final reflection. Gregory Baum seems surprised that "ordinary people who are suffering great hardship express so little impatience for the reconstruction of society." He also complains that those who wish to reconstruct our societies dramatically are very few in number, when compared with those in the mainstream who have given up their moral sensitivities. I have a possible answer to these puzzles. Perhaps the number who suffer great hardship is quite small in relation to the total society, and perhaps most of them look to future improvement; perhaps the mainstream have seen many of their aspirations approximated by the current arrangements of things. Perhaps the mainstream believe the system has been satisfactory on the whole, and that it is wiser, and perhaps just as morally compelling, to reform that system as to transform it. Given that kind of assessment, I welcome the Catholic "shift to the left" as one way, among others, to stimulate that reform.

Discussion

Edited by: Irving Hexham

Gregory Baum: It was claimed that my paper confused salvation and liberation. Salvation and liberation are indeed intertwined. But since my paper was not addressed to theologians I did not intend to clarify the interrelation between the two. Moreover, in liberation theology there is a strong affirmation of divine transcendence. Neo-conservative Christians sometimes argue that the recognition of divine transcendence relativizes earlthly issues and hence demands neutrality in regard to political conflicts. Liberation theology argues against this. Since the God of the scriptures, the transcendent divine mystery, has identified Godself with the crucified and marginalized Jesus and through Him with the poor and the marginalized, Christian faith means taking sides, means solidarity with the oppressed. At the Puebla Conference (1979) the bishops named this "the preferential option for the poor."

My paper tried to summarize a great deal of historical material. I put special emphasis on Canadian developments. What is new in Christian theology, Catholic and Protestant, is that theologians acknowledge that fidelity to the Gospel demands attention to the "signs of the times." The "signs of the times" are crucial historical events without which we cannot understand the meaning of human life in that period and hence cannot grasp the message revealed in Jesus Christ. Pope John XXIII designed as "signs of the times" the colonized people unwilling to remain colonized, workers unwilling to remain objects in the work process, and women unwilling to be treated as inferiors. Pope John Paul II designated as "signs of the times" the emergence on the political plane of people and groups that for centuries have been subjugated. These historical events produce a kind of earthquake. This is the context in which the Gospel must be read.

For many Catholics the destruction of European Jewry during

World War II is a "sign of the times." The Christian church has reflected on its own contribution to anti-Jewish sentiment and anti-Jewish symbols. The churches have rethought their position, including the Catholic church. Today Christians are summoned to be friends with Jews, to co-operate with them in matters of justice and peace, and in fact to be open to religious pluralism in general.

Speaking of human rights raises many issues. You know, you can't trust Catholics when it comes to human rights (laughter). We Catholics are recent converts to civil liberties. In the nineteenth century we rejected democratic rights as an expression of liberalism. The socio-economic rights defended by socialists were closer to the Catholic tradition. Only with Pope John XXIII do we find the affirmation of civil liberties in church documents. I had the honour to be present at Vatican Council II where we wrestled for the declaration of religious liberty. In Catholic social teaching today we find the affirmation of *two* sets of human rights, the civil rights on the one hand, derived from the liberal revolutions, and the socio-economic rights, such as the right to eat, the right to work, the right to shelter, etc., derived from the ancient Christian tradition and socialist political theory. Catholic social teaching sees itself as "a third way" between free enterprise capitalism and determinist Marxism.

Let me say a word about the expression "the third way." In Latin America, this term has been used by the Christian democratic parties to designate their own social philosophy. They advocated a constrained capitalism, oriented by strong government, accompanied by a labour code that protects workers and their organizations. Yet in moments of crisis, the Christian democratic parties always defended capitalism. For this reason, Latin American Christians who have opted for liberation say that Christian Democracy is not a third way at all.

Is there Marxist influence on Catholic social teaching? This deserves a careful analysis for which there is no time here. The radical social teaching of the Canadian bishops is strongly influenced by Harold Innis, a liberal Canadian political economist who published his famous books in the 1930s. Innis introduced the distinction between metropolis and hinterland, and argued that the metropolis always profits at the expense of the hinterland. Hinterland backwardness has economic and cultural consequences. Innis himself regarded Canada as hinterland. Economic dependency translated itself into cultural dependency. Canada relied on the cultural and scientific achievements of Britain and later of the United States. Harold Innis, though devoid of Marxist influence, developed an economic analysis of Canadian history on the basis of the exploitative metropolis-hinterland relation and offered an interpretation of Canadian culture derived from economic dependency. In this analytical context the Canadian bishops were greatly impressed by "the dependency theory" they found in the ecclesiastical documents coming from Latin America. The thrust for economic and cultural liberation which we find in many regional churches within Catholicism is not derived from Marxism. It is derived from "the signs of the times" mentioned before, from the existing struggles for greater self-reliance, from the confirmation these movements received from the teaching of the Old Testament prophets and the Messianic promises of the New Testament, and from social-scientific theories, some of which were wholly independent from Marx and others worked out in dialogue with Marx.

Imad Ahmad: I would like to take off from this phrase the "third way." It's a phrase that not only Catholics use. I hear it used by Muslims. I hear it used in various Third World environments. Yet, it seems that inevitably when the third way is looked at closely, it's always a "reformed" capitalism, or "reformed" communism. In order for something to legitimately be a third way, it has to show that it is fundamentally different from capitalism or communism. If there is a third way, it has to reconcile the two sets of rights talked about: the negative and positive rights that keep coming up. In order to reconcile those rights we have to keep in mind Meir Tamari's warning that the market is a mechanism by which people can achieve their values.

It is a mistake to say that the market provides values. People have to get their values from someplace. The market is a mechanism that has to do with negative rights. Positive rights have something to do with the values that we hold.

We cannot totally separate the free market of matter from the freedom of ideas. The free marketplace of ideas is something that can only exist in the presence of material freedom.

When you deviate from the free marketplace in commerce, you subsidize bad ideas. An example that people used earlier was the idea of discrimination. When we interfere with the free market, we subsidize people who want to discriminate. If they weren't subsidized, then society wouldn't be encouraging the hiring of people based on the colour of their skin and not on their ability to perform in the workplace.

In the beginning, the group discriminated against would get a lower wage. But there are always people near the margin. Consider these employers for whom the wage paid to the majority group is a little bit too expensive. They would not simply violate their own discriminatory premises by going ahead and hiring minorities, they would also begin to change their attitudes. And by changing their attitudes, they would be attracted to what we in this room, I assume, would consider the preferable ideology: non-discrimination.

Irving Hexham: I think there is a need to be self-conscious about something that is going on here. We've gotten into a very complex situation and I am not quite sure that we're all aware of how complex it is.

Earlier Clark Kucheman referred to persons as being very important and defined a person as self-determining. Now, that definition of person might work in America. But it wouldn't make any sense in Swaziland. The Swazi would not define a person as someone who is self-determining. All sorts of things make sense to a Swazi, but certainly not that.

One might say that this applies in a precapitalist economy. But it wouldn't work in Japan either. The Japanese are very much influenced by their tradition. A Japanese person does not expect to be self-determining in order to be considered a person.

Traditions are important. There are different ways of looking at the world. And yet, capitalism exists in Japan. This is the problem. We seem to be coming at this discussion from Catholic and Protestant traditions. We have a westernized discussion based on these Christian traditions. Unfortunately, we have thrown into this discussion Judaism and Islam. Maybe Judaism comes into it. But Islam certainly is something like a monkey wrench, because it has a very different view of authority and of what a person is.

The whole discussion of rights, which to Americans makes a lot of sense, doesn't make the same amount of sense to most Canadians. Certainly from the British tradition, talk about rights does not have the same emotive appeal. It has not the same importance as it has within the American constitution.

We need to try to focus on these problems of definition, understanding, and tradition. We need to be self-conscious about the problems we are facing in the type of debate.

Arthur Shenfield: There are, at present, over four billion people in the world. A hundred years ago there were about a billion and a quarter. Two hundred years ago, there were fewer than half a billion. The increase from less than half a billion to over four billion is definitively due to the growth of capital and the development of enterprise spreading all over the world.

It is cogently arguable that what is propounded by the Latin American and Canadian bishops in Gregory Baum's paper would inevitably produce the destruction of capital and the extinction of enterprise. Hence, it would mean a sentence of slow death for two to three billion people. Who among them has even grasped that possibility? Who has even understood that this could be a result of what is being propounded?

In this regard, I ask, Why is it wrong for a country to be a hinterland? Why is being a hinterland supposed to be evidence of colonial status? Is South Dakota unfree, and a hinterland, because it doesn't have everything that Chicago or New York has? How can it be possible for all countries in the world to be metropolises?

This idea that Canada or Brazil has colonial status is a travesty. It's a misuse of language. It simply means that Canada is poorer than the United States. Brazil is poorer than Venezuela and certainly poorer than Europe. Otherwise this concept has no meaning at all.

Richard Neuhaus: I find myself in great sympathy with Bob Benne's critique. Regarding the concept of the "new class," Irving Kristol is usually considered the originator of the current use of that term. Bishops ordinarily would not be prime candidates for membership in the new class. But, I would point out that advisors to bishops like Gregory Baum (laughter) are archetypically members of the new class (more laughter).

Comment: So are you.

Richard Neuhaus: Of course. No doubt. I am a class traitor. (laughter) But to return to my point: it is one thing what bishops sign and it's another thing as to who writes what the bishops sign.

I was distressed in Baum's paper by the almost complete absence of any allusion to democratic rights or to the role of the state. In fact, the state is barely even mentioned in the manuscript. Somehow, we, society, etc., are going to do everything. But what are the instrumentalities for this? I would suggest that the absence of any discussion of democratic rights and of the limited state is not an oversight. Rather it is inherently and necessarily part of the argument that the paper makes.

I am pleased that Baum backs away from what Benne read in his paper. Paraphrasing it as he did, "salvation is coterminous with liberation; liberation is praxis of socialism; therefore salvation is praxis of socialism." Baum said that is not what he intended to say. I would only suggest that he re-read his paper. It seems to me that this is what he is saying. Those whom he endorses in what is called liberation theology certainly are saying it. I can find it in Siegundo and Gutierrez.

The phrase used in that school of thought is the "partisan church." The "partisan church" is the one engaged in the liberation struggle of the oppressed against the oppressor. This is defined as being the substance as well as the form of gospel obedience.

I am very troubled by that. I am as troubled by it as I am by the New Right in the United States. Certain facets of the religious New Right want to theologize capitalism. They want to state that capitalism as they understand it is mandated by biblical teaching and to be Christian is to be a "gung-ho" capitalist. I think this is a great mistake. It overlooks the limits of the economic. We're dealing with a technical mechanism. It is not the source of values.

I imagine Gregory Baum would respond that I am advocating sitting on the fence when I say that the church ought to include those who say that the Christian way is socialist, communist, or even *laissez-faire* capitalism. I don't think it's a question of fence-sitting. Sometimes the church has to have the nerve to speak up and deflate the importance of *all* economic theories which purport in a very pretentious and imperious way to explain every aspect of reality.

I think the church has to operate under the postulate of ignorance. If there is some question that the gospel, or the Judeo-Christian tradition, or religion generically, simply does not address very significantly or helpfully, we must have the nerve to say that we don't know. We have to have the daring to be irrelevent to many questions in order that we attend to the questions which are properly those of religion.

Religious questions concern ultimate meaning: How the world is constructed? What is the purpose and significance of history? Is there a possibility of redemption? What is the reality of sin? This is the church's greatest contribution to public ethics. It can reinforce those values which not only make possible a free market system but which are found in a free economic system according to the will of human beings, or the persons who are most immediately affected.

Stephen Tonsor: I, too, was quite disturbed by Father Baum. I served on a subcommittee of the National Conference of Catholic Bishops and I know how these papers are written.

As a Catholic, I doubt that the church has anything significant to say in these matters, even though it has something significant to say in many other areas. Whether anyone listens to the church is another matter (laughter). Secondly, I believe that there is a fundamental inadequacy of understanding of technical economics. What Gregory Baum recommends is not a shift to the left. What has happened is not a shift to the left. Any leftist would cry out in agony if he were told that current Catholic social teaching was a shift to the left. It's rather a shift to the past. It's medievalism all over again. Except it is medievalism with a "human," or at least a different face. It is a perennial Catholic pre-capitalist social theory. And it has not the remotest contact with social and economic reality as it exists at the present time.

Ronald Preston: I want to refer to the importance of the contribution of Maritain. I think the Latin Americans are too dismissive of Maritain when they talk of the third way. Maritain ended his life in great disagreement with contemporary Catholicism as found in the Third World and among many Western intellectuals. He was a disappointed man. But he made really fundamental comments about twentieth century life. He taught me to distinguish between individual and person and to see that you cannot talk about persons without persons in community. A great deal of the discussion lying behind some of the present papers does not really recognize this important distinction, which provides a resource for a critique of economic and political philosophies.

Hanna Kassis: I agree Maritain is an enormously important Catholic philosopher. He introduced into the Catholic tradition all kinds of ideas contributed by the French revolution and liberal thought. But Maritain can't be read in the narrow context of what Christian democratic parties made of him.

Walter Block: Let me address the issue of treating people as means. If you treat them as means, then certainly we can oppose this because of the initiatory violence against the slave. But if you treat them as means in another sense I think it is unobjectionable. That is the sense in which we all deal with each other in the marketplace, where we know not who we deal with. When we buy a pencil we are treating as means all the people that made that pencil. We can only treat them as means to provide a pencil for us and us to provide money for them indirectly. That's the only option because we do not know them. Treating people who we know as means is a different issue.

With regard to Meir's point that child labour stopped because of social conscience, I believe that people in the eighteenth, seventeenth or even twelfth century for that matter had every bit as much of a social conscience as we do now. The reason we don't have child labour anymore is we can now for the first time, thank God, afford not to. And this was the result of capitalism. Not government legislation, even though parliament tried to take credit for this occurrence.

There is one aspect of liberation theology with which I agree. It helps with Indian land claims. I feel very strongly about this on the basis of Locke's theory of homesteading and private property. There is a meeting of right and left here with regard to the injustice done to Indians, and blacks in the U.S. as well. Malcolm X's claim for blacks, that they should be given some parts of certain slave societies or the land that they worked, can be justified on the Lockean principle of justice and property rights titles, as in keeping with liberation theology. So I would like to make common cause with Gregory Baum on this. I justify land redistribution based on the return of stolen property. But how does he, who opposes the concept of private property, defend this policy?

Jim Sadowsky: Liberation theologians have concerned themselves with the situation in Latin America, and indict capitalism as being the responsible agent for the plight of those areas.

But South America has been one of the areas least affected by *laissez-faire* capitalism. It is a corrupt, feudalistic society which has been called capitalist and calls itself capitalist.

But, it never had the relatively free market that characterized England and the United States. And this is particularly true for the land question in those areas. The Lockean principles for acquiring ownership of land have never been observed in that part of the world. For the most part, the Europeans went in there and just stole land, or occupied the land and prevented the land from being homesteaded.

Ludwig von Mises says that you don't have a land reform problem when the land has been acquired by way of homesteading because the amount of land possessed by people tends to be optimal.

In South America people were allowed to take ownership of idle land, keep people from that land, or from cultivating the land. That goes a long way to account for the mess in which Latin America has found itself. The market was never allowed to operate in those areas. The sad thing is that ironically the free market is being blamed for the mess.

John Berthrong: Probably the largest population growth prior to the nineteenth century happened not in the Western world but in China. Best estimates of late Ming, early Ch'ing population run to between 100 and 200 million. From the mid-1700s to the mid-1800s there was a population jump of between 550 million and 650 million.

Now, how do you explain that growth with a lack of managerial expertise? Abahai, and the K'ang-hsi Emperor were certainly not interested in the market economy. They were interested, however, in something much closer to the Canadian context; order and good government. The growth of the population probably had very little to do with capitalism, Marxism, or any kind of Western economic philosophy. It had to do with an excruciatingly fine concept of government and order within a state based on the philosophy of Confucianism.

The prosperity of the West in modern times is a very tenuous thing. It rose in the nineteenth and twentieth century. Prior to about 1850 almost anyone would have been better off in the middle and upper classes of China than in any place in the world, except perhaps during the ninth century in the Muslim heartlands. So let us try to keep in focus cases that are broader than merely the European context and European arguments about rights, duties, claims and justice.

Ted Scott: The issue of the hinterland isn't just the contrast between a rural and a metropolitan issue. That's not the issue in Canada between the West and the centre, or South Dakota, or between Latin America and other parts of the world. The issue with the hinterland is where the decisions are made that affect your life.

The feeling of the people in the hinterland is that decisions which affect their lives are made elsewhere—and that they have very little input into that process of decision-making. Now very often we assign the blame to the wrong concept. I think Father Sadowsky struggled with that point about the free market, which you have in Latin America A lot of decisions are made elsewhere that affect their life, and they assign the blame of that to capitalism and the free market, rather than the process of decision-making. And I think the difference between the hinterland and the focus where decisions are made is one of the things that underlines much of the issue that we have to get at today.

Marilyn Freidman: There has been some reference to the point in Kant about not treating people as means. What Kant said is that people should not be treated as a means only. This doesn't preclude treating people as a means. In this view, people should not be violated as ends while one is treating them as a means. If you go to purchase a ticket to go into a movie theatre you are not dealing with the ticket seller in any other capacity except as an agent selling tickets. But you don't violate him or her as a person. That leaves open the question of what it is that would count as a violation of them as a person.

Irving Hexham raised the concept of self-determination as being important. We can't presume that other peoples in the world place the same value on the concept of self-determination. We have to allow for a kind of value pluralism, which allows them to enact the values which are most important to them. When we allow that, we at the same time affirm self-determination as an important rule in our own behaviour. But we are allowing them to determine their own values.

Another issue concerns the causal diagnosis of problems and ad-

vantages in society. As a philosopher I don't have evidence and data
which allow me to be at all confident about causal diagnosis. People
who are proponents of free enterprise are expressing the claim that
free enterprise markets are responsible for most of the good things in
society.

I would ask people who put forward such causal diagnoses to sustain those claims with more evidence.

P. J. Hill: I should be glad to respond. Historically it can be shown
that the market forces were serving to eliminate many of the discriminatory practices in South Africa. In response to that situation, the
government decided to impose other constraints. The market was
serving to free the economy through the 1920s, 1930s, and 1940s.
Many of the discriminatory laws that have been instituted in South
Africa have been in response to economic and social change. In effect the South African government said, "Hey look, the market is
going to remove a lot of things like racial barriers, that we don't want
to see removed."

That becomes an empirical questions. One can go back and look at
the progress of wage rates, laws, etc. In my view there is solid empirical evidence which supports the causal diagnosis.

Now for another point. In the Canadian bishops' discussion of
economics in Baum's paper there is an interesting conflict. Many of
the things suggested by the Canadian bishops to help the poor would
probably have the exact opposite effect of really harming the poor in
the rest of the world. They object to the fact that transnational corporations are able to move units of production away from Canada to
other parts of the world where labour is cheap and unprotected.

But the jobs that are leaving Canada may well be going to other
parts of the world where people's incomes are less. If so it may be a
significant way of raising their incomes. You might respond by saying, well this is just because labour is very cheap and unprotected in
those places. It might be interesting to ask workers if they would like
to be protected, because my guess is that they would not.

So I find some very real dichotomies between the supposed concern for the poor here and proposals that if implemented would probably have some very negative effects on the incomes of poor people
around the world.

Ellis Rivkin: It is important to make a very sharp distinction between the rhetoric of liberation which has so successfully exploited the whole array of injustices which came from pre-capitalist economic systems, and actual historical process by which liberation has come about.

The history of liberationist movements is absolutely abysmal. In all areas of the world where they have successfully obtained power they have destroyed even the minimum productive systems they inherited. In addition to this, they have completely eliminated any kind of opportunity for the individual to have any input into decision-making. This is highly unfortunate.

When you come to a place like South America, you have to ask: "What would be the outcome if those who speak for the political left took power?" It would mean the displacement of one group of manipulators by another group, who will practice injustice in an even more extreme way than those they replaced.

Latin America is of great geographic strategic importance. This brings in the whole question of the relationship of the super-powers to that region; and not just the Soviet Union but the two major capitalist complexes of the West; namely the U.S. and Brito-Europe.

What is bringing the United States into such bitter opposition with Europe is intra-capitalist problems stemming from the existence of pre-existing nation states.

It would seem to me that we can demonstrate: (1) that the economic base is not ready; or (2) that the entrepreneurial talent is not available to take advantage of that revolution. There is so little mention of entrepreneurial talent as a kind of ability and a kind of gift that is in very rare supply. That is one of the reasons it costs so much to be able to make use of it. In dealing with the problems of the Third World, we have to ask ourselves whether or not the injustice that already exists would become even worse; or are we to give reign to political entities who haven't the foggiest notion how to utilize the entrepreneurial spirit to create the wealth that they promised the people?

Imad Ahmad: In Latin America, land expropriation (the prevention of people from using idle land) was done in the name of or for the benefit of American or other foreign companies. Now I agree this was not *laissez-faire* capitalism. That's how capitalism gets its bad name in the Third World, because it is associated with expropriation.

Now let me address the question about whether a free market brings about good things. Good things can be divided into two kinds:

there is material prosperity and everything else. It is generally understood why the free market brings about material prosperity. But people have many grave questions about its effects in other areas. And one of the other areas we keep hearing about has to do with positive rights.

The free market brings about negative rights because that's the definition of the free market. But it can't in itself automatically generate positive rights. The answer is that you can't get positive rights by violating the negative rights of others. What you can do is have an environment in which it is possible for people to deal with positive rights.

For example, let us say that you consider it a positive value that no one should starve to death. We can't automatically guarantee this. But in a materially prosperous society, people who have satisfied what they consider to be more pressing needs now have more money that they can apply to feeding someone who is starving to death. Those positive values are the proper province of religious ethics. In other words, the market does not instill hard values except the general negative rights that we talked about. Other values have to come from somewhere else.

Gregory Baum: Over the last decades we have witnessed a turning point in the religious history of the West. The great majority of Christians in the wealthy nations, however, have hardly noticed it. They are astounded by the official messages of their bishops. Often they do not feel an inner readiness to follow the new direction. Instead they content themselves by saying that bishops know as little about economics as they know about sexuality. (laughter)

Comment: Even less. (laughter)

Gregory Baum: What is being said about the mechanism of the free market in this room worries me greatly. It is wholly at odds with the tradition of Catholic social teaching. The free market, the popes always taught, is more advantageous for the rich, the clever, and the versatile, than for ordinary people. The free market by itself does nothing for the people who are in the margin, unless those who produce goods and own land have need of workers. In Third World countries where industrialization and the mechanization of agriculture begin at a sophisticated level, the great masses of the people are not needed in the production process as presently organized. Decades ago, Hannah Arendt, the well-known non-socialist social philosopher, expressed her fear that capital-intense industries in the Third World would make the great masses redundant and eventually manoeuvre them out of existence. Recent research has confirmed these fears. In many Third World countries the gap between rich and poor is widening; the great masses are being pushed into greater starvation so that there is a constant decline of their life expectancy. Thus in parts of Brazil, the ordinary people expect to live for less than forty years.

It has been claimed that the market is value-free and for this reason can go hand in hand with any philosophy, religious or secular. But this is not true. In sociology it has been clearly established that the free market economy has a profound impact on culture. The free market philosophy and social reality makes us look at the whole of social life as a market. It teaches people to look out for themselves trusting that some social or economic mechanism will look after others and the common good. It leads people to regard everything that surrounds them as merchandise, as having a price, as an object to be used. Even other people, especially workers (those who must sell their labour power on the labour market) begin to appear as commodities, as objects, as things.

Just recently Pope John Paul II has again insisted that in capitalism workers tend to become objects, that they are treated as if they were things, while in fact, in accordance to justice, they are subjects in the process of production and hence entitled to exercise their co-responsibility. The romantic talk about the free market in this room in no way reflects this vast critical literature. There is not even an attempt to refute these arguments. The speakers simply bracket these arguments from consciousness and repeat social positions from a previous age. This is all the more ironic since the so-called free enterprise economy, lauded by neo-conservatives, relies very largely on government support, on tax privileges, on tariffs, and on regulations of various kinds.

Richard Neuhaus wonders why I have said nothing about sacraments. Roman Catholic social teaching deals with justice in the social, economic and political order. In the wider Roman Catholic teaching, and particularly in catechesis, we deal with the Good News, the Christian message and the sacramental gifts of Christ. In the more recent books on theology and religious education, there is an attempt to integrate social concern into the teaching of faith and sacraments. The Roman Catholic liturgy is trying to communicate to people a sense of community, a new awareness of collective responsibility, a passionate yearning for justice and peace, and a conversion away from social and economic structures that hurt people, marginalize them and treat them as objects.

The language of oppressor/oppressed is not without danger. But there are situations where this language must be used, for instance when we speak of Pharaoh and the children of Israel; and there are others where it may not be used, such as the conflict between the kingdoms of the North and South in the Old Testament. I regard this as a commonplace. Oppressor/oppressed language is useful when we examine the situation of the native peoples in Canada. It is useful when we study the entire phenomenon of colonialism, that is the occupation of another country by an empire with the subsequent reorientation of the local economy to serve the interests of the empire. I do not see how we can understand Third World countries, mainly former colonies, without using the language of colonizer and colonized.

Recent Roman Catholic social teaching favours the democratization of the work place and the co-responsibility of workers for the products they have made. In other words, it favours the entry of democracy into the economic order. Capitalism operates according to anti-democratic principles. Those who labour, the many, do not participate in the decisions that affect their work. The recent terminology, "democratic capitalism," disguises this simple fact. One just has to ask people working in factories and banks whether the institutions in which they work are democratic.

As a theologian and sociologist, I am unhappy about what Richard Neuhaus said because I have the conviction that I am totally within Catholic orthodoxy. That nothing was said in my paper about sacramental life, or the mystery of God empowering is not remarkable. I simply take them for granted. These are realities within the Catholic tradition and liberationist circles. God is the mystery of empowerment stirring people everywhere to become the subject of their history.

PART TWO

CHRISTIAN SOCIAL THOUGHT

Chapter 3

Christian Political Economy:

Malthus to Margaret Thatcher

A. M. C. Waterman

On March 30th, 1978, just over a year before becoming Prime Minister of the United Kingdom, the Right Honourable Margaret Thatcher delivered "A Speech on Christianity and Politics" to the congregation of St. Lawrence Jewry in the City of London. Mrs. Thatcher declared her belief that "In this life we shall never achieve the perfect society"; that "it is a Christian heresy to suppose that man is perfectible"; and that "politics is... about establishing the conditions in which men and women can best use their fleeting lives in this world to prepare themselves for the next" (1978a, pp. 7, 8, 2). She also suggested that the system built up on private enterprise and freedom of choice had "produced an immense change for the better in the lot of all our people," that we ought not to be "tempted to identify virtue with collectivism," and that the state—in a Christian society—ought to encourage private charity rather than usurp it (pp. 7, 9). Economic freedom, she claimed, was "a necessary but not a sufficient condition of... prosperity": there must also be "some body of shared beliefs, some spiritual heritage transmitted through the church, the family and the school" (p. 9). In a subsequent article Mrs. Thatcher amplified the latter point by reaffirming the traditional conservative view of a partnership between church and state, especially in education. "Our schools should be places in which Christian belief and morality are taught." She also criticized those "supporters of the conservative cause today who would describe themselves as agnostic humanists. To my mind such people are living recklessly on the dwindling spiritual capital of our Christian culture" (1978b).

It is my purpose to show that the orthodox Christian conservative position presented with such admirable candour by Mrs. Thatcher is the intellectual heir of a tradition, generally known to historians as "Christian Political Economy," which originated with the first edition of Malthus's *Essay on Population* (1798) and closed with Thomas Chalmers' *Bridgewater Treatise* (1833). The first section describes the immediate antecedents of this tradition in the latter part of the eighteenth century. The remaining three sections deal respectively with the ideological significance of Malthus's *First Essay;* the part played by J. B. Sumner, Whately, Chalmers and others in developing the tradition; and its subsequent fortunes after a series of shocks experienced by British conservatism in the 1830s and 1840s.

I. THE CIRCUMSTANCES OF MALTHUS'S FIRST ESSAY

First British reaction to the storming of the Bastille was cautious, even mildly encouraging. Just over one hundred years previously Parliament had forced the abdication of James II and installed William of Orange. Whig and Tory alike were firmly persuaded of the merits of constitutional monarchy, and many influential voices, including that of Edmund Burke, had been raised in support of the American Revolution thirteen years before. Though the Gordon riots of 1780 far surpassed in violence and disorder the worst excesses committed in Paris in 1789, though destruction of machinery by unemployed workers had begun in Manchester some ten years earlier, there was no fear of revolution at home. Educated opinion— the only opinion that mattered at that time—was progressive, even radical. Bentham, who as early as 1776 had replied to Blackstone's conservative *Commentaries* (1765) on the law of England, introduced the utilitarian approach to government in his *Introduction to the Principles of Morals and Legislation* of 1789: in which he had been anticipated by Paley (1785) five years before. The beginnings of the anti-slavery movement date from Sharp's *Representation of the Injustice of Tolerating Slavery* (1769) and Ramsay's *Essay on African Slaves* of 1784. In 1787 and again in 1789 there were bills presented for repeal of the Test and Corporations Act, and the Dissenting interest, which strongly upheld the principles supposed to inspire the French Revolution, was then at the height of its power and influence.

It was the enthusiastic, not to say injudicious support for the Jacobins by a leading dissenting luminary, Dr. Richard Price, which began the transformation of opinion. In November 1789 Price addressed the London Revolutionary Society "On the love of our Country" and provided the occasion of Burke's extended rebuttal, the famous *Reflections on the Revolution in France* (1790). Burke contrasted the events of 1789 with those of 1688, represented the former as subversive of Christian civilization, and predicted a degeneration into tyranny and war. Though Tom Paine answered Burke with cogency in the first part of *The Rights of Man* he was overtaken by events. Within two years Louis XVI was executed and France at war with Austria, Prussia and Britain. The Reign of Terror (July 1793–July 1794) convinced waverers: opinion hardened and Burke was vindicated.

In February 1793, just as support for the Revolution was turning to opposition, there appeared the first edition of William Godwin's *Political Justice* (1793). Although Godwin rejected both natural rights and written constitutions, "the twin planks of Paine's political platform" (Locke, 1980, p. 49), and was in practice a Burkean gradualist, he was perceived by his now frightened contemporaries as a dangerous revolutionary (Soloway, 1969, p. 42). Believing in the original innocence and purity of human nature, he attacked human institutions as the source of misery, confuted the three theories of the source of political authority (force, divine right, social contract) and looked to a "true euthanasia of government." In his second edition (November 1795) Godwin strengthened the argument by deducing a doctrine of human perfectibility—always the center-piece of his political thought—from a philosophical and psychological account of the omnipotence of truth (Locke, pp. 93–7). *The Enquirer*, which Godwin published in February 1797, contained a less reasoned, more popular presentation of the same themes. Among those of his doctrines to attract the hostility or derision of the reading public were his attack on the institutions of private property and marriage, his expectation of the probable extinction of "passion" between the sexes and the indefinite prolongation of human life, and his estimate that the necessary work of society could be accomplished by able-bodied men in half-an-hour per day.

Sedition and treason

As early as 1792 the more radical British supporters of the French Revolution had become objects of suspicion and harassment to the government. In 1793 the leaders of the (Dissenting and Presbyterian) British Convention in Edinburgh were charged with sedition; late in 1795 Pitt and Grenville introduced new and more stingent Treasonable Practices and Unlawful Assembly legislation; and by 1797, in the state of national trauma created by the British naval mutinees at Spithead and the Nore, there were few left among the educated and respectable to doubt the folly and wickedness of revolution, democracy and the "rights of Man." Fear of domestic insurrection was fanned by the famine conditions of 1795–96, the year in which the Speenhamland system of poor relief was first introduced. Even moderate change was resisted lest it lead to a revolutionary landslide. Grey's ill-timed campaign for parliamentary reform was finally defeated in May 1797 and his cause set back thirty-five years.

Yet the intellectual and moral superiority still seemed to lie with the radicals. Though bishops such as Prettyman (charge to the Clergy of Lincoln, 1794) maintained that Christianity is fundamentally a religion of inequality dependent upon the exercise of "compassion, gratitude and humility" (Soloway, p. 62) their arguments were easily met and their general position undermined or at least seriously threatened by Paine, Mary Wollstonecraft, James Mackintosh, Priestly, Godwin and a host of lesser figures in the radical, Dissenting, literary intelligentsia. No major apologist for the establishment had spoken since Burke. Moreover, the more liberal-minded statesmen such as Fox, and even (Whig) bishops like Watson of Llandaff, were temperamentally inclined to attend to the Dissenters, with many of whom they had formed intellectual and social links in more peaceful days. The propertied classes "demanded that the poor be reassured that the inequities of rank, wealth and power were indeed part of a grand design to maximize human happiness" (Soloway, p. 58). But the sneaking suspicion remained that Christianity might not be so accommodating. The Dissenting attorney, Nash, had thrown out the challenge in his reply to Burke: "As I am a believer in Revelation, I, of course, live in the hope of better things; a millenium (not a fifth monarchy, Sir, of enthusiasts and fanatics), but a new heaven and a new earth in which dwelleth righteousness; or, to drop the eastern figure and use a more philosophic language, a state of equal liberty and justice for all'' (Lincoln, 1938, p. 3). It was of the utmost political importance that this challenge be met.

The publication in June, 1798, of Malthus's (anonymous) *Essay on the Principle of Population, as It Affects the Future Improvement of Society, with Remarks on the Speculations of Mr Godwin, M. Condorcet, and Other Writers* afforded the long-awaited response to this ideological need. Malthus set out to show that ''a state of equal liberty and equal justice'' could not in principle be achieved; that even if it were, it would not be the apocalyptic ''new heaven and new earth,'' nor even Godwin's Rousseauvian paradise, but rather a transitory and self-reversing condition; and that, notwithstanding the Dissenters' views of ''Revelation,'' the present state of inequality and misery was consistent with the power, wisdom and goodness of God. He brought to his task a combination of Scottish Political Economy, eighteenth century Natural Religion, Lockean metaphysics as reinterpreted by Abraham Tucker, and a long tradition of population theory running from Botero (1589), through Petty, Hale, Quesnay, Wallace, Hume, Süssmilch and Adam Smith (Schumpeter, 1954, pp. 250–58). With a sure instinct for the jugular he selected as his principal target not the superficially more subversive Paine, but the philosophic and impractical Godwin. For despite the extravagance and absurdity of much of the latter's argument, Malthus saw clearly that Godwin had got to the heart of the matter with his doctrine of human perfectibility. The primary intellectual task for the Christian conservative, then as now, was to establish the truth and the relevance of Mrs. Thatcher's axiom: ''In this life we shall never achieve the perfect society.''

II. IDEOLOGICAL SIGNIFICANCE OF THE FIRST "ESSAY ON POPULATION"

The ideological content of the *First Essay* may be summarized in five propositions.

1. The ''principle of population'' constitutes ''the strongest obstacle in the way to any very great future improvement of society'' (p. iii).
2. Were the ideal society envisaged by Godwin ever to exist it ''would, from the inevitable laws of nature, and not from any original depravity of man, in a very short period degenerate into a so-

ciety, constructed upon a plan not essentially different from that which prevails in every known state at present'' (p. 207).

3. Scarcity caused by the principle of population would (or in fact does) bring into existence those very institutions—private property, marriage, wage-labour, the state—to which Godwin ascribed human misery.

4. These institutions are, on the whole, beneficial rather than harmful, in that they provide a partial remedy for the inescapable evils of scarcity.

5. The seeming evils of poverty and inequality—shown by the principle of population to be inevitable—are necessary for full intellectual and spiritual development of the human species, and are therefore consistent with the traditional attributes of God.

The argument begins with "two postulata. First, that food is necessary to the existence of man. Secondly [as against Godwin], that the passion between the sexes is necessary, and will remain nearly in its present state" (p. 11). To these Malthus adds two other empirical assumptions: "Population, when unchecked, increases in a geometrical ratio" and "Subsistence increases only in an arithmetic ratio" (p. 14). It follows that there must be (at equilibrium, at any rate) "a strong and constantly operating check on population" (ibid). So far as human populations are concerned this check is provided by "misery and vice": the former "absolutely necessary," the latter "highly probably" (p. 15). Later, Malthus specifies the checks to human population growth as "preventive" ("a foresight of the difficulties attending the rearing of a family"), and "positive" (starvation, disease, war, infanticide, etc.), all of which, however, "may be resolved into misery or vice" (pp. 62–70; chap V passim). Because of the tendency of population to increase to the limit of subsistence, there can be no permanent improvement in the state of the poor. "No possible contributions or sacrifices of the rich, particularly in money, could for any time prevent the recurrence of distress among the lower members of society" (pp. 78–9). For the same reason, the Poor Laws "create the poor which they maintain" (p. 83). The principle of population "appears, therefore, to be decisive against the possible existence of a society, all the members of which should live in ease, happiness, and comparative leisure": which is "conclusive against the perfectibility of the mass of mankind" (pp. 16, 17).

Suppose, however, that we "imagine for a moment Mr. Godwin's beautiful system of equality realized in its utmost purity, . . . all the causes of misery and vice in this island removed" (p. 181). The existing population lives—as a prepolitical society—in healthy "hamlets and farm houses" which are "scattered over the face of the country." Land and other property is equalized, and all share equally in labour and the produce of the soil. Marriage is abolished, and the children of any and every union supported by spontaneous benevolence. In these circumstances, Malthus claims, population will double in twenty-five years: but it is most unlikely that food supplies could, even with greatly more than the half-hour of daily work estimated by Godwin. Yet, suppose they could: in another generation population again doubles, but the greatest conceivable increase in food would now be 50 per cent. "A quantity of food equal to the frugal support of twenty-one millions, would have to be divided among twenty-eight millions" (p. 189). In conditions of universal scarcity "the spirit of benevolence . . . is repressed by the chilling breath of want" (p. 190). Self-preservation leads to competition, force and fraud: "self-love resumes his wonted empire and lords it over the world" (ibid).

Best, but inadequate

With competition for scarce resources come those institutions of society which Godwin wrongly supposed to be "the fruitful sources of all evil, the hotbeds of all the crimes that degrade mankind" (p. 177). For " . . . the goadings of want could not continue long, before some violations of public or private stock would necessarily take place" (p. 194). In order to preserve peace, an agreed assignment of property rights would be required, ratified by law and sanctioned by legitimate force, even the death penalty itself (p. 197). "It seems highly probable, therefore, that an administration of property, not very different from that which prevails in civilized states at present, would be established, as the best, though inadequate, remedy, for the evils which were pressing society" (p. 198). Scarcity would also dictate a regular provision for children and a disincentive to unchecked procreation. The need to make each man responsible for his own children, combined with the (assumed) inability of a woman to support them herself, would lead to the institution of marriage. And "when these two fundamental laws of society, the security of property, and the institution of marriage, were once established, "inequality of conditions must necessarily follow" (p. 203) from a combination of inheritance with differential natural endowment, industry and luck. The poorest would be forced to a propertyless subsistence and to work as wage-labourers for the richer. Thus it appears that a set of initial conditions as prescribed by Godwin would be transformed by the principle of population, within two or three generations at most, into a political society "divided into a class of proprietors, and a class of labourers" (p. 207), based on the institutions of private property and marriage, governed by law backed by a state with power of life and death over its subjects.

Having demolished the utopian fancies of Godwin and his French allies such as Condorcet and Rousseau, it was necessary for Malthus to turn to the much harder task of justifying that *status quo* which he had shown to be inevitable. This he attempted in two ways: by demonstrating that the competition, inequality and associated institutions produced by scarcity are socially beneficent; and by providing a theological framework within which to assimilate the harsh and novel conclusions of his political economy to contemporary Christianity. His partial and sketchy treatment of the first of these, and his total failure with the second, were the cause of that development of his ideas by Sumner and others over the next thirty-five years which has come to be known as "Christian Political Economy."

Uniform prosperity, thought Malthus, tends "rather to degrade, than exalt the character" (p. 373). The social benefit of poverty derives from "the torpor and corruption" of man, "inert, sluggish, and averse from labour unless compelled by necessity" (pp. 354, 363). If bodily wants were removed mankind would "sink to the level of the brutes," rather than "be raised to the level of philosophers" as Godwin had supposed (pp. 357–8). Malthus had little to say on the benefits of inequality in the *First Essay*, but was enthusiastic about its chief corollaries, private property and self-interest. "It is to the established administration of property, and to the apparently narrow principle of self-love, that we are indebted for all the noblest exertions of human genius, all the finer and more delicate emotions of the soul, for everything, indeed, that distinguishes the civilized, from the savage state"(pp. 286–87). In all of this, however, Malthus was content merely to assert rather than to demonstrate. For "the English-speaking world of the eighteenth century read the same books and pamphlets, whatever their politics" (Robbins, 1961, p. 19), and much of the ground had been covered already by Adam Smith.

The most ambitious, and least successful, part of the *First Essay* was the concluding theological argument of the last two chapters.

The dominance of scarcity in human affairs, and the supposed social utility of greed, selfishness and competition, presented the perennial theological "problem of evil" in a new and threatening form. How can a God who is good, omnipotent and wise will scarcity for His creatures? It was essential to the ideological enterprise, in an age when even Tom Paine must publicly declare his belief in God (Paine, 1887, p. 5, Maccoby, 1955b, p. 446), that Malthus attempt to "Vindicate the ways of God to man" (Malthus, 1798, p. 349). I have elsewhere provided a detailed account of this attempt, with reasons why I believe it must be regarded (and was so regarded in its own day) as a failure (Waterman, 1983a). A summary must suffice for this paper.

"Do we want to know what God is?" asked Paine in 1797: "Search not written nor printed books; but the scripture called *Creation*" (Paine, 1887, p. 291). Whether for polemical purposes, or because, despite his Anglican orders, he genuinely shared Paine's deism, Malthus deliberately chose the same ground. Explicitly rejecting the traditional view of human life as "a state of trial and school of virtue," he concluded that "it seems absolutely necessary, that we should reason up to nature's God, and not presume to reason from God to nature" (1798, p. 350). We must "turn our eyes to the book of nature, where alone we can read God as he is" (p. 351). Basing his argument on Abraham Tucker's theory of the evolution of "mind" under the stimulus of evil (Tucker, 1768), Malthus was betrayed into a non-solution of the problem. Moreover, he came close to denying the possibility of revealed knowledge, proposed a soteriology in which Christ is redundant, rejected the doctrine of eternal punishment, and took a position which even the free-thinking Ricardo and James Mill could see was Manichean (Sraffa, 1952, pp. 212–3). Certain unidentified but "distinguished persons" in the Church of England privately persuaded Malthus to expunge chapters XVIII and XIX from later editions of his *Essay* [Otter, 1836, p. lii], and he never thereafter returned to the subject.

III. THE TRADITION OF "CHRISTIAN POLITICAL ECONOMY" TO 1833

The principal figures in the development of Christian Political Economy were William Paley (1743–1805), whose influence at Cambridge was already large when Malthus had been an undergraduate; J. B.

Sumner (1780–1862) successively Fellow of King's (1801) and Eton (1817), eventually Archbishop of Canterbury (1848), whose talents as an economist were acknowledged by no less a judge than Ricardo (Sraffa, pp. 247–8); Edward Copleston (1776–1849), Provost of Oriel (1814) and later Bishop of Llandaff (1827); Richard Whately (1787 1863), the only person in history to proceed directly from a professorship in Economics (Drummond Chair at Oxford) to an Archbishopric (Dublin, 1831) without intervening stages; and the redoubtable Scotch Presbyterian Thomas Chalmers (1780–1847) professor of Moral Philosophy (St. Andrews, 1823–28), of Theology (Edinburgh, 1828 43), leader and first Moderator of the Free Kirk secession of 1843. Their enterprise cut across traditional party, theological and denominational lines. Paley, like Malthus, was a typical Cambridge latitudinarian Whig. Copleston and Whately were high-church Oxford Tories, though Whately leaned more and more to economic, social and theological liberalism in later life. Sumner and Chalmers were evangelicals, one Anglican, the other Presbyterian. Their work was directed to three tasks: the reconstruction on a satisfactory basis of Malthus's defective theological framework, the filling in and extension of his cursory treatment of the social benefits of poverty and inequality, and the discovery of implications and corollaries of their general position.

Paley was the first to recognize both the ideological importance and the theological deficiencies of Malthus's work. *Natural Theology* (Paley, 1825, vol I), his last major work, which appeared in 1802 four years after the *First Essay*, attributed "the evils of Civil life" to the "constitution of our nature," according to the principle explained in a late treatise upon population (p. 270). Paley attempted to soften Malthus's conclusions by suggesting that the limits to growth were "not yet attained, or even approached, in any country in the world" (p. 271), and pointed out that psychic satisfactions are not subject to physical limitation. Inequality produced by scarcity is partly useful, as encouraging healthy competition; partly illusory, because of the tendency of human expectations to adjust to current levels of prosperity. Moral evil is an unavoidable consequence of human freedom (implying a doctrine of Original Sin which Paley was extremely reluctant to acknowledge explicitly), and "even the bad qualities of mankind have their origin in their good ones" (p. 274). This leaves little of the "evil" produced by Malthusian scarcity to be reconciled with the divine goodness. The residue, however, is not to be explained by the Tucker-Malthus theory of the "creation of mind." Paley cautiously ignored that entire argument having clearly seen how impossible the position into which it had led Malthus. He chose rather to reaffirm the traditional "state of probation" doctrine which Malthus had rejected (Viner, 1972, lecture iii, especially pp. 75–8). "Our ultimate, or our most permanent happiness, will depend not upon the temporary condition into which we are cast, but upon our behaviour in it" (Paley, p. 284).

Both reason and Scripture

Paley's reconstruction of Malthusian theodicy was a mere sketch, occupying the last seventeen pages of chapter XXVI of *Natural Theology*. In 1816 a younger, and very different Cambridge divine, John Bird Sumner, produced his celebrated *Treatise on the Records of Creation* (1815, 1826), "a work of large and enduring influence" (Norman, 1976, p. 43). Its second volume sought to show "The consistency of the Principle of Population with the Wisdom and Goodness of God," and is in essence a vast elaboration of Paley's brief argument. Paley's view of human life as "a state of discipline" was central to Sumner's position, but as a good Evangelical the latter looked not only to reason but also to Scripture for support. For, in sharp contrast to Malthus he held that "no other guide can enter the sanctuary where He resides" (1825, p. xix). Having shown that both reason and revelation support the "state of probation" theory, Sumner went on to argue that social inequality is best suited to "the development and improvement of the human faculties" (1816, chap III) and to the "exercise of virtue" (1816, chap IV). A benevolent creator might therefore be expected to "devise a means" of bringing this about: which He does "in the principle of population" lately set forth by Mr. Malthus (1816, p. 103).

Copleston, Whately and Chalmers accepted the Paley-Sumner reworking of Malthus and turned their attention to three other theologically significant matters: first, the futility of legislated benevolence; secondly, the teleological character of the self-regulating, market economy; and thirdly, the connection between temporal prosperity and "moral restraint."

It is logically impossible, Copleston argued in his *Second letter to Peel* (1819) to make charity compulsory, because "an action to be virtuous must be voluntary" (p. 17). The Poor Laws are therefore incongruous "with the nature of man, and with that state of discipline and trial which his present existence is clearly designed to be" (ibid.). "What is thus proved to be true theoretically, and by a kind of *a priori* argument, Mr. Malthus has shown to be deducible from the actual constitution of things." For the principle of population demonstrates "that all endeavours to embody benevolence into law, and thus impiously as it were to effect by human laws what the author of the system of nature has not effected by his laws must be abortive—that this ignorant struggle against evil really enlarges, instead of contracting the kingdom of evil" (pp. 21–2). Chalmers made use of the point in his *Political Economy* (1832), and in the *Bridgewater Treatise* (1833) developed still further the implications for conservative ideology. Copleston had noted that the poor can have no *political* rights as a class, but only *moral* rights as individuals" (1819, p. 99). But Chalmers—reflecting a notorious passage in Malthus's second edition (1803, pp. 531 2)—insisted that even as an individual a poor man has no right to "the means of existence on the sole ground that he exists" (1833, p. 234). For "if *justice* alone could have ensured a right distribution for the supply of want... then would there have been no need for another principle, which stands out most noticeably in our nature; and *compassion* would have been a superfluous part of the human constitution" (ibid.).

Self-interest

The Lakatosian "hard core" of clasical Political Economy was the idea—inherited from Hume and Adam Smith—of a market economy impelled by the unregulated self-interest of individuals. Malthus had referred to "self-love" as "the mainspring of the great machine" (1798, pp. 207, 286) but made no explanatory or ideological use of the concept. Neither Sumner nor Copleston considered the market economy. But for Whately it was the most interesting thing about economics, which he actually proposed should be renamed "catallactics" (1831, pp. 6–7). His example of the large city supplied "with daily provisions of all kinds" by individuals "who think each of nothing beyond his own immediate interest" (pp. 103–8) anticipates the most famous modern text-book (Samuelson, 1973, pp. 41–2), and was treated by him as an example of divine "contrivance" of service to natural theology (1831, pp. 109–110). Chalmers acknowledged "the observations of Dr. Whately" in his *Bridgewater Treatise* which appeared two years later, and amplified the theme with characteristic rhetoric (1833, pp. 238 40).

Malthus had noted in the *First Essay* that the subsistence wage is culturally determined (1798, p. 132): in the second and subsequent editions he drew out the implications of this by developing the concept of "moral restrant" as the chief "preventive check" and means for a permanent improvement in living standards. Paley and Whately ignored the point; Sumner and Copleston made little use of it. Chalmers developed the concept fully: it formed the centre-piece of his *Political Economy* in which the efficacy of the "moral remedy" is contrasted with the powerlessness of all other measures to increase the prosperity of the poor (1832, p. 29 and passim). Copleston had recognized the importance of parish schools in this connection (1819, pp. 102–3): Chalmers insisted that a national system of church-controlled schools was essential. For as "moral restraint" is the sole and infallible method of raising the general standard of "comfort and enjoyment," it is "a wise and beautiful connection in the mechanism of society, that the most direct way to establish it is through the medium of popular intelligence and virtue—giving thereby a practical important to efficient Christian institutions . . . " (1832, p. 32). As always, Chalmers squeezed the last drops of ideological juice from his theoretical lemon. It is precisely this "inseparable connection between the moral worth and economic comfort of a people" which demonstrates that "political economy is but one grand exemplification of the alliance, which a God of righteousness hath established, between prudence and moral virtue on the one hand, and physical comfort on the other" (1833, pp. 248–9).

IV. THE DECLINE OF CHRISTIAN POLITICAL ECONOMY

The publication in 1833 of Thomas Chalmers' *Bridgewater Treatise* marks a very definite *terminus ad quem* of Christian Political Economy. All the principal elements of the tradition had been worked out by that date and nothing of ideological significance appears to have been added since. From the 1840s modern Christian social thought began to develop in other directions.

According to Christian Political Economy, poverty and social inequality are the inevitable outcome of scarcity: more particularly of population pressures in a world of limited resources. Because of original sin and redemption by Christ, human life on this earth is to be regarded as a state of "discipline and trial" for eternity. Though poverty and inequality entail some genuine suffering—to be accounted for by the Fall—they may therefore be regarded, for the most part, as a deliberate "contrivance" by a benevolent God for bringing out the best in His children and so training them for the life to come. The social institutions of private property and marriage are economically necessary (and indeed inevitable), suited to human nature, and consistent with scriptural teaching. The combination of the institution of private property with the competition produced by scarcity results in the market economy. The efficiency of the latter in organizing human activity for the maximization of wealth is evidence of the divine wisdom and mercy in turning human frailty to socially beneficent ends. The impossibility of achieving social progress by legislation is evidence both of "design"—in the creation of the self-regulating economy—and of the moral and religious need of Christians to practise charity and compassion. True happiness in this life is largely independent of wealth and station. But in any case wealth is positively correlated with moral worth, itself a result of faithful Christianity. Universal Christian education is thus of the highest practical importance, and a vital feature of the traditional alliance (or unity) of church and state.

The reader is invited to compare this summary with the report of Mrs. Thatcher's political-theological *credo* in the first section of my paper.

"By the end of the 1830s . . . the most influential of the church leaders were all soaked in the attitudes of Political Economy" (Norman, 1976, pp. 136–7). Yet within a decade the intellectual tide had turned, "Christian Socialism" had made its appearance, and "a generation reared in the doctrines of *laissez-faire*" was well on its way to "lay the foundations of modern collectivism" (Deane, 1969, p. 215). The principal causes of this sudden revolution in theory and policy were first, the willingness of legislators to accept piece-meal reform in practice, even when it conflicted with *laissez-faire* theory; secondly, the rapidly growing incidence, during the 1840s, of conditions requiring such reform; thirdly, a revolution in the technique of government itself; and finally, the ideological consequences, in Britain, of utilitarianism, the Romantic revival, and continental socialism.

Ever since the late eighteenth-century campaigns to abolish slavery and the Test and Corporation Acts, British legislators had been growing accustomed to the idea of reform. As early as 1788 Hanway's Bill to protect chimney sweeps had been passed; Peel's Bill to control conditions of work of pauper children became law in 1802. Country squires, peers and bishops—having no particular love for the new class of industrial entrepreneurs—could generally be persuaded to legislate government intervention when presented with some flagrant case of injustice or exploitation. E. R. Norman has shown that bishops such as Wilberforce, Thirlwall and even J. B. Sumner himself, imbued as they were with the principles of Political Economy, supported Factory Acts and public health legislation as exceptional cases whilst continuing to profess their belief in *laissez-faire* (Norman, 1976, pp. 138–47). But the "recognition of exceptions to the general rule against state intervention cumulatively prepared for the displacement of Political Economy.... The advocates of laissez-faire themselves acquiesced in the reforms which pulled down its edifice" (ibid., p. 139).

The necessity for such "exceptions" came thick and fast during the Hungry Forties. Underlying most of them was an unprecedented urbanization. The population of England grew by tens of millions in the first half of the nineteenth century, and most of the increase occurred in London and the new industrial cities. A combination of starvation wages with overcrowding, jerry-building and a total disregard of private or public sanitation led to the cholera epidemics of the Thirties and Forties. The ruling class was compelled to attend. "To maintain the traditional patterns of English life" the new cities "must have drains, lavatories, paved roads, houses, policemen, nurses, schools, parks, cemetaries and churches" (Chadwick, 1966, p. 376). A stream of legislation was generated, all of it extending the responsibility and power of government for social welfare.

Economic revolution

Meanwhile, the ability of government to meet these demands had been revolutionized by the same combination of social, cultural, technical and material factors which was transforming the economy. There was "a revolution in organization and behaviour and in the personnel taking the effective policy decisions; it involved an increase in the scale of operations and in the division and specialization of labour; it was marked by a new readiness to experiment with techniques and to make practical use of developments in the natural sciences; and it developed a self-sustaining momentum" (Deane, 1969, p. 214). A quarter of a century of war had tested and fostered the power of the state. As government became a more powerful and efficient instrument for achieving social goals, more possibilities for its use naturally suggested themselves to the reformers. When in the 1830s "reforming legislation began to include provision for inspection and enforcement by means of state officials with executive powers" a "point of no return" had been reached (Deane, pp. 215,16).

Three very disparate intellectual traditions now started to converge in order to create a new, more appropriate ideology: British utilitarianism, romantic nostalgia for the Middle Ages, and socialism of the kind proclaimed in the European revolutions of 1848. The utilitarians were at first sympathetic to the *laissez-faire* principles of Political Economy for there was a close intellectual and cultural relation between the two. ".The real objective of the philosophical radicals, however, turned out to be not freedom from government but freedom from inefficient government, and efficiency meant effective and purposeful intervention in the economic system" (Deane, p. 215). Rational interventionists found unexpected support from a miscellaneous assortment of disaffected Tories and romantics ranging from Cobbett to Coleridge, united only in their hatred of the heartlessness of Political Economy and their propensity to treat Malthus as a bogeyman. Many of the clergy, including high-church bishops such as Philpotts of Exeter and VanMildert of Durham, sharing their sentiments. The temporary alliance, from 1848 to 1855, of the radical, French- educated J. M. Ludlow with the romantic Kingsley and the theologically liberal F. D. Maurice is generally agreed to mark the beginnings of "Christian Socialism" in the English-speaking world (Chadwick, pp. 346– 63; Norman, pp. 167–75).

Though Christian Socialism suffered a temporary eclipse and did not reappear until the 1870s, the vitality had departed from Christian Political Economy: as an intellectual force in the church it seems to have died with the last of its distinguished exponents, Archbishops Sumner (ob. 1862) and Whately (ob. 1863). E. R. Norman has argued very convincingly (1976, passim) that what happened thereafter was a "layered filtration" of ideas within the church. The academic clergy at Oxford and Cambridge, together with the younger and more intellectual of the bishops, tended to adopt the ideas of the most advanced section of the intelligentsia, of which, of course, they were themselves an important component. From the second half of the nineteenth century, these have been increasingly radical, secular and interventionist. Because of the time-lag in the transmission of ideas, and because of the reluctance of those who are not professional thinkers to accept new ones after their mid-twenties, the parochial clergy and the educated laity generally exhibited the opinions held by the elite of a generation before. Thus Political Economy became widespread among the literate public at about the time it was being abandoned by the most advanced thinkers. At least another generation was required before the working class and white-collar workers could absorb a watered-down version of what were the latest ideas fifty years before.

Though something of the kind has persisted into the twentieth century, the more rapid spread of ideas, together with the apparent bankruptcy of all existing ideologies, has encouraged in Christians, as in others, a more eclectic approach to political doctrine. The choice of Christian Political Economy by such highly educated and intelligent Christians as Margaret Thatcher and Enoch Powell (1977) may be less a conservative nostalgia for working-class folklore than a desperate attempt to find something that might just work.

NOTE

1. The research for this paper was supported in part by the Christendom Trust, the British Council, and the University of Manitoba. The author is also indebted to Mary Kinnear for comments on an earlier draft. Neither she nor the funding bodies are responsible for the opinions expressed, or for remaining errors.

REFERENCES

Burke, Edmund. *Reflections on the Revolution in France,* and on the Proceedings in Certain Societies in London Relative to that Event, in a Letter intended to have been sent to a Gentleman in Paris. 1790. London: Dent (Everyman), 1910.

Chadwick, Owen. *The Victorian Church,* Part I. London: A. & C. Black, 1966.

Chalmers, Thomas. *On Political Economy*. In Connexion with the Moral State and Moral Prospects of Society. Glasgow: Collins, 1832.

------. *On the Power, Wisdom and Goodness of God*, as Manifested in the Adaptation of External Nature to the Moral and Intellectual Constitution of Man (*Bridgewater Treatise I*). London: Bohn, 1853 (First edition, 1833).

[Copleston, Edward.] *A Second Letter to the Right Hon. Robert Peel*, M.P. for the University of Oxford on the Causes of the Increase in Pauperism and the Poor Laws. Oxford: John Murray, 1819. By One of his Constituents.

Deane, Phyllis. *The First Industrial Revolution*. Cambridge: C.U.P., 1969.

Godwin, William. *Enquiry Concerning Political Justice*. London: 1793.

Lincoln, Anthony. *Some Political and Social Ideas of English Dissent,1763–1800*. Cambridge: C.U.P. , 1938.

Locke, Don. *A Fantasy of Reason*. The Life and Thought of William Godwin. London: Routledge & Kegan Paul, 1980.

Maccoby, S. *English Radicalism, 1762–1785, The Origins*. London: Allen & Unwin, 1955.

------. *English Radicalism, 1786–1832, from Paine to Cobbett*. London: Allen & Unwin, 1955.

[Malthus, T. R.] *First Essay on Population* (An Essay on the Principle of Population as It Affects the Future Improvement of Society, with Remarks on the Speculations of Mr. Godwin, M. Condorcet, and Other Writers. London: J. Johnson, 1798), facsimile reprinted by Royal Economic Society, London: Macmillan, 1966.

Malthus, T. R. *An Essay on the Principle of Population*, or, A View of Its Past and Present Effect on Human Happiness, with an Inquiry into our Prospects Respecting the Future Removal or Mitigation of the Evils which It Occasions. London: Johnson, 1803 (Second edition).

------. *Principles of Political Economy*, considered with a View to their Practical Application (Second Edition). London: William Pickering, 1836 (First edition, 1820).

Norman, E. R. *Church and Society in England, 1770–1970*. Oxford: Clarendon, 1976.

Otter, W. "Memoir of Robert Malthus" in Malthus [1836], pp. xiii–liv.

Paine, Thomas. *The Theological Works*. Chicago: Belford, 1887. (Contains *The Age of Reason*, etc.)

Paley, William. *The Works of William Paley, D. D., Archdeacon of*

Carlisle. With a Life of the Author (five volumes). London: Hailes, Bumpas, etc., 1825.

Powell, Enoch. *Wresting with the Angel*. London: Sheldon, 1977.

Robbins, Caroline. *The Eighteenth Century Commonwealthman*. Studies in the Transmission, Development and Circumstances of English Liberal Thought from the Restoration of Charles II until the War with the Thirteen Colonies. Cambridge, Mass.: Harvard U.p. , 1961.

Samuelson, P. A. *Economics: an Introductory Analysis*. New York: McGraw-Hill, 1973 (Ninth edition).

Schumpeter, Joseph A. *History of Economic Analysis*. London: Allen & Unwin, 1954

Search, Edward (pseud. for TUCKER, Abraham). *The Light of Nature Pursued*. London: T. Payne, 1768.

Soloway, R. . *Prelates and People*. Ecclesiastical Social Thought in England, 1783– 1852. London: Routledge and Kegan Paul, 1969.

Sraffa, Piero. *The Works and Correspondance of David Ricardo*. Vol. VII. Cambridge, C.U.P. , 1952.

Sumner, J. B. *A Treatise on the Records of Creation*. With Particular Reference to the Jewish History, and the Consistency of the Principle of Population with the Wisdom and Goodness of the Deity. Vol I: London: Hatchard & Son, 1825 (Fourth edition, corrected); Vol II: London: Hatchard, 1816 (Xerox of what is presumably First edition).

Thatcher, Margaret. "'I Believe': a Speech on Christianity and Politics."At St. Lawrence Jewry, Next Guildhall, London, Thursday, 30th March, 1978 (Conservative Central Office, Press Release 442/78).

——. "The Moral Basis of a Free Society," *Daily Telegraph* (May) 1978.

Tucker, Abraham. See Search, Edward.

Viner, Jacob. *The Role of Providence in the Social Order*. An Essay in Intellectual History. Philadelphia: American Philosophical Society, 1972. (Jayne Lectures for 1966).

Waterman, A. M. C. "Malthus as a Theologian: the First Essay and the Relation between Political Economy and Christian Theology," in Dupaquier,J. and Fauve-Chamoux, A. (eds.), *Malthus: Past and Present*. London: Academic Press, 1983.

——. "The Ideological Alliance of Political Economy and Christian Theology, 1798– 1833." *Journal of Ecclesiastical History*, April 1983.

Whately, Richard. *Introductory Lectures in Political Economy*. London: Fellowes, 1831.

Comment

Stephen Tonsor

Professor Waterman has given us an interesting, knowledgeable and useful account of the development of "Christian Political Economy." He has been careful to place it in the historical context of the late eighteenth century and nineteenth century intellectual, social and political developments. He has raised the important question of why this effort to combine the economics of the Manchester school with the imperatives of the Gospel was so briefly successful and he has intimated that Prime Minister Margaret Thatcher's address, "'I Believe': A Speech on Christianity and Politics," on Thursday March 30, 1978 at St. Lawrence Jewry in the City of London was the last hurrah of this all but defunct and certainly misguided set of ideas. Consequently his paper is not only a statement of the historical facts; a statement valuable in itself, but it is also an opinion as to the validity and permanence of these ideas.

First, let us turn our attention to the historical analysis. I was particularly delighted to read an essay which continued the pioneering work of my former colleague, Richard Soloway. Some years ago I read his book in manuscript and though I disapproved of its tone I recognized its importance. Over the past several decades the *Journal of the History of Ideas* has kept up a barrage of articles dealing with the Scotch Enlightenment, Classical economics and "Christian Political Economy." Two recent articles bear directly on Professor Waterman's topic and while they do not diverge substantially from his thesis they do amplify and enlarge considerably the matter he is discussing. In the January–March 1977 number, Salim Rashid writes on "Richard Whately and Christian Political Economy," and more recently Edmund N. Santurri published in the April-June 1982 number an article entitled, "Theodicy and Social Policy of Malthus." More importantly, it is surely mistaken to assert, as Waterman does, that after 1789, "there was no fear of revolution at home" (England). I believe that Albert Goodwin in his magisterial study, *The Friends of Liberty. The English Democratic Movement in the Age of the French Revolution* (Cambridge, Mass.: Harvard University Press, 1979), demonstrates that there was abundant fear of revolution at home though whether or not the fear was justified is another matter.

The Romantic attack on Classical economics was in place and proved to be very effective long before 1833, which Professor Waterman describes as "the *terminus quem* of Christian Political Economy." Kenelm Henry Digby published *The Board Stone of Honor* in 1822. It became one of the most influential books in the English language in the first half of the nineteenth century. As important as its nostalgia for the Middle Ages is its attack, in page after page, on capitalism and the economy of the Manchester school. It is no accident that in 1825 Digby became a convert to Catholicism. It is well to recall too that John Stuart Mill's utilitarianism was tempered by his reading of Coleridge and that the impact of the medieval revival antedates the 1830s. I say this because I believe that pushing the date of the beginning of the attack upon the emerging industrial capitalism well back into the early nineteenth century gives us a more accurate notion of the social dynamics of the period.

Linkages

But these are quibbles and should not be construed as criticism of a paper which is knowledgeable and explores new territory. There are reasons other than the presentation of the facts of the matter which are open to criticism and debate. Whatever the merits of this paper as history, Waterman simply has not established a link between "Christian Political Economy" and Prime Minister Margaret Thatcher. Moreover, to link by implication rather than proof the ideas of the Prime Minister to a defunct and dubious set of notions, is to reject those ideas without taking the trouble of disproving their validity. There is not a scrap of evidence linking that impressive lady and her ideas to the ideas of Malthus, Paley, Sumner, Copleston, Whately, and Chalmers. Waterman argues for guilt by association. One might as legitimately argue that the eye of the squid and the eye of man have the same evolutionary origin simply because they are structurally the same. The intellectual "smoking gun" is absent and Waterman simply has not made his case.

Over a century has passed since the demise of "Christian Political Economy." Indeed, it is a century and a half since these ideas in their early formulation were taken seriously. Meanwhile "Liberal-Conservative" thought has not stood still. I doubt that the lady whose training was that of a chemist ever read Malthus, to say nothing of the lesser-known lights of "Christian Political Economy." On the other hand, I think it unlikely that she has not read von Hayek, Milton Friedman, and Enoch Powell. These men have little enough in common with "Christian Political Economy." Moreover, in the background of contemporary Liberal-Conservatism stand the two giants of the nineteenth century; Alexis de Tocqueville and Lord Acton, to say nothing of J. S. Mill and Jacob Burckhardt. To be active in contemporary Conservative politics is to have absorbed, at least by osmosis, the ideas of these men who stand between the demise of "Christian Political Economy" and the Liberal-Conservative political thought of today.

Not only has the intellectual basis of modern Liberal-Conservatism changed, but experiential reality, history, has helped to transform the ways in which men view politics and economics. Prime Minister Thatcher does not think, cannot think, in terms of Robert Malthus because her experience of the world has been so radically different from that of Malthus.

Political experience

Modern Liberal-Conservatism is based less on economic theory and social policy than it is on political experience. The fundamental fact in that political experience has been the usurpation by the state of the freedom and dignity of the individual. Margaret Thatcher, as is the case with nearly every thoughtful Liberal-Conservative of the twentieth century, is far less interested in denouncing socialism because it rests on unsound economic assumptions than because the idea of omnicompetent state and radical state interventionism results inevitably in the loss of freedom and the imposition of some form of totalitarianism. The primary experience of the twentieth century has been the experience of totalitarian socialism no matter whether one calls it Soviet Communism, National Socialism or Fascism. This experience has brought the realization that all collectivism is inherently totalitarian; that planning and intervention leads inevitably to the loss of freedom. It was this realization which led Friedrich von Hayek to publish *The Road to Serfdom* (1944). This book marks the beginning of contemporary Liberal-Conservatism as an intellectual and political movement.

To be sure von Hayek is no Christian. His devotion to freedom, however, is Christian. Lord Acton, Hayek's nineteenth century predecessor once said that "God so loved freedom that he permitted even sin." It is an odd fact that the Church in the twentieth century has generally loved liberty less than security, has loved freedom less than justice and equality. Not only has the spirit of the modern church been dominated by a pre-capitalistic mentality but the Church has been statist in its mentality.

The combination of the growth of the powers of the modern state and the quest for equality have been the chief sources of totalitarianism. Alexis de Tocqueville at the end of Vol. II of *Democracy in America* wrote:

> Our contemporaries are constantly excited by two conflicting passions: they want to be led, and they wish to remain free. As they cannot destroy either the one or the other of these contrary propensities, they strive to satisfy them both at once. They devise a sole, tutelary, all-powerful form of government, but elected by the people. They combine the principle of centralization and that of popular sovereignty; this gives them a respite: they console themselves for being in tutelage by the reflection that they have chosen their own guardians. Every man allows himself to be put in leading-strings, because he sees that it is not a person or a class of persons, but the people at large who hold the end of his chain.

Nineteenth century theories of the state which made it not only the source of life and order but the arbiter of virtue effectively extinguished both the realms of conscience and freedom. The Church, still trammeled in the Constantinian structures of establishment, accepted the omnicompetent state in exchange for exclusivity of establishment and the shadow freedom of orthodoxy. It is not surprising therefore that both de Tocqueville and Acton were unalterably opposed to established religions.

The Liberal-Conservatives of the nineteenth century were far less concerned about economics than they were about freedom. They dreamed of an economic order which would provide opportunities for expanding the area of freedom. They dreamed of a state which lacked either the power or the opportunity to destroy the freedom of the individual. Even those who reluctantly consented to state intervention did not forget the long range goal of increased freedom. J. S. Mill wrote in this vein in *On Liberty* when he remarked:

...A government cannot have too much of the kind of activity which does not impede, but aids and stimulates individual exertion and development. The mischief begins when, instead of calling forth the activity and powers of individuals and bodies, it substitutes its own activity for theirs; when, instead of informing, advising, and upon occasion, denouncing, it makes them work in fetters, or bids them stand aside and does their work instead of them.

Interventionism

It is well to recall that Mill's *On Liberty* was published in 1859. It is simply not true that an interventionist consensus existed in the second half of the nineteenth century and that intellectuals in particular were motivated by collectivist economic and social theories. If this was indeed the case, one must ignore Lord Acton and Jacob Burckhardt, William Graham Sumner and the Social Darwinists, the critics of mass society and those who worried increasingly about the growing power of the national state and its increasing drive to militarism and imperialism. No doubt these voices constituted a minority which was not adequately appreciated until the terrors of totalitarianism, the horrors of total war and the quiet and insidious power of the "Big Brother" state made them intellectual heroes. It is, I believe, this intellectual tradition which lies behind the remarks of Prime Minister Thatcher rather than the ideas of "Christian Political Economy."

Finally, it is important to ask the question of why the Church has been so tardy in developing a theology of freedom. I am not asking the Church, or the churches, to subscribe to particular economic or political systems. There has been far too much of that already and its net effect has been to corrupt the *magisterium* of the Church and to discredit it before the world. You must recall that Austrian clerical fascists of the 1930s and Father Charles E. Coughlin found approval for their particular political and economic theories in the social teachings of the Catholic church. Hanno Helbling in his recent book, *Politik der Papste, Der Vatikan im Weltgeschehen, 1958–1978* (Berlin: Ullstein Verlag, 1981), has explored the tangled accommodation of the Papacy with both Fascism and Communism.

What I am asking is that the Church consider theologically the full importance of freedom in all its aspects including economic. One cannot, it seems to me, call for freedom of conscience without affirming the importance of political and economic freedom. However, you must remember that it was not until Vatican II that freedom of conscience was affirmed by the Church and then only after the most intense debate.

Freedom, like all other dimensions of human existence, does not manifest itself as an abstract and isolated quiddity. It exists in a complex of conflicting values and human aspirations. Often it can be had only at the expense of absolute justice, security and equality. Does freedom by its nature take precedence over other values? When, if ever, may it legitimately be sacrificed in the pursuit of other values? It simply will not do to argue that freedom of conscience or freedom of religion is the only freedom important to the Christian and that under certain circumstances the political and economic tyranny characteristic of collectivism is legitimate.

Reply

A. M. C. Waterman

It was no part of my intention to disparage, or indeed to appraise in any way, either the political ideas of Mrs. Thatcher or the tradition of Christian Political Economy. The reader who looks for evaluation in my paper will look in vain. Whether my history is valid is another matter, and here I stand to be corrected by the experts, including Stephen Tonsor. For I am a mere economist.

Tonsor is probably right in saying that I have failed to prove that the ideology of Margaret Thatcher and Enoch Powell is heir to the tradition of Malthus, Sumner and Chalmers. My title bites off more than I was really trying to chew in this paper, and I deserved to get put down by the professionals. But in partial defence of my historical efforts, I will make three brief points.

1. Chalmers's *Bridgewater Treatise* is the *terminus ad quem* of Christian Political Economy not because the "Romantic attack on Classical economics" had not already begun—that is irrelevant— but because there is no further intellectual development of the tradition after that work.
2. Though Christian Political Economy made no progress after 1833 and was intellectually superseded by interventionist ideology, it retained its hold on the popular imagination for more than a century after. Edward Norman has explained why, in *Church and Society in England, 1770–1970.* Though I did not *prove* that Mrs. Thatcher derived her ideas from that source, I was entitled to *suggest* it.
3. Both Margaret Thatcher and Enoch Powell differ sharply from the "Liberal-Conservative" tradition Professor Tonsor so admires, precisely because they are Christian, and that tradition is not. Mrs. Thatcher went out of her way in 1978 (only a few months before a crucial general election!) to criticize those members of her own party who had abandoned the Christian underpinnings of British Toryism

Chapter 4

Clerical Laissez-Faire: A Study in
Theological Economics

Paul Heyne

In a recent essay on the evolution of Roman Catholic social thought in the United States, James V. Schall laments his church's failure to take seriously the productive achievements of the American economy. He writes:

> [I]n the one country wherein we might expect the most enthusiastic and enterprising efforts to relate productive economy to Christian ideas, namely in the United States, with rare exceptions, we do not find in the literature much attention to the extraordinary historical accomplishment of creating a system whereby the physical toil of man and vast natural energies of the earth could be so interrelated that what Pius XI called "a higher level of prosperity and culture" could be conceivable for all of mankind. Attention has been focused almost invariably upon abuses rather than on the essence of the system itself, what makes it productive for a whole society, what makes it grow, what makes it open to correction. There has been very little original thinking by the American Church about its own system precisely in the context of those values religion constantly announces it stands for—those of justice, rights, growth, aid to the poor, quality of life, ownership, dignity of work, and widespread distribution.[1]

A similar statement could not be made about Protestant Christianity in America, at least not by anyone familiar with its nineteenth century history. Protestant clergymen played a prominent part in the early teaching of economics in the United States, especially prior to the Civil War, and their doctrines generally lauded the productive as well as the moral virtues of the American economy. The Rev. John McVickar of Columbia University, a contender for the title of first academic economist in the United States,[2] was expressing the general conviction of nineteenth century clerical economists when he attributed the rapid advance of the United States in wealth and civilization largely to her respect for the divinely ordained laws of morality and political economy. These laws called for individual responsibility, private property, and minimal government intervention in the economy.[3] This position acquired almost axiomatic status in the second quarter of the nineteenth century among clerical economists, prompting the historian Henry F. May to speak of "a school of political economy which might well be labeled clerical *laissez-faire*."[4]

What exactly did these theological economists teach? On what were their doctrines based? And what was the fate of these doctrines? Those are the questions to which this paper is addressed.

Francis Wayland, 1796–1865

The most influential member of the school of clerical *laissez-faire* was Francis Wayland, author of *The Elements of Political Economy*, first published in 1837. Michael J.L.O'Connor, in an exhaustive examination of the origins of economic instruction in the United States, says that Wayland's *Elements* "achieved more fully than any other textbook what appear to have been the ideals of the clerical school."[5] It also achieved, in its original version and in the abridged version published for secondary school use, immediate and widespread adoption; it was by far the most popular political economy textbook prior to the Civil War. Even after its sales declined in the 1860s, its influence continued to be exerted through adaptations and imitations. Because of the authority and prestige that Wayland commanded as clergyman, educator, and moral philosopher as well as author and teacher in the field of political economy, I will use him as a paradigm case in exploring the origins, nature, and eventual fate of "clerical *laissez-faire*."[6]

The basic facts of Wayland's life may be quickly sketched. He was born in New York City in 1796 of devout Baptist parents, who had migrated from England in 1793. His father set himself up in business as a currier, became a deacon in his church, received a license as a lay preacher in 1805, and by 1807 had given up his business to become a full-time minister. Francis entered Union College in 1811 as a sophomore, graduated in 1813, and began the study of medicine. About the time he completed his medical studies, Wayland experienced a deep religious renewal and decided to study for the ministry. He entered Andover Seminary in 1816, but left after one year, because of severely straitened circumstances, to accept an appointment as tutor at Union College. In 1821 he was called to the First Baptist Church in Boston and ordained as a minister. In 1826 Wayland accepted an offer to return to Union College as a professor of moral philosophy. Before he had moved his family from Boston, however, he received news of his election as President of Brown University, a Baptist institution. Wayland took up his duties in Providence in 1827. He exerted enormous influence on Brown and on American higher education generally until his resignation in 1855. After a vigorous "retirement" devoted to preaching, teaching, writing, and active work on behalf of a variety of social causes, Wayland died in 1865.[7]

Wayland introduced the study of political economy and took on the duty of teaching it soon after assuming the presidency of Brown University in 1827, at the age of 31. In church-related colleges in the first half of the nineteenth century, it was generally the president's prerogative to teach moral philosophy to the senior class, and political economy was considered a branch of moral philosophy. The only training in the subject required of a teacher or author was the sort of philosophical background that a well-educated clergyman would be assumed to possess.[8]

In the preface to his *Elements of Political Economy,* Wayland wrote:

> When the author's attention was first directed to the Science of Political Economy, he was struck with the simplicity of its principles, the extent of its generalizations, and the readiness with which its facts seemed capable of being brought into natural and methodical arrangement.[9]

Moreover:

> The principles of Political Economy are so closely analogous
> to those of Moral Philosophy, that almost every question in the
> one, may be argued on grounds belonging to the other.[10]

Tariffs

Wayland nonetheless promised not to intermingle the principles of
these two disciplines in his textbook, but rather to argue "economical questions on merely economical grounds." He offered the issue
of protective tariffs by way of illustration.

> [I]t is frequently urged, that, if a contract have been made by
> the government with the manufacturer, that contract is morally
> binding. This, it will be perceived, is a question of Ethics, and
> is simply the question, whether men are or are not morally
> bound to fulfill their contracts. With this question, Political
> Economy has nothing to do. Its only business is, to decide
> whether a given contract were or were not *wise*. This is the
> only question, therefore, treated of in the discussion of this
> subject in the following work.[11]

As we shall see, Wayland did not consistently fulfill this promise.
It may be impossible for anyone to maintain a clear distinction between what is moral and what is wise when discussing the organization of economic life. The separation will be especially difficult to
maintain if one believes, as Wayland did, that the science of political economy presents the laws to which God has subjected
humanity in its pursuit of wealth.

It may be objected, of course, that Wayland was only making a
conventional bow to current piety when he referred to the laws
which the sciences discover as the laws of God. The *Memoir* published by his sons two years after his death, however, offers persuasive evidence to the contrary. Wayland's religious faith was
deeply and sincerely held, and he continually tested his academic
labours for conformity to what he perceived as the will of God. The
Memoir contains extensive excerpts from Wayland's personal journal, and the following extract is quite representative:

> I have thought of publishing a work on moral philosophy.
> Direct me, O thou all-wise and pure Spirit. Let me not do it

unless it be for thy glory and the good of men. If I shall do it, may it all be true, so far as human knowledge at present extends. Enlighten, guide, and teach me so that I may write something which will show thy justice more clearly than heretofore, and the necessity and excellence of the plan of salvation by Christ Jesus, the blessed Redeemer. All which I ask through his merits alone. Amen.[12]

Wayland always thought of himself as a theologian first and only secondarily as a moral philosopher or political economist.

The interesting view which Wayland held on the invariability of divine laws almost certainly affected his conclusions in the area of economics. He presents his position near the beginning of his textbook on moral philosophy:

[A]s all relations, whether moral or physical, are the result of this enactment, an order of sequence once discovered in morals, is just as invariable as an order of sequence in physics.

Such being the fact, it is evident, that the moral laws of God can never be varied by the institutions of man, any more than the physical laws. The results which God has connected with actions, will inevitably occur, all the created power in the universe to the contrary notwithstanding. Nor can the consequences be eluded or averted, any more than the sequences which follow by the laws of gravitation.[13]

We should therefore not expect to find in Wayland much sympathy for the idea that different eras, different nations, or different cultures will have their own distinct laws of political economy. Wayland's position is at the opposite pole from the historical relativism imported into American economics from Germany in the last quarter of the nineteenth century.

Wayland's political economy

Wayland apparently learned political economy largely by teaching it. He wrote the following, shortly before his death, in a reminiscence reviewing his experience as a teacher:

I endeavored always to understand, for myself, whatever I attempted to teach. By this I mean that I was never satisfied with the text, inless I saw for myself, as well as I was able, that the text was true. Pursuing this course, I was led to observe the principles or general truths on which the treatise was founded. As I considered these, they readily arranged themselves in a natural order of connection and dependence. I do not wish to be understood as asserting that I did this with every text-book before I began to use it in my class. I generally taught these subjects during a single year. Before I had thought through one subject, I was called upon to commence another. Yet, with every year, I made some progress in all. I prepared lectures on particular subjects, and thus fixed in my mind the ideas which I had acquired, for use during the next year. The same process continued year by year, and in this manner, almost before I was aware of it, I had completed an entire course of lectures. In process of time I was thus enabled to teach by lecture all the subjects which I began to teach from text-books.

The textbook he used from 1828, when he began teaching the subject to Brown seniors, until 1837, when he published his own text, was J.B. Say's *Treatise on Political Economy,* translated from the fourth French edition and published in the United States in 1821. Since Wayland rarely cites authorities or indicates a source and since the *Memoir* contains only a few paragraphs on the subject of political economy, we have no way of knowing how many other European economists influenced his thinking. We can be fairly certain, however, that he had read extensively in the work that had influenced Say: Adam Smith's *Inquiry into the Nature and Causes of the Wealth of Nations.* Smith is sometimes cited specifically. What is more conclusive, however, is Wayland's use of Smithian classifications, premises, and analyses as well as what might be called a Smithian "tone" on particular topics.

Wayland's discussion of what governments may do to promote the increase of knowledge, for example, brings immediately to mind the language used by Smith in his section "Of the Expense of the Institutions for the Education of Youth."[15] The causes Wayland lists for differences in wage rates are Smith's famous five circumstances that explain differences in pecuniary returns.[16] Wayland's extended discussion of money and banks frequently teaches notions that could only have been derived from Adam Smith's fatefully erroneous explanation of the ways in which metallic and paper money function in an economy.[17] Wayland's refutation of arguments for restrictions on imports reveals the clear influence of Smith's treatment.[18] Though Wayland, unlike Smith, preferred direct to indirect taxes, his analysis shows that he had considered Smith's arguments.[19]

The authority of Adam Smith's ideas must have been increased for Wayland by their embodiment in the "Scottish school" which exercised such powerful influence on American colleges in the late eighteenth and early nineteenth centuries.[20] In his student days at Union College, Wayland studied *The Elements of Criticism* by Lord Kames (Henry Home) and Dugald Stewart's *Elements of the Philosophy of the Human Mind*.[21] When he began teaching at Brown, fifteen years later, he used as texts both these books and also *The Philosophy of Rhetoric* by George Campbell, a member of the famous Aberdeen Philosophical Society.[22] It may also be noted that Wayland greatly admired the Scotch theologian-economist Thomas Chalmers.[23] Chalmers was one of the "heretics" who rejected the "orthodox" position of British classical political economy by asserting the possibility of "general gluts." Wayland's treatment of this topic, under the heading "Stagnation of Business," seems unclear and unsure of itself, a reflection, perhaps, of Chalmers' influence.

Ambivalence was not generally characteristic of Wayland's teachings on the subject of political economy. God had ordained laws governing morality and laws governing the accumulation of wealth, and Wayland did not expect to find contradictions between them. "In political economy as in morals." Wayland insists,

> every benefit is mutual; and we cannot, in the one case, any more than in the other, really do good to ourselves, without doing good to others; nor do good to others, without also doing good to ourselves.[24]

Wayland often pauses to call his reader's attention to the divinely intended harmony in the relations he is describing.

> All the forms of industry mutually support, and are supported by, each other;... any jealousy between different classes of producers, or any desire on the one part, to obtain special advantages over the other, are unwise, and, in the end, self-destructive.[25]

Nothing can, therefore, be more unreasonable than the prejudices which sometimes exist between these different classes of laborers, and nothing can be more beautiful, than their harmonious cooperation in every effort to increase production, and thus add to the conveniences and happiness of man.[26]

Trade, especially international trade, is a fulfillment of God's plan for amity:

God intended that men should live together in friendship and harmony. By thus multiplying indefinitely their wants, and creating only in particular localities, the objects by which those wants can be supplied, he intended to make them all necessary to each other; and thus to render it no less the interest, than the duty of everyone, to live in amity with all the rest.[27]

Individuals are thus made dependent upon each other, in order to render harmony, peace, and mutual assistance, their interest as well as their duty....

And, for the same reason, nations are dependent on each other. From this universal dependence, we learn that God intends nations, as well as individuals, to live in peace, and to conduct themselves towards each other upon the principles of benevolence.[28]

Toward the end of the book, after discussing some common causes of inefficiency, Wayland comments:

We see, in the above remarks, another illustration of the truth, that the benefit of one is the benefit of all, and the injury of one is the injury of all.... [H]e who is honestly promoting his own welfare, is also promoting the welfare of the whole society of which he is a member.[29]

Wayland is so impressed with the mutually beneficial aspects of self-interested behaviour that he has trouble recognizing or acknowledging that interests can also conflict. Don't poor harvests in one region cause higher prices and greater prosperity for farmers in other regions? Don't sellers sometimes benefit from the greater scarcity that is caused by the misfortunes of others? Wayland is reluctant to admit this. He appeals to the true but irrelevant argument that sellers benefit from the prosperity of their customers, and applies the label "short sighted, as well as morally thoughtless" to merchants who expect "to grow rich by short crops, civil dissensions, calamity, or war."[30]

Monopoly, from this perspective, is self-defeating. If the agricultural interests of Great Britain had not tried to maintain high prices through the Corn Laws, but had allowed imported grain to lower the price of food, population growth and industrial growth over the most recent fifty years would have more than compensated for the landed proprietors' loss. Wayland concludes a somewhat vague analysis with the observation:

> If this be so, it is another illustration of the universal law, that a selfish policy always in the end defeats itself; and reaps its full share of the gratuitous misery which it inflicts upon others.[31]

Wayland on the relation between economics and morality

The essential unity that Wayland saw between the laws of political economy and the laws of morality emerges most clearly in his chapter "Of the Laws Which Govern the Application of Labour to Capital."

Section I of the chapter explains how the laws on this subject are founded on "the conditions of our being," conditions that Wayland summarizes in seven paragraphs.[32]

1. God has created man with faculties adapted to physical and intellectual labour.
2. God has made labour necessary to the attainment of the means of happiness.
3. We are so constituted that physical and intellectual labour are essential to health. Idiocy or madness is the consequence of intellectual sloth; feebleness, enervation, pain, and disease appear in the absence of physical labour.
4. Labour is pleasant, or at least less painful than idleness. People crave challenges on which to exercise their faculties.
5. God has attached special penalties to idleness, such as ignorance, poverty, cold, hunger, and nakedness.
6. God has assigned rich and abundant rewards to industry.

Wayland's seventh paragraph draws the conclusion: We are required "so to construct the arrangements of society, as to give free scope to the laws of Divine Providence." We must "give to these rewards and penalties their free and their intended operation." We are bound, at the very least, to try these means first if we want to stimulate economic growth, and to avoid other policies "until these have been tried and found ineffectual." Everyone should be "permitted to enjoy, in the most unlimited manner, the advantages of labour," and all should suffer the consequences of their own idleness.

In Section II Wayland explains what is required if each is to enjoy, in the greatest degree, the advantages of his labour.

> It is necessary, provided always he do not violate the rights of his neighbor, 1st, *That he be allowed to gain all that he can;* and, 2d, *That, having gained all that he can, he be allowed to use it as he will.*

The first condition can be achieved by abolishing common property and assigning all property to specific individuals. These individually-held property rights must then be enforced against potential violation either by individuals or by society. Individual violations are held in check through the inculcation of moral and religious principles—the most certain and necessary method of preventing violations—and through equitable laws firmly and faithfully applied. Violations by society, through arbitrary confiscation, unjust legislation, or oppressive taxation, are more destructive than individual violations, because they inflict wrong through an agency that was created for the sole purpose of preventing wrong and thereby they dissolve the society itself. The best preventative is an elevated intellectual and moral character among the people and a constitution which guarantees immunity from public as well as from private oppression.[34]

The second condition is achieved when individuals are allowed to use their labour and their capital as they please, without legislative interference, so long as they respect the rights of others.[35]

In Section III Wayland shows what must be done to make sure that everyone "suffers the inconveniences of idleness." If the dishonest acquisition of property is prevented "by the strict and impartial administration of just and equitable laws," then, in a regime

of private property, "the indolent" will be left "to the consequences which God has attached to their conduct. . . . they must
obey the law of their nature, and labour, or else suffer the penalty
and starve."[36]

What about charity? Where people are poor because "God has
seen fit to take away the power to labour," God has also commanded generosity on the part of those who have wealth to bestow.
But no one is entitled to support merely by virtue of being poor, and
institutions that provide relief to the indigent without any labour requirement are "injurious."

Dependency

Poor laws violate "the fundamental law of government, that he who
is able to labour, shall enjoy only that for which he has laboured."
By removing the fear of want, they reduce the stimulus to labour
and the amount of product created. By teaching people to depend
on others, they create a perpetual pauper class. This process, once
initiated, grows progressively. Eventually it destroys the right of
property itself by teaching the indolent that they have a right to be
supported and the rich that they have an obligation to provide that
support. Poor laws thereby foster class conflict.[37]

In cases where a person has been reduced, by indolence or prodigality, to such poverty that he is in danger of starving, he should be
"furnished with work, and be remunerated with the proceeds."[38]

Section IV explains how the accumulation of capital increases the
demand for labour and the rate of wages. Section V argues for "universal dissemination of the means of education and the principles of
religion" on the grounds that intellectual cultivation and high moral
character among a people promote prosperity.[39]

In Section VI Wayland reluctantly takes up "bounties and
protecting duties, as a means of increasing production." His reluctance is due to his inability to discover how they can produce this
effect; but he knows that popular opinion holds otherwise and so he
cannot pass the subject by in silence. After presenting a careful and
quite classical criticism of such measures on economic grounds,[40]
Wayland raises the moral question: *By what right* does society interfere in this way with the property of the individual, and without
offering compensation? He declines to answer, however, on the
grounds that this question belongs not to political economy but to

moral philosophy; but he clearly thinks that no satisfactory answer can be given to his essentially rhetorical question.[41]

After stating and criticizing, again in an orthodox classical manner, the arguments in favour of legislative stimulus to industry, Wayland raises the Smithian question of whether it is not unjust for a government to abolish a restrictive system upon which people have come to depend. "To this objection," he says,

> I have no desire to make any reply. It is a question of morals and not of political economy. Whatever the government has directly or indirectly pledged itself to do, it is bound to do. But this has nothing to do with the question of the expediency, or inexpediency, of its having, in the first instance, thus bound itself; nor with the question whether it be not expedient to change its system as fast as it may be able to do so, consistently with its moral obligations.[42]

The section and chapter conclude with a brief account of what governments *can* do to promote industry and increase production. They can enact and enforce equitable laws; promote education and learning; manage strictly experimental farms and manufactures; and above all:

> They can do much by confining themselves to their own appropriate duties, and leaving every-thing else alone. The interference of society with the concerns of the individual, even when arising from the most innocent motives, will always tend to crush the spirit of enterprise, and cripple the productive energies of a country. What shall we say, then, when the capital and the labour of a nation are made the sport of party politics; and when the power over them, which a government possesses, is abused, for the base purpose of ministering to schemes of political intrigue?[43]

Wayland was not, strictly speaking, an advocate of *laissez-faire*. As we have just seen, he supported government-sponsored industrial research, and he believed that what economists today call "externalities" justified government efforts to increase and disseminate knowledge.[44] He argues that religious institutions also confer benefits upon the state and upon people who have not contributed to their support; but he refuses to draw the conclusion that this entitles religious institutions to a share of the funds from public taxation.[45] He doubts that public funds ought to be used to finance most internal improvements, such as roads, canals, or railroads; these are better left to individual enterprise, which will undertake them when they are profitable and leave them alone when they are not. There will be exceptions, however, such as works of exceptional magnitude or where the public importance of the work is too great for it to be entrusted to private corporations. Works for the improvement of external commerce, such as the improvement of coasts and harbours, are assigned entirely to government.[46]

The relief of the sick, destitute, and helpless is a religious duty, in Wayland's view, and for that reason ought to be left to voluntary efforts. He recognized, however, that purely voluntary relief would occasionally be inadequate and might in addition strain the resources of the most charitable. So he was willing to allow some provision out of tax revenues "for the relief of those whom old age, or infancy, or sickness, has deprived of the power of providing the means necessary for sustenance." For the sake of these people themselves, as well as for the sake of the economy, relief should be provided in return for labour in the case of all those capable of work.[47]

Wayland's theological economics

American economists of this period, unlike their European counterparts, were not much concerned with the Malthusian problem.[48] Wayland was no exception. Near the beginning of his chapter on wages, he takes up the possibility that human beings will reproduce too rapidly for the real wage-rate to be maintained above the subsistence level. This does occur, he asserts, and the consequences are "painful to contemplate." But after quoting Adam Smith on the high infant mortality rates in the Scottish Highlands and in military barracks, Wayland abruptly changes direction.

God could scarcely have intended so many to die in infancy from hardship and want. It therefore follows that the normal wage level for industrious, virtuous, and frugal workers will be one "which allows of the rearing of such a number of children as naturally falls to the lot of the human race." Improvidence, indolence, intemperance, and profligacy can interfere with this happy outcome; but in such cases "the correction must come, not from a change in wages, but from a change in habits."[49]

It is at first difficult to reconcile this position with Wayland's explanation of how the supply of labour adjusts itself to the demand, or his account of the relationship between the growth of capital and the growth of population. His conclusion to the latter discussion is especially puzzling:

> And hence, there seems no need of any other means to prevent the too rapid increase of population, than to secure a correspondent increase of capital, by which that population may be supported.[50]

The clear implication is that, unless God intended many to perish in infancy, capital can always and everywhere be accumulated at least as fast as the population chooses to expand.

Wayland has an escape from this strong implication, however. God is not responsible for evil that is the consequence of immoral behaviour, and the rate of capital accumulation is crucially dependent upon moral considerations. Frugality increases it, prodigality diminishes it, laws of entail diminish it, as do all restrictive laws that "fetter and dispirit industry." Above all, however, war diminishes the rate of capital accumulation:

> If the capital which a bountiful Creator has provided for the sustenance of man, be dissipated in wars, his creatures must perish from the want of it. Nor do we need any abstruse theories of population, to enable us to ascertain in what manner this excess of population may be prevented. Let nations cultivate the arts of peace.[51]

In a properly ordered society of moral persons, capital accumulation will be adequate for the number of people and "we shall hear no more of the evils of excess of population."[52]

This analysis still leaves room for paupers to blame their plight upon others, albeit immoral others. Wayland closes that door with the claim that almost all crime and pauperism in the community is caused by intemperance, and the further claim that America, which has few beggars, would have none at all if intemperance and vice were eliminated.

Wage determination

The laws that regulate wage-rates are finally beyond the power of individual capitalists or labourers to affect. The competition that will naturally exist where there are no restrictions on the mobility of capital or labour will "bring wages to their proper level; that is, to all that can be reasonably paid for them." Combinations among capitalists or workers designed to raise or lower wage-rates are "useless," Wayland asserts, because combinations cannot 'change the laws by which remuneration is governed. Without pausing to defend this *non sequitur*, he hastens to add that combinations are also expensive, because they expose capital and labour to long periods of idleness. And combinations are unjust, because they deprive the capitalist of the right to employ labour and workers of the right to be employed on terms to which the parties have freely agreed. Is this another case where moral philosophy has crowded out economic analysis? The injustice of a particular combination does not guarantee that the combination will be unable to increase the wealth of those who participate in it.

Wayland has the same sort of difficulty when he tries to explain why political economy finds laws regulating interest rates "injurious to the prosperity of a country." His first reason is that such laws violate the right of property. One could make this an "economical" rather than an ethical argument by incorporating into it Wayland's case for the dependence of prosperity on respect for property rights. If this is done, however, the distinction between questions of right and questions of expediency collapses.

The point here is not that Wayland *ought* to have maintained a clear distinction between economic and ethical arguments, but rather that he claimed to be doing so when in fact he was not. The nature of his argument is consequently obscured at important points, and the critical reader is left uncertain about the kind of evidence and arguments that would be required to buttress or to refute his conclusions.

What evidence and arguments are we supposed to consider in evaluating Wayland's claim that labour expended in the creation of a value gives one an exclusive right to the possession of that value? Or his claim that different labourers are "entitled" to dissimilar wages? Or that the liability of *all* property to depreciate in value must be taken into account when estimating the job-destroying effects of machinery? That "the act of creating a value appropriates it to a possessor" and "this right of property is *exclusive?*" That a college graduate is "fairly entitled" to a wage that will compensate him not only for the cost of his education but also for the forgone interest on the amount invested? That the capitalist comes into the market "on equal terms" with the labourer because "each needs the product of the other?'' Or that the capitalist "may justly demand" a greater interest the greater his risk?⁵³

Incorrect generalization

At one point in *The Elements of Political Economy* Wayland finds it "worthy of remark" that human ingenuity has done more to increase "the productiveness of labour" in manufacturing and in transportation than in agriculture. A generalization of that kind presupposes the solution of some rather formidable problems of definition as well as measurement. What is the common denominator in terms of which one can meaningfully compare rates of productivity growth when it is the *usefulness* of diverse products that matters? But Wayland is sure that his generalization is correct, sure enough to add these comments:

> It is, doubtless, wisely ordered that it be so. Agricultural labor is the most healthy employment, and is attended by the fewest temptations. It has, therefore, seemed to be the will of the Creator that a large portion of the human race should always be thus employed, and that, whatever effects may result from social improvement, the proportion of men required for tilling the earth should never be essentially diminished.⁵⁴

Francis Wayland apparently misread "the will of the Creator": in the United States today fewer than 3 per cent of the work force are employed in agriculture. The error in this case may be unimportant, but the problem to which it points is not. Those who look for the will of God behind concrete social arrangements thereby incur an added risk of failing to perceive the social arrangements correctly. Those who concern themselves too quickly with the moral implications of social interactions may become less able to see how those interactions are evolving. And an empirical proposition that supports an important theological or moral conviction can become extraordinarily resistant to anything as inconsequential as empirical evidence and argument.

The reaction against "clerical *laissez-faire*"

Twenty years after Wayland's death and half a century after publication of his textbook on political economy, many influential thinkers and writers still maintained that economics and religion were and ought to be intimately linked. When the American Economic Association was formed in 1885, Protestant clergymen were prominent among its founders. The dominant figure in the organization of the Association was Richard T. Ely, a young economist who insisted upon the necessity of basing economics upon ethics and who wanted to make applied Christianity the foundation of economic reform. Religious impulses played such an open and major role in the Association's early history that even sympathetic participants believed it might be interfering with the scholarly impartiality essential to a scientific body.[55]

The banner under which they organized, however, was decidedly not one behind which Wayland could have marched. The prospectus which Ely sent out in his call for the organization of the American Economic Association included a four-part platform. The first paragraph read as follows:

> We regard the state as an educational and ethical agency whose positive aid is an indispensable condition of social progress. While we recognize the necessity of individual initiative in industrial life, we hold that the doctrine of *laissez-faire* is unsafe in politics and unsound in morals; and that it suggests an inadequate explanation of the relations between the state and the citizens.[56]

The laws of God, which ordained a minimal role for government in economic life according to Wayland, required a vast extension of state activity according to Ely. How did Ely and his associates justify this remarkable about-face? How did they criticize the theological-ethical arguments that had been advanced by Wayland and his school and which were still being taught in the 1880s by prominent academics? The answer is that they did not attempt to do so.

Conflict

The most prominent exponent of "clerical *laissez-faire*" in the 1880s was probably the Reverend Arthur Latham Perry, professor of history and political economy at Williams College, author of several widely used textbooks in economics, and trusted adviser of government officials.[57] Moreover, Perry attacked Ely by name in his *Principles of Political Economy* for urging that government take a hand in the determination of wages. "The fine old Bentham principle of *laissez-faire*," Perry wrote,

> which most English thinkers for a century past have regarded
> as established forever in the nature of man and in God's plans
> of providence and government, is gently tossed by Dr. Ely into
> the wilds of Australian barbarism.
>
> There are some propositions that are *certainly* true, and one of
> them is, that no man can write like that, who ever analyzed
> into their elements either Economics or Politics.[58]

Ely was not one to steer clear of conflict. He often responded to his critics, and he took the lead in the 1880s in attacking the "old school" of political economy. Moreover, ethical and religious premises consistently played a large part in the arguments he advanced on behalf of a reconstruction of economics. Nonetheless, he never attempted a systematic critique of the theological-ethical claims of his opponents or tried to show in what specific ways his own theological-ethical premises were more adequate. His fundamental contentions were that the "old school" relied upon an obsolete deductive method, that it employed much too narrow a conception of economic science, and that it refused to take account of the results of historical research.[59]

Charles Howard Hopkins, in his history of the Social Gospel in American Protestantism, writes:

> The first advocates of social Christianity subjected the presuppositions of classical economic theory to searching criticism.
> They regarded unrestricted competition as an arrogant contradiction of Christian ethics and the inhuman treatment accorded
> the laborer as a violation of fundamental Protestant conceptions of the nature of man.[60]

But condemnations of unrestricted competition or inhuman treatment of labourers do not constitute a criticism of classical economic theory. Hopkins refers to an 1866 article by George N. Boardman as "one of the most searching utterances of its kind in this period."[61] It may be unfair to take this compliment too seriously, especially since Henry F. May finds Boardman's essay "generally in support of contemporary economic theories." But the fact remains that

Boardman's critique is far from searching; that it does not show a wide acquaintance with the literature it purports to discuss; and that the religious critics of "unrestricted capitalism" in the last part of the nineteenth century did not really address the arguments that had been advanced by Wayland or his successors. Neither the economists like Ely nor the clergymen—Washington Gladden, W. D. P. Bliss, and George Herron are more representative figures than Boardman—take the claims of the "clerical *laissez-faire*" school seriously and respond to them.[62]

Refutation?

These views, of course, have been widely repudiated, both in the 1880s and in our own time. But repudiation is not the same as refutation. Contemporary critics have generally assumed that to refute such views as Wayland's it was enough to describe them. Thus Henry F. May, after quoting Wayland on the divine imperative to labour, says: "From this simple proposition Wayland deduced the whole platform of the New England mercantile interest." A page later he refers to Wayland as one of the "simple dogmatists of the thirties and forties [who] set the tone of American political economy for many years to come." May also speaks of "the pat theories of Francis Wayland," his "all-sufficient optimistic formulae," and his "simple, dogmatic method."[63] Simple dogmatisms, pat theories, and all-sufficient optimistic formulae don't have to be taken seriously, especially if they are in reality a defence of special interests rather than an honest effort toward understanding.

One problem with this approach is that it works equally well when applied to the simple dogmatisms, pat theories, and all-sufficient optimistic formulae of Richard Ely and the clergymen who responded so enthusiastically to his call for organization of the American Economic Association. Consider the conclusions of John Rutherford Everett, at the end of his sympathetic study of the relation between religion and economics in the work of Ely and two of his prominent collaborators in the founding of the American Economic Association, John Bates Clark and Simon Patten:

> They are to be criticized ... for falling into the easy optimism
> of the nineteenth century progressivist thought. Although the
> excuse might be found in their unwitting correlation of moral

> and material progress, the error is nonetheless grievous....
> Certainly any perfectionist doctrine of sanctification has ample
> historical and contemporary disproof....
>
> Patten's analysis of selfishness as a result of deficit economics
> is superficial to the point of foolishness....
>
> It certainly looks as though the solution to the economic prob-
> lem offered by these men is nothing short of "social magic."[64]

Moreover, many of the "empirical" conclusions wielded with
such assurance by Ely and his colleagues in the 1880s now seem
quite as *a priori* as the deductive theories they condemned. And
their confident assumption that they were the "new" and
"scientific" school of political economy destined to control the future looks almost pathetic in hindsight; most of them seem to have
been completely unaware in the 1880s of the "marginal revolution"
taking place at that very time, through which "abstract-deductive"
economics would acquire a renewed and more powerful hold on the
discipline.

"Clerical school"

It would be unfair to fault May too severely, since his understanding of "clerical *laissez-faire*" and Francis Wayland was derived
from the scholarly work of Joseph Dorfman and Michael J. L.
O'Connor. Dorfman's *The Economic Mind in American
Civilization* is the indispensable source for anyone interested in
American economics in the nineteenth century. O'Connor's investigation of *The Origins of Academic Economics*, May's principal
source, is actually an examination of the origins and rise to prominence in the northeastern United States of what O'Connor called
the "clerical school." As such it was especially useful to someone
like May who was interested in Protestant analyses of economic issues but was not himself an historian of economics. The biases of
both authors ought to be kept in mind, however, by anyone using
their work.

Dorfman tends to present economic theory as a reflection of the
theorists' social circumstances, with the result that arguments are
sometimes not so much explained as explained away. This tendency
is especially marked in the case of early economists with whose

policy positions Dorfman is not in sympathy. That would emphatically include Francis Wayland, whose treatment by Dorfman comes close to cynicism.

In the ten pages he devotes to "The Reverend Francis Wayland: Ideal Textbook Writer," Dorfman tells us that Wayland studied at Union College under "the famous Reverend Eliphalet Nott, who was highly successful in acquiring a fortune for himself, in obtaining funds from the New York legislature for the college, and in teaching students the ways of God and the world." He states that Wayland received at Union "a thorough indoctrination in the Common Sense philosophy." He sketches Wayland's changes in vocational plans in a way that suggests flightiness or instability. He tells us that Wayland "took an active interest in all the movements that a respectable person should" after becoming President of Brown. His account of Wayland's position on slavery is highly misleading and seems designed to discredit Wayland rather than to present his actual views. The same might be said of his sketch of Wayland's position on the wage-fund doctrine. Dorfman seems almost to postulate bad faith and apologetic intent, as in the claim: "As the cry for tariffs and government relief became more insistent with every depression, Wayland became increasingly adept at mollifying the one and denying the other."[65] The reader would never suspect, for example, that Francis Wayland taught pacifism in his textbook on moral philosophy, raising *and rejecting* each of the standard arguments by which traditional ethical thought had attempted to exempt national governments from the prohibition against returning evil with evil.[66] Dorfman's *ad hominen* arguments are not only irrelevant but also often unfair and occasionally even false, or at least as false as innuendo can ever be.

Omission

May's principal source, however, was O'Connor's meticulously researched *Origins of Academic Economics in the United States*. Because Wayland's *Elements of Political Economy* was the most important text to emerge from the "clerical school," O'Connor presents its contents in some detail. The account is careful and balanced; but there is no systematic criticism of Wayland's economics. The reason for this omission emerges in the concluding chapter, where O'Connor lays out the lessons he would have the reader draw from his study.

The clerical school of political economy, according to O'Connor, was the social instrument of the northeastern merchant-capitalist elite, valuable to them because it taught an ideology that was useful in countering populist political pressures. These religious economists, in supporting the theory of automatic natural-law control, were in reality endorsing the social power of the merchant-capitalist groups and making it easier for that class to enjoy its privileges with a clear conscience. The clerical economists were rewarded with financial aid for the institutions they headed. Their influence lasted well into the twentieth century because cultural lag is so prominent among academics, and because they are willing to use textbooks for sixty or seventy years. The time has now come, however, to purge this obsolete but lingering ideology from economics courses and textbooks and to create a new economics that will "reflect the current social forces of the country" and enable these social forces "to play as directly as possible upon the introductory courses."[67]

In short, there is little point in criticizing Wayland or other representatives of clerical *laissez-faire* because their economics merely reflected their objective social position. The task now is not to construct an economics that will more adequately explain social reality, but to construct a system of economic education that will "command the faith of the people." O'Connor concludes:

> If cultural lags, economic barriers, and vested minority interests prevent such adjustments, the result may be that popular disillusionment which in a democracy leads to social disintegration.[68]

If what purports to be "pure" economic theory can so easily be dismissed by critics as ideology, what fate awaits an economics that is explicitly theological? O'Connor may be extreme in his willingness to reduce social theory to class-based ideology; but he is probably representative in his reluctance to take seriously any theological-ethical justification or defence of a social system of which he disapproves.

Conclusion

This paper began with James Schall's comment on the church's failure to relate Christian ideas to the productive achievements of capitalism. After examining one major effort to do exactly this, we find ourselves wondering at the end what worthwhile purpose it serves.

Does theological economics do anything more than polarize discussion? Those who already approve a particular economic system are generally pleased to read arguments showing that the system is also superior by theological and ethical criteria. Those who disapprove of the system are much less likely even to read a theological-ethical defense of it, and the likelihood is still less that they will read it fairly and sympathetically.

Theological economics or economic theology seems to possess a powerful capacity for turning conjectures into convictions and for making the rejection of favoured hypotheses seem like moral cowardice. Significant issues that could be illuminated or even resolved by careful empirical inquiry are instead "settled" on the basis of what fits most comfortably into the system. That healthy suspicion of one's own argument which is always difficult to keep alive when one is working toward a thesis seems almost impossible to maintain in theological economics. Even more serious is the tendency of those who practise theological economics to assess the cogency of their opponents' arguments by attacking imputed (and, of course, assumed) motives. It is so tempting and so easy, when we imagine ourselves to be standing on the high ground of theology or morality, to slander our opponents by accusing them of slander—or other hidden and malicious intent.

The fate of George Gilder's *Wealth and Poverty* strikes me as sadly instructive. Here is a popularly-written but nonetheless serious and well-documented attempt to examine some of the relationships between economic behaviour and religious beliefs. The book deserves the careful attention of any American who is both concerned for the health of the United States economy and convinced that an adequate economic system must satisfy important ethical criteria. The point is not that Gilder is correct: it is rather that he has raised most of the important questions in a careful and responsible way, citing his evidence and spelling out his reasoning. The sadly instructive fact is that his argument for the moral merits of capitalism has not been taken seriously by the moral critics of capitalism within the churches. The book has hardly been reviewed in the religious press. Where it is mentioned, it is usually caricatured, with some such phrase as "a bible for those who have recently come to make absolute claims for private enterprise."[69]

There is little to be learned from those who make absolute claims about economic systems, and even less to be learned from those who imagine that a caricature constitutes a rebuttal.

NOTES

1. James V. Schall, "Catholicism and the American Experience," *This World* (Winter/Spring 1982), p. 8.

2. Edwin R. A. Seligman conferred this distinction on McVickar in "Economics in the United States: An Historical Sketch," reprinted in his *Essays in Economics* (1925), p. 137. Michael J. L. O'Connor, in the course of surveying existing literature on the origins of American economics, has shown that McVickar's title is open to challenge. O'Connor, *Origins of Academic Economics in the United States* (1944), pp. 6–18.

3. "That science and religion eventually teach the same lesson, is a necessary consequence of the unity of truth, but it is seldom that this union is so early and so satisfactorily displayed as in the researches of Political Economy." John McVickar, *Outlines of Political Economy: Being a Republication of the Article upon that Subject [by J. R. McCulloch] Contained in the Edinburgh Supplement to the Encyclopedia Britannica, together with Notes Explanatory and Critical, and a Summary of the Science* (1825), p. 69. See also McVickar's notes on pp. 88, 102–03, and 159–60 and his Concluding Remarks on pp. 186–88.

4. Henry F. May, *Protestant Churches and Industrial America* (1949), p. 14.

5. O'Connor, *op. cit.*, p. 189.

6. Charles Dunbar, in a centennial review of "Economic Science in America, 1776–1876," mentioned "President Wayland's book" as "the only general treatise of the period which can fairly be said to have survived to our day." Charles Franklin Dunbar, *Economic Essays*, edited by O. M. W. Sprague (1904), p. 12. Joseph Dorfman devotes a chapter to "The School of Wayland" in *The Economic Mind in American Civilization*, Vol. II (1946), pp. 758–71. John Roscoe Turner's 1921 esay on *The Ricardian Rent Theory in Early American Economics* states: "[Wayland's] *Elements of Political Economy* (1837) was, as a text, the best work previous to the Civil War, and probably as popular as any American text on this subject. It survives, and is used as a text in some places to this day." p. 61.

7. See *A Memoir of the Life and Labors of Francis Wayland, D.D., L.L.D.,* assembled and written by his sons Francis Wayland and H. L. Wayland, originally published in two volumes in 1867 and reprinted in a single bound volume by Arno Press in 1972.

8. Gladys Bryson, "The Emergence of the Social Sciences from Moral Philosophy," *International Journal of Ethics* (April 1932), pp. 304–12.

9. Francis Wayland, *The Elements of Political Economy,* p. iii. All page references will be to the 1857 edition, (Boston: Gould and Lincoln).

10. *Ibid.,* p. iv.

11. *Ibid.*

12. *Memoir,* Vol. I, p. 380.

13. Francis Wayland, *The Elements of Moral Science,* p. 25. The edition used is the 1854 edition, (Boston: Gould and Lincoln).

14. *Memoir,* Vol. I, p. 233.

15. Wayland, *The Elements of Political Economy,* pp. 128–30; Adam Smith, *An Inquiry into the Nature and Causes of the Wealth of Nations,* Book V, Chapter I, Part III, Article 2d.

16. Wayland, *ibid.,* pp. 311–13; Smith, *ibid.,* Book I, Chapter X, Part I.

17. Wayland, *ibid.,* pp. 188–288, especially pp. 211–12, 231–32, 259–61, 278–79; Smith, *ibid.,* Book II, Chapter II.

18. Wayland, *ibid.,* pp. 145–51; Smith, *ibid.,* Book IV, Chapter II.

19. Wayland, *ibid.,* pp. 391–97; Smith, *ibid.,* Book V, Chapter II, Part II.

20. Bryson, *op. cit.,* p. 309.

21. *A Memoir . . .,* Vol. I, p. 32.

22. *Ibid.*, p. 227.

23. *Ibid.*, Vol. II, pp. 39–40, 289–90.

24. Wayland, *Political Economy*, p. 171.

25. *Ibid.*, p. 46.

26. *Ibid.*, pp. 55–56.

27. *Ibid.*, p. 91.

28. *Ibid.*, pp. 159–60.

29. *Ibid.*, p. 378.

30. *Ibid.*, pp. 176–77.

31. *Ibid.*, pp. 343–44.

32. *Ibid.*, pp. 105–08.

33. *Ibid.*, p. 108.

34. *Ibid.*, pp. 109–13.

35. *Ibid.*, pp. 113–18.

36. *Ibid.*, p. 119.

37. *Ibid.*, pp. 119–20.

38. *Ibid.*, p. 122.

39. *Ibid.*, pp. 123–32.

40. *Ibid.*, pp. 133–40.

41. *Ibid.*, pp. 140–41.

42. *Ibid.*, p. 151.

43. *Ibid.*, p. 152.

44. *Ibid.*, p. 128. For his views on how government should offer financial assistance to education, see pp. 399–403.

45. *Ibid.*, pp. 403–04.

46. *Ibid.*, pp. 184–86, 404–05.

47. *Ibid.*, p. 405.

48. George Johnson Cady, "The Early American Reaction to the Theory of Malthus," *Journal of Political Economy* (October 1931), pp. 601–32.

49. Wayland, *Political Economy*, pp. 293–94.

50. *Ibid.*, p. 305.

51. *Ibid.*, pp. 305–07.

52. *Ibid.*, p. 308.

53. *Ibid.*, pp. 19, 26, 98–99, 154, 297, 301, 320.

54. *Ibid.*, pp. 47–48.

55. For an excellent and fairly recent survey of these events, see A. W. Coats, "The First Two Decades of the American Economic Association" (*American Economic Review*, September 1960), pp. 555–74. Joseph Dorfman probably offers the best general introduction to the period in *The Economic Mind in American Civilization*, Vol. III (1949), pp. 113–212.

56. Ely reproduced the prospectus in his autobiography, *Ground Under Our Feet* (1938), p. 136.

57. Dorfman, *op. cit.*, Vol. III, pp. 56–63; O'Connor, *op. cit.*, pp. 265 66.

58. Arthur Latham Perry, *Principles of Political Economy* (1891), pp. 251–52.

59. See especially Ely's contributions to the 1886 exchanges in *Science* between the "old" and the "new" sciences of political

economy: Ely, "Economics and Ethics," *Science* (June 11, 1886), pp. 529–33; "The Economic Discussion in *Science*," *ibid.*, (July 2, 1886), pp. 3–6 (a rejoinder to Simon Newcomb); and his reply to a negative review by N[icholas] M[urray] B[utler] of his book *The Labor Movement in America*, *ibid.* (October 29, 1886), pp. 388–89. For Ely's comments on Perry, see *Ground Under Our Feet*, pp. 127 28.

60. Charles Howard Hopkins, *The Rise of the Social Gospel in American Protestantism, 1865–1915* (1940), p. 25.

61. George N. Boardman, "Political Economy and the Christian Ministry," *Bibliotheca Sacra* (January 1866), pp. 73–107; Hopkins, *ibid.*

62. The best survey of this literature with which I am familiar, covering both the social gospel and the "new" political economy, is that of Sidney Fine, *Laissez Faire and the General-Welfare State: A Study of Conflict in American Thought, 1865–1901* (1956), pp. 167–251.

63. May, *op. cit.*, pp. 15, 16, 91, 111, 141.

64. John Rutherford Everett, *Religion in Economics* (1946), pp. 143–44.

65. *Ibid.*, Vol. II, pp. 758–67. Dorfman's treatment of the slavery issue should be compared with Wayland's *Elements of Moral Science*, pp. 206–16. Dorfman accords John McVickar, the other leading clerical economist of this period, a similar treatment: *Ibid.*, pp. 515–22, 713–20.

66. Wayland, *The Elements of Moral Science*, pp. 390–95.

67. O'Connor, *op. cit.*, pp. 277–89.

68. *Ibid.*, p. 289.

69. The phrase is from John C. Bennett's lecture on "Reaganethics," reprinted in *Christianity and Crisis* (December 14, 1981), p. 340.

Comment

Martin E. Marty

Three-fourths of Paul Heyne's paper is devoted to Francis Way-land's *The Elements of Political Economy*. This apportioning of energies is extremely attractive to an historian of American religion, an event that delights the eyes of someone who too regularly sees people like Wayland left in the obscurity of the American sub-basement. Heyne does justice to the achievement and the limits of Wayland. The book was enormously influential and carefully rea-soned, and here it is accurately summarized and reasonably com-mented upon.

There is little point in my dwelling on Wayland's book or Heyne's account of it. He uses Wayland chiefly to show that once upon a time there was such a thing as respectable clerical *laissez-faire* argument— or almost *laissez-faire*, for Wayland qualified his approach, as Heyne himself notes. I take it that Heyne is less inter-ested in saying, "read Wayland," or "believe Wayland" as he is in saying, "imitate Wayland's intention" in the language of a new day.

We cannot go back to Wayland, as his commentator well knows. Heyne reminds us that Wayland cherished "the Scottish school." He was an heir of Scottish Common Sense Realism, a philosophical outlook that is simply not available to philosophers or economists today. From the viewpoint of thinkers across most of the spectrum today, his book would be an interesting period piece, a reminder that Wayland built a rather impressive structure on what is now a metaphysically condemned site. You might want to visit it now and then as a curiosity but you wouldn't, you couldn't live there.

For those who do wish to pick up Waylandian themes I suggest direct conversation with Professor Heyne, who has read the author more recently and with closer care than I have. Let me use an im-age and say that around the Wayland picture Heyne has presented a very interesting and attractive frame. I shall comment on that frame as a stimulus to further conversation between him, his audience, his readers, and the larger community of political economists and economic politicians, theological economists and economical theologians.

What Heyne is "really trying to do"

Heyne's essay, I take it, is a call or four kinds of call:

1. He would like us to appreciate if not a classic, then still an exemplar of American clerical *laissez-faire*, for the sake of its own inner integrity, so that we recognize that such a school of thought existed, and that we might take lessons from the author's intention. This point is fairly easily made, taken up, and followed if we have the will to follow.

   With this first part of his call Heyne does not try anything overly ambitious. That is, he does not commend Wayland as intrinsically awesome, as a classic. The author was a talent, not a genius. We have to decide to read it; we can be kept from it. We cannot, if we have passions in this field, be kept from the works of genius, no matter from what direction they come. Adam Smith and Karl Marx will attract friend and foe for centuries to come. After this conference Wayland will be back in the Old Curiosity Shop, having served our present purposes and merited our thanks.

2. Heyne would use the occasion to point to the dangers of theological economics and economic theology. "Theological economics or economic theology seems to possess a powerful capacity for turning conjectures into convictions and for making the rejection of favoured hypotheses seem like moral cowardice." He continues his attack on this approach for its failure to be empirical and for the temptation it brings for people on all sides to attack the motives of others. I agree with his criticism of the tendencies when the theology and economics are brought together, but shall try to show that when one gets near the zone where theology and economics meet—and there manifestly is such a zone!—"theological economics or economic theology" is inevitable. What we must do is not dismiss it but improve the rules of the game, and play by them.

3. Heyne concludes by calling for fairness on the part of a reader-

ship that approaches or should approach a twentieth century work on the elements of political economy, George Gilder's, *Wealth and Poverty*. This book is, as he says, an attempt "to examine some of the relationships between economic behaviour and religious beliefs." For some reason, however, Heyne does not go on to give us the gist or heart of Gilder. Whoever has read it will know that it is, is not ashamed of being, and aggressively purports to be a work of theological economics and economic theology. Gilder undertakes a work there that, had he been a genius and written a classic, would stand for the ages. He sets out to show that the risk inherent in capitalist ventures is a form of altruism. Therefore it is in the zone of religious sentiment and motivation. Gilder says that capitalism as he describes it is a work of faith and it demands a faith.

It is beyond my scope to say that Gilder possesses "a powerful capacity for turning conjectures into convictions and for making the rejection of favoured hypotheses seem like moral cowardice." It is within my scope to say that his genre definitely falls into the "theology—plus—economics" zone and deserves careful reading on those terms. Heyne could have chosen any number of cooler, more dispassionate, more analytical works to illustrate the idea that there can be "attempts to examine some of the relationships between economic behavior and religious beliefs."

4. It may seem condescending, even infuriating, to an author to be told what he or she is "really doing," but I mean no condescension and I hope not to infuriate Heyne by saying that what the open and close of his essay shows him "really to be doing" in his framing and framework is to ask for equal time. His quotation of James V. Schall on the first page and his reference to the treatment or mistreatment of George Gilder on the last, along with his helpful analysis of the limits of progressive or Social Gospel liberalism as theological economics make clear that what bothers him is the onesidedness of so much religious inquiry and advocacy in the field of modern economic theory.

This observation, which I hope is sustainable in the eyes and minds of other readers and which I hope will convince Paul Heyne in response, leads to the main points of my own reaction. The purpose of responses of my sort, I always assume, is to draw out the author of the original essay rather than to state a counter-thesis that obscures his. To draw him out, then, I would be explicit: "Professor Heyne, are you now, or have you ever been, an advocate of 'equal time' and 'fairness' in theological economics or economic theology—or do you really mean that the interdisciplinary field itself is so full of hazards that it should be eliminated?"

Can there be genuine dialogue in "theological economics"?

If the latter, to draw him out further, I would say I disagree. It is possible to sustain debate about economics, social thought, republican polity, and civil life without engaging at all points in what Albert Cleage has called "religiocification." Not all talk about economics has to express "ultimate concern," or have ritual and mytho-symbolic value, supported by metaphysical sanctions and implying sustained behavioural correlates. (That sentence is intended to include some of the elements of definition of "religion," the interpretation of which would be "theology.") I would resent as much as does Heyne the imperial definitions of religion that let nothing be non-religion, or of theology that allows for no non-theological zones.

At the same time, there *are* theological and quasitheological motifs in Adam Smith and Karl Marx and the many heirs of both. They make assumptions about the most profound elements of human nature and about the right use of property. Both Smith and Marx, moreover, are philosophers of history—they treat the future as if it had already occurred, for which one needs some relevation or metaphysical speculation—and thus tread dangerously close to the explicit theological economists and economic theologians.

The economic debates of our day do fall into a field that the late Father John Courtney Murray so well described in *We Hold These Truths* (New York: Sheed and Ward, 1960, p. 15): "As we discourse on public affairs, on the affairs of the commonwealth, and particularly on the problem of consensus, we inevitably have to move upward, as it were, into realms of some theoretical generality—into metaphysics, ethics, theology." Murray continues ruefully, with a line that Heyne could have written: "This movement does not carry us into disagreement; for disagreement is not an easy thing to reach. Rather, we move into confusion. Among us there is a plurality of universes of discourse. These universes are incommensurable." In the confusion, "one does not know what the other is talking about. One may distrust what the other is driving at." I take it that the purpose of the present conference and inquiry is to help us gain enough commensurability to be able to have a universe of discourse, and to move from confusion to disagreement.

How did we come to our present incommensurabilities of discourse, our distanced universes of meaning? We might accuse each other of bad faith, as some proponents of "democratic capitalism" and "democratic socialism" are wont to do. It is not hard to observe that theologians do tend to blow with the wind if it comes from a strong enough *Zeitgeist*. With Nietzsche, we can criticize them for "thinking what the day thought," for sidling up to power and the powers that be. This is what the founders of "the Scottish school" did when *laissez-faire* thought was being shaped in the eighteenth century. The early "Christian Socialists," F. D. Maurice and J. Malcolm Ludlow, tried to socialize the Christian order in an age when secular-minded folk like Robert Owen and Karl Marx were socializing without Christianity.

Unanimity

Somewhat later, in the era of Social Darwinism, (a neo-Lamarckian secularization of some Calvinist capitalist drives), almost the entire Protestant clerical establishment wrote or preached in defence of *post*-clerical *laissez-faire*. Richard Hofstadter's durable monograph, *Social Darwinism in American Thought* (Philadelphia: University of Pennsylvania Press, 1944) is eloquent testimony to the theologians' virtual unanimity. Then the wind blew from another direction, and the men to whom Heyne refers critically—Richard T. Ely, Washington Gladden, W. D. P. Bliss, George Herron (he should have mentioned Walter Rauschenbusch) wanted to *Christianize the Social Order* on progressivist, mildly socialist lines of thought then current.

They failed. In 1901 Herron had prophesied: "now is the time of Socialist salvation, if we are great enough to respond to the greatness of our opportunity." In 1925 he mourned, "I really believed... that America would... become a Messianic nation... in which there would be a new human order that would be at least an approach to the kingdom of heaven...." But it had turned into the kingdom of hell. The Age of Normalcy hardly lasted long enough for theologians to retool after the demise of the Social Gospel. But for the next fifty years most Catholic and Protestant theological economists and economic theologians were devotees of some form of welfare-minded, liberal, New-Deal progressivism. A few were socialist.

Today that epoch is over, or its assumptions are being qualified and new economic thinkers are in power in government, supported by a new generation of qualified advocates of "clerical *laissez-faire.*" This is a game that is played by innings, and a new team is at bat. At such a moment it is easy to question the assumptions of thinkers in the previous era, easier than to examine those of the school now in vogue. Heyne's essay provides an opportunity for doing both.

Rather than see theological economics or economic theology as illegitimate, it might be more advisable to ask in what ways it is legitimate and to engage in criticism of the assumptions and proposals of those who work in that discipline or interdisciplinary zone. We have no right to expect it to be merely critical, always judgmental. At least in the Jewish and Christian orbits, there are calls for support of political and economic order. God works through human structures and while humans are not to presume that they perfectly represent the mysterious divine will, they are, in Abraham Lincoln's terms, called upon to seek to discern it so far as they are able and humbly to follow it, never claiming that they thus become God or gods or arrogate to themselves divine attributes like omniscience.

Exclusion

At the same time, theological economics and economic theology does and should have a constant critical focus. God, the believer must presume, got along for aeons without either broad set of economic systems that for the past two centuries have been coded under the terms "capitalist" or "socialist." Presumably God can outlast them, world without end, Amen. He that sitteth in the heavens shall laugh at clerical *laissez-faire* supporters of princes and liberation theologian advocates of pretenders who claim to know exactly what God would do were God also in possession of economic facts. Under the conspectus of eternity, it is possible for advocates of both sides, or I would prefer to say—shunning the tyranny of possibly false and certainly confining alternatives—advocates of many, or all sides, to have sufficient identification with current economic theories to be responsible and to keep sufficient distance that they might preserve theonomous notes and a "Protestant principle" of prophetic protest. Or, more modestly, a critical principle.

James V. Schall complains that Catholicism had not developed rationales for the American system with its support of "justice, rights, growth, aid to the poor, quality of life, ownership, dignity of work, and widespread distribution." He might have noted that until a score of years ago Roman Catholics, excluded largely from the public academic dialogue and self-excluded by theological inhibition, were not producing "original thinking" on other subjects. Orestes Brownson, Isaac Hecker, Bishop John Carroll, James Cardinal Gibbons, Monsignor John Ryan—these were eloquent publicists and activists of talent in a church and state that allowed no room for genius to develop. Catholic social thinkers, we remind ourselves, were also not using the American grist to turn out socialist theological economics and economic theology.

We also lack a great Protestant tradition in this field. Wayland is an interesting figure in a gallery but no candidate for a pantheon, nor are Richard Ely and the Social Gospel thinkers. Reinhold Niebuhr, who is claimed for different reasons by both sides, or many sides, today provides some sort of a model and he bears reexamination as advocates of "clerical *laissez faire*," "liberation theology," and "democratic capitalism" or "democratic socialism" line up their pins and positions. Not always aware of his own presuppositions, capable of possessing "a powerful capacity for turning conjectures into convictions and for making the rejection of favored hypotheses seem like moral cowardice," and falling victim to ideologies of what his day thought, he did have some assets we still can use. He was aware that he had unexamined assumptions, provided tools for examining those of which he was aware, and had a theological vantage that allowed for the transcendent note both to energize responsible participation and to help analysts withhold consent and remain critics. He brought to the field a sense of irony from which Francis Wayland could have profited and from which Paul Heyne, Martin E. Marty, and, presumably, the other conferees can still learn.

Reply

Paul Heyne

Professor Marty poses the question: Am I calling for "equal time" and "fairness" in theological economics? Or am I urging abandonment of this interdisciplinary field on the grounds that it is too full of hazards to be cultivated safely?

I certainly believe in fairness; but I don't at all believe that fairness requires equal time for all points of view. As for interdisciplinary talk, I am increasingly inclined toward Frank Knight's suspicion that most interdisciplinary work represents a cross-sterilization of the disciplines. Nonetheless, here we are, engaging in interdisciplinary inquiry. I can hardly intend to reject my own efforts. Let me therefore try to state more clearly what I failed to make clear in my paper. What I learned in the course of preparing it seems, upon reflection, to have changed my underlying attitude toward theological economics.

I am *not* recommending that we imitate Wayland's intention in the language of a new day. I rather want to say: *"Abandon Wayland's intention. Do not use theological arguments to support, in debate, a social analysis."* Why not? Because, as the case of Wayland illustrates, the use of theological arguments to support a social analysis is counter-productive.

To begin with, it hardens one's social analysis and renders it less open to correction.

Secondly, it fosters alliances, and alliances subvert colleagiality. A genuine colleague will tell you exactly where she thinks you're wrong. An ally is less interested in the truth of the matter at hand than in preservation of the alliance, or the overall system, against attacks.

Thirdly, it needlessly and prematurely excommunicates those who disagree. Excommunication is inevitable in communities of inquiry if they are to become and remain effective. But excommunication is an unavoidable evil, not an outcome to be sought or hastened through the employment of theological argument.

Fourthly, theological arguments used in this way never persuade any of those to whom the arguments are directed. When the opinions of economists shifted in the 1880s, no religiously-oriented advocate of increased state activity paid a moment's attention to Wayland's theology. Contemporary scholars who are out of sympathy with Wayland's economic analysis and policy proposals refer to his theology only to caricature or ridicule his position.

Hidden theology

On the other hand, I do not want to be placed among the advocates of a purely "positive" economics.

I believe that any economics which purports to be relevant to policy-making contains a hidden (sometimes not even well-hidden) theology.

I also believe that experts should not be trusted completely: that medical doctors can be too obsessed with physiology to recognize health, that economic doctors too easily forget how little is really settled by their cost-benefit analyses, and that systematic theologians are often more eager to be systematic than theonomous. A man's best friend is too often his dogma.

And I suspect that interdisciplinary inquiry is potentially useful, but only when carried on among friends or genuine colleagues. Areas of overlap or meta-disciplinary questions can probably be explored fruitfully only between people who trust each other, who are trying to understand and improve understanding—not between people interested primarily in gaining acceptance for their own positions.

I would certainly like to take back or revise my concluding references to George Gilder. What I wanted to say is that *Wealth and Poverty* is theological economics and theological economics of substantial merit, as merit is usually measured. The author writes well, has done considerable research, and has attracted a great deal of attention to his arguments. Nevertheless, the religious press has largely ignored the book, and theological critics of capitalism have not responded to his arguments save with jibes and caricature. Isn't this evidence that theological economics promotes polarization, not dialogue or enhanced understanding?

Might it be, however, as Marty suggests, that we just haven't perfected the rules of the game? Perhaps. But when I look at what emerges from the game, I think we would be better off to abandon it. I draw a rather different lesson than does Marty from the career of Reinhold Niebuhr. Those who quote Niebuhr to support their positions seem to me to show thereby that they have missed the point. Niebuhr's sense of irony, ambiguity, and human capability mixed with incapacity are useful when applied to one's own views, but lose their point when employed in argument or when turned into a system of thought (a Niebuhrean *theology*) with which to capture or defend intellectual terrain. I recommend a careful reading of the exchange between Niebuhr and Kenneth Boulding, appended to Boulding's contribution to the Council of Churches' series on Ethics and Economic Life, *The Organizational Revolution*. It shows, I believe, that when Niebuhr distilled his insights into a "theology" for use in debate, he too tended to obscure the issues.

Value judgements

And of course, so does Heyne when he distills his conclusions into four points. But four is at least better than two, as eight would be better than four. The larger number will be more adequate and less polarizing. I think we are too eager to reduce complex, multi-faceted issues to a single question. "It all comes down to this." It probably doesn't; but even if it did, would we know how to test or assess the Big Issue? "Does the competitive economy tend to destroy itself?" That's certainly a Big Picture Question. It's probably also an unanswerable question. Useful discussions take up manageable issues, so that the conversation can focus and the participants can begin to learn from each other. A dialogue on "tendencies of the market economy" will become two monologues. Genuine dialogue requires less ambitious questions, such as "What are the causes and consequences of conglomerate mergers?" (Is that too small a question for theological economics? Are manageable questions perhaps beneath the dignity of theology?)

But what about those "hidden theologies" which I think every serious economic theory harbours? (Hidden agendas would be a less antagonizing term for those who don't agree that economic theory contains any theology.) Isn't it better that the hidden theology be explicit rather than implicit? It may be. The trouble is that not everyone who wants to explicate a hidden theology can do it effectively. Two sorts of people in particular are so bad at articulating hidden theologies that they should never foist their work upon others.

The holder of the theology is one. Gunnar Myrdal has bécome notorious for insisting that value judgements underlie all economic inquiry and that these judgements should be confessed before the economist begins his exposition. The trouble is that Myrdal's confessions become boring before they become revealing. Should we hope for anything else? We don't expect candor from the person who begins, "Let me be candid with you."

The other inept explicator of a hidden theology will be someone who wholly rejects the analysis in question, and consequently wants to *expose* the hidden theology so that its revealed absurdity will condemn the structure allegedly based upon it.

Perhaps theological economics is inevitable, as Marty says. I will continue to wonder whether that calls for us to improve the rules of the game or to make confession of our invincible arrogance.

Discussion

Edited by: Irving Hexham

Anthony Waterman: Though I am not an authority on Margaret Thatcher's thought, I don't think it necessary to prove that she read Malthus in order to be able to assert that she and her colleagues may well have been influenced by this particular tradition. Keynes has some famous, and oft quoted words in the last chapter of the *General Theory*, about politicians and people in authority being slaves of some defunct economist.

Whether we realize it or not, we say and do things which were first thought by Aristotle or somebody long before him. The climate of opinion, the sorts of things which we grow up with and take for granted, are created by all kinds of people in the past, whose existence we are not aware of.

The purpose of my paper is to bring into the open one putative set of influences upon the political thought of modern Christian conservatives. It could well be that a lot of people who call themselves Christian conservatives are more influenced by secular, agnostic, humanistic liberalism than they are by Christian Political Economy. But certainly in England, in the Tory Party, and in the case of Mrs. Thatcher, there is a large element in that tradition which is not in the least bit influenced by, or even sympathetic to, the so-called "liberal conservative" tradition that Stephen Tonsor was talking about. To illustrate my point, I want to remind you of one very important difference between the Tory conservative, which Mrs. Thatcher unashamedly is, and the "liberal conservative" of the secular, agnostic kind. It's almost an axiom of the latter that there should be a clear *separation* between church and state. But Christian conservatives, of the Tory kind, believe that there should be a *union* of church and state.

The episode of so-called Christian Political Economy is the first instance in modern, post-agrarian times, of an attempt to construct a Christian social theory which is formed by the latest, or what were the latest, scientific insights about the nature of a society itself. I am not going to pretend that it isn't open to all kinds of criticism. But I do want to suggest that since that time, in the development of Christian thought, there has been no comparable school. There has not been a school which has had such a firmly social-scientific underpinning in addition to theological insight. Why was it that in the 1830s virtually every influential Christian thinker in Britain belonged to this school, but by the middle of the century it had ceased to command the attention and respect of the British intelligentsia?

I have a hunch, based on Phyllis Dean's argument, that Christian political economy, and the *laissez-faire* approach to social policy which it sanctioned, was or seemed to be appropriate in the early part of the nineteenth century. This is because by focusing attention upon equilibrium outcomes, it drew people's attention to the fact that at equilibrium under competitive conditions the market economy maximizes welfare, subject to all the usual assumptions. Every economist now knows that the welfare predictions of economic theory are not relevant to disequilibrium. In the 1840s and 1850s, however, there were serious disturbances to equilibrium, and Christians, despite their *laissez-faire* principles, found themselves compelled to support intervention.

The basic point is this: a "market economy" type of Christian political thought may be shown to be appropriate to a society in which economic magnitudes are at or near the equilibrium values. It may not be at all appropriate when these magnitudes depart widely from their equilibrium values, because we have to live in the transition.

Paul Heyne: I have tentatively concluded that interdisciplinary inquiry should only be carried on among friends. (laughter) I am very serious about that. Higher questions can only be explored fruitfully between people who trust each other. To illustrate: Marty says he would like to see this group explore the question, "Why has this movement to the left occurred?" I am fearful of this group's taking that up, because we disagree so profoundly on whether it's a good or a bad thing. The question "why" can be discussed among people, all of whom agree it's a good thing, or all of whom agree it's a bad thing. But when you get people who believe that the church's movement to the left is a disaster, talking to people who think that it is fidelity to the gospel, dialogue does not occur.

Finally about Reinhold Niebuhr. I concluded from what I learned from him that anybody who quotes Reinhold Niebuhr has missed the point. (laughter) Reinhold Niebuhr taught the importance of irony, ambiguity, humour, the inescapability of conflict, the existence of contradictions between capability and incapacity. But when you have turned Reinhold Niebuhr into a club with which to beat somebody down, or a weapon with which to seize or hold some territory, I really think you've missed the point.

Martin Marty: A little story may condense my point. The Rabbi of Chelm is finishing his sermon toward sundown before the Sabbath. Children distract him under the window. He says, "Quick, run down to the river. There is a great dragon there. Great plates like bronze are on his sides, under which is puss, and when he breathes, the earth quakes, and inhales the river dry.

And the children think—the Rabbi told us, so they go running down to the river. And the town empties out, so the parents follow the children. And now the Rabbi is left alone in the town and it is kind of eerie and quiet, and the sun is almost setting; so he grabs his hat and runs down to the river and says, "Well, you know I only made it up, but then you never know." (laughter)

Jim Sadowsky: I just want to come to the rescue of what my good friend, Jim Sadowsky (laughter), for whom I have boundless admiration (more laughter), said. To my knowledge he does not engage in theological economics except perhaps in the sense that everybody does anyway. I have to plead innocent to that.

I want to say a word about Anthony Waterman's analysis. The question has been raised: "Why, given the alleged disequilibria in economic situations, did some people start to support interventionism?" First of all there is a problem of talking about disequilibrium. When is the economy not in a state of disequilibrium? Equilibrium is an imaginative state, like a frictionless body, it can never be arrived at. The long lasting unemployment situation in the 1920s and 1930s, was the result of government intervention in support of the trade union movement and its unwillingness to deal with the excessive wage rates that were making so many people unemployable for so long a period of time.

The situation could hardly have obtained had the government not been inflexibly supporting higher than equilibrium wage rates. Surely it's very difficult in the absence of government interference to have inflexible wage rates for a very long period; hence involuntary unemployment cannot last for a long period of time in a free market.

P. J. Hill: I don't see the very clear connection between much of Christian political economy and Margaret Thatcher's position. The connection that Anthony Waterman makes between Thatcher's views about the imperfectibility of man and the position of Malthus about God ordaining misery seems unclear to me.

To argue that man is imperfectible does not necessarily mean that God has ordained poverty. Anthony Waterman argues that, "Though poverty and inequality entails some genuine suffering to be accounted for by the fall, they may therefore for the most part be regarded as a deliberate contrivance by a benevolent God for bringing out the best in his children, and so training for the life to come."

The fact that Margaret Thatcher says man isn't perfect, and has imperfect institutions, doesn't seem necessarily to lead to the conclusion that God finds poverty pleasing or that it is necessarily ordained by Him.

Susan Feigenbaum: Professor Waterman argues that the growing efficiency of government enhances intervention. I find the causal relationship between government efficiency and government size to be problematic. If we look at the work of Jim Buchanan and others who discuss public choice theory we find that government bureaucracy and *inefficiency* lead to expansion of government. In fact it's the extension of political franchises and the impact of interest groups on the political system that leads to growing government intervention.

The argument that if there are economies of scale in government, they will be exploited, and hence government will grow, is problematic. It is certainly the case that in a *laissez-faire* economy, for-profit enterprises would exploit such economies.

However, I am not sure why we would expect, even if there were economies of scale in government, that there is any behavioural or institutional mechanism that would lead it to grow and exploit such economies.

Imad Ahmad: Paul Heyne's arguments show the danger of theological arguments about economies. But I'm not persuaded that they necessarily prohibit such arguments.

He says that theological arguments harden analyses. They often do. But I don't see that they necessarily have to. Hardening of arguments seems to be more a reflection of people's attitudes. If we take theological premises, and try to find what economic conclusions they lead to we have two choices: either to find the flaw in the reasoning or to show that the premises are incorrect.

There is a danger that if people disagree about reasoning, they will challenge arguments on theological premises when they are not really involved.

Heyne also says that theological arguments foster alliances. That's true but then so do economic discussions. People have their economic prejudices just as they have their theological biases. I'm not sure that theological alliances are necessarily as dangerous as he thinks. What theological alliances may do is cause people to give one another the respectful hearing that in the absence of common theological premises they would not be prepared to do.

Thirdly, Heyne says theological economics excommunicates those who disagree. That's certainly true. We also see it in theological physics. Whenever someone wants to maintain that their theology has implications for our view of the physical world, the Galileos get excommunicated. But why is it necessary to excommunicate someone who comes to a theologically incorrect conclusion?

Fourth, in the case of Islam different schools of thought have developed from common theological premises and they led to conclusions that affected various spheres of life. If the same is not true in Christianity, maybe that theology really doesn't have anything to say about economics.

Finally, consider Heyne's point that economic positions reflect hidden theological premises. I think it is important that theological premises be out in the open, and that people see what influences a person's reasoning rather than that their assumptions remain hidden.

Ronald Preston: There was, in fact, a collapse of the Christian social tradition which began at the end of the seventeenth century. It only revived again in the middle of the nineteenth century. It collapsed because it came from a time when the independence of various disciplines from theological control had not been achieved. When Christian social thought began to recover either it referred back to the old tradition and still didn't come to terms with what one might call the autonomy of economics or it made the autonomy too absolute.

I don't think that clerical *laissez-faire* collapsed after the 1830s. It didn't add anything new after that, but it really triumphed. It was the orthodoxy of large numbers of Christian people all through the middle of the nineteenth century.

All the issues of public and social policy go beyond the purely scientific. It's absolutely essential, therefore, that some kind of continued reflection takes place between theologians and economists.

Stephen Tonsor: I would like to suggest that the disappearance of equilibrium theory in economics is a part of the general collapse of equilibrium theories: in cosmology, in biology, in landscape architecture, in physical chemistry, etc. Equilibrium theory as a set of ideas has had its ups and downs. We're currently seeing a resurgence of anti-equilibrium theory in intellectual thought generally.

This is a part of a larger movement in Western thought which has emphasized since the beginning of the nineteenth century, conflict, catastrophe, changes, revolution, class conflict, national conflict, and the survival of the fittest. All of these are a part of a general attack upon equilibrium theory. This discussion must therefore be seen in a larger perspective rather than simply as something which is happening only in economics.

Secondly, Mrs. Thatcher's conservatism is radically different from the conservatism of Edward Heath, Harold MacMillan, Stanley Baldwin, etc., and the British conservative tradition which believed in state intervention. Nineteenth century British conservatism believed that the state had moral purposes and objectives. This radical shift in the British conservative movement is well documented. There are still old conservatives in England but they feel quite estranged from the "Thatcherite" government of the new conservatives.

Finally, Margaret Thatcher is urging that religious and moral ideas be taught in schools. This is a position which has been supported by liberal conservatives since de Toqueville's day. De Toqueville believed that religion was absolutely essential for the survival of democracy. I have no doubt that if de Tocqueville were around today he would advocate prayers in the public schools of the United States. He would support prayer in school even though he believed in disestablishment. There is no incompatibility in being a "Thatcherite" liberal conservative and supporting public religion. Such support for religion doesn't make her an old fashioned conservative.

Marilyn Friedman: When Heyne says that any economics relevant to policy-making contains a hidden theology, I assume he is using the word "theology" in a very broad sense to mean something like "value framework."

My question is: Are the theologies we normally associate with religions more dogmatic and intolerant than those theologies which don't derive their moral concepts from typically religious concepts?

Paul Heyne: Ahmad said, "Isn't it better that the theology hidden in economics be explicit rather than implicit?" I reply. "Yes, but be careful." The trouble is, there are two types of people who are no good at making their hidden theology explicit. One is the economist himself. Gunnar Myrdal illustrates this. He painfully and tediously tries to lay out all his value presuppositions and bores you to death before he reveals anything significant. He approaches his topic with all those vague values such as the dignity of the human person. But the real value assumptions that are informing him are not revealed.

The other person who's no good at revealing your hidden theology is an enemy. He's going to do it in order to show the absurdity of the structure you have erected. That is why I talked about friendly critics.

Perhaps Malthus and his contemporaries represented a group of theologians and social scientists who were friends rather than just allies. But here is a contrast. American economists of that same historical period who were clerical supporters of free markets did not form any kind of scientific community. They weren't professional enough as economists. Maybe they weren't professional theologians either. There is no evidence that they engaged in any kind of critical dialogue with one another.

In answer to Marilyn Friedman's point: the kind of theology I am talking about is whatever ultimately informs a person.

People who stand within a more orthodox theological tradition have a better opportunity to dialogue productively. They are more likely to have a community of colleagues who can criticize one another in a scholarly manner. The kind of vague theology where you appeal to something that you've vaguely apprehended which you call God is the kind of theology that's least likely to be subject to or accept criticism.

Marilyn Friedman: Do you think that people who derive their moral concepts from what are standardly called, "religions," that have some concept of the ultimate ground of all-being, perfection and so on, are worse in regard to those points you mention—hardening social analysis, and so on?

Paul Heyne: What I am trying to say is they are better. Because they are more likely to be sitting among a group of friends and colleagues who will criticize them and prevent them from running and finding God in anything they read such as this morning's editorial page. (laughter)

Richard Neuhaus: The four cautions that Paul Heyne gives for robust skepticism with respect to theological economics are well taken and very important.

Oscar Cullmann, the great New Testament scholar shortly' before his death made a well-known appeal to end what he called "generic theologies" — i.e. theology of sex, theology of society, theology of economics, theology of etc. He said that theology should get back to its proper business: how we relate to that reality we call God.

I think the cautions Heyne raises apply to "generic theologies." Some of us see economic discussion as a fourth level discussion. The main discussion is theological, the second is cultural, the third political, and only then do we discuss economics. Economic questions come in terms of what kind of economic system, or systems, or approach or bias, or whatever, is supportive of those political, cultural and theological assumptions.

This is doing economics by implication. It is economics as an ancillary reflection. I suspect that within religious communities today how scholars view economics is a very significant divide.

Robert Benne: The papers here illustrate how embarrassing it can be for theologians to claim to have identified what God wills in the world, the laws of motion, history, and so on. If that's what is meant by theological economics, it's probably a good thing that we don't engage in it anymore. Niebuhr had a very good instinct for the common ground by which one could begin to talk about theology in relation to economics, or political science. Niebuhr's strength was that he developed a doctrine of human nature or anthropology that was persuasive to people who had very different religious frameworks, and to some who had no religious framework at all.

Niebuhr did not do theological economics nor did he do theological politics. That's why he was so influential. He didn't claim to have discovered the laws of motion, of history, or God's will, or what God is doing in the world. By focusing the discussion on more penultimate questions about common human knowledge and experience we produce an approach to the interrelation of theology and economics which is much richer.

Bob Goudzwaard: Waterman's paper points to the interesting debate between Godwin and Malthus about the perfectability of man. I would like to use that debate in relation to the question about the decline of Christian political economy.

Waterman talks about the presuppositions of Malthus. Here an element of scarcity enters: "Scarcity caused by the principle of population, in fact does bring into existence those very institutions—private property, marriage, base labour, estate—to which Godwin describes human misery."

There is in those institutions, which are essential to an extensive working of the free market economy, an ambiguity because they can be seen to be caused by the existence of scarcity. They can also be seen to overcome scarcity. So the question is how far this system of political economy is destroying its own underpinnings.

Perhaps I can relate this to questions about theology in economics. One of my problems with the discussion of the presuppositions of economics is that it usually starts from the scarcity concept. Therefore it can only define economic objects as objects of use needed to overcome a power of scarcity. The other element, which you find in Aristotle and the Bible is an element of care.

The decline of Christian political economy may have to do with the image of man. It is very clear that Malthus is convinced about the imperfectability of man. Belief in the sinfulness of man is something which leads to a consistent theory in conservative political and economic thought. If you have the idea that sinfulness leads to the accumulation of power, then state intervention should be kept to a minimum.

But if in economic life there is a market institution through which self-interest brings about the well-being of the whole, then you have a system in which you can deal with the general presupposition of human sinfulness. This leads to a belief in minimum state intervention because the market economy restrains sinfulness.

Now, if in reality, the market economy leads to mass production and a decline of competition, and human sinfulness renews itself in the marketplace, then the consistency of the whole theory collapses.

I think that is one of the main reasons for the decline of the so-called Christian political economy.

John Yoder: The problem is misdefined when Paul Heyne makes the possibility of reasonable discussion a matter of theology and economics. I think it is a problem of civility in discourse which applies in all disciplines. The fundamental question is whether you can, in any dialogue, process the other person's position by giving some kind of benefit of the doubt to its integrity and frame of reference. The alternative is to say that the only way to converse is to impose my frame of reference on you, and then it's obviously only to show how silly you are.

What we are talking about is a general question of method in inter-system clashes. This question is quite independent of which discipline we are in. It also applies within each discipline. It's only a little more messy when we are between disciplines.

Now let us get back to the explanation for the waning of the American and the English schools of Christian economics. Waterman suggested that there were social emergencies that obviously required intervention even in the minds of *laissez-faire* theorists and that these crises caused the theories to fall apart. Finally, he uses the Norman thesis of intellectual infiltration as an explanation. I'm not convinced that any of these explanations fits the evidence.

Martin Marty: I would like to comment on the issue of who listens, which Paul Heyne raised. If you pose this question across the line of disciplines, there is not a lot of listening. When I joined a divinity faculty at a university, people said that's strange; you'll be irrelevant to the other disciplines. For a year or two that bothered me. Then I realized that all disciplines seemed irrelevant to each other. (laughter)

I would argue that the importance of hearing is the tie to subcultures which have political potency. This is where the theological economist of left or right or whatever has a certain political potency. You might call it a "trickle down" theory because I'm not sure that the people who make their moves know they're making the moves in the light of the academic experts who devise them.

Some years ago *Newsweek* polled adult American Roman Catholics and found that only 4 per cent were conscious of ever having made a decision in light of what their bishops said. And yet I would argue that more than 4 per cent have done so, because it's mediated through the priest, the religious, popular kinds of literature and so on.

People have to make certain moves. At a certain moment in the 1830s, 1840s, or 1850s, evidently people felt that the patterns we have described in these papers no longer worked. There were no potentials in the economic order. They needed people who could wield and transform certain symbols to give them both a sense of continuity with the tradition and a sense of innovation.

In American Protestantism, Lyman Beecher, in the Wayland era, had a very static view of the economy. He basically preached that the rich should be very self-conscious about the temptations of being rich, and the poor should have contentment with their poverty. His son, Henry Ward Beecher, in a time of an expanding middle class, ministered to the sons and daughters of the once poor who had to make a move into the middle class. To legitimate this move he used the same symbols; heaven, hell, Jesus, God, Holy Spirit, Kingdom, as his father, but in a very different context.

I would argue that this goes on today. Robert Schuller's power as a mediator of psychological theories is to teach people who didn't have it self-esteem. He advocates that they should use self-esteem as an instrument toward economic prosperity. And it works. I think it empirically verifiable that the theology of Norman Vincent Peale and Robert Schuller works if you're in an economic group that has a certain potential.

The current U.S. administration welcomes the fact that there are both pop clerics on television and "new class" clerics in the academy who legitimate some of the moves the public feels it has to make. It feels that the old system, call it the Roosevelt New Deal of fifty years ago, isn't working and we have to try something else. People need a sense that this is latent in the symbolic pool to which they are already committed as Jews, Christians, or whatever.

These are subcultures. The whole culture isn't paying attention. But the people who already believe say, "What must I do?" I think here is where George Gilder was a trial balloon for a certain section of the culture. I don't think he's been that widely read or believed, but some people wanted a theology that would legitimate capitalism as altruism instead of as competition.

On the left, Robert Heilbronner has written a script that says after business civilization collapses, America will reorganize itself economically, when somebody takes existing symbols and says this is all right.

I don't mean that it's mere ideology. I'd rather say it is normal that the public sees a new opportunity, and dares not make the complete break it demands. Professor Gellner has said that Marx would not recognize most societies that call themselves Marxist. We call ourselves Judeo-Christian, but I'm not sure "Judeo" or

Christ could recognize us as such.

However, we recognize continuities. We have to feel we're making a move in the light of our past. So we transform symbols constantly. During the Vietnamese War, American Catholic bishops and major Protestant denomination leaders said that selective conscientious objection was not incompatible with their traditions. They didn't say that tradition impells you to it. But they did say that it's a possibility. This was a move beyond the "mere pacifism" of the Mennonite, Quaker, or Church of the Brethren style.

Today's Roman Catholic bishops may be inspiring a great deal of antagonism. For them to begin to voice criticism of nuclear arms as an option within Roman Catholicism is the beginning of what will probably trickle down into a broader thing.

I think this stand is inducing everything from disdain to panic among people who realize that while the Catholic bishops may not inspire American philosophers, there is a subculture out there over whom they wield considerable, if indirect, power.

Muhammad Abdul-Rauf: I would like to emphasize the relationship between beliefs and lifestyle. If we consider preliterate societies in Africa or Asia, we discover that belief in magic and superstitious ideas do in fact interfere with and determine their way of living. Their belief in the spirits of the ancestors and how they influence their life, etc., all modify the way they live.

The other point is that even in highly developed societies, in recent years, there has been a flow of literature which demonstrates the relationship between theology and economics.

For example Michael Novak talks about the doctrine of the trinity in relation to democratic capitalism. He assumes the existence of three mutually autonomous institutions: the state, the economic institutions, and cultural, religious institutions. He also relates the development of economic capitalism to a belief in incarnation.

Moderator (Walter Block): That's a perfect point upon which to end the round table discussion. I now call upon the paper givers for a summary.

Anthony Waterman: The most important part of my paper was the question of why the British tradition of Christian social thought lost the allegiance of the intelligentsia in the second half of the nineteenth century. Granted Ronald Preston's point that it continued to persist among the public at large, it certainly lost the allegiance of the intelligentsia.

What no economist to my knowledge has yet attempted to construct is a theory of the welfare effects of the transition between one equilibrium position and another. Everybody knows that these can sometimes be serious, because sometimes it takes a long time, and a lot of human suffering, to move from one position to equilibrium to another. A coal miner in the Maritimes who's technologically unemployable will eventually become a computer programmer in Vancouver. But a lot of upset and misery may have to be borne before that new state of affairs is brought about.

Therefore I want to suggest that it is possible, in principle at least, that the difference between those here, who by and large are predisposed in favour of a free enterprise economy, and those who on the other hand are by and large predisposed against, may be merely *empirical*, and not *theoretical* at all. It could be that those who favour a competitive economy with a minimum of government interference, are those who make the empirical judgement that generally speaking the economy is at or near the equilibrium position, and that disturbances to equilibrium are sufficiently small for the painful period of readjustment to be slight, and the costs which have to be borne worth bearing. Whereas those who take the other position may be those who focus very much upon the short-run consequences of disequilibrium, and upon the human suffering, dislocation, and so forth which are involved.

Now, if that way of thinking is correct it may be at least part of the explanation that in the 1840s and 1850s in Britain, there were such violent disturbances to competitive equilibrium that even those who were most firmly convinced of the long-term merits of the capitalist system had to concede from time to time that exceptions should be made. In the name of humanity, intervention was required even though it might preclude the eventual achievement of the welfare optimum associated with full, long period equilibrium.

One of the reasons why Christians, whether predisposed to the Right or Left, have been willing in practice to favour what seemed to be interventionist or Leftist solutions, is because all Christians are obliged to take seriously the welfare of their fellow human beings, even if that violates the canons of perfect, *laissez-faire* competitive equilibrium.

Paul Heyne: I have five points. First of all, I wish I'd never mentioned George Gilder. (laughter)

Secondly, perhaps John Yoder is right in saying that the problem which worries me so much is simply civility.

Third, I think that when Reinhold Niebuhr distilled his considerable insights into a concept with which to debate, he often obscured the issue.

Fourth, Bob Goudzwaard's assertion that the market economy destroys itself—that competition leads to monopoly—is very debatable. Every economist here knows how debatable it is. I would like to suggest that this is a good example of a question that should not be taken up at a high level of abstraction. Too quickly when the economists start talking about this they are pushed into questions of the autonomy of the market system. And that's almost an impossible question to talk about. It polarizes.

Finally, I want to give a partial answer to John Yoder's question: "Why, in the American scene, did the Wayland outlook decline?" I think that one important explanation is the erosion of the belief that private property was "sacred." That is to say, that it stood above government. I think I could demonstrate that this was held by a substantial body of literate, and maybe even illiterate opinion in the early nineteenth century and that this settled the issue for Americans. But that belief changed. Why it changed is itself a complex story. I think one of the reasons was the use of the courts by business entrepreneurs to trespass on private rights. Private rights got violated in the name of economic growth. When Americans thought they had to choose between economic growth and basic rights, they lost their conviction that property rights were sacred.

PART THREE

CHRISTIAN SOCIALISM

Chapter 5

The Legacy of the Christian Socialist Movement in England

Ronald H. Preston

There are many different understandings of socialism. In 1924 Angelo Rappoport referred to thirty-nine definitions of it, and in 1975 R. N. Berki[1] found four major tendencies, in different proportions, in major socialist writings: (1) Egalitarianism and Communitarianism; (2) a Christian moralism of high ideals; (3) a Rationalism, deriving from the Enlightenment, involving expertise and a meritocracy; (4) a Libertarian and Romantic strain of an individualistic, and partly anarchic, type. The second element receives scanty treatment in Berki's book—too scanty—but at least his analysis warns us against exaggerating the legacy of the Christian Socialist movement to socialism. It may well be that it had more, if diffused, influence on the churches. Berki in fact refers only to St. Paul at Philippians 2 verses 3 and following, a passage which I have never before seen mentioned in this connection, and to Thomas More's *Utopia* of 1516. Those of whom I am now writing might never have existed. It is not clear what the qualifying term "moralism" means to him. He confines himself to saying that for Christian moralism the chief values are "social justice, peace, co-operation, and brotherhood," and that for it "capitalism is a fundamentally unjust system of society," it is "cruel and inhuman in that it sets man against man, extolling selfishness and mutual enmity in the guise of 'free competition.'"[2] We shall look more closely at this judgement in due course.

What was it that made Morgan Phillips say a generation ago, when he was Secretary of the Labour Party, that the Labour Movement owed more to Methodism than to Marx? The British Labour Party is the product of three movements, the Co-operative Movement, the Trade Unions, and the Independent Labour Party. Phillips was referring in a succinct sentence to the large number of pioneers in all three who came from a Christian background. Most of them were Primitive (not United or Wesleyan) Methodists or Baptists. Many of them, in the days before a national educational system was established, learned to read and write in a Sunday School; and even into the twentieth century it was a Sunday Bible Class in which they learned to speak in public. They carried this Christian background, sometimes considerably diluted into an ethical humanism, into the Labour Movement.[3] This was not due to the policy of the central organs of the denominations, far from it, but to the ethos of some local congregations. The result is that there has been a different ethos about the Labour Movement in Britain from that of the Social Democratic parties on the continent of Europe, such as the French or German Socialist parties. Continentals tended to talk in the language of a bowdlerized Marxism; the British in that of an ethical idealism with Christian undertones. This situation is now practically dead; an ideological vacuum is left, as neither language retains its power. The Christian concepts faded because the churches never succeeded in maintaining strong enough links with working-class life to maintain them. For a brief period there were "Labour Churches," pioneered by John Trevor of Upper Brook Street Free Church in Manchester in 1891. At one time there were nearly thirty, almost all in the industrial north of England. But all had died out by 1910 for lack of theological content, which had become lost in their socialism. Their story has never been told.

The origins of Christian Socialism in Britain

So far we have been considering Christians, mostly Nonconformists, who were active pioneers in the building up of the Labour Movement. Some Anglicans also were active, but their contribution was more theoretical and it is here that the Christian Socialists pioneered. The movement's origin can be precisely dated to the evening of April 10th, 1848. That afternoon a large Chartist march to Parliament from Kennington Common in South London had dissolved in a rainstorm.

In the evening J. M. Ludlow, who had been in Paris in February at the uprising which overthrew Louis Philippe, met with Charles Kingsley in Frederick Denison Maurice's house. They stayed up till 4:00 a.m. on April 11th writing a manifesto "To the Workmen of England," urging Chartists to join those who favoured non-violent reform, and signed "A Working Parson." The Chartist movement was not in fact violent in its aims or methods, and indeed everything it worked for has since been achieved except for annual Parliaments. The manifesto also sought to turn Chartists away from demands for political reform. Its whole tone seems condescending. It was not until 1850 that Maurice and his friends used the term "Socialist." It was a comparatively new word which had come to be used in the period of intense political and economic argument and social change after the Napoleonic wars, appearing in print in English for the first time in the Owenist *Co-operative Magazine* of November 1827.[4] Because of its Owenite origin it was associated with atheism, whereas Communism at this time had strong religious overtones. All the bolder, therefore, of the Christian Socialists to use it as (to quote Maurice) they sought to influence "the unsocial Christians and the unChristian Socialists."[5]

The Christian Socialist Movement was important because it meant the recovery of a theological critique of the assumptions behind the social order which had died out with the collapse of traditional Anglican and Puritan theology at the end of the seventeenth century. From the time of the early Fathers, Christian theology had included such a critique, though it is scarcely found in the New Testament, chiefly because of the expectation of an imminent *parousia* (return of Christ). Anglicans and Puritans continued the tradition after the Reformation, the last notable exponent being Richard Baxter.[6] The tradition probably died out because the dynamic forces of capitalism were too much for a Christian social theology which was tied in its assumptions to a static society. However the effect of its absence can be seen in John Wesley. He attacked particular abuses, and instigated some voluntary social improvement efforts, but his social theology was merely individualism writ large.[7] So it came about that the social and economic upheavals which we call the Industrial Revolution produced inchoate protest and nostalgic regret for the past, but no theological critique; and that at a time when an atomistic social and economic theory was regarded as a law of God. The Christian Socialist movement only lasted from 1848 to 1854, was unsuccessful in its practical experiments and unformed in its theories, but it did go to the root of the matter in this fundamental point, as we shall see.

Diverse socialists

The leaders were a diverse group. J. M. Ludlow had lived in Paris, and been open to the ideas of Saint-Simon, Blanc and Fourier.[8] Some of Blanc's social workshops (*ateliers nationaux*) had been set up in Paris in 1848, and all failed. To a lesser extent he was influenced by early English socialists like Robert Owen. However he was a staunch Anglican, and the doctrine of the Incarnation was more decisive for him than any of these sources. Charles Kingsley was an upper class Burkeian clergyman with a paternalistic concern for the working conditions of the poor, of which he acquired some knowledge. He it was, before Marx, who said that the Bible had been used as a book for the rich to keep the poor in order.[9] But he had few constructive ideas. E. V. Neale was a wealthy latitudinarian Christian, primarily interested in co-operation. It was his money that financed the Producers' Co-operatives which the Christian Socialists set up from February 1850, for Tailors, Builders, Shoemakers, Bakers and others.[10] They had failed by 1854, or soon after, because of quarrels with the managers, dishonesties, or the individualism of the workers.[11] It was these disasters that led the Christian Socialists to the too easy—and Pelagian—conclusion that middle class people often came to: that the workers need to be educated before they are fit to govern themselves. However Ludlow and Neale turned to give practical help to the burgeoning Labour Movement, in Friendly Societies and in the Co-operative Movement. There was early legislative fruit from their activities in the Industrial and Provident Societies Act of 1852 which, among other things, gave legal security to Producers' Co-operatives. It was F. D. Maurice who was to turn particularly to education in founding the Working Mens' College in Camden Town.

Everyone has agreed at the time and since that F. D. Maurice (1805–1872) was the leader, and that for him his theology is the key to all he did. From his Unitarian upbringing onwards Maurice is the archetype of the theologian who endeavours to hold together the many-sided mysteries of life in one comprehensive view. In his intellectual formation he absorbed influences from Julius Hare, his tutor at Cambridge, S. T. Coleridge, Erskine of Linlathen, Edward Irving, and many others, but by 1838 he had reached what in most respects was his permanent position in the best known of his voluminous writings, *The Kingdom of Christ*. He had no sympathy for the kind of social- ism advocated by the early English and French "socialists,"and in- deed was suspicious of all organizations for concrete change, so it was uncharacteristic of him both to advocate the use of the term so- cialist in 1850 and to support the Working Men's Associations. His general position was that social change must be achieved by religious means. Hence the Churches must be induced to look outwards be- cause Christ had redeemed *all* men, and his new order is already in being whether they realize it or not. The infinite love of God and the Lordship of Christ, not human sin, are the starting points of Christian theology. Christ has redeemed men in and for community with one another in God. Men seek to possess for themselves what they can only have in a community of giving and receiving. Maurice resisted all attempts to narrow the thought or boundaries of the Church. It was to him the equivalent of the Kingdom of God. Theology harmonizes the truth in every school or system of thought. He was a leading example of one who holds that men are usually right in what they affirm and wrong in what they deny. To him socialism meant the principle of co-operation in society. The various classes, Monarchy, Aristocracy, Trading, must carry out their function for the benefit of all, and a Fourth Estate is needed. Long established institutions, such as the Monarchy or the Aristocracy, are divinely intended, and social reform must be an organic growth. The *Christian* Socialist's task is to declare that the universal moral order of fellowship, which secular Socialists want to build, already exists.

What was new about Christian Socialism?

Much of this does not seem very far from Disrael's *Sybil*. Could he equally have talked of Christian Toryism? It is tempting to think so. However Toryism is partly made up of an hierarchical view of society with a stress on the duty of the higher orders of society to care for and uplift the lower orders, and partly of another element which is in- creasingly prominent. The latter is *laissez-faire* liberalism which stands, at least in theory (though often not in practice), for competi- tion and a free market as the basis of the economic order, and of such social order as it is necessary for the State to organize. To this Maurice was entirely opposed. By the middle of the nineteenth cen- tury the ideology of *laissez-faire* was dominant. The theory of the free market had ideological overtones from the time of its classic adumbration by Adam Smith, taking to itself elements from Hobbes and Locke, some Christian elements derived by several removes from certain strains in Calvinism, and more recently from Utilitarian philosophy. Its over-all interpretation of life has been called a philosophy of "possessive individualism."[12] Many Christians regarded what they called the "laws" of economics as the "laws" of God, in much the sense of the "laws" of the Newtonian Universe. This is expressed in two lines from an eighteenth century hymn.

> Laws which never shall be broken
> For their guidance He hath made.

The laws of supply and demand are akin to the law that fire burns. This was expressed particularly clearly in some Noncomformist circles, though it was widely held by Anglicans too. The Congregational journal, *The British Quarterly Review*, for instance, declared in 1846 that "Economical truth is no less divine than astronomical truth. The laws which govern the phenomen of production and exchange are as truly laws of God as those which govern day and night."[13] It was to this view that Maurice was implacably opposed. He wrote to Kingsley on 2nd January, 1850 "Competition is put forth as a law of the universe. This is a lie. The time has come for us to declare that it is a lie by word and deed. I see no way but associating for work instead of strikes."[14] And in the first of the *Tracts on Christian Socialism* later in the year he says on the first page, "Anyone who recognizes the principle of co-operation as a stronger and truer principle than that of competition has the right to the honour and disgrace of being called a Socialist." It is here that the legacy of Christian Socialism lies. The philosophy of possessive individualism, revived in recent years both in Britain and the U.S.A., is less and less appropriate to an advanced industrial society. Morevover it is an unChristian view. It has some emphases which are congenial to Christianity, a stress on personal responsibility for instance. But these are outweighed by the falseness of its overall view of life, which ignores the fact that structures of society are prior to the individuality of persons and affect their formation profoundly, for good or ill, from infancy, and that men and women are meant to live in communities of mutual giving and receiving and not in trying to be as independent of everyone else as possible.

How this is to be expressed in social and economic institutions is another question, and capitalism may well have developed some, such as the free market, which it would be folly to throw away altogether. Maurice had no grasp of the fundamentals of an economic policy, nor of its details; nor did the group get far with them in these years. Their writings are full of vague and imprecise reflections on a wide range of issues—Trade Unions, education, health legislation, the renewal of village life, the reform of the House of Lords, and many more. Maurice indeed soon parted from Ludlow on the issue of political democracy, and they went their different ways, though maintaining contact.

The Christian socialists tended too simply to favour Producers' Co-operation and education of the workers as a way of securing co-operation, instead of competition, in the process of production. It remains one serious alternative system of production which has been chiefly successful in agriculture. But it does not solve all problems. It forgets that producers have together a vested interest, an entirely proper one which needs the power of organization and representation behind it, but which also needs balancing by the organized power of the vested interests of consumers. For the rest the Christian Socialists' wider and subsequent activities provide excellent examples of how Christian insights can be, and need to be, built into the structures of social and economic life, where Christians work with their fellow-citizens of different faiths or of none. Together they need to make these structures operate in better and more human ways, and to devise new ones. Intellectually the Christian Socialists were eventually to have a long-lasting effect, mainly on a series of small groups, but partly on the Church at large. It is to this that I now turn.

Late-Victorian Christian Socialism

At first there was an interval during which the new ideas made little way. The pause was occasioned by the years of mid-Victorian self-confidence, heralded by the Great Exhibition of 1851. Later in the century things changed. 1877 saw the foundation of the Guild of St. Matthew by Stewart Headlam, with Thomas Hancock as its leading thinker; both were Anglican priests. Its aim was to "study social and political questions in the light of the Incarnation," and to stress "the social significance of the sacrament of the Eucharist." It claimed the influence of Maurice, though in practical terms it interpreted his thinking differently, seeing not co-operative production but the State as a "sacred" organ of reform. There is probably some influence of Oxford Hegelianism here. Headlam agreed with the Fabians on the role of the State. He was a member of the Executive of the Fabian Society, and in 1892 gave a lecture on "Christian Socialism" which was published as Fabian Tract 42. By 1899 the influence of the Guild was lost, though it continued until 1910. Part of the loss of influence was due to its advocacy of Henry George's Single Tax (on land values), which George had propagated in a tour of Britain in 1885. Headlam was also a child of his time in regarding the Kingdom of God as something we are to build on earth, an idea common among Liberal Protestants which also influenced Catholic-minded Anglicans. The journal of the Guild, *The Church Reformer*, was good though its peak membership in 1894-95 was no more than four hundred. At bottom it was *elitist*, as was shown by its opposition to the Independent Labour Party.

Beside the Guild of St. Matthew there was another group, led by J. L. Joynes and H. H. Champion, who began in 1883 to issue a paper called *The Christian Socialist*, influenced by Stewart Headlam and Henry George. The Guild was too Anglican for them. In 1886 their paper became the organ of an inter-denominational Christian Socialist Society, which had faded by 1892. However in 1894 another inter-denominational body, The Christian Socialist League was founded, with the prominent Baptist Minister Dr. John Clifford as President. It lasted only four years. The Quakers also had a society akin to the Guild, The Socialist Quaker Society, which lasted from 1898 to 1919. It published *Ploughshare* as its journal, and S. G. Hobson was one of its leading figures.

1889 saw the London Dock Strike, the publication of *Fabian Essays* and of the Catholic Anglican essays *Lux Mundi*, and also the founding of the Christian Social Union (C.S.U.). This last was definitely not a Socialist movement, but because of its debt to Maurice and the influence of some of its members who were socialists it must be mentioned. Bishop Westcott of Durham was the first President and Henry Scott Holland the Chairman. Westcott's social thought was inclined to be cloudy. At times he would appear to be saying that the extension of family love would be the means to sweeten (structurally unchanged) social and class relationships. The C.S.U. took from Maurice the stress on co-operation rather than competition, in other words his criticism of individualism and his denial that capitalism represented a divine ordinance for the economic order. In this it was sufficiently influential to influence the Lambeth Conference of Anglican Bishops of 1897, who spoke favourably but in very general terms of socialism. The C.S.U., like Kingsley, campaigned against sweated industries, especially in the tailoring trade. It organized a Sweated Industries Exhibition in 1907, and influenced the Trade Boards Act of 1909 which produced machinery for setting minimum wages in industries where the workers were too scattered and poor to be easily organized in trade unions. The journal of the C.S.U., *Commonwealth* was edited by Scott Holland from 1897 to his death in 1918. Two years later the C.S.U. joined with the Navvy Mission to form the Industrial Christian Fellowship, with Studdert Kennedy ("Woodbine Willie" of the first World War) as its prophet. It still exists in a minor way. The C.S.U. did not achieve much after 1909, though in comparison with other groups we are concerned with it had a much larger membership, about six thousand at its maximum, including quite a number of bishops. It was purely Anglican. And it had no working class or trade union members. The Quakers had a parallel body to the C.S.U. from 1904, the Friend's Social Union, with Seebohm Rowntree and George Cadbury among its members.

It was this lack, together with the flurry of excitement after the 1906 election which saw the landslide to the Liberals and the arrival of fifty-three Labour Members of Parliament, that led in that year to the foundation of the first Anglican society specifically committed to socialism, the Church Socialist League (C.S.L.). It was much less London-centred than most of what I have been describing, with many church radicals from the North of England as members. Conrad Noel was its paid organizer. The socialism it favoured was Guild Socialism, which by then was being discussed in some sections of the Labour Movement as an alternative to the wage system. There would be a Guild for each industry, each member would have the same status and the division between employer and employee would be overcome. The C.S.L. also continued the preference of Maurice and most of his friends for Producers' Co-operatives. At its peak in 1912 it had about one thousand members. The Socialist Quaker Society was also attracted to Guild Socialism. Once again there was a Noncomformist parallel to an Anglican society, the Free Church Socialist

League, founded in 1909. Philip Snowden, who was to be the first Labour Chancellor of the Exchequer in 1924, was a member. It soon faded.

The first Free Church book on Socialism came from the Wesleyan Methodist minister, S. E. Keeble in 1907, *Industrial Daydreams*. He was to live to write *Christian Responsibility for the Social Order* in 1922, and play a considerable part in the C.O.P. E.C. Conference of 1924.[15]

Christian Socialism since the Russian Revolution

In 1916 Conrad Noel split from the C.S.L. to form the Catholic Crusade on the basis of "the fatherhood of God, the brotherhood of man, and the sacramental principle," another interesting example of Catholic Anglicans being influenced by Liberal Protestantism. The Crusade was to welcome the Russian revolution of 1917, and then itself split after Stalin had ousted Trotsky. Those who supported Trotsky formed the Order of the Church Militant. A theological weakness is revealed in the lack of political judgement in evaluating the Soviet Union. The same defect was to be revealed by Hewlett Johnson, the "Red" Dean (of Canterbury) in his speeches and writing, and in a secularised form by Sidney and Beatrice Webb. In no case was it due to a slavish following of Marxist theory.

The remaining members of the C.S.L. split again in 1924. Another section of High-Church Anglicans formed the League of the Kingdom of God to seek a "specifically Christian Sociology." They became closely associated with an annual Anglo-Catholic Summer School of Sociology ("Christian" Sociology) which took place from 1925 for nearly forty years. V. A. Demant was its leading thinker. Behind it was the Christendom Trust which published the journal *Christendom* from 1931 to 1950 under the editorship of Maurice Reckitt. An early book *The Return of Christendom* in 1922 foreshadowed it, and another *Prospect for Christendom* was a herald of its downfall. In its desire for a distinctive social theology it distanced itself from all that was going on, indeed from all social reality. It is too simple to say that it hankered after a return to the Middle Ages, but the mediaeval strain in its thought led it to advocate a return from industrialism to rural life, the reversal of urbanization and even barter rather than a financial system. It liked neither capitalism nor the adumbrations of the Welfare State under the Attlee Government of 1945, nor did it favour State socialism, but sought for something different and distinctively Christian. It was vague as to the "natural" order to which we should return and was perhaps rather more informed on cultural than on economic and political issues. For a time its leaders advocated the Social Credit scheme of the engineer Major C. H. Douglas (as did Hewlett Johnson), which is based on a simple economic fallacy. Its activities were absorbed by the Industrial Christian Fellowship in 1957. The Christendom Trust was refounded on a new basis in 1971.

The other section of the Church Socialist League became in 1924 the interdenominational Society of Socialist Christians, changing its name in 1931 to the Socialist Christian League. It, too, talked of building the Kingdom of God on earth and of the sacramental principle. It generated some activity in local groups, notably in Stepney by John Groser, an Anglican priest who became widely known throughout the country, and a number of M.P's were members, including George Lansbury, for a time leader of the Labour Party. It continued until a re-grouping of Socialist Christian forces in 1960.

The 1930s was a decade of economic recession, the growth of Fascism and rise of Nazism, and of deepening international crisis. It was the time of the influential Left Book Club. There grew up under the same influences a group of Christian Socialists called the Christian Left. It contained a number of academics, of whom the best known was the philosopher John Macmurray. This was the first group not at all in the Maurice tradition. It took Marxism seriously in its philosophy and social analysis, unlike Conrad Noel and his associates. It seemed indeed to be Marxism with religious overtones, affirming much of what Marxism affirms but insisting that Jesus saw it first.[16] The Christian Left hardly survived the Stalin-Hitler pact. In this same decade there was an informal group, centred on the staff and senior friends of the Student Christian Movement and influenced by Reinhold Niebuhr, who believed with him that it was necessary to move to the Right theologically and to the Left politically. Rejecting the utopianism of both Liberal Protestantism and Liberal Catholicism with regard to the building of the Kingdom of God, the group sought a socialist but not Marxist political position on the basis of what seemed the most urgent events of the decade. The work of New Testament scholars on the nature of the Kingdom of God in the ministry of Jesus was a key factor in this position.[17]

Stumbling block

Then came the war. In the middle of it William Temple, who had been Archbishop of York since 1929 called a conference in 1941 at Malvern on "The Life of the Church and the Order of Society." It was a confused affair. Those on the political left tried to get a resolution passed to the effect that private ownership of the principal industrial resources of the community is a stumbling block which makes it harder for men to live Christian lives. But they could only get the phrase "*may be* a stumbling block" passed. So next year they formed the Council of Clergy and Ministers for Common Ownership, with Bishop Blunt of Bradford as President and Sir Richard Acland and Sir Stafford Cripps as influential members. The Bishop resigned in 1947 because of its uncritical support of the Soviet Union (thus recalling the Catholic Crusade, the Order of the Church Militant and the Christian Left), and was succeeded by Hewlett Johnson. In 1952 it changed its name to the Society of Socialist Clergy and Ministers, and in 1960 merged into a new Socialist Christian group, including the Socialist Christian League, after discussing with the latter its attitude to the U.S.S.R.[18] Out of these discussions came a pamphlet in 1959 *Papers from the Lamb*, and on its basis the new movement was called The Christian Socialist Movement, with the veteran Methodist minister, Dr. Donald Soper (later to become a Peer) as chairman.[19] Its journal was first called *The Christian Socialist Movement News* and later *The Christian Socialist;* it continues to be published. The Movement has some nine hundred members, with some M.P.s and some local activity

In the mid-1960s a Roman Catholic, semi-Marxist group, Slant, flourished briefly. Its impetus was the opening given by Pope John XXIII to a more constructive attitude to Marxism instead of the previous total opposition. Hitherto Roman Catholics had played little part in Christian Socialist movements (as distinct from the Labour Movement) largely because of the condemnation of Socialism in Papal teaching from *Rerum Novarum* in 1891. John XXIII deftly modified the previous blanket condemnation of Marxism by these artless words in the Encyclical *Pacem in Terris* of 1963: "Who can deny that these movements (*sc.* false philosophical teaching regarding the nature, origin and destiny of man and the universe) in so far as they conform to the dictates of right reason and are interpreters of the lawful aspirations of the human person, contain elements that are positive and deserving of approval?'' These words were a prelude to a new *Ostpolitik* on the part of the Vatican. There had been a Catholic Social Guild since 1909 which published *The Catholic Worker* and established Plater College at Oxford, a counterpart to Ruskin College, but it was not socialist. The Slant Manifesto was published in 1966. In the next decade Christians for Socialism took its place, influenced by Latin-American Liberation Theology in its Marxist tones, but it did not flourish.

The year 1975 saw three initiatives. A Quaker Socialist Society restarted, with about two hundred and fifty members. There was the launching among Anglican Catholics of a society reviving in late-twentieth century terms the concerns of the Guild of St. Matthew, the League of the Kingdom of God and the Catholic Crusade. And in reaction to the perceived inadequacies of the ''Call to the Nation'' of the two Anglican Archbishops a group called Christians for Socialism began to meet, based in Manchester. Its energies have chiefly gone into a bi-monthly journal *Christian Statesman* (a title modelled on the left-wing *New Statesman*), which has a circulation of between one and two thousand. In 1980 these groups and several others of varying degrees of radicalism began to collaborate in a loose organization called COSPEC (Christian Organisations for Social, Political and Economic Change). Indirectly related to this a symposium, *Agenda for Prophets* appeared in that year.[20]

Three father-figures

After this survey of a hundred years of small Christian socialist groups there are three men to whom it is well to refer specifically. The first is Bishop Charles Gore. He was the greatest disturber of the Church of England establishment because he would not allow awkward questions to be passed by. He was a radical social reformer rather than a socialist, though he produced a sympathetic lecture on Christianity and Socialism to the Pan-Anglican Congress of 1908. In 1913 he edited a symposium *Property, Its Rights and Duties*, which remains a fundamental treatment of Christian teaching on property. Gore was alert to the moral perils of wealth, especially the idleness of the rich, and agreed with Roman Catholic teaching in regarding a living wage as the first charge on industry.[21]

William Temple as a young man in 1908 wrote a celebrated article in *The Economic Review* which covers many of the standard themes of Christian Socialists.[22] Commenting on Ephesians 4 verse 10 he says it articulates the fullest "scheme of evolutionary socialism, so far as all fundamental points are concerned, that has yet been achieved by man." He goes on to say that the Church must be concerned with the material world because (i) the doctrine of the Incarnation means that Spirit demands bodily expression, (ii) Jesus healed without enquiring into the spiritual attitude of sufferers, (iii) the Church owns property and employs persons. The Church needs the Labour Movement and the Labour Movement needs the Church—for its inspiration and rituals. There is the need to replace the competitive basis of society by a co-operative basis, for competition is inherently a spirit of selfishness, even of hatred. It is the interest of every man against his fellows. "There is no middle path between the acceptance of Socialism and the declaration that the Gospel cannot be applied to economics. The alternative stands before us—Socialism or Heresy; we are involved in one or the other." In 1918 he joined the Labour Party, but left it some time between 1921 and 1925 (it is not clear when or precisely why). At the end of his life, however, in *Christianity and Social Order* he said "I do not simply advocate Socialism or Common Ownership," and writes of the necessity to get the best out of socialism and individualism.[23]

R. H. Tawney was a similar yet different figure. He was similar in that his social, educational and theological formation was like that of Gore and Temple; he was different in that in addition to being an academic he was intimately connected with the Labour Movement all his life. Not only did he concern himself with its educational side in the Workers' Educational Association but also in its political and industrial side, and was at times involved in policy formation.[24] No one quite like Tawney exists in the Labour Movement now, but his spirit lives on. In the malaise which has come over the Movement since the General Election of 1979 there are often appeals to recover the essence of what he stood for. The tutor of Ruskin College, Oxford, has recently produced a pamphlet from which I quote. Tawney believed "that economics raised issues of fundamental principle which could only be resolved by moral choice. History was a moral drama too, in which rival systems of belief contended for supremacy and irreconcilable interest clashed. In his (writings) . . . we are offered, in essence, a secular version of the Fall, a reverse Utopianism in which commercial forces accomplish the destruction of communal solidarities, and society as a spiritual organism gives way to the notion of society as an economic machine."[25] Although standing for a fundamental change in the philosophy of society, which in turn would lead to a new structure of economic organization, and always unwilling to conceal or evade this for temporal electoral advantage, Tawney was a moderate in Labour political terms. His fear lest it be corrupted was a fear of moral corruption rather than of semi-Marxist theorists who wanted to bind it to a programme derived from an over-simplified analysis.

Christian Socialism today

What does the "mainstream" Christian Socialist movement stand for these days? At the 1960 union it was (i) the common ownership of the major resources of the world; (ii) a classless and just society; (iii) human and racial equality; (iv) the unity of Christian people (a new note); (v) friendship between East and West (this reflects the "soft" line towards the U.S.S.R.;) (vi) abolition of nuclear weapons (a post-1945 element); (vii) disarmament and world peace. Much of this is as general as being against sin and in favour of fellowship. Discussions of common ownership have been more detailed. Here the Scott Bader Commonwealth, founded in 1963, has had a lot of influence. It is a Northamptonshire firm in the specialist chemical industry, employing about four hundred and thirty. There is a maximum wage-differential of seven to one, 60 per cent of the profits are ploughed back into the business, and as much as is distributed in bonuses to employees is given to charities. More recently the Mondragon Co-operative in the Basque region of Spain has attracted notice. An Industrial Common Ownership Movement began in 1971, and in 1976 an Act of Parliament facilitated it; and in 1978 a Co-operative Development Agency was created. But it remains small.

COSPEC also stressed five points in 1980. (i) Equality of opportunity; (ii) Workers' Ownership; (iii) Community control of wealth; (iv) A planned socialist economy; (v) Full participation in decision-making.[26]

There is a vacuum both of faith and of policies in the Labour Movement today. The reformist elements—Christian and secular— lost impetus after the creation of the outlines of a Welfare State after 1945. Now there is the defensive task of defending it against a right-wing backlash, but merely to advocate a return seems unsatisfactory, and there is doubt about ways of developing it and the nature of the economy needed to sustain it. The working class is not homogeneous.

A generation of relative affluence has increased the gap between the haves and the have-nots within it, especially between those in work and those unemployed. Trade unions and professional associations are very conservative in their attitudes. On the radical side the "idols" of the U.S.S.R. and more recently China have fallen and nothing has replaced them. Short-sighted economic nationalism is growing. Electorates do not want to be disturbed in their relatively recent affluence, and demand incompatible things; and since no government can provide them they tend to react against the one in power. It is doubtful whether governments are given enough manoeuvring room or enough time to handle the economy effectively. A question is raised as to whether our advanced industrial economies are becoming ungovernable. A further complication is caused by the powerful and often frenetic international commercial and financial forces which can shake even the largest economy. What in this situation is the legacy of the Christian Socialist movement?

Polarization

First it should be honoured for its boldness as a pioneer in grappling with the qualitatively new society which industrialism and urbanization created, and for bringing theology to bear upon it. Sometimes a debate arises as to how far intellectual developments genuinely arise out of the discipline in question and how far they arise from external factors. I do not think this is a very profitable polarization. There are many conditioning factors in thought, and the development of psychology and of the social sciences has made us more aware of them, though we can never be completely aware. We can now see that amidst their many acute internal disagreements the Victorians held in common many pre-suppositions of which they were imperfectly aware. Economic factors are the most pervasive of social influences. But conditioning factors are not determining factors. Just as we are firmly convinced that to some extent each of us can be an originator of his own decisions, so we can assume that theology has some independent influence on the thinking of those who take it seriously. It was a legitimately theological insight of Maurice to condemn the erection of competitive *laissez-faire* into a law of God and a philosophy of individualism. But the Victorian era was on the whole a confident one, and Christian Socialists tended to share the belief in the perfectibility of man rather than to counterbalance the utopian strain in socialist thought. That left Conservatism to claim that it was the "realistic" party, understanding the concept of Original Sin; although a moment's thought will reveal that it tells equally against the hierarchical and paternalistic elements in Conservatism, since no-one is good enough to exercise authority over others unchecked. This is particularly apposite in the era of multi-national companies. The Christian Socialists were often "soft" utopians in terms of building the Kingdom of God, and more recently those who owed nothing to Maurice have been "hard" utopians in accepting too simply the Marxist claim to be a "scientific" analysis of the development of society. It is the utopian element which has been one of the main reasons why Christian Socialist groups have been as fissiparous as left-wing groups in general, splitting over disputes about the "purest" form of socialism. It is the recovery of the eschatological note in the understanding of the Kingdom of God in the ministry of Jesus which has undermined the Christian basis for the utopianism. Those Christians most actively involved in the Labour Movement tended to be the least theologically-minded and the most prey to secular assumptions.

Sectarianism

The other source of fissiparousness has been sectarianism. Christian Socialist groups have been slow to learn from the Ecumenical Movement. They have had other limitations. Sociologically they have been too clerical, too middle-class and in practice too paternalistic. Politically they have been too theoretical, too suspicious of political processes. Nor has theory always come to grips with difficult issues. Christian Socialists have not seen that conflicts of interest are inherent in any society, including socialist ones; and that it is necessary to create structures which can handle them creatively and which will harness individual and group self-interest in the cause of social justice. Conflicts of interest between consumers and producers and between managers and managed are endemic. Also there are problems of government control over nationalized industries which were never appreciated in the talk of common ownership.

It is perhaps in the economic field that the Christian Socialists have been weakest. It is not just the tendency to run after popular, ephemeral and erroneous nostrums like Henry George's Single Tax or Major Douglas' Social Credit or—less fanciful—Guild Socialism, but the inability to grasp the distinction between competition and the free market erected into an overall philosophy, and the market in a properly controlled social environment as one of mankind's most useful devices for deciding a basic problem in any society, the allocation of scarce resources between alternative uses. The talk of "production for use" and not "for profit," which frequently recurs, obscures this. The assumption that there is something necessarily sinister in profits, moreover, obscures the distinction between profit as a directive and profit as an incentive, and the role of an entrepeneur in the economic order.

Nevertheless, in spite of these defects the fundamental point remains. In the Christian view the economic order is made for persons and by its effect on persons it must be judged. If its philosophy requires the treatment of labour (persons) as one factor of production just like land and capital (things) it must be condemned. Moreover in the Christian view what each person has in common under God is much more significant than any empirical differences between them; the expression of this in the social order tends towards a communal and egalitarian outlook for the sake of social fellowship. The visions of most of the Christian Socialists were on the right lines; much more practical wisdom is needed to translate them into social, political and economic policies.[27]

NOTES

The place of publications of books is London, England, unless otherwise specified.

1. *Socialism,* R. N. Berki (1975) Ch. 2. He refers (p. 10) to *A Dictionary of Socialism,* Angelo Rappoport (1924).

2. Op. cit. p. 26.

3. Cf. *Methodism and the Struggle of the Working Classes 1850–1900,* R. F. Wearmouth (1954) and *Churches and Working Classes in Victorian England,* K. S. Inglis (1963), which modifies Wearmouth on the influence of Methodism.

4. Cp. *Keywords*, Raymond Williams (1976).

5. In *The Christian Socialist, A Journal of Association*, 25th July, 1851.

6. *A Christian Directory or a Summ of Practical Theologie and Case of Conscience*, Richard Baxter (1673).

7. His famous Sermon 44 "on Money" is a good illustration.

8. J. M. Ludlow (1821–1911). Henri de Saint-Simon (1760–1825), Louis Blanc (1815–1822), Charles Fourier (1772–1831). Ludlow was to become from 1875–1891 Chief Registrar of Friendly Societies; cp. J. M. Ludlow, *The Builder of Christian Socialism*, Neville Masterman (1963).

9. Charles Kingsley (1819–76). He exposed rural conditions in his novel *Yeast*, and sweat shops in another, *Alton Locke*, and in a pamphlet *Cheap Clothes and Nasty;* cp. *Charles Kingsley and His Ideas*, Guy Kendall (1946). The quotation is from his *Three Letters to the Chartists* (1848).

10. E. V. Neale (1810–1892). The Co-operatives were set up by The Society for Promoting Working Mens' Associations, which was closed by Maurice in 1854. Neale later became Secretary of the co-operative Union, and together with Tom Hughes (author of *Tom Brown's Schooldays*) produced the first text book on co-operation, *Manual for Co-operators* in 1881. Hughes was suspicious of Consumers' Co-operation and the Co-operative Wholesale Society, Neale encouraged them; cp. *Christian and Socialism Co-operation in Victorian England*, P. N. Backstrom (1974).

11. The Tailors lasted until 1860, when it collapsed because of a fraudulent manager; and early in the 1860s the Shoemakers were taken over as a private firm. It is thought that Neale lost 40,000 to 60,000 on them. cp. *Christian Socialism (1848–1854)* C. E. Raven (1920).

12. I have dealt with this more fully in the Maurice Lectures, *Religion and the Persistence of Capitalism* (1979) pp. 69–82, 88ff.

13. Quoted in *The Nonconformist Conscience*, H. F. Lovell Cocks (1944) p. 35.

14. Quoted in *Life of Frederick Denison Maurice* by Frederick Morris (his son) (1885), Vol. 2 p. 32.

15. Details of these various societies and individuals can be found in *The Churches and the Labour Movement,* S. Mayor (1967). The C.O.P.E.C. conference, or Conference on Christian Politics, Economics and Citizenship at Birmingham in 1924, with William Temple in the Chair, with 1400 members was the first large Christian conference on the social order in Britain, and to some extent prepared for the first Ecumenical Conference on the matter at Stockholm in 1925. See *The Proceedings of C.O.P.E.C.* ed. W. Reason (1924) and the reports of its twelve Commissions.

16. John Macmurray's *Creative Society* (1935) was one expression of the Christian Left. His Gifford Lectures of 1953 and 1954 *The Form of the Personal* were to strike a rather different note.

17. I was a member of this group. The quarterly journal of the Fellowship of Socialist Christians (U.S.A.) edited by Reinhold Niebuhr circulated among us, and I was for a time the English agent. It began in 1935 as *Radical Religion* and changed its name in 1940 to *Christianity and Society*.

18. Canon Stanley Evans of Southwark Cathedral epitomized the outlook of the Society of Socialist Clergy and Ministers in his book *Return to Reality* (1955).

19. The Lamb was the name of a Public House where the group met. I reviewed *Papers from the Lamb* in an article in *Theology* for April 1960, "The Christian Left Still Lost." Lord Soper's opinions are expressed in *Christian Politics* (1977). Stanley Evans wrote another book, *The Social Hope of the Christian Church* (1965) which expresses the general outlook of the C.S.M.; the Kingdom of God is still a corporate society on earth.

20. Edited by R. Ambler and D. Haslam. I reviewed it in *Theology*, March 1981 in an article "Not Out of the Wood Yet?."

21. Gore succeeded Westcott as President of the C.S.U. His social theology is most conveniently found in an Essex Hall Lecture of 1920, *Christianity Applied to the Life of Men and Nations,* and in his book *Church and Society* (1927).

22. Vol. XIII pp. 190–202.

23. In 1917 a private group of which Temple was a member, the Collegium, produced a book *Competition. Christianity and Social Order* was a

war-time paperback; the quotation is from the 1976 reprint (p. 99f), with an introductory essay by me.

24. I have written about him as a Christian Moralist in the Maurice Lectures pp. 83–110 (note 12 *supra*).

25. *Tawney and the S.P.D.*, Raphael Samuel, a pamphlet published by the Socialist Society (1982)

26. Cp. an essay "Christianity and Self Interest" by Gerard Hughes S. J., in *Christianity and the Future of Social Democracy*, ed. M. H. Taylor (1982).

27. The sources for the Christian Socialist Movement are primarily a large number of pamphlets and periodicals. Among the useful general surveys not already mentioned are *The Social Catholic Movement in Great Britain*, A. P. McEntee (New York, 1927); *The Church of England and Social Reform, since 1854*, D. O. Wagner (1930); *The Christian Socialist Movement in England*, G. C. Bunyan (1931); *The Church in the Social Order*, C. K. Gloyn (Pacific University, Oregon, 1942); *The Church and Social Order: Social Thought in the Church of England, 1918–1939*, J. K. Oliver (1968); *The Christian Socialist Revival 1877–1914*, P. D'A. Jones (Princeton, 1968); *The Origin and History of Christian Socialism*, T. Christensen, (Aarhus, 1962). *Church and Society in England 1770–1970*, E. R. Norman, (1976) needs to be read with caution, particularly on the twentieth century.

Comment

Arthur A. Shenfield

Professor Preston offers us an extremely interesting, and for the most part truly excellent, historical survey of the development and influence of the English Christian Socialist Movement. Every character of any consequence in the Movement, major or minor, is given his place in the story, with a wealth of interesting detail. Some of these characters, though not without prominence or public recognition in their day, have now become almost completely forgotten, even amongst socialists and students of socialism in Britain. Viewed as a pure historical narrative, Preston's paper is a substantial contribution to knowledge. It deserves, perhaps, only one criticism. It ignores the influence upon Christian Socialists of some other important leading socialists or critics of capitalism whose teaching was not specifically religious—though not non-religious or anti-religious—such as Carlyle, Ruskin, Blatchford and Morris. The influence of the Christian Socialists would have been considerably less if their teaching had not meshed with that of these others. Some observations on the place in the historical record of the social Catholicism of Chesterton and Belloc would also have been to the point. Preston does bring Tawney into the record, but there were others on the socialist side who were not members of the Christian Movement whose influence assisted that of the Movement at least as much as did Tawney's.

Since he has himself had affiliations with the Christian Socialist Movement, Professor Preston is also to be commended for his awareness of the intellectual weaknesses and confusions, the naivete and mental fuzziness, which have been prominent in it. Thus for example,

> Maurice had no grasp of the fundamentals of economic policy, nor of the details, nor did the group get far with them in these years. Their writings are full of vague and imprecise reflections on a wide range of issues—trade unions, education,

health legislation, the renewal of village life, the reform of the House of Lords—and many more.

. . . . .

Westcott's social thought was inclined to be cloudy.

. . . . .

For a time its (ie. the League of the Kingdom of God's) leaders advocated the Social Credit scheme of the engineer Major C. H. Douglas (as did Hewlett Johnson), which is based on a simple economic fallacy.

. . . . .

There is a vacuum of both faith and policies in the Labour Movement today.

. . . . .

They (ie. Christian Socialist groups) did not see that conflicts of interest are inherent in any society, including socialist ones.

. . . . .

It is perhaps in the economic field that the Christian Socialists have been weakest. It is not just the tendency to run after popular, ephemeral and erroneous nostrums like Henry George's Single Tax or Major Douglas' Social Credit or—less fanciful—Guild Socialism, but the inability to grasp the distinction between competition and the free market erected into an overall philosophy, and the market in the properly controlled social environment as one of mankind's most useful devices for deciding a basic problem in any society, the allocation of relatively scarce resources between alternative users. Talking of 'production for use' and not 'for profit', which frequently occurs, obscures this.

Nevertheless, viewed as more than a historical narrative, Preston's paper is in my opinion unsatisfactory. The quotations set out above certainly show that he is a man of strong common sense, and is to a large extent aware of the problems which are inherent in the human condition and of the constraints which they impose upon us. But to him, as to many other observers, the confusion, naivete, even silliness, displayed by Christian Socialists are only warts upon what is in essentially a respectable face. Thus he concludes: "The visions of most of the Christian Socialists were on the right lines; much more practical wisdom is needed to translate them into social, political and economic policies."

The facts, in my opinion, are otherwise. The errors of the Christian Socialist Movement are not merely incidental. The Movement's ideas have been founded on myth, superstition, and ignorance. Its visions are not on the right lines, and no amount of practical wisdom could translate them into intelligent social or economic policies. Of course an accusation of intolerable arrogance may be invited by such a judgement on a movement in which there have been numerous men of moral or intellectual distinction, even eminence. I shall face this probable accusation below but first let me draw attention to what I perceive as errors in Preston's exposition.

1. Of John Wesley. "But his social theology was merely individualism writ large." Why "merely" individualism? Because individualism is supposed to be opposed to, or destructive of or oblivious of, the bonds which ought to tie men together in society. In fact individualism, properly understood, is not merely aware of the cement which binds men in a good society but actually strengthens it. The good society, its principles and practice, had nothing to fear from Wesley's life or teaching. It ought to be understood that it is precisely when the fundamental principle of society is respect for the individual, that social bonds are naturally strongest. Compare the cohesion of British and Dutch society in the nineteenth century with the fragility of other European societies which emphasized social unity. See how individualistic America could weld a united society out of disparate immigrants (the rift caused by slavery excepted), and see how that social unity is subjected to stresses and strains now that the Social Gospel urges Americans to take care of the supposedly "underprivileged" minorities. See how centrifugal forces have arisen, or if already there have been strengthened, in the United Kingdom, Canada, Belgium and elsewhere once the Social Gospel has induced the people to deride individualism and to seek their welfare from the power of government.

2. "When an atomistic social and economic theory was being treated as law of God"; and "The Christian Socialist Movement did go to the root of the matter in this fundamental point." Here is another example of the fly-blown notion that the so-called atomistic theory is incompatible with social cohesion. Of course the animus against what is envisaged as an atomistic doctrine rest not merely on a misunderstanding of the forces producing social cohesion, but also upon the simple feeling that it must favour human selfishness, contrary to overwhelming evidence of the superior moral behaviour of people living in "capitalist" societies.

3. "He (Kingsley) said that the Bible had been used as a book for the rich to keep the poor in order." Clearly Preston agrees with Kingsley on this, as do millions of other Britons who have been indoctrinated on the matter for many years. Though extremely common it is an odious slur on the best nineteenth century divines. In a free society the most destructive and counter-productive policy the poor can pursue is to seek to relieve their poverty by expropriating the rich; and the worst demagogues are those who urge the poor to do so. It was therefore correct exhortations of religion to seek to divert the poor from such temptation. The notion that this was simply a way of inducing the village labourer to tug his forelock to the squire, and the town labourer to behave submissively to his employer is a travesty of the facts. Of course the rich are naturally pleased when the poor do not assail them, and the pleasure will often be mixed with obtuseness and selfishness, but this is not the same, in a free and open society, as a desire to hold down the poor in poverty and misery. Of course it may be said that Kingsley's England was hardly a free or open society, but this is based either on ignorance of the facts or on the false notion that freedom is measured by the extent of material power or of access of material opportunities, which, if true, would mean that poverty is slavery. It is true that in Kingsley's England the working class was wholly without the franchise until 1867 and partially without it until 1884 (not to mention the exclusion of women of all classes from the franchise until 1918), but this is decisive only if the franchise is itself a decisive test of freedom. (Ask the Hong Kong Chinese if they feel unfree without it, or pose a like question to the shades of the millions of unenfranchised Britons of long ago who proudly sang "Britons never shall be slaves.") Furthermore within a generation after 1884 the working class vote began, however gradually, to be used for the self-destructive process of the expropriation of the rich.

4. "Many Christians regarded what they called the laws of economics as the laws of God in much the sense of the laws of the Newtonian universe ... The Congregational journal, the *British Quarterly Review* ... declared in 1846 that 'Economical truth is no less divine than astronomical truth. The laws which govern the phenomenon of production and exchange are as truly laws of God as those which govern day and night.' It was to this view that Maurice was implacably opposed." No doubt this view appears to

Preston as preposterous as it did to Maurice. Yet at best Maurice only half understood it. If God made the world, economic laws, supposing that there are any, are as divine in origin as physical laws. Unfortunately the mid-nineteenth century's understanding of economic laws was partial and imperfect, contrary to the opinion at that time. Even John Stuart Mill thought that no fundamental propositions of economics were left to be discovered. Hence there was hubris in declaring the contemporary exposition of economic laws to be an expression of divine law, which stands as a warning to our generation and all succeeding generations. But what Maurice and his friends objected to were those propositions of contemporary economics which were not far off the truth. Thus the contemporaries whom he criticized were to that extent closer to the "laws of God" than he was.

5. "The philosophy of possessive individualism ... is less and less appropriate to an advanced industrial society." Here we have the popular notion that policies which may have been suitable for the early capitalism of (supposedly) simple and small-scale enterprises become unsuitable for the late capitalism of (supposedly) complex and large-scale enterprises. This is a superstition, partly induced by the fact that there are indeed some differences in the application of policy. But the principles of policy are not affected by industrial change and development. Hence the truth or untruth of "possessive individualism" is also not thereby affected.

6. One may fairly assume that Canon Preston approves of the influence of the C.S.U. on the British Trade Boards Act, 1909, which produced machinery for setting wages in the so-called sweated industries. The truth is that all minimum wage legislation, whether applied under the British Trade Boards Act, 1909 or the American Fair Labor Standards Act, 1938, has injured, not benefited, the poor; and the poorer the poor, the greater has been the injury.

7. "(Bishop) Gore was alert to the moral perils of wealth ... and agreed with Roman Catholic teaching in regarding a living wage as the first charge on industry." Gore was right in the first part. There are indeed moral perils in wealth, as the divines who approved of capitalism well knew (especially Wesley). But the second part is claptrap. What is a living wage? On whom should the first charge fall, the individual employer, all employers together, or all taxpayers together? What are the effects of maintaining such a first charge? What should be done about those whose labour prod-

uct is not worth the "living wage"? These are vital questions, to which Gore and those with him had no answers which did not raise even more difficult questions.

8. "Here the Scott Bader Commonwealth... has had a lot of influence." Perhaps it has on Christian Socialists, but its influence on the public has been as close to nil as possible. Preston might also have mentioned the John Lewis Partnership, Taylors of Batley, and the few other cases of common ownership, co-partnership and profit-sharing which are all that a hundred and fifty years of preaching and example can show. This is one of the great will-o-the-wisps which men continually pursue. There is nothing in capitalism which forbids or hinders the establishment of such arrangements. If it were really true that they benefited the workers better than the more common forms of business, they would long ago have conquered the industrial field. Similarly every Briton may shop at the non-profit making co-ops if he or she wishes. But most do not, because the leading profit-making chains give better value for money. Hence private profit costs the consumer less than nothing. It is the consumer's Santa Claus, a fundamental economic fact which no Christian or other socialist has ever been able to grasp.

9. "First of all it should be honoured for its boldness as a pioneer in grappling with the qualitatively new society which industrialism and urbanisation created" (page 14). The boldness of ignorance deserves no honor. Despite the errors of the classical economists, which were to be expected in pioneers, there simply is no comparison between their level of discourse and that of the Christian socialists; and this applies even to the minor figures in classical economics, such as Torrens, Tooke, Fullarton and others.

10. "... no one is good enough to exercise authority over others unchecked. This is particularly apposite in the era of multi-national companies" (page 15). It is sad to see Dr. Preston descend to the level of the popular animus against the multi-nationals. For the most part the multi-nationals are the victims of unchecked power, not its wielders.

11. "In the Christian view the economic order is made for persons and by its effect or persons it must be judged. If its philosophy requires the treatment of labour (persons) as one factor of production just like land and capital (things) it must be condemned." Of course the economic order is made for persons and must be judged accordingly. This is exactly how economists have always viewed

it, but they see it with more informed and trained eyes than the Christian Socialist. As for the treatment of Labour, what confusions can arise here! The economic order does not treat labour "just like" land and capital. There are aspects of labour which are indeed like those of land and capital (which is why the declaration of the U.S. Clayton Act that labour is not an article of commerce is so fatuous), and there are aspects which are not: and the economic order treats labour accordingly. But the Christian Socialist cannot see that labour is in *any* aspect like land or capital, and thus his view is blinkered.

Reply

Ronald H. Preston

My paper had four purposes. The first was to summarize the history of the various Christian Socialist groups since 1848. I chose this theme partly because they have had a diffused but significant influence on Christian social thinking and were therefore relevant to a conference on "Religion, Economics and Social Thought"; partly because whilst the early history of these groups has often been told, that of recent years has not been put together before.

The second purpose was an appraisal of their weaknesses which I thought overdue. I found three. They shared too much the prevailing Victorian optimism in the perfectibility of man. They were too clerical in composition and ecclesiastically sectarian in attitudes. They did not understand the fundamental problems of any economic system arising out of the need to allocate relatively scarce resources which have alternative uses; hence their attacks on profit as immoral and competition as inherently anti-human were too simple.

Thirdly, I wanted to stress that they put their finger on one central issue, when they criticized the erection of the competitive free market into an overall philosophy of life or ideology, best called that of "possessive individualism," instead of regarding it as a useful tool for particular human purposes.

In the fourth place I wished to suggest that Christianity is *always* in search of a political and social expression, and that the radical nature of its ethic means that it will never be satisfied for long with *any* particular social order and its associated political philosophies. A stress on human imperfection is related only to one doctrine, that of "Original Sin," which is not the central one in Christian faith. (It is unfortunate that the terminology is so unsatisfactory, for it stands for what many have thought the most evident of all Christian doctrines, that there is a gulf in human lives between what *is* and what they themselves think *ought to be*, and this entail of "sin" infects all social structures, from the family upwards; so that human beings are born into human relationships which are to some extent perverted, and to some extent pervert them from infancy, long before they are able to make a personal judgement themselves. We do not start from scratch, but inherit an entail of "original" wrongdoing.) The more positive doctrines of the Christian faith concern the possibilities of renewal through life in the Christian community, created by the liberating ministry of Jesus in letting loose the power of the Kingdom (or Rule) of God, focused in his life and teaching, and continuing in the world as "leaven" in a lump. That community is one of giving and receiving in mutual support as each helps the other in growing to maturity. Because we live in two Kingdoms at once, that of the Kingdom of God and that of the Kingdom or structures of the world, we do not expect the life of the latter to be simply based on the former (and indeed it is only very imperfectly embodied in the Church itself). But it does provide criteria for a critique of political and economic philosophies. From this point of view the philosophy of the free market when turned into an overall interpretation of life, can be criticized as an inadequate understanding of what it is to be human, because it stresses the atomic and individualist aspect of life to the neglect of the prior organic and corporate aspects.

Fabian socialism

Mr. Shenfield approves of the way I have discharged the first of these aims, except that he would like some reference to the social Catholicism of G. K. Chesterton and Hilaire Belloc. This is summed up in Belloc's book *The Servile State* (1912). He and Chesterton were reacting against the state "gas-and-water" socialism of the Fabian Society, epitomized by the work of Sidney and Beatrice Webb and their famous Minority Report to the Royal Commission on the Poor Law which laid the intellectual foundations of the modern welfare state. Belloc argued that state action of this kind would turn the masses into a servile caste. Rather there should be the widest possible distribution of small-scale property, on the basis of the classical Christian defence of it found in the *Summa Theologiae* of St. Thomas Aquinas. This thinking was called Distributism. It was allied to the Guild Movement, and the weekly *New Age* founded and edited in 1906 by A. R. Orage, a dissident Fabian, but it is hardly part of the Christian Socialist tradition. It faded away in the 1929 Depression.

Mr. Shenfield's vigorous polemics are concerned with the other three aims of my paper. In detailed dissection of what I had written he makes six points, with rather more emphasis than evidence:

1. Individualism, properly understood, actually strengthens the bonds which tie men together in society. I wish he had spelled out how "properly understood" is to be taken. Instead he quotes the examples of the cohesion of the British and Dutch in the nineteenth century compared with other European societies, and that of the U.S.A. (apart from slavery) in absorbing masses of immigrants. The references are so brief that there is nothing to counteract one's astonishment.

2. The poor need to be diverted from attacking and trying to expropriate the rich. It would be to their own disadvantage, and religion should help to restrain them from doing so. Poverty is not slavery. He does not explicitly say why, but the inference is that in a free and open society the poor have the best chance of escaping poverty. Presumably some will always be rising out of it as others are falling into it. This ignores the fact that, contrary to what Adam Smith expected, wealth tends to lead easily to more wealth (particularly because of laws of inheritance), and the economic order gets more and more unequal (unless the free market mechanism of distribution is interfered with). Since it also moves erratically in booms and slumps men and women get caught in disasters which they could not guard against, and if their well-being is left to the in-

constant whims of private benevolence they could be in dire straits. To what extent and by what means the rich should be "expropriated" to deal with this is a different question.

3. Economic laws are as "divine" as the laws of physics, since human beings are faced with the inescapable necessity of choosing between scarce means with alternative uses. This seems indeed to be a brute fact of human life and part of the divine creation. But the social mechanism by which we make these choices is not determined by divine law, but rather by free human decisions. The *free market* is not a divine or "natural" institution, but a human construction for human purposes. Human beings can vary the range within which it works and decide the legal and social structure within which it is allowed to operate.

4. Minimum wage legislation harms the poor; and overlooks the fact that the economic product of some is not worth the "living wage." The first part of the statement is only true on the assumption that the free market is working on completely *laisser-faire*, atomistic assumptions; otherwise it can help the poor if we choose that it should. The second part raises the question of what we are to do with the minority who are barely employable. The living wage is one solution; a second is creating a social minimum level of benefits which are given to citizens as of right, a level beyond which they will not be allowed to fall, which is the aim of the welfare state; a third way is leaving it to private charity. The third is inhuman, and some combination of the first two seems necessary.

5. The multi-nationals for the most part are the victims of unchecked power, not its wielders. This is too big a subject to discuss thoroughly. Because they are conspicuous they are an easy target for attack, and can be made scapegoats for all social ills. But they *are* very powerful, and there have been enough scandals connected with them to serve as a warning. At their best they transcend the often petty and short-sighted nationalism of particular governments; at their worst they can be more powerful than many national governments, who find it hard to control them. In both cases they are irresponsible, in that shareholders usually have little influence, and public scrutiny is difficult.

6. There are aspects of labour which are like those of land and capital and there are aspects which are not, but the Christian Socialist cannot see that there is any aspect in which they are alike. As I acknowledged in my paper, this criticism is true of a number of

Christian Socialists who possessed a weak and often an erroneous grasp of economic realities.

I see no reason to alter the general burden of my paper. The history of the various Christian Socialist groups shows grave weaknesses, but a correct insight into the central issue. The "spirituality" which characterizes the ideology of free-market capitalism is unsatisfactory. It finds success in terms of personal rather than corporate achievements. It holds that unless everyone bears all the consequences of his own actions it is feather-bedding; that unless virtues have their personal rewards they will not be practised; that there is no place for solidarity; that public provision is only a last resort when voluntarism has failed; and that compassion, faithfulness and generosity are leisure-time activities. In their zeal to expose this outlook the Christian Socialists overlooked the value of the free market as a human institution for deciding many issues, provided it is put into a strong institutional framework and not turned into the key to all human economic relationships and to the divine ideal for man.

Discussion

Edited by: Irving Hexham

Ted Scott: Ellis Rivkin referred on several occasions to "historical baggage." Now when you talk about historical baggage or historical reality, it seems to me you have to look at the fact that risk-taking, which has been a term used and related to capitalism, never takes place in a vacuum.

Risk-taking took place in North America in the context of the development of European technology coming into a new situation that was wide open. There is a whole different context to that reality when risk-taking is imposed upon South America with a vastly larger population in another historical context or to the question of risk-taking by external groups moving in Africa, in terms of the situation there.

Issues relating to capitalism tend to focus on development within North America. But North American economic growth is part of a particular historical context and social reality. Can the North American example be transplanted to another part of the world?

It's the development of the ability to respond to those realities in the new situation that is incumbent upon those who give real support to capitalism. How do you continue a developmental situation that enables you to cope with the new realities that arise out of your actions, rather than just defend a principle from a past situation as though it is applicable in every context. I think we've tended to make that assumption much too easily in some of our discussions.

Imad Ahmad: I didn't say economics, I said "politics." I said *politics* for a reason. Economics is a science that tells you what will happen if you do certain things. As such, it's not going to be influenced by your values.

However, given that economics says, if you interfere with the marketplace, this will happen, and if you don't, that will happen, your values decide whether, once you have that knowledge, you are going to interfere or not. Those values are related to ethics. So once economics tells you what certain courses of action will lead to, you then have to make the choice as to whether you want that course of action.

So the choice we're talking about is: do we want to have socialism, or do we want to have capitalism, or do we want a third way? That's where religion comes in, at least, where ethics comes in. I would argue that religion says a lot about ethics. It definitely does in Islam.

Jim Sadowsky: I am in favour of justice but not in favour of the myth called social justice. Of course justice enters into questions of government intervention. These actions have to be judged as "just" or "unjust." The operation of the market itself cannot be just or unjust.

So justice hasn't been thrown out of the window in capitalism. But it isn't what is called "social justice." When you use the phrase "social justice," you are calling upon the mechanism itself to be just, which it cannot be, by its very nature.

Clark Kucheman: I should also like to discuss the concept of social justice. I think it does make sense to talk about social justice, if by that you mean the functioning of social institutions in accordance with human rights. When people have talked about capitalism being unjust they don't mean that it is a conscious agent. They mean that its functioning is not in accordance with the rights of human beings.

Walter Block: Once upon a time, there was a concept of justice — plain, old ordinary justice. And it meant something. I think the creation of the concept "social justice" is improper. It is merely an attempt to smuggle into the idea of "justice" something very different, while capturing the honorific element long enjoyed by this term. "Social justice" is commonly used as a synonym for "equality." Instead of favouring "social justice," it would have been more honest to come out on behalf of "equality." But this would not have worked too well public-relationswise, hence the invention of "social justice."

The analogy that comes to my mind is "rights." Once upon a time, there were things called "rights." In the classical sense rights were negative rights: i.e., the right not to be interfered with. All of a sudden, people claimed so-called "positive rights": the right to food, clothing and shelter, etc. This analogy is perfect. In both cases, ideologues attempted to latch onto a highly respected concept (e.g., rights, justice) in order to push their own agenda (e.g., income redistribution, equality).

For clarity and honesty, it would have been better, to use other terminology instead of "social justice" or "rights." But at present, the dialogue is clouded as "income redistribution" and "equality" try to hide behind the skirts of "justice" and "rights."

Imad Ahmad: The real problem is not with a concept of social justice, the problem is that the words themselves are very confusing and misleading for the reasons Walter Block has stated. That does not mean that everyone who has ever used the term social justice was not talking about a concept. I used it in my paper because there are people who use the term to mean a concept. I was referring to those people and the definition they use, but I would rather give it a new name, myself.

Gregory Baum: Schools of social thought define the term "social justice" in different ways. It is important to distinguish these differences. Otherwise we make all sorts of generalizations about "social justice" which have no basis in reality. In Catholic social teaching, we used to speak of "legal justice," "commutative justice," and "distributive justice." Pope Pius XI wanted to deal with a new form of justice, not contained in the preceding three, a new form which he called "social justice." If persons find that the existing social order does not allow them to observe the requirements of justice as previously defined, then they must engage themselves with others to change the existing order so that they may observe the requirements of legal, commutative and distributive justice. This he defined as "social justice." If a factory owner, Pius XI argued, finds that he cannot pay a just wage to his workers, then he must organize with other citizens to struggle for a transformation of the social and economic order so that just wages can be paid to workers.

Hanna Kassis: Islam has never abandoned the thought that it was a total way of life concerned with all departments of living. In fact, society can be described as just or unjust in a number of ways. This is not to say that the total society is just or unjust, but that the individual in society can be treated justly or otherwise.

In some cases, the total society can be accused of injustice. When the whole society fails to observe its duty, then the total society will be involved in sin, and will be responsible. For example, when something horrible is done and society keeps quiet, like the holocaust.

I'm in favour of keeping the term social justice if we mean by this term that the individual enjoys justice in society, is treated equally and is given equal opportunities, and so forth.

Ellis Rivkin: The religious roots of the idea of social justice really derive from such prophetic teachings as Amos, who specifically referred to a "total society" that was being brought under God's just judgement. He said that unrighteousness and evil will bring doom to the total society.

Irving Hexham: Arthur Shenfield put forward the view that a contract or market society is a good thing. One flaw with this is that people have a "folk memory." This folk memory involves a view of life where people envisage society as being like a large family. This vision of society as a family has important implications.

The point raised about Amos is relevant here. The view of society as a large family is reinforced and embedded in the Judeo-Christian-Islamic tradition. From the viewpoint of a market society this is unfortunate because if you are going to be religious you are going to keep returning to the image of society as a family.

My question to Arthur Shenfield is what do you do with Christianity, Islam, or Judaism? And what belief or religious system will replace the folk memory which is built into our religions?

Arthur Shenfield: Religion will have to be divested of that element of its folk memory. But religion must still pursue justice. There is nothing higher in the world than the pursuit of justice. If you don't understand it, you will pursue evil, and that's the real trouble.

The great insight of the philosophers and economists of the Enlightenment was that they saw that once you came to the "Great Society," the way to pursue justice could no longer be the way in which a loving father looks after his children or the chief of a clan looks after his clansmen.

The way to justice can only be the establishment and maintenance of impersonal rules. That is why we say that justice must be blind. Justice must not be a respecter of persons. A judge must not seek justice only. He must seek justice according to law. And only according to law. We all understand that. A ruler must be subject to certain impersonal rules. And a market is the best example of what this means.

But naive observers have never grasped that. And so they hate these impersonal rules. As Walter Block said yesterday, under the system of impersonal rules, we use other men as means. Critics of capitalism can never understand that that is entirely compatible with justice, because justice arises from the maintenance of impersonal rules. Once a society is properly subject to these impersonal rules the ability of individuals to be just becomes greater than in any other known society.

That is why in a society like America, slavery becomes uneconomic. It is the explanation of the fact that in the nineteenth century when there were disasters in India, Africa, or Latin America, subscriptions were always, immediately, and bountifully raised to help the victims. This did not occur in Imperial Russia, Germany, Austria, or France, but it did in America. In individualist, capitalist, America and Britain, the behaviour of people becomes more just once they understand the nature of the rule of law.

James Sadowsky: Perhaps a reconciliation is possible. The society we are dealing with in the old Testament is not the "great society." There, the situation is much closer to the family where people knew each other.

But when you go into a different situation, new occasions teach new duties, time makes ancient good uncouth. When you have this "great" or "modern" society, if you are going to avoid tyranny and favouritism you are forced to use the rule of law impartially.

Susan Feigenbaum: I'd like to suggest that the notions of family and of impersonal rules and law are not necessarily exclusive. Arthur Shenfield need not have put himself on the chopping block and thrown the family out of religion as quickly as he did. The establishment of such rules may be based on the notion of family and a willingness to forego one's individual rights or benefits in certain circumstances.

So I think that the establishment of impersonal rules — the initial allocation of property rights — from which the game begins can be consistent with the notion of family. But I agree that once such impersonal rules have been developed, according to these ethics and norms, they must be applied in an impersonal and objective manner.

John Berthrong: If you bring up such science fiction notions of law and the use of contracts and things like that, then I would simply suggest looking for an impersonal religion based upon causality. Should we convert to Buddhism? If we want an impersonal religion, let's junk the Judeo-Christian-Islamic tradition, embrace the four noble truths and analyze co-independent origination. Then happily we will go off into a market future. (laughter)

Clark Kucheman: A lot of traditional Judaic, Christian, and Islamic thought is very paternalistic in character. The images are always of the great father, not mother, but a commanding father who passes out favours every now and then, and treats us all like God's children — or sheep. It's the shepherd and the sheep. And I think that whole mentality is incompatible with the libertarian view.

Hanna Kassis: I want to take issue with the metaphor itself, and the subsequent discussion that resulted from it, in that I think it is blasphemous to speak of the fatherhood of God in Islam or in Judaism. I stand to be corrected by Muslims and Jews here. God fathered nobody in Islam. The metaphor of family does not exist as a foundation in Islam or in Judaism. What exists is not a metaphor, but a reality from the point of view of the Muslim and the Jew.

God's law has been made manifest to mankind, here on earth in time and space; and whether a man likes it or not, he is stuck with it. That's what he has to live by. He has no other option. The family metaphor is not involved here.

In other words we are dealing with "despotic leadership." I don't use the term despotic pejoratively at all. I mean it in the sense that the law of God is no longer in heaven. It is here. There is no role for fatherhood, family, love, etc., in this kind of language. There is only total obedience.

Stephen Tonsor: People ought to distinguish between a set of rules which enable men to live together in civil society and the demands of God on the individual for perfection. The justice that a Christian demands of himself always exceeds the demands of civil society. This often brings him into conflict with the civil society.

Anthony Waterman: I take issue with the metaphor from a Christian point of view. More significant than the concept of the family for Christian social thought is the concept of the Body of Christ. It seems to me that Christians are stuck with the notion that somehow or other the faithful, at any rate, are unified with Christ sacramentally in a way which in some very fundamental sense transcends their atomism — their individualism. It doesn't destroy it; but it means that they are joined with Christ and therefore with each other in a way which is quite incompatible, I think, with Arthur Shenfield's view of the just society.

Imad Ahmad: Arthur Shenfield made a mistake in thinking that Islam relates to a father figure of God, but I agree with his point about impersonal rules. The great achievement of Islam was that, long before the American Constitution, the *Qur'an* and the *Hadith* provided a set of impersonal rules that people were expected to abide by.

Richard Neuhaus: In various ways we are talking about the role of virtue, and its possible economic ramifications. Justice is a virtue. Hayek's work is a needed corrective, because people begin to speak about society as an actor, that is capable either of virtue or vice. That is simply fuzzy thinking.

Perhaps we can talk precisely about justice as an act in which there are indeed actors, individuals and groups. We can say that in some societies, the incidence of justice, or of injustice, is greater or less.

We can even go so far as to use expressions such as "a virtuous society," "a more or less virtuous society." But I agree that there is danger in this. The best we can probably do is to keep emphasizing that by justice we mean "virtue" which requires a degree of voluntarism, in which people are held as responsible actors.

The idea of virtue relates to some of the points that Ronald Preston was making. But he talked about a market leading to an atomistic rather than communally responsible society. As a matter of empirical fact, I would suspect that the virtue of community is higher in its incidence in a society that is marked by the exercise of free economic choice.

In the metaphors of judgement, fatherhood, accountability, familial attachment and responsibility, it is the Church, the believing community, that represents the exemplary degree of virtue. Therefore, the role of the Church is to stir up the capacity for exemplary virtue in society.

Let me conclude on the question of virtue. We touched on the issue of how we had gotten beyond the idea of the deserving and the undeserving poor. I'll say something that will sound terribly quaint. I think it is very unfortunate that we have dropped this terminology. For most of my adult life I have worked among the black poor in Brooklyn. These were the poorest of the poor as far as New York city goes and perhaps in all America. It strikes me as one of the greatest injustices done to these people, is that in social policy, no distinctions were made between deserving or undeserving poor. Rather, everybody was classified simply as "victim." This made them the object of abstract social policies, and those very policies reduced their initiative and incentive. They were encouraged to become irresponsible and dependent. It is one of the great indignities we do to people when we withhold discriminatory judgements.

Walter Block: I want to address myself to the distinction between cooperation and competition. Many people think that the marketplace is dog-eat-dog, vicious and competitive, in contrast to other institutions such as socialism, which exhibit cooperation. Now I agree that meaningful cooperation *can* take place in socialistic oriented institutions. But this is provided that they are *voluntary*. For example, the kibbutz in Israel, the monastery, the cooperative, the various experiments in "utopian" communal living. But even these have to be very small to succeed, and they have a long history of failure. The nuclear family is another case of non-market cooperation. Although my four-year old son and two year old daughter are sometimes not very good examples of this. They don't always cooperate with me. (laughter) Maybe what we need is more of the marketplace, even in my little tiny family. (laughter)

But certainly, the only way to get cooperation in a large society, any cooperation whatsoever, is to have a marketplace. Consider the example of this pencil I am holding in my hand. There were numerous people who cooperated to manufacture this pencil. They didn't know each other. If they ever saw each other, they might cut each other dead, or fight with each other, for all I know. And yet, through the magic of the marketplace, and I use that phrase advisedly, they were able to cooperate with each other in a way impossible had orders been coming down from on high. Large scale central planning is perhaps the *least* cooperative economic system known to man. My point is that people can, paradoxically, cooperate with each other *through* the competitive system, and that when it comes to large scale enterprise, this indirect or decentralized cooperation is actually more efficient than the supposed direct cooperation of central planning.

Chapter 6

Religious Commitment and Political Judgements: A Contextual Connection

Roger C. Hutchinson

Contributors to this symposium were asked to explore:

> the extent to which Christian (or other religious) commitment
> to a particular political and economic programme can be given
> an 'internalist' explanation (that is, can be said to be based
> upon a coherent *theological* and/or *political-economic* posi-
> tion), rather than an 'externalist' explanation as argued by
> Bryan Wilson, E. R. Norman and others (that is, it is the result
> of sociological pressures upon the clergy to be 'trendy').[1]

As requested, I will address that question to the North American
Social Gospel. I must confess at the outset, however, that the question is formulated in a way that makes it almost certain that one's
destination can be predicted from one's starting point. Since I am
sympathetic to the Social Gospel, I obviously believe that the link
between the Christian faith and radical social reform or socialism can
be based on a coherent theological foundation. A critic of the Social
Gospel or of Liberation Theology, on the other hand, could be expected to accuse social gospellers and social-justice advocates of being "trendy."

My aim is to help to move our discussions beyond stereotyped
defences and criticisms of the Social Gospel and of the link between
Christianity and socialism. Rather than focusing on how social

gospellers have *linked* Christianity and socialism, I will explore the implications of Reinhold Niebuhr's *rejection* of his earlier Marxism. As Beverly Harrison has argued, there has been a tendency to assume that Niebuhr thoroughly explored Marxism and found it lacking *on theological grounds*.[2] A more useful approach, represented for example by Martin Marty's 1974 discussion of Niebuhr's "public theology," emphasizes the impact of his empirical observations on his theological and political statements.[3] This reversal in emphasis will help us to see that the manner in which we interpret economic and social factors deserves as much attention as how we articulate or explain the theological or philosophical foundations of our differing interpretations. Compared with the sophistication and tolerance with which Christians, Buddhists, Muslims, etc., discuss one another's views of salvation, we are amazingly crude and dogmatic in our attempts to understand one another's interpretations of economic conditions and political realities.

Niebuhr's changing view of political reality

The Social Gospel movement emerged in the nineteenth century as a response to economic and social problems accompanying industrialization and urbanization. It also represented the extension of evangelical zeal from the conversion and salvation of individuals to the transformation of social structures. As a pastor in a working-class congregation in Henry Ford's Detroit, Reinhold Niebuhr both identified with the Social Gospel critique of capitalist society, and experienced the conditions which demanded a more radical solution. In 1930, he helped to launch the Fellowship of Socialist Christians (F.S.C.). According to its membership folder:

> The fellowship is committed to the belief that the social owner-
> ship and administration of natural resources and of basic means
> of production is a primary requisite of justice in our technologi-
> cal age. It affirms and supports the efforts of those who seek a
> cooperative society along socialist lines and it opposes those
> who seek to maintain the dominant contemporary system
> known as capitalism, which is characterized by private owner-
> ship of natural resources and the instruments of production.
> Capitalism... destroys the opportunity of increasing numbers
> of people to earn a livelihood adequate for physical health,
> mental and moral development, and personal freedom. It
> thereby corrupts both culture and religion.[4]

The Fellowship believed that "the workers of the world, who suffer most from the injustices of the present society, have a peculiar mission to be the instruments and heralds of this new society." Its aim, therefore, was to build a political alliance between workers and morally concerned people who themselves were not engaged in manual labour, thus creating "political forces in which human need and moral decision will be united to bring in a new economic order." It resisted both the optimistic liberalism of those who thought persuasion alone would produce the new society, and "the optimism of those Marxists who imagine that a new mechanism of social ownership will eliminate all conflict in the world and solve all the problems of the human spirit." With a Niebuhrian flourish, the F.S.C. statement concluded that, "On the basis of its Christian convictions it recognizes the inevitability of the conflict of interests in society as one of the forms in which human sin will always express itself."⁵

By the early 1940s Niebuhr's assessment of different economic systems and political philosophies had changed. According to Ronald Stone, Marxism had failed where it had been tried, especially in Russia. It was inadequate as a political philosophy since "it granted one group an absolute monopoly of power and also exaggerated the inevitable self-righteousness of man by claims of scientific rationality for its social theory." As a force for social change, the Marxist myth that utopia would follow catastrophe provided useful motivation for revolutionary action. However as a religion which absolutized its view of the dialectic of history it was dangerous:

> The illusions of Marxism ... reinforced the tyrannical tendencies of Communism. The primary illusion was its utopianism. Great evils were approved on the grounds that every act was justified which would realize the classless society.... The criticism of Marxism was in essence the same as the criticism of liberalism; both creeds were blinded by utopian illusions to the need for resolute political action for achievable ends.⁶

Stone then reiterates the view expressed in earlier comments by interpreters such as John Bennett and Kenneth Thompson: "Marxist realism had exposed the illusions of liberalism, and Augustinian realism exposed Marxist illusions." Thus, although he points out

that "an understanding of (Niebuhr's) thought is based upon grasping both the historical situation and his philosophical generalizations," he ends up implying that Niebuhr's criticisms of Marxism
flow primarily from "an Augustinian-inspired theology."[7] This
underestimates the importance of Niebuhr's empirical observations
of the changing world scene, and in particular of his American context.

Contextual judgements

Martin Marty has drawn attention to the tendency of Niebuhr's interpreters to focus on "his theological and philosophical ideas on an
almost entirely literary base of reference." Perhaps, he suggests,
this reflects the influence of "historic European theology." Or,
"Niebuhr's interpreters may be dismissing his circumstantial
thought as being the ephemeral context out of which the permanent
more abstract philosophical work emerged."[8] This emphasis on his
abstract thought and religious convictions overlooks Niebuhr's own
claim that "the gradual unfolding of (his) theological ideas (had)
come not so much through study as through the pressure of world
events."[9]

In an article called, "Reinhold Niebuhr: From Marx to
Roosevelt," William H. Becker also shifted the emphasis from
Niebuhr's theological ideas to his contextual judgements. He
pointed out that, although other interpreters recognized in a general
way that events influenced Niebuhr's thought, he wanted to give a
more precise account of how this had occurred in relation to
Niebuhr's rejection of Marxism. His main argument is that Niebuhr
"gave up his Marxist radicalism as he came to believe that social justice could be achieved within the American system." He insists that,
"the change in Niebuhr's thinking is directly attributable to his
changing view of the New Deal."[10]

Becker claims that until late in the 1930s Niebuhr believed that
capitalism "was unjust by its 'very character' and democracy . . .
was incapable of reforming it." In the 1939 spring issue of *Radical
Religion*, Niebuhr admitted that some of Roosevelt's programmes
represented real "social gains." This prompted Niebuhr to re-
examine his earlier assumptions about democracy, the role of the
proletariat, and the relations between classes.

In 1932, Niebuhr had agreed with Marx and Lenin that capitalist democracy meant that every few years the oppressed are allowed "to decide which particular representative of the oppressing classes are to represent them and repress them in politics."[11] By 1939, "he showed an appreciation of Roosevelt's role as leader which revealed his new understanding of democracy." Niebuhr admitted that a "political cause depends upon leadership to a greater degree than (he) had . . . supposed." This changed his attitude toward the role of the proletariat.

> He had believed that . . . they were to be the instrument to bring about a socialist society. But a resolute leader moving society, by steps, to socialism demotes the proletariat to a position of encouragers and supporters of the president; no longer are they the instruments of the new order, for the battle is to be eliminated.[12]

Niebuhr's belief that a class war could be averted did not mean that he abandoned his view of society as a sea of conflicting interests. In the 1940 election, "Wilkie was unacceptable because he failed to understand that government was at the center of a conflict of interests." Roosevelt deserved support for his domestic policies, as well as for his foreign policies, because he had actually brought about a degree of reconciliation between classes.[13]

Niebuhr's support for Roosevelt in 1940 was also based on his assessment of the options. If Roosevelt was not encouraged to seek a third term, "the only recourse would be the formation of a farm-labor party. Unfortunately it would take this party years to gain enough strength to win." Meanwhile, reactionaries would undoubtedly replace Roosevelt and lead the society back towards class war. "A genuine battle would probably mean the disintegration of the economic system and severe social conflict."[14] Developments in Germany and Italy prompted Niebuhr to worry that a fascist dictatorship rather than a classless socialist society would likely emerge from such a battle.

Feuds between the American Federation of Labor and the Congress of Industrial Organizations, a lack of labour union concern for unorganized workers, and the failure of labour to support Roosevelt's proposal for "an excess-profits tax on all profits six percent above those before the war," increased Niebuhr's disenchantment with labour politics. It also prompted him to conclude that "the

Roosevelt administration had more sense of justice than labor unions." By 1943 he no longer qualified his support for American economic and political institutions with the hope that socialism would eventually be achieved. In an article called "They Died for Capitalism," Niebuhr claimed that enough social control could be applied within the American system to guarantee a decent life for all without "the destruction of 'free enterprise.'"[15]

What did Niebuhr reject?

This emphasis on the extent to which Niebuhr's political judgements were related to his assessments of concrete conditions and options has a number of implications. On the one hand, it prompts us to ask again, not only why Niebuhr rejected Marxism, but whether or not he rejected all forms of socialism. As a Canadian, it heightens my interest in Niebuhr's reaction to Canadian Christian socialists in the 1930s. How seriously did he take their context? Finally, this analysis should make us more attentive to the basis upon which we decide what is going on in our own contexts and how this relates to our religious commitments. Do we assume that our understanding of the facts requires interpretation or that the disciplines we use or practice simply reflect rationality and empirical rigour? If we make this assumption, Niebuhr's ghost will haunt us!

According to Ronald Stone, "Niebuhr's critique of Marxism is a thorough-going indictment." In his view, "Niebuhr recognized that the evils of Stalin's dictatorship were partially due to contingent historical factors, but he emphasized the mistakes in Marxist theory which made such a development likely."[16] Becker, on the other hand, claims that Stalin's persecution of the kulaks and the Moscow trials did not drive Niebuhr away from Marxism as it did many intellectuals. Niebuhr "recognized the possible brutality that excessive power could beget and so was not shocked into rejecting Marx by what happened in Russia."[17] It is clear that Niebuhr did reject Stalinism and Communism, and that he roundly criticized all theories and political movements which seemed utopian or which exaggerated the human ability to know and to do what is right. It does not seem accurate, however, to assume that he rejected all forms of socialism.[18] It is also illegitimate to appeal to the authority of his theology to condemn socialism or Marxism.

Niebuhr in relation to Canadian and feminist contexts

In the 1930s a group of Canadian Christians formed a movement closely related to Niebuhr's Fellowship of Socialist Christians. The Fellowship for a Christian Social Order (F.S.C.O.) existed between 1934 and 1945. It was:

> An association of Christians whose religious convictions have led them to the belief that the Capitalist economic system is fundamentally at variance with Christian principles; and who regard the creation of a new social order to be essential to the realization of the Kingdom of God.[19]

In his review of the Fellowship's 1936 collection of essays, *Towards the Christian Revolution*, Niebuhr criticized the authors for failing to deal adequately with "the more difficult issues of the relation of Christianity to radicalism."

> These issues are not discussed because it is simply assumed that the socialist commonwealth for which the authors are striving is somehow or other identical with the Kingdom of God of Christian hopes. Is it not a little late in the day to maintain this illusion, so characteristic of the older Social Gospel?

According to Niebuhr:

> The crucial problem of every religious radicalism is how to relate the proximate goals of politics and the relative values of history to the unconditional demands of the gospel. If these unconditioned demands are merely reduced to a demand for increasing mutuality (after the fashion of John Macmurray, to whom most of the authors express their indebtedness) the result is not only a corruption of the historical meaning of the gospel but also an evasion of the actual human situation.[20]

Niebuhr's hostile reaction to the Canadians' emphasis on mutuality reflects his own convictions that the highest form of love is self-sacrifice and that the most insidious form of sin is self-assertion.[21] Although his pronouncements always reflected his own experience, Niebuhr's polemical, homiletical style often obscured the extent to which his judgements incorporated an interpretation of his own context. Langdon Gilkey points to the contextual character of Niebuhr's theology when he claims that:

> Niebuhr held to a theology of atonement, justification, and reconciliation as opposed to a messianic theology of a divine victory over evil men and evil orders, because he felt the former was a better *political* theology than the latter—and, note, better in terms of its possibilities for achieving justice, freedom, and humanity in history.... His theology... was not designed to eradicate hope for the future but precisely to eradicate the nemesis of self-destructive fanaticism and the despair that arises therefrom.[22]

In Niebuhr's context it seemed more fitting to worry about too much rather than too little pride, and about fanaticism rather than loss of hope. Feminists have observed that Niebuhr's stress on self-sacrifice and on the need to restrain prideful self-assertion is a very masculine preoccupation.[23] Women have been too passive and too reluctant to be self-affirming. In an analogous fashion, Canadians may have been too passive and lacking in self-affirmation as their nation drifted from being a British colony to an American satellite. Our main sins, it could be argued, are passivity and bad stewardship, not pride and self-assertion.

In feminist and Canadian contexts it is necessary to re-examine Niebuhr's assumption that a tolerable level of justice has been achieved within existing economic and political institutions. Niebuhr, no doubt, would agree. This would not, however, mean that he simply wanted to be trendy. It would reflect his conviction that all truth-claims are made in concrete contexts. Nor would it necessarily invalidate the central insight embedded in his theology.

Linking faith and politics in the Modern Age

Underlying Niebuhr's preoccupation with the anxious, isolated self is an insight into the nature of human existence which need not be denied in order to challenge the authority of his dogmatic utterances about sin. The spiritual condition Niebuhr was diagnosing with his emphasis on sin and anxiety has been talked about in different ways. Don Browning has pointed out that Niebuhr's position resembles William James's understanding of "twice-born" religion. In the religion of the twice-born, "one finds individuals haunted by a deep sense of risk, danger, and pervasive moral evil which runs through the world." These "divided selves" are "examples par excellance of *homo duplex*. They seem to have no natural sense of ,unity and coherence to their lives." Browning notes that, on the basis of his "pragmatic test of religious truth" and his "general philosophical psychology," James could have affirmed the fact that man is *homo duplex* "just as easily as could St. Paul, St. Augustine, Luther, or Kierkegaard."[24]

However:

> Under the influence of Kierkegaard, most post-liberal, twentieth-century theology has retrieved the Pauline-Augustinian vision of the ambiguity and dynamic duality of the human will. But the Niebuhrs, Tillichs, and Bultmanns of the neo-orthodox period could have turned to James as easily as to Kierkegaard or Heidegger. And had they done so, they would not have separated themselves from a modern world-view so profoundly as they did.[25]

Niebuhr was closer to James and to Whitehead than most of us who studied theology in the 1950s or 1960s were led to believe. Stone reports that Niebuhr "confirmed that the following quote from James represents his approach to the epistemological question":

> It matters not to an empiricist from what quarter an hypothesis may come to him: he may have acquired it by fair means or by foul; passion may have whispered or accident suggested it; but if the total drift of thinking continues to confirm it, that is what he means by its being true.[26]

Stone's further example of Niebuhr's affinity with James also illustrates similarities with Whiteheadian thought. Both Niebuhr and James

> abandoned traditional natural theology because of dissatisfaction with the arguments for the existence of God and an antagonism toward rational systems which they thought prematurely closed a developing world.[27]

It is unfortunate that these Jamesian and Whiteheadian themes in Niebuhr's thought were eclipsed by his tendency to invoke Christian beliefs dogmatically and to imply that everyday judgements about justice and political choices were secular and pragmatic.[28] It would have been more in keeping with his preferred position to have acknowledged that his religious beliefs and his political judgements were *both* either secular and pragmatic, or fraught with religious meaning. The distinction between the two ways of knowing and valuing was more important for his interpreters than it was for Niebuhr himself. In his intellectual autobiography he confessed:

> De Tocqueville long since observed the strong pragmatic inter-
> est of American Christianity in comparison with European
> Christianity; and that distinction is still valid. I have been fre-
> quently challenged by the stricter sects of theologians in
> Europe to prove that my interests were theological rather than
> practical or "apologetic," but I have always refused to enter a
> defence, partly because I thought the point was well taken and
> partly because the distinction did not interest me.[29]

Pragmatism

In his later years Niebuhr continued to hold different sub-communities and interest groups accountable for their behaviour, but he gained a greater appreciation for the "genuinely historical differences" of religious, ethnic and national communities. This led him to place even more stress on the importance of dealing concretely and pragmatically, rather than abstractly and dogmatically, with different communities. He pointed out that members of dominant groups, in particular, had to be aware of the tendency to make their "own standards the final norms of existence and to judge others for failure to conform to them."[30] It might be going too far to say that Niebuhr moved from polemics to dialogue, but proponents of interfaith dialogue can claim him as an ally.

My concluding suggestion is that the experience gained in the dialogue between communities of faith should inform future attempts at dialogue between Christians of differing political views. Respecting genuinely historical differences, resisting the temptation to equate one's own standards with the final norms of existence, and being accountable for one's behaviour, are aspects of the Niebuhrian heritage worth retrieving. We should not, however, underestimate the difficulties in the way of such conversations.

One of the ironies of the modern age is that whereas religiously-grounded beliefs have become increasingly relativized, people claiming to base their views on science have become increasingly dogmatic if not, to use Niebuhr's term, fanatical. We are comfortable with religious pluralism, yet often hear appeals to the authority of scientific experts, or of economists, as if pluralism did not exist within the empirical disciplines.

In 1966, Gibson Winter analysed the debate within the sciences and established the importance of discerning the underlying assumptions informing the differing styles.[31] The present challenge is to deal concretely with conflicting interpretations of such issues as publicly funded health care, rent control, public ownership of resources, and the impact of particular economic policies in particular contexts, for example, of monetarist policies in Chile. Out of such encounters will emerge a clearer understanding of what one's religious commitments really are and how they relate to particular political and economic programmes. This, in my view, would be more fruitful than asking who has an "internalist" and who has an "externalist" explanation of the link between their religious commitments and political judgements.

NOTES

1. Letter from A. M. C. Waterman, October 19, 1981.

2. Remarks at the American Academy of Religion Meeting, Dallas, 1980.

3. Martin Marty, "Reinhold Niebuhr: Public Theology and the American Experience," *The Journal of Religion,* 54: (October, 1974), 332–59.

4. Undated membership folder.

5. Membership folder.

6. Ronald Stone, *Reinhold Niebuhr: A Prophet to Politicians* (Nashville: Abingdon, 1972), pp. 61, 63 and 66.

7. Stone, op. cit. pp. 66, 10, 52.

8. Martin Marty, op. cit. pp. 335–36.

9. Niebuhr, "Ten Years that Shook My World," cited by Martin Marty, p. 335.

10. William H. Becker, *The Historian*, 35: (August, 1973), 539–50.

11. Becker, op. cit. p. 542: Lenin's observation was cited by Niebuhr in *Moral Man and Immoral Society*.

12. Ibid, pp. 546–47

13. Ibid, p. 548.

14. Ibid, p. 546.

15. Ibid, p. 549–50.

16. Stone, op. cit. p. 62.

17. Becker, op. cit. p. 540.

18. See Massimo Rubboli, "The Fellowship of Socialist Christians," Paper presented at the II International Congress of North American History, (Milan, Italy, June 14–17, 1979).

19. Membership Folder. For a history of the F.C.S.O. see my unpublished Ph.D. thesis, "The Fellowship for a Christian Social Order: A Social Ethical Analysis of a Christian Socialist Movement," (Toronto: School of Theology, 1975).

20. "Review of *Towards the Christian Revolution*," *Radical Religion* (Spring, 1937), 42–44.

21. For analyses of the debate between Niebuhr and Gregory Vlastos, one of the Fellowship's chief spokesmen, see my "The Canadian Social Gospel in the Context of Christian Social Ethics," in Richard Allen, (ed.) *The Social Gospel in Canada;* (Ottawa: National Museums of Canada, 1975) and "Love, Justice and the Class Struggle," *Studies in Religion*, 10; (Fall, 1981).

22. Langdon Gilkey, "Reinhold Niebuhr's Theology of History," *The Journal of Religion*, 54: 4 (October, 1974).

23. See Barbara Hilkert Andolson, "Agape in Feminist Ethics," *The Journal of Religious Ethics*, 9: 1 (Spring, 1981), 69–83.

24. Don Browning, *Pluralism and Personality: William James and Some Contemporary Cultures of Psychology* (Louisberg: Bucknell University Press; London and Toronto: Associated University Presses, 1980), p. 249.

25. Browning, loc. cit.

26. Stone, op. cit. 149.

27. Ibid. p. 149.

28. Franklin I. Gamwell, "Reinhold Niebuhr's Theistic Ethic," *The Journal of Religion*, 54: (October, 1974), 387–408.

29. Charles W. Kegley and Robert W. Bretall, *Reinhold Niebuhr: His Religious, Social, and Political Thought* (New York: Macmillan, 1961), p. 3.

Comment*

John H. Berthrong

After his short introduction, the bulk of Professor Hutchinson's paper deals with his analysis of the shifting views of Reinhold Niebuhr on Marxism and various other socialist options. It is well known to

*This Comment is an edited version of a longer article which appeared in *This World* No. 6, 1983.

anyone within Christian theological circles that Niebuhr moved from an early acceptance of Marxism to a rejection, at least in part, of Marxist theory and socialist praxis. Hutchinson finds the key to Niebuhr's theoretical rejection of Marxism or socialism not in a profound systematic theological critique of these positions, but rather in his observation of American reality. Niebuhr did not become disenchanted with Marxist theory, but rather became more impressed in the 1930s and 1940s with the seeming flexibility of the political system of the United States, which provided a tolerably just society which he could provisionally affirm.

The really key point is the question of how Niebuhr's observations of American reality helped modify his theological and political statements. This is what Hutchinson has aptly labelled a "contextual connection." In fact, the idea of a contextual connection is essential for Hutchinson's analysis of Niebuhr's changing ideological commitment. And I think it forms another common ground for ethical discussion between differing Christian theological perspectives. Hutchinson urges that we must be extremely attentive to our own context before any theoretical elaboration. This is certainly a point which a Whiteheadian Theologian can enthusiastically affirm. Whitehead once took exception to a statement by Bradley to the effect that "wolf eats lamb." Whitehead acidly noted that it was a case of *that* wolf in *that* place eating *that* lamb, and *that* lamb certainly feeling and knowing it. The context for the lamb and the wolf speaks volumes for their situation.[1]

Throughout his entire analysis of Niebuhr's evolving thought, Hutchinson continually returns to the position that Niebuhr's empirical observations always corrected his theoretical elaborations. Some scholars have argued that Niebuhr's theology is inspired by a very Protestant appeal to St. Augustine. While this may be correct, Hutchinson wants us to note how the actual transformation of Niebuhr's thought is intimately involved with the contextual connection. Niebuhr himself clearly indicated that his theological ideas came about not so much through systematic reading of the Christian texts as through pressure of world events. Hutchinson is therefore in full agreement with contemporary Niebuhr scholars who wish to emphasize the shift from a purely systematic theology to contextual judgements in Niebuhr's evolving theological reflections.

The fact is that Niebuhr clearly noted that the political structure of the United States could reform itself without transforming its economic system from a capitalist to a socialist form. Hutchinson sums up his interpretation of Niebuhr's thought when he says: "Niebuhr claimed that enough social control could be applied within the American system to guarantee a decent life for all without 'the destruction of free enterprise.'" This seems to be Niebuhr's final comment on the American social system, at least in Hutchinson's view. However, Hutchinson is not convinced that Niebuhr would have made the same judgement regarding the present Canadian situation.

Self-assertion

This is a rather interesting twist to the argument and I think we need to dwell on it for a moment. Basically, Niebuhr seems to have felt that the highest form of love, which he regards as the highest Christian virtue, is that of self-sacrifice, and that the "most insiduous form of sin is self-assertion." Hutchinson intimates that Americans have good reason to worry about pride and self-assertion, whereas Canadians should have been more self-assertive. Americans, on this reading, have seized destiny by the tail whereas Canadians have been wagged at the end of this tail. Is Hutchinson making literal claims about Americans and Canadians as individuals? Is he talking about the difference between American and Canadian contexts at the present time as well as in the 1930s? What implications does this reference to American assertiveness and Canadian subservience have for the present context of Canadian theologizing?

At this point in his paper Hutchinson moves to the question of what indeed did Niebuhr reject in terms of socialist or Marxist theory. He concludes that, "It does not seem accurate...to assume that he rejected all forms of socialism. It is also illegitimate to appeal to the authority of his theology to condemn socialism or Marxism."

We have an appeal here to an ideal of socialism without any indication of the empirical evidence of the particular context which might justify it. Some evidence ought to be provided, if nothing more than the claim that there now seems to be a relatively successful socialist, or quasi-socialist, governmental system. For example, the least controversial case may be Sweden. Sweden may not be the dream of libertarians, but it is foolish to argue that it is not a democratic state. I suspect that this is indeed the kind of social organization which Hutchinson would appeal to for empirical evidence.

In terms of Hutchinson's discussion of love as self-sacrifice,

Niebuhr himself seems to have denied at least one outstanding feature of much socialist thinking, namely the radical egalitarian strain informing a great deal of such thought. Niebuhr discussed this matter in terms of the idea of increasing "mutuality," where mutuality clearly means some kind of radical egalitarian theory. This is quite clearly linked to the concept of self-sacrifice. Carried to extremes, this ends in a radically egalitarian vision of society. A Whiteheadian can clearly affirm equality, but not perhaps on such a radical reading of social systems. For a Whiteheadian, or at least some Whiteheadians, equality must be appropriate to form. Observation of our actual context indicates that we are not all equal, in terms of being endowed either with similar talents or similar positions in the social scale.

With respect to our own country Hutchinson remarks: "Canadians may have been too passive and lacking in self-affirmation as their nation drifted from a British colony to an American satellite. Our main sins, it is said, are passivity and bad stewardship, not pride and self-assertion." I find it fascinating how Hutchinson has here linked the concept of social activity with bad stewardship. The whole concept of stewardship has become increasingly important for many Christian theologians. Here too the contextual connection is obvious. Taking one's context seriously probably demands a greater sensitivity to what Charles Birch and John Cobb have stressed as "ecological thinking."[2]

"In feminist and Canadian context," Hutchinson concludes, "it is necessary to re-examine Niebuhr's assumption that a tolerable level of justice has been achieved within existing economic and political institutions. Niebuhr, no doubt, would agree. This would not, however, mean that he simply wanted to be trendy. It would reflect his conviction that all true claims are made in a concrete context. Nor would it necessarily invalidate the central insights imbedded in his theology." This is an extremely important point, both for Hutchinson's own argument and for an emerging theological consensus reflected in the publications of the member churches of the World Council of Churches.

If any consensus seems to be emerging in W.C.C. theological circles these days, it is methodological rather than dogmatic. It asserts that theological statements must reflect the concrete context in which they are made. The widespread appeal of Liberation Theology is therefore not hard to understand. It most certainly arises out of a very specific and concrete context, and is therefore very welcome on methodological grounds. The difficulty, quite obviously, is that one is then driven to ask how the insights of that particular context are applicable to the North American and more specificaly Canadian reality. The implication, no doubt, is that both Canadians and South Americans find themselves structurally dominated by the United States. Although the situations are quite different, this one salient fact informs any analysis of the Canadian situation.

Empirical methodology

Later in his paper Hutchinson speculates on the possible relation of Niebuhr's thought to that of William James and A. N. Whitehead. While I can certainly see why he evokes the spirit of James in things empirical, I am a bit puzzled by his reference to Whitehead's noted empirical method in philosophy. He could be referring to Whitehead's own rejection of Marxism, although Whitehead himself hardly ever discussed these matters, especially during his philosophic period at Harvard. The whole Whiteheadian movement has often been rightly criticized for lacking an adequate political theory to go along with its well-defined metaphysical theory. One wit noted that you could say as much about Whitehead's ethics, political or personal, as you could about the snakes of Ireland. But even if this was a justified criticism of Whitehead's own corpus, the lack of a political commentary has certainly been remedied in the last few years within Whiteheadian circles.

For the remainder of his essay, Hutchinson continues to hammer away at the crucial importance of contextual concern within Niebuhr's evolving theological position. Quite admirably, Hutchinson contends that we too need to make the contextual situation more important for our own theological enterprise. Here again, he invokes the experience which modern theologians have gained in interfaith dialogue as an important part of learning how to do this contextual theology within the Christian faith community. He rejects any strain of dogmatism and urges us to recognize the "relative" truths of our particular context. Here a Whiteheadian must applaud Hutchinson's conclusion. A Whiteheadian thinker is always intrigued by the relative nature of truth-claims, though this does not demand that either he or she become paralyzed by the incipient relativism implied by the relational context. As with all excellent presentations, Roger Hutchinson's paper raises more questions than it answers.

But given a Whiteheadian theologian's affirmation of the radically pluralistic nature of our modern world, this cannot but be applauded. We need questions and we desperately need dialogue. Research concerning our Western religious tradition must be brought to bear on the present debate. It may be platitudinous to say so, but I firmly believe that the present political debate is too important to be left to bureaucracies and elected officials. Those of us who are in one way or another part of religious institutions must become engaged in this dialogue.

NOTES

1. Alfred N. Whitehead, *Process and Reality: An Essay in Cosmology*, corrected edition, eds., D. R. Griffin and D. W. Sherburne, (New York: The Free Press, 1978), p. 43.

2. Charles Birch and John B. Cobb, Jr., *The Liberation of Life: From the Cell to the Community*, (Cambridge University Press, 1981).

Reply

Roger C. Hutchinson

My emphasis on the relation between Niebuhr's shift to the right (or to the centre!) politically and his changing assessment of his Amer-

ican context was in part a reaction against the tendency of other interpreters to stress the role of his "deepening grasp of Augustinian theology." I wanted both to stimulate a rethinking of Niebuhr's rejection
of socialism and to draw attention to the ideological implications of
assuming that it was primarily for *theological* reasons that he had
abandoned his earlier commitment to socialism. In particular, I was,
and continue to be, concerned that Niebuhr's stature as a theologian
gave the political judgements he arrived at in an American context
more authority than they deserved when applied to a different Canadian situation.

Niebuhr's broadsides against socialism created the impression that
all forms of socialism had fallen under the scrutiny of his theolog-
ically-informed realism. We will never know, of course, whether
Niebuhr would have remained involved in socialist politics if his colleagues had been J. S. Woodsworth, Tommy Douglas, David Lewis
and the others who managed to launch a successful, politically relevant, democratic socialist movement in Canada. What is clear to me
is that the CCF/NDP tradition of democratic socialism deserves to
be assessed on its own merits in its own context. It should not be rejected on theological grounds because a theologian operating in a different context arrived at a negative appraisal of the socialist options
available to him.

I am also concerned, of course, about the fact that the same thing is
happening in our own day. Theologians of stature are invited by missionaries for free enterprise like the Fraser Institute to inform Canadians about the relative claims of capitalism and socialism. They do
not always make it clear that their attitudes towards socialism reflect
their American context. My aim is not to protect innocent Canadians
from foreign missionaries, but to encourage all of us to become more
self-conscious about the extent to which our political and theological
judgements are shaped by our particular contexts.

Dr. Berthrong wonders what kind of socialism Niebuhr might not
have rejected. The way he phrases the question is coloured by his assumption that socialism and mutuality entail a radical egalitarianism.
Rather than speculating on Niebuhr's final attitude towards different
kinds of socialism, I will simply observe that equality has a different
meaning in different philosophies.

According to Berthrong, "mutuality clearly means... self-sacrifice." As a Whiteheadian, he prefers a notion of equality which includes appropriateness to form. Vlastos insisted that the characteris-

tic feature of mutuality and socialism is sharing, not sacrifice. He started with the fact of community and the essential relatedness of human life and understood liberty and equality in the context of fraternity. Personal life in community is characterized by what Alfred Schutz called the "tuning in" relationship. It is not a Hobbesian coordination of isolated individuals.[1] As Patrick Kerans, C. B. Macpherson and others have persuasively argued, liberalism mechanized and depoliticized the relationships among persons by positing an equal opportunity to pursue individual interests which could not be assessed in terms of differential moral worth. Not all human needs, wants and goals, however, have equal claim on the community's resources or on the loyalty and respect of individuals. The kind of socialism which interests me treats this fact of differential worth as an ethical and political rather than an administrative, managerial problem. Relativizing the role of the market in allocating resources does not require a retreat to a fixed, hierarchical ordering of society, on the one hand, or the adoption of mindlessly bureaucratic management techniques, on the other. Determining priorities and making decisions involves moral and political discourse. It is no coincidence that Liberation Theologians stress participation as well as social justice.[2]

NOTES

1. Gregory Vlastos, "The Religious Foundations of Democracy: Fraternity and Equality," *The Journal of Religion*, XXII, 2 (April, 1942), p. 146.

2. Patrick Kerans, "Philosophical Barriers to Equality," in Allan Moscovitch and Glenn Drover, eds., *Inequality: Essays on the Political Equality of Social Welfare* (Toronto: University of Toronto Press, 1981).

Discussion

Edited by: Irving Hexham

Roger Hutchinson: I'll try and clarify some of the assumptions that were at work in my paper, particularly in the way I am reading Niebuhr.

First, a word about why I re-framed the question given to me about internal or external links between faith and politics. I was suggesting it was more useful to talk about contextual linkages, and to deal concretely with how faith and practice are related in concrete places rather than to debate philosophical issues.

I did that, not to escape from the discipline of rigorous analysis, but as one of the pre-conditions for dialogue. It is important to know whose context is being taken for granted in order to discuss issues on a point by point basis. So that was the main structure of my paper. The question I want to address now is: "Why did I choose to deal with Niebuhr for this seminar?"

Whether we like it or not, Niebuhr is an authority figure in the tradition of political and social ethics. I've gone through periods of feeling very unhappy about that influence. But lamenting the influence doesn't help. Niebuhr is a dominant figure in that tradition. He's an authority in the sense that his thought has influenced, and continues to infuence, many people. He's an authority in another sense: he is a vehicle for discourse about how we presently relate our religious convictions to our practical judgements.

It's in that sense that I look at Niebuhr. I certainly agree with Paul Heyne that great caution should be used by anyone who invokes Niebuhr to justify this or that point. In this context, Niebuhr shouldn't be invoked, authoritatively, to undergird an unquestioned link between freedom and responsibility of individuals and limited government intervention in the economy. That's a contextual judgement that Niebuhr would have made or rejected on the basis of an empirical assessment of what was going on.

Let us return the question to the political realm, so that we can have a political discussion about whether the freedom of individuals is best preserved through maximizing the operation of the market system, or whether it's in moving in the other direction. Such questions cannot be answered in abstract terms apart from a particular context.

My concern about Niebuhr's influence on the Canadian social gospel was that, on the basis of his stature as a theologian, his conclusion was accepted that the way Christians in the 1930s linked the Christian faith with a socialist program was based on a faulty theology.

My first thought was that I had to get rid of Niebuhr. But that didn't seem to be a practical scheme. (laughter) I then thought that the next best thing was to reread Niebuhr to see if one could somehow or other claim him as an ally. (laughter) My strategy was to return Niebuhr to his context and to stress the contextual character of his political judgements.

To be contextual in the United Church of Canada, is to realize that we have capitalists and socialists in the same organization. Therefore, unless we are prepared to read one another out of that fellowship we simply must relate to one another. But that doesn't mean that you forget that one person is a capitalist and the other is a socialist. There is a struggle going on over how the symbols of the tradition should be interpreted and applied to social issues. Socialists don't go to sleep and let the capitalist take over the symbols and capitalists aren't going to sleep either. The Fraser Institute says in its program brochure that their mission is to remind people that the capitalists have been asleep while the churches have collapsed the symbols into the socialist project.

Walter Block (Moderator): That will be enough of that. (laughter)

Roger Hutchinson: I recognize the diversity of my own faith community, and that tends to lead to a recognition of the ambiguity of our Christian symbols. So, it doesn't scandalize me that one group of people are using my symbols to justify a political program with which I disagree. I simply think it's not the most fitting way to appropriate that tradition. My main claim, however, is that it is more useful to discuss concrete issues than it is to debate the different perspectives underlying our approaches.

My plea, then, is that we become more self-consciously contextual. I don't find anything contextual about how the Fraser Institute describes its mission. It's simply announcing that the position churches have been taking is wrong. Economic dogmas now play the role Niebuhr's theological dogmas played in the 1930s and 1940s.

Gregory Baum: I am uncomfortable with the conversation about interdisciplinary studies, including the intersection of theology and social science. What offends me particularly is the claim of economists (and other scientists) that there is a single orientation in their discipline, which they in fact represent. They claim to speak for all serious economists. It is hard to believe that such people speak in good faith. In Canada, for instance, there are several economic research institutes, all of which make use of the scientific method, but they come to quite different conclusions. They follow different approaches in the same discipline.

Thomas Kuhn's work on revolutions in the sciences has shown that even in the natural sciences there are different approaches and conflicts of paradigms. In the social sciences, including economics, these conflicts are of course much greater. Here they are related to the various value-perspectives which researchers consciously or unconsciously adopt.

Obviously there is also plurality of method in theology. What is of interest to me is that in interdisciplinary studies, the approaches used in the various disciplines must have a certain coherence or affinity. Otherwise interdisciplinary study will break down or lead to contradictory results.

In my view positivism in the social sciences exercises a deadly cultural power. I define positivism as the attempt on the part of the social sciences to be assimilated as far as possible into the natural sciences. Reliance is on the scientific method alone, hence on measurement, quantity and mathematical logic. If this approach is applied to human beings, all qualities are translated into measureable quantities and all people become things or objects because their own self-understanding adds nothing to measurable science. And this applies to the dehumanizing impact of positivism whether it be adopted by mechanistic Marxism on the Left or by scientism and vulgar functionalism on the Right.

Imad Ahmad: Roger Hutchinson commented that we don't like to admit a connection between faith and politics. I'm not sure that this is a general principle. It's certainly not true in the Muslim tradition. I don't see that it should necessarily be true in any other tradition.

I think there is a necessary connection between faith and politics. Certainly our political views are in some way connected to our ethical views. Politics and political conclusions come from ethical premises. On the other hand, our ethical views are related to our religious views. Therefore, we should acknowledge this issue and deal with it explicitly.

Obviously, there are differences between the social sciences and the natural sciences, but I don't think the differences Gregory Baum is talking about are really valid. The idea seems to be that somehow it's all right to approach a social science with biases and prejudices that are allowed to interfere with your conclusions.

I've seen this in psychology where I saw a debate once over the issue of whether or not there's a statistical difference in IQ's between people of different races. People enter the discussion with the desire to believe a particular conclusion. Therefore they allow their examination of the subject to be coloured by their beliefs.

In this debate, the fellow who was arguing against the existence of an IQ difference between the races went so far as to say, "Well, ultimately, it's not a question of whether the evidence is good or not. We don't want this to be true." And, therefore it is argued that it is the duty of a sociologist if he comes across evidence that an undesirable conclusion is true, to cover it up.

This is terrible. It's terrible not just because it's bad science, but because it results in sloppy thinking in other areas. The debator had determined to defend a particular belief. His sloppy thinking had allowed him to accept the very poor concept that if there is an IQ statistical difference between the races, somehow this necessitates some difference of treatment in terms of political rights.

Regardless of what statistical differences between the races may or may not be, certainly we know there are differences of IQ's between individuals. But we must all realize that individual rights have nothing to do with IQ.

As soon as you make the distinction between the attitude that we bring to social sciences as opposed to the attitude we bring to natural sciences, you leave the door open for that kind of sloppy thinking. And no good can come of it.

Steve Tonsor: I want to consider the word "dialogue." Arthur Lovejoy suggested that in every generation there are words and phrases filled with what he called "metaphysical pathos." (laughter)

In the last generation, the generation of Niebuhr, these words were "ambiguity" and "paradox." In our generation, one of the favorite words filled with metaphysical pathos is "dialogue." I suggest that the life of the mind is not the life of dialogue. It is the life of combat. Combat! And it is true, as in a medieval tourney, there are certain rules to this combat. That constitutes its civility. We've gone beyond the point where the combat is mortal. We don't kill our opponents. But, it is combat. And to describe it in any other terms is silly.

Sartre said that the great teacher was a man who raised up successful combatants to himself. Anyone who has lived the intellectual life knows that he, the intellectual, if he is honest, carries on with himself a constant running battle, in which he continually questions his most fundamental premises. That's what intellectual life is about. It's not a nice dialogue—a tea party.

Finally, if you're going to be a successful combatant, you must, as Lord Acton said, make out a better case for the opposing side than they can make out for themselves. Unless you do that, you will never win. And I want to win. (laughter)

Ellis Rivkin: The nation state is capitalism's greatest barrier. It's a heritage from the middle ages. It's not something that capitalism brings to humankind. Quite the reverse. Capitalism is barred from being fully what it could become precisely by this inheritance from an earlier time.

Consider for a moment that Canada had actually been incorporated within the United States back in the eighteenth or nineteenth century. What would have been the consequence for the industrial phase in the United States?.

Now if that had occurred, we would not at this point be worrying about Canada-United States relationships. Nor would we be concerned about the problem of being a hinterland, which is so understandably a matter of concern for Canadians. There would simply have been a free movement of capital and labour.

One of the issues that we really have to focus on is values. The ultimate value that one is committed to, takes precedence over all other values, including economic ones. The national value is for many people an end in itself. But must we have a sovereign nation state? Must it have a set of barriers that bar it from the free interflow of capital?

Is the feeling that one must have a sovereign nation state a good one? Is it possible for ethnic and other kinds of feelings of this type to have autonomy? To have freedom? Even more freedom, perhaps simply because it does not involve the problem of two powers coming into conflict with each other, and therefore violating ethnic rights, which presumably can exist within the larger kind of framework.

Much of our problem has to do with ultimate values. If our ultimate values are a commitment to the individual then nationalism is a major barrier.

Irving Hexham: There is nothing so dangerous as underestimating one's enemy, or opponent, as Stephen Tonsor pointed out. You've got to understand their position better than your own.

In our discussion, we've been talking about a move from theoretical ideas to empirical examples. And yet the empirical examples suggested are being used as a substitute for coming to grips with beliefs that are under fire. The big issue here is socialism or, maybe more directly, Marxism and our reaction to it.

Quite a lot has been said about the failure of Marxism. But it's been said in the framework of empirical failure. Now I would like to submit that if we're going to have a fruitful discussion along these lines, we've got to recognize that in purely empirical terms perhaps Marxism can be extremely successful. I was reading Roger Munting's book *The Economic Development of the USSR*, where he argues that the Soviet economy is in fact a phenomenal success. It doesn't provide freedom and certain liberties but there are reasons to believe it has done better in the twentieth century than the American economy.

Similarly, there is an article in the *Harvard Business Review* (Vol. 60, No. 2, March/April 1982) "Tapping Eastern Block Technology" by John Kiser III, where it was argued that contrary to common American belief, the Soviets are in fact very innovative. The author of this article looked at the patents of various goods and said that many Japanese successes are, in fact, Soviet patents.

So the Soviets can't be dismissed so easily, either for economic failures or lack of innovation. We just reject them for intellectual reasons—questions of belief. This is what we need to get down to— unless we do we're going to paint a false picture and attack the wrong enemy.

I'd like to suggest that a lot of the debate about empirical success is very misleading because it is a two-edged sword. We've got to be very careful on this one. Or else, somehow, someday, a lot of young Americans may wake up and find that the Soviets aren't so unsuccessful as they thought.

In the future perhaps, the standard of living in the Soviet Union may become higher than North America. What do we do then if our anti-communism is based solely on an appeal to material welfare?

Anthony Waterman: I want to disagree with Dean Ahmad. I agree with Roger Hutchinson who does, in fact, maintain that Niebuhr's political beliefs could be detached from his theology, in the sense that they could be based upon empirical judgements about a particular context.

I want to assert, even more strongly than that, that it is actually impossible in principle to proceed from religious belief to unique political judgements. I think all political judgements necessarily involve empirical questions. And, theology, by definition, is incompetent to pronounce upon empirical questions. Therefore it is entirely possible, and frequently is in fact the case, that two persons of identical religious beliefs, and identical ethical principles formed upon those religious beliefs, will differ over some political question, precisely because they differ about the facts of the case. This point was recognized by William Temple, towards the end of his life, after having said much earlier that if one was a Christian one would have to be socialist. Temple recanted.

Christians can and may legitimately differ over political questions, because the facts of the case are not amenable to theological analysis.

Clark Kucheman: I would like to pursue that same point. It may be true that a lot of people "do" economics theologically in the sense that they have in fact a value orientation which influences their analysis.

But I would say that that is not what they ought to do. In principle, economic analysis is independent of theology.

I think ethics is also, in principle, independent of theology. You can know all about God and what God wills but still not know what you ought to do.

It seems to me, you have to make judgements independently of religious faith about what one's rights and duties are.

PART FOUR:

OTHER CHRISTIAN TRADITIONS

Chapter 7

Christian Social Thought in the Dutch Neo-Calvinist Tradition

Bob Goudzwaard

"Neo-Calvinism" is an expression which was first used by Max Weber in his contributions to the sociology of religion. He used it to describe the revival of the social and political teachings of John Calvin which took place, especially in the Netherlands, during the last part of the nineteenth and the beginning of the twentieth centuries.

The roots of that revival lie mainly in the so-called *Reveil* movement, which had its origin in the first half of the nineteenth century in Protestant—not only Calvinistic—circles in Switzerland. That movement stressed the significance of a living Christian faith: biblical studies, and prayer for the reformation of the Church and the renewal of society. The most important Dutch representative of that *Reveil* was Guillaume Groen van Prinsterer (1801–1876). Deeply influenced by German thinkers Von Haller and Julius Stahl, who were primarily within the Romantic tradition, Groen gradually developed his own approach to the social and political problems of his time, although he always remained a true "son of the *Reveil*." His main published work was a major study of the spirit of the French Revolution, *Unbelief and Revolution*. He saw the Revolution and its ideals as the driving force behind the modern unbelief of his age.

However, Abraham Kuyper (1837–1920) must be seen as the founding father of Dutch neo-Calvinism. As a theologian, philosopher, journalist and statesman, he elaborated van Prinsterer's principal ideas, but also refined them—giving them specific accents. On the one hand, he emphasized a Reformed—and especially Calvinistic—doctrine; on the other, he passionately taught the necessity of a practical—and especially organizational—implementation of those ideas.

For example, he founded the Free (Calvinistic) University of Amsterdam, the Anti-Revolutionary Party (the first democratic political party of the Netherlands), and took the lead in the formation of the Reformed churches of the Netherlands. He also deeply influenced the Dutch Christian labour movement in its formative stage. For more than thirty years he wrote daily and weekly columns in the Christian daily newspaper, *De Standaard,* which he himself founded. In addition to his prodigious academic output and his many other activities (political, social, academic and ecclesiastical), he served for many years as a member of Parliament and as prime minister of the Netherlands from 1901–1904.

More than sixty years after his death, one can undoubtedly say that the Netherlands today would be a markedly different nation had Abraham Kuyper not lived. As an illustration, my own life reflects the extent of his impact on Dutch society. Since my birth, I have been a member of one of the Reformed churches; in the sixties I was a Member of Parliament for "his" Anti-Revolutionary Party; and from 1971 to the present, I have been a professor in "his" university. I am an advisor to the 300,000-member Dutch Christian labour movement; if I publish in newspapers, I usually do so in *Trouw*—the direct successor of "his" *Standaard.* A great part of my personal life can therefore be seen as participation in Kuyper's heritage. At the same time, this personal note makes it clear that I cannot give an "objective" view of Dutch neo-Calvinism and its social thought—although I am very aware of the necessity for a critical appraisal or reappraisal of some of its features. Even in my critique, I stand in that tradition, and feel myself co-responsible for it. This is also true of the heritage of the so-called Philosophy of the Cosmonomic Idea, which was born in the inter-war period on the basis of Groen's and Kuyper's thought. This philosophy, developed primarily by D. T. Vollenhoven and Herman Dooyeweerd, can be considered as the dominant scientific tool of Dutch neo-Calvinism, although its contribution has not always been honoured in that way by the practical-institutional wing. Notwithstanding disagreement however, there is a similarity in colour and flavour—even today—between this philosophy, and the many organizations and institutions that sprang from the van Prinsterer-Kuyperian initiative.

In this paper, however, not the entire breadth of the Dutch neo-Calvinist tradition is under scrutiny, but only its contribution to Christian social thought. For this purpose, I want to distinguish between three themes in Dutch neo-Calvinism which in my opinion are not only essential for understanding that movement, but are also the most influential in the formation of its social thought: a) the theme of vocation or calling; b) the theme of antithesis and common grace; and c) the theme of an architectonic critique of society.

My plan is to discuss each of these themes. In the concluding pages, I will add some notes about their relevance for a Christian appraisal of our present bewildering, progress-oriented society.

The theme of vocation or calling

The words "vocation" or "calling" (*Berufung* in German) are used often in the teachings both of Martin Luther and John Calvin—more in the former than the latter. In vocation, one notes a reference to someone calling, addressing one "vocally." For both Calvin and Luther, He who calls is the living God.

In medieval times, vocation was also used in and by the Catholic church, but then usually restricted to God's calling of a person to leave his daily work, to enter a monastic way of life or a holy office, for instance. Luther and Calvin, however, did not hesitate to identify very common jobs in daily life with God's calling or vocation, as the "way" in which one is serviceable. Both reformers held that Christ's crucifixion and resurrection from death was a *total* victory and included the salvation of both life *and* nature. In their opinion, natural work is thereby already sanctified—holy—and does not require the prior or additional sanctification dispensed by the institutional church through sacraments. Everywhere in natural life, human beings stand and live *coram Deo*—directly before the face of the living God—who summons them to be serviceable to Him and to their neighbours, by simply doing what they must do as farmers, craftsmen, kings, housewives, or merchants. Daily work is vocation; it is giving an answer to the living God and requires no additional "spiritual dimension." Even today, the common words in Germany and Holland for one's job are *beruf* (German), *beroep* (Dutch), both of which mean "being called to."

Although Luther uses this concept more frequently, Calvin more generally points to the fact that calling also has an institutional dimension. Persons are addressed *as* bearers of an office. This means that a government as such, a church community as such, and a family as such are separate objects of God's calling. Precisely this element in Calvin's thought has inspired Dutch neo-Calvinism's unique view of institutional relations in society, characteristically expressed by Kuyper and Dooyeweerd in the principle of "sphere-sovereignty."

I now turn to a discussion of this principle. To understand its real meaning, its origins must be kept in mind. Two religious insights are at the root of this concept. The first is that because of the universal significance of Christ's redemptive work, there are no longer different degrees of holiness in natural reality. In principle, a basic *equality* exists among the different "spheres" of life in which human beings live and work together. In every "social" sphere of life—the family, state, church, school, also the business enterprise (what I prefer to call the "production-household"), the voluntary associations, such as labour unions—people are allowed to see themselves as directly responsible to God. That insight precludes any institution (whether church, state or any other) from seeing itself as the encompassing institution of society, to which the other "spheres" of life are hierarchically or spiritually subordinated.

The second religious insight is that *within* each sphere of life not only human will, but also God's calling, prevails. This gives the sphere-sovereignty principle a genuinely normative colour. The word "sovereignty," for instance, does *not* point primarily to the significance of "authority" in a specific sphere of life, and it does not point at all to the automony of the human will. It points to the sovereignty of God, who has called and still calls upon human beings to be serviceable to Him and to their fellow-men in a variety of ways. Progressing through various "spheres of life," one sees this service typically as follows: in the way of loving care for children within the family and in the schools; in the way of truthful love between husband and wife in marriage; in the way of economic serviceability and stewardship (the characteristic calling of production-households); in the way of providing just, fair treatment of workers in the case of unions; and in the way of bringing public justice to society as a whole as the characteristic norm for the state.

Moderate interventionism

Only if one keeps in mind this double foundation of the principle of sphere-sovereignty can one understand, for instance, the reason why Abraham Kuyper was in favour of some types of intervention by the state in social-economic life, though never acquiescing in the socialist programme of central, state-controlled planning of society. For state socialism would imply the elimination of the specific responsibilities of unions and production-households. Nevertheless, the first type of governmental action (carefully-planned government involvement) be-' comes necessary and fully justified if a business enterprise is not loyal to its *own* calling to be a steward of its resources; or if it behaves improperly toward people or groups, or abuses nature. If the state intervenes for these reasons, it does not violate the sphere-sovereignty of the business enterprise. Quite the opposite, the state would then honour the business's sovereignty. For, in those cases, governmental action obeys the mandate to bring justice back into public life. There is, therefore, no room for unrestrained license in Dutch neo-Calvinism. For the business enterprise there is only a normatively-bound liberty within the context of its calling.

What does this approach imply, when dealing with questions of authority and democracy within the state or other spheres of life? What will be the way of dealing with phenomena like political revolution, democracy, or social and economic co-determination by workers in a business enterprise? There is ample and interesting historical material here.

In relation to questions of *authority* and *revolution*, Dutch neo-Calvinism has usually stressed the obligation of respect for all God-given authority. Without such respect, society falls into anarchy, and to the idolatry of *ni Dieu ni maitre* of the French Revolution. From the beginning, the movement was anti-revolutionary in character, and, although it has maintained a deep awareness of the necessity of political democracy until today, it rejected fully the idea of a people's sovereignty, as proposed by Jean Jacques Rousseau for instance. But it has to be said that this is only one side of Dutch neo-Calvinism. There is also another side.

Revolutionary

That side can be illustrated with the help of a distinction made by

Groen van Prinsterer himself, between "anti-revolutionary" and "counter-revolutionary." "Counter-revolutionary" stands for the attitude of the Bourbon Restoration—of resistance to all the fruits of the French Revolution, and a glorification of authority by *droit divin*. "Anti-revolutionary" means being opposed to the *spirit* of the French Revolution. That spirit neglects the fact that for a state as for those in government, there is a divine call to do justice. The consequence of this neglect is that citizens and governments can become "revolutionary" in the deepest meaning of that word! A state becomes a revolutionary state when it systematically resists the will of God to use its power in a just, non-discriminating way. If, for instance, a government misuses its power by exploiting a nation or by denying its citizens freedom of religion, then it has become a revolutionary government in this sense of the word. Incidentally, this also implies the "right" of its citizens to resist (an expression already used by Calvin). If "magistrates"—responsible persons who are supposed to lead the nation— try to remove such a government, they should not be seen as revolutionaries. What they may have to do must be seen precisely as another way to honour the real calling of a government. Here we again encounter the second cornerstone of the principle of sphere sovereignty, namely that God's calling must have primacy over the abuse of the human will. Authority has to be honoured, no doubt, but only in the context of its calling. Both Groen and Kuyper follow Calvin in speaking very cautiously about the possibility of a necessary "revolution." There has to be a systematic, deliberate, and cruel abuse of power, and there must be care that a revolt does not lead to a bloodbath. Thus a mere collection of citizens possesses no right to resist. Power should be taken over by those who already have a political responsibility and are able to lead the nation. But in principle the right to resist is acknowledged, for having authority is not more "holy" or more "sanctified" than being subject to authority. Was Christ not among us as one who served? Here the first cornerstone of the principle of sphere-sovereignty comes to the fore: the equality in terms of holiness of all stations in life.

It follows that Dutch neo-Calvinism should also construct its own view of *democracy*. Democracy is highly valued, insofar as it expresses the joint calling of government *and* citizens to the direction of the state. It can and must be a corrective against abuse of power. For example, the choice of Elders in Reformed churches has, since Calvin's time, always been a democratic process: the congregation chooses them. But once they are chosen, their guidance and authority must be respected, unless they misuse their position for their own interests. Then their calling has to have priority, and they must be removed from their office.

From the start, the Christian Social movement in Holland consisted of a coalition of Catholics and Protestants, although each had their own institutions. Yet it is interesting, for example, that with respect to trade unionism an issue such as co-determination is viewed similarly by both groups. God calls production-households to the service of stewardship. That call is addressed not only to management, but to the whole working community. Of course the daily guidance by management has to be respected, but all have a common responsibility for the *direction* or orientation of the enterprise—just as both government and citizens have a shared responsibility for the direction of the state. And that requires institutional arrangements for co-determination. The owners of the enterprise, the share-holders, must understand that they do not own living persons or a living community. They own only the capital goods of the enterprise. If they receive their financial reward and are given a satisfactory account of what is done with their money, they must be content. They cannot assume command of this living community. To do so would be a violation of the sphere-sovereignty of a living and working human community, in which management and workers, though with different duties, share a God-given calling. If management abuses its power and exploits its employees, it must be removed. For both management and labour are *under* the one law of the Sovereign God as it applies to this part of life. The specific law which applies here has its kernel in the mandate of good stewardship over the resources entrusted to that community *as a whole*.

The theme of antithesis

Christians and non-Christians live together in a single society. Thus the evaluation of society in terms of "calling" and "sphere-sovereignty" is not generally accepted. How, then, should Christians behave amidst pluralism? Should they try to dictate the actions of non-Christians or attempt to build a theocracy?

In relation to these questions, Abraham Kuyper usually referred to what he called the *antithesis:* the radical distinction between the Kingdom of God and the Kingdom of Darkness. His use of the term, however, did not imply a state of affairs in which Christians are on one side and non-Christians on the other. Christians cannot be seen only as children of light, nor non-Christians only as children of darkness. All human beings are fallen, and God's invitation of redemption is extended to all. Therefore Kuyper—and Dooyeweerd after him—spoke of God's *common grace* given to mankind. God sends his sunshine upon all, and his call is not addressed to Christians alone.

But the concepts of antithesis and common grace do not, by themselves, solve the problem of Christian behaviour within a pluralistic society. The concept of common grace seems to permit Christian and non-Christian to cooperate as far as possible, subject as they are to the same calling and the same sin. But the concept of antithesis between light and darkness would seem to imply that Christians should withdraw into isolated communities, fleeing as far as possible from the realm of darkness. Which way did Dutch neo-Calvinism take in face of this dilemma?

One can say that Groen van Prinsterer and Abraham Kuyper, especially the former, wrestled with this problem throughout their lives. In relation to the public school issue, for instance, Groen originally held that every public school must honour the Christian faith in its whole style of education. In his view, separate schools should be erected for Jewish, Muslim or other minorities. But when it became clear that the only politically feasible outcome was that public schools would teach "generally Christian and human social and moral virtues," Groen rejected this compromise and changed his opinion. He then argued for separate Christian schools, and no longer sought to burden public schools with any religious obligation. Once a society has become secularized, he felt, no other choice can honestly be made.

Starting where van Prinsterer had ended, Kuyper founded many separate Christian organizations and institutions. Like his great predecessor, he could not and would not accept these organizations as "safe hiding-places" for a self-contemplating and complacent, Christian segment of the population. He could only accept them as the last line of defense, from which the battle for the heart of the nation would be launched. By means of their own organizations Christians must play an active role within a secular society under God's common grace. For as Kuyper himself once said, "There is no piece of this earthly soil of which Christ has not said: 'It is mine!'"

Otherness

Again we are reminded of Max Weber, who once characterized Calvinism as *innerweltliche askese*, that is, as living *in* this world but not fully being *of* this world. By their nature, Christian organizations embody the "otherness" of Christians, but in Kuyper's conception are legitimate only if they fulfill their Christian service *within* the world and *within* existing society. Exactly what is that Christian service? It is to fulfill one's calling! A Christian political party, for instance, is not meant to be a self-centred, closed meeting-place for Christians, nor a missionary undertaking to enforce a kind of theocracy. Its calling is to be a servant of public justice—for this is the meaning of all political life. This means, for example, that all must be treated as *equal* citizens of one state, regardless of their religious convictions. That seems to be a "neutral" activity, but it is not. For in this conception, the doing of justice for all is seen to derive directly from God's Law for the state. If Christianity is not to be found in the hearts of the people, the government should not try to enforce conformity. To do so would be to misuse the power that legitimately belongs to government. The battle for the heart of the nation can only be fought with spiritual weapons. But in that spiritual battle, a Christian political party can and should play an active role; pointing again and again to the fact that justice should be done in society, and upholding individual rights, as well as institutional ones, so that calling or vocation can be realized. Thus a Christian political party can play its part in the great struggle on this earth between the Kingdom of God and the realm of darkness: the antithesis.

We can understand why Kuyper would conclude his opening speech to the Free University of Amsterdam with a prayer, in which he asked God to destroy his university if it neglected the liberating wisdom of God in its concrete *scientific* endeavour. There can be no purpose for a Christian organization or institution, other than in the context of its *specific* calling. Purpose must be specific in terms of the specific norms which hold for the "sphere of life" of which the organization is a part. The norms referred to here are those which, by God's common grace, hold in a general way in the midst of a secular society.

A century later the Christian organizations of Holland are all caught to some extent in an internal crisis. Some have evolved into organizations of Christians-belonging-together, with no clear perception of their own calling in society. This is true to some extent for the Christian Democratic Appeal, cross-denominational successor of the two Protestant political parties and the Catholic party of the Netherlands. In other cases the organizations have become "open" institutions which can be joined by almost anyone. It has recently been said of Kuyper's life-work, therefore, that it was "a triumph grasped too early." His "cultural optimism" is said to have failed.

Many sincere Christians abandoned the so-called Christian institutions, either because of disappointment, or because they rejected Kuyper's view that Christians should organize separately in crucial sectors of life. What the future will bring is not clear. Will there be a revival of the existing Christian organizations and institutions? It seems improbable. Will smaller groups of Christians form new ones? Perhaps, but they will have to face the fact that, on the one hand, the "old" institutions still exist, and on the other hand, many Christians already have found their way to non-Christian institutions. An era seems to be passing away—and as one who belonged to that era, I have personal feelings of sadness. I only hope that those Christians who find their way to the non-Christian institutions in our present society will not become fully secularized, but will cherish a deep sense of their calling and that of the group, party, or organization which they have chosen to join. This last remark betrays how deeply I myself belong to this Dutch, neo-Calvinist tradition.

The theme of architectonic critique

This picture of the social thought of Dutch neo-Calvinism would not be complete without some account of a third motive: that of a critique of the foundations—the "architectonics"—of present-day society. Kuyper himself coined the word *architectonische kritiek* in a famous speech of 1891 on the condition of the working class in Holland.

Did his commitment to such a critique mean that Kuyper chose socialism? No, his critique had another basis. "Instead of honouring human society as a living organism, the spirit of the Revolution has broken up human society, and in its atomistic mischief has left nothing but the isolated, self-oriented individual." Because of that individualistic principle, Kuyper said, "Now in Europe a well-fed bourgeoisie controls an impoverished working population, which has contributed to its capital, and, when incapable of doing so, this bourgeoisie sinks into the swamp of the proletariat. . . . The rich exploit the poor....and the root of the evil is, that man is treated as though he is cut off from his eternal destiny and not honoured as created in the image of God....Our society has knelt down to Mammon, and by the spirit (incentive) of egoism it is now shaken in its foundations." Between the Kingdom of God and capitalism, according to Kuyper, "there is an absolute contradiction." "Where poor and rich stand over against each other, Jesus never chose the side of the rich; he joined the poor."

That aspect of Kuyper's thought does not mean that he approved a bloody class struggle. For such a struggle has its origin "in a hate of those who are rich and a neglect of those who are poor." Jesus did not hate the rich as such; he opposed their mistreatment of the poor and castigated their lust for money and possessions. But Kuyper adds that the position of the rich was enhanced by "a mistake in the foundation of society itself." Therefore, in his opinion the problem is not one of a lack of philanthropy, but a genuinely *social* problem.

What was Kuyper's alternative? "A Society which respects the foundations of social life, as laid down by God himself." In his view this meant two things:

a) that both State and Society had to be honoured as distinctive spheres of life, in which Society should not be seen as an aggregate of individuals, but as a living organic entity;

b) that the State, as the institution charged with dispensing justice, must intervene in Society to safeguard due respect for each sphere of life with its own place and responsibility. No sphere may exercise autonomy, but only responsibility, for "absolute ownership belongs only to God; all our property is only on loan for our use, all our administration is only stewardship" (Kuyper, *De Sociale Kwestie*, 1891).

This summary makes clear that the conception of society in Dutch neo-Calvinism is not only non-capitalistic, but also differs essentially from the reactionary, corporatist point of view. While the concept of society is organic, the idea of a state as the natural head of the organic body of society is decidedly avoided. State and society are spheres of life, each with its own distinctive calling. It is only the administration of public justice which may and should bring the state to intervene in society. For instance, if different social spheres collide, as in the exploitation of employees and their families by business firms, then government must rightly become involved.

Here the primary theme of calling in Dutch neo-Calvinism again comes clearly to the fore. Kuyper's "architectonic critique" is seen to complement the theme of calling. For such a critique is necessary to maintain families in their vocation, to recall production-households to their vocation as communities of stewardship, and to encourage the state in its calling to do justice.

This view of the state in neo-Calvinism, moreover, had concrete results. It caused Kuyper himself to design a general law for labour and working conditions (*Wetboek voor den arbeid*), compelling employers and employees to accept joint responsibilities for direction of the different branches of industry. In Kuyper's view, wages should be the outcome not of the free working of an individualistic labour market, but of negotiation between organizations of employers and employees. After Kuyper's death this came about in the Netherlands.

Relevance for our modern society

Our society is vastly different from that of Kuyper's day. The harsh features of nineteenth century capitalism have been softened by government legislation, and our economic system has changed in many other ways. New social problems have emerged. Yet these changes do not mean that the ideas and conditions that brought about the rise of neo-Calvinism are no longer valid in our time. Three illustrations may be useful here.

(1) Unemployment has grown enormously in recent years. Inflation, too, has become a structural problem. Usually, those problems are seen as temporary—caused by a lack of economic expansion on the one side, and a lack of monetary control on the other. They can therefore be treated technically, almost mechanically. We have tended to treat society like a mechanism which needs "fuel" and "help." One might ask, however, whether by dealing with our economic problems in this way, we are not exacerbating rather than solving the problem. Is unlimited economic expansion the answer to unemployment? Is this the fulfilment of our economic calling, and a proof of responsible stewardship in the use of the means entrusted to us? On the contrary, it may appear that these problems are born of a *neglect* of stewardship.

Here we have to acknowledge the reality of sin. To a large extent inflation is a symptom of an acquisitive society. Individuals and organizations are never content, but continually enlarge their desires beyond what is available. Social groups and institutions therefore shift their burdens onto each other. As this continues by means of ever-increasing wage demands, prices and taxes, the burden comes to rest on the shoulders of those who cannot fight back. The process of inflation can therefore be seen as another violation of sphere-sovereignty. Rather than rely upon mechanical devices, the government should go to the root of the problem in its fight for public justice, and discipline powerful pressure groups if they misuse their power in this way.

Unemployment

Something similar is true of growing structural unemployment. This problem is connected with the unrestrained progress of production—technology in modern society which has its origin in a worship of the idol of rising living standards. If technological progress generates an annual rise of about 4 per cent in average labour productivity, we need a demand expansion of about the same amount to maintain employment. As soon as the growth of real demand diminishes, let us say, to a 2 per cent or 0 per cent increase—due, for example, to international factors—unemployment must rise: in this case by 2 per cent or 4 per cent respectively. Those who work in more productive firms and industries drive out of employment those who can be spared: usually the weaker. Here again we observe a violation of public justice in economic life which we have already discussed in connection with Kuyper's notions of sphere-sovereignty and his "architectonic critique." We must ask, moreover, if our economic system does not lead us astray in this way from our common economic calling. The earth is not entrusted to us to provide an unlimited expansion of economic goods. If we make it so, we deplete the earth's resources and limit the economic possibilities of poorer nations and future generations.

Unless we are open to a new architectonic critique of the foundations of our present society, therefore, we shall not be able to cope with the problem of rising unemployment. The idol of ever-growing productivity has to fall *if* we want to maintain the possibility of working in a useful and serviceable way in times of decreasing demand. That is only possible in turn if society as a whole abandons its pursuit of the "holy grail" of an always-rising standard of living—what Galbraith has called "the article of faith of modern society." We find here another manifestation of the struggle between light and darkness in our times—of the antithesis as formulated by Abraham Kuyper.

(2) Where Luther and Calvin used the word "calling" in relation to *human labour*, they were emphasizing its *human* quality. Not every type of labour deserves that label. The issue here is *not* the degree of simplicity or complexity of work. Rather, it is whether or not the character of the work displays or conceals the image of God in man. The One who calls us must be honoured in the work we do.

This normative view of human labour implies that every type of work should allow choice and creativity. When God created the world, He expressed something of Himself in the work of his hands. The possibility of expressing something of one's own personality in what one does is a *basic human characteristic* of labour. Furthermore, the theme of calling implies that we should have the possibility of co-operating with other human beings, by our labour, and to serve them. Calvin once said that God did not create people with different characteristics in order to show that they are or should be unequal, but rather to make it necessary for them to help and serve each other, and to co-operate in their work. Finally, "calling" implies that work should take place in a context of Shalom—of rest and peace. The Sixth Commandment is the injunction to keep the Sabbath a day of rest, pre-eminent in the week. Only in that context of rest, or Shalom, has our human labour its legitimate place.

Progress

(3) Our society is dominated by the claims of "progress" to such an extent that the spheres of state and private enterprise are intermingled in many ways. Government itself promotes economic growth and technical progress, even sending men to the moon; private business intervenes in political processes by continual lobbying. Sometimes this intervention is welcomed by politicians. Socio-economic decision making has become a joint effort of government, employers and employees in many countries, in the context of a so-called "consensus-state." A new mass-elite division in society has arisen in this way.

Now there is, of course, nothing wrong with continual contact between government and organizations of employers and employees.

Our society is complex, and such contact can be very useful. But each participant has to be aware of his own specific calling. The norm of public justice is violated when government acquiesces in the demands of the most powerful pressure groups. Society is corrupted. Similarly, society is threatened if a government tries to rule according to the principle of "the least pain," exchanging the criterion of justice for that of utility. This may be popular in the short run, but in the longer term it creates many unforeseen problems which reveal the injustice of the act and lead to governmental rescue operations to patch up a sorry situation.

As I believe I have made clear in this paper, it is my conviction that modern society and the institutions of political democracy are deadly sick. They try to live autonomously, having lost any awareness of God's calling. But now they receive, "in their own flesh," the recompense of their sins. This is the message of neo-Calvinism. It is this that Groen van Prinsterer and Abraham Kuyper sought to explain, and that their present-day successors in Holland and North America hold out for their fellow-Christians of other traditions.

Comment

Irving Hexham

INTRODUCTION

Ernst Troeltsch (1865-1923) discusses Dutch neo-Calvinism in *The Social Teaching of the Christian Churches* (London, 1931, vol. 2, pp. 655, 660, 676, 879, 935 and 938–940), and his work is a valuable supplement to that of Max Weber alluded to in Dr. Goudzwaard's paper.

In the context of this conference it is significant that Stahl was a major influence on the thought of Peter Drucker. Stahl's major work, which greatly influenced van Prinsterer, is translated by T. D. Taylor as *The Present-Day Parties in the State and Church* (Blenheim Publishing House, State College, Pennsylvania, 1976). Van Prinsterer's work, *Unbelief and Revolution*, is at present being translated into English by Harry van Dyke and is now available from The Institute for Christian Studies, 229 College Street, Toronto. F. Vanden Berg's biography *Abraham Kuyper* (Grand Rapids, 1960) is informative but uncritical.

The Dutch Christian Labour Movement is discussed in a comparative context by M. P. Fogarty in *Christian Democracy in Western Europe* (London, 1957). For a discussion of the development of Dutch society in the late nineteenth and early twentieth century in the context of race relations, see Christopher Bagley, *The Dutch Plural Society* (Oxford, 1973).

The philosophy of the cosmonomic idea, sometimes called the Amsterdam philosophy, is the basis of a growing interest in Dutch neo-Calvinist thought among evangelical Christians in Australia, Britain, New Zealand and North America. The Institute for Christian Studies in Toronto is one institution founded to promote this branch of Calvinism. The best general introduction to the philosophy of Herman Dooyeweerd (1894-1977) is L. Kalsbeek, *Contours of a Christian Philosophy* (Toronto, 1976). Critical studies are to be found in A. L. Conradie, *The Neo-Calvinist Concept of Philosophy* (Pietermaritzburg, 1960) and Vincent Brummer, *Transcendental Criticism and Christian Philosophy* (Franeker, 1961). A recent attempt by a British evangelical to apply the insights of this tradition to social, economic and political issues is Alan Storkey's *A Christian Social Perspective* (Leicester, 1979).

The conflict between what Goudzwaard calls the "scientific" and "practical-institutional" wings of neo-Calvinism can be seen in the less than enthusiastic response of many Christian Reformed Churches in North America to Dooyeweerdian groups like the Institute for Christian Studies in Toronto. Dooyeweerd originally spoke of his work as "Calvinistic philosophy." Later he changed this to "Christian philosophy" and spoke modestly about his attempt to revive Christian philosophy. Unfortunately, many of his followers have been more lavish in their claims than either Dooyeweerd or Kuyper both of whom sought to interact with other Christian traditions.

The theme of vocation

An attempt to locate the work of Dutch neo-Calvinist thinkers in the reformation tradition is to be found in William Young, *Towards a Reformed Philosophy* (Franeker, 1952). The suggestion that Calvin saw an institutional dimension to the idea of vocation which gave institutions a calling in society is interesting. Dr. Goudzwaard should have provided more information about this, documenting the development of Calvin's thought in Dutch Calvinism.

It is important to realize the degree to which the Dutch neo-Calvinist tradition rejects mysticism and the sacred-profane distinction. It sees all secular life as holy and all religious life as secular. This is one reason why it is wrong to identify Dutch neo-Calvinism with the Puritans, evangelicals or fundamentalists. In embracing the whole of life as a religious realm the concept of the Kingdom of God is very important in this tradition.

The "principle of sphere-sovereignty" is the key to the development of Kuyper's thought and provides Dutch neo-Calvinism with a means of limiting claims to authority and power. It should be noted, however, that while both Kuyper and Dooyeweerd very clearly rejected racism, some South African thinkers have developed the idea of sphere-sovereignty as a basis for apartheid. Cf. Irving Hexham, *The Irony of Apartheid* (Toronto, 1981).

The implications of sphere-sovereignty are complicated and difficult to understand. One of the clearest expressions of the idea is to be found in Kuyper's *Lectures on Calvinism* (Princeton, 1898) pp. 108–120, where he combines an organic view of society with a mechanical view of the state. In creating his social model Kuyper acknowledges that conflict is an essential part of any human society and argues that the Christian can never hope to abolish social or political conflict but that such conflicts can be minimized when justice is made a goal. The emphasis on the calling of each sovereign sphere of society is an attempt to relativize the authority of all human institutions before the law of God. In theory this sounds great. The problem comes, however, when one wishes to identify the callings of different social spheres and set their appropriate boundaries. What, in fact, does God's calling mean in practical terms? How can a Christian businessman or labour leader implement this idea in the everyday work situation?

The principle of sphere-sovereignty is said to have a "normative colour and flavour." What does this mean? How do we derive our norms? Are they arrived at by intuition? By reading the Bible? Or by historical analysis? The problems here are similar to those faced by Karl Mannheim in developing his social philosophy when he faced the issue of relativism in his work *Essays on the Sociology of Knowledge* (London, 1952).

Soteriology

The doctrine of the sovereignty of God is basic for this development of Christian social thought. In understanding the development of this doctrine by Kuyper it is worth comparing his view of God's sovereignty with that of the contemporary British Calvinist Charles Spurgeon. For Spurgeon the sovereignty of God was related to soteriology, or individual salvation. Kuyper linked it to the doctrine of creation. Thus for Spurgeon the phrase "Christ is Lord of all" signified Christ's Lordship in terms of man's salvation. For Kuyper the same phrase was a cultural mandate which impelled Christians to take an active role in the state and society. Cf. J. Sills, *An Examination of the Social and Cultural Dimensions of the View of Life Preached by C. H. Spurgeon*, unpublished M.A. Thesis, Bristol University, 1973.

Kuyper believed that the state must intervene in society to protect the weak and maintain justice. *Christianity and the Class Struggle* (Grand Rapids, 1950) is a translation of one of his important Dutch works. Kuyper's political views are discussed by D. Jellema in "Abraham Kuyper's Attack on Liberalism" in the *Review of Politics*, vol. 19, 1957. Socialism, liberalism and Methodism were dirty words for writers in this tradition, who used them to create identifiable external enemies and thus reinforced the internal unity of the neo-Calvinist community by creating clear intellectual boundaries.

The question of central planning is a difficult one. Kuyper seems far more willing to entertain the idea than many North Americans. This needs further discussion. It is easy to say that the government's mandate is to bring "justice in public life." But what is justice? Marxists would make similar claims. The notion of justice and its practical implementation needs clearer definition and explanation. Similar comments could be made about stewardship. Goudzwaard appears to be an environmentalist. But the North American neo-Calvinist leader R. J. Rushdooney would oppose many environmental stands supported by Goudzwaard on the basis of a different understanding of the implications of stewardship.

What is the definition of "autonomous liberty"? How does this differ from "normatively-bound liberty"? Who decides which is which and how do they make this decision? The problem of authority and democracy from a perspective close to Dutch neo-Calvinism is discussed in Peter Drucker's book *The End of Economic Man* (New York, 1939). Drucker raises all the questions addressed by Goudzwaard and Dutch neo-Calvinism in what is for me a far more practical way. The weakness of Dutch neo-Calvinism is its love of theory and lack of practical application in the modern world. Drucker made his analysis, influenced by Stahl, and then in the *Concept of the Corporation* (New York, 1946) attempted to provide a solution applicable to modern society. In many ways Drucker's entire work can be seen as an intellectual debate about authority and democracy.

Popular sovereignty

Like authority, the concept of revolution needs more careful definition. For neo-Calvinists "revolution" is a theoretical term with metaphysical implications that must be related to the continual warfare between God and Satan. But while neo-Calvinists may recognize past revolutions as godly or evil I'm not so sure they can analyze the revolutionary situations of today with any clarity. The problem with talk about "respect for every God-given authority" is again the problem of definition and recognition. Were the American revolutionaries acting in a revolutionary way when they revolted against British rule or was their war of independence justified? On the basis of what is said here it would seem that they were fundamentally wrong in their actions. But many American Calvinists would dispute this conclusion. If democracy is not to be based on popular sovereignty, what is it to be based on? Isn't popular sovereignty rooted in the Calvinist tradition? The neo-Calvinist solution of God's sovereignty sounds good but what does this mean in practice? How does a neo-Calvinist, or Dutch election differ from a revolutionary, or French election? The choice of elders in Reformed Churches may have been something like a democratic process but who participated in their election? Women and some men, those under a certain age for example, were excluded.

Co-determination is a major theme of neo-Calvinist social thinkers. Its application in the North American context can be seen in the work of the Christian Labour Association of Canada. See: H. D. Ayers, *A Study of the Christian Labour Association of Canada,* unpublished

lished M.C.S. thesis, Regent College, Vancouver, 1979. We are told that government and citizens, directors of companies and their workers, have shared responsibilities. But who decides how these shares are to be allocated? Here again the theory sounds good but how does it work in practice? Further, can these deductions really be made in a consistent way from the theological doctrine of the sovereignty of God, Calvinist theology, or the Bible? Goudzwaard makes a very good point when he says that owners of the enterprises are "not the owners of living persons" only "capital goods." But what does ownership mean? Where do the owners get their goods if not from the labour of others? Here along with Keynes and the whole of modern economics Goudzwaard's position seems weakened by lack of a theory of value.

What does it mean to be "under the law of the Sovereign God"? Are the Ten Commandments being referred to? Or the Law of the Old Testament? Or the Law of Love? Or what? Again definition is needed and practical examples are lacking.

The theme of antithesis

The issue of a common society which is pluralistic is one with which few Christian groups have as yet come to terms. In attempting to implement "Christian" policies, Christians face the major problem of non-Christians who do not share their values. This need not be an issue if one believes in Natural Law but for neo-Calvinists who reject this, the antithesis is a major problem.

Anti-revolutionaries claim to appreciate some of the fruits of the French revolution while rejecting its spirit. In this way they hope to avoid becoming reactionaries. However, I fail to see how one can clearly distinguish between the good "fruits" and the bad "spirit" of the French Revolution. Surely the spirit of the Enlightenment gave birth to the fruits of the revolution. Again the problem is one of definition and the ability to make consistent distinctions. If a state is revolutionary when it fails to use its power "in a justiful, non-discriminating way" does this mean that the United States government was revolutionary prior to the civil rights legislation of the 1960s and is non-revolutionary today? A "governmental system misuses its power by exploiting a nation" and thus becomes "a revolutionary government." Does this mean that the government of South Africa is revolutionary because it exploits the Zulu and Tswana nations?

Goudzwaard says that there is a "right to resist" when "responsible persons can lead the nation." This would seem to imply that if Chief Gatcha Buthelezi were to lead a resistance of the Zulu nation against the South African government in terms of neo-Calvinist thought he would be justified. It might also be argued that the actions of Nelson Mandela in organizing South African Blacks to resist the white government was also non-revolutionary. Yet in South Africa, Afrikaners who accept the theories of Dutch neo-Calvinism would be among the leading critics of Buthelezi and Mandela both of whom are often accused of being communists. Is neo-Calvinist theory really useful if it is open to such diverse interpretations? Goudzwaard legitimizes resistance by saying "God's calling must have primacy over the (abuse) of the human will. Authority has to be honoured . . . but in the context of its calling." How do we agree on what is and what is not a true calling? I find no clear guidance as to when revolution is and when it is not legitimate.

I'm not sure what the discussion about the Kingdom of Light and the Kingdom of Darkness tells us except that we live in a very complicated world. Goudzwaard's recognition that Christians are also "fallen" is reassuring but in practice I suspect most neo-Calvinists tend to trust neo-Calvinist politicians rather than really evaluating their arguments. This may not be the case in the Netherlands but it certainly works that way in South Africa. A similar thing can be seen in the politics of the new Christian Right in America. Although the "concept of common grace" may "invite Christians and non-Christians to cooperate," in practice van Prinsterer's dictum, "In isolation is our strength" seems to prevail. The neo-Calvinist tradition encourages isolationism.

Dutch neo-Calvinism was politicized by the "public school issue." The same is true of neo-Calvinists in South Africa where the issue of Christian-National education played an important role in the creation of Afrikaaner Nationalist ideology. At present this issue is the basis for a revival of interest in politics among evangelicals in North America. What isn't usually realized is that the theories of Dutch neo-Calvinism have been popularized by writers like Francis Schaeffer to provide an intellectual justification for the actions of the new Christian Right. What ultimate impact these writers will have I don't know but it is significant that Schaeffer's book *A Christian Manifesto* (Crossway Books, 1981) sold over 190,000 copies in the six months between Christmas 1981 and July 1982.

Goudzwaard says that "If Christianity is not shared in the heart of the people, the government should not try to enforce it." Most neo-Calvinists claim to agree with this sentiment, although some like R. J. Rushdoony challenge it. However, it leaves unanswered the crucial question of what enforcement means. Are governments enforcing Christianity when they ban pornography? What about abortion? Many Dutch neo-Calvinists, such as Professor H. R. Rookmaaker, have taken a very liberal stance on these issues. But in North America, distinction is made between enforcing Christianity and upholding Christian values. This issue is far more difficult than the paper implies.

Dutch neo-Calvinist institutions arose as a result of a long social, theological and political struggle. In the first half of the twentieth century they flourished. But now they are in definite decline. Many observers argue that their decline has left the Netherlands a spiritual wasteland where religion is discredited. I would like to hear Dr. Goudzwaard's thoughts on the reasons for the decline of Dutch neo-Calvinism and its impact on Dutch religious life.

The theme of architectonic critique

Dutch neo-Calvinism is presented as making "a critique of the foundations . . . of present-day society." If this is true then we can all learn a great deal from it. Unfortunately, I do not see this claim working in practice. In the Netherlands neo-Calvinists seem to follow secular thinkers in their analysis of society. Similarly, in South Africa it was liberal and radical critics who exposed apartheid, not neo-Calvinists who have tended to accept the *status quo*. How then can such impressive claims be made?

Neo-Calvinism rejects capitalism and socialism. It sometimes sounds dangerously like fascism. Of course, Dr. Goudzwaard is not a fascist and many neo-Calvinists fought bravely in the Dutch resistance during World War II; but it needs to be remembered that others, including members of Kuyper's own family, joined the Dutch Nazi party.

Relevance for modern society

To describe inflation as "a symptom of an acquisitive society" seems to contradict history. Inflation was around a long time before industrial society, and the statement says nothing practical about its cure. It seems to me to be rather like saying the Vietnam War was caused by sin. How inflation violates sphere-sovereignty and the ways governments can prevent this I fail to understand. Goudzwaard seems to be calling for tough government action. Kuyper used the armed forces to break a railway strike in 1903. Is this the neo-Calvinist solution to social unrest?

Although he doesn't quite say so, Goudzwaard seems to see technology as essentially evil. If this is so I suggest his neo-Calvinism has strong romantic overtones. Why is a rising standard of living idolatrous? It's easy for academics to condemn labour leaders and businessmen but I'm unconvinced that declining living standards are the answer. In his comments on the depletion of natural resources Goudzwaard echoes the Club of Rome. Here I suggest we are offered a Christian attempt to follow a popular trend rather than an "architectonic critique." Popular fear of industry and environmental concerns have surfaced almost every fifty years since the onset of the industrial revolution. I believe the Club of Rome was wrong in its findings, and it could well be that its scare tactics have done more harm than good.

In attempting to re-introduce labour-intensive work, Goudzwaard wants to reaffirm the value of labour and convince us that production lines and modern methods of manufacturing are inhumane. Unlike Goudzwaard, I spent a significant part of my life in industry. His views do not reflect my own experience of industrial life but rather a popular middle-class image put forward to people who have paid short visits to the workplace. Some workers, fearing the loss of their jobs, may be against technology. But, the vast majority simply want to be sure they have a job and when that is clear, to make it as easy as possible. It seems to me, therefore, that it is a romantic gloss to talk about the meaningfulness of work. There are many jobs which can never become creative or allow the worker to feel he is making a significant contribution to mankind. Yet they need to be done. In such a situation, good pay and as much mechanization as possible seem the only answer.

OBJECTIONS TO DUTCH NEO-CALVINISM

The basic objection I have to this tradition is that its social theory rests on a series of historical contradictions. The theory is anti-revolutionary, yet everywhere it gains popularity it does so on the basis of an appeal to a religious community which has revolutionary roots. The Reformation, the Dutch revolt against Spain, the English civil war, the American Revolution, the Great Trek in South Africa and the rise of modern Afrikaaner Nationalism are all revolutionary movements. Yet neo-Calvinists accept and indeed rejoice in these revolutions. At the same time all progressive measures which can be traced to the French Revolution, the Enlightenment, liberalism or humanism are rejected as un-Christian. All I can conclude is that neo-Calvinism legitimates one revolutionary tradition by attacking another.

Although neo-Calvinists claim to make an architectonic critique of the foundations of society all I see them producing are Christianized versions of secular ideas. Two examples illustrate this. During the late 1960s and early 1970s the Institute for Christian Studies in Toronto promoted a magazine, *Vanguard,* as a forum for neo-Calvinist thought. Anyone who examines its articles during this period will see a lack of criticism and tendency to drift along with the latest cultural fad. Similarly, neo-Calvinist criticisms of apartheid in South Africa have lagged behind liberal and radical criticism by about twenty years without making any improvement on them.

Finally, this is a system which is exceptionally complicated and tends to lose itself in jargon. To my mind neo-Calvinism needs a dose of Anglo-Saxon linguistic philosophy to clarify its rather confused concepts.

VALUABLE ELEMENTS IN THE NEO-CALVINIST TRADITION

From all I have said it might appear that I am strongly anti-Calvinist. In fact I am not. I personally owe a great deal to the Dutch neo-Calvinist tradition and find the example of Bob Goudzwaard as a Christian thinker and political activist inspiring. The fact that I disagree with many of his premises and conclusions does not mean I do not respect him or the tradition he represents.

Dutch neo-Calvinism represents for me a Christian myth. Abraham Kuyper inspired his followers with a powerful vision of justice in society. His basis was the Calvinism of the Dutch people. For many Kuyper did bring justice and hope. But I'm not sure that his vision can be analyzed in the way Goudzwaard and most neo-Calvinists would like. As soon as one examines a myth it loses its mythic quality and dies. Kuyper's work held together as long as it provided a vision with the minimum of critical analysis, which is not to say that it wasn't intellectually virile and productive.

When transferred to other cultures the vision has taken on different forms. In South Africa justice for Afrikaaners in 1902 meant freedom from the devastating effects of British Imperialism and led to the development of the theory of apartheid. That this later legitimated the oppression of Blacks is the irony of a complicated situation. In North America the vision is resurrected by religious leaders of the new fundamentalism, such as Francis Schaeffer and Tim LaHaye. Here the vision has a new form but for many it offers hope in a confused and threatening world.

However we react to this tradition, I think we must all agree that it is impressive and powerful in its ability to inspire Christians. Many here may not like its right-wing associations but we must remember that Goudzwaard represents what may be seen as the left wing of this tradition, which in itself shows something of the tradition's vitality.

Reply

Bob Goudzwaard

The comment of Dr. Hexham on my paper is not only very valuable and informative (I want to thank him especially for many additional bibliographical notes), but also challenging and intriguing.

Hexham states that he owes personally a great deal to the Dutch neo-Calvinist tradition. But at the same time, he continues, he disagrees with many of my premises and conclusions. Obviously therefore, Hexham not only objects to Dutch neo-Calvinism itself, but also, and perhaps even more, to my way of interpreting it. For example, he declares, "For many, Abraham Kuyper did bring justice and hope. But I'm not sure that his vision can be analysed in the way Goudzwaard and most neo-Calvinists would like." Of course my discussant does not suggest here that he understands Dutch neo-Calvinism more profoundly than I. What he wants to make clear is that Dutch neo-Calvinism is a vision of society which hides its essence and flavour as soon as its content is analysed. This explains the astonishing number of cases in which he asks for more and sharper definitions, descriptions and identifications. He even suggests that neo-Calvinism "needs a dose of Anglo-Saxon linguistic philosophy to clarify its rather confused concepts." That seems to me to express his own conviction, that the way to the heart of Dutch neo-Calvinism is not, and cannot be, that of intellectual understanding.

I certainly agree with some of his criticism. Hexham is quite correct for instance in his remark about "love of theory"; sometimes it has even a scholastic flavour. What Kuyper wrote especially is open to a whole range of diverse interpretations. But I refuse to follow Hexham in saying that Dutch neo-Calvinism cannot be analysed at all from *within*. Hexham seems to suggest that the tradition can only escape being called "a myth," if it is prepared to define not only its *own* concepts (as I did, for instance speaking about sphere-sovereignty), but also to define and identify its "own" idea of generally held concepts such as justice, stewardship, liberty. Here I disagree. Of course I can try to make clear that a word like "justice" is used and interpreted quite differently in our tradition. In Marxian usage, for instance "justice" is a class-oriented concept; and in neo-Calvinism it refers to the basic equality of all human creatures, and to what each person needs for his or her calling. But that is not a definition. For, in my opinion, justice is a God-given norm which precedes all human activity including the activity of the human intellect. In every case in which reference is made to the ultimate norms of life, the movement has to be understood from within.

Context

Let me try to illustrate this. Where I referred to the idea of the meaningfulness of human labour, Hexham's comment is that such an expression reveals "a romantic gloss." But in Dutch neo-Calvinism the totality of life and work is nothing else than a totality in the *context* of normative, God-given *meaning,* which we either accept, reject, or ignore. Even outside this tradition Max Weber referred to the *Eigenwert*, the 'own-value' and dignity of human labour, which has to be recognized whenever production process takes place. Of course, many unpleasant jobs "need to be done"—but the question is, *how* they are done with or without creativity, co-responsibility and mutual cooperation.

This brings me to a second objection. I am sure that my discussant has a deeper insight into the *American* variety of neo-Calvinism than I. Perhaps this is also true of the South African variety, which he studied in his dissertation on the ideological backgrounds of apartheid. But my contribution concerned the original, *Dutch* neo-Calvinism. My impression is that my discussant came to the study of *Dutch* neo-Calvinism after that of the American and South African varieties. Dr. Hexham seems to follow the principle that you can judge a tree according to its worldwide fruits. How otherwise can I explain his strange remark about members of the Kuyper family joining the Nazi party? Or his statement: "Neo-Calvinism rejects capitalism and socialism. It sounds dangerously like fascism?" These comments suggest that he judges Holland with white South Africa in mind. *South-African* Calvinists indeed often spoke favourably of nazism, especially during the Second World War. But Hexham must know as well as I that the strongest protest against nazism and fascism in the Netherlands during World War II came from the Dutch neo-Calvinists. And not by accident, but precisely because of their utterly anti-fascist world-view.

How then are the South African and American versions of neo-Calvinism related to the original, Dutch tradition? As I tried to explain, Groen van Prinsterer and Kuyper used the concept of "sphere-sovereignty" as a kind of short-hand for their belief that in every situation or sphere of life, man lives and acts *coram Deo* (before the face of the living God). Their whole outlook on reality was coloured by their awareness that all—whether in authority or not—who are involved in any social relation or institution are subject to a same commandment of the One Sovereign Lord. That is to promote public justice within the State, to promote *oikonomia* (stewardship) in the firm (or production-household) and to form a community of love and truth in the family. But in the American and South African interpretations of this principle the original insight was gradually lost, and the concept was re-formulated to serve other interests. In South Africa, for instance, the principle was not only misinterpreted and misused to attach to different *races* the label of a "separate" sphere of life, but was combined with elements of German idealistic and romantic thought which referred to an original superiority of the white race and of the necessity for every "people" to survive as one Blood on one Soil. But this was and is a total subversion of all the principle stands for. The will to survive at all costs, preserving a white or Afrikaaner identity, takes the place of the original confession, that within a State everyone must be treated according to the same norm of justice.

A different deformation took place in North America. Here it occurred by way of a synthesis with individualism and conservatism. This was made possible by using the expression "sphere-sovereignty" in relation to the "sovereignty" of *individuals,* who have *authority* in one or other sphere of life. For instance, the legitimacy of almost all types of government intervention in the marketplace could be denied. Even co-responsibility of the workers in business enterprise has sometimes been interpreted as a violation of the principle of sphere-sovereignty, as an attempt to lessen the "sovereieignty in power" of individual managers or owners of the firm.

Now Hexham could possibly object here that the original concept was so vague and ambiguous that it opened the way for later neo-Calvinists to arrive at these interpretations. I am of a different opinion. No doubt Kuyper lacked clearness in his formulations; especially in his attempted distinction between the "mechanic" and the "organic" side of society which was open to abuse. But what explicitly motivated him and van Prinsterer was wilfully set aside in later times, even in the Netherlands to some extent.

Conclusion

Let me conclude with a few answers to some of Dr. Hexham's many questions.

(1) What God's calling can mean in practical terms was explained in the twenties in Gerbrandy's book *De Strijd om Nieuwe Maatschappijvormen* (The struggle for new forms of society). Gerbrandy was a true Calvinist of Kuyper's persuasion, and was the courageous prime minister of Holland during the Second World War. I discussed his contribution to some extent in my *Aid to the Overdeveloped West* (Toronto 1975).

(2) Real norms are not derived, but revealed in God's Word and in Creation. Groen van Prinsterer described them as "those truths

which are written by the Holy Spirit in the heart of the most simple Christian.'' See also for this question Herman Dooyeweerd, *A New Critique of Theoretical Thought*.

(3) Liberty in the biblical sense is not contrasted with *any* type of human control, but only with enslavement.

(4) A revolution is only acceptable for a Calvinist under extreme conditions: when a government systematically and consciously abuses its power to oppress its own people; and when, at the same time, responsible political leaders (Calvin spoke about ''magistrates'') can take command without creating chaos. The American struggle for independence was of course justified according to this view.

(5) Popular *sovereignty* is certainly not rooted in the Calvinist tradition. Groen's main work (*Unbelief and Revolution*) can be seen as one continued fight against the idea of popular sovereignty.

(6) In my opinion, the government of South Africa is indeed on its way to becoming a revolutionary government.

(7) The interpretation of Groen's statement is incorrect. He did not mean by isolation a kind of separatism, but the return to one's *zelfstandigheid van overtuiging,* (independence of conviction). See Groen van Prinsterer, *Nederlandsche Gedachten* (July 9, 1870).

(8) Enforcing Christianity is different from upholding Christian values and giving them expression in legal principles.

(9) It is not my perception that religion is yet discredited in Holland. Concerning the decline of Dutch neo-Calvinistic institutions, I tried to explain in my paper that they lost much of their original spirituality: mainly because they could not resist the temptation to become self-centred and concerned with their self-preservation.

(10) I am sorry I did not convince Hexham of the originality of Kuyper's architectonical critique, nor of its relevance for modern society. Perhaps we differ too much in our view of the problems of society today to come to a common mind. Let me only say that *of course* the desire for a continually rising standard of living can become idolatrous if it becomes the final meaning of life; and *of course* technology is not essentially evil. It becomes an evil only if the hope of a better future in terms of peace and happiness is centred on technology.

Chapter 8

Minority Themes

John H. Yoder

Most of the other papers presented at this conference are postulated upon the following assumptions:

(a) that we can see the social system as a whole well enough to talk about it realistically;

(b) that if we were to know what system were best we might be in a position to do something about bringing it into being;

(c) that what we can do we should, even at the cost of some pain and compromise;

(d) that the criteria for such a judgement are objective enough to be defined with some degree of independence from a particular political system;

(e) and are general enough to be applicable to several if not all systems;

(f) that these criteria are substantially correlated with one's theological beliefs, so as to be worthy of discussion and debate on grounds other than whim, provincial bias or personal interest.

The thin strand of Christian cultural tradition of which I speak rejects these assumptions. It should not, therefore, be thought of as entering into the same debate, but rather as beginning with a different set of commitments and therefore reaching a different set of answers.

It is rather that the people for whom I speak are involved in a different debate.

The position I describe is, and seeks to remain, quite close to that of the early Christians, or of the Jews of that same time, for whom—as for powerless minorities in most times and places—it is not possible to see the social structure whole. This is not merely because they are few and poor. The Persian Emperor, and Caesar, had much more power than they, but could not see the whole as a system either. The very notion that there is such a thing as a "system," whose characteristics one could describe (as it were) from the outside in order then to compare it with another system, was foreign to the available cosmologies of the time. Thinking about social righteousness, therefore, was not done from the perspective of the philosophically generalizing reflexes which come naturally to us. ("What if this were to be made a law?" or "What if everybody did it?")

I shall later describe in other ways how this minority view throws light on a different approach. My first point is that it calls into question axiom (a): our claim to see the system whole.

There has often been a tendency among minorities, whether racial, religious, or other, to make of their necessity a virtue. Beyond saying that their truth-system did not depend on their being able to help to run the world, they would go further and say that it called them to renounce "involvement," or "effectiveness," or "power," or wealth. This would then be a systematic negation of axiom (c), often supported by some dualistic way of defining identity and priorities, so that letting the world go to the dogs in its own way is a proper thing to do, not simply an unavoidable weakness.

Utopianism

Yet another of the axioms might be repudiated, namely (b). It might be that we see the world whole, (a), but that when we see it we learn that the way it is constructed and governed is such that there is nothing that we *can* do about it. It would then follow that the very exercise of thinking about better systems is utopian, in the bad sense of wasting effort in dreaming about the impossible (although it might also be utopian in the good sense of sharpening our minds and imaginations, and of cultivating our critical awareness).

I identify these elements of minority culture, which sustain, for the people I am to talk about, a solid scepticism about the appropriateness of hoping to make a better world, not as a basis for debate but rather as part of my assignment to situate the perspective from which the rest of my reporting can be done. I needed to label and set aside one misperception which is very difficult to avoid, namely that these traditions maintain always and only that "the virtuous person will have nothing to do with economic politics." That view I have identified as only one theme of the minority tradition.

My paper differs in another way. The tradition or heritage which I here seek to interpret does not have the shape of most others institutionally or culturally, and therefore requires a synthesis in my reporting which goes beyond ordinary historical description. Some schools of thought are represented by one master-thinker or one close-knit group; it suffices to read these authorities. Others are defined by one dominant idea or a close-knit set of interlocking assumptions. It then suffices to unpack the coherence of that set of statements, without much need to know how they were discovered or by whom. What I am to describe is more like the latter than the former, but the coherent set of perspectives can only be understood as distilled out of a long history, during which their advocates were seldom at leisure to spell them out abstractly. Those advocates were sometimes tolerated, sometimes liquidated, and sometimes able to survive in the chinks between the two, so that the actual shape their alternative perspectives took was quite different from age to age. Even the words and guiding concepts they used were often not of their own choosing, and therefore do not always cohere. This means that the challenge to my synthesis is quite different from that which faces anyone trying to write a faithful history of a single movement. I am trying to write a faithful history of a manifold movement across many centuries, discerned as a unity only by its normative source in the New Testament and by a few main lines of its critique.

Origins

Poverty has always been a mark of Christian faithfulness for some segments of the Christian community. The poor (*anawim*) were already seen in pre-Christian Jewish thought as special objects of God's protective concern. Jesus's propertylessness was not imposed on his disciples as a general law, but was held before them as a Gospel offer, which some could refuse only by rejecting him.

I do not need to review the record concerning the themes of generosity, sharing, and poverty in early Christianity. That record, in its simplicity and its variety, is the starting point for the people I am to talk about.

The oldest "alternative" theme in economics is that of distribution on the basis of need in connection with the Eucharist. The ordinary term for the beneficiaries was "widows," but certainly this caring included other people who lacked a family breadwinner. Very soon the term used was simply "the poor." Again it meant not everyone with limited resources but only those who were dependent upon such aid for survival. Meeting that category of needs, "first of all for those of the household of faith" (Galatians 6:10), was a standard obligation taught by all early Christian communities, and practised with some degree of integrity by all, so far as we can tell.

Recent New Testament scholarship has tried to guess from what social class the early Christians mostly came, and how their economic practice was determined. Though interesting, that debate is a diversion from the simpler statement that the early Christians gave status to, and cared for, the poor.

The phrase, "especially for those of the household of faith" demonstrates backhandedly that the notion of a duty to share was not strictly limited to the believing community, even though it began there. That everyone took responsibility for his own extended family's needs was taken for granted. The generalization of the responsibility to the "household" of faith (as the new extended family of the believer) was the first step. But this text indicates that early Christian benevolence was wider in its scope than the community of believers.

After accommodation

The next phase has been labelled "asceticism" by historians. This is a term which has taken on another meaning in our own time. We must therefore free ourselves from preconceptions in examining the thought of primitive Christianity.

Beginning as early as the middle of the second century, Christians found life in some parts of the Roman world quite comfortable. While the threat of persecution was always in the background, there were times when it stayed there, leaving Christians to prosper in their trades and in their family lives. Before long, there were opportunities for free time for intellectual pursuits, which we find being exercised by a few from the middle of the second century, and by several major figures within another generation. What happens decisively in the first quarter of the fourth century—the acceptance of Christianity as a religion first tolerated, then favoured by authority—was beginning sporadically and on a small scale a good century before.

This raises a new question. According to Jesus and the apostles, the life of the believer was subject to a discipline imposed by the unbelieving world. If that discipline is no longer there, should it be replaced from within? When Jesus said that his disciples would have to forsake other things in order to follow him, he had meant not only that they would be coerced into such a choice by the pressures of the world, but also that to put the kingdom first would be a normal part of sober decisiveness. If the sacrifices and losses which keep our priorities clear are no longer imposed on us by the automatic hostility of the unbelieving world, should we replace that discipline with one of our own? A businessman chooses which investments are most worthy of his capital and his imagination. A teacher chooses which kinds of knowledge and which skills need to be taught first. Thus the learning of Christian priorities, once it is no longer under pressure of direct persecution, should properly be provided with some "discipline" or "curriculum" for its own inner health.

Such a setting of priorities, not under pressure of scarcity or catastrophe, but flowing from an inner responsibility for the coherence and the directedness of the life of faith, is what is called "ascetic."

Too often the ascetic life is portrayed by those who see it from outside as if it were the product of an alien world-view which considers the body or material existence to be evil. Such ideas did circulate around the eastern Roman world at the time of the first ascetic Christian communities, and at the slightly earlier time when individuals first began to choose their own eremitic discipline of geographical isolation. Yet it would be a misunderstanding to see that kind of Gnostic or neo-Platonic explanation at the root of it. The central pastoral concern of the "ascetics" was not that material possessions are evil, but rather that they are good, proper in their place, but wrong to put at the center of one's life. A Christian community therefore needs persons and disciplines to enact the primacy of other values in regular and visible ways, not for personal salvation so much as for the sake of the whole community.

Our legalistic and defensive response to the witness of monastic poverty is to question whether its disciples really believe it possible to have a healthy culture without wealth. We then observe that the poverty of the monk is less than absolutely sweeping as a social model in two ways

(a) The fact that the celibate life is not self-sustaining, but must continue to be dependent upon families for its recruitment, implies that the acquisitive lifestyle is thereby necessary for families and hence cannot be condemned as morally wrong for all. The celibate seems to concede that parents with children cannot live under the same discipline. Therefore, poverty is a special calling for those excused from the normal duties of maintaining society.

(b) The monastery itself will with time accumulate lands and other possessions. While the *individual* has little to call his own, he shares in a level of security (and perhaps within two generations a level of comfort) greater than that of many whose participation in the lay economy is more competitive.

I have labelled as "legalistic and defensive" the procedure which tests a moral style by asking, "are all who do otherwise wrong?" Or, "can you impose that pattern on everybody?" To look at the Benedictine model with that legalistic frame of reference is to misunderstand it. The monk does not uphold an absolute moral obligation in order to be committed to condemning others who live otherwise. What he does is to respond to the Gospel in a way that takes the Gospel as *good* news, and offers it to others in the same understanding. The way of life of the monastic minority does not condemn others; but neither does it affirm in a cheaply complementary way that other ways of living are equally good, or that its distinctive commitments are only matters of taste or arbitrary preference.

The Middle Ages

Taking one great leap toward our times, we find in the eleventh and twelfth centuries a wave of renewal efforts directed towards those known to historians as "Christ's poor."

In what we call today Northern Italy and Southern France, and in the Low Countries, cities were beginning to grow out of the chaos of earlier centuries, with the resulting visible accumulation of wealth on the part of some, and a matching increasing visibility of the urban poor. Sometimes the clergy were on the side of wealth, since a parish or a diocese could own property. Since clerics could not leave goods to their children, preferment to a church office was one way for an individual to become wealthy. We observe a rising concern with the sin of "simony" (purchasing church office by means of bribes).

But the prohibition of simony is just the tip of an iceberg. As an expression of the economic discipline of the Church, it belongs with the prohibition of usury, still on the books but increasingly difficult to enforce; and with a rising number of rules about luxurious expenditure, by which the Church attempted to regulate the new affluence. The unabashed pursuit of wealth, and its proud display, were clearly seen to be vices, even though the only tools of pastoral discipline which can be found were on the surface, and failed to come to grips at its roots with this new level of offence.

The denunciation of simony is the tip of an iceberg in another sense. It becomes the rallying cry for the organization of popular protest movements, which become so strong as to have serious political weight: not by electing people to office (this is not yet the age of democracy) but by determining which of the ruling minorities in a town will be most able to govern. For a generation in the middle of the eleventh century there was a major "political party" in Milan called the *pataria* or the *patarini,* literally the rag-pickers, the people from the dump. When they called for the prosecution of bishops blatantly guilty of simony, their point was not that they were out to get bishops. They were denouncing the Church's failure to meet the challenge of this new level of economic development with an appropriate measure of pastoral discipline.

The struggle for a more valid response did not limit itself to this kind of negation. We observe the appearance of a new Christian community calling itself (or called by its neighbours) "Christ's paupers." Taking literally the words of Jesus about leaving possessions to follow him, its disciples took up a life of mendicant itineration, wandering from town to town in sizeable groups. Some settled soon into a life of residential communities, with or without formal monastic discipline.

Female leaders

Sometimes these groups were led by women. Sometimes they were accused of creating scandal by permitting men and women to travel across the countryside in mixed groups. In the Netherlands the female element seems to have been dominant. The Beguines, as they were called, seem to have more initiative, or at least to have remained more memorable in the public mind, than the masculine equivalent, the Beghards. These again were movements of economic solidarity with, and service to, the most needy.

Historical records are scanty for this period. They tell us of Arnold of Brescia, Henri of Lausanne, Peter of Bruges, without our being able to measure their impact quantitatively.

Henri is supposed to have said, "the Church only exists where the faithful confess their sins and live according to the Gospel." The phrase, "live according to the Gospel" is not a vague mood-statement but rather a technical label for mendicant itineration: it identifies the specific form of propertylessness which results from having left things behind to become a preacher of the Gospel. From this affirmation Henri and Peter derived an attack on a definition of the church in terms of ritual and architecture, and claimed that clerics excluded themselves from the church of Christ by their commitment to such stabilized ritual. What we can see in the slim record of these efforts is that this new movement of economic protest and counter-demonstration was one of the main currents of spiritual initiative from the early eleventh until the late twelfth century. It laid the foundation for a movement of more structured community-building soon to be represented by Francis and Waldo.

As a culmination of two centuries of such developments, we properly may group together a movement which was eventually rejected and one which was accepted by the Roman hierarchy. Around 1180 Peter Waldo began what Francis of Assisi began around 1200: gathering and sending people to preach the story of Jesus in the language of the common people; and (in order to do this) forsaking wealth and living by the generosity of their listeners. Both Peter and Francis went to Rome to obtain the authorization of the pope. Each seems to have received such authorization. However, when Peter returned to Lyons the local church authorities were threatened by his message and tried to stop him and his followers, whereas Francis found strong support in the bishop of Assisi. Whether that explains the ultimate difference between the fates of the two movements, the two initiatives did issue in appropriately different movements beginning from the same message. The Franciscan order, with the full complement of a male community, a female community, and a third order for penitent lay people, became the most respected form of renewal of the next two generations, and has left its traces through

Catholic religious history down to the present. The Waldensian movement, refusing to be silenced, became the oldest and strongest clandestine community, first and strongest forerunner of the Protestant Reformation, spreading as far as Moravia to the East and Flanders to the North. To the formal renunciation of wealth and acceptance of mobility, a naive imitation of a few Gospel stories, each added something more comprehensive: a culture and a sociology of evangelical poverty. The forms of preaching and education, household living and family style, were patterned after the Gospel in such a way as to be able to survive as a counter-community under the Cross.

The first Reformation

Our next leap takes us to Peter of Cheltchitz or Chelcic, the solitary lay theologian who forms a bridge between Wyclif and Hus and the failed institutional reforms of the Taborites and the Calixtines on the one hand, and on the other hand the emergence of the *Unitas Fratrum*, which grew into independent existence during the 1450s and took institutional form in 1467. The Czech Brethren are properly called by their historians, "the first Reformation." Most of the critical and constructive ideas which later come to be understood as "Protestantism" and which live on into the present in the West in forms created by Luther, Zwingli, and Calvin, were already there a century earlier in Bohemia and Moravia. The fact that we remember the latter Reformers and not their predecessors is no mystery, its causes being multiple, and mostly political:

(a) the major creative thinkers in the movement did not find powerful and reliable political support as did Luther, Zwingli and Calvin;

(b) the historians of Western Europe seldom learn the languages of Eastern Europe, and therefore neglect any history which was not lived and written in English, French or German;

(c) certain doctrinaire themes which became quintessential in Protestant scholastic polemics ("justification through faith only," double predestination) had not yet been formulated quite as radically in the Czech beginnings.

With regard to the moral and social critique of established Christendom, however, the vision of the Czech Reformers was no less radical than that of those who came a century later. In describing them, I take the most direct path of simply quoting Peter Brock:

Chelcicky saw in a society founded on class inequalities the antithesis of a Christian social order. It was as completely pagan
as the violence on which its whole structure rested. Since he
denied the need for armed force in a Christian society, the only
justification for the privileges of the nobility, whose task it was
to protect the other two estates, lost thereby its validity. The
granting of titles meant giving that homage to men which should
be reserved for God alone. The superiority of these 'coroneted
escutcheons (*erby korunovane*),' as he scornfully called members of the nobility, was based solely on robbery and violence.
Their ancestors had obtained property and titles either through
force of arms or by money. 'If they now had no money in addition to their birth, hunger would force them to drop their coats-
of-arms and take to the plough' [he writes]. 'Wealth alone,
therefore sustains the honour of their nobility and the frame of
their birth. . . . Lacking money, they would soon sink back to the
level of peasantry and, as they scorn work, they would often go
hungry.' They were at present only able to live out their lives in
idleness and luxury because of the labour of their peasants. 'If
this disappeared, their noble birth would decay miserably.'
Chelcicky denounces their whole way of life: their refined luxuries, their class education, their pride, their loose morals, their
unwillingness to suffer wrong as Christians should, their contempt for manual work, and their oppression of the workers.
Even their frequent ablutions were in his eyes an abomination,
'a burden to the servants.' The nobles were only a millstone
round the necks of the hardworking common people, 'useless
drones' who only corrupt others by the bad example of their
lives.

Serfdom, that bastion of the feudal order, is for Chelcicky a
sin against God and man. 'If your forefathers [he says, addressing the nobility and gentry] bought human beings together with
their hereditary rights to the property, then they bought something that was not theirs to buy and sell.' Christ has redeemed
mankind with his blood: how, then, do so-called Christians dare
to traffic in human lives? All their legal documents will not be of
any avail on the Day of Judgement. For there is no basis for social inequalities in Christianity, where, 'when one member suffers, all the other members suffer with him.' 'They are quite unable to show any passage from God's scriptures [he writes] why,
apart from their superior descent, they are any different from
other people.' They are indeed doubly accursed, he cries, once
through original sin and a second time by reason of their noble
birth.

Though indeed he did not expressly condemn property in it-self, apart from inordinate wealth or its improper use, the apostolic poverty of the first Christians remained Chelcicky's ideal throughout. 'If man was not deceived by avarice [he asks] why should he need property (*zbozie*) or take any heed of worldly things?' His views on property indeed, recalls Wyclif's theory of *dominium*. 'Whoever is not of God [writes the Czech] cannot truly enjoy or hold anything belonging to God, except as the man of violence unlawfully enjoys and holds what is not his own.' The whole earth belongs to God: therefore only those who were putting into practice the principle of Christian equal-ity had a real claim to the use of enough to satisfy the bare ne-cessities of existence. The path of voluntary poverty was the only way open to a true Christian, indeed the only rational course in view of the vanity of temporal things. His injunction to give alms to the poor would seem to show, however, that Chel-cicky did not advocate communism of goods—at least as an im-mediately practicable solution. In Chelcicky's opinion, it was 'difficult to sell or buy without sin on account of excessive greed,' and for him a trader was 'one who has the mark of the Beast.' 'Every kind of trade and profitmaking occupation con-nected with the town should be avoided in order not to harm one's soul.' Markets and fairs were equally immoral, as were the taverns and usurious practices always to be found in the towns. Only agriculture and certain crafts, necessary for even the simplest existence, were permissible. Chelcicky condemned the use of weights and measures as well as boundary marks, likewise produced by Cain, the outward symbols of unChristian mistrust. (P. Brock, *The Political and Social Doctrines of the Unity of Czech Brethren in the Fifteenth and early Sixteenth Centuries*,'s—Graven Hage, Mouton, 1957, pp.63ff.)

The second Reformation

During the Reformation of the sixteenth century there were several violent dissenting movements including the so-called "Peasants' War" of 1524–25 and the takeover ten years later of the city of Munster. None of these was able to overcome the defences of estab-lished government. They belong on the edge of our story only be-cause the name "Anabaptist" has been applied to them. Their use of coercion makes them closer to Zwinglians and the Crusaders.

The most thorough form of Anabaptist communism was estab-lished in 1528 among a group of refugees forced to leave the Moravian city of Nikolsburg. It was consolidated a few years later under the leadership of Jacob Hutter, and after many ups and downs survives to this day in the Hutterian Brethren colonies of the American and Canadian prairies. The rationale for complete community of production and consumption is stated classically in the *Great Article Book* of Peter Walpot, 1577, under the third article entitled, "Of True Surrender and the Christian Community of Goods." (ET in *Mennonite Quarterly Review*, January 1957, reprinted by The Plough Publishing Co., Rifton, N.Y.)

By 1577 the movement was in its third generation, temporarily tolerated, and prosperous. Walpot's exposition ranges appropriately throughout the entire Salvation story, finding support everywhere for a communal vision of life, beginning with the Mosaic legislation which had ordered that there should be no poor in Israel and which provided a Jubilee year to wipe out such inequalities as should arise. It seemed to Walpot that the provision that Priests of the Lord should need no land of their own, prefigured the status of New Testament believers as Priests.

The key conception underlying the entire synthesis is a simple polarity of "property" and "surrender." Property (*eigentum*) is related, in a way which ordinary English usage no longer makes evident, to having one's own (*eigen*) and being able to say "my." Grasping for power or independence or autonomy is the essence of the Fall. The alternative to it, which enables us to be restored as children of a gracious Father, is letting go: variously translated as "yieldedness," "surrender" (as in our text's English title in the present version), or "abandon" (as in my Spanish translation). Literally the term is an abstract noun, ending in *heit*, the rough equivalent of our English "ness," formed from the passive participle of the verb "to let." Thus etymologically the word means "having-let-oneself-go-ness." The Anabaptists did not invent the term. It was a part of the standard vocabulary of pre-Reformation mysticism and pastoral care. It did not first mean anything social or economic. For the radical Anabaptist its primary meaning still is not economic. Here is evidence of the fact that although institutionally the impetus for forming Anabaptist communities was the Zwinglian Reformation, the Anabaptist tradition took into itself many elements which had been part of other renewal movements in preceding generations. *Gelassenheit* is the "letting-go" of the mystic, who stops trying to explain and to understand the disciplines which prepare for contemplation in the confidence that God will make himself known most authentically the less we contribute to making it possible. The mystic's affirmative contribution centres in the discipline, which the tradition calls "apophatic," of pulling back or letting go.

The prophet Zechariah predicted that under the New Covenant there would be no traders or merchants in the House of the Lord. John the Baptist described economic sharing as the sign of repentance. In Jesus' temptation it is the Devil who says of the world, "this is mine." "Even so do his children, who have this deceitfulness of Belial in their hearts." Jesus called his disciples to leave their boats and fields and be among the blessed poor.

Two masters

Although these samples from a long series of references may sound like simple proof-texts, Walpot's treatise provides more systematic pastoral and ethical arguments where appropriate. Such are developed around the texts: "no man can serve two masters," and "lay not up treasures for yourselves upon earth." Even the Lord's Prayer teaches community. Christ did not teach us to say severally, "give me my bread." The Apostles' Creed requires us to confess: "I believe in the communion of saints." Jesus taught *community* by example, through the miraculous feeding of all who had come to him in the desert; and by doing it by means of the generosity of those who gave what they had. He called the rich young man to enter into that sharing. When the young man turned sorrowfully away, the disciples had learned how hard it was for the rich to enter the Kingdom.

It is obvious that the example of the Jerusalem Church is a powerful supporting argument. Yet that model is not at the centre of the argument. Nor is the Jerusalem Church taken as typical of the entire New Testament experience, or a model for all time. The churches planted in the Diaspora by Paul were no less called to fellowship, both in their internal life and in their solidarity with the Church of Jerusalem. The Hutterite case would not be weakened if the first chapters of Acts were removed from the story: it is to be found in every other strand of the New Testament.

The treatise concludes with supporting references from Philo, Eusebius, Clement, Augustine, and Chrysostom. In a way that illustrates the true meaning of *Gelassenheit*, it concludes with a quotation from the *Theologia Germanica:*

Were there no self-will, there would be also no ownership. In Heaven there is no ownership; hence there are found content, true peace, and all blessedness. If anyone there took upon himself to call anything his own, he would straightway be thrust out into Hell, and would there become a devil.... He who has something or seeketh or longs to have something of his own, is himself a slave, namely to what he desireth or hath, and he who hath nothing of his own, neither seeketh nor longeth thereafter, is free and at large, and in bondage to none.

Only the Hutterian brethren experience such combination of pressures in the 1520s and 1530s and privileges after 1550 as to make the development of the Bruderhof economy a promising and rewarding opportunity. It is not the case, however, that the other peaceable Anabaptists of the sixteenth century rejected the notion of community of goods. They had no occasion to construct large, autarchic, residential communities, but they did use the word "community" for such economic sharing and discipline as was possible in their situation. Testimony recorded by the police at Selestat in Alsace in 1534 reported, "If anyone needs it, whether it be clothing or tools for his trade, he is given money to purchase it and at the next meeting he returns the money if he can."

In 1557 a report of a meeting in the woods near Strasbourg indicates that the candidate for baptism was asked, "if he will give all his possessions and goods for this congregation, if that should be necessary to help it, and that they would never let any of them remain in need if they were able to come to help?"

Most Anabaptist congregations had a member designated from among their leadership called the "servant of the poor," whose specific responsibility it was to coordinate the distribution of material resources according to need and capacity. In troubled times this could sometimes be a sizeable economic operation. A.L.E. Verheyden, *Anabaptism in Flanders,* Scottdale, Herald Press, 1961, p.95; a report from 1597.

The British Reformation

On the left wing of the Cromwellian revolution we find Gerard Winstanley, spokesman of the "True Levellers," whose condemnation of economic inequality is based on the appeal to Creation.

In the beginning of time, the great Creator, Reason, made the earth to be a common treasure....Man had domination given to him over the beasts, birds, and fishes, but not one word was spoken in the beginning, that one branch of mankind should rule over another....Selfish imaginations, taking possession of the five senses, ruling as king in the room of Reason therein and working with covetousness did set up one man to teach and rule over another....

And hereupon the earth, which was made to be a common treasury of relief for all, both beasts and men, was hedged into enclosures by the teachers and rulers, and the others were made servants and slaves...and thereby the spirit is killed in both. The one looks upon himself as a teacher ruler, and so is lifted up in pride over his fellow creature. The other looks upon himself as imperfect, and so is dejected in his spirit....

That this civil propriety is the curse, is manifest thus. Those that buy and sell land and are landlords have got it either by oppression or murder or theft, and all landlords live in the breach of the Seventh and Eighth commandments.

With this vision Winstanley and his colleagues set out to plant a garden on St. George's Hill, as a sign of the re-establishment of equality in the Second Coming.

That which does encourage us to go on in this work is this. We find the streaming out of love in our hearts toward all, to enemies as well as friends. We would have none live in beggary, poverty, or sorrow... for by this work... bondage shall be removed, tears wiped away, and all poor people by their righteous labour shall be relieved and freed from poverty and straights. For in this work of restoration there will be no beggar in Israel. For surely, if there was no beggar in literal Israel, there shall be no beggar in spiritual Israel....

Winstanley's garden was not to last for long, but in its simplicity the Diggers brought together dramatically a vision of Eden, of the new Jerusalem, and of the next step to take in the restoration of England.

Valid generalizations?

Where does this selective narrative leave us? This is no place for the claim that the experiences of minority faith-communities "demonstrate," in the sense of "proof," anything about economic possibilities for tomorrow. It seemed appropriate, however, that I should pull from the record just enough scraps and specimens to indicate that there are sufficient resources, spiritual and intellectual, in the believing communities of earlier centuries to project a different pattern of economic functioning from that which "Christendom" has provided.

What I have described is the tip of an iceberg. This small portion of a body of beliefs and practices is as visible as it is only because there is much more of the same below the surface. Yet it permits us to identify the presence and the character of the community/poverty movement through Christian history. Every specimen I have identified is different in language and form. That could hardly have been otherwise, since each arose out of, and spoke to, its own century. The variety would have been greater still had I finished the list of well-known manifestations with Charles de Foucauld, Dorothy Day, Mother Teresa and Jean Vanier (to name only recent Catholics). What can now be said about the common characteristics within this impressive variety?

All of these movements are specifically Christian. They arise within Christian churches and appeal explicitly to the example and teachings of Jesus and the apostles. This does not mean that they are narrowly or exclusively Christian. The Renaissance, even its sectarian movements, can also appeal to the Golden Age of Greek antiquity, according to which the original state of mankind was without private property.

It would also have been possible to expand our display of models with others derived from an interchange on the frontiers of Christian mission with tribal communal economies, or with Buddhist or Hindu monasticism.

There is a continuing debate in theological ethics (going well beyond the scope of our present colloquium) about the tension between a normative Christian loyalty to Jesus, and the ability to converse with, or even learn from, non-Christians in their own language. If our agenda included that wider debate in Christian epistemology I would need to explain in more detail why I claim that the dichotomy as usually set up is false. Christian community/poverty is one social idiom in which this dichotomy is transcended, if not refuted. When encounter is at the point of the elemental needs of bread and shelter, it takes no dictionary to make visible to our neighbours, whatever their anthropological history, a new quality of redemptive community. Nor does it take a dictionary to clarify the "hard" side of the gospel:

that the price of redemption, the structural pre-condition of entering reconciling community, is readiness to throw one's "self" into the kitty.

In summary: the first claim is the broadest. The vision of Christian community/poverty represents an incarnate proclamation of the Lordship of Christ to all possible worlds in which food and shelter are needed. Because it is a proclamatory form of Christian witness, and not a set of rules to govern a special task-force or more highly specialized staff (as sometimes within religious communities), this vision will not be cooped up or penned in by non-Christian listeners or "scientifically objective" interpreters into some uniquely "Christian" pigeonhole. Overcoming self-centredness through surrender, and overcoming the destructive experience of poverty, rejection and deprivation through sharing, represent a vision of the fulfilment of human dignity that is understandable and (at least partly) operable *independently of the naming of Jesus as Lord*. That Jesus is Lord does not depend upon our naming him such, anymore than Ronald Reagan's being president depends on my having voted for him or liking him or trusting his leadership.

Fall and Redemption

The witness to community as one dimension of human wholeness, part of the original, created dignity of the race, lost in the Fall and restored in Redemption, accessible in mission even to those for whom the call is not convincing, continues to be a live perspective independently of the response of individuals or constituencies.

The advocates of this view are thus mistaken when they accept the well-meaning interpretation of "neutral observers" to the effect that this vision is relevant only to those who believe, or possible only for radical disciples. It is not a "sectarian vision" in Troeltsch's sense: that its advocates accept its rejection by all but their circle. I need to argue against this Troeltschian put-down because it sets aside the cosmic claim which is made from the inside in terms of the Lordship of Christ; and which on the outside has almost the same meaning (if not the same power) in terms of the unity of the human race.

It may seem that this excursion into wider questions of epistemology and sectarian modesty belong somewhere else than in this consultation. Its appropriateness will become clearer as we move to macro-economics. The minority community has often been seen, especially by those who intend to be tolerant of it, as one which pre-scribes no solutions for society at large. This is true in the superficial sense of not coercing conformity to one's vision, and in the instru-mental sense of being willing to move ahead in obedience without waiting for everyone else. It is, however, never granted as right that "the world" should persist in destructive acquisitiveness and glut-tony. It is never granted that "the world" *needs* avarice in order to keep the economy going, any more than it is granted by the Tolstoyan that it *needs* violence to keep the civil order afloat. The view I am de-scribing accepts the fact of not being able to coerce. It does not ac-cept that of not being heard; nor the cheap tolerance of a pluralism which votes down, unheard, major elements of the Christian witness. Therefore we do not accept being characterized as living in comple-mentary symbiosis with "normal society." We claim rather to be the bridge-head of restored normalcy, beginning to reclaim the Sover-eign's dominion over a progressively degenerating, temporarily rebel-lious, province. That we do not impose our vision on our fellows does not mean that it is only for special people. It is rather that its nature, being non-coercive, would be denied it if we were to enforce it.

There is, therefore, a constructive function in "utopian" discourse which must not be, and logically has no reason to be, set aside on the grounds that it is not immediately feasible. Neither the Declaration of Independence nor the American Constitution are immediately feasi-ble. Nor is the Reagan economic plan. No law is absolutely enforce-able, or enforced, the day it is promulgated. No moral minority accepts the backhanded Troeltschian compliment that its faithfulness is in reverse proportion to its relevance.

Frame of reference

A third general observation regarding all these models is that the economic realm is not seen as autonomous, adequately understood when looked at by itself, properly evaluated without any broader frame of reference. The economic witness is in every case the un-folding of logically coherent implications from other elements of a vi-sion of personal and social renewal. It is thus a strength, not a weakness, of this common witness that each of its forms is different, just as the worlds to which they witness are different. When renewal arises out of medieval mysticism, renunciation of property will be a part of *Gelassenheit*. If it arises in the Church of Jerusalem it will come from commitment to the personal dignity of widows forsaken by non-Messianic synagogues. In the fourth century it will be relief from the waning of persecution. In the fourteenth it will be modelling an ideal city. In the fifteenth with Chelcicky, or in the seventeenth with Winstanley, it will be reaction to the condemnation by society defending its class structure as God's intention. In Jean Vanier or Dorothy Day it is a rediscovery of the social wholeness of being at the service of the last and the lost and the least. If you stand back from these phenomena and analyse the language of each critically, their differences are self-evident. Yet in the mind of Christ, and in what they oppose, they are modulations of the same Gospel authenticity, living out the promise of the presence of the Spirit; which, according to the Fourth Gospel, was to lead us into all truth.

A parallel from the arms race may show why a position which makes different assumptions about the power gradient does not mean what it appears to people on the other side of a debate.

There are many in the U.S.A. and in Canada who say that an arms race is a stupid and evil way to take responsibility for the world. Yet we live in a society which is so structured as to give us no choice whether to be under the umbrella of the deterrent threat of mutual destruction. That such deterrence is morally illegitimate according to all classical Christian thought, that it is bad economics, bad ecology and irrational, have no power to prevent it. In this situation it is not enough for a moral person to abstain from pulling the nuclear trigger. One must speak judgementally and prophetically and creatively about ways to dismantle the MAD system. Yet one begins within the system and has no choice but to oppose it from within. This does not mean that nuclear strategy is morally acceptable. It recognizes the unacceptable as part of the landscape, in which all who care must do whatever they can to make the unacceptable less likely.

Modes of moral discourse which assume the legitimacy of control need not wrestle with paradoxes like denying the real but unacceptable, or saying that the only morally acceptable thing is something that does not and cannot exist. Yet minority communities do it all the time. We all do it all the time about nuclear and chemical war. Many of us do it all the time about the mythical being we call "the Christian family." It means, however, that our acquiescence in the world as it is must not be confused with moral approbation, or even with the "I'm OK—you're OK" language of moral escapism. In a similar sense, to say that the believing community does not prescribe an economic order for the wider world means neither that we have no notion about economic orders or wider worlds, nor that we accept in any way as morally proper the wider world's neglect of Christ's message of poverty and sharing. Change from the dominant patterns we reject can only come through nonviolent responses to its being as it is. Any violence in attempted renovation would be, by definition, no renovation, for its means would deny its end. Living a counter-cultural way in face of an acquisitive society is not a withdrawal but an aggressive protest. He who protests does not concede that he has no pointers to give the Fallen world. But the counsel he can give has only its truth power and no other sanction on its side.

Description, not advocacy

At this point we are easily led astray by the deceptive appearance of near congruence between the radical view and the pietistic one. Both speak of fleeing worldliness. Both speak of a level of spiritual and moral authority independent of the unbelief of the majority. Both speak of truths which the world does not understand, and both can live with rejection. But the pietistic spiritualization is a socially conservative move, made mostly by persons in situations of social comfort, and accepted secondarily as a palliative by persons in situations with no hope at all. They explain the inability to change the world in a direction of greater justice in terms of the spiritual/material dichotomy; the effect is to affirm the (material) world as it is. The radical, on the other hand, while using some of the same language and living in some of the same forms, projects and lives from the otherness of the kingdom of God as a concrete social judgement and empowerment for those who believe, despite its rejection by the others.

My task has been description, not advocacy. I have left to the end the reasons which might be presented in support of the tradition I have described.

I posed at the beginning a question to which I now return as more than a question. On what can one base a claim to see and comprehend the system as a whole? Generality is a nearly unchallengeable axiom of moral discourse. We are always trained to ask:

(a) What if that idea were made a matter of public policy?
(b) What if acting against that position were made a crime?
(c) Is it possible to ask that kind of behaviour of everyone?

(d) How will the social system operate if everyone behaved that way?

(e) Will you ever get people to do that?

These questions, though they differ from one another, flow together in our tendency to reason ethically for society as a whole. For any to work well we need to assume that the facts of the social system are well known. We make this presumptuous assumption in a world in which the data to be known are growing geometrically, many relating to a geometrically rising number of independent agents, each bent on guiding the system in his own way and some on misinforming others. The one thing that is mathematically sure is that nobody can see the system whole. If we were to stir into the mix a few fragments of specifically Christian anthropology, we should also be obliged to add that the claim to see as whole might itself be the root of our sinfulness.

If I am right in suggesting:

(a) that the assumption of seeing the system whole and of being able to control it is a necessary presupposition of most of the other approaches to economics, and that

(b) that is not possible,

it follows that we need to look for some new basis of moral discourse which shares the presuppositions of the tradition I have described. If I were to be its advocate in the 1980s I should not use the language of Walpot, Winstanley, or even the New Testament. Rather, I should look for contemporary language to say again, in a world with more starvation, more wealth, more waste, more economic tyranny than ever before—despite the proclaimed beneficent intentions and systemic wisdom of our latest Constantines on both the Right and the Left—that the God who put mankind in a garden to till it, has made His will most fully known in a propertyless man who shared his bread with the poor; and who, when the powerful of his age destroyed him, would not stay dead.

Comment

Richard John Neuhaus

It does not get you very far to say nice things about how provocative
John Howard Yoder is. That, he quickly responds, is intolerable
paternalism. I will nonetheless say that he is extremely provocative,
almost always so, and I am much in his debt for this paper and his
numerous other writings. And saying this is not paternalistic since I
do him the honour of quite basically and straightforwardly disagreeing with him.

Yoder is right in saying that there is a dangerous illusion of "seeing
it whole." He is also right in noting that there are quite different
political approaches which cherish this illusion and arrive at quite different ways of "guiding the whole system." While disagreeing with
his anti-property ethic, I agree with Yoder that nobody sees it whole.
Especially in the area of economics: the myriad interactions of needs,
greeds, fears, vanities and concerns which actually propel what we
call "the economy" escape any capacity to catalogue, never mind to
understand. I would suggest that in economics, as well as in many
other fields of discourse, we should begin with what might be called a
postulate of ignorance. We simply don't know. Not knowing, we
should not try to guide or control.

This is a line of thinking which could be employed, indeed is employed, in favour of something like a free-market economy. But my
purpose now is simply to question Yoder's premise that alternatives
to his own position assume the possibility of control over the whole
system, based upon understanding of it. Some alternatives, I would
suggest, are more modest than that; perhaps more modest than Yoder's property-less communal proposal.

Closely related is his argument toward the end that his opponents
assume it is necessary "to reason ethically for the society as a
whole." There is indeed a kind of false universalism in much ethical
thought accurately summed up in the questions at the end of his

paper. Such an approach denies the particularities of loyalty, affection and obligation which must inform moral reasoning. The question is not, however, whether the individual should act in bold obedience to the dominical command, regardless of others. It is rather what communities we accept responsibility for. We all make such decisions. Most of us do it, for instance, with respect to family (both the families we are given and those we bring into being). In this connection it is probably worth asking why Yoder refers to the "myth of the Christian family." It is possible that the dismissal of the family as a theologically significant community is the logical consequence of a rigorous understanding of a "believers' church," in which the only association of consequence is that between those who share a similar response to Christ's lordship.

Communities

But to continue with communities: many of us, further, accept responsibility for, "identify with," if you will, regional and national groups. One might also so identify with ethnic groups if one were Jewish or Black. In Christian perspective, it is true, one's primary commitment is to the "household of faith," but the Church in this instance is understood as the *prolepsis* or forerunner of a universal community. Certainly we would all be inclined to say that our commitment to humanity transcends our loyalty to nation. We are more hesitant when the statement is demanded with respect to family and faith. We surmise that it is through Burke's "little platoons" that more universal responsibilities are somehow to be discovered and nurtured. And, of course, Yoder has his little platoon: this community that shares a certain understanding of obedience to the propertyless Lord. Do not individuals in that community "reason for the community as a whole"? Or do they all act in relentlessly individualistic interpretations of what radical obedience requires, without reference to what this means for the community? I should think not. For the Christian, therefore, it is a matter of determining which communities we are accountable for before the judgement of God.

In a churchly rather than sectarian understanding of Christian community, there is a comprehensive embrace of myriad sectarianisms. There is indeed a tolerance (I know my friend John Yoder detests that word) of diverse understandings of the Christian imperative. Sometimes a minority may discover *the* truth which is eventually accepted by the whole community. Christian understanding of anti-Semitism and of slavery are examples of such sectarian triumphs. Christians of catholic sensibilities, however, typically warn against sectaries who believe they are in possession of *the* truth which others resist only because they "do not listen to Christ's message of poverty and sharing."

All Christians claim that their highest priority is to do Christ's will. As in any movement or institution, some participants are more serious than others. The hardest disagreement is not, as Yoder's paper suggests, between the serious and nonserious, but between the serious who have come to different understandings of what is required by discipleship. In making a decision between communities of loyalty, it might be objected that the nation, for example, is no proper object of loyalty since it does not accept specifically Christian norms. But Yoder points out in another connection, the claims of the Christian community are universal and accessible to all. Christ is Lord, Reagan is president, whether people acknowledge it or not. A Christian must be concerned for all that is the object of God's loving concern. "God so loved the *world* . . ." —not just the community of true believers.

The function of minority communities

The communitarian and other traditions which Yoder traces have an important provocative function. They do not embody the future, and it would be arrogant for them to make that claim. But they remind the rest of us that the promised future of the coming Kingdom of God has yet to arrive. They proclaim to all of us, mired in our ambiguities of moral responsibility, that none of our other loyalties can be ultimate. The celibate witness is mentioned. This witness is not compromised by its dependence upon the continuing existence of "the normal world." It is an eschatological sign reminding that "normal world" that the only acceptable normality is that promised in the Kingdom.

The whole Church is to be such a sign of the coming Kingdom. In a society such as America however, the Church does not stand "over against" society, since in sociological fact (and by a catholic theological reading) most participants in society *are* the Church. Minority groups of particular vocation (such as described by Yoder) are meant to keep stirring up the whole Christian community in anticipation of the Kingdom.

It is urged that to accept responsibility for such large terms as "the Church" and "society" is meaningless, since we cannot really change them. Over what can we really exercise decisive control? Over a small community? (How many? Ten? Ten thousand?) Within that community, presumably, there can be the rigour of accountability required for true discipleship. But any degree of psychological sophistication—not to mention other kinds—suggests that we can hardly claim such a degree of accountability even for ourselves as individuals. It seems to me quite possible that America (or Tanzania or South Africa) can be for a Christian a significant community of loyalty and responsibility. "What should I do in light of what is good for America?" seems a legitimate question. It is not the only or the most important question, of course. Church, family, other associations may take priority. But if one believes that in the big picture of world-historical change (which is, after all, the object of God's ultimate devotion in the Christian view) American influence is good for humankind, then protection, even expansion, of that influence is of urgent moral interest.

With respect to larger communities, it may indeed be true that there is little we *can* do about them. But what we feel morally bound to attempt docs not depend on an estimate of effectiveness. The catholic Christian also says, "I believe in the communion of saints," but with primary reference to the mystical communion of the Church, centred in the sacramental life, notably the Eucharist. One can say that this is mystification, and an escape from the moral obligations of real people in real community. But such a charge is of course a put-down, sometimes a paternalistic one. It ought to be expressed as forthright disagreement with classic claims about what actually happens, and about the reality experienced in the sacramental community. Along with the provocations offered by monastic and other ventures in radical communal life, the liturgical life of the Church is a "modelling" and anticipation of future communal promise. The liturgical action coexists with the experienced brokenness of the larger Christian community, and indeed of the world in which, not accidentally, that community is situated.

In a small but important way, communities of particular vocation witness to that brokenness. They may present paradigms of possibilities for all. Although it is hard to be modest when a community thinks it has that vocation, modesty is all the more required lest the claims of the community lead it to be dismissed as fanaticism. Those experiments which have often most powerfully recommended themselves are precisely those that restrain themselves from claiming too much. Mother Teresa, for example, assiduously refrains from suggesting that she and her order represent a model of broader socioeconomic significance. Dorothy Day was generally restrained on this question also, except when she felt it her mission to expound the socioeconomic teachings of Peter Maurin.

Some specific objections

I am not so sure that the Hutterite case would not be greatly weakened without the first chapters of Acts, nor that it is very strong with them. I understand the notion that property is evil, and Yoder correctly notes that it has roots in non-biblical mythology. I do not think the idea has much basis in Scripture, where notions of stewardship, reward and responsibility for the poor imply the possession (and usually, the goodness) of property. Yoder's literal approach to the imitation of Jesus (spelled out very powerfully in The Politics of Jesus) employs a particular hermeneutic which is marginal to classic Christian christology. We could ask in what ways Jesus was "propertyless," and what were his attitudes toward property; but we are not Jesus, nor are we meant to be Jesus. We do not have the competence—in the sense of both authority and ability—to do all that he did. There is little evidence in the New Testament, if any, suggesting that he is that kind of model calling for that kind of imitation. Each is called to be herself or himself in obedience to the Lord and guided by an ethic of love and promise; that ethic is notoriously short on specific directions for the kinds of decisions each must make. One requirement is that we make those decisions and act in the courage of our uncertainties—always being held accountable to communities within the Community that is the whole Church, and to wisdom that might be found outside the believing community.

Constantinianism and Christendom are terms of opprobrium for Yoder. I am not so sure. There are many ways in which "Christ and culture" have been combined, and what we call Constantinianism and Christendom were not the worst. Till Kingdom comes, the task of Christians and of the church collectively is to proclaim the promise of the Kingdom: first that the world is not that Kingdom, then that the Kingdom has proleptically appeared within history in the "Christ-event"; and finally that participation in that promised future is possible in the communion of saints. The Church proclaims this in diverse ways. One very important way is through the encouragement of communities of special vocation, even if some of their claims are outrageously (sometimes dangerously) immodest.

Yoder's minority view of existing reality might be worth discussing. Is our society, is the world for that matter, really characterized by "destructive acquisitiveness and gluttony"? This seems a generalization which, standing alone, is simply false. There are many within the Christian community who do not think that maintaining a nuclear deterrence is "evil, stupid," and the like. It is clearly very dangerous, and there are a lot of other things that might be said about the arms race. But the point is that people, including Christian people, are called to do more than simply say it is very bad. Jonathan Schell's horrifying description of nuclear warfare is a service of limited value; important to those who thought nuclear war might not be so bad. But his conclusion that we need to "re-invent politics" is of limited utility or intellectual interest.

Utopianism is extremely important. Most of what has passed for utopianism has been dangerous or irrelevant because it was not genuinely utopian. It assumed, that is, that there was a program or existing order which embodies the ultimate promise. The crucial importance of utopianism is to remind participants in every institution, including the utopian community itself, that none of these is to be identified with the Kingdom of God. That is the genuinely apophatic way, the *via negativa,* by which the present is kept open to the promise of the future.

How ought we to view minority communities?

Yoder's paper does not indicate whether there is now a specific community, or communities, practising a radical obedience to the propertyless Christ. It is hard to know what it would look like. If participants vote are they "reasoning ethically for the society as a whole"? Is there private property? If so, how is it managed in a way which recognizes that it is not *ownership* but *power* which, in the biblical view, is fraught with demonic possibilities? Can a radical Christian belong to a pension plan, or have a legal contract (enforced by the state) respecting work and income? The questions can readily be multiplied.

The Kingdom will be propertyless, we are told. I am not sure that it will be. I don't even know what it would mean, since property and person in all their parts are so inextricably interrelated. People who really believe in that Kingdom, we are further told, should live now as though the Kingdom has already come. But the Kingdom hasn't come and we're not asked to play a game of "let's pretend." People look at the radical communities Yoder advocates and say, "Yes, that's the ideal, but the rest of us aren't there yet." Yoder resents that kind of dismissal, and correctly so. I am not saying that I think "radical community" is an *impracticable* ideal. I am saying that I don't think it *is* ideal. If the biblical imagery surrounding the Kingdom suggests anything, it is that there will be much more property; we shall *all* be rich. Crowns will be passed around, and one crown will be "mine" and another will be "thine." The writer of *Theologia Germanica* will not, I think, be thrust straightway into hell for claiming what is, by the grace of God, his own. Indeed, not to claim it would be to despise God's grace. Without occasion or temptation to avarice, jealousy and resentment, the idea of property will be fulfilled, not abolished.

But for the time being, let us have *Gelassenheit*. Let us live loosely in relation to possessions, sharing generously with others, especially the poorest, and thus demonstrating that we have kept our loyalties ordered by the Kingdom and have not sold our souls to Mammon. Such a way of living does not require that we view property as evil, or embark upon an onerous and probably impossible attempt to be propertyless. For that would be a distraction from working through the difficult responsibilities that are ours in a world that is far short of what, according to promise, it will be. Those who are preoccupied with propertylessness are just as far short. Nonetheless, in our different ways of trying to walk the path of obedience, we should have a generous view of the Christian and, indeed, of the moral community; and we should try very hard to stay in conversation. There cannot be real conversation if alternative ways are patronizingly dismissed. Nor is there real conversation if disagreement is treated as a refusal to listen to Christ's message.

Reply

John H. Yoder

My assignment, as originally formulated, was to interpret the positions of persons and groups who say that it is not the concern of Christians to keep the world from going to its ruin, but rather to be morally pure on a small scale. The phrase "Christian anarchism" was used to describe this. For several reasons, that way of putting the assignment did not seem promising as a contribution to the present discussion.

Debate among Christians about denominational differences, especially about those denominational differences which were enshrined in classical vocabulary and even in classical documents, is not first of all, and usually not at all, about the question of a global economic order. Those differences need to be handled with other resources and other methods than our conversation here. They would not directly correlate with different answers on the questions of this consultation; even less with the narrower formulation of whether there are built-in class predispositions which determine how certain categories of institutional leaders think about economics when it is not their field of expertise.

If the debate among Christian groups about things more fundamental than economic order were to be relevant to the economic issue at all, it would have had to come at an earlier place in the present discussion. This is because of the questions it would address to the assumptions underlying the entire debate, about seeing the global order whole and having the duty to impose on it a global reversal. The rest of the discussion did assume that it is appropriate for us to be asking what an ideal total economic order ought to be. There has been no serious conversation about how the shape of either moral or economic discourse would be modified by resignation to the presence of a regime over which one would have no control, and of which one would fundamentally disapprove. Richard Neuhaus recognizes that this is a question, but his response does not pursue it.

But my main reason for not writing such a paper was not only that "anarchism" is not what I believe, and not what the people I have reported on believe; it is rather because of a point much more difficult to make with accuracy. I attempted to disengage what was really meant by the rhetoric which to some sounded anarchic, which the people whom such rhetoric scandalizes enjoy being scandalized by. Historic fairness means not boxing others (especially people with other languages, less complex or less literate than our own) into our reading of their rhetoric. Minority groups are obliged by definition to converse in a language not their own, speaking to options they do not accept, in a sequence of priorities fixed by someone else. It was therefore not appropriate to accept as describing them the general category of "anarchism" and then to try to exposit or advocate it.

Misplaced criticism

I agreed with conference organizer Paul Heyne instead to a task of historical reporting, passing in review varieties of positions, each of them in phase with its own world, each of which in a different way denied the characterization of "letting the world go and saving only themselves by their own purity." Each of them did, however, live within the limits of not being in control, and not being tolerated, even patronizingly, by the "classical" "catholic" powers among those who believed otherwise.

The people I describe are not the only ones who call into question the above dominant set of axioms. Any position criticizing another will raise some such questions, all the more so if it is *de facto* out-voted, even though its position be designed to provide social guidance. For my present descriptive purposes it suffices to say that one dominant Christian vision does make many of those assumptions, although often not consciously, and that the minority experience I am assigned to recount makes it easier to see through them, and is strengthened (though not "proven") by seeing through them.

I tried to report these phenomena largely in their own words, and to paraphrase or to illustrate only enough to bridge the cultural distance from their time to ours. I did not make them all the same, nor claim that what they say is the whole truth. Where I could I left the bulk of the narrative in someone else's terms.

Richard Neuhaus has criticized the paper I did not want to write:

he has not discussed the economic substance of an alternative style of Christian life, but has re-worded in contemporary idiom the systematic rejection by historic Lutheranism of the historic free church option.

My answer will belong mostly on the level of clarification. Where there is theological difference between us it is usually a matter of repeating the old debate between the historic reformation and the free churches, rather than anything directly pertinent to the present discussion. Once the choice has been made (as Neuhaus has made it) to guide a debate into stereotyped channels, it is not likely to progress far in one brief exchange. The hardening of those channels, under the constraints of the civil power exercised by one party in the sixteenth century and the ghetto status into which the other party was driven, destroyed the potential for dialogue.

A reflection of the difference between us is shown in the term chosen by Neuhaus to replace one of mine. To "paternalize" (his word) is to retain the authority which someone has, at first, by virtue of a natural responsibility and control, beyond the point where that authority should have been transformed into reciprocal respect through the empowerment of the "offspring." What the mainstream theological traditions tend to do with minority positions, in matters both of ecclesiology and social ethics is rather (my word) to "patronize"; that is to avoid reciprocity from a position of power which is neither natural nor familiar.

Scepticism

I prefaced my introduction with a warning about the claim to see the economic system whole, as a way of locating the different moral posture of the confessing minority, but did not supply an argument for it. I quite agree with Neuhaus that one reason for scepticism is a "postulate of ignorance"; yet had I been advancing an argument rather than simply locating a stance, I would have pointed out that ignorance of the whole system is not the only or the best reason for doubt about global system-management by a few rulers. In fact, the more nearly one can discern the system as a whole the better; so long as one does not derive from that vision a right to coerce others. In the passion narrative according to Luke, Jesus says of "the kings of the nations" that they "exercise dominion" while "letting themselves be called benefactors." It is this claim that the exercise of dominion is for the welfare of its subjects that makes of civil dominion something worse than mere inadequately informed manipulation. I did not "premise" that all alternatives to my "own position" assume the possibility and moral right to total control. I could hardly have held such a premise without knowing what *all* the other positions are. I do know that, at certain breaking points of dialogue, that premise has been essential. It is so, for example, with regard to the origins of the doctrine of the "just war," which is one of the five points at which the Augsburg Confession condemns the Anabaptists. The criteria of just authority and proportionality are early forms of what systematic ethical analysis today calls "consequentialism." You do not have "just war" unless the outcome you can reasonably expect by fighting would be better than that of avoiding the war. It is often the case for the "great economic debate," as Philip Wogaman* calls it. It would seem that when Neuhaus describes my topic as "a propertyless communal proposal" he is assuming that I propose communal structures for all of society. Yet, not only did I deny the ability to reason for all of society: most of the people I discussed did not even practise communal property holding for themselves. There are other ways to share and to identify with the poor than by establishing communes.

Nor is it the case that the communal patterns of the free church traditions (in distinction, of course, from those based on celibacy) "dismiss the family as a significant moral community." Except for the celibate cases in my narrative, the communal movements make more of the family than do the societies among which they live, as the context of initial moral formation. They do respect the Dominican teaching to the effect that sometimes family duties must take second place to the call of the Kingdom, but they do not ask, hope or expect always to be in that position. They do prefer extended family structures to the segregated nuclear unit, and they do deny that the family should be a privileged locus of economic selfishness. If they had been asked about a global financial system, they probably would have denied that it is appropriate that the offspring of a rich man should without work inherit the privilege his father had worked for (if he did). They did doubt that every pair of parents are qualified, in the absence

---

* Philip Wogaman, *The Great Economic Debate: An Ethical Analysis,* Philadelphia, Westminster Press, 1977.

of the wider community, to provide an adequate moral formation even for their own children.

Dismissal

This is different from the modesty about the achievements of the Christian family which was expressed in the phrase which Neuhaus misinterprets as "dismissal." That sentence says that all of us, whatever our economic or ecclesiological theory, set goals which we do not achieve, and live with the unacceptable. So at this point I was suggesting no distinction between the minority tradition and Neuhaus's own. There is no debate when Neuhaus argues that instead of choosing whether to reason for communities we have to decide which communities to reason for and by what standards to make our choices.

I must protest, moreover, at the parenthetical comment to the effect that I "detest" the word "tolerance." This is simple misrepresentation. Toleration as a mark of Western democracy is predominantly the product of the "free church" traditions; first of all on the ideal level, in that beginning at least in the fifteenth century they denied the propriety of central government dictation of the forms of faith, which official Catholic and Reformation theologies continued to advocate until they were bypassed by modernity; and secondly, because their own suffering nonconformity placed majority "Christian" governments in the position of deciding whether to continue to deal with heresy as a crime. It was Enlightenment rather than the free churches which finally pushed the separation of Church and State over the threshold into legal forms. It was not until a plurality of free churches and the break-up of Europe into competing Christian nations made it impossible to enforce religious uniformity that the churches which Troeltch and Neuhaus would call "catholic" resigned themselves to a "comprehensive embrace of myriad sectarianisms." It is because the free churches caution anyone against thinking that they have "the truth" that they deny the appropriateness of anyone's enforcing it on others through the sanctions of the civil order.

Had it been my assignment to talk about questions of political responsibility in general, rather than to describe historical patterns of contrasting economic order, which by the nature of the case arose mostly among people who had no access to political responsibility, I would have repeated the demonstration frequently made elsewhere that it is precisely the perspective of dissent that is able to change society significantly, where the "catholic" acceptance of things as they are does so less effectively. The reason is not that they are few, nor is it merely that there are many actors and we do not know about all the data. The fundamental reason for not expecting to take charge of the whole society is that most of its members do not share one's own moral commitment, and could therefore be led to conform to its prescriptions only by coercion. It is again part of customary historical slander to say that minorities are not interested in what is good for America or for Tanzania, or in how an America better than the one we have would be better for the world. What they deny is that specific selfish definitions of that "good" can be given priority which are not subjected to wider criteria of local discernment and global community.

Straw men

It is a sign of inadequate comprehension of the dialogical situation when one presents as if it were an argument a statement that is not debated. The Neuhaus comment does this repeatedly: by saying that we live in many communities and the question is how to serve which ones first; by saying that we should also try to change the larger societies, and that limited effectiveness is not a criterion which can explain withdrawal from caring. It happens again with reference to the liturgical life of the Church as a modelling of communal promise. At this last point, however, Neuhaus takes back with the left hand what he had just given with the right. After saying that the sharing of bread and the Eucharist is a model, he says that the people who share their own bread, as if they think that it is a model, are guilty of fanaticism.

Neuhaus's criticism becomes *ad hominem* when it raises questions to which my paper did not refer, such as the interpretation of Jesus. The book which Neuhaus names without responding to what it says does not say that we have the competence, the authority, or the ability to do all that Jesus did. It does compose from the New Testament witness a refutation of the claim, which Neuhaus makes on systematic and denominational (not textual) grounds, that Jesus can be appealed to in behalf of an "ethic of love" which is "notoriously short on specific directions." The question is not how "specific" may be the "directions," nor whether there is some kind of non-specific, non-directive "love" that can be disengaged therefrom. It is rather whether at those points where a consistent imperative is identifiable within scripture's witness to the Gospel, it should on other grounds be decided to give greater specific directive authority to other values. The medieval disjunction between precept and counsel, the Protestant ascription of revelatory authority to "orders of creation" identified with existing authority structures, or Reinhold Niebuhr's dichotomy between "love as impossible ideal" and "love acting as justice," are ways of doing that. Although he has not pursued the argument, Neuhaus does pay to the dissenters the compliment of granting that the argument they call for would be one based upon the interpretation of scriptures. That has not been the case with regard to most of the other Christian positions described in our consultation. To say that reading Jesus as politically relevant represents "a particular hermeneutic" is about as helpful as saying that we all belong to communities or that God cares for the world. The question is whether that hermeneutic takes account of the texts in a way that is subject to dialogue.

Literalism (Neuhaus used the yet more pejorative term "fundamentalism" orally) is a modern intellectual movement which concentrates upon the denial that there are any serious problems of hermeneutics. It claims that that denial represents classical Reformation thought, and concludes with the rejection of historical and literary critical scholarship. My *The Politics of Jesus* is a popularization of critical scholarship and a demonstration of the importance of hermeneutic problems. What it challenges is the majority, pre-critical view according to which the pertinence of Jesus for determining the social shape of the believing community is to be minimized. That view, which Neuhaus shares, is closer to fundamentalism than is my view. Neuhaus is no fundamentalist. But on this subject he says what fundamentalists say, and I do not.

Soup kitchens

Looking back over the Neuhaus critique, the most striking general impression which remains is that, while he has rehearsed the classical Lutheran rejection of the free church tradition, he has moved past this to questions regarding the economic order only in glancing ways.

It may be that the Franciscans may have accepted some of the depre-
cation of the joys of the flesh from the *Cathari* whom they were trying
to convert. It may be that Peter Walpot, in the effort to round out his
apology, drew on some neo-Platonic undercurrent of medieval mysticism. It may be that the "distributist" personalism of Peter Maurin
was less readily respected by people like Neuhaus than Dorothy
Day's soup kitchens. But at none of the points at which economic
specifics are permitted to come to the surface in the Neuhaus critique
does the challenge go beneath the surface. The text, *Theologia Germanica,* which said that since in heaven there will not be selfishness,
neither will there be property, which Neuhaus rejects, is part of the
common medieval heritage with which the Walpot text closed: it was
a text highly praised by Martin Luther, a testimony to the monastic
rather than the radical version of the communal vision.

Nor is Neuhaus relevant when he echoes Luther's phrase about
"forcing God's hand by establishing the Kingdom now." That applied to the rebellious peasants and to Huldrych Zwingli, not the non-
violent communities. The tradeoff between idealism and cynicism in
"taking responsibility for the world" is a debate that belongs elsewhere.

Here the question is not whether moral people on Christian or
other grounds, should project a distant ideal of "living loosely in relation to possessions, sharing generously." No one would disavow
such a lofty and vague idea. No one would be persecuted for it either.
The question is whether, in a world where that ideal is kept distant,
vague, nondirective, and inoffensive by majority moral discourse, the
person consciously committed to confessing Jesus as Lord either can
or should reflect those possibilities in a more concrete and costly
way, and even be called to account by his brothers and sisters for his
failure to do so. It is at that point that we must argue not about the
general ideal, but about the particular reasoning processes which especially since the third and fourth centuries have led most Christians
responsible for wealth in the power structure of society to answer this
question negatively.

Discussion

Edited by: Irving Hexham

Bob Goudzwaard: I want to explain further the main thrust of the tradition in which I stand. A person's fundamental reference is not tradition. It goes deeper. It has to do with being human in relation to the living God.

The perspective I take makes it possible for me to see the weak elements in my own tradition, especially its misuse in encouraging an apartheid ideology. At the same time, a lot of what is going on now in relation to the use of the idea of "sphere-sovereignty" is not really rooted in that principle.

My religious outlook stresses the normative element of life. It can be said that the whole of creation in which human activities take place consists of "an answer structure." There is no power which can rest in itself. Power needs to become an answer by being oriented to justice. Only in that way can it become an answer to our fellow man and to God.

The technical possibilities in creation are to be seen in a religious context. They are created to serve mankind.

So too, economic life is seen as an answer, in the aspect of stewardship: Stewardship is the careful administration of what is entrusted to you by someone who is higher than yourself.

In Aristotle you have "œconomia," which originally meant stewardship. If a man in my tradition speaks of economic life, and has some critical comments, he does not do so from the viewpoint of ethics by saying that ethics has to be related to economics. No, he points to the fact that we have to understand what economics really means. This is because we have tried to remove the normative element from the economic sphere. That's important because stewardship is more than just efficiency.

"Sphere-sovereignty" is an important element. It makes clear that responsibility can take a variety of expressions. The responsibility of a state is different from the responsibility of a family, trade union, or production unit.

And now for my last comment. In the discussion so far, we have mentioned again and again the market mechanism, production-households, and the state. In my tradition, it is stressed that the growing influence of the state can and has to be explained in terms of a diminution of responsibility in the economic sphere itself.

We would not have seen an enormous growth of state intervention if from the beginning production units had been aware of their own, direct, economic responsibility for their personnel, their environments, and the continuation of employment.

We now have an empty type of production unit, producing only for the market, oriented to efficiency. This has led to a growing necessity for the state to take over the original economic responsibilities of the production unit.

Calvinists have something to say about what is going on now in our societies. The prediction of Calvinist thought is that if we go on looking to production units in a way we will see a continuous growth of state intervention, so that capitalism will eventually end up as collectivism.

Martin Marty: Whenever I'm at a conference, I use one ear as a participant and the other as a journalist. But since I can't publish, quote or attribute anything that's going on here, I will do my journalism right now. In this regard, let me address what I think is probably the most interesting structural dimension of our dialogue on religion and economics in society.

The Liberty Fund and Fraser Institute and most of the economists here are market people, and the celebrators of reason. It seems to me they must find the language of Dooyeweerd and Kuyper extremely archaic. And Yoder sounds like a Hutterite dragged in three centuries late. (laughter) How can this be? I look around the room and anytime we think we reach a universal, on what is reason, or equality, or justice, someone speaks up for Islam, or early Judaism. We had two papers on Catholicism that an outsider or journalist would say sound like representations of two different religions (laughter), not just two different dimensions of the Christian faith.

Yoder's appeal to the public would be seen as conservative, although it is radical. Goudzwaard's people would be conservatives yet, probably almost everyone of that stripe in America voted for Reagan. And that's only the beginning.

The World Council of Churches is another of these subgroups. When Clark Kucheman speaks for Unitarian Universalism, I hear shades of eighteenth-century Enlightenment done in twentieth century fashion. In the eighteenth-century Enlightenment, everyone who opened his mouth, in that sense, thought they were talking the universal.

I am pointing to the ways in which I think the present-day market economy advocates are in very uneasy alliances with a lot of subcommunities in America. These alliances aren't going to last long unless they can penetrate the thinking of these communities. Islamic thinkers like Dean Ahmad say: "They don't care what Western reason says," and people with "sphere-sovereignty" concepts go their own ways.

Now it worked in Holland, as long as there were the *verzuiling* (pardon my poor Dutch), the pillars of society. These were columnlike divisions between Protestant-Catholic-Jew. Each subgroup then had its own territory.

But the diffusion of modernity has weakened communities. It seems to me that what the present papers are talking about is the attempt to recover the integrity of these communities. This is precisely at the moment when the market economy people are looking for universalism based on a kind of a reason that the particular communities they try to appeal to simply don't want.

Richard Neuhaus comments on the trend toward seeing things from the viewpoint of family, community, body of Christ, or whatever. And people are seeking to repeal the diffusion of modernity by trying to go back in time. That is what we are talking about doing.

These conservative, republican, evangelical folk, the Francis Shaeffers, the John Whiteheads, the John Conlans, are all influenced by the people we are talking about. They are really seeking to restore a kind of a theocracy that will either ask for subcultural theocracies, schools of their own, paid for by the state, or to transform the public schools into a particular kind of religion. The current talk is that we should legislate traditional theism as being the official religion of America.

What it all comes down to, as far as I can see, is that free-market people have come into a new sophistication and a position of power at the very moment when huge subcultures in America are trying to restore a community that doesn't welcome the language of reason to which they appeal.

What it means, I think, is that both socialists and capitalists are fighting for the heart of people in pluralist societies. They know what they have to do in the Islamic world where there is a lot of homogeneity. But what do you do in our society? I think they are going to have to find a lot more ways of penetrating these languages and communities, if they're going to win any hearts at all. Otherwise we have nothing but practical alliances.

I heard Arthur Shenfield describing what to him was simply a universal understanding of reason, purposefulness, and justice. I try to picture a Dooyeweerdian sitting there, or a Hutterite, or someone else, and they would have said, "That's very interesting, but it's a religion of its own. It's just one more down the list."

Throughout this conference I've heard two languages in collision. I welcomed both papers this morning for pointing that out. There are ways in which Catholicism and the W.C.C. look like our diffuse, generalized culture, though they have elements too that are seeking a re-particularization, but the present papers present truly radical alternatives.

To me, the strongest trend in the cultures represented in these papers is that they have given up on modernity. There is a move toward a retribalization, an attempt to understand our own language and our own community no matter what happens to the larger social fabric. That may be good or bad. It's not my point of argument right now. But I think it's not being understood how such folk hear the language of Adam Smith and the like.

Robert Benne: I'm not sure that the people who see market economic mechanisms always view them highly ideologically as a universal philosophy. That position is represented in this room but I do not see myself in that tradition. I see the market more as a co-ordinating mechanism to do some important things that have moral significance.

It seems to me that a co-ordinating system like the market can be very useful in allowing various subcultures to express themselves economically and to protect the rights of particular communal groups.

The market, along with pluralist social structures, doesn't fight against subcultures. If you view the market not as ideology but as a mechanism, it is one way to protect and celebrate pluralism. Constitutional democracies are one way to adjudicate differing interests so that they don't break into anarchism and chaos.

Roger Hutchinson: I just want to add a footnote to Martin Marty's comment. He spoke of the mainline society which is pushing forms of development that impinge upon particular communities. In Canada, those forces have an initial advantage in penetrating an identifiable subcommunity. When they wanted to locate a uranium refinery at Warman, Saskatchewan, which was a Mennonite community, Eldorado Corp. sent some of its members to the Mennonite Bible College for two years in order to familiarize themselves with that society. However, being Mennonite also gave an initial advantage to the community when it organized against that imposition.

Stephen Tonsor: The problem with the present papers is not that they present too much pluralism, but that they leave room for too little. When I read John Yoder's paper, I thought I was reading a boiled down *Readers' Digest* version in the *Magdeburg Centuries*, and that true Christianity had been lost over the centuries, except for this one, narrow, little sect.

Similarly when I read Gregory Baum's paper, with his references to the Church, I could hardly believe my eyes. The Church which he discusses is characterized by a vast pluralistic structure. Yet, the narrow, minority he represents ordains itself to the position of speaking for the whole Church. The Christian position, and to a certain extent the Jewish position, suffers from the same kind of arrogation to particular groups of the right to speak for the whole Church.

If there is one thing I think that churches need to do, it is to find commonality in their commitment and beliefs; and plurality in the pragmatic solutions which they bring to problems which arise out of those commitments and beliefs. So there's plenty of room for pluralism.

Irving Hexham: I commented on the use of words like "liberalism," "socialism" and "Methodism" in the neo-Calvinist tradition. These words were used to erect boundaries around the Calvinist community to maintain the purity of Dutch society. In South Africa, a similar thing happened. The strict Calvinists used these words to identify their enemies. So the evangelicals like Andrew Murray were described as "Methodists." They weren't Calvinists, and as Methodists they were bad. Good Afrikaaners were therefore expected to keep away from them. As Martin Marty was talking, I suddenly realized something of the appeal of the Dutch Calvinist tradition among evangelicals in Britain and North America which I hadn't realized before. The way in which the tradition has gained popularity during the early to mid 1960s is connected with what Richard Quebedeaux calls the "worldly evangelical." In this time period, evangelicals stopped identifying themselves by the old practices of not going to the cinema, not smoking, not drinking, and avoiding other "worldly" pursuits. Instead, they started to drink, grew beards, and did other things that were new to them as a religious community. But they became indistinguishable from the rest of the population. So they now have a problem of identification. It's at this point that Dooyeweerd becomes attractive.

Through appeal to Dooyeweerd and the Dutch Calvinist tradition new boundaries were created. Suddenly evangelicals could identify themselves in terms of a new language. The spoken language of this philosophical tradition rather than the body language of not smoking and not drinking, enabled them to erect new boundaries. The question is how do you maintain social boundaries? And Christian schools etc., provide a basis for communal boundaries, which are very important.

Imad Ahmad: If I've understood correctly what Martin Marty was saying, there was some reference to the contrast or conflict between universal concepts and particular religions. I think he is taking a particular case and universalizing it.

I can see why one would say that, based on the presentation we've had of Dutch neo-Calvinism, but I don't see that it necessarily applies to religions in general. It doesn't apply to Islam and I haven't seen any evidence that it applies to the other religious traditions we have discussed.

There is not necessarily any opposition between faith and reason. When we talk about economic science, and say it is value-free, we attempt to discover certain universal laws. If an analogy can be made with natural sciences, the conclusions we draw from natural science may be called "universals." And the conclusions we draw from the social sciences may also be called "universals." Thus there is no *a priori* reason to believe that a religion should necessarily conflict with them.

If one of the tenets of religion is that faith is superior to reason, then we may have problems. But in the case of Islam, reason in the natural world is one of the signs of God. Rational understanding is essentially a kind of religious knowledge.

Therefore, any religion that comes into conflict with the conclusions of science and declares itself superior to science, is creating a conflict that must be resolved. I don't think this point can be dismissed by saying, "Well, everyone thinks they're talking in universals."

A minor point on the question of pluralism is the observation that in the case of Islam you have in most Muslim societies large, functioning, and prosperous non-Muslim groups. So pluralism is respected by Islam. There is no conflict between pluralism and the absolutism of Islam.

Paul Heyne: The claim that economics is value-free is rejected by about 50 percent of the leading economists whom T. W. Hutchinson surveys. So I, as an economist, want to disassociate myself from what Imad Ahmad says.

Imad Ahmad: Really, I'm in the majority! (laughter)

Martin Marty: I agree there are no value-free economics in the view of the communities we're talking about. They would say they are utilizing paradigms that work.

It's very hard to have a transcending, national community made up of nothing but tribes who make no appeal to anything like principles of reason. People in these communities won't share that assumption, and we had better know it.

The huge legacy of Protesant neo-Orthodoxy, is just one example. Neo-Orthodox theologians have very little belief that you can connect faith and reason, or any of these things, and they're the most moderate of the groups we are discussing. So I think that keeping mechanism language as mechanism is probably one of the greatest favours the market people can do for themselves.

Ronald Preston

In Britain over the last few years a certain number of evangelicals from the Calvinist tradition have been influenced by Dooyeweerdian thinking. The effect has been two-fold. Its effect on those who are not professional economists has been to radicalize them politically, rather like the move to the left we heard about from Gregory Baum in the Roman Catholic church. Its effect on the few who are professional economists has been the opposite. There are a small number of professional economists of this persuasion and they are all monetarists. These economists want to put human beings under automatic, impersonal processes which are not subject to individual political decisions. They distrust the political process and political man, but they want to absolve economic man. In this way the same basic philosophy is having two diverse effects.

My impression is that many established theological positions can be used to work socially or politically leftwards or rightwards, to establish things or to criticize them. This indicates that one can't move directly from any of these theories to a particular conclusion without some other element entering in. So there arises an even more subtle question: what factors influence one's interpretation of empirical data?

Bob Goudzwaard: Speaking about "production-households" is a linguistic question. I use the word to include all types of human activity in production and not just those organized in a firm or corporation.

Cannon Preston's second question is very important for the whole discussion. Within neo-Calvinism there are a variety of opinions which can be described from left to right or from progressive to conservative.

This observation leads to the possible conclusion that this tradition legitimates existing ideas, and does not exercise an influence on what people think or do. That, I think, is a conclusion which goes too far.

A common element in Calvinism is to start from a deep respect for the normative elements in the Bible. Calvinists usually have a tendency to look to the Old Testament, because it is concrete, as we saw in our discussion of stewardship.

It is, therefore, possible to look at the state in relation to what public justice should mean. We can try to formulate what justice is from a biblical perspective. There is then a normative element which always will be more than just a way of thinking.

So, if you speak about justice, or stewardship, you can't say that it is only a Western type of thought and that it does not have a universal claim on mankind.

Roger Hutchinson: My main contact with the tradition that Goudz-waard and Hexham have been speaking about is the Toronto group, the Institute for Christian Studies and the Christian Labour Association of Canada. I've spent a fair amount of time with Harry Antonides of the Christian Labour Association. In particular I've used this book, *Multinationals and the Peaceable Kingdom*, in one of my classes.

Key elements in that work are "sphere-sovereignty," pluralism, and a proper ordering of society. Underlying that ordering, the image of hierarchy is very significant: children obey their parents, wives obey their husbands. In the hierarchical ordering each sphere becomes norm guided. Finally, in the Calvanist sense, the Sovereignty of God is affirmed.

This has raised the question of the role of women. How is that tradition responding to the feminist critique of hierarchical structures and basic images?

I think it's related to the question, What kind of images are our norms rooted in?

Arthur Shenfield: A quick word about value freedom and economics. Paul Heyne is right when he says that you cannot say that economics is value-free. But, I submit you can truthfully say that there are propositions in economics which are value-free. They are important and are correct.

A statement in Bob Goudzwaard's paper illustrates a deplorable confusion in the public mind. He says: "But workers and directors have a common responsibility for the direction of the enterprise. Just like government and citizens have a shared responsibility for the direction of the state."

He then asks for certain channels of co-determination through the use of a popular parallel between the state and business enterprise. I submit that this is false and dangerously false. A fatal reason is this: if the parallel were true, then it would necessitate that civil servants acting as civil servants, not as citizens, would have the right to elect a proportion of members of Parliament. If you think about that you can see it's a fundamental error.

Imad Ahmad: I think that there's a distinction to be made between economic systems and economics. Economic systems are not value-free. They reflect values. But economics, as a science, should be value-free.

Meir Tamari: The papers under consideration solved a problem which I had. I'm not sure whether the so-called minority motives in Christianity are not, in effect, a reversal to the majority Christian opinion. But the experiment to see Christianity as supportive of the market economy in the nineteenth and twentieth centuries was a sort of aberration of a tradition of Christian thought which is not only anti-market, but anti-economics and opposed to the idealization of property. Some of the points raised by Professor Sadowsky are actually an attempt by some members of the Catholic church to get on the liberal market bandwagon. What we're seeing is an attempt, not so much to go back, as to reimpose the authority of God on the marketplace.

It's not a question of a conflict between faith and science. The question is what do you do with science after you have it?

In economics, it's not a question of what we have in Calvinist, Judaic or Islamic textbooks. It's a question of how we act.

Lastly, it's very interesting that Marxism and some of the opinions expressed here have much in common in trying to depict economic forces as the major forces in life or, perhaps, the only relevant forces in life.

Anthony Waterman: Marxism and mainstream economics have something in common. I don't believe that's bad. What's interesting about the Dutch Calvinist tradition is that it makes a claim about the relation between theology and economics which we have to take seriously. I haven't yet sorted out in my mind how to deal with this claim. As I understand Dutch Calvinism, there can be, in principle, a Christian economics. Somehow or other, religious belief, or Christian belief, rightly understood, both can and ought to determine the way in which we come at our knowledge of the economy. But in both classical and Marxist economics that claim is repudiated. Both want to say that "science," including "economic science," can be epistemologically autonomous. Marxists and liberal economics may disagree about the goals of economic science, but both want to assert that theology is not queen of the sciences.

I'm not suggesting that economics has to be "value-free." What I am suggesting is that the classical and Marxist traditions can be "theology-free." The most extreme example of this was an ex-Roman Catholic nun I met in England two years ago, who is a member of the Central Committee of the British Communist Party. She said that there is no conflict between science and theology. Marxism, she argued, is the correct way to analyze the economy, therefore, she is a Marxist. But she says she is also a Christian. To my mind, the most important reason for discussing the neo-Calvinist tradition is to bring out in the open the big question: whether or not theology must be epistemologically sovereign. Must theology determine the way in which we think about reality, including social reality? Or are neo-classical, liberal, market-type economists, and/or the Marxist economists, permitted to make the epistemological assumptions they do? Can they do science independently of religious beliefs?

Susan Feigenbaum: What troubles me in the discussion of unemployment and technological change by Bob Goudzwaard is that he seems to be saying that disequilibrium situations in and of themselves are violations of the norm of public justice.

It seems to me that disequilibrium situations may, in fact, distribute the burden of such disequilibrium in ways which we may not like. We may want to share as a community with those individuals who bear that burden. But I'm not sure that I would want to say that those situations in and of themselves violate public justice. Rather, it's society's response to the burdens and the incidence of disequilibrium costs that may relate to the notion of justice.

Marilyn Friedman: This is a kind of meta-theoretical point. This session is bringing something into clear focus that I find very distressing. It has to do with the effectiveness of various intellectual systems. Martin Marty made a point about the uneasy alliances of various sub-communities in America whose only point of common commitment seems to be a certain kind of economic behaviour, but not necessarily intellectual commitment. It seems that the same behaviour gives rises to a commitment to different symbols.

Ronald Preston talked about how one and the same set of symbols gives rise to different sorts of commitment with regard to economic behaviour and systems. How effective are these various symbolic systems? Are we merely providing rationalizations for people who have already decided independently of their intellectual commitments, how they want to behave? Are we merely connecting certain people's favourite symbols to their behaviour by an acceptable sequence of conceptual links?

Some people have worried about the use of the term "justice."

Does it really express anything clear and definitive? The same worry can be expressed about the term "freedom" as it is used by different groups.

P. J. Hill: I'd like to come back to the issue of pluralism. Issues like co-determination basically run against the concept of pluralism. If as Martin Marty said, we want to try to maintain pluralism, particularly among subcultures, then it is important that we not try to impose an institutional structure upon society.

I suggest that those subcultures probably have more freedom to choose if we don't try to predetermine such things.

Yet, people might find co-determination to be desirable. If so, it can be achieved under a regime of freedom, if they so desire it. Workers can organize themselves in any sort of a pattern they wish.

Bob Goudzwaard: I do not feel that I am a member of a tribe or just a subculture. The Calvinist tradition is different from the Mennonite. The Calvinist tradition always says that you have to stand in the midst of the world. Backgrounds may be different, but Calvinists have to fully participate in scientific activities and take political responsibilities. So it is not a question of a subculture in which people try to hide themselves.

Second, the question of Christian economics is an interesting one in Calvinist thought. It can easily create a lot of misunderstanding. The point is that economics is not value-free. You cannot look at facts without selectivity, without interpretation, which are value judgements by themselves.

Next, in the present economics paradigm there is the presupposition of the infinity of human wants. This is based on an anthropology which is incorrect. The real point of Christian economics is not that you want to place a whole set of Christian normativity around economic science, but that you want to get rid of certain presuppositions which have their religious origin (in a very broad sense of the word) in humanistic philosophy. You want to get rid of false presuppositions, and have some liberty to study facts in a context which is not determined by too many narrow presuppositions. Scholars should have the opportunity to accept other presuppositions. My presuppositions are related to the finiteness of humans, and the necessity of taking care of the world.

On disequilibrium, there is a lot of economic disequilibrium in the market system which needs no government intervention because the market looks after itself. But in relation to inflation and to the unjustified use of economic power which leads to public injustice, government intervention, motivated by justice, is needed. My approach is not a mechanical one.

John Yoder: My assignment was to interpret the position of persons or groups that are thought to say that it's not the concern of Christians to keep the world from going to ruin, but only to be pure on a small scale. The difficulty as we saw is that Richard Neuhaus has answered a paper I didn't write, by dealing with questions of ecclesiology, New Testament interpretation, and systematic social ethics.

At some points his response doesn't convince me. The interesting place to start is with the shift in language he made. He talked about not wanting to be "paternalistic." I talked about the impatience of minority groups with being "patronized." As I said before, it's not the same thing.

Paternalism is the vice of somebody who has a certain title to authority and uses it wrongly. But to be a patron, or to patronize, is to assume the responsibility to put the other in his or her place, without it being clear on what ground that authority has been assumed.

That's what I see happening in mainstream social practice generally: putting minorities in their place. I'm glad that it's being done gently today; it wasn't done so kindly in the sixteenth century. But all of this still means that we haven't started conversing on the level of reciprocity. Neuhaus says, "Other views can also be modest about system control." Fine. I didn't say other views couldn't be. I said that some views aren't. I'm quite open to other views making the same assumption that I argue for, about not reasoning in terms of efficacy for the best of the total system. But most of the conversation here has still followed that line.

Another point. There is no proposal about communal property ownership in my paper. I reported on a few people who said there should be no personal property. I also discussed many people who live within the property regime. I talked about commonalities within those stances, rather than making communalism the issue.

Neuhaus says that I detest the term "tolerance." That's hardly fair. Minority groups can claim "paternity" for the notion of tolerance. We share that paternity with the Enlightenment but not with mainstream Christianity. Where we don't agree with the Enlightenment is that tolerance is an answer to the truth question. Tolerance is only an opening of the truth question.

I made the mistake in my paper of only giving examples up to the seventeenth century, and that left out things that might have protected me against this misinterpretation. The second mistake I made was that I named only few people since the seventeenth century, like Mother Teresa.

When tolerance began in the seventeenth century, as a social form in the Anglo-Saxon context, there was more freedom, political pluralism, and religious liberty than before. Then there was room for minority groups to make a contribution to system change. Because minorities think systemically, without thinking globalistically, they can exercise power as fractions within pluralism. They don't renounce reconciliation or the use of power and they become not only productive, but even prosperous. But they don't side with the rich. I could have told a separate history, of how at particular times and places, people called "sectarian"—whether descriptively or pejoratively—did more than their share in piloting new social structures, in keeping alive a critical consciousness, by creating alternative languages, and contributing to social change.

There are some historians who suggest that it was the Quakers with their concept of reliable products and stated prices that made one of the essential contributions to the market being manageable, as over-against an economy of haggling and unreliable product quality.

So it isn't the case that minority groups are not interested in the wider society, or that they fail to make contributions to it.

I would recognize in state socialism and capitalist nationalism not two serious opponents, but mirror images. Mars and Mammon are more parallel than they are contradictory, both for Jesus and in history. The way they work to oppress is not the same. They don't hurt people in the same way: but they both hurt people. More often they work hand-in-hand to oppress. So that the vision of the oppressiveness of either being decreased by cutting down the other seems hardly promising. And it certainly does not make for greater human dignity. I see no biblical validation for thinking that our suspicions about Mars and our suspicions about Mammon should be of a radically different quality.

Some people think that pessimism about human nature and its perfectibility favours one global system rather than another. That looks odd. Both systems make great assumptions about human perfectibility. The oddness is represented for me by the easy use made by some of our marketeers of words like "magic" and "miracle." We know that when we see somebody producing magic, it's usually sleight-of-hand. We have to check the operations which lie behind the claim that our system is reliable and that this way of regulating will make people's innate goodness work better than that way, or make their selfishness work against themselves, in such an effective way that we can trust the system to be ennobling.

There can be progress in taming the tyranny of the civil order. That has happened in some ways more in Anglo-Saxon cultural history than anywhere else. "Sectarians" have contributed to that. The Enlightenment too contributed, more than establishment Christians.

There can also be progress in taming the tyranny of the economic order. That may include clarifying the market mechanism. It may also include refusing to spread the market metaphor into regions where other metaphors belong.

We're not rejecting concern for the larger system. But we begin by defining moral faithfulness on other grounds than the ability to save the system. And we refuse to define ethics as utilitarian calculation about how we can help the system by making one or two basic moves.

What is the basis for the other view? Martin Marty called it "intrinsic." In different ways, Judaism or Islam could call it "law." I don't care what we call it. But it has its base in a community which is not the same as the total society, and is not derived from its ability to accredit itself to the total society. Precisely for that reason it can do something useful—not only in the minority community, but in the wider society.

Stephen Tonsor: John Henry Newman said that something was a characteristic of Christian heresy not because it was untrue, but because it was partial, that it was a truth, taken out of the context of other truths. This is characteristic of most of what we have been doing: taking truths out of the context of other truths, and commitments of faith out of the context of other commitments. Thus the science of theology is taken out of the context of other sciences; and partial views of great religious traditions are represented as being whole and absolute.

What I plead for is contextuality and a recognition of complexity within Christian orthodoxy, and its relationship to the world. Unless we accept that we don't really deal satisfactorily either with our Christianity or with the world.

Gregory Baum: I wish to say a few words about the "natural law" tradition in the Catholic church and its relation to the Gospel. In the past the Catholic church distinguished between the evangelical ideals preached by Jesus Christ and rational moral norms that apply to all people, not only Christians. Catholics believed that these rational moral norms could be discovered by people thanks to their intelligence and goodwill. In recent decades, Catholic theologians (and later the Church's official teaching) have affirmed the universality of divine grace. According to this teaching, God's summons and God's help are available not only in the Church where they are recognized and received with gratitude, but also among people outside the Church, whether they be religious or not, whenever they wrestle with the important issues of justice and truth. Many elements of the "natural law" tradition, especially those pertaining to social justice and the distribution of wealth and power, are therefore understood by Christians as related to the divine summons operative in history. Christians look upon humanists and secularists who love justice and stand in solidarity with "the least of the breathren" as guided by the Spirit.

Paul Heyne: When I read or listen to John Yoder's analysis, I'm never quite sure whether I'm listening to proclamation or argument. I say this with great respect. I always wonder whether a transformation of mind is not required before I can appropriate what he's saying. I want to make a suggestion about the nature of the transformation of mind to which I sometimes feel myself called when I am listening to John Yoder.

I find it akin to something in the romantic movement. In Rousseau's *Discourse on the Origins of Inequality*, he talks about the savage, prior to the age of calculation, prior to his ability to recognize differences; he just reacted spontaneously to everything. I can understand Rousseau when he describes lying in the boat with the universe poring in upon him; there's a complete sense of trust, of letting go. One does not have to make provision any longer for life, because it is a gift. I can understand that. I'm wondering if I'm beginning to understand the witness of John Yoder's minorities when I struggle to understand this theme in romanticism.

Roger Hutchinson: Paul Heyne's transformation of mind doesn't have to be quite that radical. What I hear John Yoder talking about is a relativization of a utilitarian framework in which it is assumed that our ethical discernments are primarily cost/benefit analyses based on calculations of consequences.

I respond to this as a member of a Social Gospel tradition which emphasizes the importance of sound analysis. One can appreciate the role of social analysis in ethics and theology around the question of discerning what's going on. The way we retrieve our theological traditions is intimately tied up to what we think is going on. If we think we're on the verge of tyranny, we call forth symbols which are resources for the struggle for freedom. If we think we're on the verge of chaos, we call from our tradition sources for recovering order and stability.

I would take a slightly different but complementary angle to Richard Neuhaus's point about seeing the system whole and acting in relation to it. It's important to locate our efforts to see and to act in relation to the question of what is going on. As Gregory Baum was saying, you must always ask the questions: "Who are the winners, who are the losers? Which side are you on? Are you on the side of the rich or the poor? And what are the consequences of this kind of policy? Who will benefit? Who will lose?"

That in a way locates me in the conflict-oriented, socialist way of seeing society in terms of conflict and contradictions, and of choosing sides. There's another aspect of being contextual that the Mennonites have been reminded about by one of their own scholars. Calvin Redekop has written about Mennonites who came to North America to escape persecution and occupied lands that were empty. But the only reason the lands were empty is that the native Indians had been kicked off. The lesson he draws from this is that when one moves on to so-called empty land one should ask the question: "What happened to the previous occupant?" By forgetting to ask that question, the Mennonites could with a good conscience set up a world-denying colony.

Settlers live in the present moment, and say, "Oh good, the land is empty, we can have our little world-denying colony." But they are already caught up in social sin.

Imad Ahmad: In our discussion, there have been three answers to one interesting question. The question is "how does one acquire a just distribution of goods?" The moderate view is you do it without coercion, but you use coercion to defend yourself. This raised the objection: "Well what about aiding the poor? How do you enforce that, without coercion?"

Another view has been: "You need coercion in order to give the poor their due." That raises the question, "Aren't you in fact creating an unjust society because there's a violation of people's rights?"

What John Yoder has done is to present us with yet a third view which says, you don't need coercion at all. If someone wants to take away material goods, let them go ahead. To this, the objection has been raised: "That purifies you, but it's not going to change society." Henry David Thoreau said he thought it was not so important that everyone should be good but that there should be some good people somewhere. Perhaps they would leaven the whole lump.

Ellis Rivkin: Historically, it seems to make quite good sense to ask what are the consequences of an economic system for minority groups. After all, it was only in those areas where we see a beachhead of capitalism expanding through the grand capitalist revolutions, the revolt of the Netherlands, the Puritan revolution and the American revolution, that we find a variety of religious options. These followed from the right of the individual to choose, and opened up the possibility of complete eccentricity on the part of an individual. He could be totally and completely associated with nothing other than what he thought was needful for himself, without being punished on that account.

Actually, it is the expansion of capitalism, alone, that opened up the possibilities for these groupings to exist uncoerced. It is preeminently in the United States that the variation and the spread of every conceivable kind of religious option has flourished with relatively little interference on the part of the state.

This is not a matter of indifference. Capitalism opened up those wider radical options that no longer involve punishment and even death for articulating them.

On the other extreme, no Marxist state now in existence allows for those kinds of options. Then there are the intermediate systems which frequently may be called socialist, but really are not socialist in that they are mixed systems. They are heir to the constitutional freedoms that were generated by the expansion of capitalism. Frequently socialism is just another name for finding ways for keeping bankrupt industries alive.

Now within mixed systems there is space also for different kinds of groupings. Therefore, one cannot really be indifferent if one is involved in a minority confession, or a minority affirmation, as to which of these systems are more likely to allow living one's life to its end within one's profession.

James Sadowsky: A lot of people seem to think that you can have something like socialism and at the same time have with it the so-called bourgeois liberties, written in such documents as the Declaration of Independence. This is an illusion, as admitted by the prominent socialist, Robert Heilbronner, in a well-known article that appeared a couple of years ago in the magazine *Dissent*. He pointed out very clearly that there is an irreconcilable conflict between bourgeois liberties and socialism.

It's also interesting that many minority groups tend to think that somehow their salvation lies in embracing collectivism and socialism—the gays, feminists, and so forth. Yet the fact is when you talk about deviant lifestyles, all the so-called "sin cities" are in the capitalistic world. (laughter) I can't imagine anybody going to Peking or Moscow to have a wild time. (laughter)

Hanna Kassis: I don't know why when speaking of socialism one has always to choose the extremes of comparing the capitalist liberalism of North America with the extreme forms of socialism of either China or the Soviet Union. I throw in the case of France, which is currently, strictly socialist. Here, not only have the so-called capitalist liberties been preserved, they have been enhanced.

Under the capitalist regime of Giscard d'Estaing, the minorities that came from outside France had literally no rights. It was under the socialist regime of François Mitterand that they suddenly acquired rights.

Ellis Rivkin: In the case of France aren't we dealing with a mixed economy? It's not a socialist country in the sense that all the means of production are owned by the state. It has a vast realm of private enterprise. The nationalization is simply a way of dealing within inefficient industries. I don't see France as a socialist society simply because Mitterand happens to be a socialist.

James Sadowsky: There is another point that could be made with regard to France and Britain. If you take a society that is beginning to go socialist, you're going to have liberties as hangovers for ·a while. And it may be that people like Mitterand want these liberties to continue.

The question is, as things develop and become more and more socialistic, is there a necessity to restrict liberties? In England, for example, in the days of the Labour government, back in the 1950s, they almost got to the point where they had to forceably freeze people into jobs.

Anthony Waterman: They had direction of labour for about eighteen months.

James Sadowsky: They had to because the price mechanism was not allowed to induce people to take certain jobs. I don't think the slave camps in Russia are an accident. If Russia were capitalistic, people would be induced to go to Siberia by enormously high wages. Where the carrot is not allowed to operate, you have to use the stick.

Ronald Preston: Simple polarizations of total structures are most inadvisable in terms of how the industrial societies in which we live are to survive. None of them are working well.

Our "social market" economies are not dealing with long-term structured unemployment. There is no chance the ideal model of a free market economy will be set up for it is not politically practicable. Other socialist economies, or semi-socialist ones, have started not from a Marxist basis, but from a social democratic philosophy. The idea that they cannot possibly develop, that they must turn into a sort of Marxist collective, seems unproven and unlikely. We are faced with the problem of how to run advanced industrial economies when none of the existing models look convincing. This is the sixty-four thousand dollar question that faces Western industrial societies.

Richard Neuhaus: We've had a very generalized discussion, as though we had just met for the very first time, about the relative merits of capitalism and socialism. We're obviously not talking about John Yoder's paper. Maybe there's a reason for that. I was somewhat dissatisfied with my response to his paper. What Paul Heyne said rang true. It's not clear whether Yoder's paper is proclamation or argument. And, that's not said critically. The paper is a declaration over-against presuppositions with which most of us are operating in the discussion of democratic capitalism, socialism, etc.

In that sense, it is dramatically in contrast to Bob Goudzwaard's paper, where he is proposing a theologically grounded way of "norming," redesigning, or raising questions about the world in which we participate.

Yoder's tradition simply says that the world in which we are participating is not the real world. It's hard to know what to say to that. But in a sense, it's like a preacher when you've listened to a sermon. You can discuss the theology of it, and so forth. But the most appropriate response is not to sit around and analyze the merits and demerits of it. You pause and think about it. You've been challenged. It is a statement of a truth that has this kind of critical, over-against, character. And meditation is a response. Or one can decide: "I want to be part of that over-against community, that radical alternative."

Gregory Baum: In these discussions we have paid no attention to the role of eternal life or resurrection in one's view of divine salvation. Eternal life and resurrection are at the core of the Christian creed. What do they mean? The preaching of life after death can have quite different political consequences. If I focus on personal survival, on what happens to me, me, me, after I die, then Christian teaching encourages narcissism and indifference to the suffering of others. If I focus on the death of the other, the oppressed other, the masses of people, victims of hungers, wars, and genocides, then the doctrine of resurrection means that the victims of history will be vindicated by God. The oppressors shall not remain victorious over the innocent victim. God raised the crucified Jesus from the dead. With this emphasis the Christian teaching of eternal life enhances our social conscience, our compassion for others, and our hope that God stands with the downtrodden, the marginal, the discarded, even the dead.

Anthony Waterman: My paper used the Christian doctrine of eternal life and resurrection to justify a very large measure of social inequality and what might, pardon the phrase, be described as "social injustice." This is because it was going to be remedied hereafter: which is a different use of the term from Gregory Baum's.

Irving Hexham: I don't think Bob Goudzwaard and John Yoder are as different as they appear, if you look at the effects of their communal beliefs. Both proclaim the evils of our society and back up their critiques with academic study. But look at what happens to the people who read their books. I've had students who have used John

Yoder's books. They read them but they don't study them. His books set them alive. Then they go out and do something. The same effect occurs with Bob Goudzwaard's books. Students get a vision and they're off as activists. Its the vision which is important. The same thing occurs with Marxists. Young Marxists who read Marx, don't study Marx. Marx just sets them alight. This is a prophetic tradition.

Stephen Tonsor: In the 1870 Prussian campaign against France, there were French men out of uniform sniping at the German troops. They were rounded up and the question was asked of Bismarck what to do with them. Bismarck said, "Shoot them. I believe in eternal life." (laughter)

Arthur Shenfield: One of John Yoder's most important points is the parallel between Mars and Mammon. But it's faulty! If I follow Mars, by which I mean that the pursuit of war is the dominant purpose of my life, then inevitably I must harm my fellow men and ruin my own soul. But, if I follow Mammon, by which I mean the pursuit of wealth, it can well be that the only harm I do is to my own soul. I may not harm my fellow man. I may pursue the acquisition of wealth, follow Mammon, by serving the wants of my fellow men more abundantly than they have ever been served before!

I make a better mousetrap, and the world beats a path to my door. I do no harm to anybody else. I do harm to my soul if my ultimate and dominant purpose in making the better mousetrap is the acquisition of wealth. That can, of course, poison my life, and make it harder for me to get into heaven than for a camel to go through the eye of a needle.

The difference, then, between Mammon and Mars is very important. The network of human beings that makes a society can tolerate a great deal of Mammon. Society can in fact live with and even prosper with a great deal of Mammon, and still remain a very good society. But you cannot have Mars and a good society.

The history of the United States is precisely that. I would say that the United States is an example of one of the best societies in the world of the nineteenth century. It had a great deal of Mammon in it. But it couldn't have been one of the best societies if it had Bismarck in it and had been serving Mars.

Imad Ahmad: The making or the pursuit or the increase of wealth as the primary occupation of one's life does not, as long as one does it by just means, constitute anything wrong, or evil. However, I also think that it may be considered a kind of calling within the Calvinist tradition. It is only when one pursues Mammon by any means, regardless of justice, that one has elevated Mammon to a God, and one becomes a Mammonist rather than a Christian, Muslim or Jew.

Paul Heyne: At the beginning of this paper, John Yoder talked about trying to see the system whole, and he worries about that. It bothers me deeply, too, when people claim to be able to see the system whole. Tillich's phrase "self-sufficient finitude" haunts me. But the economist's task is to try to see the system whole. Am I caught in *hubris?* I think the answer depends upon what comes next, when you think you've seen the system whole. Do I play the engineer and try to adjust what I see to conform to what I would like to see, thereby inevitably coercing people and involving myself in all sorts of compromises? Or do I play educator, or storyteller, and recount what I think I see in the hope that people will act differently because of the story I've told?

I think that mainstream economists overwhelmingly take the first position. They don't fully recognize it, but their concepts clearly imply that they are engineers. They think their vision of the society qualifies them to prescribe adjustments. But there are some economists—I am one—who consciously reject that and say they are educators and storytellers.

John Yoder: The last thing Roger Hutchinson said about the Social Gospel pushed me back to something I didn't say as fully as I would have liked. The approach I'm supposed to be interpreting does think systemically. It is not atomistic or occasionalist. It looks at structures and their meanings. It doesn't claim the degree of knowledge that would authorize one to make one's decisions instrumentally, or consequentialistically, in the light of the overwhelming chance that things will get better because of what we do. But we want to see as much of system as we can.

Consider the discussion we had about whether seeking to see things whole would be "value-free" or not. This means that the adequacy of one's effort to see as much as one can, as whole as one can, will be correlated with one's recognition of the *limits* within which the propositions one makes are true. Even there, the modesty of the claim to wholeness is part of its authenticity. The willingness to be an educator instead of an engineer is one sign of that modesty.

I agree with what Steve Tonsor says about orthodoxy. The people I'm interpreting never agreed with the majority and the princes. They were only a prophetic minority. They always claimed to be reading the main tradition better than the people in power. That's a debatable claim, but that was their claim. They never granted that they were outsiders with just one string on their bow. If they made just one point in the given situation, it's because it was a situation in which other points were being made by other people, whereas they were being put to death for this particular issue, so it became rather important to them. They never said that the point that had pushed them out on the edge was the only truth. Usually, when they had the time to do it, they claimed that their stance was more faithful to the scriptural documents and the experience of the Church of the preceding centuries.

What of the notion that proclamation and argument are somewhat different moral modes? I think that is what we're debating, rather than a firm conclusion. If you categorize my argument as a proclamation, that's another way of not listening to it, by saying that you'll meditate on it but that you won't grant that it has any hold on your moral accountability. You listen to it, that means, the way you listen to a sermon rather than the way you listen to meaningful discourse. That polarity itself, sometimes phrased as between realism and idealism, is just another form of what we're debating about.

Capitalism is not the only way to have a society which is tolerant. One major example, from my very modest knowledge of history, is the way in which Islam, when living up to its ideals, made a stated place for minorities. Jews in early medieval Spain and Anabaptists in seventeenth-century Transylvania were better off under Muslims than they had been under Christendom.

When you are taken in as a refugee by somebody, you tend not to be as critical of your host's social ethics as of the people who chased you out. So it isn't just that Mennonites came into North America and settled on land that was taken from the native Indians. Mennonites did that already in the seventeenth century in eastern France, and again in the eighteenth in Russia. Being the favourite of the prince, because you are a minority that is productive and not threatening, is something that both Jews and Anabaptists have experienced through the centuries in different times and places. That's one of the besetting temptations of a minority hoping to survive.

Chapter 9

The World Council of Churches and Social and Economic Issues

Edward Scott

I have taken the liberty of changing one word in the title assigned to me. The original title was, "The World Council of Churches on Social and Economic Issues," and I have altered it to, "The World Council of Churches and Social and Economic Issues." The change was small, but it was deliberately made because it enables me to write and speak more directly from the perspective and integrity of the World Council of Churches, setting forth more adequately the nature and self-understanding of the World Council so that the social and economic statements made by the Council are seen in the context of its total work. It is only when they are so seen that they can be responsibly understood and evaluated. This is not done to avoid direct questions or criticisms, but as an attempt to deal with such criticism and questions more honestly.

The nature and development of the World Council of Churches

The World Council of Churches came into existence in 1948 following several decades during which a number of efforts were undertaken to bring Churches into closer relationship, following several centuries of increasing division. A key event in this process was the World Missionary Conference of 1910 from which followed three international emphases: the International Missionary Council, The Faith and Order Movement and The Life and Work Movement. In

1948, The Faith and Order, and The Life and Work Movements came together in the World Council of Churches. In New Delhi in 1961, the International Missionary Council became a member of the Council, to be joined in 1971 by the World Council of Christian Education and the World Sunday School Association.

In 1948 the one hundred and forty-six founding Churches came, for the most part, from Europe and North America. Only thirty were from Asia, Africa and Latin America. The founding Assembly took place amid the debris of war-torn Europe. It set forth a basis for membership and other Churches were invited to join. In 1961, after long deliberations, Orthodox churches in the socialist countries became members, and now some three hundred Churches from every continent, First World, Second World and Third World, belong. The Council includes Anglicans, Orthodox, Baptists, Reformed, Lutheran, Methodist, Pentecostal, Quakers, Moravians, Disciples, Old Catholic, and also many independent Churches from Africa and other areas of the developing world, coming from over one hundred countries. These member Churches "live and move and have their being" under virtually every political, economic and social condition in the world. The World Council of Churches is, therefore, a Council which has grown out of a variety of movements within and between Churches. It still retains aspects of a "movement," and enables representatives of this wide variety of Churches of widely different traditions which exist in a multiplicity of contexts, to meet and reflect together, to interact with each other and so be influenced by each other. The World Council of Churches is not a static but a growing entity, with a great complexity of dynamic factors influencing its life and development.

Basis for membership

The decision to be (or cease to be) a member Church of the World Council of Churches, must consciously be made by each Church. The founding Assembly determined a basis for membership which is continually reviewed in the course of the Council's life and work. The Council sees itself as: "A fellowship of Churches which confess the Lord Jesus Christ as God and Saviour according to the Scriptures and therefore seek to fulfill together their common calling to the glory of One God, Father, Son and Holy Spirit."

The Council is not, nor does it desire or intend to be, a "super Church." It is a Council or community of Churches, each with its own understanding of its authority and order, through which the member Churches search for an expression of visible unity and obedience through theological study, common encounter and joint ventures in witness and service.

Structure of the Council

The structure of the Council has grown, developed and been deliberately altered as the Council itself has grown and developed. The goal (and goals are always far easier to state than achieve!) is to develop structures which enable the Council to fulfil its basic purposes as effectively as possible in ever-changing world conditions. At present, the structure may roughly be represented in the following diagram.

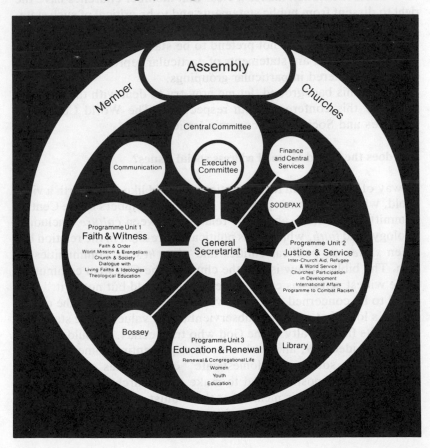

The diagram is useful because it reveals the wide scope of the work of the Council. This work is expressed in a variety of ways; through the addresses and actions of officers, staff, and members of Commissions and Units; through study documents; through reports of Units and Sub-Units; through conferences; through intensive study documents; through general publications, and through many types of public statements. The latter includes pastoral letters, messages from the presidents, and public statements issued by the Assembly, Central Committee and Executive Committee, and (between meetings of such bodies) by the General Secretary and/or Moderator of the Central Committee. The making of public statements by a body such as the World Council of Churches is a complex and very difficult process. The constitution makes it clear that member churches have the right to dissent from public statements and to be critical of such statements if this is felt to be necessary. This is a quite acceptable practice. The statements do not pretend to be statements of all the member Churches, but are statements of particular representatives of the Churches gathered in particular groupings.

Against this background, let me now try to deal with the question raised by this conference with respect to "The World Council of Churches and Social and Economic Issues."

How does the World Council address social issues?

By way of introduction to this section, I would like to set forth a view I hold, which I believe is generally shared by members of the Central Committee and staff, about the relation between *culture* (including ideology) and *faith;* which finds political expression in the relation between *states* as political entities and *churches* as communities of faith. The biblical view is that the church—the Christian community in the widest sense—is called to be "*in* the world but not *of* it." It is called to be concerned about the world as God's creation, the object of God's love; yet not to be subservient to the values of the state, but to offer its final loyalty to the God who transcends. I would contend that every ideology, and each state as representing some particular ideology, has sought to "domesticate" communities of faith to its own ideological position, and to make the Church a servant of its ideological needs. This means that there must always be tension between the State and the community or communities of faith. The degree of tension will depend upon many factors. But one of the most important is whether the state recognizes itself as accountable to that which transcends, or sets itself up as absolute, requiring final loyalty of its citizens. Since neither institutions nor persons can escape influence by the culture in which they live, it follows that Churches which make up the World Council, and representatives who form the Committees, Commissions, working groups, and staff of the World Council of Churches, will all be affected by the ideological climate of the time. It further follows that there will be tensions at World Council gatherings which arise out of the interplay between persons from different churches and from different political, economic and social systems. This interplay is found both within the various world communions, as they meet internationally, and also in the World Council of Churches. This is a very real part of the dynamic tension which is an ever-present element in World Council discussions of every kind, particularly discussions of social and economic issues. Such a dynamic is present in virtually every international gathering, such as the United Nations bodies. There is, however, a difference in the world communions and in the World Council of Churches. Here, there is a recognition that one's ultimate loyalty may never be given to a culture or to an ideology, but to God, the "I Am."

There is always a danger of separation between a theoretical position and its practical expression. The theoretical position of the World Council of Churches is that it addresses social and economic issues from the perspective of a belief in a transcendent God, who (the member churches of the Council believe) has revealed His Nature in terms that human beings can respond to, in and through Jesus Christ. How in practice does the World Council come to its positions and make public statements? How does it decide what issues to deal with and to make statements about?

Consultation and action

At each Assembly, issues are brought by the Churches, either through the work of the Units and Sub-Units or through formal representation by member Churches, for mutual consultation and action. When such issues are identified as being at the centre of the life and work of the Council, there is consultation with and between the Churches. At each Assembly, and at each meeting of the Central Committee, there are examples of business which have been introduced in response to interventions from particular Churches. Two such examples are racism at Uppsala and militarism at Nairobi. There is no special process by which political and economic issues are placed on the agenda. They are an integral part of the working procedure of the World Council of Churches. They arise out of the concerns of the member Churches. There have, inevitably, been changes in the kinds of issues which receive attention because of changes in the membership of the Council. When the Council was composed primarily of Churches from Europe and North America, the issues of central concern tended to come from those areas, and to be dealt with from the point of view of those areas. When Churches from the eastern European, socialist countries and churches from the Third World became members, new issues and new perspectives were introduced. The dynamics became more complex; the need for study, research and for dialogue in community became much more apparent. In some cases, new Sub-Units were created to attend to particular areas of concern. Statements which have political, economic and social implications can and do flow through all the Units and Sub-Units, but tend to come particularly through the Sub-Units on Church and Society, Inter-Church Aid, Refugees and World Service, the Commission on the Churches Participation in Development, and International Affairs, and from the Programme to Combat Racism. When Churches raise issues, they are usually referred for study and action to one of these Commissions for report to the Central or Executive Committees. The Central Committee has determined a number of criteria which guide the selection of matters to be placed on the agenda. These criteria include:

(1) Areas and issues on which the World Council of Churches has direct involvement and long-standing commitment;
(2) Emerging issues of international concern to which the attention of the Churches should be called for action;
(3) Critical and developing political situations which demand that the World Council make known its judgement and lend its spiritual and moral voice;
(4) Expectations of particular member Churches that the World Council should speak out;
(5) The need to formulate a policy-mandate for the World Council of Churches Secretariat.

If a statement is considered by the Central Committee, persons representing all parts of the world and all major Communions will have to vote on it. Here we get the interplay between different Churches and different political, social and economic orders. Such common statements are not easily achieved. There is a real effort to achieve consensus, to make a statement reflecting Christian insights that will be of value to the member Churches, to government agencies, and to the general public; while at the same time recognizing the situation in which member Churches have to live their lives. If at all possible, no statement is made without careful consultation with the Churches in the area whose life and work may be affected.

Sometimes some statement by the World Council of Churches is called for between meetings of the Central Committee and the Executive Committee. Such an occasion was the war over the Malvinas/Falkland Islands. Churches in both Argentina and Great Britain are members of the Council, and both expressed concern. A cable was sent to the General Secretary of the British Council of Churches communicating the contents of the message received from the Argentinian Churches, and adding the expression of concern on the part of the World Council of Churches. The British Churches were urged to keep in touch with their counterparts in Argentina. Since the World Council of Churches is a fellowship of Churches which transcends national boundaries, the attempt to achieve common witness in the social, economic and political realms can become particularly challenging and meaningful. At such times the words spoken at a provisional committee meeting at Utrecht in 1938 are tested: "We intend to stay together."

Quite apart from situations which require public statements, the very nature of the fellowship at the World Council of Churches requires careful monitoring of political and economic developments which affect the life and witness of the member Churches, and the lives of many persons outside the churches; all of whom, the Council believes, are made in the image of God and loved by God. It is not possible to express love for God without concern for the well-being of those whom God loves. Love of neighbour is an inextricable aspect of love for God. One cannot truly love one's neighbour without considering the impact of political and economic developments upon him.

"Lobbying" or "consensus?"

The question is often asked whether statements of the World Council of Churches represent a consensus among member Churches and/or their delegates, or whether they result from lobbying by activist Churches or individuals. This is, of course, a very important question. It needs to be answered on several levels.

One of the reasons for the existence of the World Council of Churches is to draw Churches into conversation with one another precisely on those points at which they do not agree. It follows, therefore, that most of the actions of statements of the World Council of Churches are directed to its member churches, and designed to engage them in further discussion and reflection, both within and among each other. The Constitution of the World Council of Churches, and subsequent explanations, make clear that only under very limited circumstances is the World Council of Churches entitled to speak or act on behalf of certain member Churches. Even a consensus of delegates could not necessarily be regarded as a consensus of member Churches. Consensus is an open and ongoing process and not the result of parliamentary voting.

This means that there may be occasions on which the World Council of Churches publicly raises an issue with its member Churches on which it is clear that no consensus exists as yet. Ecumenical discussion of controversial, social and political issues is not constrained by the consensus among member churches. It should also be added that churches are free at any time to refuse a challenge or to reject the advice or recommendation adopted by an official body of the Council.

At the same time, I know of no example where the World Council of Churches has spoken publicly without a broadly-based, prior discussion involving the member Churches. In fact, on all major areas of social and political concern, the World Council of Churches has continually attempted to arrive at an "ecumenical consensus" and has formulated a basic policy position either through Assembly or through the Central Committee, thus involving the appointed representatives of member Churches. Public statements of the World Council of Churches usually make explicit reference to this agreed policy base. Even where there are differences of opinion about the strategies of action, there is a considerable agreement in most cases on the nature of the issues involved. Before policy statements are made, therefore, we go through a process of careful consultation in which the Churches are involved. Examples of this are the positions on racism, militarism and human rights. In this connection, it should be noted that membership of the World Council includes Churches from East and West, North and South, who have been able to make common affirmations on these and many other issues which sometimes deeply divide the nations concerned. There is a process of free discussion which leaves enough room for individual Churches, groups of Churches or individuals who have particular concerns to bring these to the attention of the appropriate World Council bodies. In all these cases, the World Council of Churches provides a forum for the expression of different points of view, and any pronouncement usually is made only after attempts have been made to secure the support of the broadest possible majority of Churches or representatives concerned.

In the time that I have been Moderator, I would contend that lobbying (if it is meant in a pejorative sense) has been largely absent. Concerned Churches, groups and persons have the opportunity to raise issues for discussion and there is much very frank, direct, open debate; with ample provision where necessary for consultation between persons and groups in an effort, not always successful, to reach a common position.

Politics or the Gospel?

Another question which is often asked is whether the World Council of Churches attaches more importance to political and economic concerns than it does to traditionally ecclesiastical questions such as doctrine and worship, intercommunion, reunion, and mission. It has been my observation that this question is usually asked by those whose primary knowledge of the World Council of Churches comes from the secular press; or by those who take the position Richard Niebuhr classified as "Christ against culture" (that the Church should not be concerned about political or economic questions). There are people who are rightly concerned about an adequate balance. One of the purposes for the factual information about the World Council of Churches at the start of this paper was to indicate the wide range of its concerns. A review of its publications reveals clearly that the charge of concentrating on political and economic issues cannot be substantiated. It is true that the reports of the secular media might well give that impression. News coverage of addresses I give as Primate of the Anglican Church of Canada tend to focus on perhaps less than ten percent of what I seek to deal with in my presentations of the Christian calling today. This gives a very inaccurate view of my concerns. The problem arises partly from the media's definition of "news" and partly from my own failure of communication. It is very difficult to present information in a way that the media can use within the limitiations under which they operate. We need to develop alternative ways of communicating, in view of the fact that the secular media will never be adequately able to cover theological reflections on increasingly complex issues. I recognize that this is not a unique situation for Churches. Other segments of society face the same problem.

Another question which is raised in relation to the World Council of Churches concerns the range of theological points of view represented in its discussions of political and economic issues. This is complex indeed. Within each of the larger member Churches, there is a variety of theological viewpoints which is reflected within the World Council. Insofar as the various Churches also comprehend different theological viewpoints, these too are represented. It needs to be recognized however, that the scene is much more diverse than it used to be in the early days of the ecumenical movement. There are now few dominant theological schools. Even traditional Confessional theological positions have undergone significant change. We are in a period of theological reassessment with continuous dialogue between various traditional and contextual theologies. This dialogue influences the reflection on political and economic issues. It has led to the formulation of theological and ethical criteria which help the Churches evaluate and respond to social and political developments. Illustrations of this can be found in the guideline of the "responsible society." This has been further developed in the 1966 Conference on Church and Society In more recent times, stimulation has come from the "Humanism Study," from reflection on a "Just, Participatory and Sustainable Society," and on "Political Ethics." The World Council, therefore, is engaged in a continuous theological process of mutual questioning in which theologians and lay people from different Churches and different theological positions are involved as equal partners. This Council also seeks to involve representatives of non-member Churches, such as the Roman Catholic church and certain evangelical churches.

Representation

Questions are also asked about the principal political or ideological points of view which are represented in the Council's discussions. Since those involved in policy and decision-making bodies of the Council are official representatives of the member Churches, they are not chosen because of their political or ideological point of view. In fact they represent a very broad variety of political points of view, and the Churches they represent may also differ from one another in responding to particular political situations. Representatives come from different ideological backgrounds. Some may support and others disagree with the prevailing ideology of their particular country or government. As they engage in ecumenical dialogue, they are conscious of the fact that they speak and address one another primarily as Christians and as members of Christian churches, not primarily as representatives of particular nations or ideologies. It is with the recognition of their common commitment to Jesus Christ that they debate together, and often challenge each other. It would be a total misperception to identify members of the World Council of Churches governing bodies with particular ideological or political positions held by their states or governments. It is the freedom received in Christ that has made it possible for this fellowship of Churches to deal with some of the most difficult political and ideological differences of our time, and to speak to them as one body.

As Moderator of the Central Committee, I often am told that the statements of the World Council of Churches have a political bias, one way or another. Some people I meet, particularly in parts of the United States, make charges of a bias towards the political left. Others I meet in Europe accuse the Council and its statements of bias towards the political right. Many people in the under-developed world say that the statements are biased in favour of the developed world. Still others from the developed world say the Council's statements are biased in favour of the under-developed areas. In developing its statements, the Council seeks to combine three elements:

(1) insights from biblical witness;

(2) experiences of the Churches and the ecumenical movement;
(3) the best available social and political analysis.

The Constitution of the Council contains a reference to statements:

> While such statements might have great significance and influ-
> ence as the expression of the judgement or concern of so widely
> representative a Christian body, yet their authority will consist
> only in the weight which they carry by their own truth and wis-
> dom.

The Council recognizes that the views expressed will only have
real value if they contain truth and wisdom. They are not designed to
express ideological views, but to assist in the discovery of deeper insights into truth. There are those who suggest that a deliberate effort
should be made to ensure that such statements represent a "balance"
from a political point of view. If this were consciously done, then the
Council would be failing in its primary responsibility: to seek to be
true to its theological insights. It would, in fact, cease to be primarily
a "community of faith" and tend to become more of a "political
movement," therefore deny its own integrity. I think it is to be expected that the Council will receive criticism from every side. It
should take criticism seriously but evaluate and respond from the
basis of its own integrity, recognizing that the questions asked say as
much about the person or group questioning as they do about the
body being questioned. If a paper such as this were to be prepared at
the request of a body in a socialist country or in the Third World, I believe the specific questions they would put would differ in many
cases. They would reflect the political context or political viewpoint
in which the questions arise. This is quite understandable and the
Council should seek to respond, again from its own integrity.

Christian theology and social criticism

To ask if statements flow from a theological or from a political position is, I think, to misunderstand the essential inter-relationship of
basic concepts. Justice and righteousness, which are central biblical
words, have theological, political, social and economic implications.
The task of theological reflection is to link these implications into an
integrated whole, which is very difficult. We must therefore reject a

distinction between theological, economic or political arguments. It is concern for justice and righteousness, and the recognition of persons as relationship beings made in the image of God, that leads to critical analysis. Both the current capitalistic, and the dominant state socialist models of social and economic organization are found wanting. The World Council has so far refused to espouse any particular political, social or economic system as being the ideal expression of Christian ethical conviction. I believe it will continue to do so.

What does seem to be developing in the ecumenical dialogue is the raising of questions that are directed at the major political and economic ideological system of our time. These questions focus attention upon a deeper question which churches in all parts of the world need to address: to what extent has the Church in your part of the world become domesticated by the culture, and ceased to be leaven, salt or light?

There seems to be a growing feeling that neither the capitalist market economy nor the state/socialist approach are adequate to the challenges of our time. If this be so, if Toynbee's interpetation of history is correct, civilization as we know it may not survive. Let me be more concrete. What are some of the challenges which are not being met? Again, I want to put this in question form.

Is the capitalist, market economy proving able to close the widening gap between rich and poor among (and also within) nations? Is the consumer society which has resulted from capitalism responding adequately to the growing shortage of non-renewable resources, or has it become a society of waste? Is it satisfying the deepest needs of human beings and commanding their loyalty?

Is the state/socialist approach proving able to deal with the basic needs for food for the people over whom it holds sway? Is it proving able to address the issues of human dignity and human rights? Is it able to provide that freedom which is essential if human beings are to experience life in all its fullness?

Is either economic system demonstrating an ability to respond to the world-wide ecological crisis which is causing increasing concern? Is either able to respond to the madness of the increasing militarization of our world, with its misuse both of human and other natural resources?

The raising of questions like these within the World Council lead us to believe it should be inviting and challenging people in all parts of the world, particularly Christians, to work together for a new approach that will lead to an international order more closely approximating the ideal expressed in the Lord's Prayer, "Thy will be done on earth as it is in heaven."

Closing reflections

I recognize that I have set forth up to this point a view of the self-understanding of the World Council of Churches that readers may feel is far too idealistic. It is also the self-understanding of the member Churches and of the Council. All human beings are sinful: we all rebel against God, break covenant with our neighbours, and fail to be what we were meant to be. The World Council of Churches knows that it has weaknesses because it is made up of fallible Churches. Philip Potter has expressed it this way:

> We have sometimes made wrong-handed decisions for which we had to pay the price. We have, in the midst of conflict, sometimes hurt people one way or the other and we have had to learn how to be more patient—but patient in an impatient way, if you see what I mean. (*What in the World is the World Council of Churches?* p. 12.)

The World Council of Churches should continue to invite open dialogue and discussion with concerned groups, both within the Council and with groups outside the Council. There is a great need to learn "the difficult art of relating to each other honestly and frankly, without pulling moral rank."

This means being open to, and welcoming the process of, challenge and response; and encouraging open dialogue about issues of concern. It is for this reason that I am grateful for the opportunity to participate in this symposium.

Comment

Peter J. Hill

The paper by Archbishop Scott contains an interesting account of the rationale and mechanism by which the World Council of Churches considers social and economic issues. I find myself in basic agreement with almost all that Scott says in the paper; but suspect that if we went on to discuss the details of the World Council's position on various social and economic issues we might be in substantial disagreement.

I agree with the statement that, as a Christian, "one's ultimate loyalty shall never be given to a culture or to an ideology but to God, the 'I am.' " I also agree that such a commitment clearly points to the necessity of making decisions about culture and society. A concerned Christian should take a stand on social and economic issues, and his stand should be biblically-based.

However, in discussions such as this it is much more interesting to focus on areas of disagreement than agreement, hence I will attempt to do just that. I say "attempt" because it is not completely clear from Archbishop Scott's paper whether we are in disagreement or not, for he chooses neither to defend nor reject the World Council's position on economic and social issues. Faced with a lack of evidence I venture forth boldly, assuming that if these comments are not applicable to the Archbishop's position, they will be of some interest in discussing the position of the World Council.

Scott states that the World Council "addresses social and economic issues from the perspective of a belief in a transcendent God, Who (the member Churches of the Council believe) has revealed His Nature in terms that human beings can respond to in and through Jesus Christ . . . " As one who also holds that position, I find in that statement much clearer guidance with regard to economic and social issues than, it would seem, most of the member churches of the World Council. In the rest of my comments I will indicate how certain principles of political economy flow from such a belief, and consider the relevance of these to the basic issues of our day.

(1) To say that man is created in the image of God means to me that individuals are of infinite worth, are responsible, moral agents capable of rational choice, and as such will be held responsible for their choices. The integrity of the God-created individual means that no one has the right to control or coerce another person, except to prevent coercion. God sees all people as of equal value, and for one person to make decisions for another is to violate that equality and that sphere of influence in which God holds the individual responsible for his actions. The Bible illustrates this well inasmuch as it is basically a narrative of man's choices and God's response to those choices. However, for man's choices to have moral significance they must be uncoerced. They must represent a decision between real and feasible alternatives. Therefore, a basic issue in judging the moral quality of a society is the degree to which freedom of choice is allowed. A casual reading of Council's statements leads me to doubt whether they see the freedom of the individual as important in evaluating the moral worth of a society. Their silence about societies that are extremely coercive would imply that the degree of coercion is not a significant issue.

The foregoing does not lead to the conclusion that to be free is to be good. That clearly is antithetical to the Christian position. God's law sets out standards of right and wrong that man can choose between. I believe that choosing God's ways will lead to a more stable society of happier individuals. However, the issue at hand here is freedom of choice. God gives man that freedom. We should grant it to our fellow human beings.

(2) If part of the essence of humanity is freedom of choice, this has important implications for property rights. Without individual property rights the whole concept of a God-created individual, choosing and being responsible for his choices, is meaningless. The right to oneself implies the right to own property, to transfer it, and to dispose of it as one sees fit. To be free from coercion by others also means one is free from the claims of others on one's property. The World Council makes little distinction between societies where private property rights are respected and those where they are not.

(3) I see a clear distinction between our responsibility as followers of God to our fellow human beings, and the moral duty of the state to enforce those responsibilities. Consider, for example, the issue of

poverty. The Bible is extremely clear about our responsibility to care for the less fortunate. However, the step from arguing that individuals have a responsibility to care for their brothers and sisters to arguing that the state should *enforce* that responsibility is a large one. It is perfectly consistent to believe that those who are wealthy should share their wealth and also to believe that the state should have no power to redistribute wealth. God wants a free and loving response to His commands. To coerce obedience to His standards is to remove moral significance for actions, and God places great significance upon the act of choosing to follow or ignore His standards. One must also remember that mandatory redistribution of wealth is usually achieved only by the concentration of coercive power in the hands of a select group. To trust such power to a few means one has to trust the willingness to do good of those with power.

(4) Another theological principle becomes relevant to social issues at this point: man's fallen nature. The Garden of Eden story relates how man fell from his state of purity to one in which he became sinful, self-centred, and very much concerned with his own welfare. The rest of the Old and New Testaments develop the theme of man's alienation from God, and his consequent selfish nature. Christianity, of course, does argue that through the atoning sacrifice of Jesus Christ, man can be reconciled to God and can overcome that selfishness. However, the Bible makes it clear that even when man is in proper relationship with God there will be a continual tension between the old nature and the sinful, selfish self which will dominate for much of the time.

In view of this basic inability of mankind to act consistently in a way that is not self-centred, it seems appropriate to construct an institutional order which recognizes it. If man is selfish, if he does spend a great deal of his time concerned with his own welfare, and if he does find it difficult truly to stand in another's shoes, the basic rules of society must take account of these facts. A successful society must constrain man's selfish behaviour and encourage him to act for the good of other people. Egoism run rampant is clearly inimical to a stable society. A free society, based upon markets and private property rights, is an institutional order that takes account of man's sinful nature. It recognizes that people do not always behave for the good of others unless constrained, and it provides mechanisms for individuals to cooperate while pursuing their own ends. The price system effectively identifies areas in which selfish people can make one another better off, and market exchanges of private rights enable people to help others in achieving their goals, even while pursuing their own. Much of the World Council literature seems to deny the basic fact of man's fallen nature, and trusts instead to human institutions that assume that man is basically good rather than evil. If mankind is by nature sinful, we must be as careful to design social structures that limit our ability to harm each other as to give ourselves the potential for good. The amassing of coercive power in the hands of the state has been one of the most oft-used tools of violating God's commands about our responsibility to our fellow creatures.

(5) In respecting the integrity of the individual, the Christian should recognize that freedom of choice will mean a great deal of diversity in society. Because of the divergent mores, ethics, and values in any society, the fewer decisions which require social consensus the less strain on that society. Most collective decisions are made by majority rule. This implies that there will always be a dissatisfied minority. In order to reduce the number of dissatisfied minorities and to ease the strain on the social fabric, it is necessary to limit collective decision-making. For instance, in the United States today there is a continuing controversy over what should be taught in public schools concerning the origin of our species and our planet. The evolutionist-creationist debate is an interesting public policy issue only if we have public schools. If education were privately financed and privately controlled, we would not have to debate the "correct" view of our origins, any more than we would have to decide the "correct" position on diet, vegetarianism or non-vegetarianism. Again, I find distressing the World Council's willingness to trust the collective decision-making mechanism for so many of our choices.

Furthermore, the free society that I am arguing for here assumes no universal set of goals on the part of its members. It allows individuals to choose those goals and then respects their choices. One can disagree with those choices but still prefer the society that allows them. For instance, there is much in capitalism that I find inimical to Christian values. In a free society however, I and others of like mind, can choose to order our lives around the ethical standards we believe in. That option is not so easily achieved in a coercive society.

Now, with reference to Archbishop Scott's paper, it may appear that I think there is clear-cut positions that the World Council of Churches should take on all social and economic issues. But I do not think it is quite that simple. There are many fuzzy issues, even if one accepts the basic theological positions and their implications for social policy that I have put forth. I am most sympathetic to the difficulty of reaching a consensus among people of varied backgrounds and cultures. However, since as Archbishop Scott states, there is a common adherence in the World Council of Churches to a basic belief in a God-centred universe, there should follow from that certain basic premises about the role of the state, the importance of the individual, and the primacy of freedom of choice. I also recognize that many Christians who share the same basic theological positions as I, may not find the implications of those positions so obvious as I have argued in these remarks. However, I offer my views as a starting point for comment and discussion.

Discussion

Edited by: Irving Hexham

Ted Scott: I was concerned to study the nature and development of the World Council of Churches (W.C.C.) because I think very often it is condemned for being something it was never intended to be. The W.C.C. never takes a position on socioeconomic issues in the same way as the Roman Catholic church. By the very nature of things, the Council has wide variations. And those variations have increased since its formation in 1948.

When it was formed in 1948, the W.C.C. consisted primarily of churches from western Europe and the United States. Since that time, the Orthodox family of churches and more of the independent churches from the so-called Third World have joined.

Now with these developments there are some new dynamics. First of all, from the Orthodox side there are links with the pre-Reformation history of the Church. The liturgy and the spirituality of the East now interacts with churches from the West. We also have churches that are based and live, have to live, in Russia.

Now if we say that the Christian faith is transcendental, that its concerns are over and above the political situation, you have to ask what they have to try to stand for and work for in that context. You can't make an absolute judgement about something only in terms of the Western context when you're dealing with that kind of ecumenical situation.

The other new factor is the Third World. Churches there were formed largely under the impact of the Western Churches, but have appropriated the Christian phase out of their cultural context, with the biblical record as their primary textbook.

For most of us in Western Christianity, Christendom was formed by the whole library of classical theology. But Christians in the Third World have not had that classical tradition. So their primary textbook is the Bible.

They also deal with the Bible in a different context. They haven't dealt with it in a framework where it was used in a particular way by the Church of the Reformation, against Roman Catholics. So it speaks to them much more directly.

In fact, they raise some serious questions. Now, one of the theological debates is whether or not much of Western Christendom is not syncretism between biblical and philosophical thought, where weak philosophical thought won over biblical thought.

Most of us don't travel in those areas and are not exposed to these kinds of dynamics. That's what's taking place in much of the discussion of the W.C.C.

So when they come out with positions they are for study. They set forth an analysis in a struggle to understand. Then their considerations are presented to the churches for study.

I've been concerned since I've been Moderator that we make far fewer pronouncements and far more attempts to analyze a situation. We need to share insights so that people can grapple with them and create a consensus.

In the context of the W.C.C. public statements are questions. The interaction of the discussion is very complex, as is the interplay of factors.

A number of fundamental questions are raised. What has happened to the interplay between the Orthodox, Third World and Western Christians? How much of our expression of the Christian faith is inherently based on the nature of the faith? How many of our beliefs have been conditioned by the cultural context in which we have grown up and appropriated the faith?

We are trying to stand back from being locked into the cultural situation of being in the world and also of the world; to see where the faith elements that you hold set you in tension with the cultural context in which you live.

In this process, through the ecumenical dialogue, I think churches in all parts of the world are beginning to question their cultural contexts. Now some cultural contexts are much easier to question than others. One of the real joys and positive aspects of the culture in which we live is the freedom to criticize. I take this to be a fundamentally important freedom. Maybe the W.C.C. hasn't made clear enough its respect for the freedom to criticize. The W.C.C. is now posing some questions directly at the market economy approach in terms of some of the unanswered problems that now confront it. It is also posing some very direct questions about the socialist approach. It is raising questions about both ideological approaches. It seems to me that neither the market economy nor the operations of socialist countries have come to terms with the ecological issue. Look at some of the serious factors regarding the ecological situation. There is still an inability in the market system and socialist states to be able to respond effectively to the ecological crisis.

The other questions that neither socialism nor capitalism are responding to effectively are the use of human and natural resources and militarism. It seems to me we have problems that need to be grappled with. So the World Council raises some of the questions.

We must also do some solid thinking about what's involved in the process of coercing. How do we interpret coercion? It's very easy to see it clearly within socialist structures. But is that the only form of coercion?

I believe in both the Golden Rule and the Iron Rule. The Iron Rule is that you should never do for another person what he or she can do for themselves. You should help people to be independent and self-reliant. We are coercing any time we build dependencies which take away from the people the "right" to be responsible. There's a lot of coercion in our society in terms of both government activity and company activity.

Let me give an illustration. I worked on a mission boat running out of Prince Rupert when I was first ordained. That was the time when the Japanese were removed from the coast and there was a shortage of fishermen. The Indian people, who had not been as popular as fishermen because they weren't as systematic, as dependable as the Japanese, were in demand.

Then a problem arose. How do you keep the Indian people accountable to the cannery where they worked. The system was developed of giving them unlimited credit, and encouraging them to buy all kinds of things. So, if they went away at the end of the season owing the company money, it meant they had to come back and work for the company next year. Is that coercion?

Is it coercion to move into the homes of people in a different culture with our modern technology, to invade their privacy and family values with a whole set of alternative values? The view that life will not be full unless you have a particular product, or service is thus created by radio and television. These media often undermine traditional values by promoting greed and unnecessary consumption.

This is a religious interpretation because it says that the fullness of life consists in the things that you possess and own. That's the subtle religious message that comes over television. And that's now being focused time and time again on native Indian and Eskimo families throughout this continent.

Roger Hutchinson: A quick point on the nature of decision-making. In spite of the public's fears, P. J. Hill said that decision-making is consensual in the private sphere and coercive in the public sphere. I don't find that very credible. When INCO decided to move it's earnings from Sudbury to another town, the INCO workers in Sudbury didn't feel they had participated in that decision.

I think that there is a kind of careless rhetoric being used. Those kinds of gross distinctions claiming coercion in the public sphere and non-coercion in the private sector are not helpful.

Gregory Baum: In this dialogue I have only spoken of the Roman Catholic tradition. Yet this is only one Christian tradition among others. Anglicanism and Protestantism have also produced significant movements of social concern. I have great admiration for the World Council of Churches and its religious option to become the voice of the poor, the voiceless, the people pushed to the margin.

Roman Catholicism always stressed the common good above the private good. This corresponded to the vision of society entertained by the feudal order. Protesting against medieval religion, the Reformation often put great emphasis on the person and personal freedom. In an indirect manner this encouraged the individualism that was to spread in Western civilization in recent centuries. Reacting against this, Anglican and Protestant churches generated religious movments that emphasized the common good, the well-being of all, and preached the gospel of social responsibility. The W.C.C. has taken up this Anglican and Protestant heritage. Because the W.C.C. is in solidarity with the former colonies of Western empires and with the marginal classes and peoples everywhere in the world, it has recently come under attack. In the present, all groups, religious and secular, which advocate the redistribution of wealth and power find themselves attacked as the enemy, as subversive forces. "Blessed are those," Jesus said "who hunger and thirst after justice. Blessed are those who are persecuted for justice's sake, for theirs is the reign of God."

John Yoder: A World Council of Churches Assembly is the nearest thing I know to a high society. (laughter) It's a marketplace of six to eight hundred people who have a week together. They thrash their ideas around and make the most pertinent objections to what a small drafting committee working through the night thought most of the people would find tolerable. Whether that's a good way to work or not is a subject for separate debate. But at least it does not mean that the staff or the responsible decision-making agencies that work through the years, or all the churches, have made that statement. That document is a sounding board from the present mixed mind of the churches of the world. As such it is very valuable. But it is not a statement.

Susan Feigenbaum: How does the decision process of the W.C.C., with its emphasis on consensus, yield doctrine which is independent of time, situation or state?

John Yoder talked a little about this process, and I found it very impressive. But I also question whether it can yield doctrine which is independent of an individual's current circumstances. I hope I won't be mischaracterizing Islam or Judaism in stating that their basic tenents are independent of time and place. Therefore, I would respond to

John Yoder as follows: some religions say there is a correct position, that should not simply be determined by consensus or some kind of political decision process. Rather there are some truths above circumstances.

P. J. Hill: This discussion ignores a basic fact that somebody's in control of property. When you say that a decision is made by all, that seems to me like saying somebody else will do it. Nor will it help to call upon state decision-making. First of all, we can't assume a benevolent government. Secondly, only individuals can make property decisions, even if as part of government action.

Stephen Tonsor: In primitive societies, as Sir Henry Maine recognized in the nineteenth century, individual private property does not exist. It is the group collectively which possesses the property. The movement from custom to contract is a general movement in the development of modern societies. It was most marked in English writers in the nineteenth century who went out to India.

It's quite clear that property rights are a recent development of sophisticated modern societies. But that doesn't mean that this is not a superior way of organizing a society which gives an enclave of protection to freedom.

Roger Hutchinson: I'd like to know what Ted Scott thinks about the allegation that the W.C.C. ignores basic questions about the ownership of property. How does it relate to the way the W.C.C. actually relates to these issues?

Ted Scott: When you get into the situation of the W.C.C. taking some stand in relation to aboriginal rights you are dealing with property rights. If you are going to talk about property rights, at what point does ownership of the property begin? Is it by right of conquest?

If you are going to individual freedom and property and link those things tightly together, it seems to me you have to rethink the starting point in the situation. We are struggling with that in the world pattern. Can we go on with the kind of economy we've got on the basis of the private ownership of property? Or are we going to have to find some other way of dealing with the property situation?

The W.C.C. is trying to reconcile theories of property with the reality of the situation now. If we take seriously what we say, we have a right, a responsibility, to make contracts with aboriginal peoples. The original inhabitants of the land.

Richard Neuhaus: The W.C.C. is terribly important as bearer of the ecumenical quest for more visible Christian unity. But, I've also been very critical of it. In the current *Reader's Digest* (August 1982), there is an article on the W.C.C.'s social and political viewpoints which is highly polemical, but not unfair. The W.C.C. sent out a release to refute this article. They list some of the people who are quoted and allege that they have very vicious right-wing backgrounds and therefore are not to be taken seriously.

When they get to Richard John Neuhaus they could not say that. Instead, they say, "He is a persistent critic of the W.C.C." Period. That's enough to dismiss me because this is a community in which there is a Christian consensus for which dissent raises serious problems. I think it is a community that represents no consensus at all of any spiritual or intellectual significance. To say this is not to morally indict the individuals involved. It is in the very structure of the W.C.C.

A large part of Ted Scott's explanation has to do with the engagement of the Third World. And that this has been a new phenomenon.

But this, in fact, is not true. The majority of Christians in the Third World—Asia, Africa and Latin America—do not belong to churches which arc members of the World Council. What we have here is a classic exercise of a bureaucratic manipulation of some mythological reality, called the "Third World viewpoint." Several years ago I attended a World Council consultation in Switzerland where we spent several days on the question of multi-nationals. There were only two of us out of thirty who even thought that multi-nationals might not be unqualifiedly evil. And one such happened to be a bishop from Nigeria—very black, very indigenous, very much a native person. He gave what I thought, at least in that context, was a relatively sober and balanced statement about the negative and positive aspects of having multi-nationals operate in your country (in his case, Nigeria).

The moderator was white, European, male—and a bureaucrat of the World Council. After the bishop spoke, and had given this rather moderate, balanced statement, he said, "Very interesting, Bishop, very interesting viewpoint. That's a fine contribution. Now I wonder if we could hear a Third World viewpoint?'' (laughter) And then he pointed to a Tanzanian friend of his, whom he knew would come along with the right line.

So I cannot agree with Ted Scott's explanation the W.C.C.'s dissent from, indeed propaganda against, Western, capitalist, democratic values.

Now for another point. Ted Scott asks: Is the consumer society satisfying the deepest needs of human beings? I ask: Can any society meet all human needs? Should any society aspire to? ''Thou has made us for Yourself, oh Lord, our hearts are restless until they rest in Thee.'' Once one has accepted this viewpoint, inevitably, every society must be condemned. But just as inevitably, the only societies that will be condemned are those societies where people are free to condemn. Which is to say, our kind of society.

It is this fact that so fundamentally skews the social and political witness of the W.C.C. much to the detriment of its important and theologically mandatory mission as a genuinely global, ecumenical vision.

Roger Hutchinson: I've had some involvement with the church and society department of the World Council of Churches. Of course there are difficulties with its methodology and organization. The W.C.C. is not exempt from the difficulties all organizations have. It has the same sort of problems and the same blemishes as other large organizations.

It would be absolutely stupid to pretend otherwise. So let's take that for granted. There are going to be some flaws. But, the most important point is that ecumenical groups of people are brought together and the agenda is no longer set by the relatively well-off white churches. The W.C.C. does reflect worldwide opinion. Its leaders are not manipulating its members. The way the West thinks of things is no longer simply accepted by people of Third World countries. You don't get a consensus. It's impossible to expect the W.C.C. to reach a consensus. What it can usually do, and does rather well, is to state which issues are bothering people, and which things people really feel strongly about.

Then you can usually find a method where the major approaches to these questions are stated. Then you can say to the people: ''What are the questions that you want to address to your fellow Christians?

Have you listened to what your fellow Christians in other parts of the world, who may take another view, are saying about this? Have you done justice to their views?''

Imad Ahmad: On the matter of rights and duties. The negative right, my right not to be aggressed upon, implies that you have a duty not to aggress against me.

If you do not fulfil your duty, that is to say, if you aggress against me, I am entitled to use coercion to rectify the consequences of that aggression. If you don't fulfil such duties, that is, if you initiate violence, I may use force against you. So much for negative rights. Now consider positive rights. If you as a Christian have a duty to do positively such-and-such, then I may use coercion against you to get you to fulfil your duties. Ultimately, this leads to the kind of situation I think we are trying to avoid.

In regard to Ted Scott's list of possible forms of coercion, some of those cases involve offers. You have to be very careful and not call an offer ''coercion.'' An offer is always a situation where the person receiving the offer is, at worst, indifferent to the fact that he has received the offer. And possibly may be grateful for it. It's not proper to call that a form of coercion.

Jim Sadowsky: No person has the right to control or coerce another person except to prevent coercion. But I find objectionable the argument that a lot of libertarians use to support this statement. Libertarians claim that for men's choices to have significance, they must be uncoerced. That is, they must represent a decision between a real and a feasible alternative.

I think that is false. Your ability to gain merit, if I may use that term, or to be responsible for your choices, exists as long as it is possible for you to do the thing that you are asked not to do. The mere fact that the alternative is an unpleasant one, such as going to jail and being put to death, does not mean that you don't have a choice. It doesn't follow that there is no real moral activity.

The fact that I know that I should go to jail if I'm caught stealing, does not entail that my refusal to steal in the face of temptation is not virtuous. I can have an additional motive of refraining from stealing over and above the fear of going to jail. I don't see that in order to remove the possibility of it being a moral action, it would have to erase completely my freedom to resist.

I think it's a bad argument for not engaging in coercion. It doesn't become any better because it's commonly used.

Walter Block: It is claimed that the free market creates problems like pollution of the environment, monopoly, booms and busts, structural unemployment, inflation, etc. But in each and every one of those cases, it can be shown that this is the result not of the operation of the marketplace, but rather of government interferences with the operation of free enterprise.

In the 1840s in the United States of America, a series of ecological cases were addressed by the courts. In a typical scenario a train was spewing forth smoke and sparks, and setting the farmer's haystack on fire. Or the manufacturer was polluting and getting some women's laundry dirty.

In each of these cases, the plaintiff brought suit for an injunction against the perpetrator for nuisance, or violation of property rights. And in each case the court said, in effect, "Yes, yes yes. We agree that these are violations of private property rights; however there is something much more important than mere private property rights, and that is the public good."

This "public good," of course, consisted of subsidizing manufacturing. The courts gave manufacturers a *carte blanche* to pollute without any payment, without any limits; without any necessity to pay off people for these rights, or to homestead these rights. As a result, industry became biased toward these pollution-intensive manufacturing techniques.

Had the decision of the judiciary been in keeping with the appropriate private property rights of the plaintiffs in the first place, our industry would have been unbiased. It would have taken into account not only internal costs, but external ones as well. So to say as does Ted Scott that the pollution problem is the result of the unhampered operation of the marketplace is erroneous.

Now let us consider Ted Scott's attempt to redefine coercion so as to include offering credit to native peoples, or advertising new products and services to them. Coercion used to mean "physical invasion." In its new definition, it means advertising, or offering options, or what have you. I would suggest that this is an improper extension of the word "coercion."

If you want to use "coercion" for these new meanings, fine. But let us please keep in mind that this is a deep and serious departure from what it meant originally.

For example, take giving people credit. I think that granting credit is an ancient and honourable marketplace transaction; and I cannot see how this is akin to physical aggression. Nor can I see how advertising can be considered invasive for entering a home and offering alternative values. This is just offering people new options. This is the way we learn of new things. This is what civilization is all about. Are we to forbid this, on penalty of jail sentences (as would be appropriate for real coercion for those who seek to introduce native persons to new goods and services? Hardly.

Then there is a matter of hypocracy. Consider church advertising. Let's face it, commercial entrepreneurs are not the only advertisers. Advertising is not limited to McDonald burgers, autos, soft drinks and soaps. Religious institutions also advertise. We have spoken out in favour of freedom to criticize, and we're all in favour of freedom of speech. Well then, advertising is no more than an exercise of free speech.

Now let me address Roger Hutchinson's example of INCO moving from Sudbury to Guatemala. He characterizes this as coercive. Well, it might be coercive in this new sense of the word; but it's certainly not coercive in the old invasive sense. All it is, really, is a refusal to continue to deal with certain people. If Mr. A refuses to dance with Miss B at the Senior Prom, he is as guilty of physical invasion as INCO in moving away from Sudbury—namely, not at all.

It's a perversion of the word "coercion" to say that a refusal to deal with a person is coercive. All INCO did was pick up its own private property and take it where it thought it could earn the greatest return. Would Roger Hutchinson condemn as coercive a worker for leaving INCO to find a better job in order to increase the rate of return on his human capital? Hardly. Moreover, people in Guatemala are poorer than the people in Sudbury; so on the grounds of equality, or narrowing gaps between rich and poor, that should be considered a positive step.

Ellis Rivkin: Walter Block has brought up an issue that we have not sufficiently taken into account; that is, that by the very nature of the capitalist system, capitalists continuously find themselves competing with other capitalists. Therefore the good of one sector, let's say the manufacturing sector, and what the state ought to do on its behalf, comes into a conflict with the welfare of the homesteader, and so on.

I think there are two issues here. One is, what is the role of the state in relationship to competing capitalist interests that have to be adjudicated within the system? The second is that there is inherent within capitalism the conflict between the drive of individual capitalists to maximize their profits, and the interest of the capitalist system as a whole. There is the inherent danger that the pursuit of an individual sector's goals could, if successful, eliminate the continuation of capitalism per se.

Therefore, what is the role of the state in adjudicating the two claims? The state represents the generality and in this instance should have supported the interests of capitalism per se. That means to have decided for the homesteader as against the polluters.

P. J. Hill: With regard to Ellis Rivkin's question, it seems to me that the whole idea of a well-defined set of negative rights, coupled with the principle of nonaggression, does lend some guidance. There are some very clear guidelines that tell us when we (and the state) are acting appropriately. And it's not just a question of whose rights. I think there are some principles that can be laid out that do give some pretty clear guidance about that, namely, private property rights.

Clark Kucheman: I am bothered by the assumption here that once we know what the Christian way is, we know how we ought to organize our society. And I'd like to suggest that maybe we should have a good word for secular humanism.

Hanna Kassis: P. J. Hill said:

> It is perfectly consistent to believe that those who are wealthier than the norm should share their wealth with those who have less but also to believe that the state should have no power to redistribute wealth.

He goes on to say:

> Remember, again, that God wants a free, loving response to His commands.

I think this is a marvellous idea—a perfectly marvellous idea, if you happen to be on the wealthier side. But, if you happen to be on the side of the poor, and hungry, I don't really think you can wait until the divine miracle happens, and the wealthy change their minds and give willingly. That's why I think there has to be an authority, such as the state, to see to it that wealth is distributed, even by coercion, if need be.

Roger Hutchinson: I didn't pick up earlier on the coercion question because that wasn't my point. The point is that the decisions made in the private sector are not consensual in the way we usually define that term; and it is mythologizing to suggest they are. That was why I used the INCO example.

If we are going to talk about consensus, on what basis do we leave out the workers? That's all I meant. I wasn't saying that was coercive, and getting into some innane discussion about what constitutes coercion. It just means it was not consensual in the way this word is commonly used.

Stephen Tonsor: A major culture exerts a powerful effect. If we look at the example of Rome and Greece and their experience with the primitive peoples of Europe and the Mediterranean world, we can see the force of that culture. Incidentally, Christianity was a part of that powerful, attractive culture. And the offer, in all its variety, was there. Some Celts and Germans went on the rocks because of it. But Western society developed out of that offer and the amalgamation of cultures which took place in the period after the fifth century A.D.

So the fact that Native peoples watch television and see things on it that disturb their culture is something I would expect. It's a part of the systolic relationship between small-scale and sophisticated societies. And it has good and bad aspects.

Secondly, Archbishop Scott said one of the most intense experiences in the W.C.C. was the stripping away from Christianity of the cultural accretions of Western society; that is, of the influence of Greek philosophy and so forth.

But this argument cuts both ways. It makes us very dubious if we think of theology as interpreting, as Bernard Lonergan says, the relationship of the process of revelation to culture. When we think of it in those terms we will be very hesitant to impose on Christianity, Marxist revolutionary notions and other ideas which are quite foreign to the experience of that revelation as we find it, not in the Fathers, but in the New Testament and the Hebrew Bible.

Ted Scott: We have to deal with the question that Stephen Tonsor raised. How does a more advanced culture relate to less advanced cultures?

It seems to me that one of the obligations of more advanced cultures is to be concerned about the kind of impact they are having on less advanced peoples. New knowledge brings with it new responsibilities. We have to look at the questions: "What are the conditions we have created and developed as a result of our activities? And what are the responsibilities that follow from those new kinds of patterns?"

If we have a sense of accountability to a God that transcends, then we also have to ask the question: "What is the impact of what we are doing on other groups?" For example, in the Canadian picture, there were numerous technological studies in order to bring television to the North. But there was no major study on the possible social impact of television upon the people of the North.

We have an obligation to look at that kind of question in terms of this country. We've been talking quite a bit about the place of the state. One of the real obligations of the state has to be that of settling claims based on rights that come into conflict.

If that is true, are there any premises that, from the religious point of view, can be raised around this issue? I would like to suggest the following:

(1) The needs of the poor take priority over the wants of the rich.
(2) The freedom of the dominated takes priority over the liberty of the powerful.
(3) The participation of marginalized groups takes priority over the preservation of an order that excludes them.

These are the three premises David Hollenbauch has worked out in the question of the process of settling rights that are in conflict. I think the state should apply these premises to balance power in society. In this way we will create justice and true freedom in social life.

PART FIVE

JUDAIC SOCIAL THOUGHT

Chapter 10

Judaism's Historical Response to Economic, Social and Political Systems

Ellis Rivkin

It is pointless to ask a critically minded scholar what Judaism teaches about economic, social, and political systems.

The biblical beginnings

The Jewish people had their beginnings as semi-nomads sojourning in the land of Canaan. Their society was patriarchal, and their God was pictured as an eternal patriarch who had made a covenant with the Patriarchs to care for them and preserve them. This mode of life continued under the leadership of Moses throughout the wilderness wanderings.

During the semi-nomadic stage, the Patriarchs and Moses took for granted that tribal property rights in sheep, cattle, gold, and silver were divinely sanctioned and that polygamy and concubinage were allowable. It is also evident that the Patriarchs respected the property rights of the settled peoples, and the merchants with whom they traded.

During the stage of conquest and settlement, there was transition from a semi-nomadic to an agricultural and urban society, handled by prophetic leaders such as Joshua and Samuel. With the growing complexity of Israelite society, however, the need for an effective defence against external threats exposed the inadequacy of prophetic leadership and paved the way for the rise of monarchy. Although the United Kingdom of David and Solomon split into two kingdoms, monarchy persisted until the destruction of the Temple in 586 B.C.

Throughout this period, private ownership of land, houses, tools and personal possessions was taken for granted. For example, when Ahab confiscated the vineyard of Naboth, Elijah denounced this act as a heinous crime against God. Though Amos and Isaiah, rebuked those who ground down the poor and exploited the weak, they did not challenge the right to private property. Rather they denounced the powerful for taking away the property of others, in violation of the traditional standards of justice. No prophet ever denounced private ownership as such, or pictured the End of Days as a collective paradise. When prophets such as Isaiah envisaged the End of Days, they spoke of equity, justice, harmony, tranquillity and material abundance. But they foresaw no public ownership of land, houses or productive goods.

In the phase which followed the Babylonian exile, Jewish society was radically restructured and reorganized as a hierocratic community governed by the Aaronides, whose authority was underwritten by the Persian emperors. This hierocracy displayed many novel and interesting features. The priests owned no property, but were supported by a portion of the peasants' harvest, and by a share of the sacrifices offered by the people in public worship. The Aaronide priests built their popular support on a free peasantry. For more than two hundred years there was a flourishing and prosperous peasantry with no widespread use of slaves for agricultural purposes.

Provision was made for the welfare of the poor, orphans and widows, by setting aside corners of the field, forgotten sheafs, and gleanings for their exclusive use. Nowhere in the Pentateuch do we find the problems of the needy and the helpless solved by the collectivization of wealth, or by the expropriation of privately owned land or other possessions. The biblical record suggests that the Law accommodated itself to the economic, social, and political modes of the time.

The Law was non-Utopian. It took for granted that the poor would always be with us, and that though God promised nurturing care, His promise was conditional on absolute adherence to His laws. By contrast, the prophets pictured a Messianic age—an age in which there would be harmony among nations, collaboration between nature and humankind, equity, justice, and material well-being for all.

Thus there was in the Bible an accommodating skein of law, and a utopian skein of prophecy. The two are interwoven because both derive from the same divine source. The God who proclaimed that the poor would always be with us is the same God who will usher in a Messianic Age of abundance in which all barriers to individual fulfilment will fall. Because the source of these two skeins is the same, later Judaism wove them together in a single tapestry. Paradoxically, it was the prophetic vision which gave the people hope and courage to soldier on when the going was rough. These hopes, however unrealistic, proved to be the single most important factor in enabling the Jewish people to survive when there were no grounds for continued faith in a seemingly powerless God.

Utopian dreams were also significant because they pictured the Messianic Era as one which would be realized in this world and not beyond the grave: a fulfilment of human, not angelic, aspirations. Those who would have the good fortune to live in that age would differ from those living in Isaiah's day only in one respect: they would have committed themselves to those values which alone could sustain so idyllic an existence: justice, righteousness, compassion, and peace among nations. Individuals would then be free of the fear of hunger, nakedness, homelessness, and destructive wars. Isaiah saw the Messianic Age as one in which all human wishes would be fulfilled.

Individualism and universalism

The Hebrew Bible contains two other skeins: that of individuality and that of universality. In the first chapter of Genesis, we read that God created Man in God's image and after God's likeness, "male and female created He them." God is pictured as both male and female. This Divine Being completes His/Her creation, not with crowds, not with communities of people, not with nations, but with two individuals. It was to these and their progeny that God gave dominion over all that He had created, confident that they would bring forth from the earth all of the goodness that He had built into it. God endowed the world with abundant resources ready to yield their wealth to enterprising and risk-taking individuals. God had not doomed humankind to eternal scarcity. Scarcity was a vibrant challenge, and not a tragic destiny.

Closely linked with this focus on the individual is the focus on God as Creator of the whole universe, not as Creator of a specially favoured territory. God did not endow some part of the earth with less divine goodness than any other. According to the Book of Genesis, God looked upon His/Her total creation and was pleased with His/ Her handiwork. Indeed, it was only after God had despaired of a global solution to the problem of human evil that He called upon Abraham to father a people to whom he promised the land of Canaan.

This people, however, was to be no ordinary people. They had a divine task to perform. This was to teach the world that there was one God, who had created the heavens and the earth, and had made humans in God's image; and that this God must be recognized if humankind was to enjoy felicity. The people of Israel were singled out to restore humankind to the trans-national, trans-racial, trans-sex, and trans-class state at the time of creation.

The Israelites thus found themselves to be an anomalous people. Their most sacred book, the Pentateuch, begins not with God choosing a people, but with God creating an individual who, being in the divine image, is an individual per se. It also tells them that God is Creator of the entire universe, and that He/She chooses a particular people and promises them a particular land only because this is God's way of dealing with human free will. And having chosen this particular people, God assigns to them the task of teaching other nations that there is one God who has stamped *every* individual with His/Her image.

That God regarded all the peoples of the earth as equally precious was expressed by Isaiah when the kingdom of Israel was destroyed by Assyria and the kingdom of Judah was expecting a similar fate. Far from threatening Israel's enemies with God's unremitting vengeance, Isaiah tells both Assyria and Egypt of God's love for them:

> "In that day," Isaiah prophesied, "Israel will be the third with Egypt and Assyria, a blessing in the midst of the earth, whom the Lord of Hosts has blessed, saying, 'Blessed be Egypt my people, and Assyria the work of my hands, and Israel, my heritage.'" (Isaiah 19:24–25)

Isaiah was only echoing what Amos had proclaimed only a few years before:

> "Are you not like the Ethiopians,
> O people of Israel?' Says the Lord.
> 'Did I not bring up Israel from the land of Egypt,

And the Philistines from Caphtor.
And the Syrians from Kir?'" (Amos 9:7)

Sin and well-being

The focus on the significance of the individual is also evident in the role that the priesthood and the system of sacrifices played in the Aaronide levels of the Pentateuch. The individual was warned of the grievous consequences of sin. Sin threatened one's well-being and it threatened the well-being of the entire people. It was, therefore, essential that the individual be fastidious in seeking expiation for his/her sins from the Aaronide priests, who would sacrifice a sin-offering and secure from God a complete atonement.

The individual was thus encouraged to take responsibility for his/her acts and to reckon with the tragic consequences that might befall the community if one was heedless and neglectful. This sense of individual responsibility was heightened by the knowledge that there was only one God, who was all-powerful, all knowing, all-virtuous and impeccably just. If one disobeyed this God's commands, there was no other to whom one might fly for protection. God was also a model of human perfection.

These skeins interweave to form a tapestry which runs throughout the Hebrew Bible. They can be found in no other literature of the ancient Near East, all of which were polytheistic and mythical. For Israel alone, a single God had created the heavens and the earth and the unique individual. This God had chosen a single person to serve His/Her purposes which would find their fulfilment in historical time. The sacred literature of Israel was unique and anomalous, historical and non-mythical. It enhanced the sense of individuality because God was an individual, and because the individual was held to account for his/her actions.

Although the Bible is shot through with contradictions, inconsistencies, and incongruities, it has embedded within it values which were bound to tip Judaism's response to economic, social, and political systems in the direction of the sanctity of property and the personal responsibility of the individual.

Post-exilic developments

These values were sustained by the teachers of the two-fold Law, the written and the oral. They called themselves scribes or sages, but they are better known to us as the Pharisees. They elevated the individual beyond even the level attained in the Aaronide system. They proclaimed that God was the personal Father of each and every individual; that He so loved each one that He revealed two Laws (a written and an oral Law) which when *internalized* opened eternal life for each soul and resurrection for each body.

Pharisaism intensified the individualistic strain within Judaism so much that the very concept of peoplehood was altered. Whereas the Pentateuch offered the righteous no escape from punishment meted out to the people as a whole for collective sins, the Pharisees promised eternal life and resurrection even if the individual were the only Law-abiding one. The individual, not the collective, gained or lost the gift of immortality.

This stress on individual responsibility and internalization of the two-fold Law had powerful consequences. Guided by reality within, the individual was immune from realities without. No external force had power over the true believer. As Josephus phrased it:

> For those...who live in accordance with our laws, the prize is not silver or gold, no crown of wild olive or of parsley with every such mark of public distinction. No, each individual on the witness of his own conscience, confirmed by the sure testimony of God, is firmly persuaded that to those who observe the Law, and if they must need die for them, willingly meet death, God has granted a renewed existence, and in the revolution of the ages the gift of a better life....I should have hesitated to write thus had not the facts made all men aware that many of our countrymen have on many occasions ere now, preferred to brave all manner of suffering rather than utter a single word against the Law. (*Against Apion* II: 218–219)

Believing Jews were able to survive every kind of hardship: impoverishment, humiliation, degradation, pogroms, and expulsion. In each instance, it was the individual, not the collective, who had to decide whether reality was to be found within, or whether it was to be found without; whether the life one was now living was the only life, or whether there was a life without end where one's soul would be allotted a holy place, and whence in the revolution of the ages it would return to find in a chaste body a new life (cf. Josephus, *The Jewish War*, II: 370–375).

The shift from this-worldly to other-worldly rewards and punishments was bound to affect Judaism's response to economic, social, and political systems. The external world was a brief and transitory road to the world to come and, as such, unreal. But it was the road which each individual had to travel. It was also a winding and tortuous road with alluring by-ways which led not to salvation but to damnation. The external world might not be real, but it had to be dealt with.

The principle that underlay this teaching of the scribes and Pharisees was simple. Any system was legitimate so long as it did not block the road to eternal life and resurrection. This pragmatic approach appeared when they ruled that the payment of taxes to Caesar was allowable. A state was legitimate so long as it did not require Jews to abandon their belief in a single God or their adherence to God's twofold Law. The scribes and Pharisees pioneered the doctrine of "two realms," the one secular and the other religious, thus allowing for a peaceful co-existence between Judaism and the Empire.

The scribes and Pharisees were no less pragmatic in their response to economic and social systems. They accepted as legitimate whatever mode of production and distribution was the norm in the host society. They did not oppose slavery, nor wage labour, nor taking interest, nor making profit as practised by their Gentile neighbours, nor did they prohibit Jews from owning slaves. They had no objection to Jews employing fellow-Jews as wage-workers so long as the workers were paid the going rate and not unjustly or harshly treated. Private property was taken for granted and protected. Inequality of wealth raised no religious problem so long as the wealth was honestly come by. Only the taking of interest from a fellow-Jew was disallowed. But even this prohibition was overcome, so far as commercial transactions were concerned, by distinguishing between "usury" and profit-sharing. As for family relations, the position of women was secured by allowing them to own property and by protecting them from casual divorce: the marriage contract provided for a substantial payment by the husband in the case of divorce.

Medieval Judaism

The Judaism which prevailed throughout late antiquity proved to be pragmatic, supple, and adaptable. In relation to the non-Jewish world, it came to be summed up in the talmudic dictum of *dina de-malkuta dina*: in non-religious matters, the law of the kingdom is law.

In relation to the Jewish world, the scholar class of each generation had authority not only to preserve, alter or abrogate the law as transmitted, but to introduce new laws whenever necessary. It was thus possible to deal with unforeseen conditions, situations and problems with religious authority. As a consequence, dialectical reasoning was not only encouraged but highly rewarded. First, the Mishnah, then the Talmud, and finally the vast *responsa* literature became repositories of laws and models of how the laws could be adapted to solve problems in a realistic and constructive way.

Sealed off from the harsh facts of life by its focus on the world to come, the Judaism of the two-fold Law bred whatever variations the experience of differing societies, cultures, and civilizations required for survival. Encounter with the Sassanian-Zoroastrian civilization yielded the Babylonian Talmud. Encounter with the Ummayad and the Abassid Caliphates yielded the Gaonate, the Exilarchate, and a rich collection of legal responsa. Encounter with the Islamic culture of Andalusia produced a Golden Age of Jewish creativity. Long settlement in Christian-feudal Europe yielded Rashi's commentary on the Talmud, and the Tosaphists' dialectical-scholastic commentaries on the Talmud and Rashi. Experience of Italian city states, eastern Europe, Russia, and the Ottoman Empire further enriched the tradition of medieval Judaism. Since the economic systems of these societies differed widely, expositors of Judaism learned to adapt the tradition without compromising its uniqueness. So long as the Jews were permitted to believe in the one God and adhere to the two-fold Law, it made little difference whether the economic system was precociously urbanized (as it was in Moslem Spain in the tenth and eleventh centuries) or overwhelmingly agrarian as in Christian-feudal Europe.

There were, however, certain enduring economic and social consequences which followed from the fact that Jews in Christian-feudal Europe were largely denied the right to hold land. Jews were compelled to earn their livelihood as merchants and moneylenders. When the capitalist system emerged in Europe, Jews were already an urbanized people, though not as yet modern capitalist entrepreneurs. Their dominant *elites* consisted not of kings, nobles, or ecclesiastics, but of legal-religious scholars and the wealthier lay members of the community. Religious learning, piety, and adherence to the two-fold Law were the attributes most prized and most rewarded. The high value placed by Judaism on learning was to prove highly beneficial when capitalism reached a knowledge-intensive stage. Aristocratic values, especially those associated with military achievement, were inappropriate. When the capitalist system began therefore, Jews had no kings, nobles, or ecclesiastics to overthrow; though they did have to contend with religious *elites* which found themselves threatened by the critical spirit unleashed by the spread of capitalism.

During the Middle Ages, the Jews experienced sometimes generous, sometimes hostile treatment. Though a powerless minority, the Jews found themselves well-treated in Sassanian and Christian societies —despite religious and ideological differences—whenever these societies were experiencing economic growth. When economic stagnation and shrinkage occurred, however, they were harassed, murdered and sometimes expelled from those societies. Economic, social, and political collapse, with its attendant deterioration in the legal status of the Jews and its violent destructiveness, were viewed by Judaism as but trials and tribulations to be more than compensated for by the peace, tranquillity and joy of life eternal. Medieval Judaism, like medieval Christianity and Islam, was appropriate to the vicissitudes of human existence in a pre-capitalist world dominated by the interests of kings, nobles, and ecclesiastics.

Judaism and capitalism

The rise of capitalism in Europe posed as great a challenge to Judaism as it did to Christianity. But Judaism and the Jewish people have had a special relation to capitalism. Not because Judaism emerged out of, or along side of, capitalism. Judaism has its origins in the ancient Near East. Its subsequent development occurred, for the most part, within the framework of pre-capitalist societies. When the first great capitalist enclaves emerged in Antwerp, Amsterdam, and London, Judaism was a religion which promised to its adherents eternal life beyond the grave, and which exhorted them to pray, fast, study, and carry out meticulously the prescriptions of the Law which God commanded. Although Jews had to earn their livelihood, their ultimate concern was with the state of the soul, not the state of the body. Judaism in no way spawned the spirit of capitalism as Sombart and others have asserted.

In the sixteenth century, the majority of Jews lived in eastern and central Europe, and within the Ottoman Empire, far from modern capitalism. There were a few in Antwerp, Amsterdam, and London where it originated. The only connection between Jews and these capitalist centres in the sixteenth century was provided by Christian merchants of Jewish stock (called *Conversos*, or New Christians, or Marranos), who became Jews only when they no longer were allowed to be Christians. These first "Jewish" entrepreneurs owed as much to their "Jewishness" and their Judaism as Christian entrepreneurs owed to their Christianity. Jews were drawn into the capitalist orbit in the same way as Christians were. As capitalism penetrated central Europe, and began to appear in eastern Europe, entrepreneurially-gifted Jews, like entrepreneurially-gifted Christians, took advantage of the new opportunities.

Nonetheless, the spread of capitalism did establish a special relation between Jews and capitalism, and between Judaism and capitalism. We only have to follow the path of capitalist development from Holland, to England, France, and Germany, to see that wherever capitalism spread and triumphed, Jews were emancipated. In no instance did Jews gain emancipation before the capitalist transformation of their society. Furthermore, the degree of emancipation of the Jews was directly related to the degree of capitalistic transformation. That society least hampered by pre-capitalist ways, namely the American, was that in which Jews had never to be formally emancipated by federal law. They were singled out neither for inclusion nor exclusion. It was also in America that the Jews came to enjoy an equality of status and opportunity in practice which no other society in history had extended to them.

The relation between Judaism and capitalism, however, is highly complex. Judaism of the Middle Ages was a Judaism which proclaimed that God had revealed His will in the Bible and in the teachings of the rabbis, and that the goal of human endeavour was to believe in God, keep His commandments, and look to salvation in the world to come. Despite the individualistic implications of the Genesis story developed in the Oral Law, its broader implications were overwhelmed by the subordination of the individual to God's will which was to be found exclusively within the two-fold Law. There was no allowance either for the free play of individuality or for the critical spirit. One was bound to an external authority whose word was Law and whose teachings were sacrosanct, however unintelligible they might be. Isaiah's vision of a time when scarcity would be no more and when every individual would enjoy well-being was sacralized, its fulfilment to be brought about by the exercise of divine power and not by human endeavour. Judaism in its medieval form was not a religion for capitalist entrepreneurs, though it did not disallow entrepreneurial activity. But its central religious values were incompatible with capitalism. To be sure, there were implicit values within biblical and rabbinic Judaism congenial to the spirit of capitalism; but they were embedded within a framework which subjected the individual to an external authority, and hindered a free interplay of the critical spirit with the phenomenal world.

Reform Judaism

Jewish religious leaders in nineteenth-century Germany, priding themselves on their Westernization and enlightenment, created a new form of Judaism which proclaimed that God was always revealing Himself; that the essence of Judaism was not the Law, but ethical monotheism; and that the people of Israel were a transnational people spread among the nations of the world to be a light unto the Gentiles with no call either to return to Zion or to exercise political sovereignty. Although this new form of "Progressive" or "Reform" Judaism, originated in nineteenth-century Germany, it flourished only in the United States where the capitalist climate was favourably disposed to the right of an individual to choose his/her own road to salvation.

This radically new form of Judaism said "Yes" to modernization and westernization; "Yes" to capitalism's promise of overcoming scarcity; "Yes" to the free-choosing, risk-taking individual; and "Yes" to scientific and critical thinking. But in saying "Yes," Reform Judaism by no means gave a blank cheque to capitalism. Reform Judaism is a religion and not an economic system. Its essential teachings are that there is a single God, the consequences of Whose unique existence is the totality of the universe as it was, as it is, and as it is yet to be. It affirms that all diversity in the world is a consequence of God's unity. Reform Judaism claims that God is not only the creative source of all of sentient and non-sentient beings, but He is also the source of their capacity to be loving, compassionate, just, and wise. This variant of Judaism teaches that it is God who makes humane values possible, and God who gives the human mind the power to penetrate the mind of God Himself in knowing the laws of nature. Reform Judaism affirms that God gives free will to humankind; and is confident that goodness, love, compassion, justice, wisdom, and creativity will triumph over evil, depravity, destructiveness, cruelty, and hostility.

With access to the mind of God, we can see that other worlds beckon the human spirit. No longer confined to our planet, we need never fear extinction. Having access to other worlds, we need fear no scarcity. With moons and planets without number, we need fear no Malthusian destiny. With endless horizons beckoning, we need fear no stifling of the spirit of adventure. If humankind fails to choose wisely, then God's gamble with free will may have proved a disaster, but the disaster will have been of Man's choosing, not God's.

Reform Judaism gambles even as God "gambles." God made a good world, and He/She endowed the first humans and their progeny with the right to hold dominion over it, confident that these individuals and their progeny would realize all of its good. This confidence was misplaced, as the biblical account of the flood and the Tower of Babel makes clear. Twice "defeated," God called Abraham to father a people which would "gamble" with God, confident that humans would freely choose to build a world rather than destroy it.

These teachings of Judaism, embedded in the sacred texts, were rendered explicit for the first time by Reform Judaism, and liberated from the constraints of the ritual law. They are religious, not economic teachings, concerned with God and the metaphysical nature of reality. They evaluate economic, political, and social systems by the degree to which they are compatible with these teachings. So that when I speak of Reform Judaism's saying "Yes" to modernization and westernization, capitalism, the risk-taking individual, and the spirit of critical inquiry, it is a conditional "Yes" dependent on the nurturing of love, compassion, justice, goodness, individuality, and wisdom.

Reform Judaism could say "Yes" to capitalist development at the turn of the century, because exploitative features were more than compensated for by its liberating effects. Reform Judaism is idealistic, but non-utopian. The successes of industrial capitalism were impressive and promised more to come.

Totalitarianism

The First World War burst the bubble of confidence and hope. What occurred was so devastating that the capitalist system was shaken to its roots. Its universal and humane values were transmuted into the national, racial, and destructive values of totalitarian capitalism.

Capitalism's dynamic, revolutionary, and developmental face is congruent with the essential values of Reform Judaism. Its stagnant, totalitarian, and repressive face, however, is demonic. Capitalism is not some sturdy, unchanging entity driven by principles allowing for no compromise. It is a chamelion which becomes whatever the political climate requires it to be. It is throughly opportunist, settling for the best arrangement available. For capitalism is not a system of values, but an economic system energized by the drive for profits.

Yet on closer inspection, the unattractive side of capitalism is seen to have been caused by the accommodation to restrictions placed on its free development by the division of Europe into sovereign nation-states. These in turn were survivals of a pre-capitalist era. Capitalist opportunism was thus an adaption to historical circumstances, not an expression of its inherent drive. For when capitalist development was not barred by pre-capitalist obstructions, its thrust was towards the building of an economic infrastructure in which humane, non-economic values might flourish. Unobstructed, capitalism generates a spiral of economic and humane development, providing an economic basis for the good, the beautiful and the true.

Comment

Susan Feigenbaum

Professor Rivkin addresses two issues significant alike for Jewish theologians and practitioners. Does Judaism dictate a specific economic, social and/or political system?; and is Judaism compatible with capitalism? To the first question, he concludes that

> it is pointless to ask of a critically minded scholar what Judaism

teaches about economic, social and political systems.
A state (is) legitimate so long as that state (does) not require that
Jews abandon their belief in a single God or their adherence to
God's two-fold Law.

In response to the second, Rivkin argues that

> Judaism in its medieval form was not a religion for capitalist en-
> trepreneurs. . . .its central religious values were incompatible
> with capitalism. . . .[A] radically new form of Judaism [Progres-
> sive or Reform Judaism] said "Yes" to modernization and wes-
> ternization; "Yes" to capitalism's promise of overcoming scar-
> city; "Yes" to the free-choosing, risk-taking individual, and
> "Yes" to scientific and critical thinking.

I take strong exception to both of these claims. I will therefore offer
an alternative view of the relation between traditional Judaism and
the choice of social systems, and identify what I view as weaknesses
in the author's analysis.

Judaism and the choice of an economic, social and political system

Judaism is a religion of deeds. While the basic tenet of Judaism is the
belief in one universal, sovereign God, Judaism requires a positive affirmation of this belief by one's actions. Abraham affirms his commitment to a covenant with God not only through prayer but also
through action; specifically through *Brit Melah* (circumcision) and
Akedah (the sacrifice of Isaac). Similarly, although the first five of the
Ten Commandments are concerned with Man's recognition of the sovereignty of God, the second five require that Man sanctify human
existence through fulfilment of specific duties to his fellow man.

Indeed, the *Torah* may be viewed as a document of the development of property rights which dictates an allocation deemed compatible with the sanctification of the one, holy God. Here I use the term
"property rights" to mean not only control over physical property,
but in a broader sense rights to engage in certain actions related to
property. In every society, whether capitalist, socialist or feudalistic,
the property rights of individuals are defined, protected and limited
by social consensus. This assignment determines the distribution of
income in society and creates incentives for the use of society's resources. Changes in consensus about appropriate allocation will be

followed by changes in the assignment of rights.

The *Torah* describes a property-rights system which is consistent with the ethical code mandated by a just and merciful God, creator and protector of all life. It is a *private* property-rights arrangement, enforced by such prohibitions as "Thou shalt not steal" and "Thou shalt not murder." The initial distribution of rights is divinely made, as symbolized by the promise of land to Abraham's descendants, the Children of Israel. Property claims can be transferred only through the act of voluntary exchange and contracting, and can not be expropriated even in the name of God. Even Abraham, to whom a land is promised as part of his covenant with God, is required to honour the property rights of the Hittites and purchase from them a burial site for his wife Sarah.

Limitation of rights

A primary object of both the *Torah* and later rabbinic writings was to define and limit rights in a fashion consistent with this divinely-inspired system. For example, the *Torah* prohibited Israelite masters from working either Hebrew or non-Hebrew slaves on the Sabbath day. It forbade the complete harvesting of fields and the gathering of fallen fruits and vegetables by owners of the fields. Through the institution of the Jubilee year, pre-Exilic Israel addressed the issue of intergenerational transfer of property. Every fifty years (the approximate length of a generation), land would revert to its original owner, thereby allowing new generations the same "fair start" afforded their parents. Concern about the impoverished and the perpetuation of poverty led to no collectivization of wealth but did result in specific limitations of individual property rights. Private property was not abolished but "moralized."

As Rivkin correctly observes, not even the prophetic texts picture the end of days as a collective paradise. However, the prophets did characterize the Messianic Age as an era of material abundance, devoid of scarcity. In such a state, property rights are unimportant, since all demands may be fulfilled at no opportunity cost to society or its individual members. Only in an era of scarcity is choice of a property-rights system critical to the distribution of wealth and the maximization of social well-being. In my opinion, traditional Judaism recognized that it was through private property that Man could best act as a co-Creator with God to improve the human condition in pre-

Messianic scarcity. The *Torah* makes clear that belief in God implies
the acceptance of a divinely-inspired assignment *and* limitation of individual rights. These are categorical imperatives independent of
time or nation. While it is true that Jewish scholars throughout the
ages were charged with the difficult task of extending the rights system of the Written Law to new social and technological situations,
they were not authorized to abrogate any aspect of the Law unless its
current observance was impossible. The acceptance by the scribes
and Pharisees of slavery, wage labour and profits was no adaptation
of the Written Law, as Rivkin suggests, but the application of rights
predefined in the *Torah*. The scribes did not abrogate biblical prescriptions concerning the treatment of slaves as persons rather than
chattels, nor the prohibition against charging interest on non-com-
mercial loans made to fellow members of the Jewish community. Rivkin's conclusion, that traditional Judaism views any state as legitimate if it does not require abandonment of belief in God, imposes a
significant constraint on the rights-assignment permitted by such a
"legitimate" state.

Judaism and capitalism

Given the inextricable link between traditional Judaism and a social
system defined by private property rights, what, if anything, does
Judaism say about capitalism?

In view of the benefits conferred upon Jews by the capitalist system, one would expect that if any conflict existed between traditional
Judaism and capitalism it would be resolved in such a way as to allow
Jews to survive economically as well as to practise their religion.
Rivkin argues that such a conflict did exist, leading the development
of Progressive, or Reform, Judaism. This movement proclaimed that
"the essence of Judaism was not the Law, but ethical monotheism,"
supposed to have provided Jews with a new-found rights of free
choice and free inquiry. That such rights are critical to the development and sustenance of a capitalist system is beyond doubt. The crucial issue is whether traditional Judaism, with its emphasis on Law
and the authority of God, is incompatible with these basic human
freedoms.

In contrast to Rivkin, I contend that there is no conflict between
capitalism and traditional Judaism. There is an inextricable link between traditional Judaism and a divinely-dictated system of private
property rights. Any conflict between capitalism and traditional

Judaism must come from the second cornerstone of capitalism: freedom to exploit such rights in order to pursue personal well-being, subject only to the agreement of others whose own property rights may be infringed.

Just as capitalism emerged when the ruler was seen as the protector and regulator, rather than owner, of property rights, so too the *Torah* describes the emergence of a religious order in which the function of God is to be protector and enforcer, rather than controller, of a predefined system of property rights. Adam is given dominion over the whole of creation, to be used for his own well-being. That God does not arbitrarily rescind the rights of individuals is made clear in the Sodom and Gomorrah narrative, where God must show Abraham that His threatened destruction of the cities is not capricious but rather a response to a nation's violation of predefined limitations upon individual property rights. The existence of laws which define and limit property rights in no way reduces one's freedom to exploit these assigned rights in an unconstrained fashion. God's punishment of Sodom and Gomorrah may be interpreted as the enforcement of the bounds of such rights, rather than as an arbitrary constraint upon individual freedom. Thus, while Judaic Law dictates the bounds of an individual's property rights, it does not interfere with the ability to manage these assigned rights freely. Furthermore, traditional Judaism recognizes the individual's right to engage in voluntary exchange and contracting, and portrays God as the enforcer of such arrangements. This is the essence of the covenant between Abraham and God, subsequently ratified by the followers of Moses. God is viewed in a manner analogous to the State, as the protector and regulator of rights. Without such an enforcement mechanism, a private property-rights system such as capitalism could not survive.

Not only is Man given the freedom to dispose of his property in order to enhance his well-being, but the Torah indicates that Man is given the freedom to reject the bounds of his rights and incur the costs of his actions. Just as Adam exercised his free will to disobey God, all men have the privilege of accepting or rejecting a system of individual rights consistent with the sanctification of God. This is nowhere more evident than in the parting words of Moses:

> See, I have set before thee this day life and good, and death and evil; In that I command thee this day to love the LORD thy God, to walk in his ways, and to keep his commandments and his statutes and his judgements, that thou mayest live and

> multiply: and the LORD thy God shall bless thee in the land
> wither thou goest to possess it. But if thine heart turn away, so
> that thou wilt not hear, but shalt be drawn away, and worship
> other gods, and serve them; I denounce unto you this day, that
> ye shall surely perish, and that ye shall not prolong your days
> upon the land....I have set before you life and death, blessing
> and cursing; therefore, choose life, that both thou and thy seed
> may live....–(King James version, Deuteronomy 30: 15–19)

There is no doubt that the individual is given freedom to reject the system of property rights inspired by God and delineated through His laws. This choice is an individual one and it is the individual who must bear the consequences of his choice. The responsibility of the individual for his own actions, independent of the collective body, is reflected both in the narrative of Noah (who was righteous in his generations) and the story of Sodom and Gomorrah (where God assures Abraham that he will not sweep away the innocent with the guilty). This individualistic view of society is fundamental to the capitalist system, which allows individuals to make their own decisions concerning the disposition of their physical and human capital—and bear the total costs or enjoy the full benefits thereof—independent of any collective action.

In conclusion, let me state that I disagree with the contention that Progressive Judaism's adaptation and partial abrogation of traditional Law was a necessary response to the spirit of free inquiry that emerged from the period of the Enlightenment; or that it was essential to the development of a capitalist system founded on the principle of free choice. The central role of private property rights, the view of God as protector of these rights, and the freedom of individual choice are all aspects of traditional Judaism which are clearly compatible with the fundamental tenets of capitalism. The existence of laws which constrain these rights should not lead one mistakenly to conclude that traditional Judaism is in conflict with the freedoms inherent in the capitalist system, for the capitalist system requires a set of laws to define, enforce and regulate the rights of all individuals.

Chapter 11

Judaism and the Market Mechanism

Meir Tamari

INTRODUCTION

The treatment of the economic life of the Jew, both academically and popularly, has been to either portray a picture of a creature devoted to the sole aim of acquiring material wealth, or as a society whose economic behaviour is determined primarily by non-religious and exogenous factors.

Marx and Bauer[1] depict much of modern and primitive anti-Semitism when they present the Jew as a creature whose sole aim is the accumulation of money. This stereotype was not depicted as reflecting individuals nor as a temporary aberration caused by a specific situation; it was untruthfully held as something which flows from the very basis of Judaism itself.

Even the Judophiles adapted Judaism to bolster up their particular brand of economic philosophy. Sombart,[2] following Weber,[3] saw the Jews as prime creators of modern capitalism through frugality and hard work, the high level of Jewish literacy and education and the importance of family and community relations. Later scholars have added other factors to link the Jew with capitalism,[4] such as the political freedom associated with the free market, the effect of minority status as a spur to excellence and the ability to transcend national boundaries.

Jewish apologists, too, seem to have accepted this divorce of economic activity from Jewish religious ideology. They reason that the economic life-style of the Jew was caused partially or solely by extraneous factors. Unknowingly, they accept the anti-Semitic analysis, even though arguing that historic events deprived the Jew of a normal economic existence. Therefore, they hold, it is these events which are to blame for the commonly accepted picture of the Jew.

Independent framework

While it was obviously true that extraneous historical and social factors affected the Jewish economic history, this paper will attempt to show that there exists an intrinsic and independent framework within which the creation of economic assets, the use of material wealth, and the issues which flow from them have been handled by Jews throughout the history in all the countries of their dispersion. This paper will discuss the religious teachings and practices which are the primary constituents of this Jewish economic framework.

Although it can be shown that some 2,000 years ago the sages of the Talmud possessed a knowledge of economic mechanisms akin to that of some modern concepts, this aspect is beyond our present scope.[5] Our concern is not with the economic mechanism, nor to write a Jewish economic textbook, but with describing the ethical and religious conceptual framework within which the Jewish economic man operates.

Judaism has to be considered basically as a code of conduct rather than a creed or statement of belief. Its basis lies in the fulfilment of the divine statutes and the observance of the Commandments to a greater extent than in understanding or interpreting the will of God, important as these are. Although as in all the religions, faith is an important constituent of Judaism, man's salvation is attained through mundane actions and everyday deeds. This supremacy of action rather than of reason or of faith is one of its most distinguishing features, and, therefore, it is to the legal system, *halacha* —literally, "walking"—to which we have to turn—not for economic theories, but rather, for a code of Jewish economic conduct.

THE LEGITIMACY OF ECONOMIC ACTIVITY

In Judaism, as in all socio-religious movements, economic activities give rise to basic moral problems which have to be solved in some fashion. Broadly speaking, these problems fall into two major categories which come to define both the scope of economic activity and the moral legitimacy of such activity:

A. The status of economic activities *vis a vis* the demands of the particular religion: that a man spend time in prayer, study and meritorious deeds. In essence this is a problem of allocation of time between economic and religious acts.
B. Since the creation of economic goods and their accumulation often leads to visible inequalities, accompanied by greed, injustice, theft and, often, bloodshed, it is linked to man's evil inclinations or a sort of a *lust* which is inconsistent with the ethical and moral teachings of the religion.

At the outset, therefore, we have to consider Judaism's answer to these two serious questions in order to verify the legitimacy of the Jew engaging in economic activity if he wishes to remain true to his Judaism.

Worshipping God at the expense of economic activity.

Since time is a limited resource, man has to ration the time available between satisfying his economic needs and his religious ones. The first restraint in Judaism on the time available for economic activity, which comes to the popular mind, are those periods in the year when such activity is not permissible under religious law. The Jewish calendar is indeed replete with days when complete abstinence from labour, commerce or any other economic activity is mandatory as a major form of observance. There are 52 Sabbaths in a year, 8 major festivals; in the agricultural world every seventh year is a sabbatical one, and the fiftieth year a Jubilee year, in which much agricultural activity is limited. Furthermore, there are occasional periodic requirements such as the week-long mourning for a close relative, the week during which a bridegroom is not permitted to work, etc., which add to the number of days which automatically restrict economic activity. Measured quantitatively, however, the actual effect of these religious restrictions on economic activity is probably far smaller in the modern world than it was in ancient times. In modern Israel, farming, which is considered to be a 24-hour-a-day, 7-day-a-week occupation, is conducted by religious settlements no less efficiently than their non-religious counterparts, even though the religious restrictions are strictly observed. Modern technology has also provided the answer for many industrial plants; they are able to operate without major loss accruing as a result of religious observance.

Religious study

There is, however, a far more basic and far-reaching limitation on the time involved in economic activity which has the added distinction of being peculiar to Judaism. This is the obligation of religious study. This is an obligation binding not only on the priests, rabbis and scholars, nor limited to a special period of time in a person's life. Every individual, irrespective of age, knowledge, or economic status, is required to devote unlimited time to learning, so that one is obligated to study day and night until one's dying day. All other activities, since they detract from the amount of time devoted to learning are considered wasteful and a sign of a serious religious misconduct.

Carrying this concept to its logical, if extreme, conclusion, there developed a school of thought which views all time devoted to economic activity as illegitimate since it is time taken away from studying; and this even though generally speaking such activity was considered legitimate. God, according to this view, would provide man with the necessities and man would devote his life to study.[6] However, the majority opinion of Jewish thinkers was summed up by Maimonides when he ruled that a man should divide his time equally into three sections, one devoted to the study of Torah, one devoted to earning a living, and the third for sleeping and eating, etc.[7] It is clear, therefore, that devoting time to study is an essential tenet of Judaism even as a limitation on economic activity. This opinion has led in Jewish history to the search for such occupations as would allow one to devote time to study, either because they did not require much time, or because they could be followed in areas where there were concentrations of Jews which made such study feasible. So Maimonides recommends, for example, that a man should go into commerce, rather than farming, because commerce allows far more time for the study of Torah.[8]

Economic wealth as a form of man's evil inclination

Man's economic wants or lusts are treated by Judaism in exactly the same way as all the other basic human tendencies. They are not something which has to be destroyed, but something which man can and must sanctify, and himself be sanctified thereby. This attitude is a reflection of man's partnership with the Deity, a continuation of the process of Creation. In such a partnership, the holy sparks which reside in man transform the ordinary everyday acts into communion with God.[9] Therefore, earning and keeping of such economic assets is considered by Judaism as legitimate, permissible and beneficial, sanctified by the observance of God's Commandments, yet restricted.

The observance of God's Commandments in Judaism leads not to some ethereal other world, but to an abundance of material goods.[10] Starvation, poverty and drought are depicted as divine punishments and anger,[11] whilst a God-fearing man is characterized as one whose flocks and orchards bear their fruit in season and produce a bounty of goods.[12] The land of Israel of the Bible, the divinely defined geographic area for the Jews to live in and create a nation of priests, is not a bleak desert, but a land flowing with milk and honey.

The daily prayers of the Jews contain requests not only for divine forgiveness, for peace, for healing of the sick, etc., but also for an equitable and bountiful livelihood earned through honest and moral means. For instance, on the holiest day of the Jewish year, Yom Kippur, the Day of Atonement, perhaps the pinnacle of Jewish life, the High Priest offers a special prayer in the Temple. This prayer has as one of its major components the request for a year of plenty, a year in which the people will not be dependent on others for their livelihood, and will enjoy material plenty.

A contrast

The fact that these requests should be not only included, but highlighted in the public prayer on this important and solemn occasion stands in glowing contrast to the glorification of poverty of other faiths and creeds. The Jewish Bible does not exhort against engaging in economic activities or in the accumulation of material goods. There are no accusing fingers pointed at those engaged in normal economic activities for the earning of material goods. There are no echoes of asceticism nor of the cleansing and spiritual effects of poverty on man.

Despite the legitimacy of economic activity and man's enjoyment of material goods, however, Judaism does not allow unlimited accumulation of such goods nor an undisputed use thereof. Both the achievement of economic wealth and the use thereof are very strictly limited and channelled by Judaism, both on an individual and group basis. This does not flow from an exalted view of poverty or an other-worldly philosophy; rather, from the view that all of man's actions, including these, are to be subjected to the ethical, moral and religious demands of the Torah.

That the sphere of economic activity is a major vehicle for achieving such sanctity may be seen in the fact that well over a hundred of the 613 Commandments mentioned in the Torah as obligatory on every Jew, are related to it. This is in comparison with the 24 laws which form the basis of the dietary laws, which are such a well-known phenomenon of Judaism. The sages of the Talmud said, "He who is desirous of achieving sainthood, let him live according to the tractates of the Talmud dealing with commerce and finance."[13]

THE CONCEPTUAL FRAMEWORK FOR JEWISH ECONOMIC ACTIVITY

"The Earth is the Lord's and the fullness thereof."[14]

The most important premise behind the whole Jewish economic framework is that all wealth originates from God alone. God in His infinite mercy makes sufficient economic resources available to man. This wealth belongs to the Deity who has given it to man for his physical well-being. This is under the concept of economic steward-ship for the temporary holders of wealth. Since Judaism is a community-oriented rather than an individual-oriented religion, this means that the group at all levels—communal, national and, during periods of the loss of sovereignty, international—are thereby made partners in fact, even if not legally so, in each individual's wealth. Perhaps two biblical institutions can establish this trinity of God, individual owner and society.

1) On the sabbatical year, the land was to lie fallow and man was to eat only of the natural produce of the ground. However, over and above this, man was required to renounce legal ownership over his land, so that everything growing thereon was available to all and sundry.

Periodically, man reaffirms his belief in God's mercy by not plowing, sowing, etc., and having to rely only on the natural increase of untilled ground, not only in the seventh year, but in the eighth, as well. Even though man alone of all creatures is required to labour incessantly for his livelihood and to transform raw material into food, clothing, shelter, etc., nevertheless the Jew is taught that this economic welfare is in fact given to him by the deity and therefore has to be used according to the divine will;[15]

2) To any farmer, the first fruits of his endeavour are a special kind of crop—there is a special relationship to one's first business deal, to one's first profit, to one's first asset and even to less tangible achievements in other spheres of life. The Jew is obligated to take his first fruits to Jerusalem and to present them to the priest before he is able to eat of the new crop. However, what highlights the concept of dependence and thankfulness is not so much the bringing of the fruit, but in confession. Here, the Jew described how an insignificant little family went down to Egypt, was enslaved and persecuted. Only through the love of God and His power over the forces of nature was this family redeemed from slavery, carried through the desert, and brought into a land of its own. And it was this grace of God which gave them not only the land, but its fertility, crops and first fruits. The farmer, or the entrepreneur, was, in the final analysis, quite irrelevant.[16]

This understanding of man's dependence on the grace of God for his economic welfare and the obligation resulting from that *understanding* were translated in Judaism into legal forms and binding daily practices. Definitions were created as to what is permissible and what is forbidden, whilst regulations were promulgated governing how and when and where the permitted acts might be done. It is this definition and action-oriented legal framework to which we must turn for the implementation of the conceptual framework.

"And thou shalt do that which is righteous and just in the sight of the Lord. . . ."[17]

No society or economy can persist long without rules which limit theft and fraud. It is easy, therefore, to accept Maimonides's view of the numerous Jewish injunctions against economic crime and dishonest means of earning a living.[18] In the main, however, Judaism has viewed these concepts as far more than mere necessary social wisdom. They have been considered as part of a God-given moral, social order.[19] One is not allowed to steal simply because the Deity says so. This makes not stealing a religious act, and not merely something which flows from society's mores and concepts of economic morality. Halachik regulations consider honesty in economics as an absolute rule, not only a good, but required. Moreover, the concept of stealing has been extended far beyond that which is normal in humanistic morality. The question of theft has nothing to do with the damage done to the injured party, nor to the relative economic status of the parties concerned, so that even an item of economic insignificance is not permitted to be stolen.[20]

Misrepresentation

It is prohibited to put good fruit on top or brush an animal in order to make him look different than he really is.[21] There is an extensive code for the repair and maintenance of scales and cleaning thereof, developed so that misrepresentation should not defraud the customer.[22] One is not allowed to steal, as it were, another's opinion; in other words, many of those things that we all too often classify under advertising are forbidden.[23]

Weak and powerless members of society have to be protected in their economic activities. They might not have a full knowledge of the law, they might not have the funds or the knowledge necessary to obtain their rights, and they might be *afraid* of pushing for such rights, even where these are known. So the widow and the stranger, the poor and the orphan were singled out for protection by Jewish law. One is not permitted to oppress them, one is not permitted to defraud them either in words or deeds, and one is not even permitted to deal harshly with them in a way that takes advantage of their special status.[24] All this, of course, is over and above the usual laws of morality which apply to them as to everybody else.

There are, however, many special circumstances in which normal people need protection. The rabbinic sages, in commenting on the biblical injunction, "thou shall not put a stumbling block in the path of the blind,"[25] saw it as forbidding the giving of unwise advice; or providing, through a legal transaction, articles which lead to physical or moral detriment.[26] Professions such as counselling, brokerage, accounting, advertising, etc., as well as the legal trading in weapons, drugs or pornographic literature, would find severe restraints placed upon them by the acceptance of the rabbinic laws which flow from this concept.

Damages
A man is not permitted to use his property in a way which will cause harm or do damage to another person's body or property.[27] A tree planted alongside a neighbour's plot is in effect stealing through its roots another's wealth. Certain industries and professions through the pollution, noise and human traffic associated with them steal another's quiet, health, peace and fresh air, and therefore are forbidden or restricted to certain areas. The flesh of an ox which causes fatal damage cannot be eaten even when slaughtered ritually so as to teach the Jew the severity of causing damage to others.

It should be noted that Jewish law does not accept the Roman concept of "Let the buyer beware." Instead, it places the onus for preventing misrepresentation, damage, and loss solely on the seller. As an example, a vendor is assumed to guarantee the goods he sells even without an explicit statement to that effect, and the injured party can claim redress for fraud, irrespective of the time which has elapsed or of the value of the transaction.[28]

"And thy brother shall live with thee . . ."[29]

Not only was wealth to be earned in a moral way, but society — both as a group and as individuals — have rights with regard to private Jewish property. Although Judaism accepted the idea that man could have his own property, he is not the sole master of it. The rabbis of the Talmud, reflecting a thought process which was already hundreds of years old, claimed that Sodom's sin was its inability to share its wealth with strangers, with the weak and the poor.[30] The giving of charity is not considered as an act of kindness on the part of the haves to the have-nots. The have-nots have by right a stake or share in the property of the haves, since it was given to the latter partially for that purpose. It is no coincidence that the Hebrew word for "charity" flows from the same root as that of "justice." What is given to the poor is not an act of mercy or of righteousness, but an act of justice. Since the community has an obligation to provide food, shelter and basic economic roots for the needy, it has a moral right and duty to tax its members for this purpose. As well, it must regulate matters so as to protect the interest of its weakest members.

This wealth-sharing requirement includes non-monetary acts as well. One is not allowed to oppress in words the convert, the widow, the orphan, or the stranger by reminding them of their special situation. A creditor is not allowed to intrude on the privacy of the debtor even when he is collecting his debts. Neither is he allowed to take as security items essential for the sustenance of the debtor or for the earning of a livelihood.[31]

Unfair competition

Furthermore, the halacha produced the concept of "beyond the boundary of the law," to educate and train the Jew to forego, voluntarily, economic gains which were legally his, in order to allow weak or lesser members of society to maintain themselves. For example, many famous rabbinic personalities closed their stores after a few hours of trading so as to prevent gross unfair competition against their less learned competitors.

The duties and obligations imposed by the code towards one's neighbours went beyond the scope of charity and include acts of righteousness, acts understood in Jewish thought to be given to those who are undeserving of them. One example is the commandment to make interest-free loans. This is distinct both from the injunction against taking interest as well as from the obligation to give charity. It is an act of righteousness, granted both to the rich man who is temporarily in financial straits and to the poor man trying to improve his economic situation.[32]

Secondly, according to Jewish law a person whose land and property adjoins that of another person automatically has the first right to purchase such property (the concept of "bar-metzrah"). Since the purchase is to be at the market price, the seller suffers no loss. Yet at the same time the buyer gains, since the enlargement of his property is often an economic consideration. This is a concept of "one loses nothing and the other one gains."[33]

So a system was built introducing the demands of charity and welfare in its wider sense into the Jewish economic philosophy. These demands often lead to a deliberate distortion of the market mechanism.[34]

Pursuit of justice

A cardinal tenet of Judaism is the centrality of justice. Justice is an attribute of God, it is displayed in His conduct of the world, and its active pursuit is enjoined on man. The establishment of the legal system and courts of law is one of the Seven Noachide Laws seen in Judaism as binding on all men. This justice knows no class difference, favouring neither rich nor powerful, nor distorting itself for the poor or weak. So judges are not allowed to fear the wealthy nor favour the poor, nor succumb to bribery in all its varied and ingenious forms.

The centrality of justice provides the stable legal system which is an essential prerequisite for any economic activity. There is, however, far more than just such a legal framework contained in the Jewish concept of justice in the economic world. This justice is perfectly symmetrical. Creditors have an obligation to lend interest-free money; but the debtor has an obligation to repay the debt and not to waste the loans given to him. Employees have the right to receive prompt payment of their wages. Yet they also have an obligation, from the same source, to perform their work properly. Neither buyer nor seller enjoys special privileges in the marketplace.[35] Furthermore, there is a clear demarcation between justice, on the one hand, and mercy and charity, on the other, which has important implications for the modern welfare state.

The concept of the free loan can perhaps best serve to illustrate the separation in the economic sphere. Consider the case of a debtor who cannot repay his loan. One could argue that since the lender is presumably wealthier, he could forego his claim as a creditor. This would be an act of charity and so would seem to be the desired way to act.

A distortion

Such charity, however, distorts justice. It ignores the obligations of the debtor and foists onto the creditor society's moral and social obligation, simply because he committed a praiseworthy act by making the interest-free loan in the first place. As a result of this unpremeditated and involuntary charity, the moral basis of the debtor and creditor are distorted. The borrower on the one hand could tend to make his investments casually and "wastefully," knowing that he could perhaps evade repayment altogether. The lender viewing the loan as charity could simply be reinforcing the uneconomic behaviour of the borrower. This is a pattern often found not only in welfare states but also in economies where subsidized public sector funds are made available to entrepreneurs. The main creditor, the State, is often prepared to waive its debts or assume the debts of the defaulting corporations. This leads to uneconomic investments and their perpetuation and also to a wilful amd immoral management of public funds.

The halachic view is that the creditor does not take on himself all the social and economic problems of the borrower. Therefore the debtor has to meet his obligation even at the cost of losing all his property.[36] At he same time the community has an obligation in which the creditor shares as a member, to help the debtor socially and financially.

It is important to note that the Jewish legal system keeps a clear demarcation between crimes against property and capital crimes. Murder, adultery and idolatry were punishable by death, without any possibility of a monetary settlement. On the other hand, no prisons ever existed for debtors, and no jail sentence was imposed for theft or embezzlement; punishment was limited to restitution and fines. Capital punishment, banishment or bodily mutilation for theft were never recognized. Whilst private property has rights, which must be equitably and severely enforced, they never were considered sacred or holy.[37]

Economic mechanism

In every economy, there has to be some mechanism which determines the goods to be produced, in what quantities, and the price at which they are to be distributed. This mechanism may be the "hidden hand" of the market place or the decision of a central planning authority, or any number of variations of either of them.

Judaism is not an economic system and has no clearly defined economic theory. It is prepared to accept as legitimate any economic system which comes into being, provided it is consistent with the demands of Divine justice and mercy. Therefore it is not necessary to discuss the theoretical aspects of this mechanism, but only to present a schematic description of what the market would look like if it were conducted in accordance with Jewish legal and ethical principles.

There are many examples in talmudic and later literature of benefits of the market economy in providing society with economic goods in a manner beneficial to the majority.[38] Yet it was recognized that many distortions and injustices occur within society as a result of this same mechanism. Such distortions may lead to poverty, hunger, injustice and other human suffering. In order to alleviate and prevent these, Judaism sought to impose checks and balances on the market mechanism. Since Judaism is an "action-oriented" religion rather than a "faith-oriented" one, restraints on the market mechanism consist not of lofty exhortations to do good and to be just, but of a set of permissible and non-permissible acts.[39] Because Judaism believes that man is unable to perfect himself or sanctify his actions in any sphere of life without divinely given codes, laws and *mitzvah*s, the correction of economic injustices and immoralities could not be left to the self-regulatory actions of a market economy.[40] A network of religious obligations exists, both in legal and ethical form, which frees the divine spark in man, so that his mundane, everyday acts may become sanctified in accordance with the Divine scheme.

Price control: A "just price" and "reasonable profits"

Control of prices and profits in Judaism does not flow from an anticommercial position such as existed in Christian social thought. In Judaism, the merchant and the entrepreneur play a legitimate and even desirable role. Therefore they are morally entitled to a profit in return for their function.[41] Yet the Jewish conception of private economic activity, which sets the seal of justice, righteousness and morality on all mundane acts, requires control over prices and profits in order to prevent deviations from the Divine mandate. Jewish insistence on the centrality of justice introduces the need for full disclosure, equal rights of all parties concerned, and fulfilment of the contractual obligations into the discussion of the "just price."

We may identify the elements of Jewish price and profit control as follows:

a) Administrative, judicial and moral intervention to prevent the harming of Society (or sections of it) by deviations from "normal" market price and profits.

b) The denial of "abnormal" profits.

(1) Moral restrictions on the prices of basic commodities

Though there is nothing wrong with trading in basic commodities, the sages of the Talmud saw the increased costs caused by middlemen as detrimental to the poor and weaker classes. Enactments were cited in the Talmud which were later incorporated into the legal codes of rabbinic literature. These expressed moral disapproval of middlemen in basic commodities. "One may not earn a livelihood in the land of Israel in things which have life's soul" (basic commodities).[42] The same talmudic source mentions the injunction against earning a profit rate of one hundred percent on basic commodities, and against participation in the chain of marketing. There is further a general injunction against hoarding, or cornering the market of basic goods, which was obviously aimed at preventing speculation and raising prices of such things as oil, wine, fruit and vegetables.[43]

The rabbinic authorities saw nothing wrong with producers' withholding their products at times of oversupply in order to benefit from better prices later. Their objection was to dealers and middlemen. It would seem, therefore, that although transgressing these rabbinical dicta brought no punishment, neither social nor legal, they provided a cultural atmosphere in favour of direct producer/consumer marketing where possible, or of shortening the chain of intermediaries.

(2) Administrative and executive actions

The appointment of inspectors to enforce price control or to reduce the profit margin was a common feature of Jewish communal structure. In their price-fixing activities, most authorities allowed for normal profit, which included (in the main) recompense for capital investment, labour, and risk.[44] The prime purpose of price enforcement was to prevent speculation and monopoly profits. It is interesting to note that the rabbis overruled the opinion of Samuel that the market mechanism would force merchants to offer goods at the lowest possible price, thereby making such overseers unnecessary.[45] Jews who infringed the communal controls on prices were liable to flogging, fining, or excommunication.

Another form of price control was achieved by bringing about a decline in demand and thereby a decrease in prices. There are several examples of rabbinic action to bring down the price of goods either by forbidding their use or by changing religious rulings with regard to them. In the sixteenth century in Moravia, for instance, fishermen raised the price of fish, an important part of the Sabbath meal, which placed it beyond the reach of many. The leading rabbinic authority of that time pronounced the fish ritually unfit to eat, and the monopoly disappeared.[46] In our own day, a similar action was taken in order to reduce the price of the festive fur hats worn by members of the Hassidic sect.

It must be borne in mind that administrative attempts to impose price control were not a general concern to control all prices. Most of the time the actions of overseers and rabbis were aimed only at certain commodities thought to be essential. For example, most of medieval Jewish communities had some form of price control on the sale of wine, which forms an important part of almost all Jewish ceremonial acts. Many of them appointed special dealers who were obligated to provide this service.[47] Others limited both profit margin and price.[48] Meat and other essential articles also were often the subject of price control in medieval societies.[49] There are even a few isolated references to the subsidy of essential foodstuffs.

Generally speaking, this intervention of the community to keep prices and profits down on essential commodities would pave the way for present-day communal action when called for by suffering or distress caused by high prices. It must be pointed out that Judaism gave the communal authorities much leeway in economic legislation, provided such was in accordance with halachic rulings.

(3) The legal "just price"—*ona'ah*

In addition to an ethical restraint on the market mechanism, the religious authorities also provided redress through the legal system. The concept of a "just price" does not flow from consideration of fraud or theft. These were dealt with by the rabbinic laws on buying and selling, which operated vigorously against even the smallest instances of harmful selling practices. There is ground to consider it as a deviation from a prevailing market price which arises from lack of knowledge on the part of one of the parties or the use of undue influence by either. The "just price" as expressed by the law of *ona'ah* in the Talmud and later legislation is based on the following principles:[50]

(a) A sale is valid only if the price differs from the normal price by less than one-sixth. At that point, though the sale is still valid, the injured party can claim compensation for the difference. Beyond it, the courts can invalidate the sale completely.

(b) This protection applies irrespective of whether the injured party is the buyer or the seller. However, it applies only to the time needed to show the good to an expert and have it valued.

(c) Since the protection of *ona'ah* introduced an element of uncertainty into the market, businessmen desired as short a time-period as possible. There was an alternative rabbinic opinion that a sale could be valid even at a price up to one-quarter above normal. Naturally the business community was pleased with this ruling. Yet it preferred the majority opinion of one-sixth, since the minority opinion allowed the other party unlimited time to claim protection of the law.[51]

The protection of *ona'ah* does not apply to the sale of slaves, promissory notes, or land. It may well be that the economic reason for this lies in the difficulty of assigning a price to these articles in view of the subjective evaluation involved. Nevertheless, many authorities held that although the one-sixth restriction did not apply to land, there was a concept of exaggerated *ona'ah* (50 above market price) in which case the law of *ona'ah* would apply.[52] Promissory notes present a particular problem since we know that different investors have different degrees of risk-aversion and different methods of evaluating risk, so that a market price might not exist. There were also legal difficulties due to the fact that the signator of the note could repudiate his debt, in which case that which was sold did not really exist, which is contrary to rabbinic law. However, a discussion of the legal aspects is beyond the scope of this paper.

Maimonides, writing in the twelfth century, limited the scope of *ona'ah* to those cases where one of the parties is ignorant of the market price at the time of sale. Some of the Germanic school of rabbis, however, argued that full disclosure does not negate *ona'ah*. The injured party could claim that he was under duress of some form since he needed the goods urgently; duress voiding all sales in Jewish law.[53]

Although Maimonides also wanted to limit *ona'ah* to those goods which are basic necessities, the majority of rabbinic opinion held that as long as the goods were uniform and were not created by artisans (in which case each article acquired an individual intrinsic value), the protection of the "just price" applied.[54]

It would seem that the main application of the Jewish concept of a "just price" in a modern economy is in providing full disclosure and free flow of economic knowledge. This would impose on the community an obligation to see that all were informed about the availability of goods at the market price. The seller on his part could escape the legal consequences of evading the "just price" by making such full disclosure voluntarily. Recourse could be had to the courts to claim protection so that the "just price" could become a real protection for the ignorant or the coerced.

Encouraging competition

The sages understood that competition between sellers, in all its forms, leads to the benefit of the general public even if it means a decline in profits for some. We find rabbinic support for various methods of maintaining competition and preventing monopolies and licensing arrangements. Nevertheless, the moral issues raised by the free market, primarily in the short term, led to restricted practices sanctioned by rabbinic opinion, as discussed below.

(1) Price competition

Competition may take the form of direct price-cutting as well as methods such as prizes, gifts, and advertising. All these attract buyers, and accustom them either to buy a certain product or to frequent a specific seller. The moral question of unfairness to other sellers is raised, but the prevailing rabbinic view is that since other merchants or firms can also offer the same prizes or lower their prices, the public interest must prevail; and this is served by the encouragement of such competition.

In ancient times, majority opinion held that a firm may distribute roasted wheat or nuts to children even though this harms the business of the other traders. It was also said that "the memory of the shopkeeper who lowers prices will be blessed" (since he benefits the community by lowering prices).[55] Similarly, the sages permitted decoration of goods (provided the decoration is made known to the buyer in order to avoid any doubt of misrepresentation), an early form of advertising.[56] Yet at the same time that legal opinion was supportive of competition, a moral pronouncement was made which would limit such competition. This involved undercutting, or "forestalling," a person or firm involved in a transaction. The offer of a lower price, or better conditions, or even the expression of an interest in a transaction which had not yet terminated either negatively or positively, was construed as morally unjust.[57] Obviously such practices were to the detriment of the buyer and regarded as harmful. Although many Jews, both rabbinic and lay, followed this principle in their daily lives, there was no legal redress for the injured party. Its existence introduced a purely moral imperative into the marketplace.

(2) Free entry

Inter-firm competition is not only expressed through price, but is dependent on the possibility of free entry. This may mean the ability freely to practise various professions, establish new firms, cater to expected or actual demand, or move from one place to another to benefit from changed economic conditions. Naturally such free entry affects the firms already established in that area or industry, which can often earn abnormal profits by restricting the supply of goods, by raising the price by preventing or limiting such entry. The "closed shop" principle, licensing arrangements and immigration laws are examples of this type of restriction on competition. It would seem, however, that the general trend in the Jewish world has been towards a liberal, open-market attitude on this issue. At the same time, however, the religious considerations of mercy, justice, and the general well-being of the community could lead to limitations on the right of free entry which would cause genuine economic suffering.

Nuisance

Talmudic sources provide protection to neighbourhoods and communities against economic activity which may harm them physically or ecologically. Industries which cause pollution, noise, and congestion may be barred from a community or town by legislation. Such legislation, however, cannot prevent the establishment of new business ventures if such already exist. In modern parlance, firms cannot be prevented from establishing plants in those places where the zoning laws provide for them. The sages did not accept that the entry of new firms should be forbidden because they injure existing ones. So it is permitted to set up shop alongside shop, bathhouse alongside bathhouse, and so forth. Throughout the Middle Eastern and Mediterranean countries one can still see similar arrangements which create a far more competitive market than the shopping centres of modern town planning, with its principle of one firm for each type of business.

It is interesting to note that this ruling contradicts another talmudic decision whereby fishermen can force others to withdraw to a distance equal to that of a fish's swim from his nets.[58] However, this has been explained as a special case. Since the bait nets have already been set down, the fish may be regarded as the fisherman's property. Therefore, others would be guilty of theft. The Franco-German authorities of the twelfth century insisted, on the other hand, that customers are free to shop wherever they wish, so nobody can regard them as a captive market until the sale is completed.[59]

Free entry and competition are also dependent on the ease of population transfers and relocation of firms. The question whether noncitizens and aliens may work or establish businesses is an age-old one yet ever new. Jewish biblical commentators saw the exclusion of neighbouring tribes by the wealthy cities of Sodom and Gomorrah as their primary sin. Medieval cities limited the entry of citizens of other towns, and even today most nation-states restrict the freedom of nonnationals to work or engage in business. Generally speaking, the rabbinic authorities following a talmudical dictum held that a foreigner (or resident of another town or community) has full rights of residence, including those of an economic nature, provided he pays the taxes applicable to that community.[60] To allow freedom of entry without the tax liability would simply be immoral, in addition to being unfair. The talmudic authorities therefore favour payment of taxes by those earning their livelihood in the city but living in the suburbs.

There were, however, certain exceptions to the obligation of sharing in the tax liability in exchange for free entry. Peddlers were allowed to wander from city to city without paying taxes in order that "the daughters of Israel should not lack for jewelry and cosmetics." Out-of-town merchants were able to display their wares on market days without becoming liable for municipal taxes.[61]

In view of the religious injunction to study Torah, it is not surprising to find free movement of rabbinic scholars without the restraint of taxation.

The decision regarding the right of free entry negates the legal right of citizens of a community to exclude *on economic ground* others from entering and living in their community. It must be noted, however, that exclusion on *moral* grounds was accepted by all rabbinic authorities.[62]

Restrictive practices

In the realities of a complex economy, competition may bring in its wake human hardship and deprivation, despite the economic benefits derived. Sometimes competition is unequal, as in the case of the chain store versus the individual storekeeper, or that of the corporate employer versus the individual worker. This hardship or deprivation is also caused by large-scale unemployment, depressed or declining industries, bankruptcy, and the like. It is true that in economic theory human and financial resources are predicted to adjust *in the long run* to the changes brought about by competition. This is viewed as the market mechanism for achieving an efficient economy. In reality adjustment may often take a long time, especially when measured in terms of human life, and changes in the political or social framework within which they work may never be made. However, even if the long-term adjustment does take place, society still has to incur a human and moral cost until equilibrium is restored. Naturally, the social and moral values of society will balance the economic loss resulting from restrictive practices against the human suffering arising out of the change.

In Judaism, therefore, provisions were made for restrictive practices in order to alleviate or minimize the suffering and hardships caused by adjustment to new market equilibrium.

(1) Cartelization

The association of producers and traders into special groups, guilds or unions obviously yields economic benefits to their members by restricting competition, fixing the quantity of goods supplied to the market and so determining prices. Such associations, however, may benefit the general public by means of quality control, professional training, and mutual insurance. They also provide a mechanism for smoothing out short-run declines and booms which may occur in the market, thus preventing bankruptcy and financial hardship. Without denying the favourable effects of such associations, their adverse effects on the community must not be forgotten. It is necessary to balance the good effects of such restrictive practices against the damage in the form of higher prices and restricted entry. Talmudic authority gave the right to establish associations in which mutual agreement would limit production or determine prices.[63] However, these restrictive practices require not only the agreement of all involved in the industry, but also the public supervision of those agreements which serve as a basis for the association. The validity of trade agreements in Jewish law depends on a rabbi specially trained in this field who can serve as an arbitrator.[64] In cases where there is no such person, cases would be decided by the community council. In our own day, this would suggest the desireability of some form of rabbinic supervision over trade unions, public utilities, and trade associations. It is interesting to note that Jewish thought insisted on the supervision of cartelization and monopoly by rabbinic authority, rather than by a lay council of interested producers or consumers. The reason for this is simple. It saw the review function as an adjustment of such associations to the demands of righteousness, justice and mercy rather than economic ones.

(2) Free entry

The rabbinic opinions and rulings regarding free entry both into industries and into geographical areas discussed in the previous section were operative in a relatively free and competitive economy in which the Jews of the Hellenistic and Roman empires lived for many centuries. The economic and political conditions of Jewish life in Christian Europe, however, from the Crusades down to the turn of the nineteenth century, called into question the benefits of unlimited competiton. Some communities found themselves in situations where competition not only brought greater poverty and suffering, but often would mean the destruction of the Jewish community itself. Since the purpose of the halachic rulings had been to minimize suffering and injustice, and to further communal well-being, the social data had to be examined to see whether they met these constant religious criteria.

Medieval Judaism

Almost from the conversion of Europe down to the end of the nineteenth century, restrictive laws were placed on the Jew with regard to residence, travel and occupation. At the same time, physical persecution, expulsion and forced conversions became part of the everyday pattern of Jewish living. It is important to note that the Jew was denied the ownership of land (the major factor of production) until the Industrial Revolution. This meant that the economic existence of the Jew was peripheral to the general economic structure. As a result of these factors, the economic base of the Jewish community was both restricted and one which entailed great risk and uncertainty.

Under these conditions it was no longer true that competition was the best means of maximizing communal welfare. The contrary was true, so that morality and charity demanded a limitation on competition which manifested itself in communal edicts and rabbinic decisions. These restrictive measures on free movement are typified by two institutions: the *Herem Hayishuv* and the *marufiya*. The first limited the right to geographic entry; the second limited inter-firm competition.

(1) *Herem Hayishuv*

This was a ruling whereby veteran settlers in a town were considered to have acquired a legal monopoly on residence and trade. Outsiders were prevented from settling and trading by the threat of excommunication unless they obtain permission from the community. Unlike the talmudic decisions quoted before, willingness to pay taxes was not considered sufficient to offset the threat to the economic stability of the community.[65] The *Herem Hayishuv* was widely prevalent in medieval France, Germany, Italy and eastern Europe. In the latter, it remained until the abolition of anti-Jewish legislation at the end of the last century.

The *Herem* did not exist in the Jewish communities of Spain, North Africa and the Middle East, since in these countries the economic structure and the role of the Jews in society continued to be the free-market type which had existed in the talmudic period. Therefore competition remained the best means of achieving general communal well-being.[66] The *Herem Hayishuv* may be regarded as a temporary rabbinic enactment to prevent disruption of the fragile Jewish community by increased competition. In this case, although consumers were affected adversely by higher prices, fewer services and fewer goods, the communal well-being outweighed these disadvantages.

It is important to stress that there were certain non-economic factors peculiar to Jewish life which limited the application of *Herem Hayishuv*. These related to refugees and to the educational profession. Jewish medieval history was characterized by continual expulsion from independent cities and feudal states, sometimes temporary, sometimes permanent. The refugee has therefore been a common feature of Jewish life down to our own time.

Refugees posed two problems for the communities:

(a) how to provide for their welfare, and to deal with competition from the newcomers;

(b) how to absorb the influx without upsetting the delicate balance with the non-Jewish community.

Judaism, with its emphasis on mutual responsibility, charity and mercy, could not countenance the exclusion of refugees. Communal practice was therefore to admit refugees freely and to allow them to trade and earn a livelihood.[67]

Judaism attaches great importance to the study of Torah, not as a means of achieving knowledge for practical everyday use, but as a basic religious discipline. It is not surprising therefore to find an insistence on the free movement and unrestricted practice of rabbinical studies, even though this meant hardship for scholars and teachers already in residence in a certain town.[68]

(2) *Marufiya*

The *marufiya* (literally, "friend" in Arabic) protected the holders of monopoly rights (obtained from the Gentile authorities) from the competition of other Jews. Generally speaking these rights existed in tax-farming, public-sector loans, and the procuring of soldiers, arms, or luxury items, and were granted by the king, lord or bishop. In eastern Europe the same protection was afforded by the *Uronda,* primarily in the liquor trade, whilst in Moslem countries it prevailed in the silk trade. The moral argument for this restrictive practice, inconsistent with the free-entry principle discussed earlier, was that the holder of the monopoly right had made an investment in the grantor of the rights—had "cultivated" him, so to speak. This would suggest that rabbinic opinion might sanction monopoly rights today in such industries as public transport, communications and utilities; all of which necessitate a heavy investment which might not be forthcoming without such protection.

(3) Intangible assets

Intangible assets such as patents, copyright, trademarks or licensing arrangements are all, in effect, restrictive acts protecting the holder's investments. At the same time they may prevent society from benefiting from new technology or lower prices. Here too the moral problem of adjudicating between public benefit and private wealth applies. In the short run non-recognition of these protective mechanisms may lead to great loss on the part of both employers and employees. The rabbinic recognition of this was based primarily on the biblical injunction forbidding the removal of a neighbour's landmark.[69] Since the law already forbade theft, this injunction was understood to refer primarily to the original Hebrew settlement in the Land of Canaan.

It was not difficult to expand its application to intangible assets in medieval Jewish communities. I will limit my discussion to its application to two types of intangible assets in Jewish life: the rule of copyright and the protection of the rights of tenants.

(a) The concept of copyright involves a moral choice between two conflicting issues. On the one hand, "the jealousy of the learned increases knowledge," so that restrictions flowing from copyright should be rejected. On the other hand, products of the mind had to be protected against theft. So we find numerous examples of copyright in Jewish law, especially where publishing and printing became a major factor of Jewish economic life.[70] Often these restrictions were allowed only for a limited period in order to realize the social benefit of spreading learning as widely as possible.

(b) The Gentile authorities in most European countries restricted Jews to ghettos, or special streets, and this limited the supply of houses available to them. Yet natural increase and influx of refugees often accelerated demand for housing. Any wide discrepancy between supply and demand led to a rise in rent and the eviction of poor tenants. So by rabbinic legislation and communal decree, Jews were prevented from offering higher rents to a Gentile landlord in order to displace existing tenants.

It must be stressed that the restrictive practices enumerated in this section applied only when there was a real danger of destroying another Jew's economic well-being. The mere dilution of profits or decreasing of revenue were not sufficient to invoke rabbinic restraint. It required the destruction of an economic base to produce such intervention in the interests of charity and welfare.[71]

Summary

Although the market mechanism and legitimacy of profit were recognized by the halachic authorities, economic activity had to be regulated where the interests of the community, morality, mercy and justice demanded it. Communities were thus empowered to institute price control, and moral injunctions provided a warning against speculation in basic commodities. Redress could be had for charging above market price. It would seem that this redress was linked to the free flow of information, which became the seller's obligation. Free competition, both in prices and through advertising, is considered good for the community, and therefore not only permitted but encouraged. For the same reason, free entry is granted both to new enterprises and to foreign firms. But in cases where competition would be immoral or injurious, restrictive practices are permitted. The association of professional, commercial, or labour interests into some form of cartel is permitted provided there is supervision by rabbinic authority.

NOTES

1. Karl Marx, *About the Jewish Question.*

2. W. Sombart, *The Jews and Modern Capitalism* (1913, 1951).

3. Max Weber, *Sociology of Religion* (1964).

4. Ber Borochov, *Nationalism and the Class Struggle.* Ed., M. Cohen (1937).

5. Y. Lieberman, "Origins of Coases' Theorem in Jewish Law," *Journal of Legal Studies,* June, 1981. Also Y. Lieberman, "Elements in Talmudical Monetary Thought," *History of Political Economy,* Summer, 1979.

6. *Talmud Bavli,* Berachot 35b.

7. *Mishneh Torah,* Hilchot Deot, Chapter 5. Hilchot Talmud Torah, Chapter 1. Maimonides's Letter to his son.

8. *Mishneh Torah,* Hilchot Deot.

9. *Nachmanides's Commentary on the Torah,* Leviticus, Chapter 19; S. R. Hirsch, Horeb, Section V. 480.

10. Genesis 49, 25–26; Leviticus 26, 3–13; Deuteronomy 28, 1–13.

11. Deuteronomy 28, 16–53.

12. Psalms 128.

13. *Talmud Bavli*, Baba Bathra, 175b.

14. Psalms 24.

15. Exodus 23, 11; Leviticus 25, 2–5. *Commentary of Sepher Hachinuch and Klei Yakar.*

16. Sepher Hachinuch, Mitzvah 506.

17. Deuteronomy 6, 18.

18. Maimonides, *Shmoneh Perakim*, Chapter 6.

19. Exodus 20. *Commentary of the Malbim.*

20. *Shulchan Aruch Hilchot Geneivah*, Section 348. Also Mishnah Baba Bathra Chapter 10, Mishnah 9.

21. *Shulchan Aruch Hilchot Ona'ah*, Section 228.

22. *Mishnah Baba Bathra*, Chapter 5, Mishnah 11. Also *Shulchan Aruch Hilchot Ona'ah*, Section 231.

23. *Mishnah Baba Metziah*, Chapter 6, Mishnah 11. Also *Shulchan Aruch Hilchot Ona'ah* 228.

24. Exodus 23. 4–9. Leviticus 19, 9–10; 33–34. Leviticus 25, 25; Exodus 22, 20–21, *Talmud Babli*, Gittin 52a.

25. Leviticus, 19, 14.

26. *Commentary of Rashi* on above verse. Also Mishnah, Avoda Zarah, Chapter 1, Mishnah 2.

27. *Mishnah Baba Kama*, Chapter 2, Mishnah 6.

28. *Talmud Babli*, Baba Metzia 14a.

29. Leviticus 25, 36.

30. Malbim on Genesis 18.20. Also *Talmud* Ketuboth 103a and Baba Bathra 12b.

31. Exodus 22, 25–27; Deuteronomy 24, 10–14.

32. Sepher Hachinuch, Mitzva 66. Shulchan Aruch 97, 1.

33. *Mishneh Torah,* Hilchot Shecheinim Chapter 12, 5. 13, 14.

34. M. Tamari, *Competition. Prices and Profits.* Bar Ilan University (Hebrew).

35. *Shulchan Aruch Hilchot Ona'ah,* Section 227.

36. *Shulchan Aruch* 97, 23.

37. I. Herzog. *The Main Institutions of Jewish Law,* vol. 1, *Law of Property.*

38. Ibn Migash on *Talmud Babli,* Baba Bathra, 21b.

39. S. R. Hirsch, *Commentary on Exodus,* 20.14.

40. Sepher Hachinuch, *Mitzvah* 421.

41. *Talmud Bavli,* Baba Metzia 40b; also Baba Bathra, 4a ad menachot, 7a.

42. *Talmud Bavli,* Baba Bathra, 91a.

43. *Tosephat avodah Zarah,* chapter 5, section 1.

44. *Meiri Baba Metzia* 406; *Rosh BM,* 111:16; *Tev Choshen Mishpat,* 231:
26. Here an argument is offered for permitting foreign traders to operate
if they are selling at prices below the local ones or providing goods not
otherwise available.

45. *Talmud Bavli,* Baba Bathra, 89a (*Rashbam*).

46. *Tzemach Zeder,* Responsa 28.

47. *Pinkas* Padua, Regulation 198.

48. *Pinhas* Berlin, Regulation 240.

49. *Teshuvat HaRivash,* Responsa 195.

50. *Shulchan Aruch Hilchot Ona'ah.*

51. *Mishnah Baba Metzia*, Chapter 4, *mishnah* 3.

52. *Talmud Yerushalmi Ketubot*, Chapter 1, *Halacha* 4; *Tosaphot Baba Metzia* 47a.

53. Mordechai Commentating on *Baba Metzia*, Section 307.

54. *Talmud Bavli*, Baba Metzia 48b; *Shulchan Aruch Choshen Mishpat*, Section 227, sub-section 15.

55. *Mishnah Baba Metziah*, Chapter 4, mishnah 12. See also commentary of the *Talmud* on this *mishnah*.

56. *Shulchan Aruch; Hilchot Mecheirah.*

57. *Talmud Bavli*, Kiddushin 59a.

58. *Talmud Bavli*, Baba Bathra 21b. Comment of Rashi.

59. *Tosaphot Kiddushin* 59a.

60. *Mishneh Torah Hilchot Shecheinim* 86, chapter 6, *Halacha* 8. Also *Shulchan Aruch*, and *Tur Chosen Mishpat*, Section 126, sub-section 5.

61. *Tur Chosen Mishpat*, Section 126, sub-section 11.

62. Enactments of the Jewish Community of Canterbury, England, 12th century. (Quoted in *Select Pleas, Starrs and other records from the Rolls of the Exchequer of the Jews*, ed., J. M. Rigg. pp. 35–36.)

63. *Talmud Bavli*, Baba Bathra.

64. See Maggid Mishneh on *Mishneh Torah Hilchot Mechirah*, Chapter 14, *Halacha* 11, also Kesef Mishoh on the same law.

65. I. L. Rabinowitz, *Herem Hayishuv*. See also *Encyclopedia Judaica:* "*Herem Hayishuv.*"

66. *Responsa* of the *Rashba*.

67. Rama on *Choshen Mishpat*, Section 126, sub-section 7.

68. *Talmud Bavli*, Baba Bathra 22a. See also Rama on *Joreh Deah*, Section 145, for limitations on free entry where it actually deprived the local teacher of his livelihood.

69. Deuteronomy 19:14

70. *Responsa* of Maharan of Padua, *Responsa* 41.

71. M. Feinstein, *Iggrot Mosheh, Choshen Mishpat* 38. It must be stressed that many authorities reject monopoly rights even when there is a real danger of deprivation.

Comment

Marilyn A. Friedman

This conference has been designed to examine "the thesis that there is no necessary incompatibility or inconsistency between religious belief, properly understood, and the basic tenets of the free enterprise philosophy."[1] Dr. Meir Tamari's well-documented paper supports this thesis with respect to Jewish religious belief. In my comments on his paper, I shall reinforce Tamari's confirmation of that thesis. However, I shall also suggest that Jewish teachings show no necessary incompatibility with the basic tenets of either socialism or welfare-state capitalism. My conclusion is that we should not take the compatibility of Jewish religious belief with free-enterprise philosophy as evidence that free-enterprise philosophy is *uniquely* suited to the worldview of a person of Jewish religion.

I shall address two points. The first is a methodological point about

Jewish teachings to which Dr. Tamari has already alluded. The compatibility of Jewish teaching with a wide variety of economic structures derives both from the absence of economic theory and from their anecdotal, situation-specific orientation. Nowhere in Judaic doctrine do we find a broad, encompassing economic view which dictates a particular way of treating economic life. The second point concerns the intellectual history of the Jewish people over the past two centuries. Jews as a group have shown no overwhelming preference for free enterprise philosophy over other economic ideologies. They have displayed a great diversity of intellectual commitments regarding economic issues. It is true that this tells us nothing about the theoretico-logical consistency of any of those ideologies with Jewish religious doctrine *per se*. However it does tell us about the *living significance* of Jewish teachings for a community of people schooled according to it. It tells us about the intellectual life made possible for human beings whose background is significantly Jewish.

Methodology of the Jewish tradition

Meir Tamari believes that in Jewish teachings we find the supremacy of action rather than of reason or faith as the means for the salvation of human beings. Mundane actions and everyday deeds are the subject matter of Jewish religious teachings in regard to economic and social matters. Menachem Kellner puts the point as follows: "...Judaism is a religion which emphasizes human behaviour over general claims of theology and faith—a religion of pots and pans in the eyes of those who derogate its concern with actions."[2] The original Jewish scriptures consist largely of anecdotes, homilies, and the like—a kind of applied ethics rather than a theoretical framework. In this respect, they are a very early forerunner of business ethics and similar applied ethics specializations which have become fashionable in professional philosophy in the last decade or two.

Because traditional Jewish teachings have been silent on some of the major issues of modern times, Jewish religious leaders have had to articulate principles and concepts to guide Jews in those areas of life not covered by the traditional teachings. Judaism has had to confront various aspects of non-Jewish life and thought, and to respond to them. Its method for doing so has combined two essential ingredients: exegesis of traditional texts and interpretation of those texts in light of new material. This method has been described as one which allowed Judaism to remain true to itself while fruitfully confronting non-Jewish thought.[3]

In addition, Judaic teaching has always included a tradition which emphasized the independence of rational inquiry and the acceptance of the best arguments on an issue, rather than relying on the determination of opinion by eminent Jewish figures or revered traditions. According to one rabbinic interpretation, certain biblical passages mean that *Torah* is open to a multiplicity of interpretations. There is a deeply-rooted principle in the Jewish tradition that there is no single, unchanging way of understanding the text. Throughout most of the Jewish tradition, the principle of free exegesis prevails. For Maimonides himself, there is no authoritative prophetic teaching about the natural world held as binding on faithful Jews.[4]

Thus, Toral law sanctions the incorporation of new rules into Jewish teaching, provided only that they conflict with no other provision which is already an established part of that law.[5] For the modern Orthodox Jewish thinker especially, Jewish ethical teachings must not contradict *halakhah*.[6] The Orthodox view is that *halakhah* is a divine system, not a human system, and should therefore not develop or change in any fundamental way through historical periods. Conservative and Reform Jewish thinkers, by contrast, are more inclined to accept the essential modifiability of *halakhah*. The view of Conservative Jews, for example, tends to be that *halakhah* is "the Jewish vocabulary for approaching God." It is the human record of the revelatory experiences of God had by Jews, and therefore, as a human institution, subject to "change and historical development like all human institutions."[7]

Indirect deduction

No ancient or medieval Jewish scholar wrote economic tracts: the norms and ideals of economic and social life must be deduced indirectly from legal teaching.[8] In Tamari's words, Judaism " . . .does not have a clearly defined economic theory." Jewish law is therefore undefined for the radically different and rapidly changing social and economic conditions of our times. The population is allowed to adopt any economic system which it will, says Tamari, so long as that system is consistent with " . . .the demands of Divine justice and mercy." In this way, Judaism pledges its adherents neither to socialism nor to capitalism.[9]

Some of the specific points of Judaic teachings discussed by Tamari are more compatible with free-enterprise philosophy than with alternatives to it. These points include the acceptance of private property; the absence of a glorification of poverty; the view that there is nothing intrinsically evil about the pursuit of wealth; the association of a bountiful livelihood and material plenty with religious and moral uprightness; the encouragement of competition; the discouragement of monopolies or licensing arrangements; and the right of free entry even for foreign Jews, so long as they pay the applicable taxes.

Other points discussed by Tamari are more compatible with alternatives to free-enterprise philosophy, such as socialism or welfare-state capitalism, which permit or advocate intervention into the free-market mechanism. These include: the community orientation to property ownership and concomitant view that all members of the group are partners in each individual's wealth; special measures designed for the protection of the weak and powerless members of society; the assumption that the community is obligated to provide the basic necessities for its needy, and to tax its members for this purpose; the control of prices and profits by direct intervention into the market and by the use of the concept of the "just price"; limitations on the right of free entry into a market where this entry is seen to cause genuine economic suffering; and restrictive practices to alleviate or minimize the suffering caused by competition.

Tamari tells us that talmudic and later literature recognizes benefits as well as costs in the market economy. Judaism consequently allows for intervention by appropriate communal authorities in order that they may prevent or alleviate the poverty, hunger, injustice and other human suffering which the unchecked operation of the market may sometimes produce. Its self-regulating mechanisms are not believed capable of correcting these, or of correcting them in short enough a time. Of the three economic philosophies to which I have referred, this aspect of Jewish teaching seems most compatible with the general concept of welfare-state capitalism.

My conclusion with respect to the method of the Jewish tradition is that although Jewish teachings are indeed consistent and compatible with free-enterprise philosophy, this has minimal significance in light of the equivalent consistency and compatibility of Jewish teachings with socialist philosophy and with the philosophy of welfare-state capitalism. Furthermore, the possibility of continued interpretation of original textual materials (itself a tradition-sanctioned method for dealing with those materials) means that Jewish teachings may prove to be compatible with additional, as-yet undreamed-of, economic philosophies. This theoretical flexibility and versatility on broad social and economic matters may be one of the crucial mechanisms·which has enabled the Jewish people to survive the constantly changing circumstances of their troubled history. In any event, it minimizes the importance of any compatibility between Jewish religious belief and free enterprise philosophy.

Diversity in recent Jewish intellectual history

Jews have been prominent as proponents of free-enterprise philosophy, socialism and welfare-state capitalism. This diversity tells us nothing about the logical relation between Jewish religious doctrine and any particular economic ideology, for people of Jewish ancestry may forsake the religious beliefs of their forebears. They may also misunderstand or ignore the logical relation between their religious and their economic views. Nevertheless, this ideological diversity does display the range of positions which have been adopted by those whose background was in any sense Jewish. It therefore indicates something about the *living significance* which a Jewish religious background may have in the life of a community, the compatibility *in practice* of that background with various economic views. The evidence shows that Jewish religious belief no more leads people to ally themselves with free-enterprise philosophy than with its socialist or welfare-state alternatives.

The growth of capitalism, with industrialization, expansion of world commerce, and economic liberalism, is said by various authors to have benefited the Jewish people greatly.[10] In the words of Salo W. Baron, it "...opened broad new avenues for Jewish enterprise and imagination."[11] Jews benefited from the new occupational opportunities created by new methods of production, which obviated the restrictions placed on Jewish productive capacity by the medieval guild system and land legislation. They benefited from the new emphasis upon international commerce, something well-suited to the Jewish communities dispersed throughout the world, yet still in contact with each other through kinship and other ties. Last but not least, they benefited from the new emphasis upon individualism which allowed the Jew to be viewed more as a person than as a member of a group, as someone to be evaluated on the basis of personal merit and achievement, in particular, economic entrepreneurship.[12]

Capitalism is harmful

But at the same time, the Jewish community has been harmed by the growth of capitalism. Civil rights and economic opportunities in the surrounding non-Jewish culture, and the new emphasis on individualism, undermined the cohesiveness of Jewish community life. In addition, the reliance on human reason rather than on (putatively) supernatural revelation or socially controlled tradition has affected persons of the Jewish faith no less than their Christian neighbours.[13] Baron suggests that full liberty means, in effect, the rule of the strong; this means a tendency for economic power to concentrate in corporate enterprises. Jews have "...learned from bitter experience that for the most part economic concentration operated against them."[14] In light of these considerations, it is not surprising to find that Jews have favoured the restrictions on full liberty introduced within democratic-capitalist systems, such as antitrust, fiscal and labour legislation.[15]

Jews have participated in modern industry both as managers and employees. For example, Jewish workers coming from Europe to the New World or England at the turn of the century were pioneers in developing labour unions.[16] Indeed, Jewish unions are credited with having injected "a peculiar ingredient into the Western labour movements." States Baron:

> All through history Jewish communal life was permeated with the ideal of social justice. This, even more than immediate wage benefits or improved conditions of labor, became therefore an integral part of Jewish unionism. It has been observed that in the United States, as elsewhere, many Jewish labor leaders remained working for their unions even when they had economically more attractive alternatives.[17]

As industrial workers, Jews have been attracted by the message of socialism. Ironically, early European socialism was strongly anti-Jewish. But by the turn of the century, this had changed. The growing alliance of socialism with democracy led to recognition of the legitimacy of the egalitarian claims of the Jews. Knowledge of the poverty of east European Jews contradicted the stereotype of the Jew as capitalist. Consequently, by the turn of the century, parties such as the

German Socialist Party, and major socialist leaders, publicly repudiated any kind of anti-Semitism. This repudiation was intensified by
the increasing use of anti-Semitic slogans on the part of those who opposed socialism.[18]

Specifically Jewish socialist parties emerged within the European
socialist movement beginning in the 1870s. The Jewish Socialist
Party, the Bund, was formed in 1897, declaring its aim at first as
". . .the more effective propagation of socialism among the Jewish
masses." By 1903 the Bund had altered its position so as to advocate
national minority rights for Jews—in effect, Jewish separatism—a position which incensed the Russian Socialist Party at the time.[19]

Ambivalence

The diversity which has characterized Jewish economic doctrine in
the past exists today. Edward S. Shapiro observes that contemporary
American Jews ". . .have had an ambivalent attitude toward financial
success and commercial acquisitiveness," even though the rapid economic mobility of American Jews over the past 75 years has derived
in part from the "overwhelming" orientation toward business of east
European Jewish immigrants of the late nineteenth century. Indeed, a
contempt for business appears early among the immigrants themselves. A generally socialist ideology was common among the Jewish
labour unions and among most of the "first-generation ghetto intellectuals." Shapiro suggests that the intense union activity among Jews in
the early part of the century reflected this ambivalence, deriving as
much from the "dissatisfaction of Jewish workers at being workers at
all" as from the "wretched working conditions of the sweatshops."[20]

Shapiro identifies this same contempt for business in a recent wave
of nostalgia for the immigrant generation, and the old Lower East
Side, which appears in such writing as Irving Howe's *World of Our
Fathers* and *Fiddler on the Roof*.[21] This is how Shapiro describes this
attitude:

> For the modern Jewish intellectual, the memory of the ghetto is
> a welcome contrast to the ostentatious materialism, spiritual va-
> cuity and aimlessness which supposedly characterize modern
> Jewry. The Lower East Side is idealized because of its intellec-
> tual intensity, its socialist politics, its working class culture, and
> because the immigrant generation never completely surrendered
> to bourgeois values. It has been romanticized to show just how

far America's Jews have moved away from the ideals of their immigrant ancestors and have been enveloped within the commercialism and materialism of modern America.[22]

This one-sided view requires correction, asserts Shapiro:

> Jews will have to recognize that their history encompasses Inland Steel as well as the I.L.G.W.U., Revlon as well as Delancey Street, and Federated Department Stores as well as Jacob Adler. American Jewish identity will have to rest, in part, on the recognition of American Jewry's persistent middle class character and on the acknowledgement of the enormous benefit that America's Jews have derived from American capitalism.[23]

Shapiro's discussion is useful in the present context for the way in which it reveals the continuing ambivalence of Jewish attitudes toward economic issues. Shapiro himself is concerned with what he regards as distortion in the modern Jewish intellectuals' portrait of turn-of-the-century immigrants. It is worth noting that he does not scrutinize the reason for the alleged distortion. He does not analyze the "ostentatious materialism, spiritual vacuity and aimlessness which supposedly characterize modern Jewry." Although Shapiro may well have identified a contemporary falsification of historical fact, he has not shown that its underlying motivation is misguided. This remains an open question.

NOTES

1. Letter from Walter Block.

2. "The Structure of Jewish Ethics," in Menachem Marc Kellner, ed., *Contemporary Jewish Ethics* (New York: Sanhedrin Press, 1978), p. 5.

3. Marvin Fox, "Judaism, Secularism and Textual Interpretation," in Marvin Fox, ed., *Modern Jewish Ethics* (Athens, Ohio: Ohio State University Press), p. 3.

4. Fox, *op. cit.*, pp. 8–9, 10, 11–12, 14, 17.

5. Nachum L. Rabinovitch, "*Halakha* and Other Systems of Ethics," in Marvin Fox, *op. cit.*, pp. 99–100.

6. Kellner, *op. cit.*, p. 17.

7. *Ibid.*, pp. 16–17.

8. Salo W. Baron, "Economic Doctrines," in Nachum Gross, ed., *Economic History of the Jews* (New York: Schocken Books, 1975), p. 48.

9. Leo Jung, "The Ethics of Business," in Kellner, *op. cit.*, p. 340.

10. Jews are credited by some with a highly formative role in the growth of modern capitalism. See Werner Sombart, *The Jews and Modern Capitalism* (New York: B. Franklin. 1913, Reprinted 1969)

11. "The Challenge of Material Civilization," in Leo W. Schwarz, *Great Ages and Ideas of the Jewish People* (New York: The Modern Library, 1956), p. 413.

12. Salo W. Baron, *History and Jewish Historians,* compiled with a foreword by Arthur Hertzberg and Leon A. Feldman (Philadelphia: The Jewish Publication Society of America, 1964), pp. 49–53.

13. Barm, *op. cit.*, pp. 53–55.

14. In Schwarz, ed., *Great Ages and Ideas of the Jewish People,* p. 414.

15. Schwarz, *loc. cit.*

16. *Ibid.*, p. 406.

17. *Ibid.*, pp. 407–408.

18. *Ibid.*, pp. 415, 406.

19. *Ibid.*, p. 418.

20. "American Jews and the Business Mentality," *Judaism,* vol. 27 (Spring 1978), pp. 214–216.

21. *Op. cit.*, p. 217.

22. *Ibid.*, p. 218.

23. *Ibid.*, p. 221.

Comment

Walter Block

I want to begin by congratulating Dr. Tamari on his contribution. The interdisciplinary study of economics and religion is much advanced by his thorough analysis of the relationship between Judaism and the principles of the free enterprise system. It is a welcome addition to this surprisingly poorly developed intellectual area. Surprising, given the important role Jews have played as merchants, businessmen, and ardent defenders as well as detractors of the market system.

On a personal note, moreover, I am grateful to Dr. Tamari for bringing out the importance of study in the Jewish tradition. When my wife next insists that I study less and spend more time with my family, I shall try this argument out on her.

Before beginning my critique of the paper, I must acknowledge one shortcoming. I am unable to comment on Tamari's interpretation of Judaic law, and must therefore accept it as correct, if only for the sake of argument.

I offer the following critical points in roughly the order taken up by the author, in the hope and expectation that by so doing, he will be encouraged to elaborate his views further.

Inequality

"Since the creation of economic goods and their accumulation often leads to visible inequalities, accompanied by greed, injustice, theft and often bloodshed, it is linked to man's evil inclinations, or a sort of *lust* which is inconsistent with the ethical and moral teachings of the religion."

There are difficulties with this view. It is not the creation of economic goods that leads to inequalities, but rather the great variation in economic talents, abilities and productivities with which the Creator of the universe has seen fit to endow human beings.[1] Even if economic goods were somehow not needed, and hence not created, or created but not accumulated, the human race would *still* be characterized by vast inequalities in size, strength, speed, intelligence, beauty, etc.

Secondly, why are inequalities necessarily evil? Why should envy implicitly be elevated into a cardinal virtue?[2] While there are indeed grave evils involved in homogenization of human beings, and thus in the forced rectification of inequality,[3] it is not at all clear why inequality *per se* should be seen as evil.

Thirdly, the linkage of "greed," "injustice," "theft," "bloodshed" and "evil," all in one sentence, seems akin to the multiple choice question faced on high school exams: pick out the one item that does not belong with the others. For Adam Smith and other classical liberals, "greed" sticks out like a sore thumb. Far from a negative, in this view greed is the very source of civilization, the reason that human beings were led to carve a society out of the wilderness.[4] If the Smithian analysis is correct in this regard, and I think it is, then "greed," "uninterrupted effort," or "self-interest" should not be considered inconsistent with the ethical and moral teachings of religion.

Partners

"Since Judaism is a community-oriented rather than an individual-oriented religion, this means that the group at all levels—communal, national and, during periods of the loss of sovereignty, international—are thereby made partners in fact, even if not legally so, in each individual's wealth."

According to Dr. Tamari, all Jews are thus, in effect, business partners with each other, whether they know it or not, and whether they like it or not. It is difficult to see how this claim of communal wealth can be based on the arguments presented by Tamari regarding the practice of allowing land to lie fallow, or of thanking the Deity for crops. It is not clear moreover, how this view can be reconciled with some recent economic findings. For human capital—the skills, training, effort, health of the individual—are by far the most important component of wealth creation.[5] If Jews are really partners in each other's wealth, and wealth includes human capital, then they in effect own each other—a rather dubious proposition.[6] It is even more difficult yet to see how this view can be reconciled with Tamari's own statement that "...individuals have rights with regard to private Jewish property." If so, then how can Jews be considered to own their property in common with all fellow co-religionists?

Advertising

"One is not allowed to steal, as it were, another's opinion; in other words, many of those things that we all too often classify under advertising are forbidden."

Why this gratuitous, all too brief and unsubstantiated attack on the ancient and honourable practice of advertising? To be sure, there are advertisers who are guilty of violations of rights;[7] but so are there thieving butchers, misrepresenting bakers, and fraudulent candlestick makers. Why single out advertisers?

Advertising, for many people, has a negative aroma attached to it. Even in the economics profession, there is an invidious distinction commonly made between production costs, which are considered legitimate, and selling or advertising costs, which are not.

Such prejudice makes sense, perhaps, in a situation where information is costless, and full knowledge thus reigns. But in the real world, unfortunately, such bliss does not obtain. Here, we must struggle on, living in our vale of ignorance.

It is the task of the advertiser to alert us to opportunities we may have neglected. What is the good of producing goods and services, after all, if people are not aware of them?

But the task of spreading knowledge of this sort is no easy one. The air waves and print media are alive with competing messages. In order to succeed, the advertiser must first capture the attention of the consumer. And the fact that this is commonly done in a manner which offends the delicate sensibilities of professors, scholars, academics and other critics is no argument for prohibition. In any case their argument is not with the advertiser, but rather with the tastes of the general public, to whom he is catering.

Most important, advertising is part and parcel of free speech. Denigrating it by equating it with stealing, as does Mr. Tamari, only threatens this most vital of our modern institutions.

Harm as violations of rights

"A man is not permitted to use his property in a way which will cause harm or do damage to another person's body or property."

There is all the world of difference between *harming* a person or his property, on the one hand, and *violating rights* on the other, and the two should not be conflated. Harm may be said to befall a person when he is disappointed in virtually any way: physically, psychologically, economically; while rights violations are a very small subset of this category, limited, usually, to cases where one person physically invades, or uses force or fraud against another person or his property. A can harm B by marrying the woman B hoped to marry; by beating him in chess; by underselling him in the market and driving him to bankruptcy; by refusing to purchase from him, thereby rendering B's goods less valuable than they would have been, had A been willing to bid for them. But in all such cases, surely, A would be permitted so to act, by any reasonable code of justice.[8]

Defining property rights

"A tree planted alongside a neighbour's plot is in effect stealing through its roots another's wealth. Certain industries and professions through the pollution, noise and human traffic associated with them steal another's quiet, health, peace and fresh air, and therefore are forbidden or restricted to certain areas."

Dr. Tamari's thesis is that the free enterprise system, if left to itself, would create various types of injustices, inefficiencies, and other difficulties, and would therefore be incompatible with Jewish law; and that hence government intervention, or a mixed economy, is the only system compatible with Judaism.

But the examples offered regarding the tree, quiet, peace, fresh air, etc., are all part and parcel of the government's role in defining property rights. This is seen as a *legitimate* function of government in the view of virtually all classical liberal adherents of the free market, limited-government, democratic, capitalist system.[9] And not only as a legitimate function of government, but as one of its essential jobs.

The reason there are such difficulties in this area, then, is not because the marketplace has failed. For in the classical liberal view, the marketplace cannot function in a vacuum; it needs to be embedded within a complex legal code based on a strict and clear definition of property rights, in order to operate. The reason there are problems with pollution, property boundaries, etc., is because government has failed to acquit itself appropriately in this role of clearly defining property rights.[10]

Dr. Tamari also cites the Jewish law based on *caveat venditor* (let the seller beware) as an example of protecting the consumer. But there are great drawbacks to holding the vendor responsible for damages or losses he would refuse to explicitly guarantee in the absence of such a legal practice. Under this kind of system, manufacturers will attempt to increase the quality of their goods in order to reduce claims against them. While this might sound good at first blush (it is hard to oppose high quality) this is not really in the interest of consumers. For higher quality necessitates higher prices. Instead of being offered an array of different quality goods at difference prices, under *caveat venditor* the consumer will be able to choose only from the top of the line. Consider automobiles, for example. Would the consumer really be better off if we carried *caveat venditor* to its logical conclusion, and permitted on the road only Cadillacs, Mercedes, Rolls Royces, and other cars of such high quality? Hardly. The consumer gains by having a range of choice: relatively cheap, tiny, less unsafe-in-a-crash, low quality cars also benefit consumer welfare.

Charity

"The giving of charity is not considered as an act of kindness on the part of the haves to the have-nots. The have-nots have by right a stake in the property of the haves."

Can there truly *be* an act of charity if the poor really own (part of) the wealth of the rich? The answer would appear to be "no," for the giving of charity, surely, is over and above the call of duty. If a payment from a "have" to a "have-not" is made out of duty, it is not, it cannot be, charity; it must be merely the discharge of a debt. "Charity" and "justice" may flow from the same root in Hebrew, but not in English.

An implication of Dr. Tamari's interpretation is that the poor need not be thankful to the rich for income transfers, any more than a creditor need thank a debtor for the repayment of a loan. Both are duty-bound. The poor person, moreover, could really present the rich person with a bill, much as the restaurateur presents a bill at the end of the meal to the diner. The diner pays out of duty, not charity, for to fail to pay the bill would be equivalent to stealing the meal. Likewise, in Dr. Tamari's construal, the rich person is really stealing the legitimately owned property of the poor, by refusing to give it to him.

Could a poor person (strictly speaking) steal from a rich person? Not according to the inner logic of this position. For the rich person, in refusing to give (part of) his wealth to the poor person, is withholding what really in justice belongs to the poor person. How can it be theft to take what is rightfully one's own? Surely this should rather be characterized as "regaining one's own rightful possessions" or the "return of stolen property" (the property the rich man is presumed to have stolen merely by his attempt to keep it for himself, and out of the hands of its "rightful" owner, the poor man). In this rather fanciful example, I am of course assuming that the rich man came by the relevant property in a manner such that, were it owned by a poor man, there would be no question of theft, or of rightful ownership.

This position is so difficult to defend that Dr. Tamari himself elsewhere contradicts it when he says "The question of theft has nothing to do with the damage done to the injured party, nor to the relative economic status of the parties concerned..."; and, "So judges are not allowed to fear the wealthy nor favour the poor." But how could the relative economic status of the concerned parties "be irrelevant to theft," or "judges not be allowed to favour the poor" if the poor legitimately own (part of) the property of the rich?

Another difficulty is that the theory logically implies not placing a floor under the incomes of the poor, as many classical liberals have urged,[11] but rather absolute income equality. For, if the rich must give to the poor out of duty, this duty logically continues until the rich no longer have more money than the poor. If there are even slight income differences, there are still the rich as distinct from the poor, and they still have an obligation to transfer further income.

But not only income. Haves may be distinguished from have-nots not only in terms of money income, but ever so much more importantly, in terms of health, happy disposition, intelligence, musical ability, beauty, strength, agility, speed, etc., etc. Surely, if there were a way to equalize these endowments,[12] duty and justice would require that it be done, in Dr. Tamari's view. And if not, money incomes must be used in compensation, so that a young, healthy, happy, intelligent but poor person (in money terms), would be forced to pay off a rich (in money terms) old cantankerous sourpuss with little to recommend him besides his financial wealth.

Usury

Dr. Tamari points to the opposition of Judaic law to the practice of charging interest for loans, and allowing essential items to be used as security for loans.

It is difficulty to understand this, given the fact that these prohibitions harm mainly the poor. In the loan market, the most advantaged borrowers are the ones judged to be the least likely to default. Since ability to repay, creditworthiness, and greater collateral are usually characteristics of the rich, their desires for loans are likely to take first priority in the eyes of the potential lenders.

How can the poor compete? By offering (or being willing to pay) higher rates of interest than the rich, and/or by offering (or being willing to pledge in security for loans) valuable, precious or "essential" items. Laws that preclude or discourage these possibilities thus discriminate against the poor. With legislation or judicial findings such as those advocated by Dr. Tamari, poor people who are ambitious and anxious to join the ranks of the rich are forestalled and held back.[14]

One justification for this policy is the fear that in the free loan market, the poor will be taken advantage of: in case of default, they will have to renounce a precious possession; and their chances of success will be less, at the higher interest rates. But this smacks of paternalism: we know what is best for the poor, better than they do themselves; even though they are willing to engage in a commercial transaction, we shall forbid it—for their own good. This is to treat the poor as children; it is to add insult to injury. Presumably, it must be rejected as immoral.

The usual strictures against usury prohibit the charging of interest beyond a certain fixed and arbitrary rate. Dr. Tamari goes much further in urging a zero interest rate, or "interest-free loans." This extreme position has the additional disadvantage of even further drying up the source of loanable funds. Any prohibition against "usury" will accomplish this, but a zero interest rate will do so with a vengeance.

Nor must we only look at the interest rate as the "price" of loanable funds. It has a far more fundamental role to play, pervading every nook and cranny of the economy. The interest rate affects the rate at which stocks (income at a point in time) are traded for flows (income over a number of years). What is the present worth of the right to receive $100 per year for the next ten years? The answer to this is intimately connected to the rate of interest and to the theory of capitalized values. Why is it that wine and trees and other intermediate goods become more and more valuable the closer they are to harvestable age? Again, the interest rate. If one really wanted to control interest rates, let alone at a zero level, one would have to interfere with virtually every market transaction, for the sale prices of all goods implicitly incorporate an interest rate. This is virtually an impossible task; and to the extent that it met with "success," it would ruin the economy.

First refusal rights *(Bar-metzrah)*

We are told that neighbouring land-owners always have the right of first refusal in land sales, and that "Since the purchase is to be at the market price, the seller suffers no loss. Yet at the same time the buyer gains since the enlargement of his property is often an economic consideration. This is a concept of 'one loses nothing and the other one gains.' "

This view of *pareto optimality* is puzzling, since it implies that no one would ever pay anything to purchase an option to buy land. But options (to buy at a given price) are commonly bought and sold, so we know they are valuable considerations. Moreover, if *bar-metzrah* really implied no loss of value to the land-owner, why is the law needed to enforce this obligation on him in the first place? Surely there is a loss in the sense of alternatives that must be foregone because of this law.

The core difficulty is the assumption of a "market price," identical for everyone. Although certain economics textbook writers have concocted a "perfectly competitive model"[15] in which all buyers and sellers pay or receive an identical "market price," this has nothing whatsoever to do with the real world, or with the concept of free enterprise. (As used here, free enterprise or the competitive market system indicates enforced private property rights, free trade and minimal government interference with the economy; nowhere implied are the rigid assumptions of perfect competition: numerous buyers and sellers, homogeneous products, perfect information, equilibrium, etc.)

The market price, properly understood, is only a shorthand description of the numerous trades that take place all throughout the economy. In the land sale case we are considering, there is no reason to believe that all potential purchasers will necessarily pay the same price. If the seller is forced to give neighbours the first right to purchase, it may be at the cost of being unable to sell to a stranger who might offer more. This was recognized where Dr. Tamari saw "the difficulty of affixing a market price to [land] in view of the subjective evaluation involved." But this insight, unfortunately, was not incorporated into his analysis.

Property rights and human rights

According to our author "the Jewish legal system keeps a clear demarcation between crimes against property and capital crimes. Murder, adultery and idolatry were punishable by death, without any remission into a monetary settlement. On the other hand, no prisons ever existed for debtors, and no jail sentence was imposed for theft or embezzlement; restitution and fines were all that were imposed. Capital punishment, banishment or bodily mutilation for theft were never recognized. Whilst private property has rights, which must be equitably and severely enforced, they never were considered sacred or holy."

Strictly speaking, however, there can be no crimes against property, and private property has no rights at all. Only human beings, not property, can have rights.[16] There are no disputes between "property" and human beings; only between some human beings who own property, and others who steal, deface or otherwise destroy it. To be sure, one must distinguish between murder, rape, assault and other crimes against persons, and theft of a person's property. But sometimes property theft can be more injurious than minor bodily assault; for example, stealing water in the desert, or food or a horse in a barren wilderness.

Price controls (*Ona'ah*)

"The Jewish conception of private economic activity which sets the seal of justice, righteousness and morality on all mundane acts, requires control over prices and profits in order to prevent deviations from the Divine Mandate." Does God really command that there be price controls? Let us briefly review the function of profits and prices in a market economy, as an antidote to this view.

There are two, and only two, ways of allocating resources to their most important ends: through centralized commands (as in the Soviet system of planning) and through a decentralized price mechanism (as holds true for most goods and services in the Western democracies). All other systems are combinations of these two.

In a market economy, consumers determine what is to be produced merely by purchasing more or less of a given item. Greater (lesser) demand raises (lowers) prices; the higher (lower) the price, other things equal, the more profits (losses) will be registered by the producers. The entrepreneur is thus led "by an invisible hand"[17] to produce that which is in greater demand by the consumer, and to reduce his efforts on behalf of items which are not so heavily demanded, in order to maximize profits. Without the price and profit mechanism, the entrepreneur would have little knowledge of what people desired, less awareness of their continually changing demands, and still less incentive to suit his actions to their needs. One of the many beauties of the profit-and-loss system is that entrepreneurs can earn profits only by catering to consumer desires; but as they do so, prices come down in response to the increased supply, and profit rates level off. This indicates that the need for further efforts is no longer so urgent, and that resources can now be better employed elsewhere.

How do price and profit controls fit into all this? If prices are not free to vary by more than one-quarter or even one-sixth of what some economic czar is pleased to regard as the "market price" this interferes with the flexibility of the entire system. No longer will prices inform us as the relative demands and scarcities of economic goods and services.[18]

Tamari quite correctly sees the "difficulty of assigning a price to [certain] articles in view of the subjective evaluation involved." With regard to promissory notes, he fully appreciates that different attitudes toward risk make it impossible for a market price to exist. He fails, however, to realize that subjective evaluations and differing attitudes toward risk apply to *all* purchases and sales in the market. More important, he ignores the crucial allocative, informational, and incentive effects of prices and profits and loss. These are so basic to the operation of a decentralized market economy that price and profit controls, even if capable of a non-arbitrary implementation, would still have adverse effects. Given the misallocations brought about by price and profit ceilings, consumers often pay *more* for the controlled items when shortages, queues, and the black markets which usually arise are taken into account. We conclude then that if for some reason there must be price and profit ceilings, it would be far better for the poor and the needy if ceilings were applied only to *luxuries,* not necessities. If we must inflict these inefficiencies, need they always affect the necessities used most heavily by the more helpless members of the economy?

We cannot leave the topic of price controls without considering minimum price laws or price floors, described by Tamari as "undercutting" or "forestalling." As this too, we are told, is "morally unjust," we take note that the realm of "morally just" prices must occupy a very narrow band indeed. But Tamari's economic analysis is somewhat puzzling. In his view, undercutting is "to the detriment of the buyer." However, if buyer B is about to purchase an order from seller A, and competitive seller A[1] comes along with a lower-priced offer, this must *help* B, although it will hurt A. We are told that there was no legal redress, only a "moral imperative [introduced] into the market place." The difficulty is that if everyone refuses to "undercut," there can hardly be said to *be* a market at all. For undercutting is surely one of the essential ingredients of competitive markets.

A moral problem that arises with regard to price controls (*ona'ah*) has to do with rabbinic religious rule-changes in order to lower prices. Tamari reports that the rabbis of sixteenth-century Moravia declared certain high-priced fish to be "ritually unfit to eat," but only in order to lower prices. If the mere price of an item can determine its dietary quality, then nothing further can be said on this point. But low-priced pork is hardly kosher, and high-priced kosher food is not by that fact alone rendered non-kosher. The Moravian rabbis, it would appear, were guilty of fraudulent activity. At the very least, they were guilty of the "misrepresentation," "deliberate distortion," and "failure to fully disclose," of which Dr. Tamari warns us several times.

Middlemen

"The sages of the *Talmud* saw the increased costs caused by middlemen as detrimental to the poor and weaker classes."

If so, then the sages were seeing something that simply is not true. Suppose that A was selling to C and all of a sudden B, the middleman, arrives on the scene. The *only* way B can break into this chain is by making more attractive offers to both A and C than they are able to make to each other. How can this be done? Tamari's much maligned supermarket or shopping centre is a perfect case in point. The chain-store supermarket (B) is in a position to buy in quantity from whole-salers (A), at lower costs to the wholesaler than would be entailed by direct sales to the final customer (C). So B makes A better-off by free-ing him from dealing directly with the shopper. The wholesaler can now specialize in a more narrowly defined task and hence gain in pro-ductivity. Moreover, the supermarket can save the customer the cost of travelling to dozens of different wholesalers by providing more choice than any one shopper can provide for herself. So B also makes C better off.

If this were not so—if B ended up charging C more than the price that could be obtained from A when due consideration is given to con-venience, greater choice, and reduction of shopping costs—then C would "cut out the middleman," and "buy wholesale." The middle-man does not forestall options; he increases them. He does not *raise* prices to the consumer; he *lowers* them. [19]

The speculator

If, as Sowell states, the middleman is an economic actor long reviled by racists and anti-Semites of all stripes, then the speculator is another. It is important, not only on economic grounds, but for the sake of justice (in face of irrational anti-Semitism) to set the record straight on this matter.

Since time immemorial, speculators have been vilified for high and rising prices. This view is incorrect. In fact the opposite is true: the result of speculation is to prevent prices from rising as much as they would have done without it. [20]

To see this clearly, let us consider the example of "widgets." Sup-pose that in the absence of speculation the future supply of widgets is as in the biblical story: seven fat years followed by seven lean. Given similar demand in the two periods, the years of ample supply would result in low prices and the era of short supply in high prices. Enter the speculator. What will he do? If he has any sense, he will follow the sage counsel of profit-seeking: buy when prices are low and sell when they are high. His initial purchases will, to be sure, raise prices above the low levels that would otherwise obtain in the first period, as his additional speculative demand is now added to the demand to buy widgets for consumption purposes. But his subsequent sales will *re-duce* prices from the high levels that would have obtained, in the later period but for his efforts. This is because speculative sales, when added to other sales, must depress prices further than all other sales would have done by themselves. The speculator will be seen to be selling at high prices in years eight to fourteen. People will therefore blame him for these prices, even though they would have been higher still in his absence.

The speculator does far more than merely iron out prices over time. By damping price oscillations, he accomplishes something of crucial importance: the stockpiling of widgets during the years of plenty when they are least needed, and the dissipation of the widget inventory during times of shortage when they are most useful. Furthermore, the speculator's actions in the market signal to all other businessmen that an era of short supply is expected in the future. His present purchases raise prices, and hence the profitability of producing and hoarding now. This encourages others to do so before the lean years strike. The speculator is the Distant Early Warning System of the economy. But, as in days of yore when the bearers of ill tidings were put to death for their pains, modern day messengers—the speculators—are blamed for the bad news they bring. There is talk of prohibiting their activities outright, or of taxing their gains at 100 percent confiscatory rates. But such moves would deprive society of the beneficial effects of speculation.

There is only one possible fly in the ointment. If the speculator guesses incorrectly and sees years of plenty ahead when belt-tightening is really in store for the economy, then chaos will result. Instead of stabilizing prices and quantities, the speculator will destabilize them. Instead of hoarding during the fat years and reducing inventories during famines—and leading others to do the same—he will encourage needless saving under adversity and wasteful profligacy in good times. The market, however, has a fail-safe mechanism to prevent this sort of disaster. The speculator who guesses wrong will buy high and sell low—and incur losses, not profits. If he continues to err, he will go bankrupt, and usually very quickly. Professional speculators who have survived this rigorous market test of profit and loss can be relied upon to forecast the future with far greater accuracy than any other conceivable group, including seers, crystal-ball gazers, bureaucrats, politicians, mystics, marketing boards or swamis.

Competition and monopoly

I must also demur at Tamari's contention that Middle Eastern and Mediterranean market places, with many small shops of the same type, are "far more competitive" than Western-type shopping centres "with one firm for each type of business." For surely different shopping centres all compete with one another. As long as there are no legal prohibitions, one arrangement is as competitive as the other.

A similar analysis applies to Tamari's views on monopoly. The importance of distinguishing between the two vastly different types of "monopoly" cannot possibly be overstated.[21] In the classic sense, a monopoly is a special privilege granted by king or parliament to an individual. Thus there were salt monopolies and candle monopolies awarded to noblemen and merchants for outstanding services. A modern equivalent would be the Post Office. In all such cases, other market agents are forbidden to compete with the monopolist upon pain of fine, jail sentence or worse. Potential competitors, forbidden to compete, are unjustifiably injured. And consumers are harmed as well, since they are not able to patronize alternatives to the legally protected monopolist.

The second sense of monopoly is vastly different. Here, the term applies to the *winner* of a competitive process. Ford, IBM, Alcoa, Mozart, Rembrandt, Shakespeare, Ali were each at some time virtually the single seller of a highly valued good or service. These individuals and corporations were part and parcel of the competitive process. Far from harming consumers, as was true of the other case of monopoly, the achievement of monopoly in this sense is evidence of providing *superlative* benefits to the consumer. For how else can a company or individual become the single seller of a good or service without serving the interest of the consumer (which of course includes the poor, the elderly and the weak)?

Strangely enough, in one of the rare instances where Tamari makes this distinction, he favours monopoly in the *harmful* sense. This occurs in cases where the Gentile authorities granted Jews monopoly protection against the competition of other Jews. "The moral argument for this restrictive practice," says Dr. Tamari, is that the "holder of the monopoly right had made an investment" (by purchasing these rights from the grantor). Now this is a moral argument which is difficult to defend. For the slaveholder can make the same claim. He may well have bought the slave, made an "investment" in him, and even have a bill of sale to prove it. But does this fact constitute a moral justification for the practice of slavery? Hardly. Tamari also takes this position in his analysis of free entry. His view seems to be that when Jews are confined to a ghetto, monopoly (in the classical government-grant-of-exclusive-privilege sense) not competition, is the best means of maximizing welfare. Although he admits that granting monopoly privileges to "veteran settlers in a town" (*Herem Hayishuv*) affects the consumer "adversely by higher prices, fewer services and fewer goods, the communal well-being outweighed these disadvantages." But what were the *advantages* to communal[22] well-being of monopoly privileges for the few? Dr. Tamari does not say.

Another eccentric view of competition reported by Tamari is that if an eminent rabbi *did not* close his store after a few hours of trade, he would be guilty of "gross unfair competition" against his less able competitors. Why is it "unfair"? If the eminent rabbi closes his store early, is he not instead guilty of a monopolistic withholding[23] and therefore of ruining "communal well-being"?

Conclusion

Dr. Tamari's thesis is that democratic capitalism is so riddled with injustices and economic difficulties that it needs a strong measure of government intervention if the system is to be brought into conformity with the requirements of Judaic law. I think he has made as strong a case for this position as can be made—but that his conclusion still remains unproven.

NOTES

1. See Roger J. Williams, *Free and Unequal*, Indianapolis: Liberty Press, 1979; Murray N. Rothbard, *Freedom, Inequality, Primitivism and the Division of Labor*, Menlo Park, Calif.: Institute for Humane Studies, 1971; Murray N. Rothbard, "The Impossibility of Equality," in *Power and Market*, Menlo Park, California: Institute for Humane Studies, 1970, pp. 157–160.

2. Helmut Schoek, *Envy: A Theory of Social Behavior*, London: Secker

and Warburg, 1969; Peter T. Bauer, "Ecclesiastical Economics Is Envy Exalted," *This World*, Winter 1982, no. 1, pp. 56–59.

3. See Walter E. Williams, "A Recipe for the Good Society: A Report from the Federal Unequality Commission," in *The American Spectator*. vol. 15, no. 7, July 1982, pp. 20–22; *Discrimination, Affirmative Action, and Equal Opportunity*, ed. by Walter Block and Michael Walker, Vancouver: The Fraser Institute, 1982; Thomas Sowell, *Race and Economics*, New York: Longman, 1975.

4. Consider these quotes from Adam Smith's *The Wealth of Nations*:
   "The great advantage of the market is that it is able to use the strength of self-interest to offset the weakness and partiality of benevolence, so that those who are unknown, unattractive or unimportant, will have their wants served."
   "The uniform, constant, and uninterrupted effort of every man to better his condition, the principle from which public and national, as well as private opulence is originally derived, is frequently powerful enough to maintain the natural progress of things towards improvement, in spite of both the extravagance of government and of the greatest errors of administration."
   "It is not from the benevolence of the butcher, the brewer, or the baker that we expect our dinner, but from their regard to their own interests...." Instead of this last statement, suppose Adam Smith had said, "It is from *greed* that we expect our dinner from the butcher, the brewer and the baker...." This might have been less eloquent, more shocking and disturbing, but would it have changed the essence of this keen Smithian insight at all?

5. Gary Becker, *Human Capital*, New York: National Bureau of Economic Research, 1964.

6. See Murray N. Rothbard, *The Ethics of Liberty*, New Jersey: Humanities Press, 1982, pp. 45–46 for a treatment of this phenomenon.

7. For a more positive view of advertising, see Israel Kirzner, *Competition and Entrepreneurship*, Chicago: University of Chicago Press, 1973; Frederick Hayek, "The Non-Sequiter of the Dependence Effect," *Studies in Philosophy, Politics and Economics*, New York, Simon and Schuster, 1967, pp. 313-317; Paul Heyne, *The Economic Way of Thinking*, Chicago: SRA, 1980, pp. 34, 181–182, 188.

8. For a criticism of the doctrine that there are such things as "positive

rights," (e.g., the right to food, clothing, shelter, etc.) see "Housing Is *Not* a Basic Human Right," in *Rent Control: Myths and Realities*, ed. by Walter Block and Edgar Olson, Vancouver: The Fraser Institute, 1981, pp. 300–302.

9. Milton Friedman, "The Role of Government in a Free Society," in *Capitalism and Freedom*, Chicago: University of Chicago Press, 1970, pp. 22–36; Friedrich A. Hayek, *The Constitution of Liberty*, Chicago: Henry Regnery, 1960.

10. Edwin G. Dolan, *TANSTAAFL: The Economic Strategy for Environmental Crisis*, New York: Holt, Rinehart & Winston, 1971; David Friedman, "Pollution," in *The Machinery of Freedom*, New York: Harper and Row, 1970, pp. 139–141; Richard Stroup and John Baden, "Externality, Property Rights and the Management of our National Forests," *Journal of Law and Economics*, vol. 16 (2), Oct. 1973.

11. One explanation for governmental failure to clearly specify property rights is that in the mixed economy, it has become responsible for so many other tasks, (to which it was not suited), that it simply had not the energy nor the funds to devote to this task.

12. See Milton Friedman, "The Alleviation of Poverty," *op. cit.*, pp. 190–195 for a defence of one such policy, the "negative income tax."

13. There is! See Kurt Vonnegut, "Harrison Bergeron," in *Discrimination, Affirmative Action*, pp. 221–226.

14. Paul Heyne, *The Economic Way of Thinking*, Chicago: SRA, 1980, pp. 197, 198; Douglas Worth and Roger Leroy Miller, "The Economics of Usury Laws," in *The Economics of Public Issues*, New York: Harper and Row, 1971; Roger Leroy Miller and Raburn M. Williams, "The Economics of Sky-high Interest Rates," in *The Economics of National Issues*, New York: Harper and Row, 1972; Milton Friedman, "Usury," in *An Economist's Protest*, New Jersey: Thomas Horton and Co., 1972.

The same analysis applies to the concept of duress. If a poor man can claim duress ("since he needed the goods urgently") in order to later void a sale, then merchants will have that much less incentive to sell to poor men in general; specifically, to the extent that this concept is operable in Jewish law, poor people will have great difficulty in buying necessities they "need urgently." Does Jewish law really aim at forcing the poor to buy only luxuries?

Prohibition of interest in the Torah Pentateuch concerns charitable, not commercial, loans. "If you lend money to any of my people with you who is poor, you shall not be to him as a creditor, and you shall not exact interest from him." (Ex. 22:25) Cf. Ronald J. Sider, *Rich Christians in an Age of Hunger*, Downers Grove, Illinois: Inter Varsity Press, 1977, pp. 94, 95. (I am grateful to Mr. Doug Puffert for this citation.)

But is there a law better guaranteed to ensure that *fewer* loans will be made to the poor, for charitable purposes? In economic terminology, there is an upward sloping supply of loanable funds—for *any* purpose. The higher the interest rate, *ceterus paribus*, the more loans that will be forthcoming. And the lower the interest rate, the fewer. At zero rates, it is not likely that many loans at all will be offered.

15. Paul Samuelson, *Economics: An Introductory Analysis*, New York: McGraw Hill, 1964, chapters 3, 23, 24.

16. For a view that animals can have rights, see Robert Nozick, *Anarchy, State and Utopia*, New York: Basic Books, 1974, pp. 35–40. For an analysis of the human rights/property rights question, see Rothbard, *Power and Market*, pp. 176–178.

17. Adam Smith, *Wealth of Nations*, "By directing that industry in such a manner as its produce may be of the greatest value, and he is in this, as in many other cases, led by an invisible hand to promote an end there was no part of his intention....By pursuing his own interest he frequently promotes that of our society more effectually than when he really intends to promote it."

18. See Roger Leroy Miller and Raburn M. Williams, "The Economics of Wage and Price Controls: How to Make Cigarettes a Currency," in *The Economics of National Issues*, New York: Harper and Row, 1972; Michael A. Walker, ed., *The Illusion of Wage and Price Controls*, Vancouver: The Fraser Institute, 1976; Milton Friedman, "The Morality of (Price) Controls," and "Controls: An Exercise in Futility," in *An Economist's Protest*, New Jersey: Thomas Horton and Co., 1972, pp. 120–141.

19. See Thomas Sowell, *Race and Economics*, New York: Longman, 1975, pp. 68, 69. Sowell's analysis is so eloquent, compelling and relevant to our interests in Judaism, that I am moved to quote from him at length:

Whether in medieval society, a prisoner-of-war camp, or a modern market economy, the "middleman" essentially changes the location of things in space and time. If the same physical thing is assumed to have the same value without regard to space or time, then the middleman is simply cheating people. How this situation could persist over time, through repeated transactions, is unexplained. If A sells to B who sells to C, and B is simply cheating, then both A and C can benefit by direct transactions with each other—A charging somewhat more than he normally charges B, and C paying somewhat less than he normally pays B. Why would both then *continue* to deal with each other through a middleman? Obviously they would not.

In reality, they deal through the middleman because he is changing the value of things by relocating them, holding them to times that are more convenient, assuming various risks by stocking inventories—and doing so at *less cost* than either the producer or the consumer could. Otherwise either the producer would sell at retail or the consumer would buy wholesale, and either could perform these middleman services for himself. But given the highly fragmented nature of knowledge, those who have mastered the complexities of the production process have seldom also mastered the very different complexities of inventory management and numerous other services performed by middlemen in the process of relocating things in time and space. Consumers typically lack both the knowledge and the economies of scale needed for low cost inventory storage. Storing wholesale quantities of various goods in the home means having a bigger home, and the higher cost of a bigger home will seldom be covered by the "savings" from buying wholesale. In other words, purchasing storage space in a residential neighbourhood is almost always more expensive than purchasing storage space in a warehouse district. In short, middlemen can continue to exist only insofar as they can perform certain functions more cheaply than either the producer or the consumer. But no matter how varied and complex these functions may be, they amount ultimately to relocating things in time and space, and the physical fallacy which denies value to that operation necessarily indicts middlemen as mere cheaters.

No small part of the historic anti-Semitism of Europe (and corresponding anti-Chinese feeling in many Asian countries) is due to the Jews' role as middlemen. Legally—that is, forcibly—

denied access to many occupations in the production of goods, Jews could survive in Europe only by finding interstitial services not covered by the sweeping discriminatory bans against them. They became middlemen in the movement of goods and money over time and space—the [former] because the Catholic church's moral prohibitions against charging interest did not apply to them. The virtually universal dislike and suspicion of middlemen focused on an ethnically-identifiable group of people, separated by religion and customs from the rest of the population, and therefore a perfect target. The economic success and political vulnerability of the Jews over the centuries has been paralleled by that of the Chinese middleman minority throughout Asia. In both cases, general discrimination has been punctuated by sporadic confiscations, mass expulsions and mob violence. The history of both groups (and of other middlemen minorities in other parts of the world) has wider implications for the political vulnerability of market economies in general.

20. See Paul Heyne, *The Economic Way of Thinking*, Chicago: SRA, 1980, pp. 128–132.

21. See in this regard, Friedrich A. Hayek, "The Meaning of Competition," in *Individualism and Economic Order*, Chicago: Henry Regnery, 1948; Ludwig von Mises, *Human Action*, Chicago: Henry Regnery, 1966, pp. 273–279; Walter Block, *A Response to the Framework Document for Amending the Combines Investigation Act*, Vancouver: The Fraser Institute, 1982, p. 4; David Friedman, *The Machinery of Freedom*, New York: Harper and Row, 1980, pp. 39–60.

22. Why "communal?" Is there some benefit that adheres to the "community" that does not affect the relevant individuals? For an analysis of methodological individualism, see Friedrich A. Hayek, "Individualism: True and False," in *Individualism and Economic Order;* Walter Block, "On Robert Nozick's 'On Austrian Methodology,' " *Inquiry*, 23, pp. 299–403; Sidney Sherwood, "The Philosophical Basis of Economics," *Annals of the American Academy of Political and Social Science*, October 1897; Ludwig von Mises, *Theory and History*, New York: Arlington House, 1969, pp. 183–190.

23. This critique of "monopolistic withholding" is also made by Israel Kirzner. See his *Competition and Entrepreneurship*, op. cit., p. 110. For a reply to this view, see Walter Block, "Austrian Monopoly Theory—a Critique," *The Journal of Libertarian Studies*, Vol I, No. 4, Fall 1977, pp 271–79.

Discussion

Edited by: Irving Hexham

Ellis Rivkin: My whole approach to the development of Judaism is necessarily antithetical to Susan Feigenbaum's. This should be noted at the outset.

I have gone to great effort to try to demonstrate that Judaism is a developmental religion. It continuously undergoes significant change, in four instances, evolving quantum jumps where the Judaism becomes very very different—so different, in fact, that its legitimacy would have been denied by the previous stage.

Thus, for example, the *Aaronide* priesthood, which exercised authority for four hundred and forty-five years to the *Hasmoneian* revolt around 165 B.C., did not recognize the legitimacy of the claims of an emerging class, the Pharisees, that God had given two laws—a written and an oral law—in which God promised eternal rewards and punishments in the world to come, eternal life and resurrection of the dead. These were denounced as heretical by those who came to be called the Sadducees, who insisted that only the written law should be observed.

Even within the Pentateuch itself, we find three stages "in the evolution of Judaism": the prophetic, the Deuteronomistic, and the Aaronide.

So that you have really three stages in the evolution of Judaism within the Pentateuch itself: the prophetic, which was then modified considerably by the Book of Deuteronomy; and then the claims of the Levites.

I would deal with these texts from the critical point of view, and in no way accept them as divinely revealed, but only divine to the degree that the individual in rethinking and testing the teachings, determine that it is revelation for him or her. So if what one sees in Amos lights up as revelation, it is a personal, individual choice that one must make.

Secondly, I do not agree that law was the core of revelation. The first stage of revelation did not involve law. All the law in the Five Books of Moses is subsequent. The law itself really begins to emerge in a definitive way only with the Book of Deuteronomy and is then solidified with the end of prophesy, and the promulgation of the Pentateuch around 445 B.C.E.

I went to great effort in the paper to show some of these stages and how the basic concepts of Judaism changed over time, such as belief in eternal life. Judaism is not incompatible with capitalism, but capitalism is incompatible with a traditional authoritarian system where the individual must ultimately depend on some religious authority, like the rabbi.

I don't think the definition I give of capitalism is really crucial. I think that the crucial issue is that capitalism is itself a developmental process.

Walter Block: I want to discuss the question of value freedom in the social sciences. I think this can best be done by distinguishing between statements on the one hand and actions on the other. Let us consider a few examples of value freedom. If we saw any of the following *statements* on the blackboard, we would have to admit that they were value-free. For instance "the minimum wage law leads to black teenage unemployment; rent control reduces the supply of rental housing; tariffs harm the welfare of the poor; excess money creation leads to inflation; money is a more efficient way of running an economy than barter; usury laws harm the poor; price ceilings create excess supply, price floors create excess demand."

Now, if it can be shown that the precepts of some religion run counter to these factual statements, that is too bad for that particular religion. It is as if this religion is on record as denying that the earth is round, or that water is composed of two parts hydrogen and one part oxygen.

These factual statements must of course be distinguished from the *action* of making them. The *act* of making these value-free statements is value-laden. Certainly the fact that I choose to make these statements is value-laden. I do so because of my values. But the statements themselves are value-free, and their truth exists above and beyond or apart from religion.

One of the problems I have with Meir Tamari's paper is his view that the best way to help the poor is to enact price controls on necessities. So untrue is this claim that its very opposite is more nearly correct: price controls on *luxuries* would be more helpful to the poor. Such laws, of course, would ruin the luxury market. But the poor won't be hurt as much.

The same thing applies to usury legislation. If you want the poor to get loans, then the *last* thing you want is a law prohibiting usury. In the absence of adequate collateral, the only thing that enables the poor person to obtain a loan is his willingness to bear a high interest burden. But this is what usury laws destroy. As a result the relatively affluent will receive all the loans. I would like now to talk about the question of coercion, and minorities. This is of particular relevance to the Jews who have been dealt dirty in this regard all through the course of history. One reason Jews should favour the free market is for their own good and for the protection of their own skins. In a collectivist society there is ultimately one employer, and that is the government. If the government doesn't like you, it is difficult to find employment. When the Jews in Russia want to go to Israel, they start losing their jobs. This is a tragedy in Russia, because there are few alternatives. In the Western democracies, if you lose your job in the civil service, you can open a grocery store, or engage in a whole host of other opportunities.

As John Yoder tells us, it's true that there have been other ways for minority groups to fit within society, and he points to a few cases among the Islamic peoples.

All well and good. And God bless people who have helped minority groups—by not killing them. However, I would sooner trust to human greed than to human benevolence if my life was on the line. This is because cases of benevolence are few and far between in the course of history; whereas greed runs rampant.

This brings me to greed—and to the invisible hand of Adam Smith. I admit to a certain feeling about this invisible hand which approaches religious ecstasy for me. In my lexicon, it's up there with Mozart and Bach. It's just beautiful, the fact that people intending no benevolence whatsoever, the butcher, the baker, the candlestick maker, supply things not because they like you, or even because they know you, but rather because they want to make a buck.

This, and the fact that the market turns this greed into a benevolent thing is a paradox and a thing of wondrous beauty to me. And it's a thing to be trusted. I really trust in the existence of human greed, much more than I do in the benevolence of princes or democratic majorities. I've seen too many cases where the Jews and other such groups were not in the majority, and had their rights trampled upon. So I think we have to be very, very careful about relying, as Yoder does, on the good offices of dictators.

Now let me address the question of the middleman. According to the work of Thomas Sowell, no small part of the historic anti-Semitism of Europe (and corresponding anti-Chinese feeling in many Asian countries) is due to the Jews' role as middlemen. The Jewish people were legally, that is, forcibly, denied access to many occupations in the production of goods. Jews could survive in Europe only by providing services not covered by the sweeping, discriminatory enactments aimed against them—for instance, by becoming middlemen.

One of the chapters of a previous book of mine had the title, "The Middleman as Hero." I think that the middleman is a benevolent kind of person—at least in terms of results. The middleman lowers prices between the manufacturer and the consumer. He is not guilty of violating rights, certainly not of violating negative rights. He provides a benefit, and yet is roundly condemned by those who are ignorant of the workings of the economy.

The same goes for the speculator, another hero of mine. The Jews, and other minority group members such as the overseas Chinese and Indians, have been over-represented in this entrepreneurial class. I don't believe that the speculator raises prices. Rather he irons out or stabilizes prices.

Let me address myself to one last point, the monopolist. I think it crucially important to distinguish between two kinds of monopoly. In the first case, monopoly derives from a grant of special privilege from the state. For example, the salt or the candle monopoly during feudalism, or the Post Office in the modern era. Non-favoured entrepreneurs will be jailed for presuming to compete with such a monopoly. Needless to say, *this* kind of monopoly is evil, vicious and depraved, and certainly hurts the poor. But then there is "market monopoly," derived from the competitive system itself. Here a monopoly position is *earned* by producing a better product at a lower price. For example Henry Ford, IBM, Alcoa. There is no danger from this sort of mono-

Discussion

poly. As soon as it gets fat and sassy, someone will come in and un dercut it.

Meir Tamari: We have great difficulty in proving that something is a Jewish attitude, because we tend to think of things which are expressed by Jews as Jewish attitudes.

The onus is on somebody to prove that what he's saying has roots in Jewish teaching. It's not enough to say that it was good for Jews, or bad for Jews, or that Jews liked it, etc., etc. In order for it to be authentic, it has to be proven that it is part of a Jewish culture.

The second point is that it's true that the market mechanism operates in such a way that people offer services of various kinds in order to make a buck. However, it is also true that people kill each other, and steal from each other, and marry each other, also to make a buck. And that is the part of life which needs to be handled. It may not be a part of the market mechanism but it is a real part of life. Therefore, that part of life needs to be handled by religion.

I do not think that we can prove that there is any system in economic life which is synonymous with Jewish law. It would be very dangerous for us to say that such an economic system equals Judaism. In the course of 4,000 years, Jews have lived under a large number of economic systems. And I think that this will happen in the future as well.

In Israel, for many years it was very common to identify socialism with Judaism. This was a reaction to eastern European culture and caused a lot of difficulties.

What we want is to leave the investment decision to be considered on grounds of economic profitability. After that, we will require that the decision be examined to see whether it is a moral one or not.

I will use an example. There is a mishnah which says that one is not allowed to sell weapons to idolators, the assumption being that since they use weapons not just in self-defence, you are aiding and abetting murder. This falls into the biblical category that you're not allowed to put a stumbling block in front of the blind.

Every year, my students get up and say, "Yes, but look at Israel's balance of payments. The fact is that export of arms is one of our major industries. Cost/benefit analysis shows that if we make 3,000 tanks, each tank costs less than if we made only some for our own use. Of course, we should increase the export of weapons, etc. We try them. We prove them. We've shown that they work. We have an open market, etc., etc.''

They're technically correct, except that we have a legal obligation in Judaism to prevent somebody using the product which I am producing for purposes which are incompatible with God's will. And that's a problem. I don't have that problem when I export oranges. But from a religious point of view, it might be the other way around.

What about freedom and free choice? I think that Jewish law makes no bones about that. It is prepared to limit the rights of the individual in every sphere of life. We limit on religious grounds the right of the individual to what he eats, to what he wears, to when he works, to what he may do, and to what he may not do with his money. You have Kosher meals, you have Kosher sex, you have Kosher money. (laughter) Thus we have no problem with coercion, because the purpose of the whole structure of Judaism is the creation of a holy nation. We run into a lot of difficulties when we talk about Jews, who are a minority in another system. There, many of these things fall into disuse.

But that wasn't the purpose of Judaism. The purpose was to construct a society which would operate in a certain way. And since not religious individuals, but a religious state was the purpose of the law, the individual was to be circumscribed in whatever he did in order to fulfill the greater goal of the Jewish religion and community.

Marilyn Friedman: I would like to respond to the issue of value freedom raised by Walter Block. The concept of value-free science is a helpful and desirable ideal. I'm not convinced that it's always realized in practice. We need to analyze specific cases to see whether or not it actually exists and therefore to understand exactly how much of it we can in fact incorporate into our scientific practice.

One of the ways in which values enter scientific activity is in virtue of the way in which we organize the data in order to selectively perceive, and selectively diagnose, what is going on. So producing a string of sentences, as Walter Block did, doesn't necessarily reveal that these sentences, in actual usage, are value-free. They may in fact be defended and advocated on the basis of data which is selectively perceived, as determined by a researcher's value system.

I will take just two of his examples, and show how even the wording is not quite so clear cut. In one sentence he used the expression "more efficient." But he didn't say more efficient in doing what. And once we try to spell out what it is that is being done more efficiently, I expect that we will be launched into a value controversy.

He had another sentence: "rent control ruins housing." If the word "ruin" is not a word of valuation then I'm not sure what valuation is.

Jim Sadowsky: Let's take the statement "rent control hurts the poor." Is that a value-free judgement? I don't see why it isn't, because there are two attitudes I can adopt. If I like the poor, then of course I shall be against rent control. But suppose I hate the poor. Then of course I shall be for rent control.

Roger Hutchinson: I find it more useful, in terms of the kind of discussion we've been trying to have here, to say, "Is it the kind of statement that you can test against some kind of evidence?" Can we come up with some kind of mutually agreeable discourse, so that we know when we're making a factual claim.

Then you can go on and decide, "Now what counts as evidence?" and "Whose evidence is convincing?"

Imad Ahmad: I'm not happy with the examples Walter Block used. I would have preferred if he'd said something like, "rent control reduces the supply of housing." Saying "rent control hurts the poor" does contain some value-loaded terms. The term "hurt" may be considered to contain a value judgement. So the wording was unfortunate.

Stephen Tonsor: I see Judaism as an outsider. I think that Meir Tamari's presentation is much closer to the authentic tradition of Judaism than the reform tradition with which Ellis Rivkin presented us. One of the problems, though, with traditional Judaism, is that it is so closely associated with a specific cultural complex which has a chronological location that it is almost impossible to accommodate it to a contemporary society. The provisions for the sabbatical year, the remission of debts, etc., all raise enormous problems.

I also found Susan Feigenbaum's presentation of the history of capitalism not admissible. That's not the way it happened.

Richard Neuhaus: I was intrigued with Marilyn Friedman's opening statements. I was recently in a kibbutz in Israel and got involved in a long discussion with some people who were arguing about the fact that the socialist impulse in the founding fathers and mothers of Israel was directly related to their being emancipated or secularized Jews. That is what is getting screwed up in Israel today.

There are two stereotypes of Jews employed to great effect by anti-Semites. On the one hand, they are great capitalists, and at the centre of a grand conspiracy to run the world. On the other hand, they're a bunch of socialist, commie, wild-eyed revolutionaries. (laughter) These are not compatible stereotypes. But they're both employed regularly in anti-Jewish polemics.

The conclusion I would tentatively suggest is that really Judaism is something distinct from the economic choices that most Jews may have made. And that the religious factor is not all that pertinent with regard to the choice of economic options.

Behind that, nonetheless, religion plays a role in response to Meir Tamari's concern, that people also murder for greed; to which the answer is, "Well yes, but the greed factor only works if everyone works within the rules." You're talking about people who violate the rules.

But one has to go beyond that. There I think Tamari is right. What finally upholds the rules? I mean, is it finally a utilitarian calculus that this is going to work out better for everyone? No, I do not think, in sociological fact, that is the case. What upholds the rules is that people believe in some vague, intuitive way, they are grounded in an absolute reality which ought not to be violated. This is religious in character.

Susan Feigenbaum: I feel very strongly that we need to distinguish between Jews, economic systems, and Judaism. This gets back to the discussion of minority motives. Jews' response as a minority to different situations may be very different from Judaism's theological response to the very same situation.

Arthur Shenfield: The point about the invisible hand is that it introduces an order which directs the individual's aims to the benefit of all.

Meir Tamari recounted a number of ways in which the rabbis introduced a principle of justice in dealings between sellers and buyers. That's obviously a very important subject. But the rabbis rejected the principle of *caveat emptor*. In effect, therefore, they adopted the principle which is now becoming prevalent in Anglo-American courts of *caveat venditor*. In other words, no longer must the buyer beware. It's the seller who must beware.

I submit that the principle of *caveat emptor* was the result of the wisdom of centuries of English legal thought. It is a moral principle, a just principle, a highly beneficial principle. It is beneficial to the buyer, not only to the seller. The reason is that it enables the buyer to maximize his choice. If a buyer comes to the market and wishes to buy a technological product, the nature of which he doesn't understand, there's nothing in the principle of *caveat emptor* that prevents him from saying to the seller, "I want a warranty for this." And there's nothing in the principle which prevents the seller from actually, independently, offering warranties, in order to gain custom.

But if the buyer doesn't want a warranty, maybe he knows more about the goods than the seller himself. Then if the courts or the law impose the principle of *caveat venditor,* the buyer has to pay the price, because this will raise the price the seller will demand. Thus, the buyer is worse off. The principle of *caveat emptor* was developed largely by English judges, but you find it in Roman law, too. Nevertheless, that principle more and more accorded with the development of the free society and free economy.

Marilyn Friedman: I want to open the discussion of nationalism versus universalism. At the end of Ellis Rivkin's paper he discusses the compatibility of Judaism and nationalism. I don't believe that Judaism is a proponent of universalism. It's a proponent of nationalism.

I would also argue that capitalism, or the free market, is not necessarily opposed to nationalism or nationalistic boundaries. Restraints on trade can exist within nationalistic bounds and they can exist in universalistic nations. So Judaism is not alligned with universalism, nor does capitalism require universalism.

Muhammad Abdul-Rauf: Dr. Rivkin stated somewhere that the basis of Judaism is belief in God. Nevertheless, Rabbi Tamari states that Judaism has to be considered basically as a code of conduct, rather than a creed, or a statement of belief. I found the two statements contradictory.

Dr. Rivkin states: "Indeed, it was only after God had despaired of a global solution to the problem of human evil that He called upon Abraham to father a people to whom he promised the land of Canaan." I found it very unacceptable, even blasphemous, to say God has been unable to find a solution. If He can't find a solution, who else can find a solution?

I cannot speak of God in these human terms. Again what is the connection between His inability to find a solution to the eradication of evil and to a promised land? I found it very unclear. There is no relationship between them.

Marilyn Friedman: In response to what Susan Feigenbaum said about the compatibility between Judaism and nationalism, I recall that historians of Jewish economic history talk about the ways in which capitalism has both helped and hurt the Jewish community. When they talk about the way in which it hurt the Jewish community, they tend to mention an emphasis on individualism in the surrounding non-Jewish culture which undermines the cohesiveness of Jewish community life. That's the way capitalism hurts the Jewish community.

If that's true, what does it do to the choice of whether or not to participate in the capitalist system? How does this choice present itself to Jews, if it means a sacrifice of the cohesiveness of community life?

Ellis Rivkin: I hoped to spark off interest and debate with respect to the ultimate moral consequences of capitalism. This can be historically demonstrated through the Declaration of Independence, its appeal to natural rights, the rights of the individual, as the justification of American independence. Capitalism, an economic system, has nothing to do with the growth of nation states. It has absolutely nothing to do with nationalism. It is simply an economic system which sees the whole world as a market without any kind of barriers.

I tried to demonstrate that the American experience of society was formed with very few pre-capitalist, institutional limitations, and did not evolve as a system of national states, though the experimentation with confederacy certainly indicated that Americans were aware that this was a possibility. The consequences of capitalist development on a continental basis has indicated that capitalists do not go to war with each other simply because there are major, conflicting, competitive aspects in moving from one stage of capitalism to another.

I tried to demonstrate that Europe, through its pre-capitalist baggage and institutions, has a history of warfare that stems from existing nation states.

I also wanted to tie together the transnational aspect of capitalism, individualism, the Declaration of Independence, and the first chapter of Genesis. In the first chapter of Genesis, God creates a single individual. God does not create nations. He does not create peoples. He does not create classes or castes. Man is in the image of God as male and female. So the individual is all that there really can be. That kind of commitment to the individual is only possible with free capitalism. The ultimate concern of a capitalist state is that the individual be free, without any kind of restrictions or impediments, other than that he or she must respect the equal right of all others to be free.

Meir Tamari: How would we implement some form of economic system in Judaism as distinct from what Jews do in economics? Historically speaking, we have to separate the answer in two parts: before the French Revolution, and afterwards. It was the French Revolution that broke down the autonomy of the Jewish communities. After it, Jews had to operate in the economies of the countries in which they lived in a similar way to non-Jews.

In other words, religious belief became an individual matter. Some people observed more, others less. But even the most observant Jew followed very much a non-Jewish pattern of individual piety. Piety became a question of charity, individual charity, honesty in business on an individual basis, in exactly the same way as in other faiths in a similar situation.

Prior to the French Revolution, for close to three thousand years, the Jewish community operated a political structure in which the economic system was regulated through communal taxation (for purposes of charity, defence, education, etc.,) and by the control of profit, prices, and monopoly, where necessary. In Muslim countries, which never had the same feudalistic system as Europe, the control organized by Jewish law was much greater than the distinctive practices in Christian Europe. This was because the economic base of Jewish life was much wider there.

The independence of Jewish courts, which were able to cover economic issues, meant that economic life, trade, transactions, investment, etc., were covered by Jewish law rather than by non-Jewish law. Finally, there was an emphasis on communal welfare, the redemption of refugees, the question of provision and aid for the poor, for the sick, for study, etc.

So if we're looking for an application of an economic system, we would have to look at the autonomous Jewish communities before the French Revolution. Unfortunately, in the state of Israel today, the emphasis is primarily secular. Orthodox Jews choosing the state of Israel continue to live, in the economic sense, in the same way as in post-French-Revolutionary Europe. In other words, purely on a private basis of charity, honesty and integrity, but as individuals.

There hasn't been an attempt to mould business operation, or the economy of the country, in accordance with Jewish law. This is a prime challenge to the Jewish state, to see to what extent it can integrate Jewish thought, and Jewish teaching, into its economic system.

PART SIX

ISLAMIC SOCIAL THOUGHT

Chapter 12

Islamic Social Thought*

Imad Ahmad

Islam is little understood in the West. It would not be helpful to plunge into a discussion of Islamic social thought without first acquainting the reader with some of the terms which will be used.

The message Muhammad delivered is the *Qur'an (qur'-an:* the reading, or recitation), the Holy Book of Islam, which Muslims believe to be the actual Word of God. The text is in the form of God addressing Muhammad and Mankind. The *Qur'an* was actually written in the time of Muhammad as dictated by the Prophet to his scribes and companions, and assembled by them into its present form within a few years of the Prophet's death. The *Qur'an* is not considered authentic in translation.

Although there were Christians and Jews in Arabia during Muhammad's time, the dominant religion was idol-worship. While most of the lands around Arabia were dominated by one or another of the great empires of the day, the Arabs were organized into tribes and clans recognizing no central authority. Located as they were at the crossroads of several major civilizations and unfettered by allegiance to any single empire, they were commercially active. Yet, save for their poetry (of which they were inordinately proud) they had

---

*Abridged

no culture or science, and the pre-Islamic era came to be known as the Days of Ignorance (*al-jahiliya*).

Muhammad was a poor orphan descended from a once powerful branch of the Quraysh tribe. Until the age of 40 (c. 610 A.D.) he had been a rationalist in religious matters. He then began to report messages from God, which God bade him to take to the Arabs, and to all Mankind. This *Qur'an* is the foundation of Islam. Muhammad proclaimed that there is no god but God, and that he and all the prophets who preceded him were mere humans sent only to bring God's guidance to men; that there would be a Day of Justice (*yawm-ad-d-n*) when the good would be rewarded and the evil punished; and that all religion is one: submission to God's will (lit., *isl-am*).

The first prominent member of the tribe to accept his teachings was one Abu Bakr who later became the first *khal-fah* (successor), or leader of the Muslim community after Muhammad. Most of the tribe's established and influential members opposed him bitterly. Some like Umar ibn-al-Khattab (who went on to become the second *khal-fah*) accepted Islam before long, but most engaged in persecution against the Muslims. When this failed to stop the growth of Islam, an assassination plot was conceived against the Prophet.

Muhammad, learning of this plan, dispatched the Meccan Muslims to the nearby town of Yathrib, which had a Muslim as well as a Jewish community. He and Abu Bakr followed the others under cover of darkness on the night of the planned assassination. Their flight (*hijra*) marks the beginning of the Muslim calendar (622 A.D.).

In Yathrib, which soon came to be called Medina (the city; from *med-nat-an-nabi* —the city of the Prophet), the emigrants and local Muslims (*ansar,* or helpers) began to form a new community. A compact for the government of the city was drafted and accepted by all resident groups. This compact has been described by some historians as the founding of the first modern state. The nature of this "state," and how it differs from modern governments, is noteworthy.

Independence

Muslims were those who pledged themselves to Muhammad through the acceptance of the *tawhid* (the creed that there is no god but God and Muhammad is his messenger). Each tribe continued to govern its own affairs, independent of the "state," except that Muslim law supplanted contradictory tribal customs for *Muslims*. Jews would continue to be governed by Jewish law. They would also govern themselves, but any disputant had the right of appeal to Muhammad.

Muhammad had "legislative" authority only over Muslims. He could intervene in disputes between Jews and Muslims, but could not intervene in Jewish affairs except by invitation. If invited to rule on a Jewish matter by appeal, he would decide according to Jewish law. This is less a modern state than a Nozickian "supra-state."[1] This will become more clear when we see that the principal rule for the settlement of disputes with non-Muslims is the non-aggression principle.

Muhammad proceeded to establish a network of alliances with the neighbouring towns and tribes, some but not all of which became Muslim. The Quraysh made three attempts to wipe out the Muslims, each of which failed despite numerical superiority. When in 7 A.H. (After *Hijra*) the Muslims sought a peaceful pilgrimage to Mecca, the Quraysh agreed to a compromise, allowing the Muslims to make the pilgrimage the following year. A treaty was signed in which both sides agreed to cease all hostilities.

Two years of peace that followed saw a large increase of the Muslim ranks. When in 8 A.H. the Quraysh attacked a pagan tribe in alliance with the Muslims, the Muslims marched on Mecca with a force of 10,000. This time it was the Quraysh who were outnumbered. Lacking the fierce conviction which sustained the Muslims, the Quraysh sued for peace even before the war began. Muhammad offered a general amnesty, only excluding certain anti-Muslim propagandists.

On Muhammad's death, Abu Bakr was chosen successor by election. He and the next three successors, Umar, Uthman and Ali, are known as the four "rightly-guided" *khal-fahs,* who endeavoured to preserve the *Qur'an* and the practice of Muhammad. When Ali was assassinated, the khalifate fell into the hands of the house of Muhammad's former enemy, Abu Sufyan. This dynasty used Islam as a unifying glue for the Umayyad empire. The Umayyads held themselves to be kings rather than trustees, and themselves *kahalifat-allah* (successors to God) rather than *khalifat-an-nabi* (successors to the Prophet). Because the Umayyads produced sayings attributed to the Prophet justifying their oppression of the people, scholars began a resistance. This took the form of schools which developed principles of historical analysis for assessing the authenticity of traditions (*had-th*: lit., speech) attributed to Muhammad. Traditional Islamic law was thus codified not by the state, but by a "completely free and unorganized republic of scholars."[2]

Orthodox schools

With the overthrow of the Umayyads by the pietist Abbasids in 127 A.H. (749 A.D.), these schools flourished. With the new government's assistance, four became entrenched as the orthodox schools of Islam: the Hanafi (rationalist), the Shafi'i (moderate), the Maliki (traditionalist), and the Hanbali (fundamentalist). Each recognizes the legitimacy of all others. Of the other schools which these four considered heretical, only three deserve mention here: the Khawarij (or anarchists, who believed in no authority but God's), the Mu'tazilite (or extreme rationalists, sometimes called the libertarians because of their emphasis on free will), and the Sh-'ah (who believe that Muhammad's nephew Ali, not Abu Bakr, should have succeeded Muhammad).

The *Qur'an* is the chief basis of both Islamic canon law (*shari'ah*), and jurisprudence (*fiqh*). The Hadith are the traditions, traced through the companions of the Prophet, detailing the *sunnah* (practice) of the Prophet. They were compiled many years after the Prophet's death. Those who compiled the *Hadith* took great care to cite references to primary sources. An unbroken *isnad* (chain of transmitters) is considered by Muslims indispensable to the authenticity of a *had-th*. Additional sources of law are *ijma* (informed consensus of the community), *qiy-as* (analogy from established law), and *ijtih-ad* (formulation of law by the individual's struggle for proper understanding). My paper is chiefly concerned with social teaching based on the *Qur'an* alone.

The four schools give different relative importance to the sources of law, but all (including the "heretical" are unanimous in requiring that Islamic law be God-given and not man-created. From this perspective the "sources" of law are actually sources of *codification* of God's Natural law. As such, the *Qur'an* is the undisputed primary source, for it is believed to be the speech of God Himself. The only generally accepted secondary source for the codification of law, the Hadith, will be used here for exegesis only.[3]

From the Islamic point of view, the writings of the scholars are tertiary sources, and will be treated as such here. Most treatment by non-Muslim scholars misrepresents the Islamic position so gravely that it renders their analyses largely irrelevant.

Individual responsibility and liberty of conscience

> Say: O ye,/That reject Faith!
> I worship not that/Which ye worship,
> Nor will ye worship/That which I worship.
> And I will not worship/That which ye have been
> Wont to worship,
> ⌐Nor will ye worship/That which I worship.
> To you be your Way/And to me mine.
>
> (109:1–6)⁴

The defining principle of Islam is submission to God. This precludes both the possibility of separating politics from religion and of condoning the submission of one man's will to another's. The former would leave an area of human life outside submission, while the latter would imply partnership with God (*shirk,* the most heinous sin according to Islam).

The submission which Islam calls for is an act of the individual, and is a personal matter, though it entails social obligations. The relation of Man to God is that of individual men to God (God is "nearer to him [man] than (his) jugular vein," 50:16), and it is the *person,* not *society,* which attains grace. The Qur'an lays stress on individual responsibility.

> ...no bearer/of burdens can bear
> The burdens of another.
>
> (53:38)

> On no soul doth God/Place a burden greater
> Than it can bear.
> It gets every good that it earns,/And it suffers
> every ill that it earns.
>
> (2:286)

> Whoever works any act/Of Righteousness and has Faith, —
> His endeavor will not/Be rejected: We shall
> Record it in his favor.
>
> (21:94)

The Day of Judgement is a day of individual responsibility.

Then, on that Day,/Not a soul will be
Wronged in the least,
And ye shall but/Be repaid the meeds
Of your past Deeds.

(36:54)

Every soul will be (held)/In pledge for its deeds.

(74:38)

There is no conception of collective guilt. When a group commits injustice, God punishes each member according to his individual responsibility.

...to every man
Among them (will come/The punishment) of the sin
That he earned, and to him/Who took on himself the lead
Among them, will be/A Penalty grievous.

(24:11)

Nor is there collective virtue. No one is superior to another by virtue of sex, race or tribe.

O mankind! We created/You from a single (pair)
Of a male and a female,/And made you into
Nations and tribes, that/Ye may know each other
(Not that ye may despise/Each other). Verily
The most honoured of you/In the sight of God
Is (he who is) the most/Righteous of you....

(49:13)

And among His Signs/Is the creation of the heavens
And the earth, and the variations/In your languages
And your colours: verily/In that are Signs
For those who know.

(30:22)

If any do deeds/Of righteousness, —
Be they male or female —
And have faith,/They will enter Heaven,
And not the least injustice/Will be done to them.

(4:124)

Non-Coercion

Since no one can be forced, tricked, or brought vicariously into salvation,[5] there is no priesthood nor intercession. The Muslim may invite to salvation, but may not coerce:

> Say: Will ye dispute/With us about God, seeing
> That He is our Lord/And your Lord; that
> We are responsible for our doings/And ye for yours;
> and that
> We are sincere (in our faith)/In him?
>
> (2:139)

Pressure should neither be offered nor accepted.[6] Only God may judge in matters of conscience.

The prohibition against coercion applies as much to the Prophet as to any other man.

> It is not required/Of thee (O Apostle),
> To set them on the right path,
> But God sets on the right path/Whom He pleaseth....
>
> (2:272)

> Now then.../Call (them to the Faith)
> And...say..."For us/(Is the responsibility for)
> Our deeds, and for you/For your deeds. There is
> No contention between us/And you. God will
> Bring us together,/And to him is/(Our) final goal."
>
> (42:15)

> The Apostle's duty is only/To preach the clear (Message).
>
> (24:54)

> ...he that strays/Injures his own soul.
> Nor art thou set/Over them to dispose
> Of their affairs.
>
> (39:41)

The *Qur'an* asserts unequivocaly that reason, not coercion, is the means for the propagation of Islam:

> Invite (all) to the Way/Of thy Lord with wisdom
> And beautiful preaching;
> And argue with them/In ways that are best
> And most gracious....
>
> (16:125)

Rejection of God's message is not punishable by man, but by God alone:

> Leave Me alone, (to deal)/With the (creature) whom
> I created (bare and) alone!
>
> (74:11)

Reciprocity is demanded from the non-Muslim world. As no one may be forced to accept God's message, so no one should be forced to reject it.[7]

Choice of religion is the responsibility of the individual

> Those who believe (in the *Qur'an*),
> Those who follow the Jewish (scriptures),
> And the Sabians, Christians,/Magians, and Polytheists,—
> God will judge between them/On the Day of Judgement:
> For God is witness Of all things.
>
> (22:17)

> And dispute ye not/With the People of the Book
> Except with means better/(Than mere disputation), unless
> It be with those of them
> Who inflict wrong (and injury)....
>
> (29:46)

A distinction

A distinction is made here between those who wish to argue and those who wish to coerce. An example of how Muslims have responded to the injunction against use of compulsion in these cases is the following excerpt from a letter of Al-Hashimi to the Christian Al-Kindi, inviting him to Islam:

> ...if you reject my words and refuse the sincere advice I have offered you (without looking for any thanks or reward)—then write whatever you wish to say about your religion, all that you

hold to be true and established by strong proof, without any fear or apprehension, without curtailment of your proofs or concealment of your beliefs; for I propose only to listen patiently to your arguments and to yield to and acknowledge all that is convincing therein, submitting willingly without refusing or rejecting or fear, in order that I may compare your account and mine. You are free to set forth your case....

Therefore bring forward all the arguments you wish and say whatever you please and speak your mind freely. Now that you are safe and free to say whatever you please, appoint some arbitrator who will impartially judge between us and lean only towards the truth and be free from the empery of passion, and that arbitrator shall be Reason, whereby God makes us responsible for our own rewards and punishments. Herein I have dealt justly with you and have given you full security and am ready to accept whatever decision Reason may give for me or against me. For "There is no compulsion in religion" (2:256) and I have only invited you to accept our faith willingly and of your own accord and have pointed out the hideousness of your present belief. Peace be with you and the mercy and blessings of God![8]

That this attitude was the rule rather than the exception is attested to by the following incident from the Spanish Inquisition. One of the charges of the Archbishop of Vanencia brought before Philip II in 1602 against the "Apostasies and Treasons of the Morescoes" was "that they commended nothing so much as that liberty of conscience in all matters of religion, which the Turks, and all other Mohammedans, suffer their subjects to enjoy."[9]

This liberty of conscience extends not only to non-Muslims, but to sectarians as well:

> As for those who divide/Their religion and break up
> Into sects, thou hast/No part in them in the least:
> Their affair is with God: He will in the end
> Tell them the truth/Of all that they did.
>
> (6:159)

In succeeding sections I shall show how Qur'anic prescriptions for Muslim society manifest principles of benevolence and free trade, and how prescriptions for interaction between the Muslim and non-Muslim communities are based on the non-aggression principle. Islamic demands on individual Muslims (such as ritual and hygiene) do not belong in a discussion of Islamic social thought, except to the extent that such prescriptions may be forcibly imposed. Of that the *Qur'an* advises:

> Leave alone those/Who take their religion
> To be mere play/And amusement,
> And are deceived/By the life of this world.
> But proclaim (to them)/This (truth): that every soul
> Delivers itself to ruin/By its own acts....
>
> (6:70)

The *Qur'an* distinguishes between good and evil (enforced by God) and right and wrong (enforceable by man).

The Muslim community

> Let there arise out of you/A band of people
> Inviting to all that it good,/Enjoining what is right,
> And forbidding what is wrong....
>
> (3:104)

Respect for man's direct responsibility to God requires political freedom. But, as the American Muslim leader W. Dean Muhammad has noted, "freedom without vision is destruction."

What defines a Muslim is commitment to Islam manifested in the observance of five religious duties: (1) free and public confession of the belief that there is no god but God and Muhammad is His messenger, (2) regular prayer, (3) fasting during the month of Ramadan, (4) payment of obligatory charity (*zak-at*), and (5) pilgrimage to Mecca. The practicality of Islam as evidenced by the simplicity of these religious duties is also seen in the attention which the *Qur'an* gives to practical matters of daily living: marriage and divorce procedures, inheritance laws, contract law, rules of evidence, to name a few.

The individual responsibility of Man in the spiritual realm has its material analogue in the sanctity of private property:

> And in no wise covet/Those things in which God
> Hath bestowed His gifts/More freely on some of you
> Than on others: to men/Is allotted what they earn,
> And to women what they earn:/But ask God of His bounty.
>
> (4:32)

There are two remarkable implications of this verse. First, women have the same property rights as men. That the Qur'an gave women full property rights fourteen hundred years ago goes against the common Western perception of the role of women in Islam. Western ignorance combined with an Arab sexism has led to much misunderstanding. The pre-Islamic Arab did not believe that females had even a right to life. Female babies were murdered because of their sex. The *Qur'an* banned this practice[10] and warned against the day "when the female (infant) buried alive, is questioned for what crimes she was killed..." (81:8–9).

> ...And women shall have rights/Similar to the rights
> Against them, according/To what is equitable;
> But men have a degree/(Of advantage) over them....
>
> (2:228)

The advantages which men are given in Islamic communities are: greater weight to their testimony as witnesses (but not when testifying as interested parties); a place at the head of the household; and a greater share of inheritance. The last is balanced against greater financial responsibility for the household:

> Men are the protectors/And maintainers of women,
> Because God has given/The one more (strength)
> Than the other, and because/They support them
> From their means....
>
> (4:34)

Sexism

Feminists may take exception to the assertion that there are physiological grounds for discrimination in the family roles of men and women. Indeed, a Muslim feminist could even argue that the passage is descriptive rather than prescriptive. In any case the status of women in Islamic society is different from popular misconception. In addition to the right to property in material goods and the right to life, women in Islam have the right to property in their own persons:

> O ye who believe!
> Ye are forbidden to inherit/Women against their will.
> Nor should ye treat them/With harshness...except

Where they have been guilty/Of open lewdness....

(4:19)

I believe it is fair to say that while women are not given the same social position as men by the *Qur'an*, they are given equal human rights as individuals.

The other remarkable implication of verse 4:32 is that wealth is not seen as evil in itself. Rather, one is judged by the process by which one acquires goods:

> ...There are men who say:
> "Our Lord! Give us/(Thy bounties) in this world!"
> But they will have/No portion in the Hereafter.

> And there are men who say:/"Our Lord! Give us
> Good in this world/And good in the hereafter...."

> To these will be allotted/What they have earned;
> And God is quick in account.

(2:200–202)

This absence of dualism may seem strange to a neo-Platonist Westerner. But the ethics of Islam are often phrased in terms of the market place.[11]

The Islamic standard of merit is not how much (or how little) wealth one has aquired, but rather, how was it acquired, and how is it used? The Muslim is urged to moderation. Neither self-destructive indulgence nor other-destructive inconsideration, but free trade is the standard:

> O ye who believe!/Eat not up your property
> Among yourselves in vanities:/But let there be amongst you
> Traffic and trade/By mutual good-will:
> Nor kill (or destroy)/
> Yourselves: for verily
> God hath been to you/Most Merciful!

(4:29)

> ...nor use it your property
> As bait for the judges,/With the intent that ye may
> Eat up wrongfully and knowingly

A little of other peoples' property.

(2:188)

Profit belongs to the producer. The pursuit of profit is encouraged even on the day of community prayers (Friday).[12] It is even permitted during pilgrimage, when other mundane affairs are set aside.[13]

The basis of sound commerce is the contract, and the *Qur'an* spells out sound procedures for writing contracts in detail to eliminate misunderstandings or deceit.[14] Both theft and fraud are condemned.

> Give just measure/And cause no loss
> (To others by fraud).

(26:181)

> So establish weight with justice
> And fall not short/
> In the balance.

(55:9)

Commerce

In accord with the prohibition of fraud, contracts are inviolable:

> O ye who believe!/
> Fulfill (all) obligations.

(5:1)

> Fulfill the Covenant of God/
> When ye have entered into it,
> And break not your oaths/
> After ye have confirmed them;
> Indeed ye have made/God your surety; for God
> Knoweth all that ye do.

> And be not like a woman/Who breaks into untwisted strands
> The yarn which she has spun,/After it has become strong.
> Nor take your oaths to practice/Deception between
> yourselves....

(16:91–92)

Yet the injunction to fulfil commitments may not be used as an excuse for violation of other absolute principles. If someone swears to do something wrong in passion, he is not committed to that action, but rather to make expiation for a futile oath by feeding the hungry, clothing the poor or freeing a slave.

A distinction is made between gain through enterprise and gain through a condemned practice called *rib-a*. *Rib-a* is usually translated as usury, as in this translation by Yusef Ali:

> Those who devour usury/Will not stand except
> As stands one whom/The Evil One by his touch
> Hath driven to madness.
> That is because they say:/"Trade is like usury,"
> But God hath permitted trade/And forbidden usury....
>
> (2:275)

The actual meaning of *rib-a* has been debated since the earliest Muslim times. Umar, the second Caliph, grieved that the Prophet had not given a more detailed account of what constituted *rib-a*.

Some scholars have argued that the concept subsumes not only usury, but all interest (*rib.h*). This is reminiscent of arguments by some Western scholars that all interest is usurious. *Rib-a* comes from the root *rab-a* meaning to increase (or exceed), while *rib.h* comes from the root *rabi.ha* meaning to gain (or profit). The above verse makes it clear that profit is not a form of *rib-a*. In fact, it compares anyone who asserts that they *are* the same with a lunatic.

In the Prophet's day few loans were for the purposes of providing venture capital. The usual purpose of a loan was to allow those in deep financial need to survive until next week. The rate of interest tended to be exorbitant ("Doubled and multiplied," 3:130), resulting in further debt for the borrower. It is not surprising that scholars in early Islam perceived all interest as usury. In today's world of high finance when few borrowers are charity cases, the debate has been renewed. Is the market-clearing rate of interest *rib-a*? The matter is too complex to cover here.

Let us turn to the case of persons in distress, in desperate need of capital. Loan-sharking is forbidden. To lend money is permitted, but charity is preferred:

> God will deprive/Usury of all blessing,
> But will give increase/For deeds of charity:
> For He loveth not/Creatures ungrateful
> And wicked.
>
> (2:276)

Welfare

This brings us to the general question of welfare. Every Muslim is required to pay *Zakat*. This is a 2½ percent assessment on assets held for a full year (after a small initial exclusion) to be distributed among specified needy recipients.[15] Only Muslims are required to pay *Zakat*. Muslims receive preference in receiving it, although non-Muslims in need are also eligible.

The *Qur'an* provides for a State, with jurisdiction for settlement of disputes:

> If two parties among/The Believers fall into
> A quarrel, make ye peace/Between them: but if
> One of them transgresses/Beyond bounds against the other,
> Then fight ye (all) against/The one that transgresses
> Until it complies with/The command of God;
> But if it complies, then/Make peace between them
> With justice, and be fair:/For God loves those
> Who are fair (and just).
>
> (49:9)

This is, however, a derived authority, as Abu Bakr recognized in his inaugural address upon election to the khalifate:

> You have elected me at *khal-ifa* (successor to the Holy Prophet as temporal head of state), but I claim no superiority over you. The strongest among you shall be the weakest with me until I get the rights of others from him, and the weakest among you shall be the strongest with me until I get all his rights....Help me if I act rightly and correct me if I take a wrong course.... Obey me as long as I obey God and his Messenger. In case I disobey God and His messenger, I have no right to obedience from you.[16]

Muslims must be wary of the corrupting effect of power:

> Then, is it/To be expected to you,
> If ye were put in authority,/That ye will do mischief
> In the land, and break/Your ties of kith and kin?
>
> (47:22)

Umar took this warning to heart:

Umar asked: "What will you do if I go wrong?" One of those present stood up and shouted: "By God, we will put you right with the edge of our swords." Umar replied, "If you do not do so, you will lose God's blessing. And if I do not accept your correction, I shall lose God's blessing."[17]

When a member of a crowd demanded to know where he had got a cloak he was wearing, Umar took no offence. He answered directly, and announced to the shocked nobility around him that the people had a right to know that he acquired his possessions justly and not by graft. He practised "full disclosure."

In addition to condemning corruption in general, the *Qur'an* warns particularly against secret counsels:

Secret counsels are only/(Inspired) by the Evil One....

(58:10)

In summary I quote the observation of the Qur'anic scholar M. F. Ansari: "Islam is opposed to the mystico-ascetic approach to life and regards society as the natural framework of activity for human fulfillment."[18] The vision it provides is of a family-based society of private property and free trade, in which men and women are entitled to what they earn and deserve:

To all are degrees (or ranks)/According to their deeds....

(6:132)

Principles of justice

Nor take life—which God/Has made sacred—except
For just cause. And if/Anyone is slain wrongfully,
We have given his heir/Authority (to demand *Oisas*[19]
Or to forgive): but let him/Not exceed bounds in the matter
Of taking life; for he/Is helped (by the law).

(17:33)

One can only take life in the case of murder or heinous crime.[20] Response to aggression against person or property is covered by the rule of reciprocity. Thus, the *Qur'an* commends

...those who, when/An oppressive wrong is inflicted

On them (are not cowed/But) help and defend themselves.

The recompense for an injury/Is an injury equal thereto
(In degree):But if a person/Forgives and makes reconciliation.
His reward is due/From God: for (God)
Loveth not those who/Do wrong.

But indeed if any do help/And defend themselves
After a wrong (done)/To them, against such
There is no cause/Of blame.

The blame is only/Against those who oppress
Men with wrong-doing/And insolently transgress
Beyond bounds through the land/Defying right and justice:
For such there will be/A penalty grievous.

But indeed if any/Show patience and forgive,
That would truly be,/An exercise of courageous will
And resolution in the conduct/Of affairs.

(42:39–43)

If the perpetrator of a crime is not under jurisdiction of an Islamic government, and if his own community protects him from punishment, the law of reciprocity is to act against the community which harbours him, but only to the degree of the offence.[21]

Rights are not to be denied because of religious differences.[22] The prohibition of fraud is general and applies to non-Muslims as well as Muslims.[23] The requirements of justice and due process are binding on all, regardless of religion.

O ye who believe!/Stand out firmly
For God, as witnesses/To fair dealing, and let not
The hatred of others/To make you swerve
To wrong and depart from/Justice. Be just: that is
Next to Piety: and fear God.
For God is well-acquainted/With all that ye do.

(5:9)

External relations

Relations with the non-believers are those of mutual forbearance.

...bear them company/In this life with justice
(And consideration), and follow/The way of those who
Turn to me (in love):/In the End the return
Of you all is to Me,/And I will tell you
The truth (and meaning)/Of all that ye did.

(31:15)

Therefore shun those who/Turn away from Our Message
And desire nothing but/The life of this world.

(53:29)

God forbids you not,/With regard to those who
Fight you not for (your) Faith/Nor drive you out
Of your homes,/From dealing kindly and justly
With them: For God loveth/Those who are just.

God only forbids you,/With regard to those who
Fight you for (your) Faith,/And drive you out
Of your homes, and support/(Others) in driving you out,
From turning to them/(For friendship and protection)....
(60:7–9)

The last case constitutes a state of war, and here force *is* permitted. This is because self-defence and retaliation are allowed on the eye-for-an-eye principle.[24]

Even in war there is due process, and strict rules of war apply. To begin with, peaceful resistance is preferred to war. Avoidable oppression is no excuse for sin.[25] One needs just cause to resort to war. Thus, the *Qur'an* commends those who "defend themselves only after they are unjustly attacked." (26:227)

To those against whom/War is made, permission
Is given (to fight), because/They are wronged;—and verily,
God is Most Powerful/For their aid;—
(22:39)

Will ye not fight people/Who violated their oaths,
Plotted to expel the Apostle,/And took the aggressive
By being the first (to assault) you?/Do ye fear them? Nay,
It is God Whom ye should/More justly fear, if ye believe!

Fight them, and God will/Punish them by your hands,
Cover them with shame,/Help you (to victory) over them....
(9:12–13)

Fight in the cause of God/Those who fight you,
But do not transgress limits;/For God loveth not transgressors.

And slay them/Wherever ye catch them,
And turn them out/From where they have
Turned you out;/For tumult and oppression
Are worse than slaughter....

(2:190– 191)

Rules of war

The law of equality that applies to aggression applies also to cease-
fire and peace:

But if the enemy/Incline towards peace,
Do thou (also) incline/Towards peace, and trust
In God: for He is the One/That heareth and Knoweth
(All things).

Should they intend/To deceive thee,—verily God
Sufficeth thee....

(8:61– 62)

Fear of treachery ought not to provoke treachery. Instead,

If thou fearest treachery/From any group, throw back
(Their Covenant) to them, (So as/To be) on equal terms:
For God loveth not the treacherous.

(8:58)

Even in a state of war, terrorism is forbidden:

And fear tumult or oppression,/Which affecteth not in
particular
(Only) those of you who do wrong....

(8:25)

The innocent must be spared even accidental suffering. On this account the Muslims were forbidden to force their way into Mecca.[26]
Abu Bakr understood the implications of these verses and instructed
his troops accordingly when they set off to fight the soldiers of the By-
zantine Empire:

Do not commit misappropriation or fraud, not be guilty of disobedience (to the commander) and mutilation (of the limbs of any person). Do not kill old men, women or children. Injure not the date-palm, nor burn it with fire; and cut not down the fruit-bearing trees. Slaughter not the sheep or cows or camels except for purposes of food. You will pass by persons who spend their lives in retirement in the monasteries. Leave them in their statement of retirement.[27]

In modern terminology: no scorched earth policy.

If aggressors do not sue for peace but fight until defeated, they lose their property rights. This provides the spoils of war with which the troops are paid.[28] But the residents of the conquered lands are entitled to equality with the victors if they adopt Islam. If not, they may still remain under Muslim protection if they pay the *jizyah* or defence tax. The *jizyah* is a head tax applicable to able-bodied males of military age (non-Muslims did not normally serve in the armed forces). That it is a user-fee levied for security rather than ordinary tribute is shown not only by its small amount but also by its refund when protection could not be provided. The people of Hirah, for example, agreed to pay the *jizyah* on the condition that "the Muslims and their leader protect us from those who would oppress us, whether they be Muslims or others." In the treaty between the Muslim general Khalid ibn Walid and the towns near Hirah, Khalid writes "If we protect you, then *jizyah* is due to us; but if we do not, then it is not due." Abu 'Ubaydah once ordered the governors of Syria to refund the *jizyah* with the following explanatory message:

We give you back the money that we took from you, as we have received news that a strong force is advancing against us. The agreement between us was that we should protect you, and as that is not now in our power, we return you all that we took. But if we are victorious we shall consider ourselves bound to you by the terms of our agreement.

The Christians of Syria replied:

May God give you rule over us again and may you be victorious over the Romans; had it been they, they would not have given back anything, but would have taken all that remained with us.[29]

When Christians fought as allies of the Muslims they were not charged *jizhah,* but were given a share of the booty.

The draft

Military service was expected of all able-bodied male Muslims, but exemptions were liberal. Muhammad never denied an exemption. The theory of the *Qur'an* is that the man seeking a justified exemption should be exempted while one seeking an unjustified exemption could not be trusted in battle. In any case, God knows which is which and will Himself punish the traitors and cowards. This theory is described in Surah 9. I quote some highlights:

> If they had come out/With you, they would not
> Have added to your (strength)/But only (made for) disorder,
> Hurrying to and from in your midst/And sowing sedition
>   among you....
>
> (9:47)

> And there were, among/The desert Arabs (also)
> Men who made excuses/And came to claim exemption;
>
> And those who were false/To God and His Apostle
> (Merely) sat inactive./Soon will a grievous penalty
> Seize the Unbelievers/Among them.
>
> There is no blame/On those who are infirm,
> Or ill, or who find/No resources to spend
> (On the Cause), if they/Are sincere (in duty) to God
> And His Apostle:
>
> No ground (of complaint)/Can there be against such
> As do right: and God/Is Oft-Forgiving, Most Merciful.
> (7:90–91)

Islam and economic systems

The *Qur'an* does not prescribe the forms of government and economic system under which the Muslim is expected to live. Rather it provides an ethical base with certain political and economic implications. The discovery of these implications is a matter of much discussion among Muslims today.

Because the Islamic injunctions protecting the sanctity of private property are so strong, leftist Muslims must seek to justify their own versions of socialism from Islamic teaching about brotherly benevolence and the prohibition of *rib-a*. For example, Shaikh Ameer Ali writes in *The Muslim World Journal*, that the benevolent characteristic of Islam conflicts with "the spirit of individualism and competition—the twin pillars of present-day market economic structures." He explains:

> True, Islam encourages hard work, attributes direct responsibility to God, upholds honesty in dealing and thrift in spending, emphasizes methodical ordering of time and rational calculation and welcomes lawful earnings and material accumulation; but it also prescribes obligations and responsibilities towards the parents, the relatives, the orphans, the poor and the co-religionists. The Islamic Law of Inheritance, the institution of Zakat and in a sense even the ban on usury are built-in distributive devices to prevent wealth from circulating within a narrow circle. Hence, the true Islamic ethic is anti-capitalistic.[30]

The origin of anti-market thinking in Islam comes less from a misunderstanding of Islam than from a misunderstanding of the market.

Nevertheless, Muslim scholars have been quick to reject socialism in the narrow sense (i.e., state ownership of the means of production). They aim rather at a synthesis which incorporates the freedom of enterprise of classical liberalism and the beneficent effects of socialism, whilst rejecting what they see as the insensitivity of capitalism and the authoritarianism of socialism. Muhammad Ali wrote in his book, *The New World Order:*

> To destroy capitalism, . . .would have been an act of the greatest injustice, and it was quite foreign to the spirit of Islam. It introduced a compulsory system of charity, compulsory not in the sense that any force was employed in its collection. The compulsion was moral.

> [S]tate ownership of industry and absence of all private enterprise precludes all competition and all incentive to hard and intelligent labour; and in the end, it will, by promoting habits of indolence and apathy, lower the standard of productiveness and impoverish the nation which adopts it. . . .that the absence of private enterprise and private ownership in peaceful times will promote habits of indolence and sloth is too patent a fact to be denied, and even the Soviet Union has been compelled to modify its first views and to introduce competition in some form.

Monopoly

After noting that state ownership of the means of production would be capitalism with only one capitalist owning everything, Ali adds:

> Nay, a single capitalist in a nation would be more bearable in comparison with the state as the owner of all property and industry. An individual could be easily criticized, and he may have to mend his ways in his own interests. Not so the State which can, and often does, stifle all criticism which it thinks to be averse to its interests. There is a remedy in the world for every tyranny, but there is no remedy for the tyranny of the State, more particularly of a State which is also the sole capitalist in a country.

Ali notes that communism "carries to the extreme in practice the fascist theory by depriving the individual of both his freedom and his property." But he criticizes democracy because, despite its "high-sounding theory" its advocates have enslaved "more than half the human race."

After reading this analysis written almost forty years ago, one wonders why the so-called Islamic leaders of the world have failed to heed its warning against the nation-state. It is not that they reject his arguments, but rather that they have been guided less by Muslim ideology than by a pressing desire for rapid industrial development. Islamic principles have therefore been exchanged for whatever capitalist or socialist methods brought about industrial development. Although disregard of the wishes of those who owned and worked the land has been most flagrant under the Shah of Iran, every so-called Muslim government has succumbed to the same temptation to some degree.

This is not to say that pragmatism only has dictated the actions of Muslim political leaders. Mu'ammar Qad-afi, it is true, has unfurled the banner of "socialism" to fly over his personal interpretation of Islam. Yet, his use of the word presents no challenge to the Qur'anic view of property:

> If to be "leftist" means to oppose reaction and imperialism, well then, I am on the extreme Left: no one can be further to the left than I. If "left" means "socialism," then in God's Name I declare that socialism is an emanation of our religion and of our Holy Book.

> Socialism as we see it implies that we all participate equally in production, in work, and in the distribution of the products . . .so that this activity becomes a form of prayer, and so that the products of labor do not remain the monopoly of a single category of people. . . .

> While the word "socialism" . . .has been used in the West to designate the appropriation by society of the means of production, this same word in Arabic means association and communal work.[31]

The confusion of Islamic social justice with the Western idea of socialism is illustrated in Maulnud Kassim Nait-Belkaiem's article, "The Concept of Social Justice in Islam." He describes the difficulty Umar had in finding recipients poor enough for *Zakat,* then quotes Muhammad al-Mubarrah:

> To say that there is no socialism in Islam is to be ignorant of the nature of socialism, and to demonstrate in addition an inability to understand the teachings and objectives of Islam; to prove that one has no acquaintance with Islamic laws pertaining to the subject.[32]

Nait-Belkaiem can apply the label "socialism" to Islamic social justice *only by leaving unmentioned the coercive basis of socialism.* He openly states that his reason for doing so is to appeal to the Western-influenced young people:

> And then let this social justice be designated by whatever name one cares to choose, even that of "socialism", since it is the name that the young prefer in our days, provided that it has conferred upon it the original meaning. . . .[33]

The mainstream of modern Islamic thought is neither capitalist nor socialist, but seems to be an attempt to imitate European and North American social welfare systems by giving control of *Zakat* to the state. The advocates of this practice cite Abu Bakr's use of force to make the desert tribes recognize the obligation of *Zakat* as a precedent. But if that is the precedent, Islamic social welfare is extremely limited compared to capitalist systems, since *Zakat* is 2½ percent of assets. But the precedent is debatable, since the *Qur'an* presents *Zakat* as a duty of the individual for the purpose of aiding one's fellow man, symbolizing freedom from the worship of Mammon.

The *Qur'an* gives a very limited authority to the state. Defence and the resolution of disputes, and the enforcement of certain religious laws upon Muslims. Modern leaders who have tried to justify an expansion of state authority have turned to the *Hadith*. For example, Shaikh Zaki Yamani has defended nationalization of certain industries on a *had-th* of the Prophet to the effect that "people are partners" in water, grazing, and fire.[34]

This is an example of exegesis of the *Qur'an* on which I do not wish to dwell. Extending the concept of joint ownership of fire to include the right of the state to nationalize the oil industry illustrates the extremes to which commentators must go to bring statism under the umbrella of Islam.

NOTES

1. R. Nozick, *Anarchy, State and Utopia* (New York: Basic Books, 1974), ch. 10.

2. S. D. Goitein, *Jews and Arabs: Their Contacts Through the Ages* (New York: Schocken Books, 1964).

3. The best translation of authoritative *hadith* in English is *Sahih Muslim* (Lahore: Muhammad Ashraf Kashmiri Bazar, 1976) vols. I–IV, transl. by A. H. Siddiqi.

4. References to the *Qur'an* will be cited by the *sur-ah* and *ay-at* (chapter and verse) from the translation by A. Yusef Ali, *The Holy Qur'-an: Text, Translation and Commentary* (Washington: The Islamic Center, 1978). It is available in a paperback edition called *The Meaning of the Glorious Qur'-an* (Cairo: Dar-al-Kitab al-Masri). Another respected translation is that of Muhammad Marmaduke Pickthall, *The Meaning of the Glorious Qur'an* (New York: Muslim World League, 1977) which is available in a paperback edition without the Arabic text (New York: New American Library, 1977).

5. 4:123; conversely when one is forced to evil it is charged against the coercer and not the coerced (see 24:33).

6. 28:55.

7. 40:28.

8. Quoted in J. Morgan, *Mohametism Explained* (London, 1723–1725).

9. *Ibid*.

10. 17:31.

11. M. G. S. Hodgson notes in *The Venture of Islam*, vol. I: The Classical Age of Islam (Chicago: University of Chicago Press, 1975) that in the *Qur'an* "ethics tend to be thought of in terms of the market—thus the protection of orphans was, in the first instance, protection of their property; hence the *Qur'an* freely uses market terminology—partly by way of familiar analogy (the faithful strikes a good bargain with God), but partly by way of introducing the transcendent inextricably into daily life."

12. 62:10.

13. 2:198.

14. 2:282.

15. The needy (*mas-ak-n*) are strictly defined as those who lack the where-withal to feed themselves for a year.

16. Quoted in M. Ali, *The New World Order* (Lahore: Ahmadiyaa Anju-man Ishaat-i-Islam, 1944).

17. Chris Waddy, *The Muslim Mind* (London: Longman Grove, Ltd., 1976).

18. M. F. Ansari, *The Qur'anic Foundations and Structure of Muslim Society* (Karachi: Indus Educational Foundation, 1974)

19. *Qis-as* is essentially retaliation restricted by the limits of equity. Yusuf Ali discusses it in a series of notes to 2:178 in his translation of the Qur'an.

20. 5:35 and 2:205–206.

21. 2:178–179.

22. 3:75 and 73:10.

23. 83:1–3.

24. 5:48.

25. 4:97–100.

26. 48:25.

27. Quoted in M. Ali, *The New World Order* (Lahore: Ahmadiyaa Anjuman Ishaat-i-Islam, 1944).

28. 33:25–27.

29. Quoted in T. W. Arnold, *The Preaching of Islam* (Lahore: Shirkat-at-Qualam. 1956).

30. *Loc. cit.*, IX (Jan. 1982) #3, pp. 9, 14.

31. From M. Bianco, *Gadafi: Voice from the Desert*, quoted in Waddy, *op. cit.*

32. Quoted in A. Gaufar, *The Challenge of Islam* (London: Redwood Burn, 1978).

33. A. Gaufer, *op. cit.*

34. A. Z. Yamani, "Islamic Law and Contemporary Issues," in C. Malik, ed., *God and Man in Contemporary Islamic Thought*, (Beirut: American University of Beirut, Centennial Publications, 1972).

Comment

Hanna E. Kassis

Rather than offer a detailed critique of Dr. Ahmad's interesting and informative paper, I thought it best to attempt only two things: first, to bring into the limelight some of the salient points raised in the paper; secondly to point to certain matters that were not discussed by the author. It should be pointed out, however, that, like all other contributors to this work, Ahmad looks at his topic from a point of view *within* the faith, whereas I look at it from *outside* that faith. This offers both a handicap and an advantage.

In a discussion of any aspect of a religious tradition it is very important to distinguish the ideals and ultimate goals of that tradition from the practices and conduct of its adherents. The abyss that separates the two is, perhaps, unbridgeable. This, in my opinion, is as true of Islam as it is of Christianity and Judaism. At the same time it should be remarked that in formulating opinions and conclusions about a religious tradition the ideal is often confused with and condemned by the real. This is very true of the Western interpretation (or misinterpretation) of Islam. For the past fourteen centuries, the Christian West has failed to take cognizance of Islam, its Prophet or its Scriptures. It focused its attention on that which concerns the Christian (the person of Jesus Christ in Islam, hypothetical Jewish and Christian sources of the Muslim tradition, and so forth) but refused to accept or even consider the validity of its claim to Divine revelation. The Muslim response has been, in large measure, conditioned by this negative attitude.

Urging us to do more than simply condemn, accuse or even examine the tradition of Islam, but rather to attempt to understand it, the noted French Islamologist Maxime Rodinson sums up the reaction of the Muslims to Western attitudes roughly as follows:

The view in the Muslim East is that of a Christian West involved in an incessant attack on Islam. According to this view, which Rodinson finds to be not without justification, Islam brought about social and philanthropic enterprises to expand the realm governed by the Law of God as revealed to the Prophet—a law which is equitable, charitable, democratic and egalitarian. The reaction of the West since the eighth century has been the contempt of feudal lords, despotic monarchs and their contemporary successors. Since the Crusades, this negative attitude has not ceased to be brutal and underhanded, manifesting itself in recent times through colonialism and imperialism. Formerly, the West was feudal and despotic. It is now capitalist and self-centred. Its religious (Christian) leaders have guided, led and even blessed its soldiers and spies, and contributed to the process which attempted (and still attempts) to undermine the moral fibre of the Muslim peoples by slandering their faith, Scriptures and Prophet. Their missionary activities have always attempted to incite Muslims to commit treason (through conversion) against their own faith and community.[1]

Sadly, this bleak image of the West is not without foundation. Suffice to mention here the pioneering work of Norman Daniel in this regard, whose conclusions are very adequately documented.[2]

The record

For this reason, discussions of any aspect of Islam begins, as does Ahmad's paper, with a historical *prolegomena*. History is the record of human activity. Religious history is the record of the activities of the religious community as it attempts to realize in time and space the fulfilment of the Divine Will as it has received and interpreted it. As such, religious history is replete with "mighty acts." It is, at the same time, a record of the failure of that religious community (be it Jewish, Christian or Muslim) to realize its ideal. The failure of the Muslim community to bring about a more equitable distribution of its wealth, today as in the past, must be seen not as a condemnation of the faith, but of the community that fails to apply the laws of social justice of that faith. A historical presentation should not hesitate to underscore these failures. If Islam has a very progressive social philosophy, and I sincerely believe it does, one should attempt to explain why the ideal has failed to touch the real and change it.

I am convinced that a society shapes its destiny by the manner in which it selects and recounts the events of its history. Let me give an example. At a time when many Muslim societies seriously attempt to bring about changes in the legal and social position of women, a presentation of history would benefit more from dwelling on the social achievements of the Prophet than on his victories in the battlefield. Is it not of great significance that the first convert to Islam was a woman; Khadijah, the wife of the Prophet, and not Abu Bakr, as the paper asserts? Where would we find an episode similar to Muhammad's unquestioning trust of 'Aisha, his young and beautiful wife who accidentally spent a night away from home and who returned to her husband the following morning accompanied by a handsome young man? Muhammad's attitude and conduct in these circumstances remains a model for every man. The woman was innocent and guilt was the lot of those who suspected her or gossiped about her.[3] After the death of the Prophet, she led a rebellion against the Muslim rulers of the time whom she and her collaborators believed were straying from the Law of God. When she was defeated, she retired to the city of Mecca where her house became a meeting place for literary and intellectual activity. The dignity she acquired during his lifetime continued to flourish after his death.

In this regard, we need not limit ourselves to the life of the Prophet. Islamic history is replete with incidents that illustrate the basic attitude of Islam toward women. It is a fact little known to most Muslims that the first university in the Western world was founded in Muslim North Africa by a woman.[4] Not unlike biblical tradition, Muslim historians of the Middle Ages did not fail to give credit to women where it was due. Writers chronicling the establishment of the Almoravid Dynasty in the eleventh and twelfth centuries A.D. praise the achievements of Y-usuf Ibn T-ashf-n while pointing out that in all that he did he was guided and counselled by his wife Zaynab an-Nafz-aw-yah. Let me hasten to add that the very positive attitude of Muhammad toward women is now beginning to take effect in some, though not all, Muslim countries.

Islam (and, consequently, Islamic social thought, institutions and reform) springs from two "events": a) the "event" of *isl-am* (or submission) itself, and b) the "event" of the *Qur'-an*. The former represents the response of Man as such (free from the burden of "original sin") to the Divine call for obedience. Sinfulness or redemption, failure or success, are measured (by God) in terms of man's total and unconditional response to this call (*da'wah*). Material gain or loss are inconsequential in the light of this. For it is better to act in total obedience to God's Law and lose than to do otherwise and gain. This is best illustrated in the archetypal act (or event) of *isl-am*, namely that of Abraham's response to God's call for him to offer his son as a sacrifice (Genesis 22), the commemoration of which is the highest feast in the Muslim calendar.

The event of the *Qur'an*[5] is, for the Muslim, the Divine seal of man's life and destiny.

Divine revelation

The *Qur'an*[6] is unique among sacred books in style, unity of language and authorship, and significance in the life of the faith it governs. It is not too bold to suggest that the *Qur'an* is to the Muslim what Jesus Christ, and not the Bible, is to the believing Christian. It is the un-created Word of God, coexistent with Him since the beginning of time. No Muslim would question its divine revelation, and as a result, it has not been subjected to the same type of critical study as has the Bible. Unlike the Bible, it was revealed over a defined period of time and to one man, Muhammad. According to tradition, its canon was established under Divine guidance by the Prophet, prior to his death, and not by believers at a later time, as is the case with the Old and New Testaments. Consequently, there is no accepted body of literature in the tradition of Islam equivalent to the Apocryphal Gospels (Christian) or the Books of the Apocrypha or Pseudepigrapha (Jewish). Each of its 114 Chapters is divided into verses (*-ayah,* pl. *-ay-at*). There are two different senses to the word *ayah.* First, it is a "sign" of Divine authority in literary form, in the same sense, according to Christian belief, that the person of Jesus Christ, his words and his deeds are also "signs." Secondly, it is a literary device to identify smaller textual units within a larger literary context (as is a stanza, a pentad or a biblical verse).

The *Qur'an* was revealed to Muhammad in two different places: a) at Mecca where he first received the faith (610–622 A.D.), and to which he returned triumphantly before his death (632 A.D.). These are commonly known as the "Meccan" revelations; b) at Medina, after his Migration (the *hijrah,* Latin "Hegira"), in 622, and the establishment of the Muslim state. These are known as the "Medinan" revelations.

The tone and content of these revelations change as the community developed. One senses in the earliest Chapters—short, vibrant and rhapsodic—the mystery, fear and fascination (to borrow the vocabulary of Rudolph Otto) of the confrontation with and submission to the Divine Will. After the Migration and the establishment of the Muslim state, the *Qur'an*, while maintaining the initial themes, introduces revelations dealing with the various aspects (judicial, social and religious) of the daily life of the community under the rule of God. The Chapters, whatever their subject, become increasingly developed in style and structure. It would be wrong, however, to assume, as is sometimes done, that the rhapsodic language of the earlier period gave way entirely to the elaboration of legal formulations.

The revelations came to the Prophet in one or more verses at a time. According to Muslim belief, their content as well as the time and manner of their revelation were determined by God and not by Muhammad, who was simply the recipient and transmitter of the revelations. These revelations were memorized or written down by the believers as the Prophet conveyed them. When the "Authorized Version," the *Qur'an* in its present form, was redacted during the lifetime of the first converts to Islam, more attention was paid to the authority of the text being assembled than to the logical or chronological sequence of the contents of the revelations.

Basic document

The great degree to which the *Qur'an* shapes and governs the lives of millions of Muslims around the world is becoming increasingly evident. It is my conviction that in order to understand Islam and the Muslims, one should endeavour first to comprehend the "Word" that gave the faith its birth and continues to give the community of Islam its nourishment and sustenance. For whatever his language or background, the Muslim accepts the *Qur'an* as the basic document that governs and shapes any and all aspects of his life.

But while the *Qur'an* governs his life, the Muslim is free from the burden and benefit of an ecclesiastical order. There is no priesthood in Islam. There are no individuals who, by virtue of their ordination, installation, or consecration, acquire the authority to interpret the *Qur'an* or to initiate religious rules binding on the life of the community. The *Qur'an* is the Book of every individual and not only the gift to and guide of the community. Each person alone bears sole responsibility for interpreting and applying its rules to his own life. It is he alone who has to answer to God on the Day of Judgement for his failures. If, for whatever reason, an individual is incapable of comprehending or interpreting the *Qur'an*, he should seek the counsel of those who by their learning and piety (not their religious order or position) have a better capacity for performing these responsibilities. This, however, does not relieve him from his own responsibility before God. The learned, whose counsel he seeks and follows, do not sit in a council or similar body. The loyalty of the scholar, and hence his own responsibility, is not to a group of similarly learned men or a school to which he may belong, but to God alone. Within each of the four schools of jurisprudence referred to in the paper, there may be agreement or disagreement, as there may be as well among the schools themselves. In the tenth century the Maliki school of North Africa found it easier to deal with the Christians of Sicily or Spain than with the "heresy" of the *Sh'ah*, who challenged their conception of orthodoxy. Only if the pious and intellectual endeavours (*ijtih-ad*) of the learned could lead to consensus (*ijma'*) of the community, would an interpretation of a Qur'anic law be applicable in the life of that community. In this exercise, the learned and pious acquire a higher rank than that of the ruler or even the martyr. "A drop of ink from the pen of a learned man," Muhammad is reported to have said, "far surpasses in the eyes of God an ocean full of the blood of martyrs." The learned man, in this context, is one whose entire life and learning are to lead to a greater and deeper understanding of the Divine Will.

Religious base

Regardless of all outward appearances, the Muslim remains profoundly religious. I have discovered this in my contacts with men and women from Morocco to Uzbekistan, whose socio-political views range from the extreme Right to the extreme Left. The Muslim does not divorce his social and economic ideas and practices from their Qur'anic foundations. His inability to apply his religious aspirations to the existing social order causes him one of his greatest frustrations. The resurgence of "fundamentalism" among Muslims, especially among young intellectuals, is but one illustration of this.

In any of his dealings therefore, be they social, economic, political or personal, the Muslim operates from a profoundly religious base. His vision encompasses both this passing world, of which he is to make the best he can, and the real world, the Hereafter, toward which he should aim. "Work for this world," the Muslim is told, "as if you shall live in it for ever; but work for the Hereafter as if you shall die tomorrow." That Western man does not act likewise convinces the Muslim that the West is corrupt and morally decadent. He is enjoined to avoid decadence and corruption. He tends, albeit reluctantly, to prefer the West to the greater evil of the "material atheism" of Marxist-Leninist ideology. He is painfully aware of his dependence on the West. Painfully, because he is convinced that what he seeks from the West is already present in his own tradition, buried under his own ignorance. He is also convinced that during the centuries of the grandeur of Islam the scholars of his community had developed the ideas (based on the doctrines of his Scriptures) that could govern his modern needs and aspirations. If, as Sheikh Ahmad Zaki Yamani points out, the theory of "Social Solidarity" as developed and crystallized by Duguit resulted from the latter's life in Egypt and study of Islamic law and institutions, the learned Muslim himself should be able to derive his new ideas from the same roots.

> He who studies *Shari'ah*, feels at ease with Duguit's theory. Though the similarity between his theory and the Islamic communal concept is not absolute or complete, yet many of the ideas in his theory remind us as Moslems of our *Shari'ah*. His elements of solidarity bring back to mind the various Prophetic sayings describing the Islamic community, and what various jurists discussed regarding division of labour and the existence of the individual-collective duty. When Duguit talks of the consciousness of society we are made aware of the religious essence of the *Shari'ah* as a code of ethics strengthening legal principles and creating a subconscious respect for compliance even in those areas beyond the reach of enforcement....Duguit's theory had an important influence upon Western thinkers, and it is no doubt capable of being a subject for a more purposeful objective study. As to the communal concept in Islam, fortune has not been favoured yet with someone to expose its hidden treasures, verify its implications, and bring its scattered parts to a complete whole.[7]

He concludes with what I shall choose as my closing statement:

> When our political leaders begin to think seriously about the happiness and welfare of their people, they shall find in *Shari'ah*

a guiding proven system to achieve and fulfil their aims. The immortal principles of *Shari'ah* can be used to correct and cure our social diseases in the Islamic world. Perhaps even the West might find in it, again, a ray of light and knowledge to achieve a still more advanced civilization, or at least to preserve its existing one.[8]

NOTES

1. Maxime Rodinson, "Complexe islamo-turc et mythes occidentaux" in *Le Monde*, (23 May, 1981), p. 2.

2. See especially his *Islam and the West: The Making of an Image* (Edinburgh: The University Press, 1958) and *Islam, Europe and Empire* (Edinburgh: The University Press, 1966).

3. The episode, well-documented by early historians and biographers, is addressed in a *surah* (chapter), Surah 24, in the Qur'an.

4. I am referring to the founding of the university-mosque of al-Qarawiyin in Fas (Morocco) in 859 A.D. by Fatimia bint Muhammad al-Fihri.

5. The term here is borrowed from Kenneth Cragg, *The Event of the Qur'an: Islam in Its Scripture* (London: Allen and Unwin, 1968).

6. The following paragraphs are extracted from the Introduction to my *A Concordance of the Qur'an* (Berkeley: University of California Press, 1982).

7. Ahmad Zaki Yamani, "Islamic Law and Contemporary Issues" in *God and Man in Contemporary Islamic Thought*, edited by Charles Malik (American University of Beirut Centennial Publications, Beirut, 1972), p.72

Briefly identified, *shari'ah* is the totality of God's commandments relating to the activities of man. It touches on the whole of the religious, political, social, economic, domestic and private life of every Muslim. It is the basis for the judgment of actions as good or evil, which judgment is only in the hands of God. It is not "law" *per se*, in the modern sense of the word, because, originating from God, it cannot be penetrated or debated by human intelligence. For a brief outline, see J. Schacht in *The Shorter Encyclopaedia of Islam,* item Shari'ah.

8. Yamani, *op cit.,* p. 82.

Comment

Muhammad Abdul-Rauf

Depending, apparently, on second-hand sources, the author has repeated some historical errors that can lead to unfavourable impressions. It is not true that the Prophet Muhammad offered his capitulating enemies the choice to leave Mecca peacefully or become Muslims; or remain in the city under the protection of the Muslims in return for payment of a defence tax (*jizya*). This is incorrect and apparently an imaginary drawing by some European Orientalist. What the Prophet did, according to all reliable sources, was that he declared general amnesty to all the people of Mecca. He told them: "Go. You are all free." They were not obliged to leave the city, nor to become Muslims, nor had they to pay *jizyah*. The result of this magnanimity was that they embraced Islam. Another mistake is the author's claim that the Prophet, on settling in Medina, engaged "in guerilla raids against the caravans of the hostile Quraysh" and that "these raids resulted in three major attempts by the Quraysh to wipe out the Muslims. . . ." The impression is that the Prophet was engaged in guerilla raids all the time. The fact is that when the Prophet escaped and settled in a town on the life line of the caravans of the commercial Quraysh, it is they who were determined to wipe out the Muslims.

The first attempt by the Quraysh was preceded by an unsuccessful raid, which was provoked by the Quraysh's persistent persecution of the weak Muslims who were left behind in Mecca and could not emigrate with the Prophet. Moreover, it was not Abu Sufyan who led the persecution throughout the 13-year Meccan period and the first two years after the Prophet's epoch-making emigration to Medina. It was in fact Abu Jahl, 'Amr Ibn Hisham. Abu Sufyan assumed the leadership of Quraysh only when Abu Jahl and many other prominent Meccan leaders lost their lives in the first battle with Muslims, which took place two years after the Prophet's emigration.

Moreover, it is not clear what our author means by stating that under Islam "Each tribe continued to govern its own affairs, independent of the state." Does this mean states within the newly created Islamic state? This could not be. Arab tribes could no more conduct sudden raids against each other as they used to do. Islam united all tribes into one integrated political unit. Moreover, it is true, as the author says, that "The Jews would continue to be governed by Jewish law. . . ." and that "any disputant had the right to appeal to Muhammad"; but it is not quite correct that he then "would rule according to Jewish law," as our author imagined.

My general feeling is that the background of Islam is not given in an integrated, all-rounded picture. The doctrine of monotheism and the implication of submission to God are truly basic; but one would define Islam as a deep commitment to, a firm conviction, and an endorsement of the five basic beliefs; namely:

1. belief in the existence, unity, perfection and benevolence of the Supreme Being, the Almighty God, the Creator;
2. belief in the Divine Mission first revealed to Adam, then to a long series of Messengers of God, ending by Muhammad but including Moses and Jesus;
3. belief in the sacred books which contained the basic teachings revealed to these Messengers, especially those received by Moses, David, Jesus and Muhammad;
4. belief in the Angels, the mysterious forces who execute God's commands; and
5. belief that the earthly life is only a stage leading to a lasting and more meaningful life in which all people will be rewarded for their deeds during the earthly life.

Definition

Acceptance of, and firm commitment to these truths, accompanied by a declaration denoting this acceptance, constitute the definition of a Muslim. It is this which makes a person a full member of the Muslim community, not merely the performance of the five rituals. This commitment has to be manifested not only in the performance of the rituals, but also in upholding the Islamic moral value-system which covers the individual, social, political and economic orders.

The early Muslims were at first reluctant to compile the *hadiths* in a written form because of their concern over the integrity of the Holy Qur'an. They feared that if they should commit the *hadiths* to writing for circulation, they might get confused with Qur'anic pieces. However this fear dissipated with the passage of time, when the text of the Qur'an became too familiar to be confused with any other text, having been committed to memory and recited daily by millions in each generation. Moreover, with the rise of disputing schools of thought arguing about *political* issues, like al-Khawarij, and the Shi'a; or over *theological* issues like al-Mu'tazilah, scholars in the beginning of the second century of Islam felt the need to record and compile the authentic *hadiths* in order to distinguish them from questionable reports.

The roots of the movement of the codification of the Islamic law, or rather the *shari'a* of Islam, should be sought in the needs of the community since the death of the Prophet in 632 A.D. arising from the rapid expansion of the Islamic state, incorporating many nations within its fold, with different cultures, civilizations and historical experiences. Answers to new questions and solutions to new problems had to be sought in the light of the Holy Qur'an and the guidance of the Prophet. The first generation of Muslims, the Companions of the Prophet who survived him, and succeeding generations successfully met that challenge, and thus began the growth of the *shari'a* and the compilation of legal works by eminent jurists, some of whom inspired numerous devoted disciples and won fame throughout the Muslim world. The number of followers of these early leading jurists increased or dwindled down the generations by sheer luck, until the number of legal surviving schools shrank to four. The founders of these four surviving schools flourished during the reign of the Abbasids, not during that of the Umayyads. The founder of the first school lived under the Abbasids' rule more than twenty-two years, the founder of the second lived more than fifty years under them, and the third and fourth were born and spent their lives during the Abbasid reign.

Perhaps this is the place for me to take up the question of the authority of al-Hadith, on which the author sheds some doubt. It is certainly correct to assert that the Holy Qur'an is the basic and fundamental authority, but al-Hadith's authority is derived from that of the Qur'an. To deny this authority or try to reduce it will reflect on the authority of the Qur'an itself which calls upon Muslims to tax whatever may be given by the Prophet and avoid whatever he forbids (Qur'an, LIX, 7). The Qur'an also draws attention to the fact that the Prophet is the best model of behaviour for Muslims (XXXIII, 21). Following the steps of the Prophet is categorically praised and commanded (VII, 157 and XLII, 61). When the Prophet sent a companion to take care of a distant community, he asked him: How are you going to judge between them? He answered: According to the (teachings of) the Qur'an. If you do not find an answer? He replied: By your *sunna*, (tradition). The Prophet further asked, And if you cannot find an answer? The companion replied: I shall use my own wisdom. Our author himself, in the context of discussing the subject of *zakat* (poor alms), said it is the payment of 2½ percent of one's assets. This does not exist anywhere in the Holy Qur'an but was taught by the Prophet whose *hadith*s have their origin in the divine revelation.

The marketplace

Let us now come to Ahmad's remarks pertaining to the title of his article. Some of these views belong to the area of economics, some belong to that of political science, and others belong to the social order. These points are scattered under his three sections entitled "The Muslim Community," "Principles of Justice" and "Islam and Economic Systems."

In the context of discussing the question of property rights due to the individual, the author quotes a Qur'anic verse asserting this right both to men and women and takes this opportunity to move to the problem of sexual equality in the course of which he makes an unfortunate remark about "Arab sexual chauvinism"! One wonders in what way this alleged Arab chauvinism manifests itself.

In the same section, Ahmad, following the lead of G. S. Hodgson, makes the sweeping claim that "the ethics of Islam are often phrased in terms of the market place." Only in a few cases are the Qur'anic ethical teachings couched in metaphorical commercial style, as the following:

> O you who believe! Shall I show you the way to a 'trade' which will deliver you from a painful punishment? Believe in God and His Apostle and struggle in the way of God, sacrificing your wealth and blood. (LXI, 10)

The vast number of Qur'anic verses on moral teachings such as honouring parents, telling the truth, patience, forgiveness, good treatment of people, especially kin, neighbours, the orphan, the poor, etc., use no such metaphor.

The author's treatment of the subject of *riba*, "usury," is interesting, and his views resemble those of some modern jurists.

Treatment of the topic of *zakat*, is scanty and involves certain inaccuracies. Dwelling places, even palaces, vehicles, riding beasts, clothes, women's jewelry, libraries, and everything intended for legitimate use is not taxable by *zakat*. Likewise, tools and agricultural lands. Only five categories of wealth are taxable:

1. money kept for one year (or coming as income), 2½ percent;
2. commercial goods, 2½ percent
3. agricultural product, 10 percent (if the field was naturally irrigated — 5 otherwise);
4. excavated pre-Islamic treasure, 20 percent;
5. wealth extracted from mined material, 10 percent.

Welfare system

In that context, the author speaks of a Muslim "welfarist stream" who "attempt to imitate European and North American social welfare systems by giving control of the *zakat* to the state." He further confuses the issue by claiming that those he calls "Muslim welfarists" support their view (of giving the state control of the *zakat*) by the precedent established by Abu Bakr, the first Caliph in Islam, who used force to compel the Arab tribes to pay the *zakat* to the state. However on the death of the Prophet, these Arab tribes ceased to pay the *zakat* to the government in Medina, an action the author imagines to be debatable. The basis of the responsibility of the state to control the *zakat* is in the Qur'an itself and in the practice of the Prophet. The Qur'an reads: "Take from their wealth a charity whereby they are to be purified." (IX, 103)

Verse 60 in the same chapter counts among the lawful recipients of the *zakat* the category of people who are engaged in the administration of the *zakat*. Moreover, the Prophet instructed his emissary to the Yemen to tell the people once they agreed to pronounce the (monotheistic) word, "that there is an obligatory charity which has to be taken from the wealthy among them and to be paid to their poor one." Contrary to the notion promoted by the author, the *zakat* is not merely an individual personal matter, but is also a collective social duty. It is true that under colonial rule, governments of the fragmented territories of the Muslim people have neglected the administration of the *zakat* since the state adopted Western economic systems. The matter of the *zakat* was left to the conscience and decisions of the citizens. Nowadays there is a movement toward the revival of the state control of the *zakat*, a movement which Ahmad confuses as an attempt to imitate the West.

Ahmad's view that the Holy "Qur'an gives a very limited authority to the State" differs from what is generally believed. The Qur'an's calls upon those in power to rule with justice (III, 58), and its repeated command to rule in accordance with the revealed "law" (V, 47, 48, 49), and its severe warning against ruling differently (V, 44, 45, 47), all indicate that the burden of the state has to be very great. On the other hand, the Qur'anic call upon the citizens to obey, shows that the burden of government has to be a shared responsibility between rulers and their citizens. The state oversees the normal affairs of its people, assures justice and honest dealings for all, protects the nation's boundaries, and protects international trade. In this regard, the Prophet said, "All of you are responsible, and each is to account as to how he discharges his responsibility. And a ruler is responsible and is to account as to how he undertook his responsibility."

A framework

It is true, as Ahmad says, that "Islam does not specifically prescribe the form of government and economic system." "It rather provides an ethical base with certain political and economic implications." As it stands, this statement can be misleading. What the author calls "an ethical base" seems to be imperfect and incomplete, as it only has

certain political and economic implications. I should put it this way:
Islam provides a framework of guidance for the total human life on
earth, a flexible framework but with solid, unchangeable, peculiarly
Islamic features. Its flexibility is guided by such Qur'anic directives
as the instruction to take whatever is useful and avoid whatever is
harmful (V, 4–5; VII, 157); and its commandment that a Muslim
should partake of the good things in life in moderation (VII, 31–33;
XVII, 29; XXV, 67). But the framework has solid, permanent features that gives it its Islamic character. It is a monotheistic framework with God as its central point. In the political domain, Islam calls
for efficient organization. The Prophet said, "Even if you are three,
you should appoint one of you to be in charge of you." A ruler is the
viceregent of God and has to rule in accordance with the terms of the
Qur'an. One of the Qur'anic commandments calls for consultation
(II, 159, XLII, 38); another is to rule with justice. Consultation can
be achieved through universal franchise, or partial voting, or by seeking the views of the community leaders, *ahl al -hall wa'l-aqd,* as they
are called in this context. The distinctive feature of an Islamic state is
that it is, by definition, monotheistic and it has to rule in accordance
with the *shari'a* law. This political framework is simply Islamic; it
does not need another label, such as democratic, aristocratic, theo-
cratic, or anything else. It is thus isolated conceptually; otherwise it
is just an aspect of the total framework of guidance prescribed by Islam for an orderly, peaceful human life on earth.

At the economic level, the Islamic framework provides a stimulus
for the economic activities, as it praises work and trade and makes
such pursuits of great religious merits leading to rewards in Paradise.
It commands that a labourer should receive his fair wages before his
sweat dries; it declares that the most blessed earning is that gained by
the struggle of the hand; and promises the honest trader that he will be
in Paradise along with the Prophet and the martyrs. Work for a living
can be in a simple village workshop or in a modern highly industrialized factory in Chicago or Tokyo. All are of the same merit with God,
so long as a person is seeking the means of living for himself and his
dependents, and is at the same time, consciously or unconsciously,
contributing in any measure to the total production for the human and
animal needs. Fairness in distribution and individual liberty are cardinal Islamic principles; and moderation in consumption is the recommended Islamic mean. Wealth, as the author indicated, is not condemned but described as something good so long as it does not lead to

arrogance and does not distract from other duties. Nor is accumulation of wealth condemned so long as it is earned through legitimate methods, and all duties, *zakat* and charities are duly paid. Wealth has to be looked upon as means, not as the end of life. This simple and flexible set of teachings is framed by certain features which gives it its Islamic characteristic. These include the prohibition of usury, theft, cheating, extortion, and hoarding and the monopoly of food. They also include the obligation of payment of *zakat,* payment of the cost of living of a female child until her marriage, and of a male child until majority or completing his education; payment of the cost of living of one's wife and needy parents and siblings, and caring for the neighbour.

Guidance

Islam also provides guidance for an orderly social life. It inspires the individual with a sense of belonging to a biological, as well as a spiritual family. It inculcates in him the idea of being a child of two parents and a member of a group of sibling and kin, with mutual rights and obligations. He is also made conscious of his belonging to the large, world community of Islam. Again this fundamental social framework is another aspect of the total spectrum of Islamic guidance.

Underlying all these teachings is a fundamental Islamic principle, namely, the Islamic call for the satisfaction, in a harmonious, moderate way, of all human needs arising from the fact that the individual is a *biological, emotional, intellectual, social,* and *spiritual* being. As a *biological* being, man needs food, shelter and clothing. The individual has also to associate with a member of the opposite sex in order to procreate and meet a physiological need. As an *emotional* being, he needs the parental love and care and the sentimental support of sibling and kin, and the sustained companionship of a spouse. As an *intellectual* being, his mind needs to be nourished, first at home, then in society, then at school and through voluntary reading and researching. As a *social,* gregarious being, he needs the support of his kin, spouse, friends and his fellow believers. And as a *spiritual* being, the individual needs periodic interruption from daily routine so that he can retire and seek communion with his Creator, away from the hustle and bustle of materialistic activities. He thereby cleanses his soul and purifies his heart and feels the distinction which elevates him above the animal kingdom and brings him closer to the angelic level.

508   *Abdul Rauf*

Whereas ways and means of fulfilling other needs can largely be designed by man with some divine guidance, the terms of meeting the spiritual needs have to be prescribed fully by the Almighty God who alone knows how man should serve Him spiritually. So, God has assigned five daily periods for prayers, one month for daytime fasting and a journey once in a lifetime to His House, in an arid area, away from all the means of physical pleasures and where human activities can be purely devoted to the worship of the Creator!

However, fulfilment of all the above needs should be achieved in moderation and in a balanced harmony. Excesses are condemned. Fulfilling one aspect should not be at the cost of the others. Therefore additional worship outside the prescribed periods for prayers is forbidden. There has to be time for worship and time for work, and even time for recreational activities. In this moderate and harmonious fulfilment the individual serves his Lord best, and in it lies his salvation. Through this moderation and harmony, the individual attains his short-term objective—happiness and satisfaction on earth—and hopes to succeed when he meets with his Lord on the Day of Judgement!

In conclusion, I wish to assert that my intention is not to be too critical, but to comment on and supplement the views so very ably and eloquently brought out by my colleague, Dr. Imad El-Din Ahmad.

Reply

Imad Ahmad

I am grateful to Dr. Kassis and Dr. Abdul-Rauf for their comments. Clearly the subject of Islamic social thought is a large one in scope, and their supplementary comments are most welcome.

Dr. Kassis's points are well taken and I appreciate the Christian charity evident in his gentle expression of his criticism. Of course, some of the Gospels were committed to paper only decades after the life of Christ. The important point is that the canonical form was not established until the fourth century.

Dr. Abdul-Rauf is a man of considerable standing among Muslim scholars, an Imam whom I have prayed behind and who has graciously answered many of my questions about Islam in earlier days of my studies. I am honoured that he has made the effort to comment on my presentation.

Dr. Abdul-Rauf's knowledge of Arabic and of Islamic history are far superior to mine, and I have accepted his corrections in those areas. I will concentrate on his substantive criticisms of my analysis, which is unaffected by the corrections of transliteration and certain historical errors.

Dr. Abdul-Rauf asks whether my statement that "Each tribe continue to govern its own affairs..." means that there were states-within-a-state under Islam. He denies this with the (correct) observation that tribes could no longer, under Islam, conduct raids against each other. But raiding another tribe is not an action under the purvue of governing one's own affairs. It is, on the contrary, a case of aggressing against the affairs of others (their property, and perhaps their lives). It is precisely because *no tribe* under Islam could interfere into the affairs of another by aggression that the principle of self-government is established by Islam.

Dr. Abdul-Rauf denies that Muhammad would employ Jewish law in the judgement of a strictly internal Jewish matter brought before him on appeal. Yet in the traditions assembled by Imam Muslim we find (#4211, chapter 683) that when a Jew and Jewess accused of adultery were brought before Muhammad he inquired into the *Jewish* law on the subject, and imposed sentence accordingly.[1]

Dr. Abdul-Rauf is correct in his list of fundamental Islamic beliefs, but a community cannot determine who its members are by their *beliefs* because what a person believes (as opposed to what he professes) are known only to God. Thus men must judge men by actions.

Dr. Abdul-Rauf's point that Muslims have always looked to the actions of the Prophet for guidance is incontrovertible. I did not mean to imply that the concept of *Hadith* was a response to the Ummayad dynasty. Rather, the development of *hadith science* became a necessity under those conditions and, further, that the various schools were a counterforce against a stultifying orthodoxy such as the European Dark Ages produced. I was referring to all schools, not only the four orthodox ones. An intellectual resistance need not be "secret" to be opposed to government oppression, and even Abu Hanifa, the founder of the oldest "orthodox" school, was imprisoned for refusing to accept a position with the government.

Authority to govern

Dr. Abdul-Rauf's claim that the *Qur'an* gives some men broad authority to govern others is based on an incorrect translation of some very important verses. The word *hakama* in the verses he cites (4:58, 5:45, 47, 48 & 49) means to *judge,* not to rule. It is indeed incumbent upon all Muslim's called upon to judge to judge in accordance with justice and God's will. By no means does this give the state any authority at all to invent legislation. In fact, the *Qur'an* is quite explicit:

> ...If any one's trial
> Is intended by God, thou hast
> No authority in the least
> For him against God....

> (5:44)

If Muslims must judge with justice and in accord with God's will as expressed in the *Qur'an,* then they must condemn the actions of governments more often than endorse them. No state is mandated as such in the *Qur'an.* The requirements put upon those with authority are the same as those put upon all Muslims.[2]

Nor does the *hadith* stating that "even if you are three you should appoint one of you to be in charge of you," support the view that the state has any superiority over its citizens. The *hadith* referred to is the same as that given in Chapter 243 of *Sahih Muslim,* in the Book of Prayer:

> (1417) Abu Sa'id al-Khudri reported Allah's Messenger (may peace be upon him) as saying: When there are three persons, one of them should lead them. The one among them most worthy to act as Imam is the one who is best versed in the Qur'an.[3]

It is evident from the context that this is a statement on the appointment of a prayer leader and not the establishment of a state. Its occurrence in the Book of Prayer makes the validity of this interpretation clear.

Then there is the question of how literally one should take *hadith* prescriptions. Does the requirement that one pay a worker before the sweat has dried from his brow mean that bi-weekly paychecks are prohibited? I don't believe so. The important point of the *hadith* is that wages delayed are wages not paid in full. This conclusion is completely consistent with the analysis of riba' in my paper.

The *Qur'an* demands that believers adhere to the good and reject the evil both individually and collectively. But there is no prescription that this must needs be accomplished through the establishment of state, *per se*. The establishment of a state to achieve just ends is not prohibited, regardless of its form. But when that state practises injustice or prevents men from practising their religion (ad-Din),[4] it is the duty of Muslim to, borrowing a phrase from Jefferson, "alter or abolish it." This is *jihad* which Muhammad (peace be upon him) fought and which is incumbent upon all Muslims.[5]

NOTES

1. Muslim, *Sahih Muslim*, trans. by 'Abdul Hamid Siddiqi (Lahore: Asharf Press) vol. III, p. 918.

The question of the punishment for adultery seems to be in a great state of confusion among Muslims. In Iran it is held to be 100 lashes, while in Saudi Arabia, it is claimed, a princess was executed on that charge. I think this confusion is a direct consequence of use of *hadith* as a supplement to, rather than exegesis of, the *Qur'an*. The fact is that the *Qur'an* unambiguously prescribes 100 lashes as the punishment for adultery (24:2). References in the *hadith* to stoning as the punishment have been interpreted by some scholars as abrogating the *Qur'an*. The belief that the *Qur'an* can be abrogated is the kind of dangerous consequence that can come of an exaggerated reverence for the *hadith*. I believe that the *hadith* references to stoning for adultery are actually references to incidents such as that cited here, where a non-Muslim was tried by his/her own laws.

2. I went too far in saying, in my original paper, that the *Qur'an* prescribes a state. The *Qur'an* prescribes communal action which may, but need not, be through the mechanism of the state. See also my conclusion to this response.

3. *Loc. cit.*, vol. I., p. 316.

4. See Surah 109.

5. See 2:190–193.

Discussion

Edited by: Irving Hexham

Muhammad Abdul-Rauf Consider capitalism, or socialism, or Marxism, or communism, and other such systems which developed in western Europe. Is Islam compatible with any of them? The answer is *no*.

Muslims go back to the Qur'an which was revealed 1400 years ago.

We endeavour to understand it, and to follow its implications.

In a sense, therefore, we belong to the same generation at the very beginning of Islam. We regard ourselves to be just like them, and we try to follow the right path of God ignoring all these modern ideologies.

Some of the ingredients of capitalism, in fact, are agreeable to Islam, and Islam would promote them. For example, the notion of freedom of the individual to endeavour, and to seek, and to improve his economic condition, or to accumulate wealth. The Muslim is entitled to do so, as much as he likes, and to increase his wealth as much as he can, provided first that it must be earned through legitimate methods.

Now consider socialism. If it means charity, being good to your society, and so forth, that is good. But if it means that the state should own all the means of production, Islam is not compatible with socialism.

Islam favours individual ownership. It must be respected, as emphasized Muhammad himself. He guaranteed the protection of life and property, as well as places of worship to all peoples.

Of course the concept of ownership in Islam is different from that in other societies. It is somewhat a relative concept, because it is not an absolute ownership. The Qur'an states that the real owner of everything in the world is God the Almighty Himself. And the Qur'an states that people are only agents on behalf of God. So, human ownership is relative. It is not absolute. It is temporary. When I die, as Muhammad says, it will abandon me. It will not come with me to the grave. Only my actions or my deeds will accompany me. But basically socialism is unIslamic. It features blind coercive measures, it gives too much power to the state.

An early companion of Muhammad could be described as capitalist in some ways, because of his great wealth; but he was one of the most noble companions among those in that first generation. He did not earn money, for example, through the sale of pornography, or the sale of wine, or the sale of anything prohibited and not allowed in Islam. He earned his wealth through his legitimate endeavours.

At the same time, and this is a second condition, a Muslim must pay duties on his wealth. This is an obligation incumbent upon every Muslim. It amounts to roughly two and a half percent, but in some cases it may even be as high as twenty percent. This is in addition to other charities when needed.

So you can increase your wealth as much as you like, subject to these two conditions. And here is a third condition: your engagement in earning wealth should not distract you from the remembrance of the Almighty God. The Qur'an reads:

> Let not your wealth or your children distract you from remembering God.

So a Muslim merchant in the market, or anywhere else, must always remember God the Almighty who has provided these bounties for him, and enabled him to work, to live, to survive. As long as you remember God, serve Him, and perform your other duties, such as saying prayers, then you are entitled to increase your wealth.

In fact, Muhammad is quoted as having said:

> A thankful rich man is better in the eyes of God, than a contented poor person.

Both of them are good, but nevertheless, the person who has been rich and has been grateful to God in the sense of observing these duties, has been tested already. Moreover, he has been more useful to society because he has been applying the teachings of Islam, namely to seek to increase worldly production in the interest of other people.

Nevertheless, there is something in capitalism as promoted or advocated by Adam Smith, which is contradictory or rather inconsistent with Islam. Namely, that the aim of capitalism is to increase the wealth of nations, quite apart from the immediate motive of the individual. In the view of capitalism, the individual can try to seek his own interest, no matter what his intention might be, no matter how much he sins. The main thing is just to increase the wealth of nations.

Islam doesn't agree with this. Islam is in the interest of all nations, but at the same time, it takes into consideration the immediate motive of the individual. When you work to increase your wealth, it must be for the sake of improving yourself, providing for yourself, for your family, for the community, for your kin, and so on, and also for society at large.

But it should not be based on bad or evil motives, such as, for example, to increase your power over others, or to show that you are better than others. This would be a bad motive. The immediate motive is very essential in Islam. Even worse is Marxism or communism. Islam is dramatically, and completely, opposed to these cocepts.

Islam is just Islam. Islam is not only a creed, but a total way of life, touching on all aspects of your being—social, domestic, economic, and so forth.

In Islam, there is a strong concept of human brotherhood. A Muslim feels that he is a brother to every human being, male or female. This human bond is very basic and very important. Therefore a Muslim is one who believes in the Qur'an, who is good, and who does good.

Ted Scott: Imad Ahmad talked about the voluntary obligation to give 2½ percent of one's income to people below you, but he changed it to say, deserving people below you. What are the criteria that are used to determine "deserving people"?

Muhammad Abdul-Rauf: The poor, the destitute, those who are employed in the service of collecting the *zakat* and its distribution; slaves who are trying to buy their liberty from their masters, those who have become, or have fallen in debt as a result of their making peace and spending over that. The way of God, anything around that is for the sake of God. There are eight categories but they mainly concern the poor.

Imad Ahmad: The poor are rigidly defined in terms of people who have not the means to live for a year.

Muhammad Abdul-Rauf: There are two categories. A person who earns less than he needs and one who doesn't earn anything.

Bob Goudzwaard: Is there in Islam anything like an obligation to take care of nature, which can be interpreted as a restriction of the working of a free market?

Imad Ahmad: The Islamic view ties in very well with the point Walter Block made, about the failure of law in the United States to make it incumbent on would-be polluters not to pollute. It is just one of the rules of the market. That is a violation of other people's rights. Now Muslims would phrase it a little differently. But it amounts to the same thing. Ultimately nature, like everything else, belongs to God.

But some parts of it we hold in trust, as his agents. You cannot lay waste to something belonging to God or man. In part, this harms other people's property, but it also harms God's property.

Hanna Kassis: In terms of social practice in Islamic society, one does not throw a stone in the well from which one drinks water. Or, another rule, when there is water which is running downhill: the upper part is where you drink, the middle part is where you wash the utensils, and the lower part is where you wash the laundry. And you cannot just mix things in any fashion. Nor would you allow uncleanliness to touch the water.

For example, if the water is drinking water, you do not allow a dog, which is an unclean animal, to pollute the water.

Muhammad Abdul-Rauf: It is a sin to pollute water, to urinate in the sea.

Imad Ahmad: The enforcement of the ecological aspects of Islam was never a problem. They never had to resort to intricate court decisions and coercion, because it was understood and accepted as the natural thing to do.

Stephen Tonsor: The title of Adam Smith's *The Wealth of Nations* is borrowed from Isaiah and "the invisible hand," is a translation of the theological concept of providence. Man proposes, God disposes." *"Der Mensch denkt und der Gott lenkt."* This is an idea which unfortunately becomes, in the next generation, the magical quality of the directing hand.

So, in a sense Smith is much closer to Christian ideas than is ordinarily thought.

Imad Ahmad: One of the things that the *Qur'an* points to as proof of God's existence is the beauty of natural laws. Early Muslim scholars pointed out that this applies to the economic laws as well. It was Ibn Khaldun, in his analysis of the economic laws, who said, Isn't it marvelous that God created a physical universe that is so harmonious and beautiful? Isn't it marvelous that He created an economic system in which things like price exist to tell you automatically what is going on?

Ibn Khaldun antedated Adam Smith by four hundred years. So those people who think that the free market is somehow a cultural product of Europe, as opposed to something that's scientifically discovered in nature, are wrong.

Richard Neuhaus: Somebody, yesterday, mentioned Mike Novak's *Spirit of Democratic Capitalism*. He has a section on the division of realms and how they analogically relate to the Trinity. The Trinity is not an Islamic dogma. Islam presumably has a much more rigorously monotheistic and holistic approach to reality.

It seems to me that Imad Ahmad is talking in somewhat Novakian terms about, if not separate spheres of sovereignty, at least rather distinct worlds within worlds. That would seem to conflict with my understanding of the rigorous monotheism of Islam.

Secondly, most of us who have had any experience in the Middle East know of bartering as a form of trading. I have an awful lot of Egyptian furniture in my house that I'm not sure I really wanted. But I felt after a lovely dinner and drink, and establishing presumably great bonds of friendship with a merchant in Cairo, that I was obliged to place an order for the stuff.

Is that just very, very clever trading tactics, or is it a religiously grounded necessity to take what we would call the impersonal instrumental element out of trade and cloak it in the appearance, at least of brotherhood and solidarity?

Imad Ahmad: You asked two questions. I'd like to answer the second question first, but first I have to ask you a question. How long were you visiting this person who sold you the furniture?

Richard Neuhaus: Altogether?

Imad Ahmad: Yes.

Richard Neuhaus: Only about three hours, I suppose.

Imad Ahmad: All right. In that case, I would say it was not a clever commercial ploy to get you to feel guilty and buy his furniture. In the *Hadith*, the rules of hospitality require that during the first three days, great hospitality be extended to a visitor. Indeed, for the first day, one should actually not merely be hospitable, but make a great fuss about them. Therefore he was simply fulfilling his religious obligation to a traveller.

As far as the other question was concerned, first I have not read

Novak's book, and therefore any apparent similarity is strictly coincidental. I do not think what I have said conflicts with the holistic views of Islam. The concept of multiple worlds is something that occurs in the very first chapter of the *Qur'an*, in what is called "the perfect prayer." Words that translate into "Praise be to God the Lord and Cherisher of the Worlds," plural. Multiple worlds. In the scholars' explanations of this, it refers not only to the various planets, or the possible universes in the meta-galaxy, but also "worlds" in the sense of ways of looking at things. Worlds in every conceivable sense of the terms have been accepted by scholars as a legitimate meaning of this verse.

As far as science is concerned, the *Qur'an* is certainly not a textbook of natural science. But it keeps referring to natural science. It keeps referring to the stars, the earth, the universe. When you look at these you will see things that are wonderful, amazing, and will increase your faith in God.

On economics, the *Qur'an* actually makes some economic statements. It does say "private property is a good thing." It does say "commerce with honesty is a good thing." But, what it says about natural reality applies to sociological studies. And when you study, you not only find that the laws of economics are truly wonderful, you find they're also consistent with the *Qur'an*, which therefore confirms the premise you started from; indeed this is the Word of God.

Gregory Baum: In your tradition, do you extend the free market of goods to the labour market involving people? In other words, do you have a "just wage" teaching, as for instance Catholicism, or are wages simply determined by the mechanism of the market?

Imad Ahmad: The teaching of the *Qur'an* does extend to the labour market. There is a concept of generalized just treatment of workers. In Dr. Abdul-Rauf's paper, he referred for example to "paying the worker before his sweat has dried," which does not necessarily mean that you're not allowed to pay bi-weekly. What it says is if you're going to pay bi-weekly, you've got to reach an accommodation by negotiation that takes into account the fact that you're not paying him on the spot, which is what he's entitled to.

Paul Heyne: I was struck by the emphasis in Islam on the laws being designed to prevent the pursuit of one's own interest from destroying the community. I was also struck by the same emphasis in Tamari's presentation of Judaism. In both religions there is a concern that individuals can subvert the community, and the law tries to prevent that.

I was then driven to reflect on how many economists today studying economic development in the Third World worry about the extended family as a problem. Here you have a tension. I think we would all agree that community is vitally important. And I think we would recognize that market activity does, in fact, tend in many ways to subvert community. On the other hand, we recognize that sometimes community can be the wrong kind of community.

John Berthrong: I've been fascinated in my all too brief study of Islamic history by the extremely admirable record of the treatment of minorities within Islamic culture. The creation of pluralistic societies and the maintenance of pluralistic forms of life emerged in great periods of Islamic history.

Now, what kind of guidance would the Islamic tradition give for a Muslim living within a society where it would be fairly clear that the state would not become Islamic?

Imad Ahmad: As long as the state does not suppress the practice of Islam there is no problem.

Muhammad Abdul-Rauf: We should make a distinction between religion and culture. Religion is a well-defined matter. And there is a set of beliefs, rituals, and some basic principles for guidance, which can go with the believer anywhere he may go. He can live without disturbing the community or anyone else.

Cultural patterns may differ for Muslims from place to place. When they move from one place to another, there is no harm at all if they modify their own mode of living or culture.

We have to recognize a difference between what is Islamic and what is culturally Muslim. For example, the American way of life, the American political system, I hesitate to say is "un-Islamic" or "anti-Islamic." I would venture even to say it is "Islamic" in many ways. I mean the way of liberty, the ability to criticize, and to help guide the state, and so forth. In many ways it is consistent with Islam.

Ellis Rivkin: Within the Islamic system itself, what are the consequences for one who has come to be a nonbeliever. I'm talking about where the community was functioning as a total community in complete control. What is, or would be, the status of heretics?

Imad Ahmad: If someone denies the source of the *Qur'an*, I would say that it's not a question of heresy, but apostasy. Essentially, he's left the religion. This is debated. There are very clear *hadith* sayings in the *Qur'an* that the apostate should be put to death. However, some of the scholars have said that this is to be looked at in the context of the time in which the revelation was made. When Muslims were at war with other Arabs and the apostates were essentially people who had left to join the enemy, they were therefore seen as spies. But in a society where Islam was not under attack, the apostate would be treated like any other unbeliever.

Clark Kucheman: If I were in an Islamic country, would I be permitted to say the things that I've said?

Muhammad Abdul-Rauf: Of course. As a citizen of the state, you have almost the same rights as any Muslim citizen, except that you would be exempted from military service. And because *zakat* is an Islamic duty like prayers, you're not obliged to pay it either. But as a citizen, you are to pay some taxes, to be assessed from time to time, as a contribution to the treasury. Otherwise, in every other respect, you live as any other citizen.

Hanna Kassis: I think I can answer this question, not from the theoretical angle, but from the practical side, since I am a non-Muslim and I did live under Muslims. I was born and raised under Muslim rule. Therefore, I know for a fact, from personal experience, that it is far more advantageous to be a non-Muslim living in a Muslim country than to be a Muslim living in a Muslim country. (laughter)

Everything works in my favour. My responsibilities are fewer. For example, at one time when I was displaced and living in Jordan, I invoked a very ancient practice of not having to pay a tax to the state, because I'm a non-Muslim, a Christian. I was challenged on that, and I challenged the state using history. I said, "It's up to you to decide whether you are to adopt your methods, or Islamic methods." I was exempted. (laughter)

Gregory Baum: What comes to mind is the treatment of the Bahais in Iran. Is this consistent with Muslim treatment of non-Muslims?

Hanna Kassis: They have denied the Qur'anic rule affecting the prophet Muhammad and have proclaimed another false prophet from the point of view of Islam. Therefore they are apostates and are treated as apostates.

Imad Ahmad: I don't think that's the explanation, even from the Iranians' point of view. I don't know what's going on there either, but I can tell you what the Iranians have said in their public statements. They said that they are not acting against the Bahais because of their religious convictions, but because they have been engaged in activity against the state.

Now I don't know whether to believe that or not. I tend to be doubtful of such things.

James Sadowsky: On the taxation problem. I take it that what you're saying is that taxes in Islam are voluntary, in the sense that if I choose to be a Muslim, then I'm agreeing to pay taxes.

Imad Ahmad: As I see Islam, there is no authority for other forms of taxation. Every Muslim country has additional taxes and therefore they would all disagree with me. But, I'm giving you my conclusion based on the *Qur'an,* and my understanding of the *hadith.*

Muhammad Abdul-Rauf: The state has the right to impose additional taxation only on those who are able. That's as far as Muslims are concerned. As for the people of the book, or rather citizens who are not Muslims within the state, only able-bodied males who can afford it have to pay taxes.

Meir Tamari: I'm not very clear about the question of the individual obligations. Isn't there a contradiction between the picture you paint of everything being left up to the individual and the fact that Islam has a very highly developed religious law in economics?

And to what extent in the Muslim states of today, is the economic system any different from any other country?

Imad Ahmad: Perhaps I didn't make myself clear. I meant to point out that taxes are enforceable obligations that you voluntarily accept when you adopt Islam. In other words, you do not accept Islam because someone came and misled you about what Islam was. You accept Islam as the Word of God, therefore feel you should heed it, and follow it. You voluntarily choose to do so.

In the current situation I can only support what Hanna Kassis said in a different context. So-called Muslim states should decide whether they want to continue as they are, or whether they want Islam. I don't consider what they have now to be Islam. Although there may be some cases which come very close. I've never been to Kuwait. But I understand that the law there is very close to the Islamic norm. But other states that we hear about more often are very distant from Islamic law.

Muhammad Abdul-Rauf: One of the characteristics of Islam is that it is a universal religion. It is not nationalistic. The concept of nationalism referred to is not consistent with the Muslim concept and Islamic community on a world scale. One virtue of being a Muslim is that the Muslim is related to his brother Muslim in two ways: being human, and also being a Muslim.

As for trade, the prophet Muhammad said, "An honest trader will be raised on the day of judgement, along with the prophets and the noble people." When he went to Madinna, in fact he built or fixed a tent, and asked merchants to go and trade there. Then, the traders regarded Islam as doing a good service by bringing the goods close to the people, the consumers, who needed the goods. But Muhammad declared a prohibition on hoarding gold and silver.

Again, Muhammad from time to time used to visit the market and examine it. For example, once he put his hand on a heap of corn which looked dry and nice, he put his hand inside and got a handful of wet corn. So he discovered that the merchant was cheating. He said: "Whoever cheats us is not a member of our community." The merchant said: "The rain has come and soaked it." He said we should not hide that bad quality, and expose only the good quality on top.

In the Muslim community, as a result, there has been a special market official. His function was to oversee the rules of the market and to see that there is no cheating.

Muhammad also prohibited people from going out of town to intercept farmers coming in with their goods, and then taking advantage of them because they did not know market prices.

Imad Ahmad: When one looks at even the current understanding of Islam among Muslims, and Muslim scholars, it is never perfect. Perfection is something we only strive for. One finds an approximation to perfection in an understanding of the value of trade and commerce, of the virtues of the free and open markets, of mutual respect for rights, and so on.

Islam is very clearly and unambiguously anti-coercion. Scholars make errors because they don't understand that certain economic systems are built on coercion and are therefore un-Islamic. They don't realize that only certain practices violate this prohibition of coercion.

Finally, I would like to emphasize what I said before about economics or a free market providing a mechanism by which you can get what you want. One of the proper subjects of religious endeavour is to make sure that people want the right things, and this is not achieved by coercion. Islam offers a way by which people can be induced to want the right things. It does this not by demanding enormous and ridiculous kinds of sacrifices on their part, but only by asking from them small and reasonable things.

The *zakat* is a small and a reasonable price to pay. The restrictions that one gives up on one's personal freedom are quite modest. One is not asked to give up lust, only to put it within means that are beneficial to society. That is, within marriage—the husband and wife engage, indulge their lust with one another.

And even these small things that you are asked to give up, are not a conflict between what you want and what is good for the poor in society. It is always in your interest also, because, as Muhammad said, "every good deed you do, gets repaid ten times over."

Overview

Michael Novak

The essays, comments, and replies in this volume constitute a cornucopia of reflection. A great many points of view, probably the most representative, are included. The volume covers four great religious traditions: Catholic, Protestant, Jewish, and Islamic. It discusses the religious implications of the mixed economy, with some writers stressing the role of the economic system, some the role of the political system. As well, this volume is particularly rich in descriptive historical materials.

About specific historical movements—in the different religious bodies, in the World Council of Churches—the detail is too vast for commentary here; one would need essays at least as long as every original essay. The course I have marked out for myself, therefore, is to attempt to provide a large overview—both historical and theoretical—within which, for me, the diversity represented here may be synthesized.

One of the most striking features of these explorations is an unexpected measure of agreement. Virtually every contributor to these volumes is in favour of cultural pluralism, a democratic polity, and an economy to some extent, at least, based on private property, markets, economic growth and incentives. Even the writers who show most allegiance to democratic socialist ideals—Gregory Baum, Ronald H. Preston, Bob Goudzwaard and John Yoder, among others—do so in a relatively non-ideological way, which allows them to embrace some features of private property, markets, economic growth, and incentives. On the other hand, differences between authors are often sharp and not easily reconcilable. Moreover, *behind* the individual essays, *underlying* them, there are unmistakable differences in the magnetic pull of divergent ideals of the good society. Although in the mixed economy the democratic socialist ideal and the democratic capitalist ideal, to a considerable extent, overlap, nonetheless, the two ideals do pull in opposite directions and induce quite opposite sets of perceptions. The contrast is sharper, furthermore, if one opposes the *libertarian* ideal (represented here by Imad Ahmad, P. J. Hill, and Walter Block, among others) to the democratic socialist ideal. To put matters a little too simply, the democratic socialist ideal leads to rather more favourable expectations from state interventions in the economy, the libertarian ideal to rather more favourable expectations from the *abstention* of the state from intervening in the economy. No one denies that the state must *sometimes* intervene, on the one hand, and that the state must not intervene *too much* (becoming a tyrant), on the other hand. Debating on this very point, the two distinguished economists, Paul Samuelson and Milton Friedman, once agreed that the exact boundary between these two tendencies cannot be defined abstractly, but must be negotiated by close pragmatic observation of practical consequences.[1] The divergent tendencies, of course, continue to affect pragmatic perception and decision.

In this volume, then, I propose to offer first a historical perspective, then a theoretical one, before addressing some of the specific contributions. In the introductory essay to the second voume, I should like to address some of the more theological and more immediate issues of political economy.

Historical considerations

For the sake of convenience, it is useful to date the emergence of a new system of political economy—democratic in polity, capitalist in economy, and pluralist (Christian-Jewish-humanist) in culture—at about 1776. That is the date of the American Revolution, described on the Seal of the United States as *Novus ordo seclorum,* a self-consciously new *Ordnungsphilosophie,* and simultaneously the date of Adam Smith's *Inquiry into the Nature and Causes of the Wealth of Nations.* In his famous Manifesto of 1848, Marx spoke of a "hundred years" of bourgeois revolution, to which he attributed the greatest transformation of human life in history; so the date cannot be so far wrong.[2] Obviously, like those of any enormous transformation, its roots go very far back; I would say, myself, to the Judeo-Christian vision of the individual, the community, and human responsibility for shaping history and society. In 1776, the word "capitalist" was not yet in use: the term itself is one of Marx's coinage or, at least, popular diffusion. What is clear beyond dispute is that a new way of conceiving of human intelligence applied to economic growth had at last been hit upon. No longer did human beings feel largely passive with respect to economic circumstance, trapped in cycles of "seven lean years" and "seven fat," but able both to imagine and to effectuate sustained economic growth. From about 1780, Great Britain began to experience an annual growth of real income per head of at least one and one-half percent for nearly 150 years. The term "progress" thereby received popular validation in the rising standards of daily life.

In the year 1800, world population stood at 800 million persons. The average life-span was, worldwide, about nineteen years; and even in "advanced" nations like France, about 27 for females, 24 for males. Famine occurred regularly on an average of every fifteen years in Western nations. Even in 1820, there were not more than 220 manufacturing firms in France employing more than twenty hands. Most nations of the world were very largely agricultural.[3] The landholding class—together with the military and the clergy—was, in virtually every nation, the dominant class. Although ancient market economies were in place almost everywhere, the regnant pre-capitalist philosophy was "mercantilism." According to this philosophy, gold (in any case, coin) was the chief measure of wealth; economies served the interests of and were chiefly directed by the sovereigns of states; and the world economy was conceived of as a zero-sum game, in which the beggaring of one was a necessary condition for the enrichment of another. (Observation suggests that even today mercantilist ideas and a traditional organization of the economy hold sway in many, if not most, Third World nations. Most are neither democratic capitalist nor socialist.)

Science and invention

Led by Great Britain, the Netherlands, parts of France and Germany, and the United States, there began to occur *circa* 1776 the great transformation of which Marx wrote three-quarters of a century later. By 1850, world population had increased to one billion; by 1900 to 1.6 billion; and by 1982 to 4.7 billion. Living conditions improved in many parts of the world. By 1982, although some 800 million persons still lived in relative hunger, more than three billion lived significantly above the levels of subsistence known in 1800. Average life-span rose universally above the age of fifty. (Greater longevity is the single most important cause of population increase.)[4] It can scarce be doubted that the chief source of these humane advances was the promotion of science and invention which had become a central focus of energies in democratic capitalist societies. For the central idea of the democratic capitalist vision was to awaken human creativity, and to move as quickly as possible from invention to production. The *cause* of the wealth of nations, so went Adam Smith's central insight, is practical intellect.

Here, however, almost at the beginning, occurred three great falls in the intellectual history of democratic capitalism. Before coming to those, however, it is crucial to recognize three great contributions of the new science of political economy, of which Adam Smith was a chief, but not the only, originator.

First, Smith was the first to envisage the possibility of sustained economic *development*. (Not until Paul VI in *Populorum Progressio* did the Roman Catholic church give this idea salience in its own social thought.) He saw that the decisive question is how to produce wealth where it was absent, and to create a future better than the present.

Secondly, he was the first to imagine an *entire world* made *interdependent*, developing, and, through the imperatives of commerce and industry, pacific, lawlike, and progressive. He wrote, not of the wealth of individuals, nor even of Great Britain, but of all nations. He saw that the noble things of this world would not unite the nations, neither religion, nor the aristocracy, nor the military. Rather, the institutions despised by virtually all religions and virtually all literatures—the institutions of commerce and industry—would make the nations interdependent.

Thirdly, affected by the poverty and misery of the world so apparent to travellers of his time, he glimpsed the new moral obligation inherent in his insights: If wealth *can* be created, then, since the misery of many is intolerable, economic development is a *moral obligation*. A merely distributive justice (in a zero-sum world) is not morally sufficient. If new wealth for all can be created, it must be created. A sort of "productive justice" was born, in at least an instrumental way prior to distributive justice. It is from this vision, that political liberalism received its powerful moral *elan*. Its carriers believed that the vision which inspired them was supremely "progressive" not simply in some crass way but in a decisively humane way. "What have aristocrats, the military, and the clergy done to raise up the lot of the poor during their rule over the human race of more than two thousand years?'' liberals seemed to ask. Even in the popular mind, liberalism came to be associated not only with political liberty—although the force of that cry in a world of tyranny can scarcely be overestimated—but also with social and economic betterment for all.

I mentioned above the three great falls of liberal or democratic capitalist philosophy. Every philosophy has limits and internal errors. Concerning the internal limitations of classical liberal political economy, Joseph Schumpeter's *History of Economic Analysis* is peerless.[5] Alas, liberalism received three further blows from outside.

Division of labour

The first was the otherwise useful division of academic labours. Adam Smith accomplished his life work as a moral philosopher; but the fields he combined in his own life were later separated by the division of academic disciplines. Smith addressed the moral-cultural system in *The Theory of Moral Sentiments,* emphasizing the role of sympathy, fellow-feeling, benevolence, fair play, and due regard for the perceptions of the impartial spectator.[6] Later, in *The Wealth of Nations,* Smith addressed the economic system. At his death he was working on a book on the political system, never completed. Thus, in Smith's work, all three systems—moral, economic and political— were considered. From the middle of the eighteenth century, economists began to develop their new science, independently of political and moral-cultural factors, not in order to discard these but in order to concentrate upon a limited set of questions. Such a development is typical of every science (including theology). Here it had the unfortunate effect, however, of separating study of the economic system, eventually to be called "capitalism," from its Anglo-American matrix in a liberal polity and a humanistic ethic. The difference this makes was quickly apparent in the relative abstraction from moral and political matters visible in the work of David Ricardo, upon whom Marx was to draw so heavily.

It is not wrong, of course, that economics has developed as a specialized and separate science; the common good may well have been furthered by that advance. Still, any who would attempt to base social decisions solely upon economic considerations, apart from political and moral considerations, would be guilty of what John Paul II has called "economism." Economism is to economics what scientism is to science. The fault lies not in economics nor in economists, but in the failure of the general intellectual culture to integrate economic sophistication into political and moral considerations.

The second serious fall in the liberal tradition lies in the exaggerated emphasis which Jeremy Bentham and his followers placed upon the individual. The philosophy of "individualism" makes historical sense, insofar as it called attention to the new possibilities of the modern era, given the breakdown of the ancient order of inherited status, familism, and feudal hierarchy. In the new nation states of the liberal era, the liberty allowed individuals was unprecedented. On the other hand, philosophical emphasis upon this new reality disguised as much as it revealed. In actual fact, and contrary to the theme of individualism, the liberal era generated a new sense of the human race as one single community. Moreover, just as Smith had spoken of the wealth of all nations, so the primary institutional invention of capitalist societies was the business *corporation* and, indeed, voluntary associations of all sorts. The business corporation is not the habitat of the rugged individual in fact (as it is in the mythos of individualism), but of the cooperator, the manager, the builder of a task-oriented association. Social skills of a very high order are indispensable to the capitalist order. Nonetheless, the myth of the rugged individual appealed to the romantic sense even of those who in their working practice were most remarkable for their abilities to inspire and to coordinate great efforts from others. The so-called "robber barons" (who were neither typically barons nor typically robbers) are remarkable rather for their other-directed skills, as classically expressed by Dale Carnegie in *How to Win Friends and Influence People.* Putting together a farflung corporation is no mean social task. The actual social texture of capitalist, democratic, and pluralistic life is mis-stated by individualism and even by utilitarianism.

Survival of the fittest

The third fall of the liberal tradition, especially in its economic system, came two generations after Adam Smith, in the myth of "the survival of the fittest" which followed the discoveries of Darwin. By contrast with the fixities of the agricultural and feudal order, the competitive environment of democratic capitalism introduced uncertainties and dislocations never known before. Moreover, as new technologies replaced old, whole industries were sometimes left behind, as were those dependent on them (whaling, clipper ships, stage coaches, blacksmiths). New industries can scarcely be called "survivors," and they are not necessarily "fittest," but typically they are more efficient, more time-saving, less onerous. Material progress, in a word, is not Darwinian survival. Yet the metaphor allowed the social life of the nineteenth century—a century of *softening* manners, mores, and daily conditions of life—to be described in the terms of the jungle: harsh, mean, unfeeling, brutal. A few even came to justify amoral conduct by this wholly inappropriate metaphor.

Economism, individualism, Darwinism—these three falls in the liberal intellectual tradition—opened the way for a full-scale ideological assault upon liberalism by socialism, Marxism, Catholicism, and literary, aristocratic conservatism. This is not the place to assess the actual realities of nineteenth-century liberal societies apart from the ideological lenses through which they came to be attacked. Some of the charges, in any case, were true. The central point for the moment is that liberalism, under the three impulses mentioned, was in a poor position both for setting its house in order and for defending itself against unfair attacks. In important ways, liberal thinkers misapprehended the complex society they themselves had classically analysed.

This is the reason why Reinhold Niebuhr could write in the 1950s that liberal societies had more unarticulated strength within them than he (and others who in the 1930s had criticized them from the Left) had glimpsed.[7] That strength was there—in the political system, in the economic system, and in the moral-cultural system. It was also far too little articulated.

That unarticulated strength in self-reforming liberal societies is probably also one major reason why most democratic socialists today have slowly come to abandon the original fundamental principles of socialism—the abolition of private property, the abolition of money, the public ownership of the means of production, the nationalization of industries. In any case, most socialists today have accepted certain fundamental principles of democratic capitalism: practical reasons for private property, relatively free markets, incentives, economic growth, and inducements for savings, investment and invention. Democratic socialists still remain unusually concerned to use the *state* to address problems of inequality, poverty and disadvantage. In this sense, they remain still under the sway of the democratic socialist ideal. Moreover, they can argue, as Ronald H. Preston argues in Chapter 5 of this book, that so many of their *practical proposals* have already been adopted within democratic capitalist societies that democratic socialists prove to have been, in the main line of their moral vision, essentially correct. Whatever the most fair and exact way of putting this point, the societies of today thought of as the bastions of capitalism—the United States, western Europe, and Japan—have shown remarkable capacities for self-reform, redress of grievances, and social progress.

Theoretical considerations

I have been assuming that it is the genius of the "New Order of the Ages," as Jefferson called it, or the "bourgeois revolution" as Marx called it, to have divided social powers into three partly independent, partly interdependent social systems, three sets of social institutions: political, economic, and moral-cultural. In this way, no one person or party (nor the state itself) can come to dominate all the powers of one society. There must be a state, of course, with its own appropriate political institutions—but a state limited by the rights of individuals and their associations and bound by their consent. Secondly, this state must be allowed no power over conscience, information or ideas; hence, the churches, the press, and the institutions of intellectual and literary life must be separated from the state. Thirdly, this state must be forbidden total, direct power over the economic system; hence, large businesses, small businesses, individual workers and labour unions, and the multiple activities of not-for-profit enterprises must be allowed relative independence from state control (although not from legal and moral obligations). Such a threefold system is properly called, following the classic two-word phrase "political economy," "democratic capitalism."

Most of the 160 nations of the world today are neither democratic nor capitalist. Most are more or less traditional, authoritarian, tyrannical societies, typically ruled (as in the past) by the landed aristocracy, the military, and the clergy. Nearly fifty are totalitarian states of self-declared Marxist-Leninist design. A score or more others also call themselves "socialist," intending by that phrase not the Marxist-Leninist state but some version of *dirigisme* halfway between the ancient traditional tyranny and the ideological cover of Fabian socialism (for example, Tanzania and several other states of Africa and Asia).

It is a common mistake to think that all states which are not socialist, and which allow for private property and markets, must be capitalist. So common are private property and markets that the medieval
thinkers thought of them as derived from natural law. Virtually all
pre-capitalist, non-socialist societies (and even many which are socialist) respect forms of private property and find utility in markets.
In all of Latin America, for example, it is difficult to find a single nation which fits the ideal of democratic capitalism, except perhaps
Costa Rica. It is true that several other Latin American nations have
achieved or have been moving towards democracy. Virtually none
has a capitalist economy. In Chile, Mexico, Brazil, Argentina, and
most others, the state has immense command over the economy at
nearly every salient point. This is not a matter of "over-regulation";
it springs from a tradition of suspicion and control. Most of the large
enterprises are state-directed. Furthermore, the common ideology —
whether traditionalist, anti-Anglo, or socialist — is opposed to *liberal-
ismo*. Catholic corporatism, traditional agrarianism, Latin European
socialism, and Marxism reinforce the prevailing and pre-capitalist
tradition of state *dirigisme*.

Democratic socialism

A further comment may be needed in the classification of mixed
economies heavily influenced by the socialist ideal, such as Sweden,
Denmark, and the U.K. So long as such nations are democratic and
pluralist, and so long as they maintain the institutions of private property, the limited state, markets, incentives, economic invention and
growth, and the like, I am inclined to class them as "democratic capitalist"; and, indeed, pure socialists typically criticize them for their
"bourgeois residue." At some point, such nations may be tipped so
far over in the direction of state control that a "private sector economy" would be fiction rather than fact; that point does not seem to
have been reached. If, however, some wish to claim these nations as
examples of democratic socialism in practice — with all their current
virtues and vices, signs of decay as well as progress — I would not
waste much energy on terminological disputes. I do not much admire
the more extreme socialist components of such societies, or the doctrines which emanate from their socialist political parties. On the
other hand I admire much about these societies, as I do about the
United States.
   Finally, then, it should be clear that the conception of democratic

capitalism allows both for an active political system, for programs for the poor and the disadvantaged, and for the welfare state. It is true that democratic socialists within democratic capitalist societies keep trying to expand the powers of the political system at the expense of the economic system (and even of the moral-cultural system). It is also true that libertarians within democratic capitalist societies keep trying to reduce the powers of the political system in the name of liberty and the limited state. Both argue from the alleged benefits of their chosen practical arrangements to the common good. Since in the conception of democratic capitalism tension between the political system and the economic system is both anticipated and desired, both democratic socialists and libertarians play useful social roles. The democratic capitalist ideal is to permit neither faction to become too powerful, and to constrain both by keeping a sharp eye on practical consequences. In this respect, the democratic capitalist rejects the democratic socialist ideal of "economic democracy," that is, the politicization of economic decisions. Simultaneously, the democratic capitalist rejects the excessive restraint which the partisan of the free market imposes on the state.

Thus, it is clear, the chief arena of competition between those who try to expand the political system and those who try to expand the economic system—both in the name of the common good—lies in the moral-cultural system. This helps to explain the often noted "moralism" of Anglo-American politics. All parties couch their appeals in high moral rhetoric. "Liberty" is often opposed to "equality," "compassion" to "a rising tide lifts all boats." In a word, the religious community is one of the main target populations in the contemporary war of ideas. That is why this volume is so important. The sole defence of the free society is a fair competition of ideas. Members of the religious community can play a critical role in this debate by recognizing the sound points made by all sides to the argument, by taking care to respect the *bona fides* even of those with whom they are in most disagreement, and by trying hard to concentrate on which courses of action actually produce the consequences intended. Action in political economy is fraught with contingencies, ironies, unintended consequences, and tragic outcomes. Yet such action typically emerges, alas, from highly emotional and bitterly partisan dispute.

Particular comments

The religious community of today does not enter this argument with a completely neutral frame of mind. In general, all who have been trained in the humanities (including theology) imbibe the strongly anti-capitalist traditions of the humanities during the past two hundred years.[8] Moreover, relatively few who are trained in theology have had the advantages of commercial experience and professional training in economics. Finally, the problems of the Third World, which deeply affect universal religious bodies like Christianity, have been tremendously ideologized since World War II, almost entirely so in at least a mildly socialist direction. Common sense itself suggests, even to atheists (whom I have often heard address this point), that there is some contradiction between a religion of love and compassion and an economy based upon self-interest. Initially, a large number of theologians and churchmen will be inclined to find in democratic socialism a seemingly "natural" expression of their own religious commitments. Moreover, many central points in the political economy of democratic capitalism are counterintuitive; they represent the opposite of what seems to be *prima facie* true, and have been arrived at through close reasoning rather than through intuition. It is, in short, easier to argue the democratic socialist, rather than the democratic capitalist, point.

The papers by James Sadowsky and Gregory Baum reflect the widespread dissatisfaction with classic Catholic social thought experienced by those who enter this new field of inquiry, which I call the theology of economics. This field is far less developed than the theology of politics. Books and articles on Church and State, and related problems of politics, number in the thousands; those on Church and economy are very few. Both authors begin by noting the illiberal tendencies of nineteenth-century Catholic thought. The Church opposed ideas of progress, pluralism, Anglo-American ideas of religious liberty, the liberal polity and the liberal economy. The anti-liberal tradition was especially powerful in the Latin countries of Europe and Latin America. Baum notes how in the Second Vatican Council (1962–65), the Catholic church finally embraced significant liberal values in the sphere of political liberty (including religious liberty) and in the sphere of cultural pluralism, including ecumenism. Moreover, in the years since, Baum notes, the popes and bishops have continued to oppose Marxist-Leninist socialism for many reasons: its atheism; its materialism; its doctrine of hatred and class struggle; its call for the abolition of private property; its entrusting of the ownership of the means of production to the state; and its oppressive, totalitarian bureaucracy.

Symbolism

Baum's essay is unusually useful, however, because it demonstrates how, as he puts it, a "minority of Catholics" in powerful organizational positions—including some "ecclesiastical decision makers," especially in Canada—have seized control of the "symbols" of the Church and placed them at the source of "the Left." By this term, Baum means not only "democratic socialism" but the "non-ideological use" of "Marxist analysis," a decided hostility to capitalism, and a "long-range view" of something "beyond capitalism and socialism." Baum is able to specify rather exactly who constitutes his "prophetic" minority of Catholics: "various small communities, centres of research, action teams, pastoral projects, educational workshops, and collectives publishing newspapers, brochures, and information sheets." Baum explicitly rejects the interpretation that such persons represent "the new class" in the Church. It is clear beyond doubt that he is describing the same reality, even if he rejects the terminology.

Baum asserts that the *cause* of poverty and oppression in the world is capitalism. This is odd, since the purported effect antedates the purported cause. It is clear that "Marxist analysis" is his starting point. It is further clear that he places the hope of the poor and the oppressed of the world in institutional forms he calls socialist. But some of the actual forms he mentions—such as co-ownership of the means of production—involve private property. Further, private decision making by "workers' cooperatives" seems to imply free markets. His notions about "central planning" which is "in tension" with "decentralization" are not fleshed out. He explicitly rejects what is "practical" in the near term in favour of "symbolic adequacy" in the long term. He asserts that, since the "decisive" year of 1971— marked by Paul VI's *Octogesima Adveniens* and the Synod of Bishops—Catholic social teaching now criticizes capitalism and embraces "socialist ideals." Yet the "socialist ideals" he sketches are, on the one hand, far removed from those of classic socialism and have, on the other hand, very little political or economic content; they represent a kind of moral wish list. There is little in them that promises invention, creativity, economic growth and much in them which promises economic stagnation and the political bitterness inescapable in a zero-sum game.

A contrast

Whereas Baum asserts that, in general, the Catholic Left criticizes Catholic social thought for yielding too much to capitalism, James Sadowsky, on the contrary, criticizes it for failing even to master several elementary points of liberal economic thought. Sadowsky's essay is far more limited than Baum's, confined as it is to two central points in the thought of Leo XIII in 1891. Many more such analyses are needed of papal (and episcopal) thought since that date, on a whole range of fundamental economic points. The record of Catholic social thought in almost wholly Catholic nations—those of Latin Europe and Latin America, for example—is not a happy one, in the annals either of political liberty or of economic development. (Contrary to the casual references of Baum, however, my own researches into the record of progress made by Latin American Christian democracies from about 1950 until 1970 uncovered evidences of progress in income, literacy, education, longevity, lower infant mortality, etc., which compare favourably to any record anywhere.)[9]

There is a great danger, particularly in Latin America, that Catholic social thought will pass from illiberal corporatism, traditionalism, and conservatism to illiberal socialism, so-called "Liberation Theology," and tyrannies of the Left, without ever having paused to develop a liberal polity and liberal economy. Surely, no continent in the world is as favoured by nature as Latin America. Tiny Japan, with but a fraction of Brazil's natural resources, now produces ten percent of the gross world product, under conditions of political liberty, while vast and resource-rich Brazil struggles under illiberal political governance and debt-ridden development.

While I share Sadowsky's frustration at the failure of Catholic theologians and leaders fully to plumb liberal economic thought, and find the references to liberal values in papal social teaching most inadequate and inaccurate, I do not quite share his implicitly sanguine views about markets left entirely to themselves. History has borne him out, of course, as even Pius XI noted in commenting on Leo XIII in *Quadragesimo Anno*—in democratic capitalist nations the real wages and working conditions of the workers improved tremendously beween 1891 and 1931 (and have improved more remarkably since). Still, some of this improvement is due to efforts by the political system and by the moral-cultural system to direct economic development in fruitful ways.

Different interpretation

Finally, I should add that my own interpretation of Pope John Paul II's *Laborem Exercens* is dramatically different from Gregory Baum's.[10] The Pope's appeal to "Creation Theology" is not an endorsement of, but in opposition to, "Liberation Theology" and its "Marxist analysis." Marxist analysis is no better than its fundamental principles. It inexorably leads all who are faithful to it into illiberal political and unproductive economic praxis. The record of more than fifty nations should be clear enough. Democratic capitalist principles express a far more effective "solidarity with the poor," not only promising but delivering political liberty, sound institutional defence of human rights, economic creativity and broadly diffused prosperity. Gregory Baum embraces Bishop Romero of El Salvador, and so do I; he claims "special sympathy" for Solidarity in Poland, and so do I. Where we differ lies in our conviction about the form of political economy most likely, on the record, to raise up the poor, free the captives, and lead to liberty and justice for all.

Although I count on my colleague, John Bennett, to comment in greater detail on the Protestant discussions in this symposium, and while my own views can perhaps safely be inferred from what I have so far written, still, a few comments are in order.

The discussions introduced by Anthony Waterman and Paul Heyne carry us some little way toward two important goals. In the early nineteenth century, clergymen and lay persons of considerable distinction did argue a great deal about the obligation of Christians to improve "this world" through a new design of political economy. Much of this discussion has been bypassed by historical achievements which were sometimes invisible to those closest to them; but those old debates are often superior, in their logical and empirical clarity, to some highly emotional and uninformed discussions of today. We have much to learn, first, by studying again the arguments attendant on the rebellion of liberalism (now often called conservatism) against the *ancien regime*. In many ways, indeed, the arguments of liberals once made against the *ancien regime* parallel the arguments liberals today must make against socialist centralization. Often enough, too, especially when the attacks made against the liberal economy by socialists rest upon aesthetic, cultural, or moral grounds, socialists recapitulate many of the old aristocratic arguments. Solidarity with the poor and with workers often does entail a certain common taste, even vulgarity, as when contemporary socialists deplore the popular taste for jeans, disco music, and McDonald's. I do not entirely share Waterman's perspective (and rather harsh views about Margaret Thatcher), but I commend this and his other researches into earlier traditions; they are of great value. As always, I admire Paul Heyne's penetration of theological cant.

Christian socialism

So deeply do I share Ronald H. Preston's concern for recalling the vision (if not the impracticality) of the Christian socialist tradition that not long ago I urged Bernard Murchland to write a short history of that tradition in order that it might be better known to American readers.[11] In the trauma of the change from the *ancien regime* to a more prosperous and free political economy, much needed to be done to attend to new moral considerations. This was the impulse of Christian socialists in England. Often, to be sure, as he notes, they imparted aristocratic or upper-class imagery into their proposals; often they failed to see at least the partial merit in the new ethos which was transforming their age. One of the glories of the democratic capitalist order is that it does not insist that all join in cheering it. It quite rejects excessive enthusiasm. Two cheers is all even Irving Kristol feels it appropriate to utter in its behalf.[12] The vision of democratic socialists, carried to its own ideological extreme, does not quite work in practice and, in some respects, makes matters far worse. Still, as an antidote to a pure market orientation and as a summoning of political will and moral purpose, democratic socialism has played a significant role, and still continues to do so, in the evolution of democratic capitalism. On economic matters, as Preston seems to concede, the latter has been proved wiser in its devices; but in the political and moral spheres, democratic socialism has been the historical vehicle for many useful improvements. Those of us called (by our foes) "neoconservatives" owe much of our inspiration to it.

Archbishop Scott puts the best possible face on the work of the World Council of Churches on political economy. I admire his aims and purposes. Yet the perfect is the enemy of the good. In judging democratic capitalism according to standards that *no* mere thisworldly system, intended to function through and among sinners, can ever hope to meet, I believe he fails to judge it fairly. Moreover, he accepts far too uncritically the charges alleged against it, both in the highly ideologized Third World and among domestic critics. The fact that charges are made does not make them true. Charges about an alleged ecological crisis, a crisis of unemployment, and a crisis of inequalities between rich and poor (both among and within nations) need to be addressed at some length. At no stage of human history will any system of political economy be free of crises of this and other sorts. It is crucial to get the facts straight on which each alleged crisis is said to rest. Alas, the W.C.C. seems to me remarkably vulnerable to the most extreme and highly politicized allegations which permeate the United Nations, and to be hardly more sober than that body in sorting them out. These charges are intended to intimidate citizens of those political economies which show considerable progress in building institutions of political liberty and economic prosperity. If the political economy of Japan were a failure like others, it, too, would be part of the Third World. Dialogue is intended to be a two-way street. Citizens of successful political economies do not do enough to hold up their end of the dialogue with the Third World; by simply believing everything they hear, they patronize and condescend, and thus produce a monologue, doomed to frustration.

Roger Hutchinson does an excellent job of showing how Reinhold Niebuhr hewed closer to the facts, to questions of power and interest, and to the ironies behind easy perceptions, than most commentators of his age and ours. Niebuhr connected a powerful religious intellect to concrete contexts and proximate judgements. I do not wish to enlist him as the first neo-conservative (although his own pilgrimage was often described by his critics as a turn to the Right, both theologically and in political economy). His sympathies were in practice, even in his last years, rather more to the Left than my own now are. Yet Niebuhr himself would have been pleased to argue with those with whom he did not agree, and to direct the argument to matters of fact and proximate next steps. On such matters, it is in the nature of humans to disagree, no one being privileged to read the tapestry of future consequences and the unseen patterns of irony and tragedy inherent in all human action. In Hutchinson, there is a feel for the real Niebuhr, to whom so many feel indebted. All of us miss him so.

The Dutch neo-Calvinist tradition, especially in Abraham Kuyper, was one of the most economically sophisticated (and most perceptive about what the liberal economy was trying to achieve) of any Western nation. Max Weber himself was unable to cite serious theologians in *The Protestant Ethic and the Spirit of Capitalism;* he fell back upon a few scattered pastoral and devotional writings. So the brief historical descriptions offered by Bob Goudzwaard and Irving Hexham may serve to awaken interest in an important theological resource.

Communalism

John H. Yoder also develops a crucial and neglected theme. Within democratic capitalist societies, there is a splendid variety of communities of high and intense spiritual longing and exploration. Such communities as those he describes exert an often unseen but powerful influence upon the way we live and the way we slowly come to imagine the future. Having spent many years of my life in a religious community, not quite monastic but with a strong contemplative tradition, I share his sense of the this-worldly realism of what may seem to some an other-worldly perfectionism. In a society like ours, such communities can thrive and grow, exerting a necessary influence upon us all. They are, as it were, the powerhouses of our moral-cultural system. Indeed, many persons far too busy in the "practical" world of everyday life often and regularly seek out such communities for the good of their souls. The better problems of subsistence and political liberty are met, the larger the demand for such a form of life is likely to grow. In this respect, as in others, the "secularization" thesis has always seemed to me quite wrong.

As for the outstanding papers on Jewish and Islamic social thought, I cannot comment in an expert way. It has been my privilege as editor of *This World* and of several monographs at the American Enterprise Institute, however, to publish important essays in both of these powerful religious traditions.[13] John Locke, Adam Smith, and Thomas Jefferson thought they had hit upon "the natural system of liberty," growing out of Jewish and Christian traditions, to be sure, but universally accessible. For one thing, as we have seen, the use of markets was virtually universal in traditional societies. In Israel as in the nations of Islam, commerce was the great reality of everyday life. In both traditions, moral and religious values suffused all activities. It seems fair to say that Judaism has been more open to rapid historical change and to modernity, whereas Islam has felt the shock of modernity more recently and with greater trauma. Yet the future of a large and important part of the world depends on the shape the political economies of the Islamic nations assume in the future.

In eastern Europe, whence a large majority of American Jews migrated to the United States and Canada, the traditions of democratic capitalism were (and still are) absent. The dream of emancipation was predominantly expressed by socialism. Moreover, in the new land, immigrant Jews were often in the vanguard both of communist and socialist movements in the U.S. The language of the Old World concerning elites versus the proletariat seemed mirrored in their new status as poor immigrants. Nonetheless, observation of the actual economic and political programs of socialist parties has, over time, weakened the dream of socialism in the eyes of many American Jewish intellectuals. The so-called neo-conservative movement is predominantly Jewish (and Catholic). This movement holds that the democratic capitalist ideal is morally more attractive and in reality more productive than the democratic socialist ideal (and that the latter is inherently flawed). It holds, further, that the future belongs to the democratic capitalist ideal, which is the proven pioneer of invention and progress.

The debate about fundamental questions of political economy—in all our religious communities—has today reached an intensity unmatched for 150 years. This volume illustrates the depth and breadth of that debate.

NOTES

1. *Milton Friedman and Paul A. Samuelson Discuss the Economic Responsibility of Government* (College Station, Texas: Center for Education and Research in Free Enterprise, n.d.).

2. "The bourgeoisie, during its rule of scarce one hundred years, has created more massive and more colossal productive forces than have all preceding generations together. Subjection of Nature's forces to man, machinery, application of chemistry to industry and agriculture, steam-navigation, railways, electric telegraphs, clearing of whole continents for cultivation, canalisation of rivers, whole populations conjured out of the ground —what earlier century had even a presentiment that such productive forces slumbered in the lap of social labour?" *The Communist Manifesto* in Karl Marx and Frederick Engels, *Selected Works* (New York: International Publishers, 1968), pp. 39–40.

3. See Charles Gide and Charles Rist, *A History of Economic Doctrines*, trans. R. Richards (London: D. C. Heath and Co., n.d.), p. 112. See also F. A. Hayek, ed., *Capitalism and the Historians* (Chicago: University of Chicago Press, Phoenix Books, 1963).

4. For world population figures see *Encyclopedia Britannica*, 15th ed., s.v. "Population"; John Noble Wilford, "9 Percent of Everyone Who Ever Lived Is Alive Now," *New York Times*, October 6, 1981; and U.S. Bureau of the Census, *Statistical Abstract of the United States: 1982-83*, 103d ed. (Washington, D.C., 1982), Table 1518. The current life expectancy worldwide (both sexes) is 59 years. Of 45 countries with a population of 10 million or more, 38 have achieved life expectancies of 50 years or more (*Statistical Abstract of the United States: 1982-83*, Tables 1517, 1521). For a useful historical comparison of life expectancy for various countries, see W. S. and E. S. Woytinsky, *World Population and Production* (New York: Twentieth Century Fund, 1953).

5. Joseph A. Schumpeter, *History of Economic Analysis*, ed. Elizabeth Boody Schumpeter (New York: Oxford University Press, 1954).

6. "And hence it is, that to feel much for others, and little for ourselves, that to restrain our selfish, and to indulge our benevolent, affections, constitutes the perfection of human nature; and can alone produce among mankind that harmony of sentiments and passions in which consists their whole grace and propriety." Adam Smith, *The Theory of Moral Sentiments* (Indianapolis: Liberty Classics, 1976), pp. 71-72.

7. Niebuhr wrote, in 1953: "It was the great achievement of classical economic liberalism to gain recognition of the doctrine that the vast system of mutual services which constitute the life of economic society could best be maintained by relying on the 'self-interest' of men rather than on their 'benevolence' or on moral suasion, and by freeing economic activities from irrelevant and often unduly restrictive political controls. It released the 'initiative' of men to exploit every possible opportunity for gain and thus to increase the resources of the whole of society, at first through the exploitation of commercial opportunities and subsequently through the endless development of technical and industrial power." Reinhold Niebuhr, "The Christian Faith and the Economic Life of Liberal Society," in *Goals of Economic Life*, ed. A. Dudley Ward (New York: Harpers, 1953), p. 433; reprinted in Reinhold Niebuhr, *Faith and Politics*, ed. Ronald H. Stone (New York: George Braziller, 1968).

8. See, for example, Joseph Epstein, "The Education of an Anti-

Capitalist," *Commentary* 76 (August 1983): 51–59.

9. See my discussion of Latin America in *The Spirit of Democratic Capitalism* (New York: Simon and Schuster, American Enterprise Institute, 1981), pp. 298–314.

10. See my essay "'Creation Theology'—John Paul II and the American Experience," *This World* 3 (Fall 1982): 71–88.

11. Bernard Murchland, *The Dream of Christian Socialism: An Essay on Its European Origins* (Washington, D.C.: American Enterprise Institute, 1982.)

12. See Irving Kristol, *Two Cheers for Capitalism* (New York: Basic Books, 1978); and *Reflections of a Neoconservative* (New York: Basic Books, 1983).

13. See, for example, Muhammad Abdul-Rauf, *The Islamic Doctrine of Economics and Contemporary Economic Thought* (Washington, D.C.: American Enterprise Institute, 1979); and *A Muslim's Reflections on Democratic Capitalism* (Washington, D.C.: American Enterprise Institute, 1984); Seymour Siegel, "A Jewish View of Economic Justice," *This World* 1 (Winter/Spring 1972): 70–78.

Overview

John C. Bennett

The chapters in this volume are so informative that I am sure that readers will make many discoveries. Probably few are well informed about nineteenth-century "clerical *laissez-faire*," about Dutch neo-

Calvinism, about economic thinking in Islamic countries; or the left-ward movement in Roman Catholic thinking, or the history of Christian Socialism in England. Also I am impressed by the fact that those who represent views very different from the views of those who planned the conferences out of which these volumes have come, have abundant opportunity to present their positions and the historical background for them. Since the chapters are mainly historical and descriptive there is not as much direct debate about issues as in the companion volume, but we have reports of contrasting positions that will stimulate debate among readers. The many shades of difference in the views expressed and the very different historical backgrounds described make this volume very rich indeed.

One thing that I learned was that the relations between Judaism and the market economy are as complicated as the relations to it of Christianity, and for this reason I am much indebted to the chapters on Judaism. Two of the writers even disagree as to whether Judaism is primarily oriented toward the individual or toward the community. The fact that Jews were left little alternative but to engage in business and commerce and banking is balanced by the fact that in the past century the socialism of Jews has been far more important politically than the socialism of Christians. Socialism is an important strain in the ethos and institutions of contemporary Israel. The law of the Jubilee in Leviticus XXV is mentioned in one chapter and, even as an ideal that is never realized, this must be a challenge to that body of opinion represented in this book which is adamantly opposed to political measures to redistribute wealth.

I am surprised that so little is said about the Old Testament prophets and about their determinative influence on the social activism of Christians, except that they defended the property rights of citizens against the power of kings (Naboth's vineyard). Christian critics of capitalism have been inspired by them. The Book of Amos is a favourite with them. Liberation Theologians in Latin America make much of these words in Jeremiah XXII about the good King Josiah: "He judged the cause of the poor and the needy; then it was well. Is this not to know me?" The struggle for justice is seen as central to the very knowledge of God. As a personal observation I want to say that in the United States the minority status of Jews has meant that even when they are prosperous they tend to identify themselves politically with others who are suffering as minorities, or as victims of economic institutions. They are generally strong supporters of "liberal" social and political causes, which sometimes puts them in a camp opposed to defenders of the almost moral self-sufficiency of the market economy.

The overarching difference

The shades of difference among the positions represented in this book may make it seem simplistic to speak of an overarching difference. In spite of that warning to myself I shall try to describe what I regard as such an overarching difference which one finds in these chapters. On the one hand there are those who are defenders of what I call the "almost-moral-self-sufficiency" (awkward phrase) of the market economy and whose chief interest is in the logic of that economy's development. They do this theoretically for the most part rather than through examining particular economies as they work out in practice. They emphasize how immensely productive the market economy can be for the benefit of all and how favourable it is to freedom, not to economic freedom only but also to political and cultural freedom. For them the intervention of the state is the major threat to the health of this free and productive economy.

On the other hand there are writers in this book, and many thinkers on whom they report, who begin by asking what economies that have the free market as their main structure have done to people. Professor Preston says that the economic order is made for persons and no writer in this book would disagree with that in principle. But some would keep asking: for what people does it do most? What people does it neglect or allow to be its victims? Clark Kucheman, in replying to Father Sadowsky (whose difference from his fellow Roman Catholic, Gregory Baum, is probably the deepest difference in the book), calls attention to the fact that the relatively successful economy of the United States allows twelve percent of the people to suffer from poverty. That means about 34,000,000 people.[1] A considerable majority of the poor are women, which causes some people to speak of "the feminization of poverty." A recent study shows that about a fifth of the children in the United States live below the official poverty line. Should we not ask about the misery these 34,000,000 would suffer had there been no state intervention to provide social security, unemployment insurance, medicaid (medical aid for the poor), aid to families with dependent children, and food stamps? Yet the most stalwart defenders of the market economy are always attempting to cut back on these provisions for the poor.

I remember the Great Depression of the 1930s. I think that it was then that people in the United States became aware that fifteen million people did not suddenly become lazy but that they were victims of large-scale forces with which only the national state was strong enough to cope. Today the United States is experiencing a recovery from a deep recession and most people may be benefiting already. But if we consider the families of the twelve million unemployed it is not enough to appeal to the future benefits that will come to them if the productive market economy is given a chance. An immediate rescue operation is needed by society through the state because so many people, especially children, are being wounded and handicapped for the rest of their lives by what is happening to them now. Some of those who neglect these realities as they plead for patience with the economy which is expected to benefit everyone two or three years from now put great emphasis on what people deserve in economic terms as though that were relevant in the case of children. Also hardly noticed are the psychological wounds that result from humiliating and debilitating poverty in the presence of so much wealth. One sees these wounds in the case of the "new poor" because of unemployment, which causes people to have a sense of failure and often destroys the morale of families.

Greater clarity

I think that there are two discussions among these writers and among the many whom they represent that need to be carried on to produce greater clarity. One would be between those who go furthest in claiming moral self-sufficiency for the market economy and resist almost all intervention by the state, on the one hand, and those, on the other, who believe in the market as the main structure of the economy and yet who believe that many aspects of the welfare state are needed to make the market morally tolerable. Also, we need discussion between those who belong to the latter group and believers in socialism. In North America and western Europe the number who believe in socialism as a total system may now be quite small. Yet we see a difference in the dialogue about economic life between most of the industrialized democracies (including Canada) that have political movements with a socialist tradition, and the United States, where no such movement exists. In this contrast I think that the United States is the loser because of the narrower range of the economic debate.

I have had some difficulty in finding words to designate what I regard as faults in the main argument of those who defend the market economy against its religious critics. They are not monolithic and I have used words to suggest that their tendencies of thought have many degrees. In some cases I am critical of little more than matters of emphasis. In a few cases I see in them an absolutist ideology. Moreover, there are degrees of harshness in polemics in dealing with the critics in the churches who are believed to undermine the market economy. I shall discuss five of the tendencies of thought which for me raise serious difficulties.

Community

1. I think that strong defenders of the market economy have an insufficient sense of the importance of community. Their argument sees the world chiefly in terms of the freedom of individuals. But individuals gain a large part of the meaning of their lives from the community of which they are members. The quality of their own lives is greatly influenced by the quality of that community. They are formed by communities, especially the community of the family, and families are formed and enriched or corrupted or made miserable or denied opportunities in practice by larger communities of which they are a part. For persons of religious and moral seriousness and imagination their community has no limits short of humanity as a whole, though there are parts of that larger community for which they have immediate responsibility and which are most affected by what they do or leave undone. In principle most of the writers in this volume would probably not disagree with those statements, but I question whether all of them allow the community to be on the "ground floor" of their economic and political thinking.

The community must be distinguished from the state. The state is one of the community's structures and it is that which enables it to make many of its most fateful decisions that affect its welfare. It can implement those decisions and can enforce them, especially those that can have little effect unless all or almost all members of the community obey them at the same time. Because it has a monopoly of force, the state can be oppressive, and unfortunately this is true of the states today that control most of the world's people. This fact is a major reason for the current reaction against the power of the state. Yet we know that it is possible for a state to have built-in correctives, to provide legally, and through habit, for the balancing of powers and for the orderly displacement of those who hold political power. The state's responsibility for the welfare of the whole society is greater than that of any centres of economic power. Economic powers should be accountable to the community as a whole through accountability to organs of the state.

There is lacking in some of these chapters, which rightly stress the productive capacity of private economic entities, the realization that these entities not only make great contributions to the well-being of the community but are themselves centres of great power, direct economic power over the lives of workers and consumers, and more indirect power over the state because of their financial influence in politics. Their authors avoid any direct attack on the principle of collective bargaining and the organizing of employees. Many of their predecessors such as Francis Wayland, so well described by Paul Heyne, believed that "combinations" of workers were against the laws of the market economy and hence against the laws of God. I am glad that I do not detect adherence to that doctrine in these chapters but I wonder if it is not implied in some of them. On the other hand, the pluralism that is so much supported by all writers depends in part on the distribution of power between corporations and labour unions.

Those whose distrust of the state is greatest often appeal from the national state to local or regional government. Often this may be the best course. The principle of subsidiarity so much emphasized by Catholic thinkers is a good corrective for the tendency to increase the power of the national state, but in this area we need to be guided by experience rather than by deductions from this principle. In the United States very often appeal to "states' rights" has been an attempt to prevent change. This has been spectacularly true in race relations. More widely it has been our experience in the United States that concern about issues of economic justice have reverberated much more in the national community than in many states or smaller units of society. It has taken federal pressure to establish provisions of welfare for the poor, the sick, the elderly. Also for the young. These have usually been opposed by the business community until after they have been established. The economic well-being of people is not only a local affair. Perceptions of serious economic injustice are wounds in the life of the national community. That kind of injustice is present when, from region to region, there are vast differences in provisions for welfare, even in provisions for public education, after account has been taken of differences in the cost of living. Pride in the national community should include pride in achievements of social justice in the nation. One of the most admirable recent events in the United States was the action of the U.S. Supreme Court in annulling a law of the State of Texas that denied the right of children of undocumented workers (illegal immigrants) to have free public education. The highest court of the nation put itself alongside the weakest people living within its borders, the children of undocumented workers. I see this as a sign of national greatness.

Equality

2. My second suggestion concerning limitations in the position of the strong defenders of the market economy is that the ideal of equality seems to have no claim of its own when we think of the nature of justice. Here I am concerned with the effect of extreme inequalities—and I know that we can argue about how much is "extreme"—upon the quality of the life of the community. I am not suggesting that complete equality imposed by law is good, and I know of no one in the churches who advocates it.

There are many kinds of inequality that no form of social or political action can overcome. People are unequal in ability, in physical strength, in personal force or energy, in specific talents, in beauty, in the habits of character, or the habits of discipline and efficiency. They are unequal in their achieved merits and in the contributions that they can make to society. I am not sure that there is any equality which is given among persons except equality in ultimate standing before God, involving an ultimate reality of human dignity. There is another form of equality that is not inherent but which should be provided by society: equality before the law. Even under our constitution, that form of equality is only partly realized. In my own society persons who are both poor and members of a minority often do not in practice have equality before the police and the courts with those who have money or belong to the majority. Moreover there is the inequality before the law created by the cost of litigation.

What I have called "extreme" inequalities are a hindrance to fellowship in the community. They encourage pride and vanity on one side and subservience and self-rejection on the other. Also, extreme inequalities of condition create inequalities of opportunity. Most people in Western democracies accept equality of opportunity as an essential goal. The possibility of extreme inequalities with no limit to the wealth that can be accumulated and passed on to descendents encourages endless greed. I doubt if Walter Block can succeed in giving good connotations to the word "greed." We need a word to designate an aggressive acquisitiveness that is socially destructive and an ugly expression of character. This is not uncommon in the market economy. One of the most objectionable ideas in several of these chapters, as far as I am concerned, is the idea that taxation should never be used to redistribute wealth and income. Without that corrective use of taxation capitalistic societies are unable to overcome the forms of injurious inequality that I have mentioned. I deal more fully with the claims of equality in my commentary in the companion volume,* especially with the extent to which inequalities of condition may undermine equality of opportunity.

Freedom

3. The chief moral commitment of the defenders of the almost moral self-sufficiency of the market economy is the commitment to freedom. In this respect the arguments of both sides in this book are moral. In all of the debates between those who differ in this volume there are varying views about the claims and the priorities of freedom and justice.

The 1948 Amsterdam Assembly of the World Council of Churches, in a much discussed passage, criticized both communism and capitalism in these words:

> Each has made promises which it cannot redeem. Communist ideology puts the emphasis upon economic justice, and promises that freedom will come automatically after the completion of the revolution. Capitalism puts the emphasis upon freedom, and promises that justice will follow as a by-product of free enterprise; that, too, is an ideology that has proved false.[2]

Though I know that most writers in this volume who are strong de-

---

The Morality of the Market: Religious and Economic Perspectives, Vancouver: The Fraser Institute, 1985.

fenders of the market system differ in nuance from any absolute formula, it seems to me that the implications of many chapters are that justice will come as a by-product of free enterprise and that rarely should the community seek it directly through action by the state.

But there is an illusion about freedom among most defenders of the market economy who say that it promises freedom. They take no account of the extent to which people are not freed by the market from the tyranny of circumstance. Those who are among the 34,000,000 poor in the United States (especially those who have had a year of unemployment and have lost their health insurance and who have lost, or any day may lose, their homes) have very little freedom. They have formal political freedom and they are not arrested for advocating dissenting views. But in all sorts of ways they are subject to the tyranny of circumstances not directly willed by any political powers. I also think there is a tendency on the part of the defenders of the market economy to overemphasize the unity of freedom. The nations with mixed economies and democratic experience have maintained political freedom and civil liberties. Totalitarian governments have not resulted from incremental increases in governmental power to deal with particular problems. They have come from neglected public problems that have left large parts of the population resentful and hopeless and alienated.

Freedom is abridged or threatened by the control exercised by private economic entities over government. In the United States this control comes in part from the influence of campaign contributions to defray the appalling cost of campaigns for election of public officials. It is seen in the enormous influence of military suppliers upon the Defense Department and its allies in Congress. Particular weapons systems have their economic constituencies in the market economy and these join forces with constituencies in the armed services. Perhaps President Eisenhower's most memorable words were his warning against the power of the "military industrial complex." We can add to the military and industrial elements in this complex the influence of free foundations or "think tanks" and even universities. The market economy does make possible a degree of social pluralism and, in so far as it does so, it is favourable to democratic freedoms. But the preservation of this pluralism requires continuous vigilance both in regard to development of monopolistic or quasi-monopolistic centres of economic power, and in regard to the influence of economic powers on government.

Charity

4. I find very strange the idea that is sometimes expressed in these chapters (and much emphasized by President Reagan), that we should count on voluntary gifts for a large part of the needed aid to the most disadvantaged people. Anything but taxation! On the surface this appeal to private generosity is in harmony with Christian ethics and should always be part of the picture. There are many situations in which personal giving, or giving through churches and other private agencies, will be needed. Sometimes it has the advantage of being innovative or of quietly helping in cases of unique or unanticipated personal need. The web of family relationships or other intimate relationships often provide the best points of contact with such need. There are many religious, educational, and charitable institutions which depend for their existence on private giving. The same is true of social causes, opinion-forming and political causes which call for support in one's daily mail.

At best these forms of private giving are entirely different in scale from what is provided by the community through the state. The staggering cost of medical care and of life-maintenance for so many millions of people is far beyond anything that the most generous private giving could provide. Provisions for public education are a great drain on public resources on the state and local levels. I do not believe that any of the contributors to this book believe that private giving could become a substitute for all the public provisions which are essential for life-support of so many people.

Even if private giving were able to meet these needs, it would be wrong to depend on it. The essential well-being of people should not depend on the inevitably capricious generosity of private persons. Such a system would be too paternalistic and humiliating to the receivers of aid. It is far better for those who are in need to receive support because of the sense of justice of the community of which they are members than to receive it through the giving of private persons. It is a significant form of private generosity to vote for forms of taxation that are to one's personal disadvantage. Indeed that is often the most relevant form of generosity. I have spoken of children a good deal, though there are many others who need assistance, including the elderly, the sick of all ages, and the unemployed. But in the case of children we can put aside all questions of desert or merit. They cannot be aided without aid going to their families. Public support for children, which has long been accepted in principle in the provisions for "free" education for all, is not only a matter of caring for and justice to persons: it is an investment by the community in its future.

Property rights

5. Another weakness in the intellectual assumptions of those who defend the almost moral self-sufficiency of the market economy is that the right to property is strongly emphasized without sufficient attention to the different forms of property or to the social process by which people acquire property. I question the tendency to regard taxation as a necessary evil only and not as a good method by which society may compensate for the failure of the market in distributing property. The right of people to keep what they earn makes taxation an injustice: but this view of "right" fails to take account of the contribution of society to a person's capacity to earn. I am not suggesting that the distinctive contributions of able, and innovative, and energetic people; of courageous, risk-taking people; of people who have unique gifts for large-scale management or economic leadership, should not be rewarded with more than average compensation. I am arguing only that there should be a sense of proportion in the rewards. It is the case, moreover, that those who amass wealth because of monopolistic advantages may do so not because of exceptional creativity but because of exceptional luck or cunning. Those whose property has appreciated because of population changes owe much of their gain to the contribution of the community. Speculation may make a desirable contribution to the smooth working of the market but how far are large speculative gains earned?

I think that Pope Paul VI, in his encyclical, *Populorum Progressio,* spoke not only for his own tradition but also for the whole Christian community when he wrote the following: "Private property does not constitute for anyone an absolute and unconditioned right. No one is justified in keeping for his exclusive use what he does not need, when others lack necessities."[3] One can argue about where to draw the line concerning the need of those who possess and the necessities of those who lack possessions, but those words help to give us direction. Anyone who really believes in those words must be glad that the state helps in implementing them.

The very influential report of the Oxford Conference on Church, Community, and State (1937) emphasized the need to distinguish between various forms of property. It said the following:[4] "the property which consists in personal possessions for use, such as the home, has behind it clearer moral justification than property in the means of production and in land which gives the owners power over other persons. All property which represents social power stands in special need of moral scrutiny, since power to determine the lives of others is the crucial point in any scheme of justice." The conference also said that "every argument in defence of property rights which is valid for Christian thinking is also an argument for the widest possible distribution of those rights." This conference, which was a significant event in the development of ecumenical thought on these issues, greatly stressed the importance of avoiding identifying the Gospel or the Church with either capitalism or socialism.

Christian realism

There is one alleged difference between the representatives of the two main directions in this volume and that has to do with the extent to which they take account of the finiteness and sinfulness of human beings. I think that at this stage this should not be an intellectual difference among them. Often it is the strongest defenders of the market economy, such as Margaret Thatcher (as quoted in his chapter by Anthony Waterman, and Edward Norman in the companion volume), who accuse the critics of the market economy of naive idealism, utopianism, or perfectionism. Doubtless there are individuals on both sides who are unrealistic about human nature. Doubtless there are individuals who have not learned from the horrors of recent and contemporary history, who do not realize that human prospects are darkened by threats to the environment unknown a few decades ago, by the danger of nuclear annihilation, and by the proven difficulty of establishing governments that are effective without being tyrannical. There is no place for utopianism in any of these arguments.

Among Christians in North America, Reinhold Niebuhr has been the major teacher on this subject and his teaching has been greatly supported by events. In regard to his views on the issues discussed in this book, though he gave up his socialist commitments by the late

1940s, he never moved away from his support of a mixed economy with a considerable socialist ingredient. In politics in the United States he represented, as long as he lived, the general outlook of Americans for Democratic Action. His critical mind may not always have been on the side of particular positions taken within the "ecumenical" community. But he was closer to "ecumenical" views about capitalism than he was to that optimism about the benign effects of the market economy on the whole society which many of these chapters represent. The more conservative side claims for the support of its position Niebuhr's debunking of naive liberal idealism. The critics of the "almost moral self-sufficiency" of the market economy claim in support of their views Niebuhr's application of his insights in practice to political and economic problems. I think that they can also claim a neglected side of Niebuhr's basic theology which rejects a dogmatic pessimism and allows for indeterminate good possibilities. Niebuhr would be among the first to warn against concentrations of unaccountable economic power in the market.

Some Protestant and Catholic contrasts

I find it very interesting to compare indications about trends among left-of-centre Protestants and Catholics in the very informative chapters by Ronald Preston and Gregory Baum. Professor Preston reveals that Christian Socialism as a confident and committed movement has lost ground in England and I know that the same is true in the United States. In considerable measure the welfare state in both countries has undercut the appeal of a doctrinaire socialism, though such socialism was never strong in the United States. Preston who comes from a Christian Socialist background and still says that "the visions of most Christian Socialists was on right lines" accepts the idea that the market is very useful in "the allocation of scarce resources." He makes the good distinction between profit as "directive" and profit as "incentive" and thus makes room for the idea that emphasis on the profit incentive does increase the spirit of acquisitiveness and greed to which human nature is prone. I am not suggesting that the desire to improve the economic condition of oneself and one's family is not within limits a useful and usually needed incentive. I think that it tends to be true that Protestants who greatly stress social justice are less likely today than in an earlier period to regard socialism as a complete solution to economic problems, and that they make concessions to some of the claims of those who argue for capitalism. However, they remain far from the views expressed in this volume by those who are the strongest defenders of the market economy.

Gregory Baum by contrast writes about the increasing radicalism of much Roman Catholic thought and commitment. This tendency gets strong support from recent popes, beginning with John XXIII. Probably the encyclical *Populorum Progressio* of Paul VI is the clearest example of this trend, and Baum tells us that Paul's letter, *Octogesima Adveniens*, finally lifts the Catholic ban upon democratic socialism. It is significant that he sees the encyclical *Laborem Exergens* of John Paul II as moving in the same direction, in spite of his conservatism in internal ecclesiastical policy. The positions taken by the Catholic hierarchy in Canada on capitalism, together with the fact that the hierarchy in the United States is preparing a pastoral letter on the subject, are disturbing to strong defenders of the market economy.

The influential presence of Liberation Theology among Catholics in Latin America illustrates this leftward tendency in Catholicism. Christian Socialism in Northern-hemisphere Protestantism may have less influence but Christian Socialism among Catholics in Latin America is one of the most significant movements in contemporary theology and in the life of the Church. It goes beyond the position of the popes, but Pope Paul VI in *Populorum Progressio* provided a launching pad. Liberation Theology is a very important part of ecumenical theological conversation. All theology is in some respects contextual; even Saint Paul's epistles in terms of priorities and emphases and warnings against particular errors were strongly contextual. Many Christians in North America, both Catholics and Protestants, are stimulated and inspired by Liberation Theology even though it is not a model for their own theology in their very different situation.

Liberation Theology in part is addressed to Christians in North America because of its emphasis on the dependence of Latin America on the great industrial countries, especially the United States. Also, Liberation Theologians find themselves embattled because of the attempts of the United States to frustrate the revolutions in which they believe. Their selective use of Marxism greatly worries their critics in North America, but it must be realized that they use Marxism[6] chiefly for the analysis of their social situation and for setting the socialist goal. They are often thought to be utopian but it is almost inevitable that people involved in a costly struggle will convince themselves that if they overcome the particular oppression from which they suffer, there will be a new world with great promise. Rather than judging them from overtones of utopianism which are byproducts of struggle, it is fairer to listen to one of their most influential theologians, Gustave Gutierrez.[7] After saying that the Kingdom of God is a gift of God he says the following: "It keeps us from any confusion of the Kingdom of God with any one historical stage, from any idolatry toward unavoidably ambiguous human achievement, from any absolutizing of revolution." In any situation of costly struggle we can expect many people, including Christians, to lose the sense of ambiguity emphasized by Dr. Norman in the other volume, but it is the responsibility of the church to keep this sense alive and to prepare its members for the new temptations in the next stage of history. Professor Benne would probably not agree with all that I say about Liberation Theology but he proves himself to be a helpful mediator in this volume. After saying that he prefers reform to transformation he says the following: "I welcome Catholic social thought's shift to the left as one way, among others, to stimulate reform." In North America that may be enough, but in their context Liberation Theologians make a good case for transformation. They also make a good case for transformation in the relations between the economic institutions of prosperous countries and those of poor countries.

The World Council of Churches

The World Council of Churches has been a chief target of those who criticize forms of Christianity that are believed to be leftist and it is fitting that one of the chapters should deal with it. It is a sign of the fairness of those who planned these conferences that Archbishop Edward Scott, the moderator of the Central Committee of the World Council, was asked to write the chapter on that subject. The Central Committee is the Council's highest authority in making policy between the assemblies which meet every seven years. The Sixth Assembly is meeting in Vancouver as I write.

Archbishop Scott shows very effectively the extent of the processes of consultation that take place continually in the life of the World Council before decisions are made. Critics of the World Council seem to think that it is in the control of a few radical activists or of bureaucrats in Geneva. Actually there are many occasions for official consultations among leaders from all over the world and there are innumerable regional or specialized conferences that help to form opinion. It is often difficult for Christians in North America to realize that the World Council must be responsive to the oppressions and aspirations and convictions of people on all continents. More and more it has come to be influenced by Christians in the Third World whose experiences and insights are often so different from experiences and insights that are characteristic of churches in North America. That is the reason that the Council does at times shock people on this continent. Yet since 1948 we can see a great deal of continuity in the thinking and life of the World Council. There has been enrichment as churches in the Third World have gained influence and as new interests have gained attention. Such new interests have been emphasized since about 1970, when there came to be so much attention to new ethical issues raised by science involving the cultural effects of science and technology and the limits of the world's resources.

One of the most interesting examples of consultation and continuity is the "program to combat racism" which has provided funds to liberation movements in all parts of the world. This has been the most controversial of the activities of the World Council and probably has done more than anything else to make it a target for critics in North America. This program was established in 1969 as a result of the concern of the Uppsala Assembly (1968) that the Council do more than talk about racism. It began with grants to resistance movements especially in Africa and because some of them had the possibility of violence as part of their agenda there was a storm of criticism. The grants were always designated for education, medical care, food, and relief for refugees, and no case is known of their being used for weapons. In spite of the criticism, every year since 1969 the Central Committee of 134-144 leaders of churches from all continents has supported the program and has approved more grants to liberation movements, some of them for minorities in North America. Here is a program that was re-examined every year not by a small group of activists but by the real leaders of churches like Archbishop Scott, and has been confirmed and reconfirmed. (From time to time there have been changes in the membership of the Central Committee.) In order to be fair to churches that disagree with them the grants themselves are allowed to come only from designated gifts and not from the general funds of the World Council.

The World Council, as the Archbishop says so well, has never been a single-track organization but has always given great emphasis not only to the more publicized social teaching and action but also to the expression of the faith, to worship, to theology, to explorations leading to greater Christian unity, and to union of the churches. A better understanding of the richness and variety in the life of the World Council and of the carefulness of its processes of decision-making, of its responsibility to be the voice of Christians on all continents and not merely to be a voice of Christians in the West, may eliminate some of the emotion from the economic debates reflected in this volume as they touch the thought and life in the churches. Through the World Council, and also through the witness of the popes, churches in North America can participate in what the Catholics call the "preferential option for the poor." Many writers in this book may find those words questionable, but should they not admit that in the end the market economy which they so powerfully defend will be judged by them?

NOTES

1. On August 3, 1983 the Census Bureau reported that in 1982 the number of people living in poverty in the United States had reached 15% — 34,000,000.

2. From the report of the third section of the Assembly that had as its subject: "The Church and the Disorder of Society," Part V.

3. *Populorum Progressio,* par. 23.

4. J. H. Oldham, ed. *The Oxford Conference* (Official Report), Chicago and New York: Willett, Clark and Co. 1937, pp. 100– 102.

5. I have dealt more fully with Niebuhr's thought on these issues in an article entitled "Reinhold Niebuhr's Social Ethics: The Later Years," in *Christianity and Crisis,* April 12, 1982.

6. There is a very discriminating study of the use of Marxism by Christians

in Jose Miguez Bonino. *Christians and Marxists*. Grand Rapids: William B. Eerdmans, 1976. Probably the best overview of Liberation Theology and its background is in the same author's *Doing Theology in a Revolutionary Situation*. Philadelphia: Fortress Press, 1975.

7. Gustavo Gutierrez. *A Theology of Liberation*. Maryknoll, N.Y.: Orbis Books, 1973, p. 238.

Index